D1301457

LEARNING FROM CHANGE

LEARNING FROM CHANGE

Landmarks in Teaching and Learning in Higher Education from Change *Magazine, 1969–1999*

EDITED BY
Deborah DeZure

FOREWORD BY
Theodore J. Marchese

CONTRIBUTING EDITORS:

K. Patricia Cross
Jerry Gaff
Zelda F. Gamson
Diane Gillespie
Daniel Goroff
Kenneth C. Green
Pat Hutchings

Malcolm A. Lowther
Wilbert McKeachie
Alfredo G. de los Santos Jr.
Peter Seldin
Joan S. Stark
James Wilkinson
Barbara D. Wright

STERLING, VIRGINIA

AMERICAN ASSOCIATION
FOR HIGHER EDUCATION

Published in association with
The American Association for Higher Education

Published in 2000 by
Stylus Publishing, LLC
22883 Quicksilver Drive
Sterling, Virginia 20166

Published outside the Americas by
Kogan Page Limited
120 Pentonville Road
London N1 9JN

Compilation, Introduction, Commentaries and Conclusions copyright © 2000 by Stylus
Publishing, LLC

All rights reserved. No part of this book may be reprinted or reproduced in any form or by
any electronic, mechanical or other means, now known or hereafter invented, including
photocopying, recording and information storage and retrieval, without permission in writing
from the publishers.

Library of Congress Cataloging-in-Publication-Data

Learning from Change : landmarks in teaching and learning in higher education from
Change magazine, 1969–1999 / edited by Deborah DeZure ; foreword by Theodore J.
Marchese.
     p. cm.
     Includes bibliographical references and index.
     ISBN 1-57922-001-0 (alk. paper)—ISBN 1-57922-002-9 (alk. paper)
     1. Education, Higher. 2. College teaching. I. DeZure, Deborah. II. Change.

LB2322.2 .L42 2000
378—dc21   00-026309

First edition, 2000
Hardcover ISBN: 1-57922-001-0
Paperback ISBN: 1-57922-002-9
Printed in the United States of America
Printed on acid free paper

To Tom, Jessica, and Adam DeZure
for their loving support

Contents

Foreword

Academic newspapers and glossy magazines are piled so high on our desks today that it is easy to forget how thin the reading matter of American higher education was as recently as the 1960s. What we had at that time was a handful of official newsletters and journals. The most widely circulated of the latter, *The Educational Record*, routinely reprinted presidential speeches—no better then than now!

In the mid-1960s, as enrollments swelled and new campuses were founded weekly, a handful of New York foundations became alarmed at the state of publishing in higher education. In several Washington-area conferences, they admonished academic leaders to leave behind their "cottage-industry mentality" and recognize that they led a large, rapidly-maturing industry that needed to reinvent its media of communication. What it needed, they said, was a newspaper comparable to the *Wall Street Journal*, a magazine like the *Atlantic Monthly*, and a first-rate book publisher. By the end of the decade, entrepreneurs had the *Chronicle of Higher Education, Change,* and Jossey-Bass up and running.

Change was especially quick to get out of the starting gate. Led by a visionary founding editor, George Bonham, and fueled by millions of dollars in foundation grants through the 1970s, the magazine was an instant sensation. Nothing like it had appeared before. Here in an attractive package was investigative journalism, readable research, and highbrow opinion—about us!

By 1979, with its foundation grants expended and business affairs in a muddle, *Change* was taken over by Heldref Publications, a Washington-based not-for-profit association. Volunteer editors—David Breneman, Frederick Rudolph, and George Weathersby—kept the magazine alive, sometimes brilliantly, but *Change* was a shadow of its earlier self.

In 1984, Heldref Publications approached the American Association for Higher Education (AAHE), exploring whether we would be willing to provide the editorial leadership for a reinvigorated *Change*. AAHE president Russ Edgerton said "yes"; as vice president I voted "no," on the grounds that *Change* was diminished goods. The president, of course, prevailed; we need to think about not just what it has been, he said, but about what it could be and what the community needs. He signed the agreement with Heldref Publications—and appointed me executive editor.

Russ Edgerton was (and remains) a person of deep thought and integrity. Aided by co-editors Alison Bernstein and Frank Newman, we helped *Change* tap into the wider intellectual resources of AAHE's world and beyond. Its readership and influence grew again. Over the years, able co-editors left their mark on its pages: Catharine Stimpson, Art Levine, Zelda Gamson, and Peter Ewell.

In time, too, a tacit division of labor evolved between *Change* and the *Chronicle*. As the latter grew, it initially targeted administrative interests, then later those of disciplinary faculty. *Change*, which earlier had ranged widely in its editorial interests, increasingly focused on matters not covered by the *Chronicle*, especially the academic affairs and undergraduate reform agendas reflected in this book—teaching, learning, curriculum, assessment, diversity, faculty roles, and the pedagogic aspects of technology. The magazine attempted to open classroom doors, to look inside the "black box" of what campuses do—teach and learn. Over the past 15 years, *Change* has provided a wide-ranging forum where academic leaders came to learn about everything from service learning to the scholarship of teaching. As Danny Goroff says in these pages, its mission focused to "building shared vocabulary and understanding about academic work."

A question running throughout this volume is just how far we have come since *Change*'s founding in 1969. Is American undergraduate education better now than then? For many students—the beneficiaries of new curricula, pedagogy, technology, and appreciation for diversity—it undoubtedly is better. However, is it significantly better for most students? Probably not. For all the gains remarked upon in these pages, the undergraduate reform movement has been uphill most of the way. That is the bad news.

The good news is that these past three decades gave birth to an undergraduate reform movement. In the long history of the American college, we have had curricular movements, land-grant movements, community college movements, and so on, but never a movement aimed at our core function itself—teaching and learning. Thousands of the academy's best citizens now attend to that movement's several parts. No central, guiding hand is behind it, and no governmental authority pushes it (except for assessment); there is simply a growing professional sense that a thing that is not done badly could be done a whole lot better.

In a famous *Change* essay (1992), Parker Palmer discusses the paradox of movements: they have to step outside the logic of organizations to gather the power to rewrite their logic. For years now, people initially on the margins have been finding one another, trying and evaluating new approaches, finding allies and gathering strength. Along the way, the academy has learned from them about a host of new pedagogies; the varieties of assessment; coherent, goal-directed curricula; instructional development; and changing faculty roles—impressive intellectual capital! *Change* helped these people "go public," a critical stage in a movement's life. What these advocates of reform run up against, as Palmer predicted, is the tightly interlocked, self-reinforcing nature of the system itself, and especially its reward systems, which seem to rank, rate, and value everything but ambition in teaching.

Within this coming decade, these reformers may well carry the day, even as the journey's hills seem momentarily steeper. A booming economy and stock market have meant better times for most institutions; public cries for reform are more muted; the competitive nature of web-based markets makes cooperation harder. However, the impossible always seems so before it becomes the inevitable.

Finally, let me express my deep thanks for the imagination and diligence of this book's editor, Deborah DeZure, and for the support of publisher John von Knorring. As they have shown us, one of the best ways to think about the future is to have a good look back.

Ted Marchese
February 2000

Reference

Palmer, P. (1992, March/April). Divided no more: A movement approach to educational reform. *Change, 24*(2), 10–17.

Editor's Acknowledgments

Learning from Change represents the efforts of many generous and talented collaborators and colleagues. This book was a formidable endeavor, presenting many unique intellectual and editorial challenges. First and foremost, I wish to express my sincere appreciation to the 14 contributing editors whose prodigious efforts and expertise made this project possible: Pat Hutchings, K. Patricia Cross, Jerry Gaff, Zelda F. Gamson, Alfredo G. de los Santos Jr., Wilbert McKeachie, James Wilkinson, Daniel Goroff, Joan S. Stark, Malcolm A. Lowther, Barbara D. Wright, Peter Seldin, Diane Gillespie, and Kenneth C. Green. I am deeply indebted to them for their insight, experience, and flexibility.

The project itself is predicated on the outstanding articles published in *Change* magazine from 1969–1999 and the kind permission of the authors who consented to the reprinting of their works in this collection. These works have not only seen the rigors of the original process by which they were included in *Change*, but they also have survived yet another round of editorial review. All of us associated with this project thank the authors for their significant contributions to our understanding of higher education.

I wish to thank Theodore Marchese, Executive Editor of *Change* magazine and Vice President of the American Association for Higher Education. He has supported this project from its inception, providing sage counsel at several critical stages in its development and generously writing the Foreword for this collection.

I also wish to thank Pat Hutchings, Senior Scholar at the Carnegie Foundation for the Advancement of Teaching, my long-time mentor and guide, who gave so graciously and unsparingly of her time and talents to assist me in a myriad of ways, including her invaluable input in shaping the design of this project and her role as a contributing editor.

I give special thanks to John von Knorring, President of Stylus Publishing, LLC, who not only conceived the idea for this project but who also has been an outstanding collaborator as we have moved through each phase of this project.

I would like to express my gratitude to several of my former colleagues at Eastern Michigan University (EMU). In particular, I would like to thank Ronald W. Collins, Provost and Vice President for Academic Affairs, whose support enabled me to balance my professional responsibilities at the university and my role as editor of this project. I would like to thank Sandra Yee, Head of the Bruce T. Halle Library at EMU, and the many caring and helpful librarians who extended themselves to facilitate my work on this project. I would also like to thank three EMU students, Amanda Cable, Carla Tenney, and Connie Rowell, for their dedication and hard work on many facets of this project.

Many thanks to Constance Cook, Director of the Center for Research on Learning and Teaching (CRLT) at the University of Michigan, and my new colleagues at CRLT for their encouragement and assistance during the final stages of this project.

Finally, I wish to thank my husband, Tom DeZure; my children Jessica and Adam; and my parents Sidney and Eleanor Silverman, whose love and support have been unwavering.

Deborah DeZure
University of Michigan
February 2000

Publisher's Acknowledgments

Stylus wishes to thank the Helen Dwight Reid Education Foundation and Heldref Publications, the publishers of *Change* magazine, for their full support and cooperation, and for their kind permission to reproduce their copyrighted materials. The copyrights for the majority of the articles reproduced or excerpted in this volume are held by Heldref. Acknowledgment of each individual Heldref copyright is made at the back of this volume in the Article Index by Author.

Stylus also wishes to thank the following for their kind permission to reproduce the following articles to which they hold copyright:

Frances K. Barasch, "Learning in the Workplace: Stronger Support from the Unions"; Ernest L. Boyer and Arthur Levine, "A Quest for Common Learning: An Essay from the Carnegie Foundation for the Advancement of Teaching"; Kenneth A. Bruffee, "Science in a Postmodern World"; Harlan Cleveland, "Educating for the Information Society"; Amitai Etzioni, "A Remedy for Higher Education: A Year of Required National Service"; Edward B. Fiske, "The Undergraduate Hispanic Experience: A Case of Juggling Two Cultures"; D. J. Guzetta, "Education's Quiet Revolution: Changes and Challenges"; E. D. Hirsch, Jr., "A Postscript by E. D. Hirsch, Jr."; Florence Howe, "Feminist Scholarship: The Extent of the Revolution"; The Institute for Research in Higher Education for the article by The National Center for Postsecondary Improvement, "Gauging the Impact of Institutional Student-Assessment Strategies: Revolution or Evolution?"; Gene I. Maeroff, "Ties That Do Not Bind: The High School / College Connection"; Warren Bryan Martin, "Education for Character, Career and Society"; Frank B. Murray, "Teacher Education: Words of Caution About Popular Reforms"; Carol Geary Schneider and Robert Shoenberg, "Habits Hard to Break: How Persistent Features of Campus Life Frustrate Curricular Reform"; Emily Ann Smith, "Educating Head and Hands: Berea College's Labor Program."

We also wish to thank Peter Sacks for his kind permission to reproduce a condensed version of his article "Standardized Testing: Meritocracy's Crooked Yardstick." Peter Sacks is author of *Standardized Minds: The High Price of America's Testing Culture and What We Can Do to Change It*, 2000, Cambridge, Mass.: Perseus Publishing.

Special thanks are due to Ted Marchese, executive editor of *Change* and vice president of the American Association for Higher Education, for his advice and encouragement, and for his inspired introduction to Deborah DeZure; and to the AAHE for associating itself with this project.

Introduction

Deborah DeZure

The beginning of the new millennium has seen a torrent of retrospectives on every aspect of life in the 20th century. They have appeared in print, on the broadcast media, and on the World Wide Web. Most of these efforts endeavor to capture the *zeitgeist* of the era that we leave behind—and for good reason. The past has much to teach us about which traditions we need to honor and which to leave behind. Equally important, retrospectives often reveal fledgling efforts that require further development and those ideas that are still inchoate but rich with possibilities for a better and different future.

The best of these retrospectives offer fresh insights, the new knowledge born of hindsight and experience. They render interpretations that reconstruct the lessons of the past to maximize their relevance now as we plan for the future. Others reflect a penchant for nostalgia and sentiment, often for a world that never existed for the majority of us, a Normal Rockwell painting of the "good old days." Such retrospectives satisfy our need to believe that life was once comfortable, secure, and uncomplicated. They offer us an illusion that provides momentary succor but few solutions for a world changing faster than we can possibly anticipate.

Still other retrospectives provide glimpses of the past without context or commentary. They presume that documents speak for themselves without further explanation of the events portrayed: why they happened, when and to whom, the forces at work, and what happened next. They do not offer the causes and the effects, the continuities and the discontinuities. They do not help us see the synergy that occurs when events from different arenas of thought and action coalesce to lead to change. This change is sometimes revolutionary but most often evolutionary, modest but cumulative, leading us forward one small step at a time.

This collection is indeed a retrospective. It attempts to emulate the best of this genre by offering a guide through the past with commentaries and implications for the future. It focuses specifically on issues of teaching and learning in higher education during the last 30 years of the 20th century as seen through the discerning lens of *Change* magazine.

Change Magazine

Founded in 1969, *Change* has long been the vehicle by which members of the academy and those outside of it have voiced their concerns about higher education and the constellation of issues that surround it. George Bonham, editor of *Change* from its founding until 1980, clarified its intent:

> . . . *Change* is an opinion magazine, a child of journalism rather than of scholarship. From its inception, *Change* was meant to be a new kind of forum on the central issues of human development and the future of higher education. . . .
>
> *Change* is not an extension of the academic world; it is a public institution. . . . It is precisely at these junctions between the academy and the 'real world' that much of the future of higher education will be determined. . . .
>
> I'm occasionally asked why *Change* is called *Change*. . . . [H]igher education remains challenged by the need for a prolonged period of constructive adjustment to new national circumstances.
>
> In a field that to a large extent still looks at itself introspectively and distances itself from the mainstream concerns, *Change* has become a surprisingly

influential sounding board for American thoughts and ideals. And in this context our objectives are well laid out for the foreseeable future. Most of these objectives have to do with stimulation and encouragement of a pattern of education that will be more diverse and more serious, more at ease with itself politically and ideologically, more effective in the use of available resources, and less defensive about its social and pedagogical purposes. The task is not easy, of course, for fiscal as well as intellectual reasons. . . . Few people now agree as to the fundamental purposes of education. . . .

. . . Much is expected of us, often too much. We cannot build new roads where old ones have been. But we can erect road signs. . . . And we are committed, to use an old-fashioned word, to widening the idea of *Change* as a national town meeting on the education enterprise. . . .

(1976, p. 13)

Goals

The title of this collection reveals its purpose: *Learning from* Change. Its goals are threefold: (1) to capture the richness of the conversation in this ongoing national (and now international) "town meeting" about teaching and learning; (2) to illuminate these "conversations" by tracing the continuities, discontinuities, and changes over time; and (3) to suggest ways in which these trends offer lessons, opportunities, and inspiration for the future as we step into the new millennium.

Why Do We Need This Collection Now?

For the last decade, higher education has been under attack for failing to produce graduates with skills required for success in the workplace and for active participation in a democratic society. All too often, graduates cannot communicate effectively, use higher-order critical-thinking skills, work well with others, and demonstrate ethical responsibility. The charges have been harsh and inclusive, attacking the leadership, the faculty, and the students; the curriculum; the organizational structure and infrastructure; the models for evaluation of faculty, students, and institutions; the methods of instruction; and the speed and the slowness of integrating technology. These are not issues at the macro level of higher education administration or of governance. These issues are about teaching and learning: about the specifics of what we teach, to whom, why, how, and with what effects. They strike closest to the lives of teachers and students and the complex, collaborative, and communal process we call "teaching and learning."

These charges are sometimes warranted but often reflect misconceptions. One response is to clarify where we are in higher education and how we got there. This approach is not designed to perpetuate the process of laying blame; rather it is intended to help us to better assess the roots of our complex and long-standing dilemmas.

These problems will not be solved with a quick fix or with the infusion or denial of funds. The challenges reflect changes in the larger society and forces both within and without the academy that confound easy solutions. For every force and good intention that propel us forward, there are countervailing forces with different but often good intentions that resist change. Indeed, the dialectics of change, of thrust and counterthrust, of active and passive resistance, and profound structural impediments are central to every one of the "conversations" about teaching and learning over the years. The articles in this collection bear witness to these struggles, particularly those in "Curriculum," "Methods of Teaching," "Assessment," "Instructional Technology," and, most clearly, in "Promoting a Culture of Teaching," whose subject is cultural change in higher education.

Change has been exploring issues of teaching and learning for 30 years. The treatment of those issues offers a rich source of insight into the complexities of the problems and the solutions, many of which have been tried and even heralded — over and over again — but not heeded or supported. Readers of this collection will find that many of the solutions that educators find most compelling today were offered to us in the pages of *Change* decades ago, some at regular intervals. Their fate offers more than a cautionary tale. Their fate helps us to anticipate the pitfalls — the places where we must shore up the walls, remove the roadblocks, or create new pathways — if these "innovations" are to survive the next time around.

Fortunately, higher education has not stood still — sardonic metaphors of graveyards, glaciers and dinosaurs notwithstanding. There have been changes, many small but significant ones, which together now form a critical mass, enabling us to move forward, albeit slowly. These changes are chronicled in these pages and clarified in the Commentaries. They offer hope that the mighty efforts of so many have not been in vain. Together these readings offer the rich lessons of history, the ones that most bear repeating in the light of all that has changed. In the words of George Bonham, they offer "road signs" toward the future we want to create.

Intended Audience

This collection is designed for audiences both inside the academy and outside its increasingly permeable walls who want to understand key dimensions of teaching and learning in higher education. Because of the journalistic roots of *Change*, the articles are written in a style that is accessible to a wide range of readers. These include individuals within institutions of higher education — administrators, faculty across the disciplines, specialists in higher education, faculty developers and staff. In addition, this collection will assist leaders and policy makers in disciplinary, professional, and accrediting organizations, funding agencies, state and federal governments, and the media, whose understanding of higher education is crucial for its ongoing support and for informed decision-making.

Format

This collection presents over 160 landmark articles and excerpts from *Change*. They are organized into 13 broadly defined topics that capture the many voices and themes that have emerged over these 30 years. These sections are introduced in Commentaries by recognized experts in the field who contextualize and frame the articles for current readers.

These experts served as contributing editors, fulfilling three crucial roles in this endeavor: they selected the articles in their sections from among dozens on the topic that have appeared in *Change* over 30 years; they identified significant excerpts that captured the heart of an argument or a telling example; and they crafted the Commentaries to illuminate their selections and offer an integrative perspective on them.

The book concludes with an analysis of trends that thread throughout the sections and across time. The analysis traces the ebb and flow of movements, their elaboration, and their interaction with other developments in higher education and in the larger society.

Process

From the outset, this book has been a collaboration among many people. They include Theodore Marchese, editor of *Change* magazine since 1984 and Vice President of the American Association for Higher Education (AAHE); John von Knorring, President of Stylus Publishing, who conceived the idea for the collection; 14 contributing editors, all national experts in their respective fields and long-time members of AAHE; and myself.

As editor of the collection, I read all 30 years of *Change* magazine, selecting over 750 articles that addressed key issues in teaching and learning broadly defined. I identified categories and categorized articles by primary, secondary, and tertiary topics. I refined the initial 20 categories, arriving ultimately at the 13 categories that constitute the sections of this book.

Theodore Marchese, Pat Hutchings, formerly Director of the Teaching Initiative at the AAHE and now Senior Scholar at the Carnegie Foundation for the Advancement of Teaching, and I identified potential experts who were invited to participate as contributing editors for specific sections. Every one of them has a distinguished record of academic achievements and is heavily committed to numerous activities in higher education. They all graciously signed on to this project as an opportunity to review and comment on areas they have long studied and promoted and to support and recognize the significant contributions made by *Change* to the ongoing public discussion of key issues in higher education.

Approximately 20 percent of the articles fit equally well into two or more categories, in which case more than one section editor received them. Some categories had significantly more articles than others. Accordingly, some sections have more articles but shorter excerpts in an effort to accommodate the wide range of views and subtopics. In the final set of 160 articles in this collection, eight articles were selected by more than one contributing editor. These eight articles are reprinted in only one section.

Explicit criteria were used both by the editor and contributing editors to evaluate all articles. The criteria for evaluation included:

- Importance of the article in historic context
- Relevance of the article for us today
- Perspective was prophetic or predictive
- Quality of writing

Articles were rated: "high priority to include," "include if possible," "low priority to include," "don't include." If an article was recommended, reviewers were asked to indicate what portion should be used, ranging from "all" to a "small segment." The contributing editors then prioritized their selections based on the criteria for evaluation as well as additional factors, including representation of key issues in the ongoing conversation over time and diverse perspectives.

Did this process render the "best" of *Change*? Not necessarily. Would another panel of editors choose other articles, organized into other sections? Very likely. This collection does not purport to identify the "best" articles; rather it aims to capture highlights or "landmarks" in our public conversations over time about key issues in teaching and learning in higher education, and it accomplishes *that* goal very well indeed. The process relied heavily on the input and expertise of the contributing editors, who bring their own perspectives, considerable wisdom of practice, and integrative skills. In higher education, we have a long tradition of respect for expertise, and it was on the basis of their expertise that these articles were selected, organized, and interpreted.

As in many scholarly efforts, the final product reflects compromises among competing needs. Perhaps the most serious of these compromises was the use of excerpts. All of the editors, including myself, would have preferred to provide complete articles. To do so, however, would have limited opportunities to capture the range of conversations over time. We made the decision to use excerpts — some long, some short; but regardless of length, we endeavored to represent the intellectual position of the author(s) as accurately as possible.

Some excerpts were selected to capture a single powerful point; others for their rhetorical fervor; and still others for a particularly predictive or relevant comment for us today. Longer segments were included when it was critical to understand the logic of the argument as well as the thesis; in some cases, whole articles appear. Excerpts can never do full justice to the articles they represent. Readers are encouraged to obtain back issues of *Change* for the complete texts. Full citations are located at the back of this collection to facilitate that effort.

Overview of the Sections

I will close this introduction with a few comments about each of the 13 sections in this collection.

In "Promoting a Culture of Teaching," Pat Hutchings offers an interpretive framework for this collection, using the concept of "culture" to help us make sense of the evolution of higher education with regard to issues of teaching and learning. There are several topics under this broad umbrella, including faculty roles and rewards, infrastructure and epistemological issues that both define and limit change, teaching as community property, faculty development as a communal endeavor, and the redefinition of scholarship with particular emphasis on the scholarship of teaching.

In "Portraits of Students: A Gallery Tour," Patricia Cross guides us through four galleries that capture the portrayal of student issues in *Change* during the past 30 years: the student protest movement of the late 1960s, open admissions, affirmative action, vocationalism, and the student-as-consumer, each with its own trajectory.

In "Curriculum," Jerry Gaff describes the full menu of curricular options and approaches during the past 30 years: the core curriculum; the major as it reflects the hegemony of faculty specializations; and the advent of multiculturalism, with black studies, ethnic studies, women's studies, and global studies. He leads us through the "culture wars." He identifies the trends in developmental education and the quest for higher-order critical-thinking skills, and he concludes with a focus on liberal education.

In "The Origins of Contemporary Learning Communities: Residential Colleges, Experimental Colleges, and Living-Learning Communities," Zelda Gamson traces the origins of contemporary learning communities from their roots in colonial America's "collegiate way of living," through living-learning communities, experimental colleges, and residential colleges, often embedded within larger institutional models. She identifies characteristics that link all of these models and their newest incarnations in current learning communities, including first-year programs and on-line discussion groups. The articles describe institutions and programs that have attempted to integrate their institutional mission, curriculum, methods of teaching, community connections, academic affairs, and student affairs. These programs had varying degrees of success and longevity, but they all provide instructive case studies as we explore the potential of learning communities today.

In "Work, Service, and Community Connections," Alfredo G. de los Santos Jr. traces four related themes during the past 30 years: inclusion of adult learners and life-long learning; work and work/study as part of the collegiate experience; increased community connections, including high school/college connections; and service learning, both co-curricular and academic service learning, as part of efforts to renew a commitment to civic life.

In "Philosophy, Psychology, and Methods of Teaching," Wilbert McKeachie takes us from broader issues about the goals of college teaching to studies that debunk widely held myths about effective teaching. He underscores the efficacy of the paradigm shift from an emphasis on teaching to learning and concludes with two productive instructional methods: discussion-method teaching and cooperative learning.

"Methods of Teaching" features articles that discuss "generic" principles of teaching. In contrast, the next three sections include articles that locate the discussion of teaching and learning in a disciplinary context.

In "Visiting Across the Disciplines — *Change* and the National Teaching Project," James Wilkinson focuses primarily on the National Teaching Project. Supported by a FIPSE grant and the disciplinary associations, *Change* published several issues devoted to exemplary models of teaching in specific disciplines.

"Science Education Reform — Getting Out the Word," by Daniel Goroff, traces the evolution of the public conversation on reform in science and math education that began in the 1980s. The articles in *Change* in these decades emphasized science and math education, reflecting in part the national sense of urgency about the declining recruitment and retention of students in these discipines. These articles, intended for a wide audience of both scientists and non-scientists, are journalistic in style and readily accessible.

An important exception to the post-1970s focus on articles on science and math is seen in "Professional, Graduate, and Teacher Education: Criticism and Reform," by Joan S. Stark and Malcolm A. Lowther. They note that, while these three areas are not synonymous, they do have common issues that benefit from discussion together. The commentary places professional, graduate, and teacher education in a larger context, responding to factors inside and outside of higher education, including accrediting agencies, assessment, national reports, mandates, and the marketplace.

In "Assessing Student Learning," Barbara Wright traces the development and continuity of the assessment movement in higher education. We see efforts to define and promote the assessment movement, identify forces of resistance, discuss mandates, and examine struggles of implementation as well as success stories, concluding with studies that tell us how we are doing. In the area of assessment, in particular, *Change* has not only reflected the key issues but also taken a leadership role in defining the terms of the debate.

In "Evaluating College Teaching: Myth and Reality," Peter Seldin addresses prevailing myths that continue to dominate perceptions in higher education despite the considerable body of research about teaching effectiveness and productive ways to assess it. The articles chronicle the evolution from concern and confusion about the validity of evaluating college teaching to evidence of the widespread use of evaluation practices today.

In "Teacher Narratives," Diane Gillespie contextualizes the articles in this section, most of which are stories about the authors' experiences as teachers. They represent a unique genre, appearing frequently in the early 1970s and again in the 1990s. In one sense, they represent efforts to "go public" with one's teaching, but beyond that they often reveal a personal quest that shares the author's transformation as a teacher and as a person when confronted with the challenges of teaching. These narratives have a special place in this collection, just as they have had in *Change*, because they personalize and validate the human dimensions of social and educational change.

Last, but certainly not least, is the section on educational technology. In "Media and Technology: *Plus ça change*," Kenneth C. Green takes us through 30 years of technology, from experiments with media and television to distance learning, computers, and the Internet. Although many of us think of technology as one of the great revolutions of the last 30 years, Kenneth Green underscores the recurrence of similar challenges and pitfalls with the introduction of each new form of technology. He reminds us as scholars to use the rich literature on higher education, including the literature on educational technology, to learn from the lessons of the past lest we continue to repeat the mistakes of those who went before us. The articles in this section are rich with suggestions and solutions, the "road signs" that George Bonham promised us two decades ago.

Infusion of Topics

Two topics of vital importance in higher education do not have their own sections in this collection. Indeed, they are so important and so central to teaching and learning that they appear in all sections: "Faculty Issues" and "Commitment to Diversity."

In the case of "Faculty Issues," faculty perspectives are ubiquitous. Even the section entitled "Portraits of Students" integrates faculty views of students. Faculty are central to the teaching/learning enterprise, and no section was needed to ensure that their voices would be heard.

The decision about whether to create a separate section on "Commitment to Diversity" raised different issues. Infusion of diversity into higher education is a battle that continues to be fought on campuses and in the courts. Diversity in higher education is not assured, and diverse voices are not always heard. To segregate diversity issues into a separate section had the potential to marginalize and parse it out too neatly and too easily from the rest of teaching and learning. As editor, I had a stack of articles categorized as "Diversity Issues," but every one of those articles had one or more other designations, including "Curriculum," "Students," "Methods of Teaching," "Assessing Student Learning," and "Service Learning." The advantage to creating a section on "Diversity" was that it would have enabled us to see more readily the range and evolution of articles on this topic, but it also would have systematically removed all or most of the articles on diversity issues from the rest of the collection. In the end, the decision to infuse diversity articles throughout the collection was an intentional, symbolic, and strategic choice to underscore the conviction that diversity is not the discrete responsibility or domain of any one sector of higher education. Because the commitment to diversity is one that belongs to all of us, you will find articles on "Commitment to Diversity" in every section of this collection—where we think they belong.

Reference

Bonham, G. (1976, June) Notes from the editor. *Change,* 8(5) 13.

PROMOTING A CULTURE OF TEACHING AND LEARNING

Pat Hutchings

When the American Association for Higher Education (AAHE) launched its Teaching Initiatives program in 1989, those of us involved in shaping the effort announced that our work would aim "to foster a culture of teaching." The phrase was not new, certainly; the idea that culture was an important aspect of an organization or community was increasingly in the air, and it seemed a productive way to think about higher education. The AAHE program encouraged a culture in which teaching would be "talked about, inquired into, documented, reviewed, and continuously improved." Our use of the term was broad, a synonym for "climate" or "environment." As evidenced by the title of this section, the term has had some sticking power. Perhaps that is because it is a convenient catchall, capacious enough to contain whatever topics we care about. Indeed, in his recent Charles Homer Haskins lecture, Clifford Geertz calls "culture" "not only an essentially contested concept [but] a multiply defined one, multiply employed, ineradicably imprecise" (1999, p. 9). However, my thesis is that the "culture of teaching" has stayed with us as a phrase (and a goal) because it is beneficial to look at teaching through the lens of culture; in doing so, we learn lessons and see possibilities we otherwise might miss.

First, to look at teaching through the lens of culture is to shift our focus beyond method and technique. I do not mean to suggest that method and technique are not worthy topics; they are where most of us enter the conversation and where as faculty we focus our energies on a daily basis: What is the best way to get my students talking about the novel I am teaching this afternoon? Can I adapt what my colleague down the hall has been doing with small-group techniques? If I go this route, what is the right principle for constructing student groups? And so forth. However, looking through the "culture lens," one might step back and ask a different set of questions: how teachers think and make decisions about method, the degree to which we share frameworks and goals for doing so, how we exchange with colleagues what we know and do as teachers, whether and how our knowledge and practice are made public in ways that can be built upon. These are "bigger" questions than those of method, questions about the web of beliefs and behaviors that shape what faculty members actually do in the teaching and learning settings that constitute their work. Although this aspect of culture is not new, it has assumed growing prominence in recent decades, as *Change* witnesses. The themes of being more public about teaching, of communities for exchange and knowledge-building about teaching and learning both within and across fields, are long-standing motifs. It is interesting, for example, to note that some of the scholarly societies were writing about them several decades ago.

A subset of these larger cultural themes—one that figures heavily in the pages of *Change*—is the reward system. One may debate the power of different kinds of motivation, but it is hard not to see that the weight of teaching in promotion and tenure affects the amount of intellectual energy and time faculty are willing to spend on the educational enterprise. This aspect of the culture of teaching has been increasingly front and center for the past decade as campuses examine faculty roles and rewards and struggle with ways to bring more attention to teaching and learning—through new policies for evaluation, more robust forms of evidence and documentation, the introduction of peer review strategies, and changes in promotion and tenure guidelines.

A focus on culture also points to the larger curricular context for teaching. When we think of teaching, what's typically conjured up is the drama (or, on a bad day, the boredom) of that time between 9:00 and 9:50 on Tuesday morning; we think, that is, of the classroom and about what goes on inside it on any given day. But the reality is that teaching—and learning—is a process that unfolds over time as students move through a designed set of experiences, be it a single course or a set of courses in a program or departmental curriculum. A culture of teaching thus brings into focus not only what happens in the classroom but also course and curriculum design, program context and goals, and the learning that results for students as they move through the educational experience, over time. It's a bigger picture than the one traditionally conjured up by the word "teaching."

At the same time, culture points us toward the "small picture"—the particulars of teaching and learning to which anthropologists might attend as "local knowledge." Though we often talk about teaching in generic terms, it is always a here-and-now phenomenon: a particular teacher, with particular students, in a particular time and place, engaged with particular material and ideas and purposes. Attending to these particulars is a counter to the recent raft of good-practice principles and criteria checklists for effective teaching—not that these are not helpful but that they are made richer when complicated by the concrete realities of practice. Indeed, one might say that teaching excellence means making choices informed by an exquisite sense of the particulars of the occasion. Not surprisingly, then, stories, cases, ethnographies, and other narrative forms are, for many readers, the most vivid, telling accounts of teaching. Capturing rather than washing out the particulars reminds us that there are many teaching cultures, rather than a single one.

Finally, the concept of culture is important for understanding the process of change itself. The emergence of "the scholarship of teaching"—a phrase that appears increasingly in the pages of *Change* and that Lee Shulman and I describe in the September/October 1999 issue—is a process that entails "a kind of 'going meta,' in which faculty frame and systematically investigate questions related to student learning: the conditions under which it occurs, what it looks like, and how to deepen it, and so forth—and do so with an eye not only to improving their own classroom but to advancing practice beyond it" (p. 13). The interesting question is how this idea—which embodies a number of themes highlighted above—has emerged.

The answer, for many in higher education, is the 1990 report by Ernest Boyer, *Scholarship Reconsidered*, setting forth a broader definition of scholarship that includes teaching. Arguing that excellent teaching entails the same habits of mind that characterize other types of scholarly work, Boyer states that teaching should receive greater recognition and reward—an agenda significantly advanced by the 1997 followup report *Scholarship Assessed* by Charles Glassick, Mary Taylor Huber, and Gene I. Maeroff. Clearly these two Carnegie publications have been key catalysts; their language has entered our lexicon. However, it is important to see that their effect is a function of other developments as well. For starters, one might mention Donald Schön's (1995) work, which also tackles and attempts to broaden our conception of scholarship, looking especially at the epistemological implications of this shift.

A different line of development focuses on a conception of teaching. The argument here (Lee Shulman is its clearest proponent in *Change*) is that teaching is best understood not as technique but as an enactment of the teacher's understanding of what it means to know the field deeply—and how that understanding develops. As such, teaching needs to be reconnected to scholarship and to the scholarly communities through habits of documentation, exchange, and peer review; such processes are not only essential to a greater valuing of teaching but to the advancement of the profession and practice of the field as well.

Another stream of work (drawing on both Boyer and Shulman) is peer collaboration and review of teaching. Most notable here, perhaps, is the multi-campus national initiative undertaken by the AAHE from 1994–98. Entitled "From Idea to Prototype," the AAHE project brought together teams of faculty members who developed nine strategies for making their work as teachers available to one another, whether for individual growth and improvement or for personnel decision-making. As reports from the project make clear, for many faculty the opportunity to talk with colleagues about their teaching and their students' learning, to be part of a "culture of teaching and learning," and to find colleagueship around this important aspect of their professional lives met a deeply felt need. These faculty members do not necessarily talk about their work as the scholarship of teaching, but they are clearly moving in that direction: looking carefully at their practice, learning from it, and sharing what they are learning with their scholarly peers.

The scholarship of teaching also has been shaped by student outcomes assessment, particularly that aspect of assessment that focuses on the classroom. Though many faculty members have been skeptical about external mandates for assessment at the institutional level, the principle that we might be more purposeful about whether our students are learning what we think we are teaching has caught fire in many settings. Indeed, assessment has helped to make the idea that faculty might examine their own practice in its relation to impact a natural, even inevitable, idea. It has in this way helped shape the language of the current Carnegie Foundation program, the Carnegie Academy for the Scholarship of Teaching and Learning.

My point here is not to spin out a full-blown history of the scholarship of teaching but to show that this emergent concept and practice draws upon *multiple* histories. The scholarship of teaching (and, yes, learning) is not a story of systemic reform, or of some single, powerful action-forcing event, agency, or charismatic leader. Rather, it is the story of a gradual convergence of themes from multiple sources and lines of work. Parker Palmer might talk about its emergence as an example of what he calls "a movement approach to change" (1992, p. 10). Larry Cuban, from his recent study of research and teaching at Stanford, might invoke "strategic incrementalism"—"a series of small but high profile improvements" aimed at a common purpose (1999, p. 204).

More to the point of this essay on the culture of teaching—as I am reminded by my colleague Mary Huber, an anthropologist—one might invoke Clifford Geertz's famous definition of culture as "webs of significance" we ourselves have "spun" (1973, p. 5). In this sense, culture is both what makes change difficult and a process of development (as in "cultivation," or the kind of "culturing" that goes on in a petri dish) in which we are agents. Seen in this way, the kind of work featured in this section must be understood as long-term, requiring patience, even doggedness. To put it more graphically, it is, as someone once told me, like "nailing jello to the wall," messy, non-linear, never finished. Most important, promoting a culture that values teaching and learning must be understood as collaborative work, the power of which lies not only in the particular developments featured in this section but also in our ability to connect them, to weave the various strands together, to see the whole—which is, of course, precisely what *Change* has helped us to do.

References

Boyer, E. L. (1990). *Scholarship reconsidered: Priorities of the professoriate*. Princeton, New Jersey: Carnegie Foundation for the Advancement of Teaching.

Cuban, L. (1999). *How scholars trumped teachers: Change without reform in university curriculum, teaching, and research, 1890–1990*. New York, NY: Teachers College Press.

Geertz, C. (1999). *A life of learning*. Charles Homer Haskins Lecture for 1999. American Council of Learned Societies Occasional Paper, No. 45.

Geertz, C. (1973). Thick description: Toward an interpretive theory of culture. In *The interpretation of cultures*. New York: Basic Books.

Glassick, C. E., Huber, M. T., and Maeroff, G. I. (1997). *Scholarship assessed: Evaluation of the professoriate*. San Francisco: Jossey-Bass. Carnegie Foundation for the Advancement of Teaching.

Hutchings, P., & Shulman, L. S. (1999, September/October). The scholarship of teaching: New elaborations, new developments. *Change, 31*, 11–15.

Palmer, P. J. (1992, March/April). Divided no more: A movement approach to educational reform. *Change, 24*, 10–17.

Schön, D. A. (1995, November/December). The new scholarship requires a new epistemology: Knowing-in-action. *Change, 27*, 26–34.

January/February 1971

Who's in Charge?

Peter Shaw

The agitation for teaching reform which has followed the student disturbances of the past few years bears the credentials of a long and respectable university tradition of bettering the lot of students. The youthfulness of many of the faculty reformers, however, and their consuming dissatisfaction with their own teaching performances, suggest that this movement has more to do with the needs of the junior faculty themselves than those of the students. When those needs are translated into teaching practice, they express themselves in an encounter group or group therapy atmosphere that bears little educational utility beyond exorcizing part of the young professor's guilt at having so recently joined the "Establishment." The young reformer's indictment of himself, one understands, is meant to stand as an indictment of the entire system, and the reader is expected to admire the confessant for his candor rather than to abuse him for his former incompetence. But to my mind, though he thinks of himself as a critic of the system and something of a rebel, his proposals, which have been all too sympathetically received, have little to do with education.

His indictment of college teaching, significantly enough, is usually delivered in the form of an autobiographical memoir: the young reformer characteristically does not write tracts, pamphlets, or even essays containing formal proposals, but rather personal reminiscences. His testimonial recounts, in the manner of a reformed alcoholic, his past degradations, his awakening, and his more recent conversion. He candidly admits the difficulties of living the reformed life: his failures to function effectively, the absence of the old gratifications, his occasional nips of the old academic brew, and even binges of returning to accepted values and coherence.

The memoir begins in graduate school. During the 1950s, as a graduate student, the young professor was seduced into accepting the "Establishment" method of scholarship and study in his discipline. In the course of time, he became dissatisfied because, he now believed, the traditional approach prevented him from relating his own interests to the interests of his students. After having served for several years as a graduate assistant, and junior faculty member teaching introductory courses, he began—just when he was permitted to add one or two advanced courses to his program—to find his teaching "dull" and devoid of "relevance."

At this crisis, he devised an experiment with one of his classes, at the end of which he asked for written evaluations from his students. He is by no means entirely satisfied with the results, for, as some of the adverse comments by his students which he forthrightly quotes suggest, the course occupied much of its time floundering in search of a subject and in lack of student-teacher and student-student communication. However, he offers a description of this experimental semester as his contribution to the crisis caused by what he takes to be a general university dissatisfaction with the way in which classes are usually taught. To begin with, he threw open his class to student initiative. He emphasized his own role as that of an occasional umpire and guide, though he did at the outset present materials which he thought the class would find relevant. Though he believes that he attempted to let the students work out their own scheme of values, he "confronted" them often, and made them "relate" to one another in a personal way. He is aware of the growing interest in group dynamics—sensitivity sessions and the like—and he incorporated some of their techniques in this class.

Looking back on his experiment, he has to conclude that, for all its longueurs and discontinuities, it represented the most genuinely satisfying teaching experience, and he hopes, learning experience for his students, of his life.

The question that raises itself about teaching experiments such as these is not so much how small or great a contribution they represent as it is that of why such experiments have become popular at just this time. For the most remarkable feature of the new educational reform lies in its historical timing. The generation of young professors who were educated during the fifties studied under the most progressive conditions then known in American education. They taught, during the sixties, under still more permissive conditions. Before their time, college instruction lay in the hands of a small and undistinguished class—an elite, if not an elite of merit. With few exceptions, college instruction reflected the disengagement from life of hoary, pedantic specialists, most of whom seemed to be cast-off younger sons of the wealthy, or social misfits of one kind or another.

. . . Given their experience as students, and the regard in which they are held by their students, how is it that a group of younger academics has come to such disaffection with the academy at just this moment? Ostensibly, they have reacted to the failure of the university to effect pressing, necessary changes in American foreign policy and American society. Yet the terms in which their disillusionment expresses itself are invariably personal, having to do with a feeling of impotence in the classroom.

If their feeling of ineffectuality has persisted despite the politicizing of the university, its cause may be traced to the nature of the teaching experience of today's young faculty. As the years necessary to gain a Ph.D. have stretched out and candidates have begun to come from families which could not independently support them, colleges have had to find alternate ways to support candidates for the degree. The main solution has been to award teaching assistantships, whereby the graduate student could earn a salary by conducting the introductory course in his field while working part-time toward his degree. Not surprisingly, to teach such courses for a number of years, without the leaven of the more satisfying advanced courses given to full-time teachers, eventually proves discouraging. By their nature, introductory courses offer much in the way of new concepts and new information to the student, with correspondingly less time for original thought than in advanced courses. The basic course in English, the field from which the preponderance of experimental reforms have come, is the most frustrating of all, and its frustrations in particular have influenced teaching reform.

Freshman English has baffled instructors for a hundred years. Though each new generation of teachers has experimented with one or more new approaches to it, no one has ever come up with a satisfactory formula. Consequently there have been periodic demands that Freshman English be abolished. The university at large, however, has continued to require it on the grounds that it improves student writing. The university has been right, in this case, and so have the teachers. It does seem that no matter who teaches it, and no matter how it is taught, Freshman English, as long as the students continue to write between six and ten themes per semester, results in improving student writing. . . .

. . . The personalizing young instructor, who accuses himself of having been an authoritarian before his conversion, remains authoritarian in his implied demand that everyone in his classes participate in his experience and his vision. Nor does the new system of enfranchising student-group values diminish his authority. He has gone from his original method of undercutting conventional wisdom by submitting the world to his personal judgment to undermining it by submission to the judgments of his pupils. But in both cases he has been the one to decide where value stems from, and each time he has affirmed that its source lies in subjectivity.

By now it should be apparent that we are dealing not with a movement for reform, but with a form of self-expression. In lower education, proposals to concentrate on teaching quality and techniques would have to be taken seriously. There, the first can be controlled through practice teaching and observations of class sessions, the latter through centralized curriculum planning and checks on teachers' plan books. No such intrusion is possible on the conduct of college classes, either in the manner in which they are conducted or the content of their curricula. The experimenter-reformers, then, are not seriously calling for change, since change of the sort they advocate is impossible. They are rather advertising their own sensitivities and concerns.

It is true that the academic freedom which prevents interference of the sort that could impose these reforms has come under attack by the politically engaged. But their very attack is best calculated to hurt the interests of those who mount it. Without academic freedom, the teaching experiments which the young reformers describe would never have been allowed to take place.

Ultimately, the proposals of the young reformers reduce themselves to an attack on excellence. Whatever a teacher may know is evaluated not by the test of argument, but by the sole judgment of those who have come to learn from him. The subject and its texts in which he has prepared himself are rejected in favor of readings that appeal not to any general standard of value but to the presumed popular tastes of his students (though why they should be taught what they already understand better than their teacher, remains a mystery).

There may seem little to choose between the hide-bound traditionalism that continues to beset much of university teaching and the mindlessness of what proposes to replace it. Yet one is led to wonder how the university can have survived under its old system, even to producing the present generation of reforming faculty. On what theory and in what actuality did those incompetent, cast-off younger sons conduct their classes without utterly crushing everyone who passed through them? The answer is simple. They taught the major texts of the Western tradition. If a student was lucky enough to read those texts under an inspired professor, so went the old thinking, so much the better. But if he had to read them with one of the incompetents, the results could not be terribly bad, since the primary business was to read those books. The new uneasiness about what goes on in the classroom is not a symptom of dissatisfaction with the workings of the educational process; it reflects a loss of faith in the Western tradition. . . .

. . . To say that the proposed reform of teaching in higher education stems from the grievances of younger faculty rather than the interests of students should not dismiss the subject. For the grievances of the younger faculty are real, and they deserve better than the emotional translation into "reform" which they have so far received. The issues of working conditions and pay, to begin with, need to be resolved. Secondly, younger faculty should be given more opportunities to teach advanced courses. They now spend several years in training to learn how to conduct academic research, only to find themselves confronted with the teaching of a demanding elementary course. In return for assuming this burden, they deserve some of the compensations that are so enviably a part of the senior faculty's prerogative: time, dollars, and advanced courses in which the scholar can come closer to working with the materials of his own research.

To dismiss the reforms offered by younger faculty is not to suggest that teaching may not be improved. Even an academic conservative like myself may conduct an experiment. Mine has been to join my class once a week with that of a colleague whose class is following the same reading list as mine. At that meeting we have a discussion between the two professors. This plan has the opposite tendency from current reform. Rather than pitching the discourse to the students' level, it attempts to let the professors speak in, and the student attend to, a style of talk closer to that which the professors use among themselves than the classroom usually permits. Some would say that such a proceeding will create a class atmosphere to exacerbate the already baleful influence that the "old" have on the young. My colleague and I, in contrast, look to its possible beneficial effects. Such differences of opinion promise to continue between those who are questioning and those who are defending the traditional disciplines. The reformers, however, threaten academic freedom when, in effect, they advocate the imposition of their own approach on others. The two parties must learn to live with one another, which in this case means that the young reformers will have to turn their attention from the ambience of the classroom to more substantive concerns. Otherwise, they are embarked on a campaign of coercion, not reform.

Community Colleges
Helping Teachers Teach Better

Leslie Purdy

Helping teachers improve their skills is becoming an increasingly complex task . . .

One of the serious flaws in in-service training is its one-sidedness — administrators are telling faculty members that "you have to change your techniques." In-service is too often based on a "we-they" approach: "we," the administrators (often with the help of outside consultants), are telling "you," the faculty, what "you" should do to improve instruction. Rarely have faculty been given an opportunity to define their problems and find solutions. . . .

What are the components of a faculty development program which aims to support and encourage growth of professional faculty? I completed an in-depth study of the faculty members at a community college that revealed some characteristics of faculty as individuals and as group members that may provide clues to effective faculty development programs. . . . First, a high degree of teacher colleagueship was found to exist on the campus. Personal friendships among the faculty provided both support and ideas for experimentation in teaching approaches. Faculty would often ignore information on innovative practices presented at an orientation session or workshop unless a colleague had tried the new machine or technique and gave a personal recommendation.

Thus, the college that would generate change would do well to provide opportunities for frequent interaction among teachers who are willing to experiment with new ideas and techniques. These instructors will both challenge and support each other as well as be models or stimuli for others. . . .

The Sociology of Teaching and the Teaching of Sociology

Lawrence J. Rhoades and Hans O. Mauksch

One of the perplexing problems confronting any attempt to improve undergraduate teaching is the absence within academic disciplines of collegial communities based primarily on teaching. Though such communities abound among researchers and scholars, teaching appears to be largely an individual enterprise rather than a collective one. The explanation for that seems to be in the social organization of academic disciplines, where the paramount value is the production of knowledge for consumption by the disciplines' own members. This value has been institutionalized in the authority, status, and ranking systems of these professions. Consequently, disseminating knowledge to laymen becomes merely a byproduct of the more fundamental process in which academic disciplines are engaged, and this situation has important ramifications for undergraduate education. Although laymen frequently assert that academicians live in ivory towers, professors are realistic enough to recognize the career implications of the academic value system. Career mobility depends not on teaching excellence but on research and publication, for only these can be converted into a visible professional reputation.

Informal and formal communication channels among teachers, however, are notable by their absence; teachers are isolated, largely invisible. This lack of significant external reward and collegial interaction means the teaching effort must be based on intrinsic rewards. Unfortunately, teachers find it difficult to maintain their motivation because of the negative feedback they receive from colleagues and students. Colleagues complain because teaching is not seen as directly supporting highly valued activities, and they point out that "one should not break his back to become a second-class citizen." Students are disgruntled because teachers, lacking the necessary skills, are frequently inept in the classroom; teaching skills are not formally acquired because they are regarded as natural endowments rather than learned capacities. In addition, working conditions faced by most teachers are so far from the idealized professional atmosphere and student relationships they have experienced in their graduate training that they become disillusioned.

Several years ago, the Council of the American Sociological Association (ASA) recognized this situation and its own responsibility to stimulate and improve instruction in sociology. As a result, the Council encouraged the development of a Section on Undergraduate Education as a first step toward increasing the recognition of teaching as an intellectually stimulating, professionally worthy, and constitutionally required activity of the Association. In addition, the Council later provided financial resources for a workshop aimed at creating a proposal to improve undergraduate instruction. . . . The ASA Project on Teaching Undergraduate Sociology has been a going enterprise ever since. . . . The Project has sought to (1) organize an extensive network of interaction among sociologists committed to teaching; (2) develop institutionalized communication channels for teaching-related information; (3) assist, support, and recognize teachers of sociology; and (4) promote the development, production, and distribution of teaching materials.

January 1980

Inside Room 307

Teaching: A Profession of Possibility

Theodore L. Gross

. . . When I began my graduate studies at Columbia University in 1955 and my teaching career at City College in 1958, the traditional distinction was still made between scholarship and teaching. My contemporaries and I read deeply and broadly in our fields and tried, as far as possible, to bring our learning into a classroom of students whose career goals, largely in civil service and teaching, were far more clearly defined than they are now.

At City College of New York in the late 1950s a typical course load for a young English instructor included three writing classes and one in the history of British and American literature. Elective courses were taught by senior faculty to students preparing to be schoolteachers and college professors. We rarely taught the subjects we had studied intensely in graduate school. At the outset there was a clear division between teaching and the scholarly publication efforts upon which our careers depended.

The external prestige of the department naturally depended on scholarship. Indeed, a rather ordinary teacher who served the department and the college in a perfunctory way but published with some distinction could advance to the full professorship with little difficulty. But within the department there was extraordinary pressure to be an impressive teacher—extraordinary precisely because it was not formally codified or measured. One received tenure after three years of full-time employment. There was no union and the members of the appointments committee, especially the chairman, exercised momentous power. They visited classes and evaluated teaching seriously. A sizable number of faculty spent endless hours with students at the expense of their personal scholarship and they created an informal hierarchy of values. If a young professor wanted the respect of his colleagues, he taught well. Denial of the value system meant exclusion from honor students and from a social and moral and professional community. For a novice seeking acceptance into this circle, the price of concentrating on self-centered scholarship was too dear.

The system worked fairly well because most of us had dissertations that could be converted into first books or extended articles, earning us tenure and at least two promotions. Then we took some time off to complete a new book for the full professorship. The system also succeeded because the faculty really did care about their students. Every department had its cadre of majors and something like a connection could be made between the world of learning and the world of work. English majors became schoolteachers or professors; English majors chose prelaw or premed. In 1970 there were 700 English majors in a college of 20,000; in 1978 there were 70 out of 15,000. Throughout the fifties there was a system of controls—department-wide examinations in basic writing and in literature, a department-wide syllabus, common texts—that monitored teaching and inevitably resulted in comparative judgments of every teacher's competence.

In the early 1960s these conditions began to break apart. When the number of required courses diminished, controls of measurement were relaxed. When individual paperbacks replaced larger texts in the classrooms, another control was gone. Then a graduate school was established in the academic megalopolis called the City University of New York and divided loyalties between scholarship and teaching were further strained: Local control of faculty, with its stress on classroom teaching, was loosened still more. The graduate school matched those of Columbia and New York University in its application of rigorous standards and served ultimately to underline the need for scholarship in each of the senior and community colleges. Graduate students found early employment in the colleges of CUNY and the system seemed large enough to accommodate the needs of both administrators and students.

But in this same period a student revolution was brewing that called into question the strict training of graduate schools. Those whom the graduate students taught wanted relevance—and so did the new crop of graduate students. The needs of undergraduates began to change too. With the advent of open admissions in 1969 the classroom teacher confronted far more foreign-born students, minorities, and young people who needed to learn basic skills. The distance between the professional preparation of graduate students and the actual profession they would practice—more often characterized as a job—widened significantly.

Academic schizophrenia resulted as the classroom teacher found himself caught between competing demands. At City College of New York we attempted to narrow the gap between personal scholarship and the public classroom by holding seminars on the pedagogy of basic writing for PhD candidates and by creating a master of arts in teaching for the new scholar and teacher in urban education. Some PhD candidates, intensely involved with basic writing, changed their dissertation topics to reflect their classroom experiences; subjects dealing with rhetorical problems became more evident. But the teaching of a new student body between 1970 and 1976 was so demanding that the connections could not be wholly made. Throughout their struggle toward tenure these graduate students and young teachers were measured in the most conventional way. An article on Spencer's *Faerie Queene* in *PMLA* still counted far more than one on pedagogy in *College English*.

How confused our so-called standards had become was dramatized by the brief but brilliant career of the late Mina Shaughnessy. The most impressive figure in the field of basic writing at City College—and, in the eyes of most scholars, at any college—she did not have a PhD. Hired at City College in 1966, she became the administrator of a prebaccalaureate program, then of the entire basic writing program, and finally of the CUNY-wide writing program. Throughout the late sixties and early seventies she wrote long memos that clarified the classroom problems of basic writing teachers; these memos eventually resulted in her book, *Errors and Expectations*. But her efforts met with great resistance in the rewards system of the college, even though her work was directed at the heart of the problem confronting most colleges in this country. Finally she was promoted, but largely because of her unusual superiority and because the college needed her so badly. She became the exception rather than the rule.

Let us not delude ourselves. The conditions for genuine basic research in any field exist in only a few wealthy major universities. Most institutions cannot afford professors who work only with doctoral candidates. Most colleges cherish those few scholars who manage to do impressive original work despite the taxpayers' demands of teaching and service; but the vast majority of professors are not given the time or the resources to labor at the frontier of the profession. To the extent that a college permits only conventional scholarship to determine advancement, professors will too often sacrifice teaching, churning out tedious writing in esoteric journals that help very few people — certainly not the students who come every day to class.

The majority of writing by college teachers is, after all, secondary research: commentary, reflection, criticism. When it enhances classroom teaching, it can be extremely valuable. But we have come to a strange pass in the history of education when administration, scholarship, research, college and community service — almost *anything* — carries greater prestige than the classroom experience. We have created an odd distortion in higher education, with swollen administrative bureaucracies and countless extracurricular activities. Yet it is the classroom, the give-and-take of people learning, on which everything else depends.

Teaching is a selfless art. One surrenders to an experience that seems evanescent and difficult to measure. No series of books stands on the shelf at the end of a career to say, I accomplished this at 30, that at 40. What remains — if one is lucky — is a returning student who might remember to say, "You changed my life — you influenced me. . . ." But most students forget — so that what really remains, beyond praise and recognition, is the deeply satisfying sense that one's profession matters.

That profession may be frustrating. Students may become truants or grow bored or turn disruptive — but everyone, especially the teacher, knows that this profession matters to the survival of our communities, to the fundamental health of our society. There is something pristine about the relationship between teacher and student; Mark Hopkins's famous observation — that a university is a teacher and a student at two ends of a log — still carries a truth that everybody recognizes.

Teachers may have varying views on unions and affirmative action; they may attribute the decline of prestige in classroom teaching to different forces in our society — television, the breakdown of authority in the family, drugs and violence, the politics of education, racial tensions; one can draw up a list of grievances that seems endless. But anyone who ever had a measure of idealism as he entered a classroom, who felt a flutter of fear as he faced a group of students, knows how rewarding it is to achieve success in that room and how gratifying to provide deep insight for someone who wants to learn. At that moment each of us digs into his own character for those qualities that inform great teaching and tries to bring to the surface these attributes of his performance as a classroom teacher.

September/October 1990

What We Talk About When We Talk About Teaching

Robert Hahn

When we talk about teaching, what are we really talking about? What do we learn about our subject, about ourselves, from listening to what is said and not said, the words we use and the silences behind the words? What we hear, expressed in an interplay of meanings, are our doubts and our aspirations, the fears that plague us and the hopes that sustain.

. . . When we talk about teaching, we talk about art as if it were science; about the devalued as if it were esteemed; and about defeat as if it were victory.

These substitutions may occur separately or in conjunction. For example, when we give the Teacher of the Year Award (with banquet, speech, and standing ovation) to a person who is overworked, underpaid, and undervalued both in the specific community (where colleagues look disdainfully at a lionized teacher), and the larger community of our corporate culture (which is indifferent), we do our best to talk about the devalued as if it were esteemed. When we talk about accountability, about evidence that learning outcomes are achieved, in the face of declining literacy and uncertain results, we try to clothe our anxieties in the language of a possible victory.

When we describe an art in the language of science, we cloak our own doubtful efforts in words evoking esteem: the language of empiricism, evidence, and data. We take a random, groping, intuitive process and drape it in words evoking a realm of the precise and the fixed: the language of "hard" science (at least to the ears of envious non-scientists), blended with the language of "management science," from the top-down, nononsense world of setting goals and getting results. . . .

. . . What we find are languages borrowed from business and management; from engineering and architecture; from laboratory science and experimental psychology. It is a language of objectives, goals, and measurement, a language of the controlled experiment, of variables held constant, a reassuring world structured to assure results. . . .

Nevertheless, the world this language tries to envision (let's call it, summarily, "the circumstances that create effective teaching") is a world in which the variables are famously variable: intuition and inspiration, accident and chance, magic and passion. . . . Who does not remember at least one occasion in one course, when sitting in the classroom filled us with some of the awe and total attention usually reserved for the church, the theater, the first glimpse of the Acropolis, or the love-at-first-sight candle-lit dinner? It is an experience we remember all of our lives—that magic class with a great teacher—and we remember it because it was so rare. Who knows what impossible mix of training, experience, knowledge, honesty, skill, passion, money, textbooks, architecture, class-size, timing, weather, and luck it took to make the experience possible. . . .

When we use a language of management and science to speak of teaching that reaches for such inspirational moments, we do so not out of blindness or mere fashion but out of need. We know that effective teaching is at base dependent on the artful and the intuitive, on passion and chance, but we know also that the enterprise of teaching in its largest sense is too essential to depend on random encounters. Thus we do, whether we like it or not, need to manage, motivate, and design environments; we need to know what we're doing, and demonstrate that we do, and use a language that communicates to appropriate audiences. This is the functional, operational reason for some of the ways we talk about teaching.

But if the language we use—or the interplay of languages—is thus understood as meeting a pragmatic need, it also has a transformational burden, meeting emotional and psychological needs (for consolation, and for a sense of control). While the words we use to talk about teaching help us perform real-life tasks (set an agenda, establish goals, manage change), they also labor to transform reality, and thus have a magical or alchemical quality. It is as if our language were struggling to transform base metals into gold. . . .

July/August 1991

Changing the Culture of Teaching

Mathematics at Indiana, Chicago, and Harvard

Ursula Elisabeth Wagener

W hat will it take to change the ways in which mathematicians teach their subject and recruit undergraduates? America not only faces a shortfall of mathematicians—but general math illiteracy. The number of math Ph.D.s granted today is two-thirds the number awarded in the 1960s, and student achievement is below that of other countries. Yet, the teaching of math is still geared to memorizing routine skills with little room for reflection and logical thought. By the time students reach college, they are bored, passive, hostile, and full of complaints.

It is hardly startling, then, that math educators and professors have taken a new interest in teaching. At the national level, major organizations have issued reports calling for changes in American attitudes toward mathematics and the ways in which the subject is taught. At the university level, several mathematics departments have taken steps to change their culture of teaching: More professors teach undergraduates; doctoral students apprentice to master teachers; smaller classes allow for interactive pedagogy in math classrooms; and teaching-learning communities are used to recruit undergraduates.

These efforts deserve examination because they open the possibility that our approach to teaching undergraduate mathematics and training graduate students will change. This article looks at initiatives within the mathematics departments at the University of Indiana at Bloomington, the University of Chicago, and Harvard University. These universities have taken steps in the right direction. The responses are positive, but incomplete, and they bring with them their own warning signals.

Changing the Culture

The mathematics departments at Indiana, Chicago, and Harvard are directing their attention to teaching much more so than ever before. How has this occurred? For one, each of the departments has taken advantage of the complaints about

teaching and the pressure to recruit new scholars and majors to inject "new blood" into their ranks. These are colleagues with particular pedagogical skills and competence in teaching undergraduates. At Chicago, Diane Herrmann was recruited specifically as associate director of undergraduate studies and as organizer of the College Fellows Program. Indiana recruited Greg Peters, an outstanding high school math teacher, to run its teaching seminar for doctoral students. Harvard created a joint position with the Danforth Center for Teaching and Learning and hired two senior preceptors known for their teaching skills.

The new appointments have signaled that teaching is valued. One Harvard graduate student reported: "I went to Deb Hughes-Hallett's class of 200 students. This gave me confidence. With a fair amount of preparation, I can do a very good job. Hallett and [Robin] Gottlieb are intimidating. They spend all their time teaching, and teach superb classes." As well as serving as role models and, not incidentally, providing superb teaching, the new pedagogical experts offer other faculty members a language—a basis for conversation— about teaching.

The quality of the new faculty inhibits the likelihood that what they are doing will be a mere "add-on." Their effectiveness is heightened by the extent to which they work with faculty and involve them in doctoral training. A Harvard faculty member talked about the faculty's involvement: "The department tries to ensure that all faculty teach calculus every once in a while. When they [professors] teach calculus, they usually have an apprentice and get involved in talking about teaching." At its best, the hope is realized, but it is a struggle.

A second way in which the departments have modified their cultures is by introducing graduate students to the dilemmas of teaching the discipline. Most professors learn to teach by the seat of their pants: Anyone who knows the discipline can teach it. The limitations of that model quickly become apparent once attention is directed toward teaching. The new teaching assistant or professor quickly discovers that establishing authority in the classroom, learning how to construct and grade examinations, and knowing what material to use and how to cover it are not immediately obvious. To communicate with students, a teacher must walk in a student's intellectual shoes and be able to comprehend diverse modes of thinking and analyzing.

Mathematics professors face an additional difficulty. Mathematics is a tall subject — that is, each level of learning depends upon mastery of previous levels. Preparing students for the next level almost invariably becomes an end in itself. Mathematics teachers succeed to the extent that they provide successive blocks of knowledge for their students efficiently and quickly. This increases the pressure to complete the syllabus, a process that often leaves little time to explore the discipline, a phenomenon uniformly criticized in introductory college calculus courses. Memorization quickly becomes the most efficient way to get through the course, leaving everyone dissatisfied in its wake.

Efforts to change the culture of teaching in mathematics departments have focused on confronting the dilemmas of the discipline — recognizing the need to teach mathematics not only as a series of building blocks — a prerequisite to other studies — but also as an act of creative imagination and exploration. By making these dilemmas part of mathematics graduate training, the traditional divorce of scholarly inquiry from pedagogy is being challenged.

A third way in which the mathematics departments have tried to affect their cultures is through the establishment of teaching-learning communities, though there are substantial differences between wealthy private institutions like Harvard and Chicago and a large public university like Indiana. At Harvard and Chicago, small classes, professors teaching undergraduates, and an environment that encourages conversation, meetings, and study groups — characteristics commonly associated with liberal arts colleges — all contribute to the teaching-learning community. At Indiana the task is made more difficult by the sheer numbers of students, though a larger proportion of faculty are teaching undergraduates than previously.

Finally, each department has taken advantage of presidential initiatives on the campus and of existing institutional support to improve teaching.

At Harvard, President Derek Bok launched the Harvard Assessment Seminars to discover how much Harvard students learn. The initial outcome was a plea to faculty to institute relatively simple changes in their teaching to improve student learning. Bok also has supported the Danforth Center for Teaching and Learning, founded in 1975. Initially involved with teaching assistants, videotaping classes, and helping graduate students analyze their teaching, the center's clientele and budgets have grown substantially — $450,000 annually, a nine-member staff, and a research agenda on teaching. Center staff now work directly with 44 departments, challenge Harvard faculty to treat pedagogy as an intellectually rewarding enterprise, and view active learning as necessary to knowledge retention.

At Chicago during the 1980s, President Hanna Gray initiated a series of commissions to study graduate life and graduate student teaching. Building upon one of the commission's recommendations and using money provided by the Fund for the Improvement of Postsecondary Education, Chicago established the Chicago Teaching Program. Considerably smaller than the Danforth Center at Harvard, with a $100,000 budget and three staff members, the program offers graduate students opportunities to discuss course design, instructional strategies, and how to incorporate disciplinary knowledge into appropriate general education courses. Experienced faculty members work with novice teachers to develop critical perspectives on their emerging teaching styles. More recently, Gray has pushed for greater investment in teaching through the establishment of a Council on Teaching, a permanent group of 10–15 faculty members from across the university, chaired by Wayne Booth of the English department. The council's task is to study and implement ways to improve teaching on the campus.

Indiana's reputation is as a teaching institution; its mandate is to educate the citizens of its state. Like many other universities, however, Indiana is striving to establish itself at the front ranks of research, with increasing emphasis placed on faculty research accomplishments. At the same time, the university has taken steps to improve teaching. President Thomas Ehrlich has appointed a Faculty Colloquium on Excellence in Teaching composed of 50 outstanding faculty members from each of the branches of the university. The colloquium, which convenes each year for a three-day retreat, develops ideas about how to promote better teaching, and its members discuss these ideas with faculty on their own campuses.

Indiana's Teaching Resources Center provides limited services. With a budget of $8,000 and one full-time professional, the center's activities are limited to a lecture series and individual consultations with faculty and graduate students.

In the Indiana, Chicago, and Harvard mathematics departments, the developments cited have begun to modify institutional cultures so that the quality of teaching begins to receive the attention it deserves. Yet questions remain, alerting us to the need for caution before we conclude that quality teaching is just around the corner.

Cautions

Without corresponding changes in incentive and reward systems, teaching *practica* only go so far in changing graduate student attitudes and values toward teaching. Mathematics students are recruited for their research interests and skills and enroll in doctoral programs in the hope of becoming recognized scholars. The implicit and explicit messages that Ph.D. students get from many faculty reinforce a disinterest in or negative stance toward teaching. The central message is: "Don't let teaching get in the way of your real work—your dissertation." Everyone knows that research credentials are the avenue for upward mobility, and acts on that assumption.

Second, knowledge of subject matter still constitutes the overwhelming core of graduate education today. Professors offering graduate instruction typically forget that the students they teach will soon function as classroom teachers themselves. Regular courses within the discipline do not include explicit consideration of pedagogical issues. For example, graduate students are never asked, in paper assignments or examination questions, to construct and justify undergraduate syllabi on a given subject.

Third, few tenured or tenure-track faculty are centrally involved in appenticeship programs or practica. This is least obvious at Chicago and most obvious at Indiana. All three universities face the potential problem of creating reliance on a second tier of teaching faculty. The new experts on teaching imported to head the teaching practica all hold lecturer or quasi-administrative positions, rather than tenure-track positions that are central to the professoriate.

Changing or modifying a culture is not easy. But at Indiana, Chicago, and Harvard, the first steps have been taken. What remains is to convince more students and faculty that teaching issues are intellectually interesting and integrally tied to thinking about a discipline—that they are worthy of a scholar's attention and deserve the highest rewards. When and if these changes occur, teaching will have achieved the central place it deserves at the university.

March/April 1992

Divided No More

A *Movement Approach to Educational Reform*

Parker J. Palmer

As I travel the country talking with faculty about the reform of teaching and learning, I meet many people who care about the subject and who have compelling visions for change. But after we have talked a while, our conversations take an almost inevitable turn. "These are wonderful ideas," someone will say, "but every last one of them will be defeated by the conditions of academic life."

That claim is usually followed by a litany of impediments to institutional reform: Teaching has low status in the academy, tenure decisions favor those who publish, scarce dollars will always go to research (or to administration, or to bricks and mortar), etc. No matter how hopeful our previous conversation has been, these reminders of institutional gridlock create a mood of resignation, even despair—and the game feels lost before play has begun.

The constancy of this experience has forced

me to think more carefully about how change really happens. I have found myself revisiting an old but helpful distinction between an *organizational* approach and a *movement* approach to change. Both organizations and movements are valuable, worthy of leadership, and channels for change—and a healthy society will encourage symbiosis between the two (indeed, reform-minded administrators often welcome movement energies). But when an organizational mentality is imposed on a problem that requires movement sensibilities, the result is often despair. I believe that some of us are making precisely that mistake when it comes to the reform of teaching and learning.

The organizational approach to change is premised on the notion that bureaucracies—their rules, roles, and relationships—define the limits of social reality within which change must happen. Organizations are essentially arrangements of power, so this approach to change asks: "How can the power contained within the boxes of this organization be rearranged or redirected to achieve the desired goal?" That is a good question—except when it assumes that bureaucracies are the only game in town.

This approach pits entrenched patterns of corporate power against fragile images of change harbored by a minority of individuals, and the match is inherently unfair. Constrained by this model, people with a vision for change may devote themselves to persuading powerholders to see things their way, which drains energy away from the vision and breeds resentment among the visionaries when "permission" is not granted. When organizations seem less interested in change than in preservation (which is, after all, their job), would-be reformers are likely to give up if the organizational approach is the only one they know. . . .

The Movement Way

But there is another avenue toward change: The way of the movement. I began to understand movements when I saw the simple fact that nothing would ever have changed if reformers had allowed themselves to be done in by organizational resistance. Many of us experience such resistance as checkmate to our hopes for change. But for a movement, resistance is merely the place where things begin. The movement mentality, far from being defeated by organizational resistance,

takes energy from opposition. Opposition validates the audacious idea that change must come.

The black liberation movement and the women's movement would have died aborning if racist and sexist organizations had been allowed to define the rules of engagement. But for some blacks, and for some women, that resistance affirmed and energized the struggle. In both movements, advocates of change found sources of countervailing power outside of organizational structures, and they nurtured that power in ways that eventually gave them immense leverage on organizations.

The genius of movements is paradoxical: They abandon the logic of organizations in order to gather the power necessary to rewrite the logic of organizations. Both the black movement and the women's movement grew outside of organizational boundaries—but both returned to change the lay, and the law, of the land. I believe that the reform of teaching and learning will happen only if we who care about it learn to live this paradox.

What is the logic of a movement? How does a movement unfold and progress? I see four definable stages in the movements I have studied—stages that do not unfold as neatly as this list suggests, but often overlap and circle back on each other:

- Isolated individuals decide to stop leading "divided lives."
- These people discover each other and form groups for mutual support.
- Empowered by community, they learn to translate "private problems" into public issues.
- Alternative rewards emerge to sustain the movement's vision, which may force the conventional reward system to change.

I want to explore these stages here, but not simply in remembrance of things past. By understanding the stages of a movement, some of us may see more clearly that we are engaged in a movement today, that we hold real power in our hands—a form of power that has driven real change in recent times. Knowing our power, perhaps we will have less need or desire to succumb to the sweet despair of believing that organizational gridlock must have the last word.

Choosing Integrity

The first stage in a movement can be described with some precision, I think. It happens when isolated individuals make an inner choice to stop leading "divided lives." Most of us know from experience what a divided life is. Inwardly we feel one sort of imperative for our lives, but outwardly we respond to quite another. This is the human condition, of course; our inner and outer worlds will never be in perfect harmony. But there are extremes of dividedness that become intolerable, and when the tension snaps inside of this person, then that person, and then another, a movement may be underway.

The decision to stop leading a divided life, made by enough people over a period of time, may eventually have political impact. But at the outset, it is a deeply personal decision, taken for the sake of personal integrity and wholeness. I call it the "Rosa Parks decision" in honor of the woman who decided, one hot Alabama day in 1955, that she finally would sit at the front of the bus. . . .

I suspect we can say even more: Rosa Parks sat at the front of the bus because her soul was tired of the vast, demoralizing gap between knowing herself as fully human and collaborating with a system that denied her humanity. The decision to stop leading a divided life is less a strategy for altering other people's values than an uprising of the elemental need for one's own values to come to the fore. The power of a movement lies less in attacking some enemy's untruth than in naming and claiming a truth of one's own. . . .

I meet teachers around the country who are choosing integrity in ways reminiscent of Rosa Parks. These faculty have realized that even if teaching is a back-of-the-bus thing for their institutions, it is a front-of-the-bus thing for them. They have realized that a passion for teaching was what animated their decision to enter the academy, and they do not want to lose the primal energy of their professional lives. They have realized that they care deeply about the lives of their students, and they do not want to abandon the young. They have realized that teaching is an enterprise in which they have a heavy investment of personal identity and meaning — and they have decided to reinvest their lives, even if they do not receive dividends from their colleges or from their colleagues.

For these teachers, the decision is really quite simple: Caring about teaching and about students brings them health as persons, and to collaborate in a denial of that fact is to collaborate in a diminishment of their own lives. They refuse any longer to act outwardly in contradiction to something they know inwardly to be true — that teaching, and teaching well, is a source of identity for them. They understand that this refusal may evoke the wrath of the gods of the professions, who are often threatened when we reach for personal wholeness. But still, they persist. . . .

Corporate Support

But the personal decision to stop leading a divided life is a frail reed. All around us, dividedness is presented as the sensible, even responsible, way to live. So the second stage in a movement happens when people who have been making these decisions start to discover each other and enter into relations of mutual encouragement and support. These groups, which are characteristic of every movement I know about, perform the crucial function of helping the Rosa Parks of the world know that even though they are out of step, they are not crazy. Together we learn that behaving normally is sometimes nuts but seeking integrity is always sane. . . .

While stage one is strong on many campuses, stage two is less well developed. Faculty who have decided to live "divided no more" are often unaware of each other's existence — so weak are the communal structures of the academy, and so diffident are intellectuals about sharing such "private" matters. It is difficult for faculty to seek each other out for mutual support. But it is clear from all great movements that mutual support is vital if the inner decision is to be sustained — and if the movement is to take its next crucial steps toward gathering power.

Where support groups do exist, they assume a simple form and function. Six or eight faculty from a variety of departments agree to meet on a regular but manageable schedule (say, once every two weeks) simply to talk about teaching. (The mix of departments is important because of the political vulnerability faculty often feel within their own guild halls.) They talk about what they teach, how they teach, what works and what doesn't, and — most important of all — the joys and pains of being a teacher. The conversations are informal, and, above all, candid. . . .

Going Public

The third stage of a movement has already been implied. As support groups develop, individuals learn to translate their private concerns into public issues, and they grow in their ability to give voice to these issues in public and compelling ways. To put it more precisely, support groups help people discover that their problems are not "private" at all, but have been occasioned by public conditions and therefore require public remedies. . . .

I am using the word "public" here in a way that is more classical than contemporary. The public realm I had in mind is not the realm of politics, which would reduce us to the manipulation of organizational power. Instead, to "go public" is to enter one's convictions into the mix of communal discourse. It is to project one's ideas so that others can hear them, respond to them, and be influenced by them—and so that one's ideas can be tested and refined in the public crucible. The public, understood as a vehicle of discourse, is pre-political. It is that primitive process of communal conversation, conflict, and consensus on which the health of institutionalized power depends.

Many would argue, of course, that our public process is itself in poor health and cannot be relied upon for remedies. These critics claim that there is no longer a public forum for a movement to employ. But historically, it is precisely the energy of movements that has renewed the public realm; movements have the capacity to create the very public they depend on. However moribund the public may be, it is reinvigorated when people learn how to articulate their concerns in ways that allow—indeed, compel—a wider public to listen and respond. . . .

Even more remarkable, the movement for educational reform has been joined by publics far beyond the walls of the academy. Parents, employers, legislators, and columnists are calling for more attention to teaching and learning, and their calls are insistent. Recently, a coalition of major accounting firms used the language of collaborative learning to press the agency that accredits business schools toward the reform of business education. At moments like that, one knows that "going public" can make a difference. . . .

By giving public voice to alternative values we can create something more fundamental than political change. We can create cultural change. When we secure a place in public discourse for ideas and images like "collaborative learning," we are following those reformers who minted phrases like "affirmative action" and made them the coin

of the realm. When the language of change becomes available in the common culture, people are better able to name their yearnings for change, to explore them with others, to claim membership in a great movement—and to overcome the disabling effects of feeling isolated and half-mad.

Alternative Rewards

. . . In stage four, a more systematic pattern of alternative rewards emerges, and with it comes the capacity to challenge the dominance of existing organizations. . . .

What are the alternative rewards offered by a growing movement? As a movement grows, the meaning one does not find in conventional work is found in the meaning of the movement. As a movement grows, the affirmation one does not receive from organizational colleagues is received from movement friends. As a movement grows, careers that no longer satisfy may be revisioned in forms and images that the movement has inspired. As a movement grows, the paid work one cannot find in conventional organizations may be found in the movement itself. . . .

As we explore this fourth stage, where movements return to intersect with organizations, it is important to recall that a healthy society is one in which organizations and movements are related symbiotically—as the case of black and feminist scholars will show. Without movements, such scholars would not be bringing new life to organizations; without organizations, such scholars would not have found ways to sustain careers. . . .

. . . The movement will persist until the obvious is acknowledged: Teaching has as much right to full status in the academy as any other academic function—research, athletics, administration, lobbying, fund-raising—and it may have even more right than some! Teaching simply *belongs* in the academy, and there is no need to defend that claim.

The defense, if any, must come from those who have promoted a concept of higher education so bizarre that it can ignore the question of how and why we teach and learn. We are at a moment in the history of education when the emptiness of that concept is clear—a moment when real progress on reform is possible. There is much to be done that I have not named here, from revisioning teaching as a legitimate form of scholarship (building on the superb work of the Carnegie Foundation) to developing more sophisticated strategies for change. But in the midst of those complexities, we must remember that all great movements start simply: A few people feel the pain of the divided life and resolve to live it no more. In that resolve is the power to live our moment to its full potential. . . .

July/August 1993

The Re-examination of Faculty Priorities

Russell Edgerton

Beginning in 1990 and accelerating in 1991 and 1992, university presidents and provosts across the country began charging task forces to re-examine various aspects of the faculty reward system — from the obligations faculty are expected to perform, to the ways teaching and service are evaluated, to the bases for promotion and advancement. What set off this re-examination? What issues have campuses decided to take on? Are campus leaders just engaging in a public relations stunt or are they really raising fundamental questions about the academic cultures of their institutions?

With these questions in mind, last fall I began poring over materials generated by over 50 campus task forces. Many of these were collected by Ernest Boyer, president of the Carnegie Foundation for the Advancement of Teaching, as background for a forthcoming Carnegie Foundation report on the assessment of scholarly work. Others were collected by the American Association for Higher Education's (AAHE's) new Forum on Faculty Roles and Rewards. While some interesting campus studies undoubtedly escaped our nets, I think we caught a broadly representative sample of what the "first wave" of campus re-examinations was all about.

What Set Things Off?

Three ingredients are often present in the "making" of a public issue. 1) Conditions change, creating materials out of which issues emerge. 2) Leaders step forward and, by their words and actions, draw attention to the need to respond. 3) A study, report, or other precipitating event ignites these materials into a national issue. With respect to the emergence of faculty priorities as a national issue, all three ingredients are present.

Changing conditions. The laundry list of changing conditions includes new and sharper public expectations for quality; an ebb in nearly all the major sources of revenue for higher education; and a more elusive but quite real erosion of public trust in higher education. As Derek Bok has pointed out in *Change* (July/August 1992), sloppy accounting procedures, athletic scandals, neglect of undergraduates, and many other abuses now so widely aired in the press have actually existed for years. What's different today is that these abuses have an audience they never had before.

These conditions have prompted campus leaders (especially leaders of complex research universities, at which much of the criticism is aimed) to pay more attention to undergraduate education and to look for ways to nudge their campuses into responding to the needs of their surrounding communities. From here, it's but a short step to taking on the issue of how to elevate the priority faculty are giving to the functions of teaching and service.

This said, it would be a mistake to assume that the re-examination of faculty priorities is powered only by pressures from *outside* the campus. Conflicts over what priorities faculty should pursue are occurring *inside* our campuses as well.

For example, the campus reports and surveys I studied reveal tensions between younger and senior faculty as well as between the interests of minority and feminist scholars and traditional notions of disciplinary rigor. Many mid-career and senior faculty clearly feel caged in by the reigning definitions of what scholarly work is valued. New technologies for communicating scholarly work are posing yet another set of issues about how to evaluate work that appears in forms other than published articles in refereed journals.

Leadership emerges. In 1990, three campuses took initiatives that made waves across the country.

First, there was Syracuse. With a modest $25,000 grant from the Sears Roebuck Foundation, Vice Chancellor Robert Diamond decided to survey faculty, department chairs, and deans, asking what they thought about the balance between teaching and research. Each constituent group responded that the university's priorities were tilted too heavily toward research. What was even more interesting was that most respondents assumed that they were alone in their beliefs, that their colleagues favored a stronger emphasis on research. When the survey results were released, revealing the number of "closet" teachers there actually were on campus, the balance between teaching and research became an issue for the entire university.

Knowing that universities rarely strike out in new directions without looking over their shoulders at peer institutions, Diamond then turned his survey into a national project. During the fall of 1990 and spring of 1991, with support from the Lilly Endowment, he and his colleagues convinced 46 other research universities to administer the survey, consisting of eight items about the relative importance of research versus undergraduate teaching. *Every* campus favored a more equitable balance between the emphasis on teaching and research.

While the Syracuse initiative was unfolding in a low-profile way, there was nothing low-key about Stanford University President Donald Kennedy's address on April 5, 1990, to the Stanford faculty, billed as a "vision for Stanford's second century." Kennedy called on the Stanford faculty to recognize that teaching was "the first among our labors"—and came down hard on the need for a recommitment to teaching. On March 3, 1991, he followed with a second major address calling for changes in the faculty reward system including: 1) ending quantitative standards for measuring research productivity in order to cap "the overproduction of routine scholarship"; 2) broadening the definition of scholarship to include creative work beyond that reported in peer-reviewed journals; 3) peer review of teaching effectiveness; and 4) more flexible approaches to faculty careers.

Then, in September of 1990, University of California President David Gardner established a universitywide Task Force on Faculty Rewards, chaired by Karl Pister, then professor of engineering science at the University of California-Berke-ley. The Pister report, issued in June, 1991, called for a new balance among categories of scholarly activity, respect for broader forms of scholarship, peer review of teaching, and other themes that paralleled the Kennedy address.

The catalytic report. When Berkeley stirs, others wake up. By the fall of 1990, re-examinations were under way on perhaps 30 campuses. The trains had left the station. But the destinations of these re-examinations, and the decisions by many other campuses to embark on similar trips, were enormously influenced by the release, in January 1991, of *Scholarship Reconsidered: Priorities of the Professoriate*, a report by Ernest Boyer. Scores of campuses placed bulk orders for the report, which soon became the best selling "special report" the Carnegie Foundation had ever issued.

Instead of describing faculty roles in terms of the familiar trilogy of teaching, research, and service, *Scholarship Reconsidered* argued that faculty were responsible for four basic tasks: advancing knowledge, synthesizing and integrating knowledge, applying knowledge, and representing knowledge through teaching. This formulation, originally proposed by Eugene Rice, then a Scholar in Residence at the Carnegie Foundation, spoke to faculty not as "professors" (with obligations to their employing institutions for teaching, research, and service) but in terms of their deeper identities as "scholars" (with obligations to their peers in the field). The formulation invited faculty to take responsibility, *as* economists, biologists, and so forth, not only for advancing the knowledge base of their fields but for *representing* that knowledge base to others. It presented teaching and service, not as *add-ons to*, but as *expressions of* their scholarly work.

Spurred by *Scholarship Reconsidered*, the re-examination of faculty priorities became a nationwide phenomenon. At our own annual meetings of AAHE in 1991 and 1992, sessions on topics about the "reward system" drew overflow crowds. In order to channel this interest into productive lines of work, we established, with support from the Fund for the Improvement of Postsecondary Education, a Forum on Faculty Roles and Rewards. The Forum's first annual conference, January 28–30, 1993, drew a capacity crowd of 550. We turned away several hundred others.

So what is this re-examination all about? With apologies to both Woodrow Wilson and J. Edwards

Demming, I find it useful to put my observations into "fourteen points." Five are about changing expectations; five are about changes in how faculty are evaluated; and four are about shifts in faculty incentives and rewards. Readers should remember that these observations are drawn from materials that come from four-year institutions that must balance complex missions of teaching, research, and service. I do not presume to characterize what's happening at campuses where teaching and service are the exclusive missions.

Setting New Expectations

1 *The master issue is not how hard faculty work but what tasks faculty should work on, and how clear the signals are about this . . .*

2 *Nearly everyone, including the great majority of faculty at our most prestigious universities, agrees that teaching is undervalued and that the status of teaching should be elevated . . .*

3 *Campuses are not simply giving more weight to teaching; they are redefining the roles faculty perform.* Many campuses start off by embracing the formula of Scholarship Reconsidered, *then invariably return to the traditional categories; but in the process they come to more inclusive definitions on what both teaching and research entail . . .*

4 *"Service," in all this, is typically treated like the country cousin. The status and definitional issues of service are as muddled as ever . . .*

5 *The good news is that the scholarly societies are getting into the act and beginning to redefine the expectations and rewards for members of their communities . . .*

Evaluating Performance

6 *Lots of attention is focused on when faculty in various ranks should be reviewed and on what expectations are appropriate at each review stage. Campuses are moving toward continuous evaluation throughout the faculty career cycle, and toward standards that acknowledge different stages in faculty careers . . .*

7 *A second recurring theme is that campuses are insisting on better evidence to justify recommendations and decisions about faculty performance, especially in the area of teaching . . .*

8 *A third theme is that student evaluations are not enough; the faculty themselves must play a stronger role in the evaluation of teaching. Put differently, campuses are coming to accept the prop-* *osition that teaching, like research, should be subject to peer review. But what is endorsed as a goal has yet to be put into practice . . .*

9 *A number of campuses have seized on "teaching portfolios" as a vehicle by which faculty can present their teaching for review. But not much thought is being given to what teaching portfolios should contain, or how the process of preparing and reviewing portfolios can be used to promote understanding and reflection about what good teaching really is . . .*

10 *The perceived need for new evaluation criteria and methods seems to be limited to the domain of teaching. Few campuses seem to be rethinking the criteria and methods for evaluating research, or holistic approaches to evaluating all the dimensions of scholarly performance . . .*

Rethinking Recognition & Rewards

11 *In this latest round of concern for teaching, universities are beginning to address the really gut issues, such as how central teaching is regarded to be in the decisions departments make about faculty appointments, promotion, tenure, and salary . . .*

12 *While teaching awards to individual faculty are increasingly seen as a token gesture, some institutions are contemplating interesting steps that could strengthen the role and impact that teaching awards can have . . .*

13 *In the commendable focus on re-examining their formal reward system, campuses may be neglecting opportunities to foster the intrinsic interest faculty have in teaching and professional service . . .*

14 *There is new talk of shifting the focus of evaluation and accountability from individual faculty to groups of faculty, especially academic departments. But most campuses are sneaking up on this agenda rather than tackling it head on . . .*

The Next Round

Looking back on these past three years, skeptics will say that nothing really has changed. The Pister report has come and gone, and daily life down in the chemistry department at Berkeley remains the same.

This is true, but too harsh. The *climate* has changed. The fact that faculty task groups are now *saying* things—like acknowledging the need to strengthen the role of faculty in the review of teaching—is an important gain. The Pister report and other such reports have *legitimized* the faculty reward system as a topic for serious academic discussion.

But it's also true that the real work still lies ahead. What are the prospects that the re-examination of faculty priorities will move out of the provost's office and campus task forces and into the real decision-making at the departmental level? Will there be a second round of reform, and if so, what will its character be?

We can count on the fact that the underlying conditions to which institutions are responding will not only stay with us, but intensify. And I believe we can count on the fact that the catalysts for action will shift. *Scholarship Reconsidered* challenged faculty on a personal and professional level to rethink their scholarly identities and aspirations. It was a fortunate way to begin. But the next wave of conversation won't be so friendly. Issues will be framed in terms of how to respond to external pressures to legislate productivity, regulate workloads, and so on. How the next wave plays out will come down, as usual, to the kind of leadership for cultural change that emerges — both inside and outside higher education.

Within higher education, three distinctive kinds of leadership are needed. First, academic administrators need to muster the political will to go into the second and tougher round. Universities are organized into what *appears* to be an academic "chain of command," from presidents, to vice presidents for academic affairs, deans, and department chairs. But we all know that things don't really work this way; that it takes administrators with strong personal conviction to overcome the decentralized character of our institutions. I was at an occasion recently where a colleague was asked what he thought of Henry Rosovsky's "farewell address" as Harvard provost, lamenting the decline of faculty citizenship at Harvard. He replied, "Great statement." Then he added, "Too bad he didn't say it *during* his time in office."

Academic administrators must not only gauge reactions of their own faculty; they must also look over their shoulders at peer institutions. If university X picks up on Lee Shulman's idea to ask candidates for faculty positions to give a "pedagogical colloquium" and finds itself all alone in doing so, it has much more difficulty making the practice stick. So, in this next round, it will also be important for peer institutions to get together and create consortial approaches to reform.

The second level of leadership must obviously come from the faculty, department by department. This is the toughest issue of all, but not — as is too often alleged — because faculty don't want reform. It is tough because of the lack of incentives for faculty to engage in reform.

In changing these incentives, we must keep in mind the message of *Scholarship Reconsidered* — that faculty, especially in research universities, can best be reached through the scholarly communities where they live out their professional lives. Teaching can be cast as an obligation owed to the universities where they work. It can also be cast as a responsibility, as a member of a scholarly community, to involve the next generation in the great conversations of one's discipline. Deep reform will turn on how deeply involved the learned and professional societies become in the reform movement. Parenthetically, funding agencies such as the National Science Foundation and the National Endowment for the Arts and Humanities will, in turn, have much to say about this.

Progress also will depend on a third level of leadership — that provided by the reflective practitioners and experts who put their minds to *how* reforms can be implemented. Strong administrative leadership and the right faculty incentives are necessary but not sufficient conditions for progress. To actually *do* the practical reforms now on the agenda, for example, to practice peer review of teaching, to define and evaluate professional service, to evaluate and reward departmental performance, requires a know-how that is not yet invented. *With* exemplary practices and prototypes in hand, universities can — and will — make real progress. Changes in practice can, and will, pave the way for changes in attitude.

Finally, there is the matter of leadership beyond the campus. Faculty-bashing is becoming a growth industry. Without denying the important role faculty can play, we need to remember that faculty also are caught up in a larger system of rewards and incentives. Faculty priorities are shaped by decisions of departmental colleagues, colleagues across the country, larger university faculty, central administration, the student marketplace, state governments, the federal government, accrediting and testing agencies, and more. In the 1950s and 1960s, all these constituencies had a hand in creating the system we now have. They all must now take part in bringing about change.

November/December 1993

Windows on Practice

Cases about Teaching and Learning

Pat Hutchings

... What Are Cases?

... [C]ases are detailed, story-like accounts of classroom incidents designed to raise issues about effective teaching and learning. Long-time Harvard University case writer Abby Hansen points out that (like much that happens in real classrooms) cases also have "an irreducible core of ambiguity" that makes them especially powerful for prompting lively conversation among teachers. ... Cases vary in length, focus, point of view, even in medium (most are written but interest in video and interactive media cases is on the rise), and the form is evolving based on emerging practice. But whatever the form, the purpose of their use is not to give answers but to raise questions, to encourage problem solving, to call forth faculty experience and judgment, and to promote more effective teaching practice.

Cases are especially well suited to these ends because, in the words of two faculty members at Monash University in Australia (whose work I'll come back to), they open "windows on practice," through which — in contrast to the bloodless writing about teaching one typically gets — we see teaching that lives and breathes, that's full-bodied, robust, complex, concrete . . . and *interesting*.

That cases are more lively than a lot of the discourse about teaching is, all by itself, an argument for their use. But it's not the only one. On campuses that have begun using them as part of an effort to strengthen teaching, cases are bringing four important benefits:

- *Cases put permission in the air to talk about teaching. . . .*
- *Cases recognize and honor the experience of teachers. . . .*
- *Cases can help reconnect process and content. . . .*
- *Cases foster a view of teaching that leads to improvement.*

Whether efforts at improvement take hold or fail depends in part on how faculty think about teaching, and a final benefit of cases is that they promote a view of teaching that's particularly potent for improvement. We've seen several aspects of this view: that teaching is public, that it's experience-based, that it's not just about process but about ideas and their transformation. But beyond — or perhaps beneath — these particular points, cases represent teaching as a complex, intellectual endeavor, *and* — following Ernest Boyer's now well-known work, *Scholarship Reconsidered* — as a scholarly one.

It's notable that Boyer's phrase, "a scholarship of teaching" is in widespread and mostly approving use today. The meaning of the phrase is still, in my view, being invented, but one thing that's sure is that it does not describe the current view of teaching on most campuses, which seems to be focused largely on method and technique. The evaluation of teaching on most campuses, for instance, still looks primarily at process and classroom-management issues; programs aimed at the improvement of teaching typically focus on the need for new and better "instructional technology," more up-to-date tools and strategies for, say, active learning or the use of small groups. These are important topics, of course, and good teachers want and need to know about broad matters of method and technique.

But if improvement stops with technique, teaching loses. It loses in a way illustrated by the story . . . about the organic chemist who doesn't want to be told that he has to teach his classes through role-playing. Technique doesn't "speak to" this person, or to many others, because it gets disconnected (in perception if not in fact) from the knowledge and values faculty most care about — their own disciplines and students. As a consequence, teaching itself is diminished, for if teaching is mostly a matter of technique, it is not, after all, a subject for serious, scholarly attention — the very thing it needs for ongoing, real improvement.

Cases can help counter this diminished view

of teaching. Their use is predicated on a view that the knowledge that effective teachers bring to their work (or need to be able to bring) is not simply a knowledge of methods, but one of substance and ideas—about one's field, about students, about learning, and about the complex relationships among these "particulars" in real classrooms. The case for cases is not, in this sense, that they will tell you what to do on Monday but that they promote *a way of thinking about teaching*, one that recognizes teaching as a complex, intellectually engaging process of adaptation and decision making in hard-to-fathom, ambiguous situations.

In short, cases give teaching its due as an intellectual activity. In doing so, they speak not only to "already converted" faculty who care about teaching (and show up for every teaching workshop) but also to those who have traditionally eschewed the topic—and without whom widespread improvement cannot occur. . . .

November/December 1993

Forum: Teaching as Community Property

Putting an End to Pedagogical Solitude

Lee S. Shulman

At the end of the June commencement ceremony at which I received my graduate degree, George Beadle, then president of the University of Chicago, turned to those of us baking in our robes in Rockefeller Chapel and proclaimed, "Welcome to the community of scholars." Perspiring though I was, a chill went through me because this was something I had aspired to—membership in a community of scholars.

As the years have gone by, I've come to appreciate how naive was my anticipation of what it would mean to be a member of a scholarly community. My anticipation contained two visions. One was the vision of the solitary individual laboring quietly, perhaps even obscurely, somewhere in the library stacks, or in a laboratory, or at an archaeological site; someone who pursued his or her scholarship in splendid solitude. My second vision was of this solitary scholar entering the social order— becoming a member of the community—interacting with others, in the classroom and elsewhere, as a teacher.

What I didn't understand as a new PhD was that I had it backwards! We experience isolation not in the stacks but in the classroom. We close the classroom door and experience pedagogical solitude, whereas in our life as scholars, we are members of active communities: communities of conversation, communities of evaluation, communities in which we gather with others in our invisible colleges to exchange our findings, our methods, and our excuses.

I now believe that the reason teaching is not more valued in the academy is because the way we treat teaching removes it from the community of scholars. It is not that universities diminish the importance of teaching because they devalue the act itself; it is not that research is seen as having more intrinsic value than teaching. Rather, we celebrate those aspects of our lives and work that can become, as we say in California, "community property." And if we wish to see greater recognition and reward attached to teaching, we must change the status of teaching from private to community property. I would suggest three strategies that can guide us in this transformation.

First, we need to reconnect teaching to the disciplines. Although the disciplines are easy to bash because of the many problems they create for us, they are, nevertheless, the basis for our intellectual communities. Like it or not, the forms of scholarship that are seen as intellectual work in the disciplines are going to be valued more than forms of scholarship (such as teaching) that are seen as non-disciplinary.

Notice that I say non-disciplinary, not interdisciplinary. (I would argue that most modern disciplines are in fact inter-disciplines.) The distinction is not between disciplinary and *inter*-disciplinary but disciplinary and *non*-disciplinary. Look, for instance, at the way the improvement of teaching is *treated* in most of our schools. Institutional support for teaching and its improvement tends to reside in a universitywide center for teaching and learning where many of the TAs are trained, and where faculty — regardless of department — can go for assistance in improving their practice. That's a perfectly reasonable idea. But notice the message it conveys — that teaching is generic, technical, and a matter of performance; that it's not part of the community that means so much to most faculty, the disciplinary, interdisciplinary, or professional community. It's something general you lay on top of what you *really* do as a scholar in a discipline.

Similarly, in most of our institutions, the student evaluation forms are identical across the disciplines, as if teaching civil engineering and teaching Chaucer were the same. But of course they're not. We would never dream of sending out examples of someone's research for peer review to people at another university who were on that other university's faculty *in general*. The medievalists evaluate the research of other medievalists; research by civil engineers is reviewed by other civil engineers. Not so with teaching.

The first strategy I would argue for, then, in attempting to make teaching community — and therefore *valued* — property, is that we recognize that the communities that matter most are strongly identified with the disciplines of our scholarship. "Discipline" is in fact a powerful pun because it not only denotes a domain but also suggests a process: a community that disciplines is one that exercises quality, control, judgment, evaluation, and paradigmatic definition. We need to make the review, examination, and support of teaching part of the responsibility of the disciplinary community.

The second strategy I would propose is that if teaching is going to be community property it must be made visible through artifacts that capture its richness and complexity. In the absence of such artifacts teaching is a bit like dry ice; it disappears at room temperature. You may protest, "But that's so much work!" Notice that we don't question this need to document when it comes to more traditional forms of scholarship. We don't judge each other's research on the basis of casual conversations in the hall; we say to our colleagues, "That's

a lovely idea! You really must write it up." It may, in fact, take two years to write it up. But we accept this because it's clear that scholarship entails an artifact, a product, some form of community property that can be shared, discussed, critiqued, exchanged, built upon. So, if pedagogy is to become an important part of scholarship, we have to provide it with this same kind of documentation and transformation.

The third strategy is that if something is community property in the academy, and is thus deemed valuable, this means we deem it something whose value we have an obligation to judge. We assume, moreover, that our judgments will be enacted within the disciplinary community, which means, I'm afraid, that the terrifying phrase "peer review" must be applied to teaching. Think what this would mean: if your institution is like mine, the principle of peer review is best expressed not as an inverse-square law but as a direct-square law. The influence of any evaluation of someone's scholarship is directly related to the square of the distance from the campus where the evaluator works. So for Stanford faculty, a Berkeley review is pretty good, but Oxford is *much* better. (I haven't checked to see whether the curve continues as you go to Australia or if there's a plateau, but this is the sort of thing higher education researchers would probably enjoy studying.) My point is that the artifacts of teaching must be created and preserved so that they can be judged by communities of peers beyond the office next door.

This kind of peer review may seem far-fetched on many campuses; it is far from the norm. But one of the sources of pleasure I have had at Stanford is serving on the universitywide Appointments and Promotions Committee and thus reviewing promotion and appointment folders for the business school. In our business school, and I suspect in a number across the country, the promotion folders look very different from those in, say, history or biology. The portfolios of business school faculty are often just as thick in the domain of teaching as they are in the area of traditional social science and business scholarship. Included in them are samples of instructional materials developed by the teachers, cases they have written, and detailed essays in which candidates gloss and interpret the course syllabi that are included in their portfolios. Most impressive of all, one finds reviews by colleagues who visit their classes and critique their case-based teaching, and reports by faculty at other business schools who examine their teaching materials and their cases. What a contrast to the promotion dossier that provides three sets of student ratings and two letters that say, "She must be a good teacher, she sure gives a good talk!"

There's an important corollary point to mention here too. We should evaluate each other as teachers not only with an eye to deriving accurate measurements of our teaching effectiveness — though of course we must have precision. Our evaluations should also have positive consequences for the processes and persons being evaluated. We are obliged, that is, to organize the evaluation of teaching so that the very procedures we employ raise the likelihood that teaching gets treated seriously, systematically, and as central to the lives of individual faculty and institutions. This means we are obliged to use procedures from which faculty are likely to learn how to teach better. I like the way the chair of the English Department at Stanford put it: "What we're trying to do," he said, "is to create a culture of teaching, one in which the conversations, the priorities [and, I would add, the rituals and kinship systems] of the department have teaching at their center."

No single change will produce this culture, but let me end with one suggestion that would, I think, take us a long way toward it. If we really want a different kind of culture, we ought to change our advertising. By way of example, I've drafted an ad for *The Chronicle* announcing a new position in 20th Century U.S. History at Shulman College. "We seek a new faculty member who is good at both research and teaching" — the ad says the usual things along those lines. But then it goes on to say that candidates who are invited to campus will be asked to offer two colloquia. In one colloquium, they will describe their current research — the usual research colloquium. In the second, which we'll call the *pedagogical colloquium*, they will address the pedagogy of their discipline. They will do so by expounding on the design of a course, showing systematically how this course is an act of scholarship in the discipline, and explaining how the course represents the central issues in the discipline and how in its pedagogy it affords students the opportunity to engage in the intellectual and moral work of the discipline.

Think of the impact on our doctoral programs if we knew that there were colleges and universities out there that had agreed to employ the *pedagogical colloquium* as a regular, central portion of that mating ritual we call recruitment. We could begin to change the ways we think about preparation for a life or career of scholarship. Moreover, the public nature of this *pedagogical colloquium* would change the culture of the institution doing the recruiting. We could begin to look as seriously at evidence of teaching abilities as we do at research productivity. We would no longer have merely to pray that this good young scholar can educate. We would have evidence of his or her abilities as an educator-in-the-discipline.

To change academic culture in this way will not be easy. But colleges and universities have always taken justifiable pride in their commitment to inquiry and criticism in all fields, even those where dogma and habit make real scrutiny uncomfortable. Now we must turn this tough scrutiny on our own practices, traditions, and culture. Only by doing so will we make teaching truly central to higher education.

Good Talk About Good Teaching

Improving Teaching through Conversation and Community

Parker J. Palmer

After 25 years of teaching undergraduates, graduates, and older adults, I am still trying to fathom the mystery of how people do and do not learn. I have been edified by research on the subject and by experts who share what they know. But, like most college faculty, I have often been deprived of a deep reservoir of insight about teaching and learning. Faculty, unlike many other professionals, lack the continuing conversation with colleagues that could help us grow more fully into the demands of the teacher's craft.

No surgeon can do her work without being observed by others who know what she is doing, without participating in grand-round discussions of the patients she and her colleagues are treating. No trial lawyer can litigate without being observed and challenged by people who know the law. But professors conduct their practice as teachers in private. We walk into the classroom and close the door—figuratively and literally—on the daunting task of teaching. When we emerge, we rarely talk with each other about what we have done, or need to do. After all, what would we talk about?

This privatization of teaching may originate in some misguided concept of academic freedom but it persists, I believe, because faculty choose it as a mode of self-protection against scrutiny and evaluation. Ironically, this choice of isolation leads to some of the deepest dissatisfactions in academic life. I visit dozens of campuses each year to lead faculty workshops on teaching and learning, and I often hear about the "pain of disconnection" among faculty, the pain of people who were once animated by a vision of "the community of scholars" but who now find themselves working in a vacuum.

This pain takes quite specific forms. For example, many faculty suffer from the common institutional practice of evaluating teaching with a standardized questionnaire—one that forces all teaching into a Procrustean bed by reducing it to ten dimensions on a five-point scale. The nuances of good teaching cannot possibly be captured this way. But if we insist on privatizing our work, how else can administrators evaluate us except by tossing some questionnaires over the transom at the end of each term and hoping that students will make marks on them?

Privatization creates more than individual pain; it creates institutional incompetence as well. By privatizing teaching we make it next to impossible for the academy to become more adept at its teaching mission. The growth of any skill depends heavily on honest dialogue among those who are doing it. Some of us may grow by private trial and error, but our willingness to try and to fail is severely limited when we are not supported by a community that encourages such risks. The most likely outcome when any function is privatized is that people will perform the function conservatively, refusing to stray far from the silent consensus on what "works"—even when it clearly does not. That, I am afraid, too often describes the state of teaching in the privatized academy.

The good news is that the academy's resources are considerable, a fact I rediscover on virtually every campus I visit. Much of what we need in order to foster good teaching can be generated by any faculty worth its salt—and there are many—through continuing, thoughtful conversation. The question is, how can we help that conversation happen? . . .

Our Need for Leadership

On a recent visit to a college that bills itself as a "teaching institution," I found, as I often do, that this phrase has its limits. This college hires people who care about teaching, it gives student opinion real weight in making decisions about promotion and tenure, and its official rhetoric is full of exhortations about teaching and learning. But the college does not have regular occasions for its faculty to explore teaching with each other, except for an annual workshop where the emphasis is on learning from an outside expert rather than from colleagues.

When I observed a need to create more opportunities for "good talk about good teaching," one person spoke, with all earnestness, what seemed to be the mind of many: "I'd like to talk with my colleagues about teaching, but I feel awkward about walking into someone's office and saying, 'Let's discuss the various learning styles among our students.'"

What strikes me about that comment (in addition to the evidence of privatization it provides) is how subtly it reveals the weak culture of leadership in academe. The comment assumes that cultivating a conversation about teaching depends entirely on the wills and wiles of individual professors; there's nary a hint that academic leadership might play some role in fostering such conversation. The comment reveals a kind of silent conspiracy between faculty who do not want to be led and executives who find it safer to administer than to lead.

But very little talk about teaching—good or otherwise—will happen if presidents and provosts, deans and department chairs, do not expect and invite it into being on a regular basis. I choose my words carefully, because leadership that tries to coerce conversation will fail. Conversation must be the free choice of free people. But in the privatized academy, conversation will happen only as people are surrounded by expectations and invitations from leaders about new ways to use their freedom. The most powerful kind of leadership is to offer people pathways and permissions to do things they want to do but feel unable to do for themselves. That sort of leadership evokes energies within people that far exceed the powers of coercion. . . .

Of course, this kind of leadership depends on our ability to look beyond the masks people wear and into their true condition. Some faculty may wear a mask of indifference about teaching, but the best academic leaders know that beneath the mask there may be real concern—if only because most faculty spend so many hours in the classroom that self-interest cries out for those hours to be made more fruitful. And beyond narrow self-interest, there are reasons to care about teaching that are rooted deep in the human soul. "Teaching" is simply another word for the ancient and elemental bond that exists between the elders of the tribe and their young. When the bond is broken, both groups feel fearful and incomplete, and both will wish to reweave the relationship, no matter how profoundly alienated they may be.

Experience tells me not only that there is a deep reservoir of insight about teaching among faculty, but also that faculty have a deep need to draw upon that life-giving source. The reservoir waits to be tapped by leaders who perceive its presence, who expect and invite people to draw upon it, who offer excuses and permissions for the dialogue to happen—and who can help make that dialogue less woeful than it sometimes is and as winsome as it can easily be. . . .

July/August 1994

Overcoming "Hollowed" Collegiality

Departmental Cultures and Teaching Quality

William F. Massy, Andrea K. Wilger, and Carol Colbeck

Since publication of Ernest Boyer's "Scholarship Revisited" in 1992, much of the effort to improve undergraduate teaching has focused on faculty reward systems. While this work is compelling, we believe that reward structures offer only a partial explanation for the lack of effective undergraduate teaching. Of equal importance are broader questions about the *organizational context* within which undergraduate teaching occurs. The most crucial such context is the academic department.

Our research attempts to dig into conditions within departments that support or inhibit faculty members' working together on undergraduate education. The project consists primarily of interviews with faculty at 20 colleges and universities about the contexts for their work. So far, we've conducted some 300 interviews across eight research institutions, four doctorate-granting institutions, and three liberal arts colleges, talking with roughly equal numbers of faculty in science, social science, and humanities departments.

Our initial results indicate that many faculty do indeed encounter conditions that hinder their ability to work together on issues of undergraduate teaching and learning. Certain patterns emerge from the data, patterns that cross institutional type and disciplinary lines. The descriptions that follow represent our best qualitative judgments based on the weight of the evidence we've studied so far.

Faculty Isolation and Fragmentation

Three key features of academic departments constrain faculty in their ability to work together on teaching. First, fragmented communication patterns isolate individual faculty members and prevent them from interacting around issues of undergraduate education. Second, tight resources limit opportunities and strain faculty relationships. Third, prevailing methods of evaluation and reward undermine attempts to create an environment more conducive to faculty interaction. . . .

Departments That Support Effective Teaching

A few departments in our study have found ways to support undergraduate education despite the negative pressures just described. Faculty in these departments genuinely value teaching, and active discussions about it continually reinforce their beliefs. What has made the difference? We searched for patterns in faculty members' descriptions of their departments and found some interesting contrasts with other departments in our study. . . .

The exemplary departments are distinguished by their supportive culture for undergraduate teaching, frequent interaction among faculty, tolerance of differences, generational equity, workload equity, and course rotation. Also important are peer as well as serious student teaching evaluation, balanced incentives, consensus decision-making, and, above all, effective department chairs.

Supportive Culture

"I think that the faculty feel teaching is a cooperative thing."

Faculty in our exemplary departments expressed an overall favorable attitude about the value of teaching. They take teaching seriously, even when their department is nationally ranked in research. One professor at a research university stated, "It would be hard to be a member of this department and be a poor teacher." Respondents pointed out that when faculty in a department care about teaching, their concern is contagious — it permeates the entire department. New faculty quickly learn that the quality of their teaching is important. . . .

Frequent Interaction

"I know that this department meets a lot compared to other departments — once a week for at least an hour. Now, we don't always do 'business.' "

Faculty in departments that support teaching talk with each other frequently — in formal department meetings, in curriculum review sessions, in the corridors, and by the copying and coffee machines. While the subject is not exclusively teaching, in departments where faculty have frequent face-to-face interaction — those departments where faculty regularly schedule and attend meetings, colloquia, or retreats and where they hear each other present their latest research findings — they seem to have a healthier sense of their colleagues' qualities. . . .

Tolerance of Differences

"We have disagreements, but those disagreements don't translate into divisions. They don't translate into destruction of collegiality."

The veneer of civility that permeates so many departments in our study is absent in those that support teaching. Faculty hold significantly different opinions about theory, methods, and the direction of the discipline. These differences, however, do not paralyze the department or prevent it from discussing important issues. Faculty respect their colleagues; they appreciate their differences. . . .

Generational Equity

"Of course, junior faculty get to comment on senior people."

The gulf between junior and senior faculty appears to be much narrower in departments that support teaching. Communication between older and younger faculty is frequent. Senior faculty view their younger colleagues as representing the future of the department and appreciate the ideas they bring with them. Senior faculty consider the voice of junior faculty as equal to their own; new professors are "taken seriously" and "involved" in major decisions that affect the department. In addition, senior faculty expressed admiration for assistant professors, who must meet increasingly high standards for both teaching and research in order to attain tenure. . . .

Workload Equity

"We have a very egalitarian system here. It doesn't really matter how famous you are or how many prizes you have—you still teach. No one is ever brought in with a lighter teaching load."

Sharing the joys as well as the burdens of teaching is important to faculty in departments whose culture enhances teaching. These departments "strongly discourage" buy-outs of teaching time with research grants. Not only do all faculty teach the same number of classes, but faculty also teach at all levels, from introductory and service courses to advanced seminars.

. . . In another exemplary department, junior faculty are explicitly kept away from large introductory courses. The department, recognizing the work involved and the difficulty of teaching these types of courses, assigns them to senior faculty. The situation is viewed as positive for everyone— junior faculty are given the opportunity to develop their teaching skills in smaller classes, and new students are given the opportunity to work with the best-known faculty in the department.

Course Rotation

"When you're assigned a new course you've never taught before, you go talk to the person who is teaching it now, or somebody who has taught it before, and say 'What textbook did you use? Did you like it? Is there a better one? What topics did you cover? Can I borrow your notes?' "

Although teaching the same course year after year may be a way of saving time in course preparation, faculty in departments that support teaching do not feel the savings are worth the price of potentially stale teaching. Some require regular course rotation: no one teaches a course more than three consecutive times. All faculty take their turns at teaching freshmen, upper-division students, and graduate students (if their department has a graduate program). Faculty report these policies produce a cohesive and up-to-date curriculum and help keep their teaching fresh. . . .

Faculty in one department have formalized a way to facilitate communication about courses. After their third time teaching a course, they complete and file a report on it. This report includes the syllabus, discussion notes, written opinions about the text and other course materials, and a statement about what worked and what did not. These reports provide a wealth of information for faculty who subsequently teach the course. In the case of courses that have been taught for many years, the reports constitute the department's pedagogical history. Faculty members with more than 20 years' experience were just as likely as junior faculty to tell us that they benefit from regularly consulting this file.

Peer Evaluation of Teaching

"When somebody is teaching a new course, or they're teaching a course for the first time, we'll have another faculty member sit in on one or two lectures and take notes and critique what the person is doing. We just give advice—it's not something that's used in any formal sense. It's just simply a collegial way of providing some feedback."

Faculty in departments that support teaching appear to be less intimidated by peer evaluation than their colleagues in other departments. The style, purpose, and range of peer review varies in these departments. In some, the purpose of peer evaluation is to help junior faculty identify teaching weaknesses so that they have ample time to improve their skills before critical promotion and tenure reviews. In other departments, faculty seem more interested in the overall quality of departmental course offerings. One or more colleagues visit and critique each new course, regardless of the rank of the professor teaching the course. . . .

Student Evaluation of Teaching

"The other thing we are trying in terms of educational quality is to meet regularly with our honors students to get their input on curriculum, advising, teaching, and so on."

Faculty in departments that support teaching appear to take student evaluations seriously. While they recognize that students sometimes criticize faculty for things unrelated to teaching, these faculty believe that the process has some merit. One chair stated that faculty in his department listen to students because they provide an accurate "sense of the quality of the course and how well the professor is communicating." The department has instituted "spot checks," immediate peer visits to classes prompted by "rumblings" from students. The goal is to help faculty make mid-course corrections instead of "always correcting after the fact." Another of these departments has just "radically redone" its student evaluation forms to include extensive written comments, which faculty believe are critical to improving teaching.

Balanced Incentives

"We are scrupulous in promotion and tenure decisions about the evaluation of teaching. We insist that teaching be very good. We review faculty members on a set schedule. Assistant professors are reviewed every two years, associates every five years, and full professors every seven years. The review includes both teaching and research, as well as service and other contributions to the field."

While teaching is not weighted as heavily as research even in the departments with cultures that support teaching, it is becoming a more significant factor in tenure decisions. These departments scrutinize their junior members' teaching skills and offer guidance and assistance before crucial decision points.

. . . The change even affects senior faculty. The chair of one of these departments told us, "If you're a crummy teacher, at least during my time as chair, it's unlikely you will get hefty salary increases no matter how stellar your research."

Consensus Decision-Making

"Well, I guess I'd have to say that most of our decisions are made pretty informally. The chair or someone else will bring up an issue at a meeting or in the office and we talk about it until we reach a decision that everyone — or at least most of us — can live with."

Those interviewed described decision-making processes in these departments as "consensual," "collegial," "informal," or "participatory." All (or most) departmental faculty were involved in key decisions. Although absolute consensus is generally not possible, members of these departments are willing to take the time to discuss issues at length and formulate compromises that most faculty can accept. . . .

Effective Department Chairs

"He [the chair] is very nurturing. He sees our success as his success and lobbies hard for faculty and money from the institution. He is a real advocate for junior people. He makes a good impression on all the faculty."

The chair may well represent the single most important factor in determining whether or not a department actively supports teaching. Interviewees cited the crucial role the chair plays in creating an environment conducive to effective teaching. . . .

Collegiality
. . . The distinctive characteristics of our exemplary departments — an emphasis on teaching, frequent interaction, tolerance of differences, generational and workload equity, peer evaluation, and consensus decision-making — reveal a pattern widely recognized in higher education: *collegiality*. . . .

"Hollowed" Collegiality
The collegiality we observed in the majority of departments we evaluated brings a sense of fairness to some departmental processes and permits faculty to economize on the effort required for certain tasks. It furthers civility and equity, and maximizes faculty discretionary time.

Despite these trappings of collegiality, respondents told us they seldom led to the more substantial discussions necessary to improve undergraduate education, or to the sense of collective responsibility needed to make departmental efforts more effective. These vestiges of collegiality serve faculty convenience but dodge fundamental questions of task. This is especially the case, and is regrettable, with respect to student learning: collegiality remains thwarted with regard to faculty engagement with issues of curricular structure, pedagogical alternatives, and student assessment.

We believe these vestiges of collegiality are superficial or "hollowed." And it is this hollowed collegiality that stands in the way of improved departmental functioning and breakthroughs in student learning. Ironically, it can also stand in the way of a more satisfying professional life for a department's members. . . .

November/December 1995

The New Scholarship Requires a New Epistemology

Knowing-in-Action

Donald A. Schön

If we intend to pursue the "new forms of scholarship" that Ernest Boyer presents in his *Scholarship Reconsidered*, we cannot avoid questions of epistemology, since the new forms of scholarship he describes challenge the epistemology built into the modern research university.

In addition to basic research—Boyer's *scholarship of discovery*, which "has come to be viewed as the first and most essential form of scholarship, with other functions flowing from it"—Boyer envisions three new forms of scholarship.

■ The *scholarship of integration* gives meaning to isolated facts, "putting them into perspective . . . making connections across disciplines, placing the specialties in larger context, illuminating data in a revealing way, often educating nonspecialists, too. . . ."

■ In the *scholarship of application*, "the scholar asks, 'How can knowledge be responsibly applied to consequential problems? How can it be helpful to individuals as well as to institutions?' "

■ The *scholarship of teaching*, which "begins with what the teacher knows," means not only transmitting knowledge but *transforming* and *extending* it as well. . . ."

If integration, application, and teaching are to be taken as "forms of scholarship" in other than a Pickwickian sense, the new scholars must produce knowledge that is testably valid, according to criteria of appropriate rigor, and their claims to knowledge must lend themselves to intellectual debate within academic (among other) communities of inquiry. But what are these kinds of knowledge, claims to validity, and criteria of appropriate rigor? And how do they stand in relation to the "old" scholarship of discovery?

I argue in this article that if the new scholarship is to mean anything, it must imply a kind of action research with norms of its own, which will conflict with the norms of technical rationality—the prevailing epistemology built into the research universities. Drawing on my experience studying MIT's Project Athena, I illustrate what this kind of action research could be like in at least one instance and suggest the epistemological, institutional, and political issues it raises within the university.

Institutional Epistemology

Like other organizations, educational institutions have epistemologies. They hold conceptions of what counts as legitimate knowledge and how you know what you claim to know. These theories of knowledge need not be consciously espoused by individuals (although they may be) for they are built into institutional structures and practices. . . .

The dilemma of rigor or relevance. In the varied topography of professional practice, there is a high, hard ground overlooking a swamp. On the high ground, manageable problems lend themselves to solution through the use of research-based theory and technique. In the swampy lowlands, problems are messy and confusing and incapable of technical solution. The irony of this situation is that the problems of the high ground tend to be relatively unimportant to individuals or to society at large, however great their technical interest may be, while in the swamp lie the problems of greatest human concern. The practitioner is confronted with a choice. Shall he remain on the high ground where he can solve relatively unimportant problems according to his standards of rigor, or shall he descend to the swamp of important problems where he cannot be rigorous in any way he knows how to describe?

Nearly all professional practitioners experience a version of the dilemma of rigor or relevance, and they respond to it in one of several ways. Some of them choose the swampy lowland, deliberately immersing themselves in confusing but critically important situations. When they are asked to describe their methods of inquiry, they speak of experience, trial and error, intuition, or muddling through. When teachers, social workers, or planners operate in this vein, they tend to be afflicted with a nagging sense of inferiority in relation to those who present themselves as models of technical rigor. When physicists or engineers do so, they tend to be troubled by the discrepancy between the technical rigor of the "hard" zones of their practice and the apparent sloppiness of the "soft" ones.

People tend to feel the dilemma of rigor or relevance with particular intensity when they reach the age of about 45. At this point, they ask themselves, "Am I going to continue to do the thing I was trained for, on which I base my claims to technical rigor and academic respectability? Or am I going to work on the problems — ill-formed, vague, and messy — that I have discovered to be real around here?" And depending on how people make this choice, their lives unfold differently.

What are the sources of the dilemma of rigor or relevance?

The dilemma depends, I believe, upon a particular epistemology built into the modern research university, and, along with this, on our discovery of the increasing salience of certain "indeterminate zones" of practice — uncertainty, complexity, uniqueness, conflict — which fall outside the categories of that epistemology. . . .

The new scholarship implies action research.

The new categories of scholarly activity must take the form of action research. What else could they be? They will not consist in laboratory experimentation or statistical analysis of variance, nor will they consist only or primarily in the reflective criticism and speculation familiar to the humanities.

If teaching is to be seen as a form of scholarship, then the practice of teaching must be seen as giving rise to new forms of knowledge. If community outreach is to be seen as a form of scholarship, then it is the practice of reaching out and providing service to a community that must be seen as raising important issues whose investigation may lead to generalizations of prospective relevance and actionability. If we speak of a scholarship of integration — the synthesis of findings into larger, more comprehensive understandings — then we are inevitably concerned with designing. The scholarship of application means the generation of knowledge for, and from, action. Indeed, Boyer's proposition, "New intellectual understandings can arise out of the very act of application," is a fairly exact formulation of Lewinian action research.

The problem of changing the universities so as to incorporate the new scholarship must include, then, how to introduce action research as a legitimate and appropriately rigorous way of knowing and generating knowledge. . . .

Project Athena at MIT

. . . Project Athena, begun in about 1982, was MIT's attempt to introduce computers into undergraduate education, and, in the process, to reestablish itself at the leading edge of institutional computing . . .

Athena began with several key premises. One was that the computer held the potential for revolutionizing undergraduate education. It would do so, as the dean of engineering put it, by increasing educational effectiveness and efficiency . . .

Another of Athena's premises was that faculty members would invent educational software. Funds were made available for this purpose, and faculty were invited to ask for grants to develop educational software for subjects of their choosing . . .

Is developing educational software a legitimate form of research? . . . Shaler was . . . an engineer working as a junior faculty member in the field of civil engineering. He had developed two programs for computer-assisted instruction. One of these, Program A, was conceived as an intelligent tutor designed to help civil engineering students learn statics. It would administer problems, register the correctness or incorrectness of the student's proposed solutions, and for incorrect answers, would diagnose the errors in question, provide the correct principles, and re-administer new problems that posed the same kinds of difficulty. Program B, on the other hand, was conceived not as an instructional program but as a "design tool." It made it possible to draw a structure on the CRT screen—a bridge or truss, for example; specify its dimensions and materials; and apply a load of a given magnitude. The program would then instantly display the structure's deflection in response to the load.

When we interviewed students who had used both programs, we found they hated the intelligent tutor. They thought it dull and boring and used their MIT smarts to subvert it so that it simply spat out the right answers (thereby deriving some educational benefit, I suppose). But Program B, which was intended to function only as a "design tool," turned out to be extraordinarily educational for about a third of the students who used it in their design projects. These students would draw and load their structures in the virtual world of the machine, expecting a certain kind of outcome, and would often be surprised to get something else entirely. They would ask, for example, "How could this structure become stiffer when I take something *away* from it?" And because these were confident MIT types, they did not respond by questioning their aptitude for engineering. Rather, they said, "Wow!" and tried to find out what was going on. They would revisit Statics 105, which they'd taken in their freshman or sophomore year, and would discover that the formula that applied to the phenomena was one they already knew. But they would say: "I knew the formula, but I never understood how the damned structure behaved until I tried this program."

It happened that Bob Shaler . . . came up for tenure. When his case came before the Academic Council, they found that his work did not look like high-quality research to them. They also asked, "Who can read this stuff and critique it? How can we judge it?" Shaler was denied tenure.

Because this process was going on in the midst of our study of Athena, we were able to look into what was happening. We found that members of the committee judged Shaler's research to be of poor quality—or even more damaging, unable to be evaluated. But we also found that Shaler, although he knew how to design software and get it to work in the design laboratories, did not know how to make "research" out of it—that is, to read into his inquiry a question that could be subjected to empirical research.

Shaler was surprised by how the students used and reacted to his two programs. In my view, this surprise could have been a springboard for research. Shaler could have gotten interested in what the students were actually making of his software, how they used it, what it meant to them. Indeed, I think all educational software designers should get interested in this question, for they would discover that the object they designed often takes on a meaning in use that differs from their design intention, and they might be led to think differently about the "knowledge" they intended to convey . . .

Conclusion

The basic argument of this paper is simple, although its consequences are far from simple. The new forms of scholarship call for a new institutional epistemology. If the scholarship of synthesis, application, or teaching requires that the scholar contribute to knowledge according to norms shared and developed within a community of inquiry, then the new scholarship cannot achieve legitimacy within an institution exclusively dedicated to technical rationality—the epistemology around which the modern research university was originally established and which still underlies its key institutions.

The new forms of scholarship advocated by Boyer and others lie much closer to practice. They proceed through design inquiry, in the Deweyan sense. They are infused with a tacit knowing that their practitioners usually cannot describe (at least without observation and reflection devoted to that purpose), and they are inimical to the conditions of control and distance that are essential to technical rationality.

The epistemology appropriate to the new scholarship must make room for the practitioner's reflection in and on action. It must account for and legitimize not only the use of knowledge produced in the academy, but the practitioner's generation of actionable knowledge in the form of models or prototypes that can be carried over, by reflective transfer, to new practice situations. The new scholarship calls for an epistemology of reflective practice, which includes what Kurt Lewin described as action research. But in the modern research university and other institutions of higher education influenced by it, reflective practice in general, and action research in particular, are bound to be caught up in a battle with the prevailing epistemology of technical rationality.

In my admittedly special example of MIT's Project Athena, I have tried to show how the introduction of the kinds of inquiry inherent in the new scholarship are likely to encounter a double impediment: on the one hand, the power of disciplinary in-groups that have grown up around the dominant epistemology of the research universities; and on the other, the inability of those who might become new scholars to make their practice (of teaching and curriculum development, in this instance) into appropriately rigorous research.

In order to legitimize the new scholarship, higher education institutions will have to learn organizationally to open up the prevailing epistemology so as to foster new forms of reflective action research. This, in turn, requires building up communities of inquiry capable of criticizing such research and fostering its development. The story of Project Athena also suggests how the growing interest in design and its teaching, and in the educational potentials offered by computer, may be used as occasions for introducing and legitimizing the epistemology of reflective practice that underlies the new scholarship. . . .

July/August 1996

Socializing Future Faculty to the Values of Undergraduate Education

Jerry G. Gaff and Leo M. Lambert

Any serious discussion about socializing future faculty to the values of undergraduate education begins with a simple fact: 102 universities produce 80 percent of all U.S. doctoral degrees awarded annually. These few universities operate as a funnel through which the vast majority of faculty members in America's 3,500 diverse colleges and universities must pass. The majority of "hiring" institutions — liberal arts colleges of varying selectivity, comprehensive universities of different sizes, technical and community colleges, and other special colleges, such as women's and historically black institutions — have missions, values, cultures, and conceptions of faculty roles and responsibilities far different from those of doctorate-granting research universities.

A serious, long-term consequence of this funnel effect is that doctoral graduates are socialized into the values of the research university and frequently remain out of tune with the values and real work of institutions where they are likely to be employed. Too often, the graduate faculties responsible for preparing the future professoriate are unaware of the values of different types of academic institutions or, occasionally, are even hostile to the very places their students will seek jobs. Doctoral education is a powerful enculturation process, but is sometimes disconnected from the realities of jobs available to new faculty.

Both graduate faculty and graduate students often operate as if the academic positions that newly minted PhDs secure will resemble those in the research university. In fact, fewer than 10 percent of PhDs end up in other research universities. One major university (with generally high-ranking departments), awarded 419 doctorates in the arts, humanities, and social sciences during the most recent three-year period, and 25, a mere 6 percent, took jobs at other research universities.

Anyone associated with undergraduate education knows that preparation for research is a necessary but insufficient qualification for academic employment. A provost at a leading liberal arts college in Minnesota told us,

"As someone who has interviewed about 200 new PhDs for positions here over the last four years, I know the country needs to provide

encouragement, support, and training for those graduate students interested in becoming faculty members. Very few of those I interviewed knew what life would be like on our campus, and all had been discouraged from applying to a small liberal arts college."

New college faculty are typically confronted with a need to design new courses, teach a diversity of students, advise about education and careers, contribute to institutional initiatives ranging from internationalizing the curriculum to using technology, and serve on faculty committees—none of which they are typically prepared to do.

The Values of the Hiring Colleges and Universities

Let's look more closely at five specific values of hiring institutions.

1. Expectations and Definitions of Scholarship

Institutions hiring new faculty value scholarship and other creative expressions as a key dimension of professional life. But scholarship at a comprehensive university, for example, may have a broader definition appropriate to the institution's mission, in contrast to the traditional research university definition of scholarship. . . .

2. The Primary Commitment to Undergraduate Teaching

At most "hiring" institutions, undergraduate teaching is the top institutional priority, and demonstrated success as a teacher of undergraduates is the single most important criterion for promotion and tenure. Understanding this reality is sometimes an epiphany for PhD students who view teaching as unconnected to other aspects of professional life, see excellent teaching go unrewarded (or even harm professional advancement), seldom discuss teaching in any great depth with faculty or graduate student colleagues, and may have witnessed faculty at some research universities give short shrift to teaching. . . .

Another key aspect of professional life learned early on by new faculty is that hiring institutions often require heavy teaching loads, typically three or four courses per semester. Thus, learning to handle teaching responsibilities, make progress on one's scholarly agenda, and participate in other

aspects of the academic community is a struggle for many first-year faculty.

3. The Values Inherent in the Curriculum

Another key dimension of academic life at a teaching-oriented campus concerns the values inherent in an undergraduate curriculum. Today, many campuses have incorporated ambitious goals into general education programs, such as teaching world cultures and promoting multicultural understanding, fostering interdisciplinary courses, incorporating service-learning, promoting discipline-based writing classes, and encouraging instructional approaches that actively engage students in their learning.

While doctoral students routinely have experience teaching introductory courses in their disciplines (and perhaps an undergraduate course in their specialty area), seldom do they have the opportunity to examine the continuity of the undergraduate curriculum in their fields, to understand the philosophical underpinnings of a general education program, or to think about a body of curriculum as a coherent form.

4. Faculty Governance and Service Roles

At many employing institutions, faculty assume a host of responsibilities related to departmental and university governance and service. These may include advising a student organization, serving on departmental and university committees or on a faculty senate, or using their professional expertise to solve community problems. These are important functions; university communities depend on faculty "volunteers" to get such tasks accomplished. Performing these well is part of fulfilling one's responsibilities as a faculty colleague and community member.

5. Graduate Education at Master's-Level Institutions

Many new faculty members find themselves at comprehensive universities and liberal arts colleges with master's degree programs, and some will discover that they have immediate responsibility for advising master's theses and teaching graduate courses and seminars. Ironically, little attention is given to preparing future faculty to be mentors and advisors to graduate students, aside from imitating the (hopefully) positive behaviors of their own graduate teachers and mentors. New faculty must learn what constitutes a good master's thesis, how teaching a graduate seminar differs from teaching an undergraduate course, and the general roles and function of graduate faculty.

The five topics above may be dealt with (however briefly) in the search process and in new-faculty orientation programs. But much more can and should be done in graduate school to acquaint future faculty with the real work of their chosen profession. More importantly, graduate students, even talented ones from the "best" universities, are not able to secure academic positions unless they exhibit at least a modicum of sophistication about these matters.

New Approaches to Graduate Preparation

Today many institutions and organizations are developing innovations to socialize future faculty with a different set of values, ones more in keeping with the values of hiring institutions. Here is a list of recent initiatives.

■ Public universities of Washington, Texas, Ohio, Illinois, and Colorado have played lead roles in developing programs to orient and support graduate teaching assistants and to share their approaches nationally through biannual conferences.

■ Private universities such as Brown, Duke, Emory, Loyola, Rochester, and Syracuse have completed successful demonstration projects to enhance graduate students' teaching effectiveness, often in collaboration with partner undergraduate institutions.

■ Colleges such as Connecticut, Guilford, Illinois Benedictine, and St. John Fisher have provided opportunities for graduate students to teach courses and experience faculty life on their campuses.

■ Pilot projects conducted by the Association of American Colleges and Universities and the Council of Independent Colleges have demonstrated ways to incorporate teaching and service components into doctoral study and to provide graduate students opportunities to work with teaching mentors at predominantly undergraduate colleges. . . .

■ Learned societies, including the American Academy of Religion, American Sociological Association, American Historical Association, and American Council of Learned Societies, have featured conference sessions on new approaches for preparing future faculty.

■ The New England Board of Higher Education (NEBHE), the Southern Regional Education Board (SREB), and The Western Interstate Commission for Higher Education (WICHE) have launched a "Compact for Faculty Diversity" to help ensure a continuing stream of students of color who are committed to careers in college teaching.

■ The professional literature on the career development of graduate students and new professors—and programs to support them—is growing.

These efforts may be small-scale, scattered, and diffuse, but collectively they add up to an impressive alternative to traditional ways of socializing faculty. Many of the demonstration projects have documented the benefits of their approaches, creating a new base for changes in the preparation of the future professoriate. . . .

Preparing Future Faculty Project

Perhaps the most ambitious effort to change the "culture of preparation" is the Preparing Future Faculty project (PFF), a joint effort by the Association of American Colleges and Universities and the Council of Graduate Schools supported by The Pew Charitable Trusts. Each of 17 research universities works with a cluster of "hiring" institutions. Each cluster includes a small number of diverse, primarily undergraduate teaching institutions—liberal arts colleges, comprehensive institutions, and community colleges.

Through numerous approaches, the PFF projects expose graduate students to a variety of teaching experiences. In the words of Robert Schwartz of the Pew Trusts, the PFF arrangement brings the "consumers" of PhDs to the table with the "producers" to discuss the qualities desired in new faculty, and it gives opportunities for graduate students to gain experience with faculty members, students, and academic values at various kinds of institutions beyond the research university. The project includes a total of 85 institutions—13 community colleges, seven historically black colleges and universities, six women's colleges, and scores of liberal arts and comprehensive institutions, along with 13 land-grant universities and nine members of the Association of American Universities.

PFF programs take many different shapes, depending on local situations, but a configuration of principles animates them. Perhaps the most generic is that graduate students should enter the academic profession as competent professionals who have already begun a process of growth as scholars, teachers, and members of an academic community. This marks a significant departure from the usual approach of focusing nearly exclusively on research, with the possibility of modest experience as a teaching assistant. Graduate students, we believe, should be regarded as "colleagues-in-training" and receive opportunities to have first-hand experience with the full spectrum of faculty roles.

The more specific principles are these:

1. The graduate experience should include a) increasingly independent and varied teaching responsibilities, b) opportunities to grow and develop as a scholar, and c) opportunities to serve the department and campus.

2. Apprentice teaching, research, and service experiences should be planned developmentally so that they are appropriate to the student's stage of development and progress toward the degree. These experiences should be thoughtfully integrated into the academic program and sequence of degree requirements.

3. PFF programs should build upon and go beyond teaching-assistant orientation and development programs. While TA orientation is crucial, graduate students should not be sent the message that preparation is a one-shot activity. The establishment of ongoing, discipline-based professional development seminars, the involvement of graduate students in departmental governance and decision-making, and the development of active strategies for advanced graduate students to find academic employment are examples of ways departments, and PFF, may build upon the most common teaching assistant training activities.

4. The graduate program should include a formalized system of mentoring in teaching and other aspects of professional development. This should be as integral to the degree as the supervision of the dissertation.

5. Graduate students should learn about the academic profession and have direct and personal experience with the diverse kinds of institutions that may become their professional homes.

6. The graduate experience should prepare future faculty for the classrooms and campuses of tomorrow. This includes becoming familiar with the role of technology in the delivery of instruction, dealing with the diverse needs of students, and using some of the more active and collaborative methods of teaching and learning.

None of these ideas is new or radical. What is new is that they are becoming operational in actual graduate programs and are beginning to make a difference in the education of students. And they are spreading: PFF principles can now be seen in similar programs at Indiana University, North Carolina State, and the University of New Hampshire.

Since the clusters of institutions in the PFF program were each encouraged to develop programs tailored to their own particular needs and circumstances, no generic program can be described. Institutions apply the above principles in various ways. But a flavor of the programs can be seen in illustrative activities in three loci.

■ *Universities* are doing such things as offering a course on college teaching and learning, designing forums on issues of faculty life and careers, and helping graduate students to prepare portfolios documenting their expertise in teaching, research, and service.

■ *Departments* are offering a course on the teaching of their subject, providing a sequence of supervised teaching experiences, and holding forums for faculty to discuss their professional histories, career paths, and lifestyles.

■ *Partner institutions* are assigning a teaching mentor to work with a graduate student in teaching a segment of a course, inviting students to department or faculty meetings, and including graduate students in a faculty development activity.

Although programs differ, all incorporate a broader vision of graduate preparation and provide graduate students with experience in institutions markedly different from their own graduate universities. . . .

Taking Learning Seriously

Lee S. Shulman

What do we mean by "taking learning seriously"? . . .

When we take something seriously, we often talk about *professing* it. . . .

A more contemporary meaning of the word . . . is to profess one's understanding, one's expertise: to be professional, or to be a "professor." Members of professions take on the burden of their understanding by making public commitments to serve their fellow beings in a skilled and responsible manner. "Professors" take on a special set of roles and obligations. They profess their understanding in the interests of nurturing the knowledge, understanding, and development of others. They take learning so seriously that they profess it. This brings us to the topic of *learning*.

Professing Learning

. . . When I began teaching learning theory, our conception of learning was fairly simple. For any given learning situation, the "inside" of the learner was treated as more or less empty; learning was understood as a process of getting the knowledge that was outside the learner—in books, theories, the mind of the teacher—to move inside. We tested for the success of learning by giving tests to look inside the heads of our students to see if what had previously been outside was now there. I exaggerate, but there was a comforting simplicity to our psychological behaviorism in those days.

We now understand that learning is a *dual* process in which, initially, the inside beliefs and understandings must come out, and only then can something outside get in. It is not that prior knowledge must be expelled to make room for its successors. Instead, these two processes—the inside-out and the outside-in movements of knowledge—alternate almost endlessly. To prompt learning, you've got to begin with the process of going from inside out. The first influence on new learning is not what teachers do pedagogically but the learning that's already inside the learner.

David Ausubel was one of the pioneering cognitive educational psychologists. He wrote a lovely epigraph at the beginning of his 1968 textbook, *Educational Psychology: A Cognitive View:* "If I had to reduce all of educational psychology to just one principle, I would say this: The most important single factor influencing learning is what the learner already knows. Ascertain this and teach him accordingly."

We've come to understand more clearly the extent to which learners construct meaning out of their prior understanding. Any new learning must, in some fashion, connect with what learners already know. Of course, that is an oversimplification, but it is what I mean by "getting the inside out." As teachers, unless we can discover ways of getting the inside out and looking jointly at their prior knowledge with our students, taking seriously what they already know and believe, instruction becomes very difficult. Our first principle, therefore, begins with the assertion that we must take seriously what the students have already learned. To take *learning* seriously, we need to take *learners* seriously.

An interesting surprise is that once what is inside gets out, it seldom just sits there; in a setting where serious activity and/or discussion is possible, that knowledge is enriched and elaborated by social interactions with people who have also experienced their own processes of getting what's inside out. Thus, learners construct their sense of the world by applying their old understandings to new experiences and ideas. That new learning is enriched enormously by the ways in which people wrestle with such ideas on the "outside," before they bring those ideas back inside and make them their own. This explains why one of the most important remedies for combating the illusion of understanding and the persistence of misconceptions is to support learners in the active, collaborative, reflective reexamination of ideas in a social context.

Learning is least useful when it is private and hidden; it is most powerful when it becomes public and communal. Learning flourishes when we take what we think we know and offer it as community property among fellow learners so that it can be tested, examined, challenged, and improved before we internalize it.

... We have finally begun to recognize that when we confront serious problems in education, we must embark on systematic research to help us cope with them. ... The sobering news is that although we can learn a great deal from traditional forms of research at the level of general principles, education is not a science; it is a complex set of practices that is grounded and principled but not rule-governed. As the late Donald Schön wrote eloquently, the principles of technical rationality are necessary for this work to proceed, but these principles must be joined with reflective practice.

Far too many interpreted Schön's writings as advocating a rejection of scholarly research in the professions or applied fields. Far from it. The strategy we must pursue is an approach to scholarship that legitimates more than one kind of research. Research that renders one's own practice as the problem for investigation is at the heart of what we mean by *professing* or *profession*.

At the very core of any field that we call a profession is an inherent and inescapable uncertainty. ... Professions (like teaching) deal with that part of the universe where design and chance collide. One cannot resolve that uncertainty by writing new rules. The way forward is to make that collision, that unpredictability in our fields, itself an object of individual and collective investigation. ... We can develop new forms of inquiry that both learn from and support the "wisdom of practice."

Taking Teaching Seriously

... [W]e must commit ourselves professionally to a scholarship of teaching.

What do we mean when we call something "scholarship"? Certainly, all acts of intelligence are not scholarship. An act of intelligence or of artistic creation becomes scholarship when it possesses at least three attributes: it becomes public; it becomes an object of critical review and evaluation by members of one's community; and members of one's community begin to use, build upon, and develop those acts of mind and creation.

Think about what happens in the scholarship we create when we're doing traditional forms of research. We publish our findings and ideas because we have a responsibility to make our acts of mind available to our colleagues. Yes, a few of

us want to get promoted, too. But the real reason that publication is important is that scholarly acts must be made available for public scrutiny. They have to become community property or they will not contribute to the larger profession, as scholarship must.

We cannot treat all acts of scholarship indiscriminately. We have to ask which of them meet certain standards and genuinely contribute to knowledge. We care about standards of quality because we recognize that scholars are engaged in work that none can accomplish alone. Since we can't do it alone, we depend on the scholarship of others as the building blocks for our own scholarship. Thoughtless critics often ridicule the fact that our acts of scholarship usually end with long lists of references. A list of references is a set of thank-you notes. It is our way of acknowledging that, without the people whom we reference, we could not have done the work we did. We are members of a community of scholars. References permit our readers to trace our research back to its sources.

For a scholarship of teaching, we need scholarship that makes our work public and thus susceptible to critique. It then becomes community property, available for others to build upon.

How many professional educators, when engaged in creating a new course or a new curriculum, can turn to a published, peer-reviewed scholarship of teaching in which colleagues at other colleges and universities present their experiments, their field trials, or their case studies of instruction and its consequences? Where is the scholarly literature through which higher educators study exemplars of teaching and can build upon that work? With precious few exceptions, we don't have such a literature.

In this respect, the scholarship of teaching is dramatically different from the scholarship of investigation. It's one of the reasons why any sort of progress is so hard to come by pedagogically—because blindness and amnesia are the state of the art in pedagogy. We just don't know what our colleagues before or elsewhere have done. We don't even document and analyze our own efforts. Indeed, we often don't know what our colleague in the next office is doing pedagogically, although we are thoroughly familiar with the research of colleagues a continent (and an e-mail click) away.

We are committed at the Carnegie Foundation

to infusing into academic culture a profound commitment to the scholarship of teaching. This scholarship is a way of recording, displaying, examining, investigating, and building more powerful

pedagogies for dealing with the challenges presented by the pathologies of learning, which are pandemic in our classrooms and institutions. . . .

September/October 1994

The Decline in Undergraduate Teaching
Moral Failure or Market Pressure?

Gordon C. Winston

It appears to be a consensus of the mid-1990s that the quality of undergraduate teaching in the United States is in decline—or—if it's not getting any worse, it's already bad enough to justify public concern. And there is a near consensus, if not always explicit, that the root cause is a moral failure of American professors; they simply have too much power and they pay too much attention to their research and consulting and graduate students and too little attention to their undergraduates and lectures and advising and caring.

At its crudest, the argument is Charles Sykes' in *ProfScam*, which identifies all problems of U.S. higher education with a spoiled, devious, and venal professoriate. Or Martin Anderson's *Impostors in the Temple* or Richard M. Huber's *How Professors Play the Cat Guarding the Cream* or. . . . Such criticism has been a cottage industry of the early '90s. At its most recent, the argument is made in *The New York Times'* 1994 survey of higher education by William H. Honan. At its most gentle, it is implicit in William F. Massy and Robert Zemsky's (1992) argument that points to the complicity of administrators who let academic departments press for "discretionary time" on behalf of their faculty and then let the envy of faculty in other departments ratchet up those costly advantages through egalitarian appeals. An endless spiral of reward-equality-reward-equality results in increases in discretionary time, and hence, higher instructional costs all around and reduced attention to undergraduates and teaching. . . .

I want to take a different tack in getting at the question of why undergraduate teaching is in decline, one that complements the Massy-Zemsky observations but recognizes that there's a deeper structure to the problem—that there's an impor-

tant *context* in which all this is operating. I doubt, quite simply, that there's been a general corruption of the moral fiber of America's college and university teachers who no longer keep the bargains with society they once honored. . . .

What's going on appears, in significant measure, to be the working of an active *market* for faculty—a national market—in which prestige-seeking colleges and universities compete with each other to build institutional excellence. They do it, in important part, through the faculty they hire. Institutions vie for both faculty superstars—the Nobels and potential Nobels—and the best of the new PhDs. They bid with money to some extent—healthy salaries—but more importantly, they use the subtler coin of discretionary time that Massy and Zemsky identify, time for which the faculty recruit will be paid but time she won't have to devote to *undergraduate* teaching and advising. She can use it for graduate students and her "own work"—for research and consulting. From the leading schools in national markets, these pressures ripple out to affect much of higher education.

If the market context is, indeed, an important aspect of the issue, two results follow from the characteristics of competitive markets. First, individual faculty members are pawns in this process—pampered pawns, perhaps, but pawns—and, second, individual colleges and universities are pawns, too. Institutions can refuse to play by the market's rules but only if they're willing to put their "institutional excellence" at considerable risk. . . .

. . . But why has discretionary time become the coin of the realm? Why not money or even the chance to teach and advise *more* undergraduates?

The answer appears to be that the colleges' interests in institutional excellence and individual faculty members' interests in professional advantage come together powerfully in discretionary time. Scholarship and publications "travel" well and broadly—they signal to the world an excellent faculty and, by implication, an excellent school. The article about a scholar's work in *The New York Times* or *U.S. News* or the segment on "Nova" or the Nobel itself are the stuff of which prestige is made, for both the school and the scholar. The great undergraduate course, in sharp contrast, gets *local* kudos—not national acclaim—so it can have only narrow impact on the school's or the teacher's reputation. There can be national publicity *about* an outstanding teacher's course, but unlike outstanding research output, the teaching can be experienced and appreciated only on her campus. The local, ephemeral, personal, real-time nature of good teaching—versus the durable, portable atemporality of good research—reduces the value of teaching in the faculty market. And so far, good teaching has not been much changed by new technologies in ways that will alter this. The taped lecture might travel well, but it can't convey the sensitive, inspiring, personal interaction with a live teacher that occurs in a classroom. It's no accident, in a related arena, that live theater thrives in an age of movies and video. The two experiences are very different. So the technologies that might once have been hoped to give teaching the same mobility and durability—and respect—as scholarship haven't done much to change the balance. . . .

Resources

Bok, Derek. "Reclaiming the Public Trust," *Change*, Vol. 24, No. 4, July/August 1992, pp. 12–19.

James, Estelle. "Product Mix and Cost Disaggregation: A Reinterpretation of the Economics of Higher Education," *The Journal of Human Resources*, Vol. 12, No. 2, 1978.

James, Estelle. "Decision Processes and Priorities in Higher Education," Chapter 4 in Stephen A. Hoenack and Eileen L. Collins, *The Economics of American Universities*, Buffalo, NY: State University of New York Press, 1990.

Hansmann, Henry. "The Role of Nonprofit Enterprise," Chapter 3 in Susan Rose-Ackerman, *The Economics of Nonprofit Institutions*, New York: Oxford University Press, 1986.

Honan, William H. "New Pressures on the University," *The New York Times*, January 9, 1994, *Educational Life*, pp. 16–18.

Lapin, Lisa. "Hard-pressed UC Finding Cash in Its Invention Patents," *The Sacramento Bee*, October 25, 1992, p. 1.

Massy, William F. and Robert Zemsky. "Faculty Discretionary Time: Departments and the Academic Ratchet," Stanford Institute of Higher Education Research, Discussion Paper 4, May 1992, inter alia.

September/October 1994

EDITORIAL: **A National Market for Excellence in Teaching**

Russell Edgerton

G ordon Winston's article . . . adds an important perspective to the national conversation about elevating the status of teaching in academe, especially in the prestige tier of research universities and selective liberal arts colleges. But at the end of his engaging analysis, he leaves us stranded—passive victims of large, impersonal market forces over which we have little control. I'd like to offer a happier ending.

Winston argues that efforts to improve teaching often ignore the fact that both individual faculty and single institutions operate in a context of powerful national markets. Campuses earn national reputations by attracting faculty who have themselves developed national reputations through their scholarship and publications. In the bidding wars for these faculty, the coin of the realm is a reduced teaching load, or—if this doesn't suffice—a carte blanche to teach courses that match one's research agenda (whether or not these courses add to a coherent curriculum). In the process, the quality of undergraduate education gets traded away.

It's wishful thinking, Winston states, to expect individual faculty or individual colleges, acting alone, to buck these market forces. And the prospect that institutions can get together and act collectively to change the rules (e.g., agree not to raid each other's faculty) are slim. The best we can hope for, Winston concludes, is that students and their parents—the biggest market of all—might gradually become more discerning customers.

I would rewrite this script at the point at which Winston diagnoses what it is that faculty national reputations are based on in the first place. He draws sharp differences between teaching and research. Teaching is "personal," "ephemeral," "appreciated on one's own campus": in short, *"local."* Research is "durable," "portable," "atemporal": in short, *"national"* (and international). Hence, teaching a wonderful undergraduate course brings only "local kudos," while writing a book can prompt articles in *The New York Times* and episodes on NOVA. Moreover, Winston adds (pounding the final nail in the coffin of teaching), teaching is a lot harder to judge. Teaching is assessed locally while research is judged all over the world.

Well, yes; all this is true. At the moment. But must it forever be so? Is there something *intrinsic* to the nature of teaching and research that forever confines excellent teaching to being a local phenomenon, while research brings wide renown? Do national reputations inevitably depend on scholarly publications? And, if so, how do baseball players and other performers who don't write books acquire their national reputations?

I'm willing to concede that excellent researchers have a significant edge. But before we condemn excellent teachers to the Siberia of being "locals," let's look at what it would take to enable excellent teachers to earn national reputations as well. Three elements are essential.

The first is a *visible product*. Since research is typically reported in a publication of some sort, our attention is focused on this final product. (We talk about evaluating "research," not "researching.") But to evaluate the quality of a scholarly project such as a research experiment, we actually ask questions about *intentions* (i.e., is this a significant undertaking?), *enactment* (i.e., is the proj-

ect cost-effective?) and *results*. All these factors go into an assessment of a scholar's performance. Writing up "the findings" is often the last task that a researcher does.

Suppose we viewed the teaching of a course as a scholarly project, not unlike the undertaking of a research experiment. The syllabus gives evidence of intentions. Lesson plans, assignments, videotapes, classroom observations by colleagues, and many other artifacts provide evidence of how the course was taught. Samples of student work, student interviews, test scores, etc., offer evidence of what student learning resulted from the course. What's missing is simply that faculty aren't in the habit of writing up the results of their "teaching experiments" in a way in which they can be shared with colleagues.

Various "write-ups" of what goes on inside our classrooms will never make the best-seller list. But they would suffice to enable the second key element to be put into play: *peer judgment*. There are hundreds of faculty with national reputations for research who have never been "read" by anyone outside their field. Rather, their work has been judged as significant by their disciplinary colleagues, and their reputations spread from there.

Teaching could be similarly judged. Indeed, if the various scholarly disciplines would regard teaching as they do research—as an activity that draws on and entails the discovery, synthesis, application, and representation of ideas—they would conclude that judgments about quality *require* peer review. Students are perfectly reliable witnesses of the mechanics of teaching. But only faculty can reliably judge whether the substance of a field is being represented in creative and appropriate ways.

Nor is there any reason why the peers rendering such a judgment need be from the same campus. Departments reviewing a colleague for tenure routinely turn for expert opinion about the candidate's research performance to colleagues in departments on other campuses who are specialists in the same area. Why should these comments be limited to research? Are there not aspects of teaching that would benefit from a similar review?

The third element we would need to have in place is a system for new *forms of public recognition* of teaching. Scholars who do excellent research have dozens of ways to achieve public recognition for their work. They get grants, awards, invitations to become members of privileged societies, and so on—and all these indicators of status show up on their résumés. Why not the same for teaching?

Actually, this is the easy part. Once teaching performance becomes visible, portable, and subject to peer judgment, new vehicles for recognizing this performance naturally follow. Models are everywhere. The national medical boards are the model for a new venture, the National Board of Professional Teaching Standards, that is trying to bring professional recognition to teachers in elementary and secondary education. Soon, school teachers will be able to stand for demanding, performance-based examinations and be certified in various specialty areas. Phi Beta Kappa represents an alternative model—where local chapters are authorized to anoint individuals into membership according to certain guidelines. The baseball farm system is a third model of a loosely coordinated system where players surface in one league and get invited into the next.

Within higher education, things are already moving in this direction. Last year, the faculty senate at the University of Wisconsin voted to establish a "Teaching Academy" for the Madison campus. Membership in the academy will be limited to around 100 faculty who have made significant contributions to the improvement of teaching. Ohio State University has a similar proposal under consideration. With some luck, these academies will soon be a force for teaching improvement within their universities—and mechanisms for giving national visibility to the individuals who are academy members.

In short, excellent teachers don't have to live out their careers as unknowns, victims of a national market that only recognizes scholars who write publications. With effort, we can put the elements in place that will enable the market to favor excellence in teaching as well.

The hardest part is to figure out ways to capture what goes on in the classroom and display it for review by peers. Where will the motivation come from? If the motivation is simply self-justification—putting together the brilliant portfolio for promotion or tenure—I doubt we'll ever get from here to there.

But there is another, more promising possibility. More and more faculty are coming to regard their teaching as a form of scholarship. They are beginning to invent ways (writing cases, developing portfolios, etc.) of documenting and displaying their teaching for colleagues. They are doing so not because they are gearing for promotion but because they feel a responsibility, as scholars, to communicate to their colleagues what they are learning about their teaching. They want to be part of scholarly communities that are concerned not only with the discovery of new knowledge but the ways this knowledge can best be represented to and learned by others. . . .

. . . These faculty are not pawns. They are inventing a new currency—a currency that recognizes teaching as a scholarly activity. With projects like this, we can change the market itself.

September/October 1995

EDITORIAL: Getting Smarter About Teaching

Ted Marchese

. . . Why is our rhetoric of change so externally referenced and threat-driven? Why, indeed, is it said that change comes in higher education only when outside forces impel it?

The full answer, could we know it, would have multiple facets. Our tendency, like anybody's, is to resent outsiders' threats. Our tradition is to "conserve and transmit" knowledge—hardly an agenda for change. Analytic caution is bred in our genes.

Large, bureaucratic systems constrain initiative. Reward systems honor business as usual.

Even as these reasons are enumerated, the thought persists that something is missing internally in our attitude toward change and improvement itself . . . especially with regard to teaching. In research, faculties continuously push forward the frontiers of knowledge and practice; in teaching, it's hard to discern a comparable ethic.

So it is, for example, that the few changes in undergraduate education we've seen over the years have been far more a function of markets and funders than of any internal dynamic. There's no clear ethic in our value system that says a college's ability to educate undergraduates should regularly and systematically improve — that my teaching, my college, or higher education itself should get smarter and better all the time at prompting student learning. . . .

Three years ago in *Change* Derek Bok observed that "teaching remains one of the few human activities that does not get demonstrably better from one generation to the next." One consequence is that undergraduate education remains in a rut — as ever, a terrific experience for some students, a failure for many others, not much of a dent on the large group in the middle. Despite the past decade's flood of commission reports, foundation grants, new pedagogies, curricular innovations, and shelves of research, it's hard to say whether American undergraduate education has improved that much. Indeed, looking across years

of data on student attainment, it's possible to argue we've slipped a bit. . . .

How does a teacher (and her department) get "smarter and better" at prompting student learning? Up front, getting smarter and better has to be your goal — it all starts with an ethic of continuous improvement. Then the means follow: with clarity all around about the intended learning; with data and close observation at the classroom and curricular levels; with constant, experimental adaptation of best practices from elsewhere; with deep reflection and public conversation about results; and by making students more self-aware and responsible in their role as learners.

Teaching and learning, in this paradigm, are inseparable — like inhaling and exhaling, as one conferee put it. They describe an activity and an ethic of faculty and students alike.

. . . Good teachers, I found, reflect upon and seek constantly to advance their craft, thus to claim better futures for students, for the society we serve, and for ourselves as a profession.

July/August 1999

The Academic Calling

Creating Spaces for Spirit

Diana Chapman Walsh

. . . If great teaching requires inspiration, what can we do to foster the expression and expansion of spirit in the academy — in teaching, scholarship, and service? What can institutions do to support faculty who want to continue to grow? Let me suggest five possible approaches.

First, we can reconnect faculty work to the fundamental purposes of a liberal education. Last September at Wellesley, at a surprisingly popular conference on spirituality and education (we'd expected 200 attendees; we had to close off registration at 800), students read a Unitarian-Universalist prayer that pictures the learning environment we need to restore:

"Come into this place of peace and let its silence heal your spirit.

"Come into this place of memory and let its history warm your soul.

"Come into this place of prophesy and power and let its vision change your heart."

As Donald Kennedy writes in *Academic Duty*:

The university is above all else about opportunity: the opportunity to give others the personal and intellectual platform they need to advance the culture, to preserve life, and to guarantee a sustainable human future. Could anything possibly matter more than that?

In short, the first and most important thing we can do for faculty morale is focus on our fundamental purpose.

Second (a corollary and a crucial one), we can hew to our primary goal — inspiring lifelong learning — and not allow the demands, lures, and metaphors of the market to impel us to move lesser concerns to center stage. We have seen that the stories students tell about teaching that changed their lives turn on low-tech interpersonal connections, subtle transfers of commitment that would be difficult to measure objectively or codify formally.

The key to inspiring teaching (as opposed to, say, efficient or entertaining teaching or even teaching that promotes learning of specific course content) lies in sustaining an intellectually vital and engaged classroom. This, in turn, requires nourishing the inner lives of the professoriate. We risk reducing the profession to a set of skills or sensitivities by promoting other agendas for faculty—mastering technology, evaluating outcomes, developing learning contracts. We must take care that these skills and sensitivities enliven the academic agenda without deflecting the attention and sapping the spirits of teachers who are also scholars and whose scholarly excursions infuse their teaching with deeper meaning.

Third, we can reward a range of gifts and contributions, instead of being rigid or doctrinaire about faculty roles and responsibilities. Gary Krahenbuhl's article in the November/December 1998 issue of *Change* makes a cogent case that the learning environment can be impoverished by inflexible faculty workload practices that ignore the full complement of faculty activities, and that overlook the variety of ways—in and out of the classroom—for faculty to ignite student learning over the course of an evolving career. Faculty go through cycles in which generating, applying, and transmitting knowledge come in and out of focus.

What a different place the academy would be if all of us were to define our essential task as discerning our colleagues' and students' particular abilities at a given point in time and helping see to it that they were encouraged to contribute to the good of the whole.

What a different place the academy would be if we were to shake loose Procrustean notions about teaching effectiveness. Csikszentmihalyi describes his college design professor, a man who—despite his being a "terrible teacher"—made an indelible mark on many lives.

He could not explain what he wanted from us, nor did he try to; he did not demonstrate how to do things; his feedback to students

was erratic and arbitrary. We were in a constant state of uncertainty and confusion in his classes. He violated all the rules of rational transmission of information; he was the exact antithesis of a well-designed teaching machine. Yet what a great professor he was! His concern for good design, for the integrity of vision and execution, was clear to everybody; it was etched in the lines of pain on his face when confronted with a facile drawing, or the look of exultation that—alas, much more rarely—passed over his features when someone broke away from a conventional cliché. It was clear that he enjoyed every minute of his work, even though most of it was painful. He could not fake enthusiasm, conviction, or belief either for our sake or for his own, but this very submission to the rules of art generated enthusiasm, conviction, and belief on our parts.

We can guard a place in the academy—always—for "terrible teachers" like that.

Fourth, we can fight deadening perfectionism, which kills off the spirit, and instead welcome into the academy the messiness of real life. We can be light and accepting of our human fallibility and open to learning from our mistakes and from what others have to teach us. As Steven Brookfield argues, a culture of trust and openness in which students will make themselves vulnerable in these ways is one in which everyone is willing to "go public with [his] learning." If we are all willing to risk being public learners, we will suspend our harsh critical judgments more of the time and listen with empathy, listen deeply in the ways that encourage the spirit to expand.

Please don't misunderstand. I am not arguing for a retreat from standards. Nothing is more corrosive of faculty morale than the sense that someone is asking them to lower their standards, dilute their syllabi, spoon-feed their students, and dumb down the curriculum to make sure that students are always feeling chipper and having fun. If we keep our eye on our essential purpose, as I am arguing we should do, we'll tighten, not loosen, our standards, be clear about our expectations, and respect the very best of which each of the students is capable.

Fifth, and finally, we can create time and space, as we did at our conference last fall, for faculty, students, and staff to honor their inner lives, when, if, and how they choose—not on command, not invasively, and ever respectful that professional scholars must be autonomous. They must be free to pursue their causal chains wherever they may lead, to seek truth through confirmation rather than revelation. The freedoms we scholars treasure need not be threatened by opening ourselves to the spiritual dimensions of teaching, learning, and knowing, need not deny the possibility of a kind of knowing that comes from the heart and soul. These forms of knowing should be sought not *instead* of the intellect but in *partnership* with the intellect, in all its beauty and power.

We know what it feels like when we are engaged in helping our students discover places of deep knowing within themselves; perhaps it's our "flow," to borrow Csikszentmihalyi's concept. When we are engaged this way, we are alert to students' intellectual travails and attuned to their inner conditions. We listen intently for what's being said and for what's still unsayable, ask gently probing questions that open avenues to self-awareness, strike a careful balance between nurturing and challenging, and encourage and support thoughtful reflection on experience. What I'm suggesting here is that we can make an effort to create opportunities—and a cultural ethos—to be those kinds of good teachers, not just to our stu-

dents, but also to ourselves and to one another within the academy.

If those of us who are called to be educators in these times of great ferment and change can support one another in our efforts to cultivate our own inner resources, then we can create healthy learning environments. Our students will benefit in two ways: directly from the effects of the healthier environments we create, indirectly from the influence of the healthier, more balanced role models we project—models of adults who have their priorities straight, who know who they are and what they love, and who find the deep meaning that animates their work.

Inspired faculty—faculty who are not dispirited and whose morale is high—are indispensable in meaning-making (surely part of what an education is about). They can build the relationships, forge the connections, bind together the pluralistic global learning communities that will provide undergraduates with models to carry throughout their lives, models that inspire lives of purpose and commitment to causes larger than themselves.

We owe it to ourselves to take heart. That is the lesson we must learn over and over. We must learn it, and we must learn how to do it. And that learning is—perhaps—the most important lesson we model for the future.

September/October 1999

The Scholarship of Teaching
New Elaborations, New Developments

Pat Hutchings and Lee S. Shulman

... What *is* this thing we're calling "the scholarship of teaching"? This is not, it turns out, merely a routine question but a marker of how this topic has evolved over the past several years. Five years ago, say, the scholarship of teaching was typically used as a term of general approbation, as a way of saying that teaching—good teaching—was serious intellectual work and should be rewarded. This was, after all, the powerful message most readers took from *Scholarship Reconsidered*. We must, Boyer wrote, "move beyond the tired old 'teaching versus research' debate and give the familiar and honorable term 'scholarship' a broader, more ca-

pacious meaning," one that includes four distinct but interrelated dimensions: discovery, integration, application, and teaching. Boyer thus sought to bring greater recognition and reward to teaching, suggesting that excellent teaching is marked by the same habits of mind that characterize other types of scholarly work.

What Boyer did *not* do was to draw a sharp line between excellent teaching and the scholarship of teaching. Now, however, we've reached a stage at which more precise distinctions seem to be wanted. Indeed, we sense a kind of crankiness among colleagues who are frustrated by the ambiguities of the phrase. How, they're asking, is excellent teaching different from the scholarship of teaching? If it is, why should anyone care about it? Is there a useful distinction to be made between the scholarship of teaching and "scholarly teaching"? Where does student learning fit in? These, in fact, are the very questions that campuses in the Campus Program are responding to as part of their process of stock-taking. They're important questions—to be taken up not in the name of creating yet another set of terms but as a way of being clear about our ends and the strategies necessary to reach them.

In this spirit, we would propose that *all* faculty have an obligation to teach well, to engage students, and to foster important forms of student learning—not that this is easily done. Such teaching is a good fully sufficient unto itself. When it entails, as well, certain practices of classroom assessment and evidence gathering, when it is informed not only by the latest ideas in the field but by current ideas about teaching the field, when it invites peer collaboration and review, *then* that teaching might rightly be called scholarly, or reflective, or informed. But in addition to all of this, yet *another* good is needed, one called a scholarship of teaching, which in another essay, we have described as having the three additional central features of being public ("community property"), open to critique and evaluation, and in a form that others can build on:

> A scholarship of teaching will entail a public account of some or all of the full act of teaching—vision, design, enactment, outcomes, and analysis—in a manner susceptible to critical review by the teacher's professional peers and amenable to productive employment in future work by members of that same community (Shulman, in *The Course Portfolio*, 1998, p. 6).

A fourth attribute of a scholarship of teaching, implied by the other three, is that it involves question-asking, inquiry, and investigation, particularly around issues of student learning. Thus, though we have been referring here to the scholarship of *teaching*, our work is with the Carnegie Academy for the Scholarship of Teaching and *Learning*. Indeed, our guidelines for the Carnegie Scholars program call for projects that investigate "not only

teacher practice but the character and depth of student learning that results (or does not) from that practice."

And with this, we believe, the circle comes full round. A scholarship of teaching is *not* synonymous with excellent teaching. It requires a kind of "going meta," in which faculty frame and systematically investigate questions related to student learning—the conditions under which it occurs, what it looks like, how to deepen it, and so forth—and do so with an eye not only to improving their own classroom but to advancing practice beyond it. This conception of the scholarship of teaching is not something we presume all faculty (even the most excellent and scholarly teachers among them) will or should do—though it would be good to see that more of them have the opportunity to do so if they wish. But the scholarship of teaching *is* a condition—as yet a mostly absent condition—for excellent teaching. It is the mechanism through which the profession of teaching itself advances, through which teaching can be something other than a seat-of-the-pants operation, with each of us out there making it up as we go. As such, the scholarship of teaching has the potential to serve *all* teachers—and students.

This vision will not be easily reached. And it will not be achieved except over the long haul. It is important to stress that faculty in most fields are not, after all, in the habit of—nor do most have the training for—framing questions about their teaching and students' learning and designing the systematic inquiry that will open up those questions. Indeed, one of the fundamental hurdles to such work lies in the assumption that only bad teachers have questions or problems with their practice. Randy Bass, a faculty member in American Studies at Georgetown University, and a Carnegie Scholar, writes,

> In scholarship and research, having a problem is at the heart of the investigative process; it is the compound of the generative questions around which all creative and productive activity revolves. But in one's teaching, a "problem" is something you don't want to have, and if you have one, you probably want to fix it. . . . Changing the status of the problem in teaching from terminal remediation to ongoing investigation is pre-

cisely what the movement for a scholarship of teaching is all about ("The Scholarship of Teaching: What's the Problem?" *Inventio*, 1998–99, online journal at www.doiiit.gmu.edu/inventio/randybass.htm).

Even faculty like Bass, who identify "problems" they want to explore and have the intellectual tools for doing so, face the reality that they live and work in a culture (on their campus and/or in their scholarly or professional community) that is only beginning to be receptive to such work. Doing it is a risk, both in terms of tenure and promotion and in terms of wider impact on the field, since there are as yet few channels for other faculty to come upon and engage with this work in ways that will make a lasting difference. And, of course, there's the issue of time. In short, the scholarship of teaching runs against the grain in big ways.

Moreover, there are hard intellectual questions yet to be hashed out. One is suggested by a recent e-mail we received from one of the Carnegie Scholars. "Personally," he says, "I can be perfectly content in my own world to continue doing this kind of work because it helps me develop pedagogical expertise and I think students will benefit from that. But I wonder whether this work and the knowledge it 'creates' will be credible with others. Presently I believe that it will not be well received by those in my discipline because it does not use 'credible' methods of inquiry." At issue here, as readers will see, is not only this individual's motivation to do the scholarship of teaching, but also a larger set of issues related to methods and rules of evidence, and therefore to issues of rigor and credibility. Put simply: Will this work "make it" as "scholarship"?

One of the things we have learned from the work of the Carnegie Scholars is how hard it is for faculty, regardless of their own field and its rules of evidence, not to assume that credibility means a traditional social science model of inquiry. Part of the attractiveness of the social sciences comes from the fact that they cover a lot of methodological ground these days, having been extended and transformed over the years through the influence of fields such as anthropology, linguistics, and hermeneutics. They have been transformed, too, by the fact that most of the questions about human behavior we most want answered

are not, in the end, "science" questions, ones that lend themselves to immutable general truth, but rather questions about phenomena as they occur in local, particular contexts (like classrooms!). But to get at the fullest, deepest questions about teaching, faculty will have to learn and borrow from a wider array of fields and put a larger repertoire of methods behind the scholarship of teaching.

Which brings us to a second challenge: the need to keep the scholarship of teaching open to a wide set of inquiries. One of the things we have observed thus far is that many faculty gravitate to questions that might be described as "instrumental": Does this new method I'm trying lead to more or better learning than the traditional one?

Such questions are eminently sensible, the very ones, we suspect, for which there is a real audience on campuses, where faculty (and their deans) want to know whether a given approach is likely to be more powerful than another and whether it is therefore worth the time and resources to make the change. But the scholarship of teaching can also make a place for "what" questions — questions in which the task is not to "prove" but to describe and understand an important phenomenon more fully: What does it look like when a student begins to think *with* a concept rather than simply *about* it? How can we describe the character of learning in a service-learning site? There must be a place, too, for questions that allow for more theory-building forms of inquiry, and for the development of new conceptual frameworks.

Indeed, if the scholarship of teaching is to advance as a field, there must be inquiry into the process of inquiry itself. We think here of a wonderful paper by Deborah Ball and Magdalene Lampert in which they discuss their teaching in an elementary school classroom, not "to highlight our practice" (which others wanted them to do) but to draw on "our knowledge of investigating practice." Understanding their topic as a problem of representation and communication, they "realized that if we could represent practice, then the possibilities for investigating and communicating about teaching and learning — by different communities — would be enhanced" ("Multiples of Evidence, Time, and Perspective: Revising the Study of Teaching and Learning," in *Issues in Education Research*, ed. Ellen Condliffe Lagemann and Lee S. Shulman, 1999).

Third, there are issues about the most appropriate forms, media, and "genres" for making the scholarship of teaching available to the field. The word "scholarship," for many academics, conjures up the image of a traditional published article, monograph, or book. But as illustrated by the selection of examples in a "baseline" (that is, "where-we-started") bibliography on the scholarship of teaching developed for CASTL (and available to readers on the Carnegie Web site: www.carnegie foundation.org), a much wider variety of forms is now emerging. . . .

Finally, there is the issue of sustainability, which matters since the impacts of a scholarship of teaching will be achieved only over the long haul. It is heartening to see individual faculty developing examples of the scholarship of teaching; these will become prompts for a next set of efforts (just as they built on work from the several traditions that converge in the scholarship of teaching). But what's needed as well is a culture and infrastructure that will allow such work to flourish.

Among the many infrastructures that might be imagined, we end this article by focusing on just one possibility—a possibility appropriate to the need and available to many of the campus leaders who read this magazine. It is this: that campuses should think about redefining the work of their institutional research offices. Traditionally, these offices have been treated as a kind of company audit, sitting outside the organization's inner workings but keeping track of its "effectiveness" as witnessed by graduation rates, student credit hours, faculty workloads, and so forth.

Imagine, instead, a kind of institutional research that asks much tougher, more central questions: What are our students really learning? What do they understand deeply? What kinds of human beings are they becoming—intellectually, morally, in terms of civic responsibility? How does our teaching affect that learning, and how might it do so more effectively? These are, in fact, questions that the assessment movement (at its best a kind of cousin to the scholarship of teaching) put into the picture on some campuses, but they're hardly questions we've finished with. If we reconceived "institutional research" to be about such questions, in the service of its faculties, led by faculty members, then the scholarship of teaching would not be some newly conceived arena of work, or a new route to tenure, but a characteristic of the institution that took learning seriously.

The scholarship of teaching draws synthetically from the other scholarships. It begins in scholarly teaching itself. It is a special case of the scholarship of application and engagement, and frequently entails the discovery of new findings and principles. At its best, it creates new meanings through integrating across other inquiries, negotiating understanding between theory and practice. Where discovery, engagement, and application intersect, there you will find teaching among the scholarships.

STUDENTS:
Portraits of Students —
A Gallery Tour

K. Patricia Cross

Presenting an overview of what has been written about students over the past 30 years is, in many ways, similar to mounting a retrospective of paintings. The task of a docent leading a tour through the galleries of student portraiture is necessarily limited. Impressions are shaped by what the artist/author intended to convey, by what the curator/editor chose to display, and by what the docent/reviewer selects as representative or interesting to discuss.

As in art retrospectives, there are schools of style and messages displayed in the portraits of students over the 30 years of this exhibit. I have identified four galleries of portraits, each gallery representing a different era. The first gallery contains portraits from the 1960s and early 1970s. It contains pictures with heavy restless movement and vivid swirling colors. The era represented is variously described as the time of student unrest, discontent, activism, and radicalism. The portraits reveal idealism, rebellion, and confusion. The second gallery is the Gallery of Open Admissions. It pictures students who gained admission to higher education despite poor past performance in school. The portraits in this gallery are often confused with those in the next gallery—Affirmative Action, but the two contain rather different portraits. The Open Admissions Gallery pictures first-generation students who are mostly the white sons and daughters of blue-collar workers; the Affirmative Action Gallery pictures students of color. Finally, in the fourth gallery are the portraits of "students as consumers," who are comparison shopping to find the options that best serve their needs.

Gallery of Student Protest

In retrospect, we tend to look upon the decade of student unrest with something between admiration and benign nostalgia. However, the artists of the time painted a rather different picture. Bruno Bettleheim, a distinguished professor at the University of Chicago, was alarmed. He found striking "similarities between the present student rebellion in this country and what happened in the German universities to spearhead Hitler's rise to power." "Politically," he wrote, "the German rebels embraced the extreme right, while the dissenters embrace the extreme left, but what is parallel is the determination to bring down the establishment" (1969, p. 18).

While Bettleheim's analysis seems extreme to us today, his dark and angry mood is reflected in the work of even such esteemed artists as Fred Hechinger, long-time education editor of *The New York Times*. Hechinger found "Academic freedom on the American campus . . . as embattled today as at any time in the present century, including the McCarthy era" (1970, p. 32). "It is embattled," he wrote, "not only by the hostility of the repressive right-wing throughout the country, but also by the coercive and occasionally violent radicalism within academia" (p. 33). "When left-wing professors and right-wing trustees—brothers under the skin—reward students and teachers, not for academic accomplishment but for political orthodoxy, Left or

Right, then the exercise of free expression becomes a matter of martyrdom. This is hardly an environment in which academic freedom can flourish" (p. 35).

While much of the anger was directed at the student radicals, much of the concern was over the potential for overly repressive reactions from the universities. From the perspective of 30 years, many of the portraits in the Gallery of Student Protest seem overwrought. As we stroll toward the exit, the portraits become noticeably less troubled. Andrew Greeley, of the University of Chicago, wrote in 1972 that, "The word is out that the Movement has had it. . . . At best," he said, "it was a splendid display of energy, enthusiasm, altruism, and commitment . . . at worst, the Movement was simplistic, self-righteous, naïve, romantic, and inept" (1972, p. 19).

While the Movement left an imprint of greater openness and a lowering of barriers between social classes on the activists themselves (Niblett, 1973), it had little impact on the universities it tried so hard to reform. It is in the Gallery of Open Admissions that we find strong and effective, albeit unintended, pressures for reform.

Gallery of Open Admissions

This gallery could not be more different from the Gallery of Student Protest. The scenes shift from university campuses with their architecturally distinctive buildings and green, well-tended lawns to urban colleges, commuting students, and run-down buildings in the midst of crowded cities. If Berkeley was the poster campus of the 1960s, City University of New York (CUNY) was the poster campus of the 1970s.

Robert Marshak was the eighth president of City University of New York when open admissions was mandated by the Board of Higher Education in 1970. In a diptych, descriptively entitled "Open Access, Open Admissions, and Open Warfare," (1981) he painted a vivid picture of how an urban university moved almost overnight from rigorously selective admissions to open admissions.

The Gallery of Open Admissions contains two distinctive types of portraits. Symbolically, they face off against each other: faculty portraits hang on one wall, student portraits hang opposite. Students are pictured as anxious, insecure, eager to make it academically, but lacking the skills for doing so. Edward Quinn, Chairman of the English Department at City College, declared that the one thing that open admissions students had in common was that "most of them have not been particularly successful people. They lack the social ease of those whose parents went to college, the confidence of those who have always been near the top of their class, and in many cases the elementary sense of feeling at home here — 'here' being not only at the City University of New York but the United States of America" (1973, p. 30).

Some of my own portraits of students hang in this gallery. I noted that the "pervasive experience with failure" in the American public schools characterized most of the students who gained access to college through open admissions (Cross, 1973). It should have come as no surprise that students who had never been particularly successful in school approached traditional learning tasks with a certain lack of enthusiasm and confidence. Nor was it surprising that faculty members, used to teaching students who had been selected for college precisely because they were already successful students, should have approached their new task with trepidation and uncertainty.

Faculty members are pictured as confused, hostile, and faced with a challenge that they were not prepared to meet. President Marshak observed that the faculty "were driven into opposition to open admissions when it confronted them with a life crisis" to teach types of students that they had never been prepared to teach.

Professor Theodore Gross painted a dramatic portrait of a faculty facing open admissions: "What really gnawed away at our innards and left us hollow," he wrote in an article in the *Saturday Review* entitled, "How to Kill a College," "what coursed in our bodies like an incurable illness was our growing realization and fear that in middle age we no longer had a profession" (Gross, 1978).

Among faculty members who found a new and challenging profession, however, was Mina Shaughnessy, a remarkable professor who taught remedial English at CUNY. In her classic book, *Errors and Expectations*, she showed that under the messy surface of the writing of students who had little experience with written expression was coherence and meaning. The chaos that appeared to traditional teachers to be "errors" could in fact be used in writing laboratories to improve student writing. Other faculty members also soon discovered that teaching students who really needed good teachers could be the most rewarding career of all.

Gallery of Affirmative Action

While the Gallery of Open Admissions contained largely the portraits of white students—often white ethnics—the Gallery of Affirmative Action is distinctive for its portraits of students of color. This gallery is clearly unfinished. On one wall hangs a huge collage consisting of "swirling rhetoric, confusion, and the lack of common understanding about the meaning of diversity" (Levine, 1991, p. 4). The collage consists of many messages such as the following: "I realize that I avoided educational institutions because I didn't trust them" (Giddings, 1990, p. 14). "The fact that faculty and administration approached Afro-American and black studies with the same reserve and circumspection they brought to all important matters, shook my confidence in the scholarly process" (Porter, 1977, p. 36). "What troubled me and what troubled many of my friends was that we could find no relevance between what we found in the white classroom and what was occurring in the black community" (McSwine, 1971, p. 31). "Everyone, or so it appeared, discussed books that I had not read. No one discussed the books I had read" (Porter, 1977, p. 36).

Frank Wong painted a picture of doubt about whether the messages in the collage were getting through to colleges and universities. Arguing about affirmative action, he said, is like a "duel in the dark" with arguments stabbing thin air and anger and frustration mounting. The very term "multicultural community" he said, "may be an oxymoron; 'many cultures' is likely to mean many communities" that will fail to bring about a shared sense of purpose. He concluded that, "It is not a multicultural community that we seek; it is an intercultural community, where different groups engage each other with united purpose" (Wong, 1991, p. 53).

Gallery of "Student as Consumer"

This abbreviated tour of the major galleries of student portraits from 1969–1999 would not be complete without a brief glance into a gallery of mixed media. The portraits in this gallery are a mixed bag. They were mostly painted in the 1980s but seem to grow out of some combination of the pragmatic vocationalism of students who entered college under open admissions, general disillusionment with the social activism of the 1960s, and the decline of the campus as a focus of student life. If there is a central theme in these portraits, it is that of student as consumer. Arthur Levine's computer-generated picture derived from surveys of student attitudes toward their education looks like this:

"Higher education is not the central feature of their lives, but just one of a multiplicity of activities in which they are engaged every day. For many, college is not even the most important of these activities. Work and family often overshadow it.

"The relationship these students want with their college is like the one they already have with their banks, supermarkets, and other organizations they patronize. They want education to be nearby and to operate during convenient hours. . . . They want easy, accessible parking, short lines, and polite and efficient personnel and services. They also want high-quality products but are eager for low costs. They are very willing to comparison shop — placing a premium on time and money" (Levine, 1993, p. 4).

Krukowski painted a related picture. "What do students want?" he asked. "In a word, the answer is status, especially the status that is attached to a prestigious institution" (Krukowski, 1985). Other portraits in this gallery show students as docile and conservative (Gross, 1981), self-absorbed and fatalistic about society, but optimistic about their personal chances to make a good salary in a high-prestige profession (Levine, 1981), performing poorly, more materialistic than spiritual, and more concerned with themselves than with others (Winn, 1985).

A Personal Reflection

Usually, the docent ends the tour at the last gallery, hustling people toward the exit without attempting to summarize what viewers have seen or felt. However, I will risk a brief personal reflection.

One does not come away from this exhibit without reflecting on the severe challenge of change. The road to the democratization of higher education has not been smooth; indeed, it seems to have had more than its share of bumps along the way. As one who has been professionally involved in each of the eras depicted in this set of articles published in *Change*, I confess that I was surprised by the adversarial tone of much of the writing of the time. It should be remembered, however, that the mission and editorial policy of *Change* is reflected in its name; it is to question the status quo. Thus, the articles were neither written nor published with the intent of encouraging readers to bask in the comfort of tradition and tranquility. Moreover, some descriptions of students appear critical when viewed through the lens of traditional academic values, as in, for example, "students unprepared to do college work," and "students more interested in status and careers than in learning." Viewed through the lens of student expectations, however, they appear quite different. The issues embedded in such descriptions remain unresolved. What can colleges expect of students, and what can students expect of colleges? In CUNY, for example, where the revolution in Open Admissions made headlines in the 1970s, the removal of remedial courses is making headlines today. Is it the responsibility of the university to prepare students for college level work through remediation, or should the university wait until students are prepared before admitting them?

As we look back over a relatively short period of 30 years of *Change*, perhaps the real story is to be found in how rapidly a huge, hard-to-steer conglomeration of diverse institutions has responded to the varying needs of changing student populations. However, each challenge for change has been met in a different way. The student protest era did not change universities as much as it changed students. Open Admissions was accomplished more through the creation of community colleges designed and dedicated to a new mission than through change in existing institutions. Affirmative action is slow-going because it really does require change in society as well as in all institutions. Meeting the needs of consumer-oriented students is being accomplished through market-place competition — some from attractive alternatives offered by profit-making entrepreneurs, most by innovative traditional institutions.

Although resistance to change has been the predominant theme in each gallery, higher education ultimately has been transformed by the necessity of responding to each new wave of students.

As for the next 30 years, we can safely predict more changes. A new style of educational artist is interested in designing genuine communities of learners. Service learning, student/faculty collaboration on research, learning communities, and joint K–12 programs are all growing phenomena, and they picture students, faculty, and community agencies working together for an improved 21st century society.

References

Bettleheim, B. (1969, May/June). The anatomy of academic discontent. *Change, 1*, 18–26.

Cross, K. P. (1973, February). The new learners. *Change, 5*, 31–34.

Giddings, P. J. (1990, March/April). Education, race, and reality: A legacy of the 60s. *Change, 22*, 10–17.

Greeley, A. (1972, April). The end of the movement. *Change, 4*, 42–47.

Gross, T. (1978, February 4). How to kill a college. *Saturday Review*.

Gross, T. (1981, March). Where have all the flowers gone? *Change, 13*, 25–29.

Hechinger, F. M. (1970, November/December). Academic freedom in America. *Change, 2*, 32–36.

Krukowski, J. (1985, May/June). What do students want? Status. *Change, 17*, 21–28.

Levine, A. (1981, March). Today's college students: Going first class on the *Titanic*. *Change, 13*, 16–23.

Levine, A. (1991, September/October). The meaning of diversity. *Change, 23*, 4–5.

Levine, A. (1993, September/October). Student expectations of college. *Change, 23*, 4.

Marshak, R. E., & Wurtemburg, G. (1981, November/December). Open access, open admissions, open warfare I. *Change, 13*, 12–19, 51–53.

McSwine, B. G. (1971, May/June). Black visions, white realities. *Change, 3*, 28–34.

Niblett, W. R. (1973, March). Jottings. *Change, 5*, 63–64.

Porter, H. (1977, February). The visible man II: Reflections of a black son. *Change, 9*, 34–39.

Quinn, E. (1973, Summer). The case for open admissions: We're holding our own. *Change, 5*, 30–34.

Winn, M. (1985, May/June). The plug-in generation. *Change, 17*, 14–20.

Wong, F. F. (1991, July/August). Diversity & community: Right objectives and wrong arguments. *Change, 23*, 48–54.

Academic Freedom in America

Fred M. Hechinger

The wheel has come full circle. The original revolt, begun at Berkeley in 1964, triumphed under the banner of the Free Speech Movement. But apparently only its subdivision, the Filthy Speech Movement, gained a lasting victory. Speech on campus, though unabashedly filthy and often uncivil, is demonstrably less free than it was a decade ago. Implicit or explicit loyalty oaths either to the New Left student guerrillas or the Old Right trustees are becoming preconditions for the license to hold, and express, views on campus. . . .

The present situation would be far less alarming if intellectual opinion were not so confused. Many liberals, in and out of the academic world, find themselves emotionally incapable of taking seriously a threat to campus freedom as long as those who appear guilty share their own aversion against the war and social injustice. They honestly fear repression, as well they might; but they refuse to believe that a totalitarian Left, particularly when represented or led by students, can jeopardize liberty as directly as the hardhats of the Right or the anti-democratic forces of the "law and order" stripe. . . .

It is surely wrong to conclude that, because the radical student minority and their professional camp-followers have no chance of taking over the country, it is tolerable to let them terrorize the university and diminish its internal freedoms. To fight the right-wing threat of repression but to ignore the more pinpointed left-totalitarian designs against freedom on the campuses is a peculiarly anti-intellectual stance. It puts a low value on the universities, makes them, at least temporarily, expendable. Perhaps the left-totalitarians, aware of the intellectuals' readiness to appease them, are willing to limit their war to the attack on the universities. But only those who foolishly or deliberately underestimate the universities' importance could consider this a limited war, or write off academic freedom as a luxury to be sacrificed for an uneasy campus truce.

The End of the Movement

Andrew M. Greeley

The word is out that the Movement has had it. The cyclotron at Stanford may have been damaged by a bomb. The American Association for the Advancement of Science may be incapable of maintaining freedom of speech at its meetings. An occasional confrontation may still occur on campus. But these are the last dying gasps of the social phenomena that not so long ago many observers thought represented the wave of the future.

Young men and women attend football games, study for their exams, worry about whether jobs will be available for them to begin their careers, and concentrate on their personal relationships.

Law school graduates come to job interviews with their hair cut, their faces shaved, and their clothes pressed, and speak respectfully to their future employers. The use of drugs is declining. The hard drugs are dangerous, we are told, and marijuana isn't that much fun. And beer is rediscovered as a way of escaping from one's problems. The Jesus people replace the SDS as the interesting campus phenomenon of the year; black students still are under pressure to keep to themselves, but enrollment in black studies programs declines. Politicians draw a small crowd, and many young people have yet to register for the 1972 election. Only the women's lib segment of the Movement retains vitality, and even this seems to be undergoing a transformation. The "Revolution" ended almost as soon as it began. . . .

The collapse of the Movement has created astonishment in certain quarters of the journalistic profession, and reporters are scrambling around the campuses of the country trying to find out what happended. But anyone who looked at the serious research done on young people could not have been surprised. . . .

First of all, there is no such thing as a generation gap. Overwhelming research evidence indicates that most young people are like their parents and that even a considerable number of the radicals come from families where the ideological atmosphere has predisposed them to radical action. Furthermore, those who set the tone and the atmosphere of the campus at any given time are a small minority. Most young people, like their predecessors and like their successors, are interested in studies, career, marriage. The elite, because it is elite, sets the tone, attracts a larger body of mildly committed fellow-travelers, and, on occasion, but only on occasion, can command mass support. To interpret those occasions of mass support as turning points in human history is utter foolishness. . . .

At best it was a splended display of energy, enthusiasm, altruism, and commitment. The Peace Corps, the civil rights movement, the early days of the anti-war protest, the strong vision of the possibilities of a better life—all of these were part of an interlude in American life of which no one need be ashamed.

But at worst the Movement was simplistic, self-righteous, naive, romantic, and inept. It preached relevance and commitment and yet when the going got tough, it abandoned politics. It preached high moral standards and yet decided that stealing was all right when it was called "ripping off," that violence was all right because other people practiced it, that promiscuity was all right because bourgeois marriage was dull, that freedom meant the right to disrupt other men's freedom of speech, that oppression was justified in the name of liberty, and that those who disagreed with the Movement's form of dissent were not to be permitted their own dissent. It decreed that drugs were all right and indeed virtuous, because other Americans drank alcohol and swallowed aspirin. It preached love, but despised hard-hats. It preached peace but reveled in violence. It argued in the name of rationality but unleashed the irrational. It denounced virtually everyone else in sight as immoral but never questioned its own behavior. It wanted to remake the world, but it never had time to formulate clearly its own vision of what the world ought to be, much less to articulately communicate this vision to others. It claimed political sophistication, but demonstrated incredible naivete about how you convert other human beings to your cause. It was absolutely certain that it was the wave of the future and was confident that it would survive even after the end of the Vietnam war. But the war is not yet over and the Movement is gone. . . .

The collapse of the Movement is not merely or even principally the result of the fact that some young people have changed, though obviously many have; what has changed is the student body on the college campus. Today's freshmen and sophomores were in high school at the time of the Cambodia-Kent demonstrations; perhaps half the current college students in the country did not experience the electric atmosphere of that tumultuous week. If there is one iron law of changing generations, it is that one year's freshmen are likely to be extremely skeptical of what was popular with last year's seniors. Yesterday's Movement is old hat today.

The New Learners

Changing Perspectives on Quality Education

K. Patricia Cross

What is quality higher education? There was a time when people thought they knew. It was typified by bright students, a faculty distinguished in research and writing and affluent and successful alumni.

To attain such heights a college selects students of known academic accomplishments, recruits faculty with big names and proven records, and assures itself of successful alumni through placing its sought-after seal of approval on its graduates. Somewhere between entrance and graduation it is assumed that students gain a "quality" education. But all we know for sure is that the best way to graduate a bright class is to admit a bright class.

Up until now higher education has been a low-risk venture. You get out about what you put in. So sure are people of this formula that most research and careful application of the findings reside in the admissions office—not in the classroom. Probably the closest thing to science in the practice of education lies in predicting the winners—and losers—of the academic race.

Despite all the hue and cry to the contrary, the science of academic prediction is decades ahead of the science of education and learning because in accuracy of prediction lies the promise of institutional success. But a new day is dawning. It looks very much as though quality education in the future will be measured in terms of value added, and that means we will have to look at the process of education itself—at what happens to the student between entrance and graduation.

A recent case study illustrates the issues involved in the transition from the relatively easy task of prediction and selection to the infinitely more difficult task of education. S. Resnik and B. Kaplan, the authors of an insightful and sympathetic analysis of the open-admissions policy at the City University of New York (CUNY), discovered to their "amazement," since they had "started out with an initial distrust of such tests," that the Cooperative English Test was uncannily predict-ive of student dropout and of independent teacher judgment about student performance. A very high percentage (fifty out of sixty) students with low test scores "were dropped or left the program voluntarily during the first year, and most of the remaining ten left in the second year."

The findings illustrate the tension between the old and the new. The task of the old selective admissions approach was to find the most promising young people and to educate them for roles of leadership in the society. When technology was young and educational resources were scarce, it seemed logical and efficient for the growing nation to educate a cadre of elite leaders who would use their training and knowledge to raise the standard of living for everyone.

Now there seems to be an unending supply of the comforts and luxuries of technology. The problem for the future is not so much in the generation of new technology and new products as in better distribution systems, broader-based knowledge and greater concern for individual development. The way to raise the standard of living for everyone is no longer to train leaders but rather to educate the masses to their full humanity.

Certainly we will continue to educate leaders; we will always need intellectual leadership. But institutions like CUNY have taken on an additional and much more difficult assignment. The task of the new CUNY is not to predict who will fail, but to make life better for every student crossing its threshold.

The "amazing" success of the Cooperative English Test isn't so amazing after all. It shows two things. First, that failure on a traditional test predicted failure in the traditional curriculum with high accuracy. Second, that the traditional curriculum did not do anything to educate the nearly 100 percent of very low-scoring students who dropped out. The test, the curriculum and faculty judgments about performance are all irrelevant to the task of improving life for everyone through education.

This change in philosophy about the purposes of college and who should attend will probably have more impact on educational methods and procedures than anything that has ever happened in higher education. Just as soon as a college agrees to do what it can for all comers, it forgoes the luxury of selecting students who fit its way of life, and it takes on the obligation of adapting itself to the needs of students.

That is where many colleges are today.

Thousands upon thousands of students who would never before have considered college are on our doorsteps, and we don't know how—or if—we can do anything to help them develop their talents to become happy and productive citizens. We face the task of gearing up to serve a new clientele.

The new clientele for higher education in the 1970s consists of everyone who wasn't there in the 1940s, 1950s and 1960s. There are four distinctive but overlapping groups: (1) low academic achievers who are gaining entrance through open admissions; (2) adults and part-time learners who are gaining access through nontraditional alternatives; (3) ethnic minorities; and (4) women who are gaining admission through public conscience and Affirmative Action.

I have written extensively in *Beyond the Open Door* about low academic achievers as New Students in higher education. It is this group that epitomizes the problem of education beyond high school for the masses. It is not too difficult to accept adults—to deliver education in new ways, to credential adequate academic performance and to permit part-time students to earn degrees. It is slow and sometimes traumatic but not impossible to abolish discrimination and grant ethnic minorities and women college degrees. But to deliberately set out to accept people who "can't do college work" as it is presently defined is an altogether different matter.

The greatest single barrier to college admission in the 1960s was not ethnic identity or socioeconomic status per se. Rather it was lack of demonstrated academic ability—as that ability is nurtured and measured in the schools.

Although black and brown and red students are overrepresented among this group of New Students, a great disservice has been done to ethnic minorities in equating skin color with low academic achievement. Actually, most of the students flooding into colleges poorly prepared to undertake traditional college work are the white sons and daughters of blue-collar workers. Almost two thirds of the community colleges in this country report that less than 25 percent of the students enrolled in remedial courses are members of ethnic minorities. Numerically it is whites, not blacks, who have gained educational advantages through open admissions. But regardless of skin color, there is a powerful relationship between social class and academic achievement. Over two thirds of the lowest third of high school graduates are first-generation college students; their parents have never experienced college. So much ignorance of what college is all about among family and friends of entering college students will probably never be present again in this country. In California, for example, with its extensive development of public postsecondary education, 80 percent of the high school graduates are continuing their education, and they will be able to pass some firsthand experience on to their children.

It is not, however, the racial and socioeconomic characteristics of New Students that ought to concern educators most. Rather it is the pervasive experience of New Students with failure in the American school system. Most students who graduate from high school in the lowest academic third of the class have been poor students all of their young lives. Thus it is not surprising to find research that shows that they don't approach traditional college learning tasks with enthusiasm and confidence (see "New Students of the '70s," *The Research Reporter*, The Center for Research and Development in Higher Education, University of California at Berkeley, Vol. 6, No. 4, 1971). There is no reason to think that colleges will do a better job with these students than high schools have done as long as they use the same methods to teach the same materials. Research that repeats the tiresome statistics that a few (but not usually very many) "high-risk" students survive the first year of college should convince us that colleges are not making their adjustment to universal postsecondary education very smoothly.

We might do well to give up our preoccupation with correcting the "deficiencies" of New Students and concentrate instead on developing the new range of talents and interests that they bring to higher education. "College-level" work need not mean higher and higher levels of abstraction; it might well mean higher and higher standards of performance. In any event, our new educational purposes suggest that we begin with the student and help move him toward the development of his abilities. It does not suggest that we try to make him into a pale carbon copy of the academically elite leader of bygone days.

Under the new purposes of higher education adults too have a claim to education that helps them develop their abilities and fulfill their lives. They may not be young enough to meet the old criteria of furnishing fresh leadership to a growing technology, but they are able, eager and interested students. In a research survey of the learning preferences and experiences of adults conducted for the Commission on Non-Traditional Study, sponsored by the College Board and Educational Testing Service, we found that 77 percent of the people between 18 and 60 in this country would like to learn more about something.

Although adults have been considerably more restrained about it than have some of the young people, it is quite apparent from the data that they too are demanding relevance in education. The message is clear that they want to learn how to *do* things—as opposed to how to think about things. Dedicated liberal arts advocates will be disappointed to learn that adult males are most interested in returning to school to improve their vocational and professional skills, whereas women are most interested in sewing, cooking, crafts and gardening. And those interests are in the lead for college graduates as well as for the general population. Adult learning priorities seem to be dictated by the usefulness of the learning. Highest in priority are those skills that are needed by all adults in the course of daily living—vocational skills, investment and home repair for men; home and family skills for women; sports and leisure-time activities for both men and women. Next in order comes learning that will foster personal development and community responsibility—humanities and the arts (especially for women) and public affairs and community problems. And finally at the bottom of the list of preferences, endorsed by fewer than 10 percent of the potential adult learners, are the basic academic tools of social, biological and physical sciences and English language. Once again, college graduates aren't much

more interested in learning more about these staples of academe than is the general public. The problem is not that the social and physical sciences are inherently dull or unimportant, but that they are taught as background for professional scholars—and not many of the new clientele have any interest in becoming professional scholars. The physical and social sciences, after all, form the backbone of the new curricula in ecology and urban studies that are extremely popular with young and old alike. But these courses of study have a problem-oriented focus. They are taught in order to solve problems—not to perpetuate the discipline into graduate school.

So adult learners do challenge the heart of higher education—the curriculum. But equally important—and more likely to succeed—is their challenge to the time and place requirements of traditional education. It is this battle that the nontraditional studies movement has taken on. No one can put forth a very strong argument that four years, chopped into 120 credit hours delivered to people who can present themselves physically in a room set aside for "classes," makes much sense as the major strategy of education. A concept of education for all the people requires new methods of delivery to take education into prisons, homes and industrial plants. We need new measures of competency that acknowledge that what is learned rather than how it is learned is the true measure of education. And we need new flexibilities that can begin to make lifelong learning a reality.

More attention has been given to the educational needs of ethnic minorities and women than to other groups of new clientele. And yet their challenge to educational tradition as preserved by the academic disciplines and by institutional procedures is not nearly so great as that presented by New Students or adults. True, the demands for equality of educational opportunity on the part of ethnic minorities and women has struck a deep emotional response in the white, male-dominated system of higher education. Affirmative Action is a personal threat to ruling faculty, administrators and students too. But minorities and women are not a threat to the content and form of traditional education except as they constitute highly visible segments of the New Student and adult populations.

It is hard to talk about curricular or classroom needs that are based on skin color or sex. But the assumption throughout this article has been that education is broadly interpreted to encompass the full development of individual potential. Given that interpretation, the educational problems of ethnic minorities and women are profound.

The influx of ethnic minorities and women into all segments of postsecondary education is increasing rapidly, as the Carnegie Commission report *American College and University Enrollment Trends in 1971* shows. In the single year from 1970 to 1971, the total undergraduate and graduate enrollment of women increased 5 percent (compared to a 3 percent increase for men). The increase for blacks was 17 percent and for those with Spanish surnames 19 percent. The most dramatic increases occurred where one might expect—in the previously closed graduate schools. Women made a 6 percent gain (compared with 4 percent for men), but blacks showed a 38 percent gain and those of Spanish descent a 31 percent increase. Spanish Americans are just beginning to get their message across with a force equal to that of the blacks. First-time graduate enrollments increased 36 percent for Spanish Americans, 11 percent for blacks, but only 5 percent for women.

As these data show, ethnic minorities, and to a lesser extent women, are assuredly part of the new clientele. Society looks to education to improve the lot of its citizenry, and the failure has been painful in the case of groups whose appearance marks them as targets for discrimination. As Martha Peterson, chairman of the American Council on Education, remarked recently, "The shame of Affirmative Action is that HEW had to get into it at all."

The problems, however, are more than legal or even moral. Racial segregation on campus is a growing phenomenon that no one knows how to deal with (see *Time,* November 27, 1972, pages 44–45, and "The New Black Apartheid," *Change,* October 1972, page 8). Highly sensitized women and ethnic minorities are becoming increasingly aware that it is easier to deal with overt discrimination that can be fought head-on than it is to deal with covert and frequently unconscious discrimination on the part of well-meaning people.

The full meaning of universal postsecondary education has probably not been understood, and certainly not accepted, by the majority of people whose life work is education. The most common position among faculty who consider themselves enlightened is that higher education should be open to all those able and willing to do the work in the manner and form in which it is now offered. A second position is taken by a growing minority of misguided liberals who are willing to "lower the standards" of academic education in order to get credentials in the hands of the "disadvantaged" so that they can obtain the material and social benefits of society.

Neither position is adequate for these times. The purpose of education is not to certify (especially not falsely) nor is it to prepare a band of elite intellectual leaders (except perhaps in graduate education). It is to maximize the potential of each person to live a fulfilled and constructive life. And to accomplish that end, we need not lower standards. Quite the contrary, we should organize education around the premise that we must demand of each student the highest standards of performance in the utilization of his or her talents.

The New Vocationalism

James Hitchcock

Almost every institution in American society has suffered confusion and demoralization in the past decade. Probably none has suffered more than the university, precisely because it is expected to provide enlightenment and leadership, to stay on the path of wisdom when everyone else has strayed. Now the universities have confessed that they no longer see clearly where the lamp of reason is leading, and it is ironic that they have undertaken to prescribe the remaking of society at a point in time when they seem to have no clear notion of their own purpose. . . .

The key to present educational confusion is the fact that, for all the ridicule that has been heaped upon the concept, there is no longer any pedagogical absolute except relevance. "Relevance," however, is indefinable, since it is whatever the individual perceives as meaningful to himself, and such perceptions are constantly changing. . . .

From the election of John F. Kennedy until the Democratic convention of 1968, relevance tended to be equatable with political awareness. Students were said to be impatient with studies remote from social needs. . . .

As political concerns began to wane . . . relevance tended to change its meaning also—from the objective, outward-looking scrutiny of society to the intensely subjective scrutiny of self.

The greatest irony of the educational history of the past decade is the fact that relevance has now turned full circle and is coming to apply precisely to what five years ago almost everyone agreed was fundamentally the wrong function of higher education—"processing students for the System." In short, the newest version of relevance is vocationalism.

When student rebellions first erupted on the campuses, almost all commentators . . . accepted . . . that young people were tired of being forced to spend years in school during which they were treated like IBM cards, solely in order to fit into an occupational slot marked out by the capitalist-technocratic society. Education, according to the rebels, was supposed to be humanistic and humanizing, divorced from occupational requirements, so that students would have leisure and space to think, experience and criticize.

This view of education, which was consistent with the philosophy of the traditional liberal arts if not always with their practice, still survives, just as do the older notion of the liberal arts and the notions of education for radical political activity and for personal probing. The dominant voices in education, however, now increasingly speak of vocationalism as the necessary way of the future, the path the universities must follow if they wish to make themselves relevant.

It is a point of view articulated, for example, by Joseph P. Cosand, United States Assistant Commissioner of Education. . . .

Since Cosand . . . is an official of a conservative Republican administration, it is tempting to speculate that neovocationalism, cloaked in a radical rhetoric . . . is part of a general conservative reaction against the present state of the universities. The new emphasis on vocationalism no doubt builds on the awareness that, in general, students training for a specific career were much less likely to rebel or to become radicalized a few years ago than those in the liberal arts who contemptuously rejected vocationalism as an educational goal. Career orientation, with a realistic prospect for gainful employment at the end, might be an effective way of ensuring a permanent return to tranquillity on the campuses. It would also ensure a greater measure of outside control on the universities, since they would be educating students in accordance with the demands of the market. . . .

It would, however, be a serious mistake to regard neovocationalism as solely the program of political conservatives. The tendency of recent educational radicals to take student desires as the ultimate criterion of correct pedagogy works to the same end, because by definition one cannot tell a student what is relevant to him. . . .

The democratizing of higher education through the admission of more students from minority groups, and the general penetration of higher learning by the white working class through community colleges and state university branches, tends especially to this end. Radicals of the 1960s assumed that the admission to college of large numbers of the disadvantaged would force higher education in the direction of radical political activity, to the point of encouraging exotic and revolutionary programs in black studies, for example. It is now clear, however, that minority students want and need a practical education, either for personal advancement or community leadership. As in the past, students from a disadvantaged background generally prefer educational programs that appear to promise tangible career benefits rather than those emphasizing personal development or knowledge for its own sake.

There are other ways too in which radical attitudes of the past now tend to support conservative educational goals. Many young people whose consciences were aroused in the 1960s are concluding in the 1970s that passion and acute theoretical understanding are less valuable than specific skills—law, medicine, engineering—for dealing with social problems ranging from racism to pollution. If conservative businessmen and the ambitious children of the poor tend to regard the traditional humanities as expensive irrelevancies, many white social activists do also. . . .

There is a widespread conviction in the universities that liberal arts education has failed and needs to make way for something else, whatever that might be. Rather than having failed; however, it is possible that the liberal arts are the victims of their own success. In the 1950s professors railed at students to shake them out of their unquestioning, career-oriented complacency; in the 1960s they reaped the whirlwind. Obviously a generalized humanistic education was not the sole or perhaps even the major cause of student idealism in the past decade, but it was undoubtedly an important contributing factor. An education oriented toward questioning, toward social awareness, toward a concern for great problems, certainly bore significant fruit in the 1960s, even if not all of it was sweet. The "irrelevancy" of the humanities lies in that, having brought students to perceive social problems, they appear able to contribute little to the problems' solution. Their value, however, has always been in the attitudes

and habits of mind they create, the spirit they engender, and not in their practical usefulness. It is worth asking what society will be like if, even at the university level, there is a retreat from the ideals of humanistic education.

That there will be such a retreat seems evident, despite the disclaimers of the apostles of vocationalism. The removal of all or most course requirements by many colleges does not, for the most part, enable students to follow imaginative, personally tailored programs of self-development but allows them to pursue rather narrow and often rigid career objectives. . . . Cosand acknowledges the possibility that the new vocationalism may foster a narrow provincialism. His remedy is a pious hope that the student has "the intention of picking up a broader education later."

There is, however, a good deal to be said on behalf of vocational education, whatever its dangers. It is a dubious procedure to force into the academic mold young people who have little taste for intellectual things, although humanities professors also know that some members of this captive audience are awakened in the process. Many students will in the long run probably be happier and wealthier if they settle on a reasonable career and follow it. . . .

Perhaps unintentionally, the apostles of vocationalism may also intensify class distinctions in higher education. It is unlikely that the most prestigious schools will commit themselves to vocationalism to any significant degree; a general education will continue to be the hallmark of the most privileged students. The greatest demand for vocational training, and the greatest response, is likely to be in the community colleges, the state schools and lesser private schools struggling to survive. There may come to be a division between academic and vocational institutions at the highest level comparable to that which has long existed at the secondary level.

The resurgence of interest in vocationalism coincides with reports of a new conservatism, or at least a new quietism, on the campuses. To the degree that vocationalism proves acceptable to students, it will help to bury yet a little deeper the many myths circulated about "the young" in the 1960s, especially their alleged rejection of the goals of money and success. . . . Student interest in vocational education is in large measure stimulated by the poor employment prospects that now face liberal arts graduates. . . .

The abandonment of the liberal arts as the core of higher education has implications far beyond mere pedagogy. The tradition of liberal arts education rested on the assumption that Western culture has a common base, a common tradition that should be accessible to all persons living in the culture, so that communication and a sharing of common values and perceptions are possible. It was considered the individual's necessary starting point in his search for self-definition. Now this assumption is both explicitly and implicitly denied in favor of a radical individualism that sees each person as hopelessly locked within himself, able to articulate only in terms of his own feelings, his own perceptions, his own ambitions and desires.

The frantic search for "community" often masks a deeply rooted self-centeredness. The universities were perhaps the last institutions that kept alive the older ideal of meaningful and civilized discourse founded on a common culture. The educational changes of the past half decade— whether predicated on the individual's need to discover who he is or merely on his need to find a suitable job—proclaim an end to that ideal. On the campus as elsewhere, each person is now left to do his own thing, while the forces of the whole culture touch and mold him in ways he can only dimly understand and scarcely at all control.

Summer 1973

"We're Holding Our Own"

The Case for Open Admissions

Edward Quinn

. . . [A]s teachers involved in open admissions we are asked, "Is it working?" The truth is, we have been too busy trying to keep the casualty rate down while we capture one stronghold at a time to have given the matter much reflection. Nevertheless it's a reasonable question and it deserves an honest answer—provided of course that the interrogator is a member of the Wehrmacht rather than the Gestapo.

I cannot give a quantitative answer to the question. But I shall try to give a qualitative one— describing the impact of this experience on the lives of our students and on ourselves—lest the quantitative be seen as the sole determinant of success or failure. Statistics, no doubt, have an important role to play, as safeguards against romantic illusions, natural prejudice or simply sloppy thinking. . . . Nevertheless it has to be kept in mind that these numbers—reading levels, SATs, math achievement, dropout rates—are to the educational enterprise what the score is to the game. They measure and judge and discriminate, but they are not the game itself. I say this not in the spirit of sour grapes. I have no reason to believe that the score is going against open admissions: I suspect we are holding our own. But win or lose, it is critical that we not become enslaved by numbers. . . .

. . . The failure shows up in the statistics, the success in the life of the student. . . .

What sort of people [are these students?] Young, to be sure, but beyond that the generalizations don't hold up very well. Except to say that most of them have not been particularly successful people. They lack the social ease of those whose parents went to college, the confidence of those who have always been near the top of the class, and in many cases the elementary sense of feeling at home here—"here" being not only the City University of New York but the United States of America.

They have come with considerable anxiety and insecurity, in many cases even with guilt. Until relatively recently they had no expectations of going beyond high school, and as a result their high school performance has been lackadaisical. Those—over half—who come from white working-class families discover that their acceptance in college frequently creates more hostility than pride. Their families interpret their undistinguished grades as evidence that they have not earned the right to go to college. Added to this is the fact that continuing their education creates an economic burden. Even when there is no cost for tuition, college students are adults who are not bringing money into the house. Often in the eyes of their working-class families they have joined the ranks of welfare recipients and foreign countries — "freeloaders living off the government."

Under pressures like these, the impulse to drop out of school and into a job is strong. . . .

Many of these are old City University problems, not at all unique to open admissions, but what is new is the coupling of them with academic insecurity. So that walking into the classroom you sense the students' strain, their mistrust, their faintly articulated desire to make it — to make it in the academic sense: achieving the pleasure that comes from knowing something well. Some of them, of course, have given up already and there is no strain, no desire. They are just hiding out here, like Ensign Pulver in *Mister Roberts*, hoping not to be noticed by the Captain. Most of them, however, are believers. They haven't read the articles proclaiming open admissions a hoax or a failure or the politicians' sellout. For them it is simply a break, and you may have noticed that people who think that they have just gotten a break are nice people to be around. "Nice people," my colleague, a well-known Joyce scholar, was saying the other day. He is teaching his first open-admissions class and is pleasantly surprised to find that he likes them. He finds them interested in literature and even more so in learning. I suspect they're also interested in him because he happens to be the real thing: a genuine scholar who is also a good teacher. A man who knows something well.

These two stimuli — the fact of simply being in college and the influence of good teachers — contribute to a third: a growth in self-awareness. You see this primarily in their movement from passivity to activity, in their willingness to take a chance and risk an opinion. Sometimes that movement releases anger, but just as frequently it produces clarification. I recall my experience teaching a class in the SEEK program, the vanguard of open admissions, a few years ago. The course had not been going well: I found myself

unable to penetrate the pervasive resentment in the class. About halfway through the semester, a delegation of students came to me after class. They knew I was a specialist in Shakespeare and that in the SEEK class I had taught in the previous term I had included some Shakespearean plays. My failure to include these this term — the result of a misguided experiment on my part — had been interpreted by them, quite correctly it now seems to me, as patronizing. They had arrived at a point where they could trust themselves and care enough to express that concern. They wanted the best I had to offer and wouldn't settle for less.

That was the first important lesson I learned from these students: patronize and you perish. What the students learned was that becoming aware of what they wanted and articulating that desire is an essential aspect of education. What all of us learned was that all of us had a lot to learn. . . .

. . . Summarized simply, they are likable, intelligent young people who for one reason or another have not been reached by the educational system we have now. We can see that failure in their lack of basic skills and of an intellectual frame of reference we have come to regard as essential for college-level learning. Consequently, such students are forced to do double duty: they have to play catch-up on the elementary mechanics of composition and math at the same time their intellectual energies are absorbed by the concepts and ideas they encounter in regular courses. But it is one thing to be answering an essay question on the importance of the Alliance for Progress to the Latin-American farmer and another to be striving for an answer under the added pressure of writing correct English. Everyone feels this pressure to some degree, but for these students the problem is intensified by the distance between academic discourse and their own linguistic experience. The result is partial paralysis, the painfully self-conscious attempt to write examinationese. What usually happens is that they achieve neither correctness of expression nor adequacy of response, and this indecisiveness presents the major obstacle to their success. . . .

For us, the faculty, the encounter with these students has brought with it the knowledge that if they are on trial, we are as well. That knowledge has been slow in coming, and even now many of us are unwilling to accept it. For one thing, such an admission looks like the latest form of liberal self-flagellation, and most of us have had enough of that. For another, many of us feel that openly acknowledging our self-doubts will deflect attention from the problems of understaffing, overcrowded classrooms, inadequate facilities, political hypocrisy and public indifference that threaten to overwhelm our best efforts. Nevertheless we are painfully conscious that we are being asked to use muscles we never knew we had. And some of us are fearfully out of shape.

After all, until fairly recently teaching was one of the few nonproblem areas of our lives. We conducted our classes in the best professorial manner: casual erudition, tolerance of disagreement, high irony. Students — at City College at least — were aggressive, hard-working, occasionally brilliant and almost always respectful. We fancied that our classrooms were the last bastions of civilized discourse.

The balloon burst in the late sixties. They stopped reading [and] stopped coming to class. . . .

For a while it seemed they could do nothing wrong and we could do nothing right. . . . We watched them turn the university on its ear, transform the culture, almost even stop the war. They were off in pursuit of limitless possibilities. . . .

. . . The students of the sixties awakened in us a romanticism that had been vexed to sleep in graduate school, and they forced us into a self-examination that, for all its excesses, made possible the adaptation to open admissions. Our self-image had been permanently altered. Even those who felt that the Revolution turned into a Reign of Terror — even those who disapproved from the very beginning — are not the same. Five years of Nixon, budget cuts and recession have not been able to restore the old serenity.

The advent of open admissions is an index of the change. Here was an opportunity to focus — as we had in the past — on the students' inadequacies and failures rather than on our own. But after two years we have learned that our capacity for sustained effort and imagination is being tested. So be it. Most of us, I think, are willing to accept this reading — not out of a desire to play the martyr but largely because one side effect of open admissions has been a renewed interest in education itself. As recently as ten years ago, education competed with economics for the title of dismal science, and college professors were openly contemptuous of educational theory. Now the process of helping people to learn occupies the center of our concern. . . .

Another consequence of this new interest has been the emergence of a debate about the purpose and goals of a college education at this time. Our experience with these new students is forcing us to see these goals as falling within three categories: vocational, intellectual and ethical. Ideally conceived, these three are not only *not* mutually exclusive but so closely interrelated as to be mutually dependent. The critics of open admissions wish to establish intellectual achievement as the exclusive category, or at the very least the primary one. Their position presumably is that a certain level of cognitive achievement is a necessary precondition for appropriate functioning in jobs and professions limited to college graduates. Even these critics would grant that this is not universally true, but they hold to it as a general operating principle. However, long before open admissions the intellectual criteria applied to no more than 15 percent of the graduates — those who moved on to professional study. For the rest, college provided not so much intellectual training as a complicated array of attitudes, aspirations, habits of mind, social postures and a sense of self that this society values or thinks it values. The college graduate is not a measurable entity but a style, and most people have always known this.

Furthermore, the students who come to us through open admissions can draw on experiences that are unusual in the classroom and exceedingly valuable there. . . .

. . . People on welfare, on the other hand, have a healthy respect for the objective world. Their experience has left them more open to the perception of one of the crucial insights provided by a college education. . . .

. . . I find it difficult to understand how extension of this activity to people who have not had access to it could have inspired such vehement opposition. Perhaps the source of that opposition is not mean-spiritedness but a compulsive inability to keep one's eye off the scoreboard while missing all the action on the field. From its very inception, open admissions has been the object of one evaluation after another. To characterize them as premature is to be kind. These instant judgments are, I suppose, inevitable products of the contemporary mania for locating everything in what Northrop Frye calls "those two great dialectical categories . . . lousy and swell."

But open admissions is too complicated and too important for simplistic judgments. It will be at least ten years before it can be accurately measured. Meanwhile we know that a myth of freedom is sustained and renewed by contact with those who need it most. The open-admissions student needs to believe in himself and in the process of higher education. We need to believe in his belief. . . .

February 1977

Reflections of a Black Son
The Visible Man

Horace Porter

There comes a time when every young man leaves his father's house. I left my home in Columbus, Georgia, on the second of September in 1968. It was a day marked by three extraordinary events in my life: I boarded a plane for my first flight; I left the South for the first time; and that afternoon I walked across the campus of Amherst College.

Late in the day I met my roommate from Grosse Pointe, Michigan. After the usual introductions and small talk, Brian asked me about my religious views. I told him I was a Baptist, a Christian. He stated emphatically that he was an atheist. We assured each other we would not allow the difference to lead to conflict. That night, however, in a scene reminiscent of Queequeg and Ishmael at the Spouter Inn, I got down on my knees to say my prayers. Brian asked if something were wrong. I told him that I was saying my prayers. He nodded, amazed. That was the first and the last night I said my prayers on my knees at Amherst. I reasoned it was time to bring to an end that particular practice of my southern boyhood.

Yet I pondered the events of the day for several hours after my prayers. I thought of my parents. Like many southern blacks born during World War I, neither had made it through high school. Neither had, of course, gone north to college. And neither had heard of Amherst until I spoke about it. At boarding time that morning, they had assured me that they would pray for me, and they asked me to pray and trust in the Lord. As I lay awake, I wondered why my parents had found it necessary to pray. I had expected them to be as ecstatic as I was. I was not, after all, like many of my unfortunate friends, on the way to the battlefields of Vietnam. I was going to college. . . .

I needed my prayers. Amherst was like a foreign country those first few months. . . .

The students all appeared wealthy, articulate, and atheistic. Clad in faded bell-bottom jeans and wire-framed glasses, they discussed the war and the coming election with what seemed to me expertise. Everyone, or so it appeared, discussed books I had not read. No one discussed the books I had read. . . .

. . . Everyone, it seemed, had already met Godot. I had read some Sartre, but God knows I had not heard of Marcuse. Menaced by my sense of intellectual insecurity, I read books and examined journals and periodicals with a diligence I have not since been able to surpass. It was during that unforgettable season of intellectual passion that I read Ralph Ellison's Invisible Man, a novel that shook me with the force of an earthquake. Given the temper of the times, I readily identified with the nameless protagonist who proclaims: "I was my experiences and my experiences were me. . . ." I was driven to explore my own hidden name, my own complex fate.

I read W.E.B. DuBois, James Weldon Johnson, Carter G. Woodson, Jean Toomer, and numerous other Afro-American scholars and writers. Theirs was a valuable legacy for me. In times more trying than my own, they had worked and thought well. Some, like DuBois and Woodson, lived and wrote during the heyday of what came to be known as "scientific racism." The notion of the innate inferiority of the black race suffused the air they breathed. But by dint of their indefatigable wills and their discipline, they wrote novels and histories that spoke eloquently of the souls of black folk — long before my time, even before the time of my parents.

Ironically, those black writers and thinkers helped to bring about the first long, snowy winter of my discontent at Amherst. Only a few Amherst professors had even heard of them when I arrived. No one on the faculty was primarily committed to a study of the Afro-American experience. The one black member of the faculty was a mathematician. That greatly disturbed me. After those initial months of awe and a trip home at Christmas, I began to consider the social and political dimensions of my love for books, words, and ideas. What, I wondered, was in store for me if I decided to make my love my profession? What peculiar problems would I encounter as an Afro-American intellectual? I asked myself what was the real beast in the Afro-American intellectual jungle. My attempt to answer those questions led me to the realization that I owed my soul to the Bible, the Constitution, and the Declaration of Independence, to Shakespeare and Melville, to Freud and Marx, and to the English language in which I thought, spoke, and wrote.

This awareness proved very troubling at the time because of the obsession among black students with all that was unique to the Afro-American experience. Black pride was regarded as inextricably bound with a black consciousness, a black aesthetic, and black English. Intellectually, the assumption was, of course, highly problematic. But discussion was rarely dispassionate during those years. In fact, if one were black and did not use the black vernacular from time to time, one ran the risk of being labelled a "Negro." That was one of the most pejorative epithets a black student could use to describe another brother or sister, an elegant variation of the "oreo" of a decade later. On a deeper level, the question was whether Afro-Americans were being forced to learn what — in many cases — amounted to an alien tongue. It was frequently pointed out to me that many Afro-Americans speak a variant of American English. I knew, of course, that my family's English was very different from the English of Amherst, that each time I boarded a plane to return home for a short spell, I had to weed out of my vocabulary much of the verbal flora I had cultivated. I did not want to sound like a guest in a strange house. I had to get down, as it were, into the black vernac-

ular. I had to tune my ears to a different subjunctive and accept, once again, the fact that inflections really can be marvelous adverbs. . . .

I flew back to Amherst after those trips, back to a room of my own, back to the quiet and comfort of the Robert Frost Library. I felt somewhat guilty because there was no black community in which to work or play in the town of Amherst. I began to take perhaps too seriously the charges of militant black nationalists and other critics of the American society who argued that black students at prestigious colleges and universities were being bought, that our loyalties were being subtly besieged by the "system," that life in ivory towers was a luxury we could not afford at such a late hour, that it was the responsibility of my generation to destroy "Faulkner, Dick, Jane, and other perpetuators of evil."

Those arguments, along with the fact that the faculty and administration approached Afro-American and black studies with the same reserve and circumspection they brought to all important matters, shook my confidence in the scholarly process. To be sure, I had learned the value of reasoned discourse. I knew how precious the goals of academic freedom and objectivity were to the academy. But I also realized that courses concerning Afro-Americans were no different from others; any course could become partisan or ideological depending on the teacher and the students. I recognized too that some scholarly and artistic work necessitates years of contemplation, but I reasoned that a commitment to the black struggle was not necessarily incompatible with such endeavor. I wanted the Afro-American presence asserted at Amherst. I wanted the Afro-American voice heard immediately. . . .

American society at large was as much a cause of my malaise as Amherst College. There were so many palpable evils to be eradicated. To speak out and rebel seemed, at the time, the only right thing to do. I became one of the more prominent members of the Amherst Afro-American Society. I petitioned and protested. I signed angry letters addressed to the Amherst administration and the world. I encouraged the rebellious imperatives of my newly politicized self: I went on strike, I sat in, I fasted, I wept, I prayed. . . .

Every year the student body faced a series of crises and rallying causes. One after another they came in, in lockstep: Kent State, Jackson State, Mylai, Calley, Carswell, Angela Davis, George

Jackson, Attica. And the war that went on and on led along with the other crises to numerous expressions of moral outrage. We had two moratoria my first year and a major "takeover" by black students and a general strike my second. We sat in at Westover Air Force Base during the spring of my last year. Moreover, the state of things, the times, forced a number of my classmates and other students away from the college. Some did not return. Others tripped on drugs and never really came back. I, too, was frustrated and tired. I longed for a nonpolitical space for myself.

I grew nostalgic at times. Columbus, Georgia, had been a world of black and white (though sometimes unpleasant) certainties. I missed the communal warmth and encouragement of relatives, friends, and neighbors. I missed Sunday mornings in Columbus—New Providence Baptist Church and the hours of praying, singing, and shouting. Those Sunday mornings had shaped my sense of myself and the world. Yet I now had to admit grudgingly that Sunday morning had been robbed of its hallowed traditions. My singular compulsion had become the Sunday issue of *The New York Times*. I communed quietly with Russell Baker, and the whole galaxy of New York literary personages. Thus, my Sundays became a symbolic critique of my religious past. I now looked at the world with new inner eyes. Furthermore, I was forced to admit that my parents' Christian vision was limited, that had been impaired by history, circumstances, and time.

But as Faulkner reminds us, our pasts are never really past. In spite of my intellectual attempts to become something other, Christianity was in my blood. My father and grandfather are Baptist deacons. So when I communed with my own heart each Sunday morning at Amherst, I sometimes felt like a sinner—or worse, a backslider. Something deep within told me that it was neither right nor sound to turn my back on the traditions of my forebears, that I was not only being a prodigal son but also a foolish one. I was reminded, too, to use my grandfather's oft-quoted expression, that my arms were too short to box with God. . . .

. . . But I was unhappy much of the time too. For I had come as one of the last black delegates of the Civil Rights Era, an era brought symbolically and dramatically to a close by the assassination of Martin Luther King, Jr., a few months before. I had come, that is, with a definite sense of personal and historical purpose. Thus, I readily internalized and was willing to act upon Amherst's motto: *Terras irradient*. The behavior of my peers was at times disheartening. They will do nothing to change America, I often thought and said. Yet I remained because I saw that in its own groping way Amherst was about changing our collective mind and heart. I saw, too, something of the possible beauty and glory of life there. I learned the value of critical and dispassionate discussion. I came to treasure most forms of artistic expression. I experienced the pleasure of leisure time. Many sunny afternoons I leaned and loafed with my friends on the grass of Memorial Hill. Many snowy nights, I danced until dawn. Yet my love for Amherst was tortured by an inarticulate hate, my hate by an undeniable love.

My feelings were similarly contradictory on commencement day. . . .

Amherst College was sending forth another class of its sons to "illumine the land." And those purple-ribboned diplomas had great significance. They mean that one's sensibilities had been caressed by some of the finest minds in America. They meant that one had been taught some of the best that had been thought and said. They meant that one had experienced profound sweetness and light. But they did not mean that one had an understanding of those brutal truths taught by the university of adversity. They did not mean that one had intimate knowledge of the "fires of human cruelty" or that one had gained an acute awareness what it means to be disadvantaged, both by law and custom. Perhaps Amherst could never teach that. Perhaps no liberal-arts college could. I did not know. But the world of my father's house had taught me much about those particular facts of life. That knowledge distinguished me from most of my classmates. And my mind seized the moment to make it clear.

Then it was my time to stand. I stood and turned, catching my mother's eye. And as I walked toward the platform a poem by Langston Hughes I had memorized years before mysteriously came to mind. . . .

So boy, don't you turn back.
Don't you set down on the steps
'Cause you find it's kinder hard.
Don't you fall now—
For I'se still goin', honey,
I'se still climbin',
And life for me ain't been no crystal stair.

Today's College Students:

Going First Class on the Titanic

Arthur Levine

. . . Throughout the seventies, and now eighties, commentators have described the nation's campuses as in the throes of a 1950s revival, which seemed about right.

That it is not right is the unmistakable conclusion of surveys of 95,000 undergraduates conducted in 1969 and 1976, a survey of a representative sample of 600 colleges and universities carried out in 1978, interviews with student leaders and student groups at twenty-six institutions in 1979, and annual studies of the nation's college freshmen and high school seniors.

The survey results present a clear picture of today's thinking on campus. The overriding mood of today's undergraduates might be described as a "Titanic ethic." . . . Put simply, today's college students are optimistic (91%) about their personal futures, but pessimistic (59%) about the future of the country.

When asked what they are apprehensive about, undergraduates list everything under the sun — and that, too, if one counts solar energy. They are fearful of the economy, pollution, crime, morals, energy, and nuclear war. They are concerned about drugs, money, foreign policy, corruption, illegal aliens, and the right wing. They worry about permissiveness, increased regulation, self-centeredness, reduced standards of living, the environment, and the justice system.

There is a sense among today's undergraduates that they are passengers on a sinking ship, a Titanic if you will, called the United States or the world. Fatalism and fear of becoming one of the victims is widespread. And there is a growing belief among college students that if they are being forced to ride on a doomed vessel, they owe it to themselves to make the trip as lavish as possible and go first class. This attitude permeates their educational, social, and political lives. . . .

In the course of this research, nearly two thousand people were asked how college students had changed since the 1960s. By far the most common answer was that undergraduates are more career-oriented today. . . .

When undergraduates were asked in 1969 what they regarded as most essential to get out of a college education, they ranked learning to get along with people first and formulating values and goals for their lives second. By 1976, these aims had been replaced by getting a detailed grasp of a special field and obtaining training and skills for an occupation. Top among the reasons freshmen give for attending college today is to get a better job. . . .

A Recommendation

What can one conclude about current college students? Most generally, that they form a special generation — like all others. More specifically, that on the average they are:

- self-concerned and me-oriented
- nonideological
- disenchanted with politics
- moderate in political attitudes
- liberal in social attitudes
- weak in basic skills
- career-oriented
- competitive
- diverse in lifestyles and background
- concerned with personal development (physical and spiritual)
- optimistic about their individual futures
- pessimistic about the future of the country
- interested in material success
- friendly and pleasant
- pragmatic

This generation is no better nor worse than any other; it is different. And from generational differences flow generational needs. The post-sixties college generation is in serious need of education with at least four distinctive qualities:

- They need education that teaches basic skills, problem solving, "crap detecting" (identifying the drivel, exaggerations, and untruths that we hear and read each day), and surviving (coping with a rapidly, and perhaps not pleasantly, changing world). These skills are critical for an estranged generation weak in the three R's and already mired in cynicism.

- They need education which emphasizes our common humanity and which is concerned with our common problems and the ways that we together can solve them. This is ever so important in mitigating the self-concern that more than any other characteristic stands out in this generation.
- They need education which stresses issues of values and questions of ethics. For a pragmatic,

competitive generation with a Titanic ethic and a propensity for taking shortcuts, this is essential.
- And they need education which enlarges upon the vocational preparation they seek. That education must act as much as the label on a bottle of medicine — telling when specialized learning should be used, when it should not be used, and what the consequences of its misuse are likely to be.

Colleges have a vital role to play. Many creative approaches to improved education are possible, and any number of them can show that the education needed for today can be vibrant, attract students, and get students jobs. . . .

November/December 1981

Open Access, Open Admissions, Open Warfare
Part One

Robert E. Marshak with Gladys Wurtemburg

. . . A History of Humanistic Service

City College was founded in 1847 as the first free municipal institution of higher education in the United States, in order to serve the children of the burgeoning working class in New York City. The humanistic mission of the college was defined clearly by its first president, Horace Webster, when he said:

The experiment is to be tried, whether the highest education can be given to the masses; whether the children of the people, — the children of the whole people, — can be educated; and whether an institution of 'learning of the highest grade' can be successfully controlled by the popular will, not by the privileged few but by the privileged many.

For over a century, City College discharged its humanistic mission with rare distinction and consummate sensitivity. As immigrants and workers generally were attracted to a rapidly growing New York, so did City College offer their children an education suitable to their backgrounds, their

hopes, their professional and cultural aspirations. It accepted the economically and socially disadvantaged students from New York City with whatever training they received in the public high schools — subject only to the constraints of space — and, through rigorous curricula, provided the graduates with the intellectual training, professional skills, and academic credentials that enabled them to climb quickly up the ladder of social mobility and post-graduate achievement.

Perhaps no one has better expressed the nature of the City College experience through World War II than the late Yip Harburg, a 1918 alumnus, who said on a television program in 1963:

As I look back I am struck by the knowledge that City College served as a unique bridge between the people who came from the Old World and the America that was in the process of being built. And I think that no other college — the Harvards, Yales and so-called Ivy League Schools — has that particular climate for that kind of person, the person who is trying to make an adjustment in America.

The teachers at City College were aware of this need and reacted to their students accordingly. I might say that my language became the English language because of people like Professor William Bradley Otis. I also learned about economic problems and social problems from the teachers. But they weren't intellectual exercises as at other colleges. You lived in those social conditions and you lived in those economic conditions; that is the great heritage of City College. I think it continues to persist because it still must serve as the gathering place for people from lower echelons of the economic and social system. That is what makes it a unique college, a democratic college.

With the end of World War II, several developments on both the national and city levels, becoming increasingly urgent in the sixties, produced severe strains on the historic humanistic mission of City College. The first development derived from the rapid changes in the demography of New York City itself—with large numbers of blacks and Puerto Ricans entering the City and settling in the neighborhoods that the rising and departing white middle classes were abandoning. The second important development was a rapid deterioration in the quality of New York City's public school system such that academic disadvantagement became closely correlated with economic and social disadvantagement (a correlation that was not so close in earlier decades). A third factor was that the socioeconomic conditions in the inner city have always been unconducive to proper study habits and have placed inordinate work burdens on the young people. All of these developments took place at a time when hundreds of black and Puerto Rican high school students became keenly aware that a college education . . . could offer tickets out of the ghetto, out of inequality, out of truncated futures.

As the sixties unfolded, student unrest became prevalent through the City University (CUNY). Intensified by the assassination of Martin Luther King, Jr., in 1968, this unrest finally erupted in the black and Puerto Rican occupation of the south campus of City College in the spring of 1969.

. . . The takeover led to the introduction of open admissions into the entire CUNY system by September 1970 . . . signalling the urgent need to update the humanistic mission of City College. . . .

Open admissions for City College was a misnomer from its very inception. . . . The open admissions policy . . . did *not* guarantee a place at City College . . . to every graduate of a New York City public high school. Under open admissions policy, students who maintained an 80 percent average or better, *or* who finished in the top half of their graduating class, could enter a CUNY senior college. High school graduates with lesser grades or class rank (an average below 80 percent *or* in the lower half of the graduating class) could enter one of the CUNY community colleges. . . .

. . . The real difference and challenge implicit in the CUNY version of "open admissions," as contrasted with those tried in the past, was that through tutoring, remediation, and counseling, a genuine attempt was being made to keep the CUNY program from becoming a revolving door through which large numbers of students with ability but with inadequate preparation would be admitted and then dropped indiscriminately without a chance to demonstrate satisfactory performance. The guiding principle was that while CUNY could not guarantee that all students with deficiencies would overcome their handicaps, each student was given a chance to prove himself. . . .

New Responsibilities for Faculty

. . . Open admissions was the university's bold attempt to integrate "open access" and to bring a mix of all kinds of students directly into the mainstream of its senior four-year colleges. A noted poet who taught in CCNY's Basic Writing Program during the first years of open admissions said of her students:

The highly motivated but ill-prepared Black student, the Asian student channeled toward the sciences and with severe English-language deficiencies, the alienated second or third generation White student from parochial school, may all be the first of their families to enter college, may all have problems with writing and with college-level reading; but their relationship to almost everything has been different—to America, to family, to the educational system, to the police, to the standard English dialect. Openness and emotional accessibility differ, ways of surviving in a classroom differ, responses to stimuli differ. . . . How we work with these and many more strands to design a writing course that can liberate these diversified groups into control of the American language and genuine articulation of their needs, becomes a more and more challenging question. . . . (Adrienne Rich, "Final Comment on the Interdisciplinary Program," 1972). . . .

A Remarkable Teacher

Scattered among these critics of all kinds were a few faculty who tried in a systematic way to discover in their new students clues that would lead to new education. Among these faculty was a remarkable person, the late Mina Shaughnessy, who taught remedial English at City College to SEEK students. Fred Hechinger, of *The New York Times,* a City College graduate, described Mina Shaughnessy's moment of discovery:

A crucial moment in Shaughnessy's progress came in 1972 when she was teaching in the City University's SEEK program (at City College). . . . One day the administration dumped 15 cartons containing 4,000 placement essays in her office. Instead of despairing of the task, she analyzed more than 2,000,000 words of student writing, trying to find out what was going on in the authors' minds. She concluded that all was not mere chaos and ignorance. Under the messy surface she detected a coherence in the students' mistakes. In many of the misspellings she discovered a pattern based on what students had misheard, or a particular formulation that came from a non-English usage. . . .

With increasing understanding of these writing problems . . . Professor Shaughnessy communicated her findings to a wider audience in a classic work, *Errors and Expectations,* a book which De-Mott terms in the same article "a social and moral breakthrough." DeMott concludes his tribute to Mina Shaughnessy with one of the most sensitive defenses of open admissions that has ever been written:

Few will urge that the term remediation carries round it a nimbus of glamour. But to be distracted by the plainness of plain labels is absurd: remediation is intimately connected with the grand project of this society, that of democratic realization. . . . Our duty is to grasp that, because of the character of the society, sometimes even because of its peculiar corruptions, we are placed periodically to advance in knowledge of our brothers and sisters, to feel our way forward into a deeper and more consequential fraternity with one another than hitherto achieved. Caught up in condescension, irony, muckraking, or despair, we often miss the step that our best democratic selves have been attempting, amidst chaos, to learn to take. But such failures of vision need correcting. Leaving them uncorrected, indeed, may well seem to the historian, in the longest run, the only "New York tragedy" worth recording.

Mina Shaughnessy was a remarkable person. Her dedication to the new student was emulated by all too few faculty colleagues—at least during the early years of open admissions. . . .

Thus City College, because of its location and perhaps because of its very reputation as the "open access" college among New York's disadvantaged, was selected as the first choice college more often by just those students in the lower high school average ranges who were also members of the poorer black, Hispanic, and immigrant Asian groups in New York. . . .

Achievements and Shortcomings

. . . One must first acknowledge that the open admissions experience brought about invaluable educational changes at the college. Many of the remedial programs added measurably to the college's ability to bring poorly prepared high school students through the difficult transition to the intellectual demands of a college education that would meet traditional graduation requirements. The relaxation of "entrance" requirements was not accompanied in any significant fashion by a relaxation of "exit" requirements. What is true is that the attrition rate *before* graduation increased substantially—especially in the freshman and sophomore years—not a surprising result if graduation standards were to be maintained. . . . Key alumni not only understood the moral and human issues involved in the open admissions policy in City University but also appreciated its socioeconomic significance. ... Dr. Herbert Bienstock, then head of the New York office of the Bureau of Labor Statistics ... said: "This investment in open admissions is going to produce a population that consumes fewer services and earns more income, and will give us a head start on the manpower needs of the coming 'knowledge society.'"

... The experiment must be judged a success. ...

... The college not only survived open admissions but showed how to turn it to academic innovation as well as social good. ...

May/June 1988

The Undergraduate Hispanic Experience
A Case of Juggling Two Cultures

Edward B. Fiske

... For many Hispanic students the most serious problems are not those they confront getting into college but those they face once they get there. The problems range from the anxiety of breaking close family ties to the loneliness and tensions inherent in finding their way in institutions built around an alien culture. Some Hispanic undergraduates complain of subtle or not-so-subtle discrimination. Even those from secure and privileged backgrounds are often thrown off-balance by finding themselves identified as belonging to a "minority" group for the first time.

Culture shock is a reality for many, if not most, Hispanic college students when they first set foot on an American college campus. For some the shock comes simply from being thrown on their own in a large institution. Ron Lopez grew up in Pacific Palisades, a middle-class suburb of Los Angeles. ...

"UCLA was overwhelming," he says. "It was just big. I had to work and live on my own. It was a real shock. My first two years were outrageous. I was working so hard at the academics and at my job—I was spending at least twenty hours a week at the job—that was just hardship, serious hardship."

Add to that the cultural differences. Angelina Medina, a 21-year-old marketing major at the University of Texas at San Antonio, observes that Hispanics from the barrios on the south and west sides of the city are readily identifiable in a university where most students are middle-class whites. "They dress differently," she says. "They drive different cars, low to the flow."

Since curricula rarely reflect Hispanic interests, even the classroom can contribute to a sense of alienation. "We validate other cultures by studying them, but we don't extend that same validation to Chicanos," observes Maria Meier, a senior international relations major at Stanford University who would like to see aspects of Latino culture worked into that university's controversial general education program.

Since Hispanics often come from weaker high schools, failure in the classroom is a frequent occurrence. ...

Academic disillusionment can come in other forms. Hispanics who reach colleges are used to being considered part of an elite—which they are. "The Mexican-American students that come to the University of Texas think that they have it made, because they were stars in high school," says Consuelo Trevino, a counselor in the dean's office at UT. "When they start competing, they realize that they're competing with stars. It's a big shock."

Hispanic college students say that discrimination is pervasive in American colleges and universities, sometimes in subtle ways, sometimes overt. The stereotypes of Hispanics fed by television and the movies persist. ...

"I've been stereotyped out the wazoo," says Jake Foley, a 22-year-old Mexican-American accounting student at the University of Texas who grew up in the Rio Grande Valley. "People will joke ground—at least, I hope they're joking—and say, 'Oh, he's Mexican, hide your wallet.' " . . .

Many Hispanic students feel themselves under pressure to continually justify their presence on a college campus, in part because of the existence of affirmative action programs. "We carry a stigma in a sense," said Irma Rodriguez, a 21-year-old senior at the University of California at Berkeley. "When I first came here as a freshman, a white undergraduate said to me, 'You're here, and my friend, who is better qualified, is not.' "

Mr. Mendez of UCLA says that he has heard the arguments against affirmative action over and over and takes the position that majority students just don't understand the situation. "What they don't realize is that we have to fight other barriers than they do," he observes. "We're from a different culture. We have pressures on us not to lose our culture, while maintaining a status quo in this culture. That's a big pressure. Some people don't think it is, but it is. You lose your culture. You get branded as a sellout. People who argue against affirmative action often aren't aware of our backgrounds or how we feel. They don't understand where we're coming from. If they did, they'd realize that affirmative action has helped a lot of people."

The problem of how to balance participation in two cultures is a continuing one, and each Hispanic student must make his or her own decision. Some join Hispanic social or political groups and affirm their heritage as overtly as possible. Others become "coconuts"—brown on the outside, white on the inside—but this leads to charges of "selling out."

Juggling two cultures is never an easy task. "I think I'm always swimming against the current," says Lupe Gallegos-Diaz, a 26-year-old graduate student at Berkeley. "I feel as a Chicana that I always have to perform. I have to know my material, then deliver it in a forceful, articulate manner. Otherwise, you're stereotyped as not being able to cope." Even the most successful students are not immune from subtle forms of racism, says Mr. Lopez. "Sometimes that will take the form of someone's saying, 'You say you're Chicano, but you're not really like them. You're not the way they are.' "

Scratch a Hispanic college student, and you'll probably find someone in his or her background who showed a special interest in them, who took them aside and gave them the aspiration and encouragement to go on to higher education. For Jorge A. Ontiveros, a student at Our Lady of the Lake College in San Antonio, it was the Hispanic doctor down the street where he grew up in Dallas. "He told me that I had to go to college," he says. . . .

Hispanic students say that they feel the absence of "role models" once they get to predominantly Anglo colleges and universities. Julie Martinez, a senior at Stanford who is from a predominantly Hispanic working-class high school in San Antonio, wants to become an anthropology professor and says that the biggest improvement Stanford could make would be to have more Latino faculty members. "Just having them here makes a big difference," she observes. "They serve as role models. Before I came here, I had never seen a Mexican-American in a position where I wanted to be in ten years."

Not surprisingly, Hispanic college students are conscious that they, too, become role models for their siblings or other younger Hispanics. . . .

A universal theme among Hispanics in American colleges is the need for adequate support systems. This starts, of course, well before college. "Many Hispanics are first-generation college students with very little knowledge of exactly what the heck they are getting into," says Jose Anaya, a Mexican-born student from East Chicago at Indiana University and president of Latinos Unidos, a campus Hispanic group.

Mr. Anaya came to Indiana through the Groups Special Services Program that takes students who might not be considered college material and puts them through a summer program to help shore up their academic and nonacademic skills. "I was scared and a little timid," he recalls. "I decided to find out if I could survive a large campus. The Groups Program offered me an opportunity without throwing me in the waters and saying 'swim or drown.' " . . .

This tendency to stick close to other Hispanics and to Hispanic campus organizations is not unusual. . . .

This may be one reason why Hispanics typically end up majoring in the humanities and social sciences. "It might have to do with the fact that there are already more Latinos in social science or that are interested in literature," suggests Mr. Lopez of UCLA. "One thing that has characterized the Chicano movement in general is a great deal of continuity." Being part of a minority group can also have a profound effect on academic choices. "Perhaps it has something to do with growing up in a marginalized cultural group," he comments. "Maybe we study cultural things as a consequence of that. When you grow up in a marginalized group, even if you're becoming an intellectual, you're interested in understanding that."

One of the great strengths of Hispanic culture is the close family relationships that it fosters, and these have a profound influence on the experience of Hispanic college students. Many will tell you how hard it was to break away from their families to come in the first place. "I have a lot of friends back home who are smart enough to be here and who could afford it through scholarships and their parents," says Alicia Estes, a 19-year-old Mexican-American at the University of Texas. "But because of the close family ties they have, their parents didn't want them to come." . . .

University administrators tell stories of students going home for Christmas vacation and not coming back, and Hispanic students seem more willing than students in similar economic situations to put aside their academic plans to help earn money for their family. . . .

Hispanic cultural values sometimes come into conflict with those that make for academic suc-cess. For Hispanics, looking someone in the eye is seen as a sign of disrespect, even if that person is standing in front of you in a classroom. "You're taught to be more humble and not to question authority," says Sylvia Gacza at the University of Texas at San Antonio. "It's real hard to ask questions."

This can translate into a tendency not to make use of the academic resources available. "Minority students, and Hispanics in particular, are not prepared by high schools to be assertive enough, to make use of all the services this university has," says Alberto Torchinsky, dean of Latino Affairs at Indiana University. . . .

Hispanic students are also increasingly conscious that, for all the obstacles they face — inferior schools, insensitive high school counselors, stereotyping, and the like — a college education is worth the effort. "To me, being a Latino student means trying to succeed, using all the resources within my grasp," says Mr. Mendez of UCLA. "It means meeting others' expectations — peers and family members — to achieve what other Latinos were unable to achieve."

Miss Medina of the University of Texas at San Antonio, the youngest of four children, all of whom have gone to college, put it best. "Our family doesn't have money or a business to pass down to our children," she says. "All we have is education. And that's something that no one can ever take from you."

March/April 1990

Students on Campus

Sex, Race, and Diversity Tapes

Alison Bernstein

I n September 1969, a desire to study, write, and teach about American history led me to graduate school at Columbia University. . . .

. . . I was a member of the last class to graduate from Vassar that was all women. Yet I hadn't given much thought to the differences between the campus climate for women at Vassar and that which awaited me at Columbia. Initially, there were minor adjustments to be made: none of the restrooms in Fayerweather Hall, where the history department was located, had the word "Women" on the door. (Columbia did not officially "go educational" at the undergraduate level until 1980.) That omission did not deter emerging feminists, but it reminded us that Columbia didn't have "women's rooms" even if it did have room for women in its graduate school.

I felt uncomfortable at Columbia, but I did not attribute this discomfort to issues of sexism or gender inequality. Looking back, I realize that I never encountered a single woman faculty member in the department. As it turned out, there were two—a tenured Africanist and an untenured historian of British history—in a department of over 20 full-time faculty. There were no full-time black historians at Columbia when I started, and I do not recall a single black graduate student in any of my first-year American history seminars. There were, however, as many women in my first-year seminar as men.

The equal numbers of women and men in Columbia's graduate history department presaged a demographic revolution in higher education more broadly, as the number of women students in the 1970s grew from 41 percent of the total enrollment in 1970 to 49.9 percent in 1979. In 1980, for the first time in the history of higher education in this country, women constituted over 50 percent of total college and university enrollments. And this trend continued: by 1985, 52.5 percent of all students were women.

To get some idea of the magnitude of this change, consider that between 1974 and 1984 the enrollment of women in higher education increased at a rate *nine* times greater than that of men.

The twin but distinct issues of sexism and gender equality were ones that dominated the extracurricular life at Columbia and countless other traditionally male institutions in the early 1970s. Women students discovered consciousness-raising as a developmental, intellectual, and personal instrument of self-discovery. In "CR" groups, women students read for the first time Simone de Beauvoir's *The Second Sex*, Germaine Greer's *The Female Eunuch*, and, of course, *The Feminine Mystique*, Betty Friedan's 1963 analysis that by 1970 had become both a classic and surprisingly outdated.

I remember how excited I was to discover that Kate Millett's bestselling book, *Sexual Politics*, was actually a revision of her Columbia master's thesis. The media hype surrounding her controversial literary analysis and her affirmation of her bisexuality testified that, in 1970, sexual mores were rushing to keep up with the reality of women's lives.

In October 1969, two months into my first semester of graduate school, I received a phone call from the chairman of the Vassar board, inviting me to serve as Vassar's first "young trustee."

. . . I was probably their token feminist as well, since I was not afraid to use the term and accept the label.

Like so many other women's colleges, Vassar's relationship to feminism was complex, and not an easy one. Although over 92 percent of all undergraduate women students were then enrolled in coeducational institutions, the women's colleges, especially Seven Sisters schools like Vassar, were important symbols of women's intellectual achievement. They had been founded in the late nineteenth century to provide an education equal to that of men at the Ivy League colleges; they offered environments supportive of women's needs but not overtly challenging to the gender-ordered status quo. By the 1950s and '60s, many women's colleges were dominated by male faculty, who may have had the same assumptions about and low expectations for women students as their counterparts at all-male institutions. Moreover, while women students were discovering the women's movement in the late 1960s, Vassar was preoccupied with an intensive self-examination to determine whether it should become coeducational.

In 1970 Vassar was the first of the long-established and prestigious women's colleges to admit men into the freshman class. During the decades of the 1970s and '80s, scores of other women's colleges followed Vassar's lead. The total number of women's colleges dropped from 233 in 1960 to 90 in 1986, a decline of over 60 percent. This period of decline roughly corresponds to the emergence of the second women's movement.

Some feminists applauded the trend toward coeducation because they viewed these single-sex institutions as victims of patriarchy and, as such, anachronistic; women students did not need separation from men to declare their equality. Other feminists, among them Gloria Steinem and Betty Friedan, both graduates of Smith College, criticized their alma maters for their lukewarm support of the women's movement during the 1960s and '70s. . . .

. . . What is interesting about Vassar's relationship to feminism now, as opposed to 20 years ago, is that, by and large, it's a more openly feminist institution today. With a student body that is 45 percent male, there is greater acceptance of feminist scholarship in the curriculum, there are coeducational student groups that proudly use the "F" term, and the college seems much less concerned about being labeled a "feminist" community.

Back in 1969, however, white women students

were largely apolitical with regard to sexism in the curriculum or toward the subtler forms of gender inequality at the college. After all, the college existed to serve their needs. Black women, on the other hand, were convinced this wasn't true regarding their needs.

I received my first test as a Vassar trustee mediating between "hairy youth and hoary age" in November 1969, when a half-dozen black women students took over the administration building. . . .

Their demands were really not demands per se. They simply wanted to focus attention on a range of issues affecting blacks on campus, including the need for curricula in black and urban studies. Unlike Columbia, Vassar has a bucolic campus, quite removed physically from anything urban, even Poughkeepsie. Black students wanted new courses, outreach to the local black community, and a downtown facility to bring the campus into the life of the city. Moreover, black students questioned Vassar's commitment to issues of equity on the faculty and in administrative positions. (Words like affirmative action and cultural pluralism were not used in those days.)

I recall thinking that these students were more committed or just plain more risk-taking than I was. They could easily have been expelled. As it turned out, they were not. They left the building peacefully, and they even cleaned up afterwards. Perhaps they knew that several key trustees agreed with their critique, although those same trustees were not prepared to move so swiftly to redress the grievances. . . .

If I had a button on my word processor like I do on the VCR, I'd "fast forward" the next 15 years, to 1990. . . .

I found myself once again on the Columbia campus last month. This time I was trying to take the measure of the campus climate with regard to racism, sexism, homophobia, and a range of intergroup issues. Columbia College is now fully coeducational; approximately 8 percent of the un-

dergraduates are black, and a smaller but growing percentage of students are Latino. It feels like a different place from the university without a women's room in Fayerweather Hall. For example, there is an active gay and lesbian students' organization. Unlike blacks and women, 10 percent of Columbia's undergraduates were probably gay back in 1969, but they were invisible then. Latino and Asian American students have their own groups and political agendas. Yet, the more things appear to change, the more they stay the same: there are fewer than a handful of tenured black faculty in arts and sciences.

And, yes, the university is still sorting out what it means to be an internationally recognized research university in a troubled urban setting. One black student reported that, even though he flashes his student I.D. whenever he enters a university facility, like the gym, he is frequently asked by campus security to justify his presence as a student. Blacks, he laments, are admitted to Columbia, but they do not belong. A Latina from Miami in her senior year at Columbia tells me that she and her "sisters" recently formed a human wall to try and stop other women students from entering a fraternity house party. A rape allegedly occurred at the fraternity, and these women fear that an unsuspecting younger student might be a victim of a similar act of violence.

Are universities and colleges healthier institutions now than they were in 1969? My answer is yes. Is the task finished? The answer is no. The challenge of diversity is one legacy of the last 20 years that we cannot ignore. This time it's not a matter of "doing the right thing" for those nontraditional or under-represented students. Today, in most colleges and universities, nontraditional students—whether they are women, part-timers, commuting students, or people older in age—are the norm. In many institutions, minority students together have become the majority. Colleges and universities must embrace diversity because their survival as centers of excellence and democracy-enhancing institutions depends on it.

Diversity & Community

Right Objectives and Wrong Arguments

Frank F. Wong

. . . What do I mean when I say that cultural diversity advocates have the wrong end of the argument with respect to community? A community needs a shared sense of purpose. It also needs a set of shared activities that rest upon a broader sense of the possibilities of shared human experience. Something in common needs to exist for community to flourish. This something in common is what we often call tradition. Diversity cuts in the other direction. Diversity divides, it fragments, it attacks tradition, it will often undermine a sense of common purpose.

We may wish to believe, as I heard it said at a recent conference on "Making Diversity Work," that the more diversity you have, the fewer problems you have. But on campuses where hate crimes have escalated, where student ethnic groups have begun to attack each other, where arguments over the traditional canon have made enemies of colleagues, it is not convincing. We cannot fall into the trap of arguing that diversity in and of itself is good and ignore the importance of commonality, coherence, unity, connectedness, and community.

Those of us who support cultural diversity will often argue for a multicultural community without acknowledging that the very term may be an oxymoron; "many cultures" is likely to mean many communities, and a rhetorical conjunction of the terms will not bring about a shared sense of purpose. Our arguments tend to imply, even if we do not explicitly state, that every culture has its own validity; when we argue for cultural pluralism it comes dangerously close to cultural relativism. . . . We argue that tradition and meaning must be deconstructed into many traditions and many meanings, but neglect to reconstruct anything in their place. . . .

We will often argue, correctly, for the inclusion of the new scholarship in women's studies, ethnic studies, and international studies, but our rhetoric sometimes echoes the exclusionary tones of those whom we oppose. So we label our adversaries as Eurocentric, reactionary, or backward looking, and by creating these stereotypes we do unto them as they have done unto us. . . .

When we complain about the exclusion of our fields of study and the exclusion of our groups from positions of influence, we are inclined to make it an issue of power, which in some respects it certainly is. But our complaints about power conflict with concerns about community, so inadvertently we find ourselves again on the wrong side of the argument, even though our concerns are right. Challenging the power of those in power does not contribute to a sense of community.

What then are the right sides of the community argument that our adversaries make so wrongly? The academic conservatives argue that our colleges and universities should be concerned primarily with truth rather than power, understanding rather than political advocacy. . . . For an academic community, it is more appropriate to build a sense of shared purpose around the pursuit of truth than around the pursuit of politics.

Academic conservatives are also on the right side of the argument when they associate truth with universalism rather than relativism. The ultimate test of truth is that it applies to everything everywhere anytime, which is to say that it is universal. . . .

. . . Our quest for more limited truths is still driven by our impulse to find order, explanation, coherence, unity, and ultimately some proximate universalism.

The problem with relativism is that it leads all too easily to separatism. If each group has its own truth, and each group's truth is equally valid, and there are no wider standards to deal with the differences, you will then have difficulties in creating a sense of community. At UCLA, where every student ethnic group has its own newspaper advocating its own separate cause, some of these difficulties have surfaced.

The inherent pluralism of American society, bred by the multiple immigrant origins of its people, has avoided separatist anarchy through a larger universalist vision of human rights applying to all people regardless of religion or racial origin. This vision was established in the Declaration of Independence and institutionalized in the Bill of Rights.

Allan Bloom is on the right side of the argument when he suggests that Western civilization has set the standard with its insistence that cultural claims be universal, applying to all civilized human beings and not just to those in a particular time and place. But he and other academic conservatives argue this case wrongly when they presume that their view of the Western tradition is equivalent to universalism. . . .

The hypocrisy of this approach is similar to the hypocrisy that has occurred in the history of this nation when the principles of equal opportunity enunciated in the Declaration of Independence and the Bill of Rights are extended to some groups but not to others, even though their application is claimed to be universal. . . .

The feminist philosopher Elizabeth Minnich neatly punctures the universalist claims of conventional wisdom in the social sciences when she points out that what is defined as normal for human beings is said to be similar to what is defined as normal for males, while what is called abnormal for human beings is similar to what is called abnormal for females. The false equation between male behavior and all human behavior is unmasked. Carol Gilligan makes the same case when she shows that moral development theory from Freud to Kohlberg is essentially male moral development theory—theory that does not adequately account for or explain female behavior with respect to moral response. The Gilligan and Minnich challenges are based on the failure of earlier theories to be inclusive of the experience of women; they assume that truth should be universal and not relative. . . .

Academic conservatives are on the right side of the argument when they stress the importance of maintaining high and consistent standards of quality as our student population becomes increasingly diverse in its cultural backgrounds. But as in the case of their emphasis on truth, their argument is defective when they concern themselves only with standards in the abstract and not with how those standards are applied and whether their application is truly universal and therefore equitable. To advocate consistent admissions standards

is entirely appropriate; to assume that SAT scores and high school grade point averages are a fair and equitable measure for all students, including those with different cultural backgrounds, is inappropriate.

Standards, like truth, should be inclusive rather than exclusive. Wise advocates of cultural diversity like John Slaughter recognize the importance of associating diversity with quality rather than pitting diversity against standards of excellence. Diversity, says Slaughter, is the point at which excellence and equity intersect.

Capturing Community for Diversity: Finding the Highest or the Lowest Common Denominator?

In setting out to capture the flag of community for the cause of diversity, it is important to recognize that at many, if not most, institutions of higher education the traditional sense of community no longer exists. Even before the issue of cultural diversity became the topic of the day, for at least a quarter of a century colleges and universities were breaking up into subcultures that had nothing to with gender, race, or ethnicity—indeed, breaking away from collegiality that had shaped the mythic ideal of the academic community. The forces that caused this erosion of the academic community include the increasing professionalization of the faculty, the specialization of academic research and graduate training, and the bureaucratization of administrative functions. The domination of the curriculum by professionalized and increasingly autonomous departments led to the fragmentation of the curriculum, which in turn led to a call for coherence in the form of the general education movement.

Indeed, the hallmark of American higher education has been its diversity—intellectual, social, and institutional—as the country reached for broader, more democratic access to our colleges and universities. Given this history of increasing, pervasive diversity, it is reasonable to ask, Why is it that the additional diversity, represented primarily by women and ethnic groups, is now so troubling and vexatious to the academic community?

Perhaps it is because this new cultural diversity more directly challenges a traditional culture of academe, a culture shaped by Anglo-European influences. African-American studies, women's studies, Hispanic-American studies, and Asian-

American studies have raised serious questions about the inclusiveness of that Anglo-European tradition in ways that did not occur when higher education admitted war veterans after World War II or when federal and state financial aid opened university doors to families with limited financial means. While earlier new groups to higher education willingly accepted assimilation on the traditional academic culture's terms, the new groups have refused to do so. Instead, they have argued for the right to contribute to the redefining of that tradition on the terms of their own insights and arguments about their own experience.

If our institutions already have an eroded sense of community and now confront a more contentious and fundamentally challenging diversity, what hope can we have that the flag of community can be captured by the cause of cultural diversity? . . . Let me suggest three ways in which we might regard this situation as an opportunity and not just as an overwhelming problem.

First, we should regard the challenge of cultural diversity as a crisis confronting our institutions in their entirety. It is a crisis of such urgency and complexity as to require the cooperative efforts of all major parties within our institutions. No institution can effectively address these issues without the involvement of faculty, students, administration, and staff. The faculty must take the lead in clarifying the intellectual issues, in reshaping the curriculum, and in devising new pedagogies; no academic department is without responsibility or opportunity in this area. Students must help to reshape the social climate so that minority students do not feel devalued and segregated. Administrators must keep the issue on the university agenda, order priorities accordingly, and provide needed resources. Student life offices, athletic departments, admissions and financial aid, academic support units, cultural programming offices — all must be involved in addressing the new cultural diversity. Staff have their own special role in conveying the style and attitude of the institution as they serve students.

There are many problems confronting universities that can be resolved by one office or another, one sector of the university or another. But cultural diversity is not that kind of problem. Because it is a community-wide problem, it must summon the coordinated efforts of *all* sectors of the community. In the process of doing so, it may just serve to restore some sense of common purpose, something of the lost community still envied by our collegial instincts. The climb up the mountain will be more successful if it is a community effort. The need to climb together can generate a community focus not present without the challenge of the climb.

Second, we should not think of cultural diversity as an end or good in itself. We should think of cultural diversity as a necessary means to a larger purpose. Increased cultural diversity will happen; it is written in the demographics. Of course we must insist that access to all levels of our institutions be fair and equitable so that the diversity is pervasive and not segregated. But as many campuses are now learning, increased access creates new problems, not the least of which is our inability to unite around larger goals. Our own rhetoric may contribute to that inability when we talk about "celebrating diversity" or "affirming differences."

What we need is a way of talking about diversity within the context of those things human beings share in common. We need to pursue an understanding of diversity within the imperatives of universality. With such a perspective, the end and objective of confronting diversity on our campuses is a higher and more integrated community. It is not a multicultural community that we seek; it is an *intercultural* community, where different groups engage each other with united purpose. We seek not a community of the lowest common denominator, where differences are tolerated and sometimes sullenly accepted, but a community of the highest common denominator, where difference is an enriching resource that leads us to a fuller understanding of what is universally true.

We need to create an academic community where people with different cultural backgrounds view each other as having similar needs, similar aspirations, and similar problems but with different ways of manifesting them. In this kind of community, different clothes, different accents, different music, different habits, different skin color, and different self-presentation are viewed with interest and curiosity rather than hostility and suspicion. In such a community, cultural differences are regarded not as a dehumanizing stereotype but as an intriguing variation that we seek to understand. In so doing we enlarge both our understanding and our humanity.

Such a community would rest upon the insight of the artist who seeks the expression of the universal in the particular. It is the insight revealed by Toni Morrison in *Beloved*, when we understand the humanity of the slave through her writing, even though we are not black nor have been enslaved. It is the insight we gain from Manuel Puig in *Kiss of the Spider Woman*, when we understand the humanity of homosexuals, even though we have no such experience. It is the insight we learn from Maxine Hong Kingston in *Woman Warrior*, when we understand the humanity of women struggling for respect in a male-dominated society and of immigrant families torn across two cultures.

But communities require more than shared, high-minded objectives. They also require shared daily activity. It is here that we find our third opportunity. In seeking to create a new academic community out of cultural diversity, we should turn to the activities that are most widely shared and address the cultural diversity issues within them. Because it is the faculty that sets the intellectual tone for a university, we should focus on their primary shared activity: teaching. It is in the classroom that faculty and students engage each other, where teaching and learning, the primary functions of the university, converge.

We need fresh ways to present our subject matter so that the conceptual pitfalls around cultural diversity do not become embedded in the way students learn. Social science courses that purport to describe human behavior in general should be critically examined to see if they describe behavior only in a particular culture. Studies of culture should not take place in isolation or in separation, but in either a comparative context or in relationship to other contemporaneous cultures. We need more courses in comparative religion, comparative history, comparative literature, comparative politics, and comparative psychology. In such courses the tests of difference and commonality should be jointly applied so that students gain a

vision of the variations of common humanity. The spirit that infused Joseph Campbell's approach to mythology should underlie our study of humanities and social sciences.

We need fresh ways to understand how the way we teach may adversely affect the way students from different cultural backgrounds learn. We should be mindful of Uri Triesman's discovery that the performance of African-American students in math classes at UC-Berkeley was more a result of how they were taught than the level of their intellectual ability. If students feel socially alienated, their learning is impaired.

The teaching that we do is like giving students the techniques for climbing the proverbial mountain of truth. In familiar terrain, students will be able to climb alone; in unfamiliar terrain, the security of the group is important if not essential. Both in climbing and teaching about climbing, we should have the appropriate humility that our condition requires. We should no longer confuse our foothills with the mountain. We should know that the climb is difficult and still ahead of us. And we should know that there may be many paths that lead to the same mountaintop, and we should not confuse the paths for the place to which they lead us.

A Conclusion in Five Epigrams

Let me conclude with five epigrams that summarize my observations. First, diversity without community becomes anarchy. Second, community without diversity becomes fantasy, if not anachronism. Third, community with diversity is an act of creation rather than an act of tradition; perhaps it is an act of recreating tradition. It is more an act of morality than an act of politics. Fourth, mountain climbing takes great individual effort but is fundamentally a team sport. Fifth, it is up to us to finish our story—not as a fairy tale, but as an allegory.

September/October 1993

New Students—New Learning Styles

Charles C. Schroeder

... Faculty nationwide are bewildered and frustrated with the students they see in their classrooms today. Unfamiliar with many of the new characteristics, they see contemporary students as hopelessly underprepared, or less bright or motivated than previous generations. Clearly, the way contemporary students view knowledge and derive meaning are vastly different from those of their instructors. These differences may be one of the causes of the low morale, sense of discouragement, and tendencies toward despair that are recounted across the country when faculty gather to discuss their roles as teachers. ...

Learning Characteristics of New Students

For the past 15 years, my colleagues and I have been fascinated by Pat Cross's observations concerning new students. We have been struck by the similarity between the characteristics of Cross's new students and those entering our institutions. During this period, we obtained a variety of information on approximately 4,000 entering students, all of whom were administered the Myers-Briggs Type Indicator (MBTI), a widely used instrument based on Jungian typology.

The MBTI has been a very useful tool in contributing to our understanding of the role of individual differences in the learning process. Scores obtained from the MBTI indicate a person's preference on each of four dichotomous dimensions. The first two dimensions are particularly helpful in understanding learning styles: extroversion (E) versus introversion (I) indicates whether a person prefers to direct attention toward the external world of people and things or toward the inner world of concepts and ideas; sensing (S) versus intuition (N) indicates whether a person prefers perceiving the world through directly observing the surrounding tangible reality or through impressions and imagining possibilities.

In our initial studies, we focused most of our inquiry on two very broad learning patterns associated with sensing and intuition. The results indicate that approximately 60 percent of entering students prefer the sensing mode of perceiving compared to 40 percent who prefer the intuitive mode. The learning styles of those who prefer sensing are characterized by a preference for direct, concrete experiences; moderate to high degrees of structure; linear, sequential learning; and, often, a need to know why before doing something. In general, students who prefer sensing learning patterns prefer the concrete, the practical, and the immediate. These students often lack confidence in their intellectual abilities and are uncomfortable with abstract ideas. They have difficulty with complex concepts and low tolerance for ambiguity. Furthermore, they are often less independent in thought and judgment and more dependent on the ideas of those in authority. They are also more dependent on immediate gratification and exhibit more difficulty with basic academic skills, such as reading and writing. The path to educational excellence for sensing learners is usually a practice-to-theory route, not the more traditional theory-to-practice approach. Because these students find security in both structure and clarity, they often request specific information on the length of writing assignments, the content of examinations, and what they should know from lectures. This seemingly constant need for clarity and specificity can be a source of frustration and concern for faculty.

Contrast the sensing learning patterns to those of the intuitives. They are generally global learners, "big picture" types, who prefer to focus their perceptions on imaginative possibilities rather than on concrete realities. Intuitives love the world of concepts, ideas, and abstractions. Their path to excellence is from theory to practice, and they often prefer open-ended instruction to highly structured instruction. They usually demonstrate a high degree of autonomy in their learning and value knowledge for its own sake. Compared to their sensing counterparts, intuitives prefer diversity in ideas and learning options and are not uncomfortable with ambiguity. These learning characteristics are quite similar to those of most faculty who value critical thinking, independence, depth and originality of thought, and the ability to grasp abstract ideas. . . .

The results of these various studies led us to speculate that there is a very strong link between students who prefer the sensing learning pattern and the learning styles exhibited by new students. In comparing our results with data obtained from the Center for the Application of Psychological Type in Gainesville, Florida, we found that on many campuses students who prefer the sensing learning pattern are now in the majority. This is particularly true for relatively non-selective institutions that do not place a premium on entrance examination scores. One might wonder why so many students with the sensing preference are entering college. The reason is fairly obvious when we consider that approximately 75 percent of the general population has been estimated to prefer the sensing learning pattern. As the egalitarian movement emphasizes greater access to higher education, the college population is beginning to reflect the makeup of the general population. . . .

Faculty Characteristics and New Students: A Mismatch?

Colleges and universities today show an increasing disparity between faculty and students, between teacher and learner. What suffers as a consequence is the learning process itself—an observation that pervades in numerous national reports on the status of higher education written in the 1980s. Unfortunately, the *natural differences* in learning patterns exhibited by new students are often interpreted by faculty as *deficiencies*. What may be happening, then, is a fundamental "mismatch" between the preferred styles of faculty and those of students.

When comparing the preferred learning patterns of faculty to those of students, it is not surprising to find that faculty prefer the abstract reflective (IN) pattern. MBTI data collected over the years on faculty on numerous campuses reveal that over 75 percent of faculty prefer the intuitive learning pattern, with the vast majority of these preferring the abstract reflective (IN) pattern. On many of these campuses, fewer than 10 percent of the faculty prefer the concrete active (ES) pattern.

Concrete active (ES) learners come to class seeking direct, concrete experience, moderate-to-high degrees of structure, and a linear approach. They value the practical and the immediate, and the focus of their perception is primarily on the physical world. Their IN instructors, on the other hand, prefer the global to the particular, are stimulated by the realm of concepts, ideas, and abstractions, and assume that students, like themselves, need a high degree of autonomy in their work. In many ways, the contrast between the ES learner and the IN teacher characterizes the kinds of frustrations experienced between many students and teachers; and it may be that this basic incongruence is the root of the dilemma in today's college and university classrooms. As faculty, we often create classroom environments that are rewarding to us and to students like us, but these settings can be extremely frustrating for the new students. . . .

There are many ways to create a better match between new student learning styles and faculty approaches to instruction. In general, these can be categorized primarily as *active* modes of teaching and learning. For students who prefer the ES pattern, experiential learning that actively engages their senses in the subject matter is often highly effective. Examples include small group discussions and projects, in-class presentations and debates, carefully monitored experiential learning, peer critiques, team projects, service learning, field experiences, developing simulations, and utilizing the case method approach. . . .

Finally, new students, compared to their more traditional predecessors, prefer a high degree of personalism. Because they are often unsure of themselves, they want a great deal of feedback from their teachers. They adapt quite well to group activities and collaborative learning. Carefully reviewing assignments, classroom methods, and tests according to how well they match up with the way students learn can be an effective learning process for faculty. . . .

CURRICULUM

Jerry G. Gaff

One impression from reviewing 30 years of articles about the curriculum in *Change* is the prevalent and unapologetic usage of the term "liberal education." During its early years, *Change* published many attempts to define, improve, and celebrate liberal education; it included many examples of how it could be translated into instructional programs and institutional settings. One striking phenomenon of the times was the creation of new colleges, both free standing and colleges-within-a-college, most with a number of educational and organizational innovations—Hampshire College, University of California at Santa Cruz, University of Wisconsin at Green Bay, and many more. During the next several years, the idea of liberal education was assaulted by a host of changes in the academy and in society, and it lost the centrality it once enjoyed.

Reviewing these articles drives home the point that the curriculum changes reflect larger social changes, even over as short a time as three decades. One notes the social turmoil and student protests of the late 1960s and early 1970s, hears the slogan of the time: "Don't trust anyone over 30," and almost sees graduation requirements and curricular structures falling. When a recession followed the oil boycott starting in 1974, colleges and universities saw a dwindling pool of students, and institutions began developing new, more practical courses of study designed to appeal to what Patricia Cross called "the new students." The "new vocationalism" (though indistinguishable from the "old vocationalism"), ushered in a wave of career-oriented programs. Liberal education for most students was reduced to general education requirements. As the student body became more diverse, new studies were launched around issues of concern to women, African Americans, Asians, and Hispanics, and in most places these programs proceeded to gain a stronger foothold. Programs for working adults also proliferated, sometimes providing a lifeline to otherwise struggling institutions. All of these changes challenged the old subject matter of the liberal arts and sciences and questioned whether it was appropriate for the new students.

By the 1980s, the academic major had moved into the open spaces created by the erosion of liberal education and the relaxation of graduation requirements, and it became the central feature of the undergraduate curriculum. Curiously, only one article in 30 years, that by Jonathan Smith (1983), focused on the major, unless one includes those dealing with the professions. Rather than celebrate it, however, Smith asserted that the major often is as lacking in educational focus, structure, and coherence as is general education. As Frederick Rudolph's (1984) article indicates, the faculty had become committed to professionalism and specialization, defined in terms of their academic disciplines. Thus, the major came to dominate the attention and claim the allegiance of both students and faculty.

Even so, interdisciplinary studies, integrative education, and synthesis of disparate elements held an allure for many faculty, students, and authors in *Change*. Throughout the years, from the new experimental colleges to the institutions of today, interdisciplinary studies have been championed for their wholeness, their ability to address real world problems and issues, and their power to motivate students in a way that the curriculum carved up into separate disciplines does not. Although a perpetual argument has been made for interdisciplinary studies, it has largely been a losing one. Interdisciplinary courses and programs are found in nearly every institution, but they remain on the periphery of the prevailing disciplines.

Given the prevalence of loose distribution requirements that freed students and faculty from strictures of a tighter and more purposeful curriculum, many students found ways to navigate the requirements to avoid whole areas of knowledge and to skip demanding courses that emphasized development of intellectual skills, such as critical thinking and writing. The growing awareness that too many students could not think well or express themselves clearly and that they lacked "cultural literacy" led to a wave of "national reports" and calls for reform. The dialogue between Wayne Booth (1988) and E.D. Hirsch (1988) went to the heart of this debate.

A well-educated work force was increasingly seen to be a strategic economic asset, as the 1983 publication of *A Nation at Risk* claimed, and another revival of interest in general education ensued. By the end of the decade, as many as 90 percent of the four-year colleges and universities claimed to have reviewed or revised their general education programs, and great numbers of curricular experiments were spawned, many of them discussed in *Change*. By the end of the 1980s, general education programs were becoming more purposeful, higher in quality, and a bit more coherent, although progress was more than a little uneven.

During the 1990s the nation embarked on an astounding economic expansion, taking advantage of opening markets and new sources of cheap labor in former communist and other developing countries. Growing national awareness of human interdependence meant greater need to understand other peoples abroad and to respect diverse populations at home; these social changes were paralleled on campus by education for diversity. Concerns for multiculturalism, political correctness, and diversity dominated both popular and academic rhetoric and curricular practice. Neoconservatives attacked what they saw as a loss of standards, the neglect of "great books," and a general "dumbing down" of the curriculum; liberals defended the expansion of the curriculum to include previously excluded voices, an expansive scholarship of diversity, and more complete understanding of history and culture.

The incorporation of technology into all courses of study, remedial education to help those who need a boost to succeed, service learning to enhance classroom instruction, and global studies across the curriculum—all helped to complete the transformation of the undergraduate curriculum away from the circumscribed, fairly defined version of the 1960s. By the end of the 1990s, the undergraduate curriculum had come closer to fulfilling the dream of Ezra Cornell, who founded an institution "where any person can find instruction in any study" (Rudolph, 1977, p. 1).

We have come full circle. In their 1999 essay, "Habits Hard to Break" and their 1998 essay on which it is based, "Contemporary Understandings of Liberal Education," Carol Geary Schneider and Robert Shoenberg urged that rather than abandon this important tradition we adapt it to today's circumstances. To those who regard liberal education as general and lacking in purpose, they see it as serving specific educational ends. To those who regard it as impractical, they see it as central to a successful career and integral to a full professional preparation. To those who believe that liberal education is removed from the world, they see it as engaged and as a means to social improvements. In short, they assert that liberal education is the very definition of a quality education: an essential part of the higher education of every student and of every academic specialization. They point out that the curricular structures created a century ago—departments as silos, the separation of general education and the major, isolated courses and credits—get in the way of a high quality, truly integrated, liberal education. Can the old ideal of liberal education be resurrected? Can it serve as a viable educational vision in an age that approaches near-universal postsecondary education? The jury is still out on these questions.

The late JB Hefferlin observed (1969, p. xx), "the curriculum is the battlefield at the heart of the institution." These readings document that point, as well as show the dynamism that is involved in the curriculum. As Frederick Rudolph (1977, p. 3) declared in his classic study of the curriculum since the founding of Harvard College in 1636, ". . . change in the course of study has been constant, conscious and unconscious, gradual and sudden, accidental and intentional, uneven and diverse, imaginative and pedestrian." The excerpts that follow illustrate this assertion.

References

Booth, W. (1988, July/August). Cultural literacy and liberal learning: An open letter to E. D. Hirsch, Jr. *Change, 20,* 10–21.

Hefferlin, JB. (1969). Dynamics of academic reform. San Francisco: Jossey-Bass.

Hirsch, Jr., E. D. (1988, July/August). A postscript by E. D. Hirsch, Jr. *Change, 20,* 22–26.

Rudolph, F. (1977). *Curriculum: A history of the American undergraduate course of study since 1636.* San Francisco: Jossey-Bass.

Rudolph, F. (1984, May/June). The power of professors: The impact of specialization and professionalization on the curriculum. *Change, 16,* 12–17, 41.

Schneider, C. G., and Shoenberg, R. (1998). Contemporary understandings of liberal education. Washington, D.C.: Association of American Colleges and Universities.

Schneider, C. G., and Shoenberg, R. (1999, March/April). Habits hard to break: How persistent features of campus life frustrate curricular reform. *Change, 31,* 30–35.

Smith, J. Z. (1983, July/August). Why the college major? Questioning the great unexplained aspect of undergraduate education. *Change, 15,* 12–15.

U.S. National Commission on Excellence in Education. (1983). *A nation at risk: The imperative for educational reform.* Washington, DC: U.S. Department of Education.

Educating for Survival

A *Call for a Core Curriculum*

Ernest L. Boyer and Martin Kaplan

Throughout human history, education has mirrored the state of civilizations. The education of Americans—what is taught and what is learned—speaks to the conditions of our times. If much of the content of our education now seems atomistic, "value free," and without a common center, it reflects to a large degree the American condition—now culturally dispersive and devoid of shared assumptions.

Can the American Experiment survive, in the long run, without exposing our people educationally to their common bonds? Or is it possible to reveal to our citizens, with their thousand varied roots, some core of educational experience that may help assure social continuity rather than further outward dispersion? We believe that social survival in this and the next century is more likely when a common sharing of our human voyage is rediscovered by our educational leaders. We believe that we are indeed in a race for social survival and that some return to a core of learning is crucial to the larger national goals of America's third century.

To build a core curriculum today might seem a hard, perhaps impossible task. Everything—the vanished consensus, the spread of knowledge, institutional inertia—argues against it.

Yet while diversity necessarily and correctly affirms the individual, education for independence is not enough. Education for interdependence is just as vital. Only a common core of study confronts the fact that isolation and integration are both essential, that social connection points are crucial for greater understanding and survival. Loss of spirit, lack of inspiration, the clash of special interests, the decline of common loyalties—all these must now give way to an awareness based on new global relationships of mutual dependence. . . .

"Our own social and cultural condition" calls out for a new core curriculum; and while the task of creating one may be hard, it is not impossible. Further, we are convinced that a common educational core need not mean common repression. The central focus of our quest is community.

The growth of diversity stands as an honorable component of American history. To claim that our nation is not one culture but many, to assert the rights of minorities, to protect individual liberties from mass tyrannies, to protect the right to dissent, even to disobey—these are all keys to liberty; and, to the extent that they have flowered in our midst, Americans may be justly proud.

But this story has an unhappy sequel. Diversity's undertow has pulled us far from shore. Democracy requires a tension between self and society, and yet today the broadening social vision seems in full retreat. The human agenda that we all confront is global; the issues are transcendent. Yet social structures are beginning to break apart, and humans tend increasingly to isolate themselves. Self, privatism, "your own thing" are the new ruling tides. . . .

Every core curriculum of the past was guided by the vision of commonality.

Clearly, students must be free to follow their own interests, to develop their own aptitudes, and to pursue their own goals. But truly educated persons move beyond themselves, gain social perspective, see themselves in relation to other people and times, understand how their origins and wants and needs are tied to the origins and wants and needs of others. Such perspectives are central to the academic quest. . . .

A college curriculum that suggests that students have nothing in common is as flawed as one that suggests that all students are alike. The new common core curriculum is built on the proposition that students should be encouraged to investigate how we are one as well as many; the core curriculum must give meaning, in a democratic context, to *e pluribus unum*. What are these experiences all people share? And which of these common experiences should be studied by the college student? Within the answers to these questions will be found the new common core. . . .

I. We Share a Common Heritage

Colleges have an obligation to help the human race remember where it has been and how, for better or worse, it got where it is. All students must be introduced to the events, individuals, ideas, texts, and value systems that have contributed consequentially to human gains and losses. An understanding of this past from which all of us spring should be required of all students. . . .

. . . [N]o attempt should be made to worship the deity Coverage. One could do worse than to learn less about world history and more about the world. To choose a few things carefully; to study them intensively and across disciplinary lines; and through them to see our own times—these goals may well be adequate for the new core. . . .

. . . [A] component of the core curriculum's approach to heritage should be concerned with change, with shifts of historical paradigms, with sets of events viewed from different vantage points. . . .

Finally, no look at the common and changing past would be complete without a look at the most traditional idea of commonality enforcing our historical inventory, the concept of "human nature"—its limits and its possibilities. . . .

II. We All Confront the Challenges of the Present

. . . The new common core should ask students to look at the contemporary world and to understand the processes in which, as social creatures, they are engaged. . . .

All students should be exposed to a broad range of issues raised by our common existence in a world of messages. They should have an awareness of how languages develop, of the symbols we use, of the process of receiving and interpreting messages, of breakdowns in communication, of the search for an international language. They should strive for "comprehensive literacy"—an ability to spot the hidden presuppositions behind an act of communication, to infer the intent and suasive designs of a message. . . .

We are shapers of institutions and are shaped by them. Living in modern society means interacting with institutions. Understanding our common plight means developing institutional literacy; no educational enterprise has done its job if it has not acquainted its students with the roles, rights, and responsibilities of the principal institutions—public and private—that make up their world. . . .

We all produce and we all consume. For too long colleges have neglected the ways in which society is defined by the common activities of getting and spending. Except for a handful of individuals, no one can choose not to work; and everything we know about society suggests that work choices are overwhelmingly important in shaping the values, culture, and social relations of a time. . . .

III. We Are All Making the Future

. . . [T]he future must be a part of the curriculum to be studied. If consideration of the past and present emphasizes American society's internal connectedness, looking ahead will underscore complex global interrelationships. And to inquire about that is to wonder not only whether the future will resemble the present, but also whether there will be a future. . . .

IV. We Are Partisans, We All Make Ethical Choices

As a capstone to a core curriculum, we propose a very strong and forward look at the moral and ethical considerations that guide the lives of each person, a kind of forum in which personal beliefs could be discussed. Everyone "believes," everyone continually makes value-laden choices, and no one holds values wholly unrelated in origin and impact to the values held by others. . . .

The core curriculum . . . must encourage frank and searching discussion about the choices people make and why they make them, about religious beliefs and ideologies. It must bring students into contact with people who hold explicit ideals, people outside the university, people who can talk carefully and thoughtfully about their own commitments, and who are capable of pursuing questions like, When should values change? When should partisanship be revised?

In this way, the core could even become a forum for its own self-examination. What are the assumptions from which other approaches to the core have arisen? What presuppositions underlie a free-elective system? What tenets give rise to an approach based on commonality? Such questions could provide an occasion for fruitful revision of the rationale and content of the core. . . .

Growing Down

Julius Lester

Black studies carries the burden of its beginnings. It was not invited into the curricula of colleges and universities because it was thought to have something new and vital to offer the humanistic body of knowledge. Indeed, it was not invited into curricula at all. It fought its way in through demonstrations in the sixties and seventies. Black studies was born because a man named King was assassinated.

It is not surprising, therefore, that few white academicians perceive black studies as legitimate. It is a political pacifier, a badge of liberalism universities wear to prove they aren't racist. . . .

All too many white academicians make assumptions about black studies and mistake their assumptions for knowledge. Seldom do they engage in that enterprise which is the alleged cornerstone of the humanities—inquiry. If they did they might learn that the generation of black students and faculty responsible (with important white support) for the creation of black studies was demanding that the university cease being a reflection of white, Western realities and values only. Black studies was demanded as a corrective to the exclusive whiteness of higher education. . . .

. . . [B]lack studies should exist "on terms of equality." Black studies has an existence and legitimacy of its own. Black studies is more than putting previously excluded information into the curriculum. It is not a psychological bromide for angry black students, and even if there were not black students at a university, black studies would have a place. . . . Black studies represents a different point of view from that of the "traditional" disciplines, and for that reason black studies has the potential to revitalize and transform higher education. . . .

Black studies is not only the study of the history, culture, and lives of blacks. It is the point of view that comes from a reality so tenuous that one did not own even the very breath of his or her life. This reality is the heart of black studies. As W.E.B. Du Bois said almost 50 years ago:

> Instead of the university growing down and seeking to comprehend in its curriculum the life and experience, the thought and expression of the lower classes, it almost invariably tended to grow up and narrow itself to a sublimated elite of mankind.

Black studies offers higher education an invitation to grow down. . . .

Black studies offers a challenge to higher education far beyond the inclusion of black subject matter in the curriculum. Its challenge is how we view human existence itself. The question is, whose lives do we value? Black studies begins with the lives of black people and reaches out to all humanity. . . . Within black literature, history, and culture lie truths about America that can be found in no other place. I knew, because universal truths lie within the black experience as certainly as these truths reside in the experiences of any people. Unfortunately, white academicians resist growing down into the black experience because to do so means an inevitable confrontation with the underside of America—racism. Yet, what more appropriate place for such a confrontation than the classrooms of universities and colleges? . . .

Basic Skills: Closing the Gap

Fred M. Hechinger

Remedial education for underprepared college freshmen has become a major academic enterprise. It is the natural consequence of a radical change in the American view of higher education from the old concept of a privilege to something very near a right. Open admission formalized that change. If everybody with a high school diploma is entitled to be admitted to college, what is the college's responsibility toward helping everybody to succeed?

Public attitudes have changed radically on that point: While most of the midwestern state universities have operated under the principle of open admission for a long time, in practice their open door tended to be a revolving door through which the under-educated exited almost as fast as they entered. In the past decade, however, the burden of responsibility has shifted from the student to the university. Admission alone is no longer enough. Once the student has arrived, teachers are expected to provide the pedagogical support to pave the way toward graduation.

There can be little doubt that the most powerful impetus for this change has come from the admission of great numbers of minority students. The very fact that they were generally classified as "culturally disadvantaged" provided the rationale for remediation: If it is the culture's fault that certain young people are disadvantaged, then it is the culture's responsibility to erase the disadvantage. It would nevertheless be misleading to view remediation as a novelty created to deal only with the academic problems of certain racial and ethnic groups. Long before compensatory education was invented, there were a variety of provisions, such as "bonehead English" or even—in the case of the highly selective City College of New York in the 1930s—English for Engineers. Moreover, when open admission let in a flood tide of students at such institutions as the City University of New York, the underprepared included great numbers of lower-class white students who needed as much remediation as their black or Puerto Rican contemporaries. . . .

Teachers' attitudes toward the new task of remedial education vary greatly, from the old-line contempt for doing the grade schools' work in college to pride in the opportunity to unlock the capacity of intelligent students severely handicapped by their academic deficiencies. . . .

The ways of doing it differ greatly. But it is fair to say that the earlier approach of simply returning to the laborious teaching of the three R's—or rather their reinforcement—has generally been scrapped as unsuccessful and demeaning. . . .

There are many reasons for such a dismal preparation in the most simple basic skills. Growing up in essentially inarticulate homes is one, unfamiliarity with middle-class English may be another; but the paucity of English instruction within the schools—particularly in the area of writing—compounds the handicap. Increasing numbers of high school students, moreover, have learned to skip English instruction altogether by taking "more interesting" courses such as film. . . .

Whatever the specific methods used by remedial writing teachers, the common denominator was defined by Mina Shaughnessy: "There's no way of learning to write unless you write, and since the high schools don't require a good deal of writing, there's no particular reason we should expect students to be able to write." Most of the remedial writing programs have in common their emphasis on writing, writing, and more writing. . . .

. . . Successful programs, moreover, cannot readily be replicated in different settings; they are at best broad guides about ideas and strategies that *might* be helpful, provided they mesh with the personality and the goals of the program's managers and, more important, the teachers. In the end remedial instruction depends on faith and commitment—faith in the students' ultimate capacity to rise above their deficient preparation, and commitment on the part of teachers and administration to help them succeed.

Education and the World View

George W. Bonham

... For all of America's long years as a world power, for all of its engagements—peaceful or otherwise—in virtually every nook and cranny of this globe, we now witness an entirely new stage in world development; and yet we hardly see it at all. We fail dismally to unhook ourselves from ideologies that are no longer consonant with the new motor forces of world events. We stubbornly cling to easy dichotomies—East-West; Capitalist-Communist; the haves and have nots—and we fail to see the true world of vast new multiplications of cultural forces in which the old ideologies are not only incorrect, but keeping them may lead to disastrous consequences. ...

... We live in a world that is increasingly anarchical, increasingly unpredictable, and increasingly a world not of American choosing or of America's imagination. ... The role that education must play in the years ahead is inexorable and plain to see. The word has unalterably changed, and so must American education.

What is at stake here is a major sea change in the way we must perceive global events, in the relationships of nations, and in understanding new strategic consequences. ... Unless the major institutions in this very rich country—and especially education, the communications media, and our public agencies—resist the easy answers and prepare us for a world of vastly diffused power, our bad public arguments in regard to international order must inevitably become bad public decisions. ...

... Whatever the educational offering, it should not be mounted in the service of one ideology, but should represent a substantive reading of a globe where virtually every answer now promises to be exceedingly complex and beyond the social imagination of most of us. ...

... The reshaping of that world order is now occurring before our eyes, but only a firmer understanding of the likely shape of things to come will give us any sense of control over our destinies. A firmer educational footing of this global understanding is the first essential step in developing prudent political sensitivities. In dealing with other cultures, it will pay us to listen more carefully. We have usually asked others to listen to us. To listen carefully to viewpoints other than our own, alas, is not generally taught well in our universities.

I have placed international understanding into the larger political framework in order for us to better understand the true educational challenges. ...

The Council on Learning's Education and the World View project is a carefully defined public project of two years' duration to encourage serious curricular reconsiderations in our schools and colleges in view of the new realities of the world. ...

A Quest for Common Learning

An Essay from the Carnegie Foundation for the Advancement of Teaching

Ernest L. Boyer and Arthur Levine

General education has become the spare room of academic life. Like most spare rooms it is chronically in a state ranging from casual neglect to serious disrepair. Efforts at dusting, rearranging, and sprucing up absorb a great deal of effort and bring little in return. . . .

The one positive sign we see is a growing willingness within the academic community to take a fresh look at general education. Most of the schools we visit these days seem to be revising their curriculum in one way or another. . . .

Indeed, general education is touted on campuses from coast to coast as the answer to almost every educational and social problem we confront. . . .

On campus, general education is embraced as the answer to the decline in academic performance, especially in language and mathematics. It is also viewed as a palliative for the "new vocationalism," the increasing career orientation and declining interest in the liberal arts of today's undergraduates. At the same time, it is sought as a remedy for academic overspecialization, the rising concentration in major studies which resulted from the elimination of general requirements in the 1960s.

General education is greeted too as a solution to the growing problems of campus management. . . . More positively, general education is regarded as a vehicle for revitalizing the faculty member who is overspecialized or too remote from undergraduates. . . .

To a remarkable degree, these successive general education reforms did reflect the social concerns of their respective eras. Each movement occurred in a period of social drift and personal preoccupation. The movements were the products of times when war destroyed community, when political participation declined, when government efforts to set a common social agenda weakened, when international isolation was on the rise, and

when individual altruism decreased. And a careful look suggests that, despite apparent conflicts and contradictions, general education activity from 1914 to the present reveals a significant, recurrent theme. Each general education revival moved in the direction of community and away from social fragmentation. The focus consistently has been on shared values, shared responsibilities, shared governance, a shared heritage, and a shared world vision. To us, this is an important point. It suggests that the ebb and flow of general education is, in fact, a mirror of broader shifts in the nation's mood.

During each revival, general education spokesmen consistently have been worried about a society that appeared to be losing cohesion, splintering into countless individual atoms, each flying off in its own direction, each pursuing its own selfish ends. They have been convinced that our common life must be reaffirmed, our common goals redefined, our common problems confronted. The specific agenda—the preservation of democracy, the promoting of a common heritage, the development of citizen responsibility, a renewed commitment to ethical behavior, the enhancement of global perspectives, the integration of diverse groups into the larger society—has varied. But the underlying concern has remained remarkably constant. It reflects the neverending tension between the individual and the group, between freedom and control, between independence and interdependence. . . .

The perennial tension between the individual and the community is mirrored in the college curriculum. The elective portion of the curriculum acknowledges individualism—the right of each person to act independently and make personal choices. So does the academic major; here the student, within limits, is permitted to decide what he or she wants to study.

General education is a different matter. This

portion of the curriculum is rooted in the belief that individualism, while essential, is not sufficient. It says that the individual also shares significant relationships with a larger community. In this manner, general education affirms our connectedness. It is the educational tool we reach for in our search for renewal of the frayed social compact. Through general education on the one hand, and majors and electives on the other, the college curriculum recognizes both our independence and our interdependence. It acknowledges the necessary balance between individual preferences and community needs. Just as we search politically and socially to maintain the necessary balance between the two, so in education we seek the same end. . . .

A Proposal

We offer a modest proposal for the reform of general education. . . . General education should concern itself with those shared experiences without which human relationships are diminished, common bonds are weakened, and the quality of life is reduced. It should focus on our areas of interdependence, as members of the human family and of a specific society. In short, it should concentrate on those experiences that knit isolated individuals into a community. . . .

. . . [W]e have identified six broad subject areas that we believe to be the proper concern of general education. All students should come to understand that they share with others the use of symbols, membership in groups and institutions, the activities of production and consumption, a relationship with nature, a sense of time, and commonly held values and beliefs. It seems quite clear to us that an exploration of these connections is indispensable if students are adequately to understand themselves, their society, and the world in which they live. . . .

In Conclusion

At bottom we must recognize that general education is not a single set of courses. It is a program with a clear objective, one that can be achieved in a variety of ways. And while there may be great flexibility in the process, it is the clarity of purpose that is crucial.

January/February 1983

Education for Character, Career, and Society

Warren Bryan Martin

The Trilinear Curriculum

Amid the currents and cross-currents, with some colleges trying to hold the line against the encroachments of professional education, . . . a college of character offers a curriculum that explicitly provides for humane studies and skills training to start out together, without sacrificing their separate functions; remain in balance and run on parallel tracks; then later come together in advanced general education and integrative studies.

Two of three main themes featured in this curriculum are familiar: general education and vocational education or, as stated above, humane studies and skills training. The third theme, integrative education, is widely lauded but seldom achieved. Its function is not that of general education any more than it is vocational education. Its service is cross-disciplinary, involving the interconnectedness of things.

One useful way to carry out this integrative function is through seminars, classes, and independent study dealing with the moral and ethical ramifications of both general and vocational studies. . . .

Faculty in a college of character are willing to assume the heavy and dangerous responsibility of working together to determine what is taught, rather than leaving such a decision to the individual or to chance or to external pressure groups. They are willing to determine how what is taught can be used not only to help a student learn one subject well and to prepare for a vocation but how to integrate and synthesize that knowledge in order to apply it to sociopolitical, moral, and ethical issues.

At the heart of integrative education in a college of character is a concern for moral challenges and responses. Stated even more uncompromisingly: Integrative education capable of meeting contemporary needs is moral education. It is education for character. . . .

Questioning the Great, Unexplained Aspect of Undergraduate Education

Why the College Major?

Jonathan Z. Smith

The college major is the great unexamined aspect of undergraduate education. Despite its fairly recent introduction into the curriculum, its purpose and design have come to seem all but self-evident. While there are periodic convulsions in institutions of higher learning over general education and its requirements, there has rarely been discussion of the major, say when a particular major is introduced at a given institution and seeks license. In principle, general education is everybody's business—hence, it all too often becomes nobody's business especially after the thrill of constructing a new program subsides. But the major is the daily business of a small quite particular, and often well-organized group of faculty—hence, no one else's business. To be busy about someone else's major is to be a busy body indeed!

Although majors consume more than half of a student's college career and more than half of a faculty member's teaching effort, the major is held to be largely unaccountable to the wider faculty or institution except in the most ceremonial sense. It remains the privileged responsibility of a small group within the institution as well as, to some degree, the larger profession without. The prime issue confronting the integrity of the baccalaureate degree is faculty governance, and the assumption of corporate responsibility for the totality of the degree. The failure to assume such responsibility is most evident in the major. . . .

. . . The major, we are told, was introduced to bring focus and depth to what was perceived as an unfocused (elective) and over-generalizing curriculum. But rarely was the question asked, depth and focus for what? . . .

. . . While the pattern varies, general education requirements are most usually fulfilled through patterns of required distribution with these distribution courses most frequently introductory departmental courses, i.e., courses introductory to the major. (They are, in fact, perceived by many departments as recruitment devices for the major). In many instances, sample distribution patterns are "recommended" by the various major programs. As students are asked to make increasingly early decisions with respect to their major, the major determines both the shape and content of their general education courses. . . . The power of the major is preeminently political for the major is coextensive with departments. . . .

In most cases, departments and majors lack coherence because they are neither subject matters nor disciplines. Rather than the principled stipulation of a domain of inquiry (a perfectly legitimate endeavor), they are the result of a series of gentlemen's agreements. . . .

Lacking principled stipulation, most majors are incoherent. This is especially noticable at the middle range. While the first course is frequently a well-organized survey, and the last course an individualized research project, what comes in-between is political rather than substantive: a course with each of the major professors. . . . It would be difficult to articulate in most instances in what respects they bring depth study. . . .

. . . [T]he curricular choices . . . ought to be a conscious faculty decision which may well presume other modes of faculty governance than the present federation of departments. The implication is that these goals are public, that they may be tested by the faculty as a whole, rather than owned by some sub-set. For it will be the goals and choices which generate the components of the curriculum. . . . we may demand that they be articulated, and tested for, and that the goals be explicitly built into every course of study and not left for accidental discovery by a student. . . .

Let us have an end to passing off our responsibility to our students and their high schools. It is not the careerism of our students that has disfigured liberal learning, but our own, and that of our colleagues. It is not the deficiencies of secondary education students that has weakened liberal learning, but rather that of graduate schools, domi- nated, as they are, by departmental concerns, which train our faculty and which we ... control. . . .

May/June 1984

The Power of Professors
The Impact of Specialization and Professionalization on the Curriculum

Frederick Rudolph

. . . David Riesman and Christopher Jencks have spelled out . . . the academic revolution that propelled the university into its position as a central institution in American life, moving higher education from aristocratic to meritocratic values and styles and making it ultimately responsive, not to politicians, philanthropists, businessmen, trustees, or students, but to "the assumptions and demands of the academic profession." Whether they know it or not, the power that the professors hold over American higher education, and, therefore, over American society and the social order, is awesome. In the end, therefore, if anything is going to be done to confront the crisis in American education, it is going to be done by the professors or it is not going to be done at all. They captured the curriculum when they went professional, and before long they were not only creating the knowledge that underwrote new professions but they were also providing the practitioners of the professions with the credentials that established their status in American life. . . .

Professionalism among the professors, their narrow specialization, the complete neglect in their training of any concern with teaching or with any professional responsibility other than to scholarship, are conditions that inhibit optimism about whether even liberal arts colleges can in fact teach liberally. Too many teachers of liberal subjects are so far gone into specialization and into the scientific understanding of their specialties that the challenges of teaching, of bringing students into a humanistic relationship with their subjects, are beyond their interest or capacity. And, these days, the uncertainties of the academic job market and the territorial behavior that goes along with academic departments all but disqualify the professors from thinking creatively and responsibly about what a comprehensive and coherent college education ought to be. But, this is where any reform must begin. The professors have the power. They must be encouraged to use it responsibly.

Educating for the Information Society

Harlan Cleveland

. . . The Informatization of Society

. . . The revolutions that began with Charles Babbage's "analytical engine" (fewer than 150 years ago) and Guglielmo Marconi's wireless telegraphy (not yet a century old) started on quite different tracks. But a quarter of a century ago, computers and telecommunications began to converge to produce a combined complexity, one interlocked industry that is transforming our personal lives, our national politics and our international relations.

The industrial era was characterized by the influence of humankind over things, including nature as well as the artifacts of humankind. The information era features a sudden increase in humanity's power to think, and therefore to organize.

The "information society" does not replace, it overlaps, the growing and extracting and processing and manufacturing and recycling and distribution and consumption of tangible things. Agriculture and industry continue to progress by doing more with less through better knowledge, leaving plenty of room for a knowledge economy that, in statistics now widely accepted, accounts for more than half of our workforce, our national productivity, and our global reach. (*The Economist* recently estimated the information sector at 56 percent of the U.S. economy.) . . .

If information (organized data, refined into knowledge and combined into wisdom) is now our "crucial resource"—that's how Peter Drucker describes it—what does that portend for citizenship, and for the education of citizens? The answer has to start with a close look at the inherent characteristics of information considered as a resource. These provide some clues to the vigorous rethinking that lies ahead for all of us:

Information is Expandable. In 1972, . . . John McHale came out with a book called *The Changing Information Environment.* . . . McHale argued that information expands as it is used. Whole industries have grown up to exploit this characteristic of information: scientific research, technology transfer, computer software . . . and agencies for publishing, advertising, public relations, and government propaganda . . .

Information is not Resource-Hungry. Compared to the steel-and-automobile economy, the production and distribution of information are remarkably sparing in their requirements for energy and other physical and biological resources. . . .

Information is Substitutable. Information can, and increasingly does, replace capital, labor, and physical materials. Robotics and automation in factories and offices are displacing workers and thus requiring a transformation of the labor force. . . .

Information is Transportable. Words and numbers can be transmitted at close to the speed of light. As a result, remoteness is now more a matter of choice than geography. . . .

Information is Diffusive. Information tends to leak—and the more it leaks the more we have. . . . the leakage of information . . . is wholesale, pervasive, and continuous. . . .

Information is Shareable. Shortly before his death, the great British communications theorist Colin Cherry wrote that information by nature cannot give rise to exchange transactions, only to sharing transactions. Things are exchanged: if I give you a flower or sell you my automobile, you have it and I don't. But if I sell you an *idea* or give you a *fact*, we both have it.

An information-rich environment is thus a sharing environment. That needn't mean an environment without standards, rules, conventions, and ethical codes. It does mean the standards, rules, conventions, and codes are going to be different from those created to manage the zero-sum bargains of market trading and traditional international relations.

Power And Participation

Knowledge is power, as Francis Bacon wrote in 1597. Therefore, the wider the spread of knowledge, the more power gets diffused. . . .

In an information-rich polity, the very definition of control changes. Very large numbers of people empowered by knowledge ... assert the right or feel the obligation to make policy. ...

More participatory decision making implies a need for much information, widely spread, and much feedback, seriously attended—as in biological processes. Participation and public feedback become conditions precedent to decisions that stick. That means more openness, less secrecy—not as an ideological preference but as a technological imperative. ...

Education for Citizenship

... Education is the drivewheel of citizenship in the informatized society. With information now America's dominant resource, the quality of life in our communities and our leadership in the world depend on how many of us get educated for the new knowledge environment—and how demanding, relevant, continuous, broad, and wise (not merely knowledgeable) that learning is. ...

... What we need now is a theory of general education that is clearly relevant to life and work in a context of the information age—a rapidly changing scene in which uncertainty is the main planning factor. Perhaps, in the alternating current of general and job-oriented education, it is time for a new synthesis, a new "core curriculum". ...

... [W]e could construct a new "core curriculum" from ... these:

- Education in integrative brain-work—developing the capacity to synthesize, for the solution of real-world problems, the analytical methods and insights of conventional academic disciplines. (Exposure to basic science and mathematics, to elementary systems analysis, and to what a computer can and cannot do, are part, but only a part, of this education.)

- Education about the social goals, public purposes, costs, benefits, and ethics of citizenship—to enable each educated person to answer for himself or herself two questions: "Apart from the fact that I am expected to do this, is this what I would expect *myself* to do?" and "Does the validity of this action depend on its secrecy?"
- A capacity for self-analysis—through the study of ethnic heritage, religion and philosophy, and art and literature, leading to the achievement of some fluency in answering the question, "Who am I?"
- Some practice in real-world negotiation, in the psychology of consultation, and the nature of leadership in the knowledge environment.
- A global perspective, and an attitude of personal responsibility for the general outcome of public life—passports to citizenship in an interdependent world.

The fusion of computers and telecommunications, and developments in bio-technology, are the basis for a legion of new activities, new things to do, new "jobs," on Earth, in the oceans, in the atmosphere and outer space. The number and quality of "jobs" will be a function not of physical constraints but of the human imagination. Will we use our imagination to create full employment at fulfilling work? In the words of Barbara Ward: "We do not know. We have the duty to hope."

There are two predictions to which I would assign a high probability value. The first is that people who do not educate themselves—and keep reeducating themselves—to participate in the new knowledge environment will be the peasants of the information society. The second is that societies that do not give *all* their people an opportunity for relevant education, as well as periodic opportunities to fine-tune their knowledge and their insights, will be left in the jetstream of history by those that do.

The Skillful Baccalaureate
Doing What Liberal Education Does Best

Gary A. Woditsch, Mark A. Schlesinger, and Richard C. Giardina

... What the baccalaureate does best ..., *is educate liberally. ...*

... College catalogues tell us that liberal education produces capable thinkers, communicators, problem solvers, and decision makers; people with a capacity for rehearsal, reflection, and review that enables them to perfect their response to the changing issues they confront.

It appears—perhaps surprisingly—that liberal education *can* have such effects. And there is more than anecdotal evidence that liberal skills of this sort in fact correlate well with effective career performance. ...

Clearly, in terms society finds relevant, the non-specialist baccalaureate is doing something worthwhile. ...

... It is in their *approach* to subject matter—not so much the subject matter itself—that the liberal and the specialized instructor tend, almost necessarily, to differ. Daniel Bell (1968) makes the point nicely:

> The relevant distinction, I feel, lies in the way a subject is introduced. When a subject is presented as received doctrine or fact, it becomes an aspect of specialization and technique. When it is introduced with an awareness of its contingency and of the conceptual frame that guides its organization, the student can then proceed with the necessary self-consciousness that keeps his mind open to possibility and to reorientation. ...

Two insights emerge that can usefully inform any effort to develop intellect. The first, though it is not often clear in instructional literature on intellectual development, is that such development is *recursive*. ...

Skilled thinkers, consequently, do not always think skillfully. But they do have the choice; and the more places good thinking has served them,

the more they may be inclined to try it elsewhere.

What this recursive quality underlines is the futility of viewing thinking skill as something education can pedagogically install, check, adjust, and then leave on automatic. Given that good thinking occurs only in context, the baccalaureate should demand *throughout* its breadth and depth the exercise of intellectual skill. Curriculum becomes more than a sequence of courses; in this light, it becomes an orchestrated sequence of summonings for the student to think skillfully.

The second insight involves the kind of mental activity we count as evincing skill. Many of the skills ... involve the active formation of concepts—skills that apply the abstract connections (cause and effect, action and consequence, contingency, proportionality and so on) that fix ideas. But there are other ways to handle concepts. In a far removed sense, concepts are the stuff of a typical course; they are put before the student to learn. Education needs a new self-consciousness about the kind of concept-handling it promotes.

The "new case for the liberal arts" is built on *operant* measures. Winter, McClelland and Stewart carefully distinguish between such measures of intellectual skill and those that typically occur in higher education. The latter "respondent" measures emphasize recall and reiteration. Liberal arts colleges can promote adult competence to the extent that they require students to "operate" on information, rather than simply retain it.

Dominant modes of assessment suffer particularly from the fact that good thinking is an activity, not a product. How does one differentiate between, say, the student's thinking conceptually and his or her reiterating concepts? The answer isn't immediate in the conventional products of the educational encounter: responses to classroom and test questions, essays and the like. It lies in the *process* by which the student operates on information. A completed essay is a far less reliable indicator of that process than is observation of the student's thinking en route.

In sum, liberal education should invoke these two extremely important notions:

1) Thinking skills mature recursively—educators need to supply context and sustain motive for that recursion; and

2) to be guided, thinking skills need to be caught in action, not just surmised from their outcomes.

There are programs afoot that strive to apply these insights. If we sketch a composite based on them, we can see what a baccalaureate program seriously intent on fostering thinking skills might look like.

Our model baccalaureate will not eschew any of its traditional missions, but three insights will orchestrate everything it does. First and overarchingly, it will expect students to employ their intelligence more powerfully and effectively when they leave than when they come.

Second, it will build and maintain a window to the students' thinking processes so that students themselves, peers, and instructors may grow conscious of what transpires there. It does this because with consciousness comes the possibility of guidance and self-modification.

Third, it will govern pedagogy with the recursive nature of intellectual growth in mind, which means each advance in skill will be sequenced and exercised so as to encourage the next.

We must emphasize that our baccalaureate will wield these insights *programatically*. They will cut across course and department lines and define much of the interdependence among the program's various parts and phases. . . .

Good liberal educators transform novices at intelligence into intelligent novices. They do it because they know beyond question that the only significant mark of the liberally educated is the Intelligent Mind at Work.

July/August 1988

Cultural Literacy and Liberal Learning
An Open Letter to E. D. Hirsch, Jr.

Wayne C. Booth

. . . Dear Don:

. . . [A]fter reading your challenging book several times, I find that a short answer is not possible. For one thing, I agree with much that you have to say, and I can't see how to express my troubles without putting them into the context of the ground we share.

Let me begin . . . with points on which I think we agree. Surely no one will quarrel with your claim, as quoted from Benjamin Stein, that too many young Americans "are not mentally prepared to continue the society because they basically do not understand the society well enough to value it." Some of us would want, of course, to extend the indictment to include most Americans, old *and* young. . . .

As you put it, we should hope for citizens who "are able to grasp the meaning of any piece of writing addressed to the general reader"—in other words, who can enter all debates of general importance to our nation. You and I thus would pursue similar kinds of universal competence. . . . We are thus both heirs of the noble American experiment in "mass" education: we hope for a nation of mutual "understanders"—a genuine community able to debate their ends and means profitably together. We don't limit our goal to improving the quality of education for an elite; we seek an education that will improve the quality of our national life. . . .

But here endeth the list of our harmonies. Though you state powerfully your minimal goal of a literate citizenry, you seem to me to make crucial mistakes that are likely to vitiate any effort to achieve that goal, *if* the effort is based on your analysis.

First you give so much prominence to the minimal goal—"to *possess* the basic *information* needed to thrive in the modern world" (my italics)—that you either ignore or mislead us about what it might mean to "thrive" as a human being in this or any other culture. You are quite explicit about this emphasis: your book is not about the higher goals of liberal education, but about the necessary substrate of literacy upon which, as you claim, every higher goal must depend. You do acknowledge, toward the end, that in addition to the "extensive" education in cultural information that every reader requires—that list or something like it—schools should also engage in an "intensive" education: not just the "transferring" (your term) of what you yourself call necessarily vague, superficial information, but the actual reading of novels, poems, plays, essays, speeches, philosophical and historical works: reading them, discussing them, engaging with the ideas and emotions they induce. To this "intensive curriculum" you devote slightly under three pages (pp. 128–30). It is as if you said, "of course it is necessary to go deep, part of the time, but don't go deep until you have covered all the necessary surfaces." . . .

When you report on the obvious necessity for a rich supply of "schemata" that we absolutely depend on in all reading, you again slant your report toward inert possession of "information." Of course you are acquainted with the research that shows that our conceptual worlds are not given but taken, not poured in but sucked in. Each mind actively constitutes its world. But you consistently underplay that point, and in doing so I think you badly misread the significance of much of the research that you report on. As I read it— no doubt we each look for what confirms our prejudices—most current research tells us that the schemata are actively created. Those that do real work for us, from day one through kindergarten and on through life, are not inert bits or things but active patterns of experience. Everything that we experience, of course, carries with it what you call information, but no information is ever sucked in unless charged by some motivated experience. You rightly mock the effort of some "skills" enthusiasts to teach skills as broken-down units, skill by skill, on the mistaken assumption that skills are simply transferable, independent of what they are

exercised on. Why do you not then acknowledge that teaching bits of deliberately superficial information will be subject to the same corruption: information that is picked up to satisfy factitious experiential demands, such as a threatening test, will seldom last beyond short-term memory; what sticks is what we can *construct* into a context, one that provides a reason for attending to it. More important, if students are led to see learning as something that others *give* them, they will become permanently passive—indifferent, like too many of their parents and, no doubt, too many of their teachers—to any further learning; curiosity will die. . . .

In short, we forget most of what we learn, and almost all of what we have no continuing use for. "Continuing use" for what you call cultural literacy is discovered primarily in continued reading and in thinking about what is read. Those who do not get engaged early in continuously expanding reading, and in conversation about it, will quickly forget everything they have "been taught" and will put their minds to whatever seems to be useful in whatever "worlds" they enter. And no child will ever put his *mind* to learning a list, even when you have added the encyclopedia of explanations for each term that you have promised. . . .

. . . [Y]ours is a very strange analysis of causes and effects on the American educational scene. Suppose we grant, one last time, that knowledge of a vast range of background stuff of some kind is required for any complex reading activity; it does not follow that such *necessary* stuff can be treated as a *sufficient* cause of literacy, or that stuffing it in will take care of more than a fraction of what in fact causes our present deficiencies. In short, like too many educational theorists, including many of those "skills people" you attack, you seem to reason like this: "What are the elements discernible in an educated person? They are such and such. Then surely we should teach those elements, as elements, in order to produce an educated person." But education just doesn't work like that, as the fate of the Bereiter-Engelman curriculum materials should have taught us.

One good test of adequate writing about educational problems is the degree to which it recognizes the relevance of causes from at least four sources—what Joseph Schwab has called the four "commonplaces" of education: the student or "child"; the teacher; the subject matter or curriculum; and the circumstances — political, social, and physical — in which education occurs. Even if you had not reduced curriculum to information transfer, I find it hard to understand how you could blithely ignore the other three major sources of our woes. . . .

Finally, then, though you and I both want a democratic education, we part company on what that would be: for you the goal seems to be a nation of *knowers* who can talk with each other about what they know. For me it is a nation of learners, a nation in which teachers, students, parents, and the great public would all be engaged in self-education — all eagerly reading and talking together about matters that matter. We desperately need a national educational program that would, by its very nature, educate us to the complexities of our great democratic experiment. . . .

There are indeed hints in your book that you hope for that kind of liberally-educated nation of learners.

Cultural Literacy has the great merit of challenging hundreds of thousands of readers to think about education. But it offers invitations for the mean-spirited and under-educated to develop just one more mechanical obstacle to kill the spirit.

Nobody knows enough about many of these matters to speak with great confidence, but one might hope that you and I would spend time finding out about them rather than pursuing a simplistic, single-cause analysis of why so many Americans, even those who have a kind of cultural literacy, fail to pursue a liberal — that is, a liberating — education.

July/August 1988

A Postscript by E. D. Hirsch, Jr.

E. D. Hirsch, Jr.

. . . I shall decline the easy but tedious task of dealing with Booth's observations point by point. Everyone, including the readers of *Change* and Wayne Booth, will be better served if I undertake the more rewarding task of stating the underlying issues in a way that is appropriate to the readers of this magazine devoted to higher education.

Although the main focus of *Cultural Literacy* is on grades K–6, its reforms *will* affect college-level education. I predict that its reforms will result in a greater percentage of high school graduates who are qualified to go to college, and also a greater number of students who are able to do distinguished work after arriving there. That is a quite definite prediction. This postscript will explain why it would be foolish to bet against it.

The research finding that literacy and learning depend on specific shared background knowledge raises a difficulty that is peculiarly American. The easiest way to achieve shared background knowledge among all students is to institute a national core curriculum. . . . But a national core curriculum is not in the cards. It goes against our traditions. Most people in the United States oppose establishing a set of universally required texts — not because creating a core curriculum is inherently undemocratic, since most democracies in the world use core curricula, but because it's a very un-American idea. . . .

When the performances of American students are compared with those of students from democracies that use core curricula, American students perform very poorly — in fact, near the bottom. . . .

The true measure of reading skill is the ease and accuracy with which a person can understand diverse kinds of writing. The emphasis falls on diversity. All valid tests of reading ability consist of short samples taken from several different domains. One long passage would be an adequate test of reading only if reading were a formal, generalizable skill. But, in fact, reading is not a generalizable skill. If a young boy knows a lot about snakes, but very little about lakes, he will score well on a passage about snakes and less well on a passage about lakes. To get a fairly accurate picture of his overall reading ability, one has to sample how well he reads about a variety of subjects.

This variability of performance shows something of utmost importance about reading ability. To have high reading skill, one needs to know about a lot of different things. If you know about lakes and snakes, and so on, you will have higher reading skill than if you just know about snakes. Doesn't that simply mean you read better if you have a large vocabulary? Of course. But consider what it means to have a large vocabulary. Words refer to things; knowing a lot of words means knowing a lot of things.

That is the first, critical step in understanding the correlation between reading skill and learning ability. High literacy requires knowledge of a wide range of subjects, and the same is true of learning. It is a basic axiom of learning that the quickest way to learn something new is to associate it with something old. If our minds are stored with a lot of old information, we find it easy to make analogies that enable us to accommodate new information quickly. In short, both learning and reading depend on background knowledge. Thirty years ago, the College Board discovered that the best indication of overall performance in school is a score on a simple test of general knowledge. Reading ability and learning ability both show a high correlation with general background knowledge.

But reading and learning skills depend on something more definite than broad background knowledge. They depend on *specific* knowledge, because reading is not just a technical skill but also an act of communication. Good communication between writer and reader depends on their sharing unspoken information. To read with understanding is to grasp both a text's literal meanings and its implied meanings, which latter can only be understood when reader and writer share precisely relevant background knowledge. The quality of learning and of reading is critically affected by the amount of background knowledge that is shared between writer and reader, and, analogously, between teacher and student. That is why the skills of reading and learning are deeply connected with shared literate culture. No active reading researcher—that is, no one who is thoroughly conversant with the relevant empirical data—has challenged this analysis. . . .

Opposition to teaching shared knowledge has been expressed by Wayne Booth and educationists who favor the teaching of "critical thinking skills." They caricature the cultural literacy project as mindless memorization and see it as inimical to critical or independent thought. That would be true if literate content were in opposition to critical thought, or if critical thought were possible apart from specific literate content. Neither position is tenable. Those who stress the importance of skills must come to realize that literate content is absolutely essential to the higher skills of reading, learning, and thinking—on precisely the technical sort of grounds that educationists invoke.

The reason for this technical correlation of critical thinking and literate culture is as follows. All intellectual skills depend on rapid deployment—the faster the deployment, the greater the skills. The correlation of skill with speed is explained by a fundamental limitation of human short-term memory. If an intellectual operation takes more than a second or two before it can unify five or six elements, the mind forgets some of the critical components involved in the problem and has to start over and over, tediously, no matter how many skills one has learned to apply. The only way around this bottleneck is to have one's mind well stocked with specifically relevant knowledge. That allows the mind to deal with a few integrated *chunks* instead of many atomistic elements in each new problem. Thus, it isn't enough to learn habits and techniques, important as they are; it is also necessary to learn the specific background information that enables one to *have* intellectual skills within a culture. Knowledge is not just power; it is also speed.

The real test of any educational idea is its usefulness. The teaching of core knowledge will be a useful, even an essential, tool. But I hope and expect that no school, or teacher, or student will conceive of core knowledge as a final educational aim. It is a necessary but not sufficient attainment of an educated person. Background knowledge is shallow; true education is deep. Yet the fact that specific knowledge is required for reading and learning suggests the paradox that broad, shallow knowledge is the best route to deep knowledge. Because broad knowledge enables students to read and learn quickly, easily, and with pleasure, it is the best guarantee that they *will* read, and learn, and deepen their knowledge. True literacy has always opened doors—not just to knowledge and independent thought and economic success, but also to other people and other cultures. . . .

Time, however, may be on the side of the ideas behind the cultural literacy project (not to mention common sense and the results of empirical research). The letters that the Cultural Literacy Foundation has received from hundreds of schools make it obvious that many teachers find merit in these ideas and wish to put them into effect. That may be exactly what Booth fears. But he would be brave indeed if he were willing to state with absolute confidence that these schools, by focusing explicitly on literate content, will not make improvements in all dimensions of education, including the development of independent thinking.

July/August 1989

General Education at Decade's End

The Need for a Second Wave of Reform

Jerry G. Gaff

The public talk about education this decade has not been kind to America's colleges. Our students, by press accounts, display multiple illiteracies; our faculties have "closed minds"; and "Western Civ" has been sold down the river. Less visible to the public, however, is the fact that a curricular reform movement went forward on campuses through these same years, focusing on general education and touching, by survey account, 90 percent of all two- and four-year colleges. To be sure, in most of those colleges the "reform" started and ended with "strengthening" degree requirements "relaxed" in the '60s. But many important new emphases came to the fore in the '80s, too (see below).

Even so, my own monitoring of these developments and most recent round of inquiries tell me that the reform of general education may be running out of steam and what we now need is a Second Wave of reform as a basis for next improvements in the '90s.

There should be four goals for this Second Wave. First, it should broaden existing reforms and embed them more firmly in the life of the college. Second, it should engage the larger number of colleges that have thus far neglected or only flirted with reform. Third, it should attract new individuals to the movement, and through them raise new perspectives and strategies for improvement. Finally, it should confront more candidly the very real campus barriers to devising, approving, and implementing actual reforms and develop more sophisticated strategies for overcoming them.

Much of the debate till now has been dominated by the content question: What should students study? . . . We have to move beyond content—as important as that is—to consider other critical elements, including the students, teachers, and circumstances within which education occurs. . . .

I suggest that a conceptual focus for the Second Wave be the idea of the college culture. More specifically, I raise as an issue the *integrity* of the college culture as it relates to the goal of providing a general education for all students. . . .

The essential first step for a college, . . . is to decide what it stands for by way of undergraduate education. What qualities do we want our graduates to possess? . . .

The next step is to assume, in the words of Willamette's Jerry Berberet, that "everything that happens on a campus has curricular implications." This means working to assure that not only the formal curriculum but also extracurricular life, admissions practices, publications, faculty hiring and evaluation, and budgeting will further agreed-upon learning goals. . . .

. . . A college's core values have to be reinforced in student activities and campus events, in faculty personnel policies and a dozen other areas, and not simply stand alone in a core curriculum.

What matters, then, is not just "integrity in the

curriculum," in the words of one national report, but integrity between the curriculum and the college's larger culture. A college of integrity says what it does and it does what it says, not just in the curriculum but in *all* of its activities. . . .

Curriculum Trends of the '80s

1) *Higher standards, more requirements.* This development, like the others, plays out in different ways at different institutions. Among these 13, it is the most common. Higher admissions requirements, mandates that students pass an exam to be eligible for upper-division study, and more stringent graduation requirements are variations on the theme.

2) *Tighter curriculum structure.* The trend is away from loose distribution requirements that students may satisfy with any of a large number of courses, and toward curricula consisting of a limited set of courses that meet specific purposes, a common core of the same courses for all students, or some combination of the two.

3) *Fundamental skills.* Skills such as writing, speaking, logical or critical thinking, foreign language, mathematics, and academic computing are increasingly emphasized in curricula today.

4) *Liberal arts subject matter.* The liberal arts — the most fundamental and useful bodies of knowledge, methods, and perspectives devised by the human mind — are taking a more prominent place in the curriculum, even in professional and preprofessional programs.

5) *The freshman year.* Freshman topical seminars, stronger advising, and greater attention to the intellectual and personal development of students are themes common to new freshman-year programs.

6) *Global studies.* Given the growing interdependence of economic systems, environmental problems, and security needs, colleges are emphasizing the study of other peoples.

7) *Gender and ethnic studies.* Another trend is heightened attention to cultural pluralism in America and the West and the incorporation of new scholarship on these topics into the core curriculum.

8) *Integration of knowledge.* Integration is what is "higher" about higher education, according to Harlan Cleveland; thematic, interdisciplinary, and "capstone" courses are found in many of the new curricula.

9) *Moral reflection.* More than technical expertise is expected of an educated person; colleges are re-emphasizing values through the study of different cultures, controversial issues, and the implications of science and technology.

10) *Extension through all four years.* Rather than being concentrated in the first two years, general education now extends throughout the entire span of college as a context for specialization.

11) *Faculty development.* Faculty are the key to implementing any change in curriculum; colleges serious about reform provide seminars, retreats, workshops, travel, and other assistance to help faculty acquire new knowledge and pedagogical tools.

12) *Administration.* Several colleges have established greater central authority over the core of the curriculum by creating an administrative position (such as a dean or director of general education) and a collegewide faculty committee to provide oversight.

13) *Assessment.* Assessing student learning is increasingly common, to determine the extent to which a new curriculum is effective and identify problems that call for change.

Multi-Culturalism

The Crucial Philosophical and Organizational Issues

Patrick J. Hill

... Diversity ... is not new. ... In Western thought, four major frameworks have been employed in the analysis of diversity:

1) *Relativism,* which in one way or another regards all knowledge-claims as self-contained within particular cultures or language communities, and which recognizes no higher or commensurable ground upon which objective adjudication might take place.

2) *Perennialism* or *universalism,* which see commonalities or constancies in the great variety of human thought, and which frequently (as in the influential work of Frithjof Schuon) regard those constancies as the essential and more important aspect of diverse historical phenomena.

3) *Hierarchism,* which attempts to sort or rank the multiplicity by a variety of means, among them establishing criteria or methods of inquiry that divide knowledge from opinion, or interpreting world history and human development in such a way that certain opinions and behavior are progressive, developed, and/or mature while others more or less approximate those ideals.

4) *Pluralism,* which in its democratic version is central to the analysis of this article. ...

Democratic pluralism. Within the context of a commitment to democratic values, the diversity of the world's peoples is to be welcomed, respected, celebrated, and fostered. Within that context, diversity is not a problem or a defect, it is a resource. The major problem within all pluralistic contexts (including relativism) is less that of taking diversity seriously than that of grounding any sort of commonality. It is the problem of encouraging citizens to sustain conversations of respect with diverse others for the sake of their making public policy together, of forging over and over again a sense of a shared future.

Conversations of respect and the making of public policy in a democracy cannot be based on mere tolerance—on the "live and let live" or "to each his own" attitudes of individualistic relativism. ... It is impossible to respect the diverse other

if one does not believe that the views of the diverse other are grounded in a reality—the democratic version of reality—that binds or implicates everyone as much as do our own views.

Conversations of respect between diverse communities are characterized by intellectual reciprocity. They are ones in which the participants expect to learn from each other, expect to learn non-incidental things, expect to change at least intellectually as a result of the encounter. Such conversations are not animated by nor do they result in mere tolerance of the pre-existing diversity, for political or ethical reasons. In such conversations, one participant does not treat the other as an illustration of, or variation of, or a dollop upon a truth or insight already fully possessed. There is no will to incorporate the other in any sense into one's belief system. In such conversations, one participant does not presume that the relationship is one of teacher to student. ... The participants are co-learners. ...

... Higher education, judged by the standards of democratic pluralism, does not take seriously even the diversity within its walls, much less the diversity outside its walls. The diversity of disciplinary or ideological perspectives is muted by what the recent national study of the major conducted by the Association of American Colleges called "the ethos of self-containment." Even in institutions that take interdisciplinarity seriously, the diversity most frequently worked with is not the challenging diversity of unshared assumptions or excluded peoples but the congenial diversity of presumed complementarity. Wedded as most of higher education is to the notion that the point of teaching is to transmit what we already know, few agree with Gerald Graff in seeing a positive pedagogical function for exposing our students to unresolved conflict. ...

Meaningful multi-culturalism ... transforms the curriculum. While the presence of persons of other cultures and subcultures is a virtual prerequisite to that transformation, their "mere presence" is primarily a political achievement (which different groups will assess differently), not an intellectual or educational achievement. Real educational progress will be made when multi-culturalism becomes interculturalism.

What might such an exploration in intercultural education look and feel like to the student in a democratically pluralistic university? . . .

Such persons have immersed themselves in a sustained learning community, a community that is intercultural and interdisciplinary. They have studied something of great human significance and have experienced how their understanding deepens with the additions of each relevant perspective of another discipline, culture, or subculture. They have mastered or at least internalized a feeling for more than one discipline, more than one culture. They know the value and indeed the necessity of seeking many and diverse perspectives, most particularly the inevitable *partiality* of those perspectives. They have mastered the skills of access to those perspectives. They have mas-

tered the skills in understanding and integrating these diverse perspectives. They are comfortable with ambiguity and conflict. Tolerance, empathic understanding, awareness of one's own partiality, openness to growth through dialogue in pluralistic communities — all of these things have become part of their instinctive responses to each novel situation they encounter. (They might even characterize those who proceed otherwise as uncritical thinkers.) . . .

If higher education were to take as its role the creation of new structures of dialogue and invention and cooperative discovery (i.e., structures appropriate to an inchoate world), there may indeed emerge a new world order. I speak not of an order in which technologically powerful Americans try to bring the diversity of the world to heel, but of a new world order that empowers hitherto excluded peoples of our and other nations to contribute their experience on an equal footing to our collective understanding of ourselves, society, and the world.

September/October 1991

Pluribus & Unum

The Quest for Community Amid Diversity

Carlos E. Cortés

. . . I am an E Pluribus Unum (EPU) Multiculturalist. That is, I see the Diversity Revolution's opportunities and challenges in terms of the historical American Pluribus-Unum balancing act described incisively by R. Freeman Butts in *The Revival of Civic Learning*. Such Pluribus values as freedom, individualism, and diversity live in constant and inevitable tension with such Unum values as authority, conformity, and commonality. Constructive EPU Multiculturalism involves responding thoughtfully to both powerful Pluribus and necessary Unum imperatives, as well as carefully setting limits to Pluribus and to Unum when they become poisonous to climate and destructive to community.

The United States has been involved in this Pluribus-Unum balancing act since its inception.

That's what federalism and the separation of powers are all about. That's what much of the Constitution, myriad laws, and many Supreme Court decisions have addressed. But the Diversity Revolution has added a major new dimension to the Pluribus-Unum relationship. . . .

The challenge of building campus community in a multicultural society involves balancing Pluribus and Unum imperatives, avoiding Pluribus and Unum extremism, and rejecting the prophets of polarization. For the complex dilemmas raised by the Diversity Revolution, there are no simple solutions. However, as Einstein pointed out, "the formulation of a problem is often more essential than its solution."

By providing a framework for weighing and responding to both Pluribus and Unum as basic, sometimes conflicting values of our society, EPU Multiculturalism can help colleges and universities reformulate, clarify, and thereby more effectively address these perplexing issues. Moreover, it also provides an educational vision for better preparing college students to participate more constructively in what will inevitably be a multicultural future.

March/April 1999

Habits Hard to Break

How Persistent Features of Campus Life Frustrate Curricular Reform

Carol Geary Schneider and Robert Shoenberg

As we write, hundreds of colleges are struggling to update or reform the liberal arts component of their curricula. . . .

Over and over again, however, faculty design teams soon come face-to-face with organizational realities that frustrate their high hopes. Almost whatever plan for integrative, practice-oriented learning they envision, there are structural features of the academic environment that work silently but powerfully to undo it. . . .

The Discipline as Silo

The 20th-century educational model is ostensibly . . . built on a conceptualization of knowledge structured by "discipline." . . .

If "department" and "discipline" ever were synonymous in the ways the model implies, they certainly are no longer so. The degree to which a discipline represents a paradigmatic structure of knowledge that provides, in and of itself, a viable organizational principle for undergraduate learning is called into question by the increasing "interdisciplinarity" of both student interests and faculty behaviors, not only in their teaching but in their research as well. . . .

General Education and the Major

As long as general education was conceived predominantly as study of a range—or "breadth"—of subject matters, with study in a designated major providing "depth," the conventional sharp division between general education and the major made some sense. But with today's educational focus on helping students develop intellectual skills, understand a range of epistemologies, and increase their ability to negotiate intellectual, cul-

tural, civic, and practical topics and relationships, the assumed dividing line between general education and the major is no longer useful. . . .

Courses and Credits

The dysfunctional dichotomy between general and specialized education is discernibly beginning to erode. The challenge, of course, is to replace it with an educationally viable alternative. But standing in the way is another familiar structure, the system of courses and credit hours, which remains in place as strongly as ever. . . .

Credit Transfer Practices

The equating of course titles with learning becomes even more problematic in the context of student transfer. . . .

The Undefined Baccalaureate Degree

The ultimate problem with this entire system of courses and credits is the way it comes to define the baccalaureate degree itself. As course credits become a surrogate for learning, we allow ourselves to shirk responsibility for developing a rigorous definition of what the baccalaureate degree should mean.

. . . [T]he academy is insufficiently focused on the kinds of educational outcomes it is trying to achieve. . . .

The Faculty Reward Question

Hanging over all this need for rethinking inherited structures is the thorny question of how faculty members will be rewarded for the considerable efforts required to change and assess educational programs. . . .

Moving from Here to There

. . . It is not concepts and practices we lack, but a practical consensus about the purpose of baccalaureate education that will encompass them.

We believe an emerging framework for such a consensus exists. It emphasizes a range of intellectual skills; epistemological and research sophistication; global, societal, and self-knowledge; relational learning; and making intellectual connections. It requires seeing undergraduate education as a whole as opposed to splitting it between general and specialized learning. It also argues strongly for aligning the goals and emphases of K–12 education more intentionally with those of collegiate education.

This emerging direction for undergraduate learning is well served by instructional strategies that reflect the resurgent emphasis on the student as learner, with the teacher as mentor rather than sage. The development of problem-solving skills, both as an individual and in collaboration with others, is essential to this pattern, as is experiential learning in its many forms. Institutions' choices of educational technologies ought to reflect this learning-centered, intensively "hands-on" approach.

Connecting Goals with Practice

What we need next for collegiate reform is the parallel embodiment—in a variety of four-year undergraduate programs—of curricula purposely directed toward goals campuses avow. These models should do more than simply reorganize existing individual courses; they should be integrated structures of carefully related learning experiences that pay systematic attention to developmental sequencing and concomitant student assignments. For a variety of practical reasons, the curricula may need to be presented in the standard form of semesters and courses and credits, but the rationale for and instruction within ought to become far less atomistic than in current practice.

To meet fully the challenges of this approach, faculty members will have to give up some old habits of thinking, most significantly the idea that they are sole owners of the courses they teach. Offering their courses within integrated, intentional sequences will require them to acknowledge the stake that their departments and the institution as a whole have in each course and in the student outcomes it is intended to produce.

Faculty will have to teach toward some goals about which there has been mutual agreement and around which there is some sense of collective accountability.

This need not mean what faculty most fear— externally imposed constraints on the actual content of a course. But it should mean that designated categories of courses work intentionally and accountably, through the kinds of assignments students undertake, to foster specific capacities and intellectual skills. Models for this combination of flexibility and focus already exist in some fields (the health sciences, for example). The challenge is to build on available examples.

Given the transience of students, particularly within regions or state systems of higher education, some broad agreements within the higher education community about educational goals and what they mean operationally will also be important. If the emphasis is on the mastery of particular intellectual practices rather than on a simple passing of named courses, then faculties within institutions among which students regularly move should be able to negotiate some common understandings about appropriate assignments. Educational goals should not simply be imparted to students; they need to become a continuing framework for students' educational planning, assessments, and self-assessment.

The difficulty of articulating important educational goals across institutions and getting faculty to acknowledge them in what and how they teach, while maintaining a high level of institutional and faculty autonomy, is not to be underestimated. Such coordination requires enormous amounts of educational insight, negotiating skill, and good will. Yet making sense of education for the large numbers of students who increasingly move from institution to institution, and for whom a coherent, purposeful curriculum can never be predesigned at a single campus, would seem to require the effort.

This emphasis on student outcomes rather than on course credits and curricular features implies a wider user of assessment. The assessment will be more appropriate and effective if it is embedded in coursework or grows naturally out of it, rather than taking the form of short-answer instruments created solely for the purpose of external reporting. Ideally, assessment should provide opportunities for students to advance, integrate, and correct their understandings at key junctures in their course of study. Assessments that provide no useful feedback to students themselves defeat what should be an important goal of the assessment effort.

Moving forward with a framework for learning that expects broad, deep, and complex accomplishments for every student is a challenge that invites the participation of the entire array of higher education stakeholders, from the public and its elected representatives to each individual institution, and including accreditors, state higher education agencies, university system offices, learned societies in the disciplines, testing agencies, federal education agencies, and so on. The groundwork for success has already been laid in the form of an emerging consensus about what matters in undergraduate education and some promising pedagogical strategies for getting there. We need to seize the opportunity for building the more purposeful, powerful, and integrative forms of undergraduate education that the consensus now makes possible.

THE ORIGINS OF CONTEMPORARY LEARNING COMMUNITIES: Residential Colleges, Experimental Colleges, and Living-Learning Communities

Zelda F. Gamson

From [the] beginning in Massachusetts Bay, American higher education was concerned not only with the training of minds, but also with the molding of character; the 'Collegiate Way of Living,' with its common residence, structured community life, shared intellectual exchange, and spiritual purpose and practices, was the path to those complementary goals (Ryan, 1992, p. 30).

The one idea most commonly agreed upon [at Black Mountain] was that 'living' and 'learning' should be intertwined. Education should proceed everywhere, not only in classroom settings which in fact . . . are among the worst learning environments imaginable. . . . A central aim was to keep the community small enough so that members could constantly interact . . . at meals, on walks, in classes, at community meetings, work programs, dances, performances. Individual life styles, in all their peculiar detail, could thereby be observed, challenged, imitated, rejected—which is, after all, how most learning proceeds. . . (Duberman, 1972, p. 32).

[T]he overwhelming concern for anomie . . . pushed the planners [of Santa Cruz] in the direction of the physical plan and the search for intimacy and community. . . . The larger and more difficult issue was and remains that there is no single, coherent answer to the question of what a liberal education means in contemporary American society. [L]iberal education has never been able to push its way completely out of the exclusive and elitist tradition of genteel learning and the suspicion that the knowledge it imparts has more to do with sophistication than with active and equal membership in democratic culture (Adams, 1984, p. 27).

Communities of practice are . . . essential and inevitable building blocks of society. . . . It is the practice and the concepts they share that connect members of a community, not a warm glow of communitarian fellow feeling. So we are not claiming, as communitarians do, that it would be useful to form communities and that universities are good places to form them. Rather, we claim that communities, with all their strengths and shortcomings, grow inevitably and inescapably out of ongoing, shared practice (Brown & Duguid, 1996, p. 14).

These quotations from four of the articles excerpted from *Change* over the years carry the argument of this section on the origins of contemporary learning communities. The "Collegiate Way of Living," which brings students together in the same residence in a family-like community that can support their moral, emotional, and intellectual development, goes back to the very founding of American higher education. This ideal, increasingly marginalized by the growth of disciplines, specialized research, and the universities that grew up to support them, waxed and waned throughout the nineteenth and twentieth centuries. The collegiate ideal, however, never disappeared. Repeated rumors of its demise were premature.

The collegiate ideal led to the founding of residential colleges across the country. In the 1930s and 1940s, it was stretched in unpredictable ways by an extraordinary generation of experimental, often utopian, colleges. These small alternative communities differed in their politics, curricula, attitudes toward traditions, and styles. Antioch and Goddard were based on the progressive and communitarian perspectives associated with John Dewey. In contrast, Black Mountain and Bennington were more individualistic and oriented to experimentation in the arts. The Hutchins College at the University of Chicago and St. John's were designed around traditional and prescribed curricula. In the 1960s and 1970s, the collegiate way of living found its expression in the universities themselves, in residential "cluster" colleges, "living-learning" communities, and new university campuses structured around colleges.

The collegiate ideal rested on the existence of a place—a college, a dormitory—in which students gathered together to study, play, and live. These students were still in adolescence. As higher education in the United States expanded in the post-World War II period, community colleges and four-year colleges and universities were founded or redirected to serve commuting, older students. The collegiate ideal was not thought to apply to commuters and their institutions, by definition, and these students did not receive the benefits of a strong community or the holistic, personal attention lavished on younger, residential students.

As time passed, however, the link between a common on-campus residence and shared learning weakened. Ideas and practices from traditional residential colleges, experimental colleges, cluster colleges, and living-learning communities were adapted to students who commuted to campus and were older.

What are these ideas and practices? First is the crucial idea that the best learning happens in a small **community**, where the participants spend a lot of time communicating with one another on a variety of subjects and in a variety of aspects of life. The great insight of the current generation of innovators in undergraduate education is that a community can be created without shared residence—in a set of classes clustered together (such as learning communities at Evergreen State and many other institutions, including community colleges), in individual classrooms set up as learning communities (using cooperative and collaborative, inquiry-based learning), or in short, intense residential periods punctuating individual study online and offline (for example, the Goddard Adult Degree Program and other adult programs with residential components).

Second is the commitment to a **larger world** beyond higher education itself. From the experimental colleges of the 1930s and 1940s came a deep connection to different worlds: progressive social change at Antioch, avant-garde art at Black Mountain, the labor movement at Brookwood. Some of the more traditional colleges also held enduring connections to larger worlds: the Quakers at Earlham, Appalachia at Berea, the Jesuits at the College of the Holy Cross.

Third is the growing realization that the best kind of education is **constructed** out of the interaction between tradition and experiment, between the disciplines and the professions and, most important, between the academy and the larger society. Here, the battles of the 1960s and 1970s carried into higher education by political activists in the civil rights, antiwar, and women's movements and by the social and spiritual countercultures had a profound influence. The new colleges such as Evergreen, New College in Sarasota, Hampshire, and the Residential College at the University of Michigan, set up so that their students could become self-directed learners, rested on the assumption that educators could no longer claim to possess the sole authority to determine the "received knowledge" that students should learn. Rather, educators should engage students as active participants in the construction of knowledge as a social act (Belenky, Clincy, Goldberger & Tarule, 1986). Only from "communities of practice," as discussed in Brown and Duguid's article, could real learning take place. (See Brown & Duguid, 1996).

From these three elements—a **community** committed to a **larger world** and engaged in **constructing knowledge**—grew the learning communities of today. For a sampling of the emerging models, see Gabelnick (1997) for a discussion of learning communities in the context of efforts to promote an engaged citizenship, and Singleton, Garvey, and Phillips (1998) for a discussion of a first-year program, both in this section; Arches et al. (1997) for an exploration of learning communities built around service learning and diversity in the section on Work, Service, and Community Connections; and Johnson, Johnson, and Smith (1998) for a summary of the research on cooperative learning in the section on Philosophy, Psychology, and Methods of Teaching. These learning communities are more oriented toward understanding and contributing to the larger society than were their predecessors. They are less oppositional and less utopian. Not as invested in battling the disciplines, research, and universities, they live in larger institutions that sometimes barely tolerate them, while at the same time offering them as evidence of institutional investment in undergraduate education.

Contemporary learning communities may never command the name recognition as the older colleges and living-learning communities included in this section. They may not be as enduring as some (but hardly all) have been. Yet many of these contemporary communities vibrate with the excitement, energy, and power of the best of the collegiate ideal. They are built on sophisticated educational and social structures that encourage serious learning. They go a long way toward addressing Adams' critique of Santa Cruz for not moving liberal education from its aristocratic social and philosophical foundation to a democratic one. They do so for a far more diverse student body, in the heart of the higher education system, and probably cost less in dollars and in faculty and administrative wear and tear.

We need to pay our respects to the rich and innovative past captured in this section by hearing about its new incarnations across the country. These incarnations have grown from and given rise to a rich literature created by philosophers, sociologists, psychologists, mathematicians, biologists, and practitioners of other disciplines. Some of this literature has appeared in *Change*, and several articles are excerpted in this volume in the sections on Work, Service, and Community Connections; Philosophy, Psychology, and Methods of Teaching; Teaching in the Disciplines; and Media and Technology. [See also works by Gabelnick et al. (1990) and Gamson and Associates (1984).]

References

Adams, W. (1984, May/June). Getting real: Santa Cruz and the crises of liberal education. *Change, 16,* 18–27.

Arches, J., Darlington-Hope, M., Gerson, J., Gibson, J., Habana-Hafner, S., & Kiang, P. (1997, January/February). New voices in university-community transformation. *Change, 29,* 36–41.

Belenky, M., Clinchy, B. M., Goldberger, N. R., & Tarule, J. M. (1986). *Women's ways of knowing: The development of self, voice and mind.* New York: Basic Books.

Brown, J. S., & Duguid, P. (1996, July/August). Universities in the digital age. *Change, 28,* 10–19.

Duberman, M. (1972, Summer). Reflections on a pioneer living-learning community: Black Mountain. *Change, 4,* 30–46.

Gabelnick, F. (1997, January/February). Educating a committed citizenry. *Change, 29,* 30–35.

Gabelnick, F., MacGregor, J., Matthews, R. S., & Smith, B. L. (Eds.) (1990). *New directions for teaching and learning, No. 41. Learning communities: Creating connections among students, faculty, and disciplines.* San Francisco: Jossey-Bass.

Gamson, Z. F., & Associates. (1984). *Liberating education.* San Francisco: Jossey-Bass.

Johnson, D. W., Johnson, R., & Smith, K. A. (1998, July/August). Cooperative learning returns to college: What evidence is there that it works? *Change, 30,* 26–35.

Ryan, M. B. (1992, September/October). Residential colleges: A legacy of living & learning together. *Change, 24,* 26–35.

Singleton, Jr., R., Garvey, R. H., & Phillips, G. A., (1998, May/June). Connecting the academic and social lives of students. *Change, 30,* 18–25.

The Living-Learning Community

Judson Jerome

. . . The Residential College

Because undergraduate education has been neglected in the academic revolution, with its sponsored research-swollen pressures toward graduate studies and professionalization, many universities are creating the atmosphere of a private liberal arts college in enclaves like the Residential College at the University of Michigan. This atmosphere has an immediately recognizable spirit of community largely missing from the oceanic university surrounding it.

At Michigan, an old dormitory was converted into a living-learning center. More variety was introduced into the living quarters — singles, doubles, apartments with kitchens and suites for four or more students. Sexual segregation was relaxed. Lounges and other public areas were used for classes. A small auditorium was built for lectures, musical and theatrical performances. Basement areas were converted to language laboratories, ceramics and silk-screen workshops, conventional classrooms, offices and coffee shops. Faculty offices were distributed through the building.

Ineluctably the image of the Residential College has become that of the counterculture. . . . But when you write for an application blank and get a set of love beads sent with the form, there is an inescapable message conveyed. Students are attracted by the College's offering the "best of two worlds," the large university's facilities and activities and the small college's greater intimacy. Three times as many apply as can be admitted, and those who are chosen seem to be the more intellectually inclined students. Significantly, studies have shown that the Residential College students resemble "honors" students in personality patterns much more than do the typical students of the large university, though they may not achieve at "honors" levels. . . .

The economics of higher education, especially in the public system, are inescapably involved. Because appropriations to the school are made on the basis of credit hours offered, a record evaluated in terms of the student's recorded progress toward the degree. Unless time can be accounted for in terms of "formal" learning, evaluated and credited, it cannot be used to justify faculty salaries and other funds. Educational, even moral, choices are colored by the stain of this reality. Those ways of spending time which accumulate credit are regarded as more "worthwhile" than others which might be more richly relevant to learning and personal growth. . . . It is astonishing that as much community spirit as is present in the Residential College can persist under these conditions, for it is specifically social, informal, exploratory activity — rapping, working together at common tasks, meetings, festivities — that build communal bonds.

But the hunger for community is so great among faculty, students and administrators that it occurs. . . .

"Once you get used to this way of learning," a young woman said, "it spoils the classes outside for you." By "this way," she meant active participation, a shared responsibility for the quality of the classroom experience, and an amiable informality. Class meetings tend to run over the scheduled hours, and extra meetings are requested.

Old dorms are best for such programs, places which the maintenance department has more or less surrendered. Mattresses can be put on floors . . . and a little creative carpentry on university facilities is not a heinous offense. . . .

But the taste of freedom is a taste for blood. Colleges may expect that, in freer programs, restraints which are perceived as arbitrary or artificial will be relentlessly tested and rooted out. It may be that the learning compelled by requirements is good in itself, but the method of compulsion vitiates that value. The traditional liberal arts core curriculum eroded at the Residential College, for example, into diverse offerings, with a wide choice in satisfying requirements. . . .

Tensions within the colleges seem minor compared to those between the College and the large university, a factor which may help maintain fairly high morale within. The faculty feel like and are treated like second-class citizens in regard to tenure and promotion. Since much of the academic work in the college is upgraded — grades being replaced by paragraph evaluation—matters such as scholarship aid and honors become problematical. The college's students and faculty are likely to be seen as intellectual dilettantes by outsiders in the University, many of whom measure seriousness by commitment to preparation for graduate school. In the College, however, undergraduate education is concerned with enduring kinds of growth—"changing attitudes or the way you look at things, or relate," as the dean put it, rather than the "self-contained series of mosaics" in learning associated with the acquisition of specific knowledge and skills.

College students can do just about anything they want to as "independent study" if they can find a faculty sponsor—and the prevailing friendships between students and faculty probably make it difficult for faculty to turn down student requests. They can also take "furlough" semesters for credit; students are in India, Budapest, Barcelona . . . . Creative writing majors are required to take an off-campus semester, and work-study is an integral part of the urban studies major.

Such arrangements rely on a high level of trust such as is possible only when students and faculty feel themselves to be part of a community. It is clear that the responsibility for education is on the student. Though you technically cannot fail on independent study, as the grade is either S or U, you can fail yourself or let down a relationship with a faculty friend—and that is in many ways a more terrifying control than externally imposed discipline. . . .

REPORTS: **Washington's Evergreen College**

Kenneth Gehret

Evergreen State College is . . . a handmade, one-of-a-kind model. . . .

. . . Evergreen's planners started with the concept of a student-oriented college. This meant in effect placing the student in charge of his own education, though not without guidance and assistance. "Our basic assumption is that the sooner we get the student into a position where he is a self-directed learner, the sooner a student gets on with individualized education at his own pace and takes responsibility for his own learning," explains Dr. David G. Barry, Vice-President and Provost.

The Evergreen approach places a heavy burden on students, administrators and perhaps most of all on faculty. It relegates professors to a position secondary to that of students. . . .

. . . Evergreen has no departmental organization, no faculty senate, no standing committees and no faculty tenure. The distinction between students and teachers is played down; professors are thought of as co-learners with their classes.

Whether or not faculty members view themselves in this light, they are indeed required to go on learning by the nature of the Evergreen program. For the curriculum consists of a number of unrelated multidisciplinary courses. Five faculty members combine as a team to devise and instruct each such course and are responsible for no other courses or students. Approximately 100 students sign up for a given course, which constitutes the core of their studies. Classes meet twice weekly in seminar style and once weekly on a large-group basis.

The class of 100 breaks into five sections for seminars. This means that each faculty member teaches one seminar, not necessarily in his specialty. He has to make himself familiar with relevant aspects of each discipline represented in the course. The incentive to continue learning, and in a field other than the one in which he has been trained, is clearly built in. . . .

. . . Rapport with students appears strong. "One big, happy family" . . . is probably closer to the truth than at most colleges and universities. . . .

Face-to-face communication is easy at Evergreen. "I'm never too busy to see a student" is more than a slogan among administrators and faculty. And students take it as a matter of course that their voices should be heard. . . .

The eleven multidisciplinary courses now offered are problem-themed and embrace from five to seven disciplines each. . . . In addition to seminars and other meetings, each course requires extensive reading. This in fact is the basis of each course and the focus of seminar discussion.

Evergreen also emphasizes "contracted studies"—independent study meant primarily for upper-division students. It consists either of research projects or work experience in business and industry, government, schools, and community agencies. . . .

Learning is self-paced at Evergreen. . . . Readiness to graduate will not be determined by the annual credits, nor by examination, letter grades or numerical averages, but by "portfolio." All of a student's reports, projects, contracts, assessments by on-the-job supervisors, etc., go into this dossier, which attests to his achievements on and off campus while at Evergreen.

. . . Some youths obviously are not ready for the degree of freedom and responsibility that Evergreen thrusts upon them.

College officials say incoming students must know what the college is all about and must "really want to come." . . .

June 1972

Innovation on Staten Island

Leonard Quart and Judith Stacey

. . . Integrated Studies, . . . is a product of Richmond College, an upper-divisional unit of the City University of New York. It represents one of the early joint attempts by students and faculty in a major urban public university to create a student-centered educational program. . . . The underlying assumption is that learning occurs best and most joyfully when the teacher rejects his traditional role of power and domination.

Although in philosophy and practice Integrated Studies may not differ dramatically from familiar experimental programs at elite private institutions like Goddard, the fact that it attempts experimental education with working-class students in a public institution makes it a unique undertaking with its own very special problems. . . . To many of Richmond's first-generation collegegoers, schools represent a lifetime of frustration and failure; there a sense of mediocrity is repeatedly reconfirmed. . . .

. . . Those who taught in the program attempted to reduce institutional authority, hoping that responsibility would evolve from a collective of students and faculty. To encourage this sharing of power, a weekly Colloquium was instituted where students and faculty met to hammer out governance and policies. A freer, more humane atmosphere was developed in and out of the classroom. The goad of grades and course requirements was generally given over to students; formalities of classroom seating, dress and deference disappeared; doors opened for students (generally without appointments) to walk in and out of offices; faculty could constantly be found in the cafeteria in rap sessions with students; and all were on a first-name basis, making it difficult to distinguish faculty from students.

Though these instances may seem superficial, they represent a profound change in the nature of human relationships within an institutional setting. For example, expression of emotion has become more spontaneous and direct: faculty publicly argue and accuse each other of ego tripping and manipulation; faculty and students touch and embrace one another and occasionally engage in deep personal relationships. Because the quality of classroom participation has become more open and intimate, students feel freer to relate their personal experiences in depth to the material discussed. . . .

Integrated Studies has also created a wide-ranging and imaginative curriculum which avoids any semblance of educational or political homogeneity. Courses use diverse educational materials and techniques, from great books and popular arts to consciousness raising and community action. Films, books and personal experience have been used to explore racism, madness, the self and the nature of capitalism. Other courses involve students in building food co-ops, engaging in community action and sensitivity groups, keeping personal journals; they have dealt with arts and crafts, body movement, media and political and sexual consciousness raising. One course brought the study of alternative social structures to its logical end by renting a house and setting up a commune. . . .

Even if Integrated Studies has been a significant departure from the conventional forms of schooling, it does not break with them completely. Learning is still focused on classrooms, credits and courses. Grading, while less oppressive, remains an institutional reality. The major success of Integrated Studies has been in raising the level of student and faculty consciousness about the whole teaching and learning process: relations with students, the nature of governance and the concept of knowledge. . . .

. . . [I]t may be naive to expect a publicly controlled institution to grant real power to radical educators. . . . But no matter what the fate of Integrated Studies at Richmond College, the idea of a humane, communal, student-centered education for more than the elite will survive.

Summer 1972

Reflections on a Pioneer Living-Learning Community: Black Mountain

Martin Duberman

To the extent that Black Mountain is known today it is as the site of a now defunct experimental community located in the foothills of North Carolina, the forerunner and exemplar of much that is currently considered innovative in art, education and life style. It is known, too, as the refuge, in some cases the nurturing ground, for many of the singular, shaping talents of our time: John Cage, Merce Cunningham, Buckminster Fuller, Willem de Kooning, Franz Kline, Charles Olson, Josef Albers, Paul Goodman. . . .

A full history of Black Mountain is . . . the story of a small group of men and women—ranging through time from a dozen to a hundred, . . . who attempted to find some consonance between their ideas and their lives, who risked the intimacy and exposure that most of us emotionally yearn for and rhetorically defend, but in practice shun. . . .

At its best Black Mountain showed the possibilities of a disparate group of individuals committing themselves to a common enterprise, resilient enough to absorb the conflicts entailed, brave enough, now and then, to be transformed by its accompanying energies. . . . For others Black Mountain provided a glimpse—rarely a sustained vision—of how diversity and commonality, the individual and the group, are reinforcing rather than contradictory phenomena. . . .

(from the introduction to *Black Mountain*

John Andrew Rice was . . . the indisputable leader of the Black Mountain community . . . [from] its founding in 1933. . . .

. . . "The College," Rice wrote . . . "is for the present content to place emphasis upon combining those experiments . . . which have already shown their value in education institutions of the western world; but which are often isolated and hampered from giving their full value because of their existence side by side with thoughtless tradition." . . .

The one idea most commonly agreed upon was that "living" and "learning" should be intertwined. Education should proceed everywhere, not only in classroom settings which in fact, at least as usually structured, are among the worst learning environments imaginable. A favorite slogan at Black Mountain was that "as much real education took place over the coffee cups as in the classrooms," and a central aim was to keep the community small enough so that members could constantly interact in a wide variety of settings—at meals, on walks, in classes, at community meetings, work programs, . . . whatever. Individual life styles, in all their peculiar detail, could thereby be observed, challenged, imitated, rejected — which is, after all, how most learning proceeds, rather than through formal academic instruction. "You're seeing people under all circumstances daily," as Rice put it, "and after a while you get to the point where you don't mind being seen yourself, and that's a fine moment."

All aspects of community life were thought to have a bearing on an individual's education — that is, his growth, his becoming aware of who he was and wanted to be. The usual distinctions between curricular and extracurricular activities, between work done in a classroom and work done outside it, were broken down. Helping to fight a forest fire side by side with faculty members, participating in a community discussion on whether the dining hall should serve two or three meals on Sundays, discovering that a staff member was a homosexual . . . —all these and a hundred more experiences, most of them the more vivid for being unplanned,

contributed at least as much to individual awareness as traditional academic exercises. . . .

. . . [M]any at Black Mountain believed that differences in age need not preclude communication, that interests could be shared, that the perspective of the young also had value. It meant, too, that while information, analytical skills and reason were prized, they were considered aspects rather than equivalents of personal development; they were not confused, in other words — as they are in most educational institutions — with the whole of life, the only elements of self worthy of development and praise.

It was hoped that a double sense of responsibility would emerge out of the varied contacts and opportunities Black Mountain provided: that which an individual owes to the group of which he is a member, and that which he owes to himself — with neither submerging the other. Black Mountain emphasized the social responsibilities that come from being part of a community, yet tried to see to it that personal freedom wouldn't be sacrificed to group needs. . . .

September 1972

Let a Hundred Antiochs Bloom!

Gerald Grant

Horace Mann, who left Massachusetts for . . . Ohio in 1853 to become first president of Antioch, moved boldly to put it in the company of those few radical colleges of the day that dared to admit women and Negroes. . . . Perhaps his greatest legacy to the college was an aphorism that remains near the heart of Antioch's philosophy today: "Be ashamed to die until you have won some victory for humanity." . . .

. . . Arthur Morgan . . . had headed the Progressive Education Association before he became president of Antioch. . . . He was a student of utopias and saw them as essential blueprints for the bettering of human society. . . .

Morgan dreamed of a college "such as never had existed." Antioch should be "a lever to move the world . . . a great adventure, standing for radically different patterns of life." It was important

to provide an "education in life as well as books," and for the students to develop "life aims and purposes." Rather than seek piecemeal reforms, Morgan totally reorganized the college by juxtaposing work and study. He originally planned short alternating cycles of two weeks of campus study followed by two weeks on a job within commuting distance of Yellow Springs. . . . [W]ork-study became a three-month cycle. But the basic work-study plan — so successfully developed at Antioch, although not, as widely believed, invented there — continues to be one of the most important characteristics defining the College. . . .

Consistent with Arthur Morgan's Dewey-like faith in learning by doing was his espousal that students participate in their own governance. . . . Morgan laid the groundwork for a unique system of governance. It centers around an Administrative

Council of six faculty and three students, of whom six are elected principally by the students. Three of the faculty members are elected by the faculty, the other six members by the entire campus. The president and the dean complete membership on the council. . . . It has been a unique blend of faculty and administrative authority legitimated by student participation. . . .

. . . Grades were abolished several years ago, and a student's record shows only his credits, not his failures. And among a small minority of the faculty, there are no failures because they believe, as one said, that the "judgmental process interferes with the teaching relationship." Faculty are asked to submit written evaluations, but these are often superficial . . . as former Associate Dean Yates Hafner pointed out in an essay which stimulated a revision of evaluation procedures. . . .

Pressure to improve evaluations also came from students, who complained both about their quantity and quality. A number of universities had notified Antioch that they would not accept its transcripts. Now, all evaluations are put on a computer and professors are required to list in some detail the conditions for granting "credit" in their courses in terms of readings, projects and papers required. Faculty must report a letter grade if asked to do so by students; this is happening increasingly. . . .

Intellectual achievement alone has never been a source of contentment at Antioch. During his presidency, Morgan was never entirely pleased with the mere intellectual success of students who increasingly headed toward traditional graduate school and professional careers. . . . [H]e was disappointed that students and faculty did not generate enough "creative discontent" to break the old molds. The tensions that underlay Morgan's presidency still haunt Antioch. They are the tensions between those who seek the scholar's "quiet niche" and those who precipitate the turmoil of social reform. . . .

Until the late 1940s, the faculty mirrored Morgan's search for mavericks and utopians who rejected specialism. . . . These faculty are gone, but they continue to exert a powerful influence through a few contemporary faculty and administrators. . . .

. . . [T]he middle and most numerous layer of faculty . . . might be called liberal professionals . . . . Traditionally trained, they were personally drawn to an experimental setting in which to teach. Under Gould, they battled with the old-guard mavericks, seeking to raise intellectual standards and to cut back the work program, especially for students bound for graduate school. . . .

The cultural radicals and educational experimenters seek new forms and methods of education ranging from encounter groups to filmmaking, broadly interpreted field work, and independent study. They see themselves as resources who should adapt to changing student interests, rather than as specialists eager to induct students into a field of inquiry. Summarizing his differences with more traditionally inclined faculty members, one avid experimenter said: "They blame the administration for producing the kind of student who will not buy the traditional package, instead of recognizing that they ought to change to meet student demands." Some faculty have become converts to the counterculture. A professor of engineering, for example, faced with dwindling classes, plunged into a whole new field of media studies. . . .

Battle lines for the current conflicts were drawn in 1965 when the new experimenters pushed through the First Year Program at Antioch. Freshmen were assigned to preceptorial groups of 15 under faculty—mostly the experimenters themselves—who volunteered as preceptors. Grades were abolished, all requirements were suspended for freshmen, and—most controversially—students received automatic credit for the year even if, as some chose, they did nothing. . . . To its supporters, such abuses of freedom are worth the benefits that they believe will follow—freely chosen, self-directed, and hence more meaningful educational engagement. . . .

REPORTS: Goddard's Adult Degree Program

Richard Goldberg

G oddard calls it the Adult Degree Program (ADP), a pioneering curriculum launched back in the pre-Berkeley calm of 1963. At that time the college was seeking to devise a format for people over age 26 who had once started but never completed work toward their BA degrees. It was to be an alternative for those not free to attend college on a full-time basis and who rejected formal, institutional modes of learning. Not only would it have no lecture halls, required courses, texts, or grades, but it would also spurn the conventional wisdom which decrees that students must reside physically on a campus all year.

It was Goddard's basic outlook and commitment to educational experiment which made it a logical site to launch this program. . . . Goddard viewed living and learning as processes that were tightly bound together; it sought to liberate education from a strictly classroom setting. Because of these views, it has developed over the years into a school for undergraduates who both engage in unstructured study on campus and participate in accredited work/learning experiences off campus. It was not surprising that many of these approaches would be incorporated into the Adult Degree Program. . . .

. . . Twice a year they are required to come to the Plainfield campus for a two-week residency. During that period they interact in intense group sessions and relaxed seminars, evaluate past work with the faculty, plan new study projects, and mix with other students. They then return home to carry out their studies and projects and return six months later for another residency. Ultimately, they graduate (or "culminate," as Goddard people prefer to say), receiving BA degrees and a good chance to restructure their lives. . . .

. . . The important thing is that learning is freed from a campus base. . . .

A Retrospective on St. John's

Stringfellow Barr

T hirty-seven years ago, at the age of 40, I accepted the presidency of St. John's College in Annapolis with the stipulation that I would liquidate the elective system and replace it with a curriculum based on the study of some hundred great books from Homer to the present. My stipulation was based on 13 years' experience of teaching in the elective system, 12 at the University of Virginia, and 1 at Chicago. At Virginia the late Scott Buchanan and I had served on a committee that had unsuccessfully proposed St. John's Program for honors students. Buchanan and I went to Chicago because the chancellor, Robert M. Hutchins, had teamed up with Mortimer Adler to run an undergraduate seminar on the so-called "Great Books." . . .

. . . Buchanan constructed the college's list of "Great Books" based on experience at Columbia, in adult education in New York, the abortive effort at the University of Virginia, and the course that Hutchins and Adler taught at Chicago. As dean, he taught the 20 freshmen who had chosen voluntarily to follow the program. The second year no freshmen were admitted into the old program, or elective system, and in four years the elective system was gone.

I have had no reason to lose faith in the St. John's Program during the 37 years it has been taught. I'm asked if I still consider it more exciting and more useful than the American elective system, but they are, on the whole, incommensurable. They have different prime purposes. The elective system is chiefly concerned with course offerings in "fields" of human knowledge. These course offerings in large part provide information. The St. John's Program is a return to what liberal education meant for more than 2,000 years: an education that develops the intellectual virtues or habits.

Throughout the history of Europe and its colonies these intellectual virtues were taught by "the seven liberal arts" because the practice of them liberates the human intellect. . . .

Many of those men who founded the American Republic used these liberal arts in drafting a constitution that would foster not mere "law and order" but laws designed to help human communities achieve the common good, laws to foster true "commonwealths." The founders knew that it takes good politics to support good ethics. . . .

Two hundred years later, as we approach the bicentennial of our Declaration of Independence, we have to ask ourselves again whether "government" is merely a euphemism for naked force and fraud or a necessary device for achieving justice and liberty in a society. But we shall ask such questions well only if we once more practice the liberal arts well. And both the best and the speediest way to master those arts is to read books by writers who used them so superbly that their works will still teach us how to talk and listen and read and write. Children learn to speak by listening to their parents speak. Undergraduates learn to use the liberal arts in their speaking and writing by "listening" to books that great artists wrote. If American freshmen read Plato's dialogs, for example, and discuss with each other what they have read, the same miracle happens, sooner or later, to them too. And after that miracle they will never

again speak as sloppily or as emptily as they had before. . . .

. . . [A]t St. John's I watched a small group of adolescents transform itself into a profoundly human community. I watched the guffaws yield the floor to sly smiles and quiet wit. And I suddenly realized that these college students were doing, on a high level, what very small children do: they were learning to talk!

One Friday evening, a member of a freshman seminar that I was co-leading rushed up to me, his face radiant, and cried: "Mr. Barr, I was able to follow the lecture this evening!" "Haven't you been able to follow any of the other formal lectures?" I asked. "No sir," he answered, "but I followed this one." He wasn't mortified by his late arrival in port. He was too happy he had made port at last to lament his tardiness. . . .

What should our standards be? How high a mountain must our students climb? Not necessarily very high and not necessarily the same altitude for all climbers. It was continuous motion that Buchanan and others were after and St. John's tutors are after it still: the continuous motion otherwise known as intellectual growth. A year or two ago I heard a freshman seminar at St. John's argue over Aristotle's *Metaphysics*. Along with most other persons who have read it, they had found it difficult. But they never flagged. Large bones are not given to small puppies for them to eat; the puppies are persuaded to try to eat them and thereby to sharpen their teeth. On the same visit I gave a Friday night lecture and came away thanking God for intellectual puppies. I find that those pups who go on to graduate or professional schools are admired for their intellectual bite. That most professors on most campuses would probably continue to shake their heads over the courses "St. Johnnies" missed does not alarm me in the least. No cook wants his dishes left untasted.

New College

The Noble Experiment That . . . ?

David Riesman

The American South, which includes Florida geographically and in part culturally, has made a strong effort to "overtake and surpass" Northern accomplishments in higher education. . . . Sarasotans, some miles south of Tampa, wanted to have a college of their own. . . .

. . . The chamber of commerce commissioned a market survey which concluded, . . . there was indeed a need for a college. . . .

Probably the main energizer of those who envisaged not simply an available college but a visionary one was Philip Hiss. . . . [He] concluded that a small, selective college might do something to upgrade what he regarded as Florida's inert educational record. . . .

In this early stage, excellence and innovation were not seen as antithetical: Innovation was to be on behalf of excellence, defined in traditional terms. . . . Interdisciplinary curricula were . . . a way toward the reorganization of knowledge in the liberal arts along lines pioneered at Chicago and Columbia. . . .

. . . On the assumption that only very gifted students would be recruited, grades and credits were to be dispensed with; however, assessments were to be provided by a college examiner who, in the Chicago style, would supervise comprehensive examinations at the end of the first year and serve as an institutional researcher to report to faculty on student attitudes and progress. There were to be no departments, but three major divisions — natural science, humanities, and social science — and the entering student would be required to take work in all three areas, as well as study a foreign language. Gustad deprecated survey courses in favor of modes of thought or analysis. In the second year the student would specialize, while in the third, final year students would do a research project and, in addition, everything would be integrated in a common seminar. This hope for synthesis is something which, in studying experimenting colleges, turns up again and again. . . .

. . . [T]he most advertised innovative feature of the initial plan was the three-year baccalaureate, obtained in 11-month academic years, with faculty supposedly given a respite not only in August but also during the interim terms set aside for independent study. . . .

. . . [S]tudents were attracted by the blank Rorschach card named New College. . . . They liked the promise of freedom . . . and the notion of moving at their own pace in independent study.

. . . But experience at New College and elsewhere makes perfectly clear that motivational factors are, if anything, even more important than cognitive ones: the ability to endure frustration, with a minimum of narcissism, as well as sufficient independence of character so that one does not desperately fear even momentary dependence on a mentor.

The students were told . . . that they were the best and the brightest, or in the phrase then used, first-class minds. The immediate result was to put New College on the academic map. . . .

Indeed, the relative isolation of most faculty and of students from the outside community and cultural life facilitated what has always characterized New College: the intense relations of some eager students and dedicated faculty. The latter . . . were zealous teachers. . . . And many students . . . opened up to faculty who could move them quickly to the frontiers of their subject matter, notably in biology and other natural sciences. . . . At its best, New College developed an intellectual as well as academic intensity which, in fact, served the charter class well when it won outstanding national fellowships and awards for graduate work — an intensity again that one can find elsewhere, . . . but in most other colleges it is a minority. In New College it had embraced a large proportion, and given students a legitimacy as intellectuals they often missed in their previous milieux. . . .

... For a time, New College experimented with a contract system as an option, with some students working with a mentor to write a contract both for short-term and long-term goals, while other students could simply pile up satisfactories at the rate of three courses or tutorials a term. It was on the whole the scholarly, more academically oriented faculty who decided to eliminate the non-contract option, so that every student would be required to declare his or her aims at the outset and tell how he or she proposed to reach these aims in both curricular and noncurricular efforts. . . .

For a minority of faculty, innovation represented something at once more ambitious and more subtle. It did not mean experimentation with new techniques of teaching. . . . Rather, as David Smillie, professor of psychology, has written me, " 'Innovation' has covered a concern to provide young people with an experience which will make them feel whole and human and happy. Particularly during the late sixties and early seventies . . . there was a desperate sense of things falling apart. I was interested then, and am still interested, in the students' involvement with R. D. Laing as social philosopher, since I think that this interest expressed their own feeling of having been betrayed by society and by their parents. As 'innovators' we faculty were their parent surrogates attempting to provide a Laingian therapy. . . . The methods utilized were a removal of external constraints, the attempt to establish close working relationships with the student, the introduction of existential themes . . . into the course content." . . .

Alexander Astin, who in *Change* has listed New College as among the most selective in America, would probably maintain that New College recruited bright students and that the later scholarly attainments merely reflect this fact. . . . Nevertheless, I would contend that the more academically oriented and concerned enclaves of the students' subcultures and the faculty who were at once scholarly and therapeutic helped bring out and support the value already there, and hence gave it further impetus. . . .

November 1977

REPORTS: **Freedom and Identity at Hampshire College**

Nancy Frazier

... Although the first students did not arrive on campus until 1970, Hampshire has been widely regarded as part of the experimental college movement of the 1960s. . . .

During its early years Hampshire benefited from its antiestablishment identification and enjoyed the reputation of being in tune with the youth movement. . . . [O]ne of Hampshire's most important chores now is to remind itself and others of its intellectual foundations. These were rooted in the educational malaise of the fifties rather than in the anxieties of the sixties and were based on the premise that students learn best by learning how to teach themselves.

"The New College Plan" for Hampshire was formulated way back in 1958 by the University of Massachusetts, Mount Holyoke, Smith, and Amherst. It came on the heels of "the drastic increase in college-age population." . . .

. . . [T]he idea for a new college lay dormant, or at least snoozing, until 1965. . . .

. . . [A]nyone reading "The New College Plan" quickly sees that the enthusiasm for executing the design went far beyond these original rationales. The authors were really going after the development of "new departures in educational methods and techniques." They wanted to free students from the tyranny of The Course and liberate faculty from the tyranny of The Department. From the outset, they abolished departments as well as survey and required courses. There were to be none of the usual measures: no grades, no prerequisites for majors and minors to graduate, and no required attendance at specific classes. . . .

A Hampshire education follows a European rather than an American tradition. Students move from division to division by successfully completing six examinations. At least one exam will be in each of the four schools (which replaced conventional departments): Arts and Humanities, Natural Sciences, Social Sciences, and Languages and Communications. They assume responsibility for devising and designing their own exams and for inviting other students as well as faculty and professionals to judge their work. . . .

At Hampshire independence and independent work are presumed. That is central to its educational philosophy. Though seminar-type offerings can be chosen from the catalogue, apart from the examinations there is nothing that students have to do. Perversely, that can make the pressure to do something unbearable — and often paralyzing. Perhaps that accounts in part for the College's high dropout rate — between 30 and 40 percent. A lot of students go through a period called "floundering" (so widespread that it's now part of the College lingo), trying to deal with the frustration built into the system. . . .

Teaching at Hampshire can be "marvelous" because so many of the students are "people capable of inner evolvement, and it is a wonderful place for creative initiative," one member of the faculty said. But you can be "eaten alive" by students hungry for help and suffering keenly from a sense of personal isolation. The faculty dropout rate is about 30 percent. . . . "Some kids see us as a way-out, artsy place while others see us as an Ivy League school," said John Runyon. "We have our own specific reality."

That "specific reality" now includes a healthy dose of intellectualism. Hampshire is proud to point out that the last graduating class included some exceptional scholars. . . .

. . . (Having no grades to submit with applications, Hampshire students submit their portfolios.)

In one important way the Hampshire student is not taking such a great risk. Students at other experimental colleges have had tougher odds against them because of their isolation. However, the academic back-up in the western Massachusetts area allows for boosting morale and credentials with traditional courses and grades at any one of the nearby institutions. There is a five-college transportation system and Hampshire students benefit by the proximity.

Some of the graduates this year were fretting that Hampshire was losing its revolutionary image. "We congratulate those who are off to law or medical school; but . . . ," a former student said. And the "but" was an important one. They reminded their colleagues of their responsibilities. "We don't need geniuses or great leaders. We need people who are prepared to undertake the incredibly difficult task of working with others to create new institutions, new lifestyles, new ways of thinking. . . ." . . .

September 1979

Reed College: The Intellectual Maverick

Barry Mitzman

. . . A number of adjectives one repeatedly hears applied to Reed: serious, demanding, single-minded, uncompromising — and excellent. It is a small college . . . that . . . has changed little in its nearly 70-year history. . . .

It is a college of the highest academic distinction. . . . Alumni are most notably distinguished as scholars and scientists. . . .

Reed students are well prepared for graduate school by an unusually intense curriculum, demanding of both hard work and self-discipline. "We see our job as one of providing enough information so students can work and think in an area," says Larry Ruben, a professor of biology at Reed since 1955. "We try to provide opportunities for students to do independent work." . . .

. . . [U]nusual academic policies have proved durable. Grades still are not normally released to students, though they may now be seen on request. All students still are required to pass a junior qualifying exam and to write a senior thesis and defend it orally. The thesis requirement, in fact, was reaffirmed by the faculty just last year. Rejecting a proposal to rule the thesis optional, most faculty agreed that it "makes educational policy sense" and "is, perhaps, the one distinctive feature of a Reed education." At other colleges honors students must write a thesis, but Reed alone requires it of everyone. "Reed has always operated on the premise that all its students are honors students," says Marvin Levich. One result of the college's high expectations, he says, is that "a lot of our students do better than they're presumably able to do because it's expected of them."

Reed similarly carries on its requirement that all freshmen and sophomores take the same series of humanities courses — the kind of core requirement to which other colleges are just now returning. . . .

From the humanities sequence has grown Reed's distinctive conference system of instruction, now a part of most courses. A teacher and a few students gather around a seminar table to discuss their reading, with the burden placed clearly upon the students to conduct the discussion, make sense of what they've read, and explain and defend their responses. "That may sound idyllic, but often it works that way," says Gail M. Kelly, a Reed alumna who has taught anthropology there since 1960. . . .

November/December 1981

Brookwood Remembered

An Unheralded Educational Experience

Arthur Levine

. . . Brookwood Labor College was founded in Katonah, New York, in 1921. It closed its doors sixteen years later. . . . But Brookwood is worth recalling today. Its accomplishments deserve to be celebrated and its experiences are worthy of study. . . .

. . . Brookwood's supporters and champions included John Dewey, Jane Addams . . . Reinhold Niebuhr . . . to name just a few. Sinclair Lewis once called it "the only self-respecting, keen, alive, educational institution I have even known." . . .

Brookwood Labor College's sole reason for being was to educate labor leaders. Its mission, in the words of its founders, was:

> [to] serve American labor with trained, responsible liberally educated men and even from the ranks of the workers . . . [to] closely cooperate with the national and international labor groups, also with the various local colleges and schools that send to it working men and women who show promise as to need further education in order to best serve the labor movement and through it society.

Brookwood did a surprisingly effective job of achieving this goal in spite of its brief life. It educated a number of the best-known labor leaders in the country. . . . Perhaps most importantly, Brookwood educated the corps of middle-level staffers behind the great leaders. More than 80 percent of its graduates went on to work in the labor union movement, a far more impressive accomplishment then than it would be today. . . .

What distinguished Brookwood most definitely from other colleges was not its physical plant, but its students. Usually numbering about fifty or somewhat less, they came from coal mines, factories, and a polyglot of other trade occupations. . . . Slightly more than half the students were native born. About a third were women. All came from industrial families. They averaged in age from twenty-one to thirty, though few were younger and many were older. . . .

Brookwood offered these students a two-year program, later a one-year option, designed to teach adults who knew something, how to say it. There were never grades or report cards, and the curriculum shifted gradually and continually throughout the history of the college. But there were some constants. Always the program included basic skills instruction — courses with titles like "How to Study," and "The Use of the English Language." For some, even the native-born student, it was necessary to teach English as a second language. There were classes in speech. . . .

At the core of the Brookwood program was a liberal arts curriculum with a labor flavor, . . . always with an eye to how the subject affected workers.

. . . Brookwood was, above all else, a community—a labor community and a college community. Service was a requirement for all. Faculty and students alike were expected to perform college chores. . . . They remembered a lot of laughter. Community meals, community sings, and community hikes were truly popular events, . . . and all the frivolity of college life were an essential part of Brookwood, too.

. . . It offers higher education a number of important lessons. . . .

First, Brookwood showed that adult and nontraditional students deserve to be treated seriously. . . .

It shows too that adults and nontraditional students have educational needs that differ from those of eighteen- to twenty-one-year-olds. K. Patricia Cross has written that adult learners need education with six distinctive characteristics: 1) it must raise self-confidence levels, 2) it must build positive attitudes toward education, 3) it must meet the goals and expectations of learners, 4) it must respond to the life transitions of learners, 5) it must create learning opportunities and remove learning barriers, and 6) it must provide useful experience and skills. This is precisely what Brookwood did and there is much that higher education can learn from its experience.

A second lesson from Brookwood is that liberal arts education provides vocational training. Brookwood Labor College was occupation-specific in purpose. It sought only to train labor leaders; nothing more, nothing less. But it attained that goal by providing students with a broad liberal education. . . .

Study after study has shown that narrow technical training gets students a first job with greater ease and larger benefit than a liberal arts education, but it offers students thereafter little mobility. It is the combination of liberal and career education that spells the difference between a job and a career. . . .

A third and final lesson from Brookwood is that quality means more than survival. Brookwood Labor College closed after only sixteen years. There was no shame in its demise and a legacy of accomplishment remains long after its death. . . .

March 1982

Innovation—Bloodied but Unbowed

The Legacy of the Sixties

Warren Bryan Martin

Whatever happened to the agitation and . . . innovation of the sixties? . . .

What happened, if the truth be told, is that most of the reforms associated with the student movement of the sixties, particularly the educational reforms, did not die as quickly as they were born. They were, instead, slowly incorporated into the policies and procedures of the majority of American colleges and universities. Those innovations have been institutionalized. . . .

One cheer for . . . co-optation.

A distinction must be made between the student movement and the counterculture. The student movement of the sixties was mainly directed toward educational reforms. . . . The students wanted personal respect, good teaching, free speech, and an opportunity to participate in the formulation of policies that influenced their education as well as their personal lives.

Two cheers for student leadership in expressing educational concerns. . . .

. . . [A]s the war in southeast Asia expanded, . . . the student movement saw the need to couple the reform of the university with the reform of political and social institutions, especially in the area of the university's involvement with the military-industrial complex. Thus a second front was added for the student movement and, understandably, for many people, the educational concerns slipped into the background. . . .

... [T]he civil rights movement was gaining momentum. ... The student movement reached out to connect with civil rights—supporting the demands of minorities and the poor.

Three cheers for the movement's extension ... to endorse the use of political, educational, and moral force to improve the status of misused Americans.

While the student movement was going forward on these three fronts, behind the lines the counterculture was rapidly developing. ...

It was the counterculture that lashed out in all directions at once—hippies, yippies; sit-ins, People's Park; National Guard, tear gas; Haight-Ashbury, communes; drugs, theft; alienation, death. Attempts at social revolution displaced educational reform, the counterculture replaced the student movement. ...

Three cheers, again, for the best of the student movement, and especially for the educational reforms that it helped to bring into the mainstream of higher education: Individualized programs of study, alternative grading and testing procedures, off-campus work/study, shared governance arrangements, living/learning facilities, relevance— personal, social, political—in curricular offerings. ...

The student movement did not, obviously, move without prior impetus and available antecedents. Almost all of the educational reforms had established track records—at Bennington, Reed, Berea, Goddard, Black Mountain; at CCNY, Chicago. ... The notion of cluster colleges—smaller units within a larger organization, where more individualized and flexible teaching and learning would occur, where a sense of community and sharing could be achieved—found expression in the sixties at Michigan State, ... Santa Cruz, ... and a few other places. ...

As for staying power, or the ability of the reform movement to keep moving in the seventies and eighties, the educational innovations of the sixties have shown the least endurance where they were made the centerpiece of a separate operation. ... But the majority of institutions, those described as traditional, have been able to incorporate innovations and have become broader, more inclusive colleges and universities for having done so.

To repeat, those colleges created in the sixties or seventies for the purpose of promoting innovations, or even those places that became identified with sixties' innovations, have of late found the going very hard. The Evergreen State College, the several cluster colleges, New College Sarasota, Shimer and Bard and Goddard—these and other schools are either undersubscribed or have gone under. The publicity attending their problems has contributed to the erroneous conclusions that nothing enduring and influential came out of the student movement of the sixties.

Another factor in the confusion leading to the premature announcement of the demise of innovation in education has been the unpopularity of certain innovations that, in fact, had more to do with the counterculture than with the student movement. An example is "nonpunitive grading," often expressed by the removal of the grades of D and F. This innovation was motivated by social egalitarianism, not educational improvement. As the traditional grading system has been reaffirmed in the late seventies and early eighties, and the D and F reinstated, there has been a tendency for observers to conclude that the loss of the penalty grades battle by forces identified with innovation meant that innovation had lost the war.

Nonsense. Remember the one cheer for co-optation. And the two cheers for legitimate student concerns. And the three cheers for a reform movement that brought together educational, sociopolitical, and racial changes. There was too much that was too good in the movement for all of its features to be discarded, despite the problem of guilt by association with stuff that was little in spirit and short on substance. ... [E]ducational innovations of the sixties have been brought into otherwise conventional institutions and have made contributions there.

Here are examples of this phenomenon in one university and one college—Kent State University and Manhattanville College. ...

Kent State University ...
- Credit by examination
- Pass-fail grading option
- Grades other than A to F ...
- "Forgiveness policies" affecting probation
- Individualized majors
- Nondegree programs
- Interdisciplinary certificate programs
- Cross-disciplinary majors
- Weekend and evening colleges ...

Manhattanville College
- "Portfolio"—comprehensive assessment . . .
- Cooperative programs—BA/MD, BA/MS, . . .
- Off-campus study . . .
- Pass/fail grading option . . .
- Study skills center . . .
- Credit for "life experience," . . .
- Program for older adults . . .

At community colleges, innovations are not merely among program options, they have become the heart of the enterprise. . . .

One conclusion, then, is that many of the educational innovations endorsed by the student movement in the sixties have survived for a decade or longer in colleges and universities of all types. . . .

A second conclusion is actually an inference: The spirit of innovation that swept across academe, pushed along by the student movement, made possible an attitude of receptivity toward other innovations—for example, college credit for high school students for classes taken within their schools, offered at Syracuse, New York. The rapid development of individualized programs of study for older adults is also a popular phenomenon that shows obvious connections with earlier innovations.

A third conclusion, another inference, is that the student movement and the educational innovations promoted by that movement were sufficiently persuasive that many of the most traditional and aloof universities felt compelled to design and implement variations on reform themes for their own use. Stanford University is, for example, much more responsive to student rights, to the importance of effective undergraduate teaching, to the recruitment and encouragement of minority students, and to the social responsibilities of the university, than was the case before the rise of several influential developments, including the student movement. . . .

. . . The student movement promoted educational innovations, that is, new means to established ends. The counterculture promoted sociopolitical experimentation, that is, new means to new or unknown ends. The student movement succeeded. The counterculture failed. The educational innovations have survived, bloodied but unbowed. The cultural experimentation has succumbed, remembered but abandoned.

May/June 1984

Getting Real

Santa Cruz and the Crisis of Liberal Education

William Adams

. . . Though it was first conceived in the late 1950s, long before there was any suggestion of student activism at Berkeley, the Santa Cruz experiment was the creature of the same political vision and social theory. When it became clear that the University of California would have to expand to keep pace with the burgeoning enrollments of the postwar era, [the principal architects of Santa Cruz . . . Clark Kerr and Dean McHenry] were convinced that one of the new campuses should be committed principally to innovative, undergraduate education. Their criticisms of the multiversity guided their designs. Above all else, the bureaucratic and centralizing momentum of the research-oriented university would have to be contained. A predominantly undergraduate campus should be kept intimate and personal, encouraging a "sense of belonging," in McHenry's words. Faculty and students would be kept in regular contact; authority would be decentralized, visible, and humane.

To these ends, Santa Cruz was planned as a system of small, independent colleges, nestled within the research and professional facilities of the conventional university, intended to define both the social and intellectual substance and boundaries of undergraduate student life. Students were to live and study in the colleges, thus cementing the personal, social, and academic dimensions of thinking and learning. Faculty, too, were to be incorporated into this model. Each faculty member was made a fellow of a particular college, and was expected to serve in both its intellectual and social life. The key word in all of this was community, although, clearly, the collegiate inspiration owed something to an Oxford ideal. Each college was envisioned as a distinctive intellectual and social body, to which its members would belong in meaningful and lasting ways.

The colleges were also intended to serve a novel and more precise intellectual function. In Kerr's and McHenry's understanding, the multiversity had warped the meaning of the liberal curriculum. . . .

The earliest plans for Santa Cruz argued that there should be no academic departments on the new campus. Instead, the colleges would define coherent and independent undergraduate curricula, based upon distinctive thematic definitions of liberal education, and emphasizing interdisciplinary courses and innovative teaching techniques. The colleges were thus intended not only to foster a sense of belonging and community, but to develop particular styles of intellectual life uniquely suited to the needs of undergraduate teaching and learning.

Something less original and more complex actually happened. The university eventually built eight colleges, all of them, originally, with distinctive core programs for freshmen and sophomores (Cowell College, Western Civilization; Stevenson College, Culture and Society; Crown College, Science and Society, etc.). All but one of the colleges, the last, were given carefully and individually designed physical facilities. But "boards of study" were also created to provide a disciplinary or departmental component within the university. The boards shared in personnel decisions, and were allowed to organize traditional courses of disciplinary study and set requirements for disciplinary majors. Typically, faculty members belonged to both a college and a board of study.

This dual structure was clearly awkward, but for a number of years the faculty accepted the additional demands and ambiguities it brought with it. In its first five years of exuberant growth, the institution did appear to be "decentering" itself in the steadily expanding college system. There were unusually large numbers of interdisciplinary courses, including the core programs, which drew on a wide range of faculty expertise and support. And there was tremendous energy and enthusi-asm, drawn from the widely shared belief that something intellectually novel and important was happening at Santa Cruz.

A fair portion of this energy was generated by the conjunction of the founding of Santa Cruz with the cultural and political radicalism of the sixties. Not all of the founders identified with that radicalism. Indeed, Dean McHenry . . . fretted publicly over the impact of . . . "politicals" . . . on the balance and character of the university. The institution was nevertheless profoundly influenced by the new politics and culture. . . . [T]he experimental momentum of the sixties pushed the innovative structure of college curricula in more extreme, and also unpredictable, directions than they might have otherwise pursued. The campus was also thoroughly politicized. . . . Student activism at Santa Cruz appeared more typically in the concern for relevance and in remarkably broad interest in critical political thought and social policy programs like community and environmental studies.

But the influence of the sixties on the university was in the long run paradoxical. . . . If the multiversity's ideal of knowledge was abstract, technical, and impersonal, then a new, humanized form of knowledge would be intensely personal, immediate, and emotional. Curricular experiments pushed to the extreme limits of that inversion, including the Kresge College core program in humanistic psychology, would later be used as evidence that the old Santa Cruz was soft and lacking in standards. More important still, the student demand for "relevance" made it more difficult for the colleges to define and maintain coherent and substantive programs that could effectively challenge the primacy of a curriculum conceived along disciplinary lines. . . .

The tensions between tradition and innovation, and finally between teaching and professional work, were bearable so long as the university continued to attract students, and especially students who could cope with the inevitable ambiguities. In 1973, remarkably, fully one-sixth of all majors at Santa Cruz were either independently designed or interdisciplinary in nature. But all of that began to change in 1975. Falling applications meant that junior college transfer students, already settled in disciplinary majors, soon outnumbered freshmen enrollees. Above all else, the student conception of relevance was dramatically, and ironically, shifting. What now seemed relevant . . . [was] how well that curriculum prepared the vocationally anxious for advanced professional training. Like so many institutions, Santa Cruz began its own long, mutinous march back to the familiar lines of academic respectability.

The recovery of respectability required sweeping structural changes at Santa Cruz. . . . In 1978, chancellor Robert Sinsheimer, one year after his appointment, initiated a second and far more massive reorganization of the campus. The new organizational matrix stripped the colleges of all curricular authority and any real leverage in the personnel process. Finally, in 1980, after much debate and the intense lobbying of the dean of admissions, the faculty narrowly approved a letter grade option for all university courses. . . .

The character of these reforms has followed the bureaucratic logic of standards. A more efficient, coherent administrative organization was needed if more exacting and truly normative measurements were to be applied across the entire campus. Given the history and standard political form of the university, that meant the restoration of the authority of the disciplinary departments and, of course, the central administration. From the point of view of standards, the decentralized structure of the collegiate system had worked almost too well. . . .

. . . From the outset, the colleges were envisioned as communities within the larger political and intellectual framework of a conventional university, a scheme which ensured that the real levers of power, including personnel and operating budgets, would remain under the control of a centralized administration. The contradictions of such a mixed regime were at least implicit in Kerr's challenge to McHenry—to build a university that would "seem small even if it grew large." This overriding concern for the appearance of intimacy meant that the democratic and decentralized potential of the collegiate system was only partially, and finally inadequately, realized.

. . . [T]he colleges at Santa Cruz never really resolved the pivotal question of the meaning and structure of the liberal curriculum. More accurately, they were not given the time, institutional independence, and economic resources to do so. In this respect, the problem at Santa Cruz was in part that the criticisms embedded in the original plans were not radical enough. There is a substantive, fundamental tension between the professional interests of the academic disciplines, and

the kind of critical intellectual culture that leads to membership in contemporary American society and which is, or should be, the larger goal of a liberal education. A coherent and genuinely innovative definition of the liberal curriculum should begin with a clear statement of that tension. . . .

. . . The larger and more difficult issue was and remains that there is no single, coherent answer to the question of what a liberal education means in contemporary American society. The collegiate system was implemented at Santa Cruz at the very moment the standard definitions of the liberal curriculum were being called into question with the first stirrings of the student revolt at Berkeley. What that revolt made breathtakingly clear was the extreme disjunction between the genteel tradition of humanistic learning and the complex and rapidly shifting realities of the contemporary world. The technical, scientific, and pragmatic requirements of the technological order are pressing and apparent, and the public university has learned to respond quickly and coherently to those requirements. But precisely how and where the critical and imaginative values of the humanities and social sciences figure in daily membership in that order is not nearly so clear. That is a problem for teachers and philosophers of education, but it is also a political and social problem, tied to the structure and character of American society.

It is one of the ironies of American history that the liberal curriculum, in spite of its commitment to political and critical knowledge, has never been claimed decisively by democratic actors and movements. When democracy has laid claim to higher education, it has done so chiefly in terms of useful knowledge, in technical and vocational fields that have an immediate economic payoff. The critical and democratic potential of the liberal curriculum has been spurned most by those who, in theory at least, it most clearly serves.

In part because of that history, liberal education has never been able to push its way completely out of the exclusive and elitist tradition of genteel learning and the suspicion that the knowledge it imparts has more to do with sophistication than with active and equal membership in democratic culture. Santa Cruz has lived out that paradox and all its consequent tribulations. As a public institution committed to general education, the university in principle invites a wide diversity of cultural and social groups. In practice, it has always attracted an almost exclusively white and relatively affluent group of students, and it is threatened precisely because of that narrow band of interest. . . . At the moment the university in general, and Santa Cruz in particular, faces increasing pressure to develop new and deeper links with technology and industry, and when the need for a revitalized critical and imaginative culture is the greatest, the traditions of higher education best suited to respond to that need are the most threatened and irrelevant.

The call to standards will not significantly alter the fragmentation and uncertainty that is the deeper crisis of liberal education. For the real problem is not a lack of discipline but a lack of focus, and a clear sense of the substantive connections between the traditions of criticism and imagination and the everyday contemporary world. The sorts of intellectual values and skills that are essential to political, cultural, and personal life in contemporary American society have not been established in clear curricular terms, let alone passionately and persuasively argued before a skeptical public. What is happening instead, precipitously at Santa Cruz, less dramatically elsewhere, is that the question itself is being surrendered.

July/August 1989

Requiem for the Hutchins College
Recalling a Great Experiment in General Education

F. Champion Ward

During a brief period in the '40s and early '50s, higher education witnessed a great experiment in general education. Under the guidance of its chancellor, Robert Maynard Hutchins, and a succession of deans—including F. Champion Ward—the undergraduate college at the University of Chicago offered its students a departure from the specialization of the traditional bachelor's degree.

. . . [It] was called "the Chicago Plan" or just "the College" . . .

. . . The Hutchins College was explicitly designed as a standing critique of liberal arts education as organized and conducted elsewhere in the nation. What were the sources of the College's distinctiveness? . . .

■ The ideal time for "general, higher education" is the period between the middle of the high school years and the middle of the college years; that is, between ages 16 and 20.

■ It is possible and necessary to decide what kinds of knowledge and competence all students, whatever their individual bents, ought to acquire before going their separate ways, and to prescribe a common course of study to that end.

■ Such knowledge and competence are best acquired by actively examining and discussing exemplary works, leading ideas, and central issues in the various fields of disciplined human inquiry.

■ Because students are far from equal in skills and knowledge by the time they have had 10 or more years of schooling, they should be tested on entry to college with the results used to place them appropriately in the prescribed curriculum.

■ Acquisition of the required knowledge and competence should be demonstrated through performance on comprehensive examinations and should be recognized by the award of the Bachelor of Arts degree.

■ Even college and university presidents should be permitted to have and express ideas concerning the ends and the means of education. . . .

Ten years after resigning as dean of the College, . . . I wrote at some length about the College: . . .

The College offered a balanced and prescribed program of studies in the humanities, social sciences, and natural sciences [three 3-year sequences], mathematics, writing, and foreign languages [3-year courses], with culminating efforts to employ history and philosophy as means of integration [2-year courses] . . . The overall end of this education was to teach students "how to think." In a free and increasingly complex society, men and women are confronted constantly by diverse statements purporting to be true, by alternative courses of action claiming their adherence, and by individual works of art inviting their admiration. The College sought to give students the knowledge and intellectual competence to choose wisely and live well in such a society. . . .

. . . [T]he business of liberal education in a democracy is to make free men wise. Democracy declares that 'the people shall judge.' Liberal education must help the people to judge well (*op. cit.*, The Staff, Social Sciences 1, University of Chicago Press, Chicago, 1949, Vol. 1, p. vii).

How can liberal education help people to judge well? . . .

In the College we sought to achieve this aim by subordinating the lecture in favor of critical discussion. In half of the College's courses there were no lectures at all, and in the others lectures were secondary. When faculty gave lectures, they were not talking textbooks devoted to laying out the subject. Instead, teaching and learning occurred in discussion classes of approximately 25 students, usually meeting three times weekly.

In those discussions, students were expected to attempt to answer questions raised first by their teachers and, as the discussion proceeded, by other students and themselves. Frequently, the initiating question would ask, à la Plato's Socrates, about an apparent contradiction or other puzzlement in the day's text. . . .

How distinctive was the College in teaching students how to think? Can't all liberal arts colleges make the same claim? Yes, and no. Most strong liberal arts colleges tend to give pride of place to the preparation of future scholars and scientists; the College was more mindful of the importance to American society of men and women who would bring to a wide range of vocations and many areas of American life a capacity to deal discriminately with statements and issues characteristic of "fields" other than their "own." . . .

Given a single curriculum leading to a single degree, it is possible to place students within that program at points appropriate to their skills and knowledge upon entry. This we achieved with placement tests correlated with the College's various courses and year-end examinations. . . .

In the College, the single curriculum itself defined the bachelor's degree, and we allowed students to present themselves for the comprehensive examinations whenever they believed that they were ready to take them. Moreover, students proceeded toward the degree at paces determined by their competence on entering and the rate at which they prepared for and passed the comprehensive examinations. . . .

. . . [T]he only unavoidable College requirement was successful performance on the comprehensive exams. . . .

In spite of this limited independence of the comprehensive examinations, substituting them for the usual course grading had a number of advantages: 1) taking courses was seen as only one way of preparing for the examinations; 2) it was no good studying or cultivating one's teachers, who were seen not as final arbiters but, like Oxford tutors, as aids in acquiring the knowledge and competence needed to survive the examinations; 3) preparing the examinations helped the teachers of a given course to define more clearly the knowledge and competence that they sought to instill. . . .

When Hutchins died in 1977, David Broder wrote as follows about the College:

Those of us who went to Chicago in those years . . . knew that in that great research-oriented center of graduate studies . . . Hutchins had created an undergraduate college with a single shared liberal arts curriculum and a faculty dedicated to teaching over everything else. It was an unconventional college, which disdained the rituals of course credits, attendance taking, and academic bureaucracy. It took students without high school diplomas and granted them degrees with no pretense of preparing them for a profession.

But there was an excitement of intellectual discovery, a sense of shared adventure there, that even now, 30 years later, remains tingling in the memory. . . .

Residential Colleges

A *Legacy of Living & Learning Together*

Mark B. Ryan

... [M]y purpose is to reflect on the historical roots and educational meaning of [the] polarity [between "college" and "university"], and to advance a few thoughts about what it might mean to universities today.

... [T]he Puritan magistrates ... may have named [Harvard] ... after the great English university several of them had attended. But the model for the school they had in mind was not the multifarious collection of institutions by the River Cam, but one of the units within it, which they called a "college." The colleges they had known—Emmanuel, Trinity, Christ's—had grown up out of the medieval universities, first as mere boarding houses, then gradually gaining ascendancy as the centers of teaching and learning. The early universities of Europe provided no lodging—but students clearly required it, and benefactors, especially in England, saw a need for structured social institutions to provide for young scholars, both in body and soul.

Perhaps the earliest was Merton of Oxford, founded in 1264 by the Bishop of Rochester to take care of the "temporalities," as he said, of students—and perhaps not incidentally, to assure the good behavior and proper development of his nephews. The buildings of Merton were grouped around a chapel, where students worshiped daily; its statutes, establishing the seminal "Rule of Merton," prescribed diligence, sobriety, chastity, and other personal virtues. Merton and its early imitators were not teaching institutions, but with the founding of New College, Oxford in 1379, older fellows of the college began instructing younger ones, and by the middle of the next century, the teaching functions at Oxford and Cambridge lay almost entirely in the hands of college lecturers. Unlike the university, the colleges governed student life beyond instruction: they attempted, we might say, to manage a student's full development.

That was the model the magistrates of Massachusetts Bay had in mind when they set out to build an institution" to advance Learning," as they put it, "and perpetuate it to Posterity." Some of the more practically minded observers suggested that the school, after the manner of universities in, say, the Netherlands, simply hire ministers to read lectures—leaving the students to fend otherwise for themselves. But as Cotton Mather later retorted, "the Government of New England was for having their Students brought up in a more Collegiate Way of Living." From that beginning in Massachusetts Bay, American higher education was concerned not only with the training of minds, but also with the molding of character; the "Collegiate Way of Living," with its common residence, structured community life, shared intellectual interchange, and spiritual purpose and practices, was the path to those complementary goals.

To support the "Collegiate Way," the early Colonial institutions—reflecting their passion for this ideal—erected the largest buildings in the English colonies: Old and New Colleges at Harvard, the Wren Building at William and Mary, Nassau Hall at Princeton. In those ambitious structures were a hall for lectures and dining, a kitchen, a buttery, a library, and chambers for students and tutors. In those halls and rooms students heard lectures together; they demonstrated their mastery of ideas through recitations and disputations with one another. They followed a rigorous daily discipline of prayers and study, meals and recreation—and in their intellectual and personal development, pursued for four years in close community, they formed lifetime bonds with one another. ...

... [T]he most notable formal defense of ... "the Collegiate School" [was] the seminal "Yale Report of 1828." The focus of that report was curricular: it defended the classical curriculum—the study of what was called "the dead languages" and mathematics—as well as a prescribed, common study of other, newer subjects chosen by the faculty. But it also defended the close community and residential arrangements of the traditional American college. The young students of that era needed, in the words of the report, "a substitute

... for parental superintendence ... founded on mutual affection and confidence" between students and their teachers. "The parental character of college government," the report stated, "requires that students should be so collected together, as to constitute one family; that the intercourse between them and their instructors may be frequent and familiar."

That goal, the report noted, required suitable residential structures and resident faculty who knew the students individually and well. These arrangements allowed not only for providing information to students through lectures—what the report called the "furniture" of the mind—but also for the "daily and vigorous exercise" of what it called the "mental faculties," on which it based its psychology. The intellectual exchange in the community, then made formal with daily recitations and disputations, was a crucial educational tool. The aim of all of this—both curriculum and college life—was "to lay the foundation of a superior education" and, as the report stated it, to "produce a proper symmetry and balance of character."

Take note here that the rationale for the Residential College had moved, over two centuries, from one that was primarily spiritual (protecting the moral welfare of the students) to one that was more psychological (encouraging students' full human development, both intellectual and personal). The rationale remained, as before, student-centered, but it was grounded now less in a theological understanding of human nature than in human psychology as it was then understood. Educators of that era found this rationale convincing: graduates of these institutions in the East set out to found colleges across America—by the eve of the Civil War there were some 250 of them, many of them aspiring to the educational ideals of the Yale Report. The residential ideal was reinforced by an American habit of placing these schools in rural settings, away from the temptations of the cities, where other residential arrangements would have been available, often in towns with names such as "Athens" and "Oxford."

Nevertheless, this collegiate ideal, as expressed in the Yale Report, had a fundamental weakness. From the beginning, it had been associated with a common curriculum, and even a unitary view of knowledge. That curriculum was derived from the early Renaissance reconciliation of classical learning with medieval Christian theology, in which every intellectual endeavor had its place in a larger framework. The intellectual history of American higher education can be viewed as a progressive breakdown of that unitary view of knowledge, under the pressure of secularization, new perspectives, and new fields of inquiry.

By the time of the Yale Report, that process had begun to tear at the very structure of the American college. The explosion of new knowledge from Europe, especially in the sciences, had begun to crowd the curriculum, making it seem cursory, or to antiquate it, making it seem irrelevant. Democratic, newly industrializing America wanted more practical, vocational subjects, and an educational elite, looking at the intellectual advances of Europe, called for the study of modern languages, political economy, and the blossoming diversity of natural sciences. Such subjects could be incorporated only if students could *choose* from among various course offerings.

With the attack on a common curriculum often came an attack on the close-knit community life associated with it. Reformers such as Francis Wayland, president of Brown, took as their model not the old English colleges but the very different, non-residential universities of Germany, with their emphasis on independent and graduate study and on faculty research. Wayland called for the study of new subjects, an elective system, professional and vocational study, and—striking at the heart of the old college—for the abolition of residences and of the college's role in what was called "parental superintendence." Without the burden of residences, he argued, the school could devote its resources to academic purposes, to professorships and libraries—with the added benefit that students might not so readily lead each other to moral perdition (a point that some of us who live among them must, I'm sure, from time to time entertain).

These thoughts did not bear fruit until the flowering of the university movement after the Civil War, funded by the new wealth of American industrialism. By the 1870s, great public universities and land-grant colleges had begun to rise up in the Midwest, built to accommodate a much-expanded university population and a more service-oriented, utilitarian curriculum. Johns Hopkins was founded as a graduate research institution on the non-residential German model, and, fortified by an elective curricular system, greatly expanded universities began to emerge out of some of the old colleges. Frequently, these creations and expansions entailed the abandonment not only of a prescribed curriculum, but of chapel, community rules, and dormitories as well.

Surely the great spokesman for the expansion of the old American college into the new American university was Eliot of Harvard, who assumed his post as president in 1869 and kept it through the first decade of this century. At the heart of Eliot's reform was the elective system—free choice from a wide range of course offerings. He built his case on a radical individualism: because students were not uniform, he argued, neither should be the curriculum. It must not only change with new knowledge and social conditions, but it must allow for wide variation in students' tastes and talents— for, as he put it, vast "diversities of . . . minds and characters." . . .

For Eliot, building the university implied de-emphasizing the residential nature of the American college and its supervision of student life. A large university could not, as he phrased it, seclude students "behind walls and bars." He favored urban campuses, with many students living in the city. If the sense of the college as a close community suffered in the process, then so be it; community was not his goal. . . .

. . . In one of the more vitriolic debates among American college presidents, Noah Porter of Yale and James McCosh of Princeton attacked Eliot's university pretensions, defending prescribed study and the supervision and moral guidance of students in residential halls. Referring to the relinquishing of institutional control over students' behavior and course of study, McCosh fumed, ". . . if we cannot avert the evil at Harvard, we may arrest it in the other colleges of the country." But even at his and Porter's own institutions, electives took over more and more of the curriculum, and a smaller proportion of resources went into the building of dormitories. The residential collegiate ideal was clearly in retreat.

By sometime during the first decade of this century, however, a backlash took hold. Many educators and observers—the likes of Charles Francis Adams—were not enamored with increased specialization, with the focus on research rather than on teaching and on graduate and professional schools instead of undergraduate education. They

had profound reservations about an unstructured undergraduate curriculum, about a laissez-faire attitude toward student morals and character, and about the separation of intellect from other aspects of development. The collegiate ideal began to revive within the new university.

A leading figure in that revival was Woodrow Wilson of Princeton. As university president, he spoke of the need to join "intellectual and spiritual life" and to "awaken the whole man." Princeton, he said, was "not a place where a lad finds a profession, but a place where he finds himself." Wilson moved Princeton away from the free elective system back toward a more structured curriculum; and with the construction of residences, he attempted to rebuild the sense of community he thought the university had lost. "The ideal college . . . ," he said, "should be a community, a place of close, natural intimate association, not only of the young men . . . but also of young men with older men . . . of teachers with pupils, outside of the classroom as well as inside of it" (Laurence Veysey). For architectural inspiration, Wilson looked back, once again, to the English Residential Colleges, with their closed quadrangles. . . .

The fulfillment of that vision took place elsewhere: it awaited the philanthropy of Edward S. Harkness, Yale Class of '97, who in 1926 proposed to fund such a comprehensive system of colleges. . . .

Both . . . [Yale and Harvard] then mustered . . . one of the great enterprises in the history of American higher education: the creation of collegiate units *within* the modern university and, through that, the joining of collegiate and university ideals. Officials from Harvard and Yale went scurrying across the Atlantic to examine the Oxbridge Colleges on which their new units were supposedly to be modeled—but what they needed to build, of course, was something quite different. The British Colleges were autonomous sovereignties, self-governing and independently financed, agents of instruction with their own faculties. The American units, grafted on to an existing, centralized university, would be something new, something between a British College and an American dormitory.

Thus began the enterprise to which today's Residential Colleges are the heirs. The initial phase, I believe, was a moment of inspired creativity. In fashioning these units, the planners at Harvard and Yale faced—without American precedent, and with great care and resources—the fundamental issues shaping discussions today: issues such as the optimal size of these units; their staffing; the functions of their officers; their architectural configurations; forms of faculty involvement; their educational as well as social functions; their relation to existing units of authority, especially departments of study; their relation to the extracurriculum; the forms of their student governance; and even such symbolic concerns as names, titles, and heraldry.

Looking over this broad history of collegiate tradition, we see two basic characteristics: it accepts the educational value of community life, and it strives to develop the whole student psyche. . . .

. . . [T]he Residential College aims to promote the enduring elements of . . . "the Collegiate Way of Living." In promoting cohesive communities within the university, the collegiate ideal embraces the principle that informal contact in structured community life is a significant element in the learning process—contact between students and instructors, and among students themselves. We attempt to give meaning to the old ideal of mentorship, to the value of what the Yale Report would have called "mutual affection and confidence" or "frequent and familiar intercourse" between students and faculty. Some modern commentators point with passion to that need. As Page Smith puts it, "there is no decent, adequate, respectable education, in the proper sense of that much-abused word, without personal involvement by a teacher with the needs and concerns, academic and personal, of his/her students" (*Killing the Spirit*, Viking, 1990). This implies that a Residential College should provide for a strong faculty presence—for formal and informal avenues of advising and counseling, of listening and affirmation.

The collegiate ideal also accepts the principle that students educate each other just as much as they are educated by the faculty. They may absorb information in the classroom, but it is in exchanges with one another that students internalize that information, take the measure of what rings true, relate it to their experience and intuitions, and assess how it has meaning in their lives. Further, in their diverse backgrounds and tastes and experiences and perspectives, they expose one another to sometimes infectious insights and interests, to rich if sometimes painful personal histories and experiences. The educational value of that exposure argues for college communities that reflect the full diversity of the university population.

The second enduring element in the collegiate ideal is that it attempts to look after the whole student psyche, to promote the development of character as well as intellect. This is a persistent theme, from the Yale Report's psychological portrait of the student to Woodrow Wilson's concern that a Princeton student find not just a vocation, but also himself. The college must seek to create an atmosphere in which students are supported in their full personal growth. The college community supports that growth by serving as witness to it; appreciating it; providing a forum in which all student concerns, especially personal and developmental ones, can be given a full hearing. For college officers, this implies, I think, that what we might call human sensitivity is every bit as important a credential as scholarly achievement. College officers should be skilled as personal counselors, and they have an obligation to familiarize themselves with the major issues of personal development in the college years.

A traditional element in this focus on character in the collegiate ideal, from the founding of Merton College, is an emphasis on values we call moral and spiritual. Obviously, that does not mean for us what it meant for Cotton Mather, but the terms crop up in the whole history of the Collegiate Way, through the rhetoric of Woodrow Wilson and Lawrence Lowell. Their meaning, for us, I would say, is twofold: it lies in community ethics and in personal awareness. Ethical concerns should be at the heart of the college's community life. In their interactions with each other, in the creation and enforcement of college regulations, students must constantly be encouraged to look to the community's harmony and welfare and to consider how the virtues and values that thus come to play are expressed—or not expressed—in the larger society.

As for the spiritual element, perhaps colleges in the modern secular university must be content to let it emerge from the bonds of affection formed in the group—and to encourage a place for inner, personal exploration. If the concerns that we call spiritual are rooted, as I believe they are, in compassion—in the cultivation of sincerity, mutual acceptance, even love—then they can begin with the ties and mutual understanding formed in college life. To make the most of that, colleges must,

I believe, find ways to encourage in students a deepening awareness of personal experience, a "trust in [one's] own subjectivity," as Vaclav Havel recently has phrased it, "as a principal link with the subjectivity of the world." Through that, they can encourage some attention to the life cycle, some concern for the largest context of human life.

The educational value of community life and the development of the whole student psyche — is carrying forward these enduring ideals of the Collegiate Way, we as heirs to the collegiate tradition can promote, in the fragmented university of today, a student-centered vision of education that, in a way appropriate to our times, both builds characters and sharpens minds. . . .

January/February 1997

Educating a Committed Citizenry

Faith Gabelnick

. . . Curricular Models

The educational landscape of the past 20 years reveals a series of patterns, themes, and educational initiatives that have created a philosophical curricular trend that is changing the way we think about learning. While the "sage on the stage" is still the common pedagogical mode, other philosophies of learning are now present on college campuses in the form of learning communities, general education programs, experiential learning programs, women's studies programs, ethnic studies programs, service-learning projects, undergraduate research, and ethics centers. These enabling, democratic initiatives are flourishing even as the public demands more evidence of competency and as access becomes more problematic.

Present in all types of institutions, these programs are used for different types of institutional renewal and contribute directly to a civic stance within the university and at the intersection of university and community: they teach important leadership skills by incorporating collaborative learning experiences within classes. They also shift the locus of authority from the teacher to the interactions among teacher, student, and other resources; they imbed in the curriculum ideas of social justice, community responsibility, and respect for difference. For example, learning communities intentionally restructure the course unit through different types of linkages or connections and engage faculty and students in reconceptualizing social, economic, political, and multicultural issues.

Using themes such as "The Individual In Society" or "Technology and Human Issues in Democracy," students work together to build knowledge and insights that they could not learn independently. Learning communities that are called Linked Courses, Clusters, Coordinated Studies Programs, Freshman Interest Groups (FIGS), or Federated Learning Communities are used primarily to build cross-disciplinary coherence into general education programs at freshman levels, but increasingly are being used at upper levels for both general education/capstone purposes and for building more connection within majors. . . .

Student retention in learning communities is high because students feel they are active participants in their education. They can confront each other, create meaning jointly with other students and faculty, and discover and experience how group work deepens individual insight. Learning communities move students and faculty into a collaborative learning arena. Faculty appreciate the opportunity to discover new connections across disciplines and to break out of the isolating class unit. These experiences can translate into other community efforts, breaking down the idea of learning alone, being alone, teaching alone.

Many general education programs now address issues such as social responsibility, ethical action, gender politics, multiculturalism, and global awareness. For example, in Occidental College's general education program, which is called "Cultural Studies," students take such courses as "Women of Color in the United States," "Technology and Culture," and "The Great Migrations."

In these classes and through their assignments, students study issues of race, gender, and class, as well as the social, political, and economic realities in California and in the United States as a whole. . . . Engaging in difficult dialogues about race, class, and gender, they are learning a more complex view of civic responsibility and engagement that connects them vitally with our nation's most important issues.

Over the past 10 years, general education programs, learning communities, and other types of curricular reform that are focused on engaging faculty and students on hundreds of college campuses in building community responsibility have been supported by major grants from the U.S. Department of Education including the Fund for the Improvement of Postsecondary Education (FIPSE), from the National Endowment for the Humanities, and from the National Science Foundation. Jerry Gaff, Alexander Astin, Zelda Gamson, and others have argued that learning in community not only strengthens our educational vitality and decreases alienation in the educational workplace, but prepares students to be competent leaders in professional work environments.

A plethora of writing on pedagogy, experiential learning, and community service has emerged to accompany these new approaches in higher education.

For the past 12 years, the Washington Center for the Improvement of Undergraduate Education has engaged almost all of the universities, independent colleges, and community colleges in the state of Washington to promote educational reform in the context of civic and social responsibility. The center has sponsored important conferences on learning communities, critical thinking, diversity, and curricular reform. Administrators and faculty have participated in sessions to assess learning and to take the learning into the community. . . .

Through these and other programs, students find themselves in a variety of field experiences, as well as undergraduate research, community service, and social/political projects. In so many ways, on so many campuses, students are invited to learn by doing and to reflect on their learning with faculty and other students. It is an exciting time to be a student, and an exciting time to be a faculty member. Our educational landscape has been ignited by a "common fire" of civic involvement and change. . . .

May/June 1998

Connecting the Academic and Social Lives of Students

The Holy Cross First-Year Program

Royce A. Singleton, Jr., Robert H. Garvey, and Gary A. Phillips

Academic reform is seldom bold or daring; it rarely entails radical change. Yet, in spite of itself, the College of the Holy Cross, a Jesuit liberal arts college in central Massachusetts, seems to have planted the seeds of revolution among its students and faculty. . . .

Beginnings

The program came at the end of an intense, decade-long self-examination. In the 1960s and 1970s, Holy Cross had experienced fundamental changes, including a shift to coeducation, a sharp

decline in the number of Jesuit faculty, and an increasingly research-oriented faculty. Given these transformations, in the 1980s the college crafted a mission statement that sought to identify common ground for a predominantly lay and largely non-Catholic faculty, an overwhelmingly Catholic student body, and an institution with a strong Jesuit tradition. According to that statement:

> . . . To participate in the life of Holy Cross is to accept an invitation to join in dialogue about basic human questions: What is the

moral character of learning and teaching? How do we find meaning in life and history? What are our obligations to one another? What is our special responsibility to the world's poor and powerless?

. . . The College is dedicated to forming a community which supports the intellectual growth of all its members while offering them opportunities for spiritual and moral development. . . .

Soon after the mission statement was drafted, two committee reports, one examining student life, the other the overall curriculum, were prepared for the college's 10-year re-accreditation visit. . . .

. . . Both committees called upon the faculty to become more knowledgeable about student life; and both committees endorsed the idea of a first-year program. . . .

Components of the Program

The First-Year Program (FYP) at Holy Cross is built around a central theme, which takes the form of a question adapted from Tolstoy's *A Confession*: "How then shall we live?" This question provides an ethical orientation intended to bring relevance and coherence to everything that goes on within the program.

Tolstoy's question helps faculty pose fundamental issues. The "we" part makes purely individualistic answers problematic; it implies interdependence and community. . . .

Finally, the "then" part may be interpreted in many ways. . . .

The faculty who teach in the FYP do not try to force students to arrive at a particular interpretation or answer to this question. Their goal is to help students realize that this is a question each of us must ask him or herself throughout life. . . . This is what makes the FYP distinctive: the readiness of faculty to make the moral and ethical question a legitimate academic concern and to engage students in a collaborative search for answers.

Each year, seven to 10 faculty members are selected from a pool of volunteers to plan and carry out the program. The faculty team is chosen to represent all areas of the curriculum. . . .

Each year, the responsible faculty place the theme's core question ("How then shall we live?") in a specific context, such as

- " . . . meaningfully in a world with so many claims of what is true and good?" . . .
- "In a world bounded by convention, . . ."

They then cluster the other FYP components around this refined theme. For students, these components include

- taking one FYP seminar . . . of 16 students;
- reading three books each semester in common with the other FYP students;
- participating in . . . co-curricular events . . .
- living with all other FYP students in the same residence hall.

Faculty members design new courses that will both introduce the instructor's discipline *and* address the FYP theme. . . .

The faculty team coordinates the reading of the common texts with major co-curricular events in order to tie together classroom and outside-of-class experiences. . . .

Altogether, the FYP sponsors about 10 or 12 co-curricular events each semester, three of which are designated as major events that all FYP students are expected to attend. Each event is tied to the FYP theme, and is discussed in class immediately afterward.

The final component is a common residence. All FYP students live in the same residence hall. . . . Living in a single building enhances opportunities for intellectual discussion, as students have ready access to others in their FYP classes as well as fellow students reading the same books and attending the same events. The building serves as a convenient site for FYP events. Also, to break down further the barrier between the academic and social spheres, some FYP faculty have held classes and have scheduled office hours in the residence hall. Most importantly, having all FYP students living in a single building enables the FYP theme—*How then shall we live?*—to come alive concretely in the shared experience of living together. . . .

Evaluating the Program

. . . The evaluations show at every turn that the program has been a resounding success among the participants. . . . FYP students in their first year

- were thoroughly engaged in the program; . . .
- expressed very favorable opinions about facets of the program; . . .
- evaluated their residence life experience more favorably than did other first-year students; . . .

- behaved more responsibly outside the classroom than other first-year students; . . .
- were more likely than non-FYP students to assume campus leadership positions; . . .
- achieved significantly higher grades than non-FYP students.

By the same token, nearly all faculty participants agreed that teaching in the program

- was intellectually invigorating and renewed their enthusiasm for teaching; . . .
- . . . enhanced their appreciation for the connection between students' social lives and their performance in the classroom; and
- created an unprecedented opportunity for faculty development, as faculty worked together to address issues of teaching and learning. . . .

The FYP in effect created what Willimon and Naylor call a "learning community," with open communication among students and faculty and commitment to shared values. Moreover, the effects of this community extended well beyond the first year, as FYP students moved to other residence halls and faculty returned to their academic departments.

The program engendered a love of learning that led FYP students to seek out other intellectually stimulating programs, and it fostered a sense of caring that made FYP students feel personally responsible for the campus and larger community, so that they became active in student governance and social action. Similarly for faculty, teaching in the program was rewarding and liberating, leading many to reconsider what and how they teach; it also created a feeling of camaraderie within the faculty teams, which reinforced a sense of community and commitment to the college. . . .

. . . The program calls on students to think of themselves as members of a community and, in that context, to reflect on the moral consequences of their choices about how to live. The result—for students and faculty—is a richer, more integrated intellectual experience.

WORK, SERVICE, AND COMMUNITY CONNECTIONS

Alfredo G. de los Santos Jr.

For many years, institutions of higher education have tried various ways of forging connections with segments of the communities they attempt to serve and with the world of work. These connections extend well beyond the responsibilities that faculty members perform in their traditional functions in research, teaching, and service (the last of which has been defined primarily but not exclusively as service to the institution itself).

There have been persistent claims that higher education remains in its ivory tower aloof to the pressing social problems that prevail outside its walls. While such claims are often valid, the articles in this section challenge that perception. They document successful efforts to create connections to the community and the world of work and advocate for greater responsiveness to and involvement by higher education to engage actively in civic life.

The articles reflect four interrelated threads: 1) inclusion of *adult learners* and students with diverse backgrounds in higher education, 2) efforts to integrate *work* as part of the collegiate experience, 3) increased *community connections* manifest in areas as disparate as high school/college connections and town/gown relations, and 4) a resurgence of interest in *service learning* both in the curriculum and the co-curriculum as meaningful educational experiences that also support civic and social needs.

The first of these topics—inclusiveness and openness of higher education to adult learners—is certainly not without precedent. Land-grant universities, the GI Bill, and community colleges have all responded to the interests of adult learners to pursue higher education. What we see in the articles in this section is an explicit valuing of adult learners for the life experiences they bring to the classroom, the social and economic good that would derive from providing them with access to further education, and the pragmatism of engaging the huge market segment they could bring to higher education.

Maclure's 1971 article on England's Open University (included in the section on Media and Technology) chronicled efforts to reach the adult population through the outreach of distance education. Although the United States has a long history of distance learning in the context of extension programs in primarily agricultural communities, England's Open University combined outreach to the adult population with the use of television on an unprecedented scale, resulting in the doubling of England's university population within a few years, anticipating the current dramatic growth we see in distance education today. It also anticipated and promoted the increasing openness of higher education to part-time students whose access was limited due to time, financial circumstance, and geography.

In the United States, a result of Open Admissions in the early 1970s was the entrance of large numbers of working adults with diverse backgrounds and skills into higher education. The City University of New York broke new ground when it opened its doors to all high-school graduates in the early 1970s, assuring admission to one of its community colleges. In "Education in the World of Work" (1973), Peter Binzen described the efforts of LaGuardia Community College, established to absorb the influx of new students, to respond to the interests and needs of the local community by integrating work as a meaningful part of the curriculum. It also reflected the emergence of community colleges as a significant model for higher education that continues to grow in ways that are both innovative and responsive to community needs generally and to the needs of adult and part-time learners in particular.

The model of integrating work in the curriculum was a long-standing feature of Berea College. Its Labor Program (Smith, 1982), which is central to the educational mission of the institution, not only allows students to exchange their labor for the cost of tuition but also provides mentoring and active learning in the context of their work responsibilities. These efforts all support the goals of a liberal education through a unique combination of labor, interpersonal support, and academic challenge, attending to hands, heart, and head.

One other group of learners already fully engaged in the world of work includes adults who seek continuing education through the workplace itself as a benefit of employment and union participation. Emily Barasch in "Learning in the Workplace" (1981) described the status of workplace education as a significant trend and opportunity for higher education that is more recently being challenged by organizations outside of higher education to provide the training and education that workers want. This challenge to higher education from for-profit training groups was the focus of D.J. Guzzetta's (1982) wake-up call to higher education to attend to its growing competition.

Educators and politicians alike saw the need to provide greater access to adult learners not only for a college education but also for opportunities for lifelong education for our citizens. Walter Mondale's essay, "The Next Step: Lifelong Learning," (1976) articulated both the escalating interest in lifelong learning and the benefits for us as a society in supporting it.

All of these models affirmed and celebrated the human potential of all of these "new" students to benefit from higher education, to succeed, and to bring back their education to their communities. Broadening access has been one of the most dramatic and productive changes we have seen in higher education in the past 30 years, but it is a work-in-progress; many more groups in our communities have not yet been included.

Access to education is only one aspect of community connections. Several articles in this section advocated for more rigorous efforts on the part of higher education to fulfill its mission to serve society, to rebuild civic life and commitment to citizenship, and to assume responsibility and leadership roles in addressing social problems (Parks Daloz et al., 1996; Gamson, 1997). Gene Maeroff (1982) focused specifically on the role higher education should take in supporting K-12 school reform through high school/college connections and elaborates on the consequences of the absence of higher education in providing support, input, and leadership. He identified productive models of high school/college collaborations, including LaGuardia Community College's Middle College High School, which served as the prototype for many similar efforts based on its success in retaining students through high school and into college.

Service Learning is one manifestation of the call for greater civic involvement. Beginning in the mid 1980s, the call for community service appeared with renewed vigor. It is a call that is cyclical, recurring every few decades; in this case, it reflected a confluence of factors, including a concern for the ardent vocationalism of students, social needs, and a political agenda that advocated greater citizen participation in redressing social problems.

The arguments for service learning take many forms. Together, they made a compelling case that is being heard, although not without a struggle. The evolution of this struggle was captured in articles by Newman (1987) in his inspiring interview with students committed to community service; Bojar's (1989) case for "Broadening Community Service" to engage low-income students; Etzioni who saw it as "A Remedy for Overeducation" (1993); Arthur Levine's (1989) interview with Robert Coles, one of the movement's articulate proponents, as well as Levine's overview of "Service on Campus" (1994); with the more recent trends articulated by Edward Zlotkowski (1996), who advocated moving service learning from a voluntary co-curricular activity to a curricular commitment of faculty, and Arches et al. (1997) who examined the challenges of integrating the twin missions of service learning and commitment to diversity.

As a group, the articles in this section anticipated many of the trends we see today in higher education: the increase in adult and diverse learners in higher education, the proliferation of distance learning, the integration of work and work/study opportunities in which hands, hearts, and heads enrich the education of students, and the increasing commitment on the part of institutions of higher education to address social issues, from school reform to socio-economic and environmental challenges. Service learning appeared to both promote and reflect a resurgence in the commitment to civic life (Parks Daloz et al., 1996) and the leadership role that higher education can and should play in society (see Gamson, 1997).

However, the struggle to increase access and to integrate community service, service learning, and work in higher education continues. Although there are signs that the reward structure for faculty work is beginning to change, faculty and staff involvement in these activities remain marginalized and are potentially high-risk endeavors for untenured faculty. Since the infrastructure of most institutions does not provide for ongoing support of these initiatives, they are vulnerable to changes in funding, political agendas, and the presence of advocates on each campus who will champion these causes. These challenges were present three decades ago when *Change* first began to feature articles about these initiatives, and each of these initiatives is far more accepted and widespread today than ever before. Their acceptance, however tentative, is due in no small part to the foresight and efforts of *Change* magazine and the leadership of the AAHE, who have kept these initiatives before our eyes, giving them a chance to take root.

References

Arches, J., Darlington-Hope, M., Gerson, J., Gibson, J., Habana-Hafner, S., & Kiang, P. (1997, January/February). New voices in university-community transformation. *Change, 29,* 36–41.

Barasch, F. K. (1981, April). Learning in the workplace: Stronger support from the unions. *Change, 13,* 42–45.

Binzen, P. (1973, February). Education in the world of work: LaGuardia Community College. *Change, 5,* 35–37.

Bojar, K. (1989, September/October). Broadening community service to include low-income students. *Change, 21,* 22–23.

Daloz, L. A. Parks, Keen, C. H., Keen, J. P., & Parks Daloz, S. (1996, May/June). Lives of commitment: Higher education in the life of the new commons. *Change, 28,* 11–15.

Etzioni, A. (1983, May/June). A remedy for overeducation—A year of required national service. *Change, 15*, 7–9.

Gamson, Z. F. (1997, January/February). Higher education and rebuilding civic life. *Change, 29*, 10–13.

Guzzetta, D. J. (1982, September). Education's quiet revolution—Changes and challenges. *Change, 14*, 10–11, 60.

Levine, A. (1989, September/October). Learning by doing through public service for students and professor alike. *Change, 21*, 19–26.

Levine, A. (1994, July/August). Editorial: Service on campus. *Change, 26*, 4–5.

Maclure, S. (1971, March/April). England's open university: Revolution at Milton Keynes. *Change, 3*, 62–68.

Maeroff, G. I. (1982, January/February). Ties that do not bind: The high school/college connection. *Change, 14*, 12–17, 46–51.

Mondale, W. (1976, October). The next step: Lifelong learning. *Change, 8*, 42–45.

Newman, F. (1987, July/August). Students in public service: Honoring those who care. *Change, 19*, 19–27.

Smith, E. (1982, November/December). Berea College's Labor Program: Educating head & hands. *Change, 14*, 32–37.

Zlotkowski, E. (1996, January/February). Linking service-learning and the academy: A new voice at the table? *Change, 21*, 21–27.

Education in the World of Work

LaGuardia Community College

Peter H. Binzen

In the fall of 1970, New York City's Board of Higher Education put into effect an "open-admissions" policy guaranteeing places in the City University of New York (CUNY) for all interested city high school graduates regardless of their academic records. . . . Fiorello H. La Guardia Community College . . . opened a year later to help handle the crush of students that took advantage of CUNY's open door.

Long Island City is . . . one of New York's eleven poverty areas. . . .

About 80 percent of its population is white, largely of Italian, Irish, German and Greek extraction. . . .

. . . Both of the academic high schools ranked among the six lowest on reading scores out of sixteen schools in Queens. The proportion of students from these two schools applying for college was substantially below that in the borough and city. . . .

It was clear to CUNY's planners that Long Island City needed a community college, but they weren't sure that it *wanted* one. The young people there surpassed their parents' level of formal education just by completing high school. "Since many of them come from low-income families," their study explained, "the short-term gain of 'money in my pocket' through employment immediately after high school cannot fail to be attractive. Consequently, it appears that an intensive information and recruiting program will be needed to get many of these students to apply to colleges.". . .

So Fiorello H. La Guardia Community College had to tailor its appeal to Long Island City's skeptical ethnic whites. To do so, the planners decided that the college would operate out of a converted factory once used by Sperry Rand and surrounded by other factories and light industry. More important, its students would not just go to classes; they would also go to work. CUNY's top administration recommended that La Guardia try some kind of work-study program. Joseph Shenker, the 31-year-old president, and his staff went one

better than that. They decided to try something that, to their knowledge, had never been tried before: an "all co-op" community college.

Cooperative education at the college level is about 65 years old, but the usual practice is to limit the co-op program to one department or division of a college or university. . . .

At La Guardia Community College, the decision was made to require all students to participate. All would work at full-time outside jobs for three of the eight quarters they attend La Guardia. For this work they would receive nine credits towards the sixty-seven they needed to graduate, and the jobs were expected to pay about $2 an hour. Shenker and his staff believed the educational advantages would be at least as important as the plan's economic advantages to the students. They were determined to integrate off-campus and on-campus learning. . . .

. . . The college quickly won support among adults and young people who had never before given much thought to postsecondary education.

"There's no doubt in my mind that parents in this community like this kind of college," said Sheila Gordon, associate dean of cooperative education. "They're ecstatic about the idea of kids making money while working for degrees. The kids are excited, too, some because they need to make money and others because they don't know what they want to do and welcome a chance to sample jobs.". . .

Long before the start of school, La Guardia administrators set to work to "humanize the education process." After its first class had been selected, La Guardia staff members went to the sending high schools and spoke individually to about 80 percent of the incoming freshmen. . . .

Unlike all other units within CUNY, La Guardia runs on a twelve-month basis. Students get one week off at the end of each quarter, but there is no summer vacation. First-year students take courses for two quarters and then have jobs for one of the next two quarters. In the second year they alternate jobs and course work, each taking two of the four quarters, so that half the class is in school and half out on jobs at all times. (About half of La Guardia's students have part-time jobs of their own that are unrelated to the co-op program.) . . .

Yet, clearly, La Guardia's major innovation is its cooperative education scheme. And here the big test is just beginning. La Guardia intends to match students with work in their areas of interest. Women students taking the secretarial science course are to get secretarial jobs. Those studying business, accounting, retail management and data processing are lined up with positions in those fields. Liberal arts transfer students uncertain of their job interests sample various areas.

The true test of co-op education comes when the students attempt to integrate what they learn on their jobs with what they are learning in the classroom. "Co-op is not something that can be hooked onto the academic program," says Martin Moet, an assistant to Shenker. "Teaching here may be difficult. The faculty will face challenges from students who may say, 'Look, what you just told us isn't what I learned outside.'"

When I visited La Guardia at its opening in September 1971, the first work experiences were still six months away. Eight full-time staffers were seeking internships among sixty to seventy employers, including banks, stores, factories and public agencies, and joint appointments had been made in La Guardia's co-op and business departments. . . .

The administration at La Guardia recognizes that its central challenge is directly to link what students learn on the outside with what goes on in the classroom. They plan a series of tie-ins. Co-op advisers will visit all the interns at least once at their places of employment. Every week interns will return to the college for meetings with co-op staffers and faculty members. Faculty members themselves have been directed to adapt their courses to the outside work experiences. Sheila Gordon, who heads a staff of twelve who line up jobs for students, says, "Students are much more mature and surer of themselves after the work experiences." . . .

October 1976

The Next Step: Lifelong Learning

Walter F. Mondale

Part of America's strength as a democratic society has historically rested on an enlightened citizenry. The accomplishments of our system of higher education in opening learning opportunity to ever larger segments of society have been and should be a source of national pride. But times have changed, and we must now return to the job of providing greater access to learning for all Americans regardless of age or social and economic position.

We have obviously not finished this task when according to a recent study, one in five persons cannot read well enough to understand a help-wanted ad, one in three cannot figure out how to read a newspaper grocery ad, and one in six cannot perform the most basic of writing skills. And there remain untold millions, often in mid-career, nearing retirement, or past retirement age, for whom learning is as crucial a need as for those of traditional college age.

It is thus a unique time for the advancement of lifelong learning. . . .

. . . the State University of New York, like many other state institutions, now offers courses free to all students over 60; and on campuses around the country it is becoming more and more common for the elderly actually to move into dormitories with younger students. Inspiration for the movement in this country has come from Europe as well, where several countries are experimenting with on-the-job education, paid educational leave, and similar mixes of living/learning experience.

What these programs and the people involved in them have in common is that they all believe that education is something that can take place outside of school, and in the minds of those older than 21; that the process continues throughout one's life; and that as we increasingly encounter changing career and social demands, we must shape education to help us meet them.

I see the concept of lifelong learning as inclusive of many separate programs and concepts that have developed in recent years. These include adult basic education, occupational training, independent study, parent education, education for personal development, remedial education, continuing education, and education for groups with special needs. Schools, factories, shops, homes, churches, and just about anywhere people gather or live can and should be the sites of such activities.

Lifelong learning is a concept that demands the very best thinking of our most creative educators and social philosophers. It is a concept that, if implemented, offers a hope that all of us will be able to participate fully in and contribute to our society throughout our lives. And it offers a hope that each one of us can continue to grow— to achieve his or her full potential—and to avoid getting stuck in occupational and educational ruts that can lead to alienation and downright boredom. . . .

But lifelong learning has ramifications for all

of us. It will help us, for example, to find solutions to the deep and pervasive problems of work roles. Both the labor movement and a number of corporations have tried to humanize working conditions in America, and one of the most promising aspects of this effort is the increase in educational opportunity. . . .

These new arrangements may also encourage institutions of higher learning to respond more fully to the growing numbers of part-time learners. . . .

The lifelong learning movement is also responding to the technological revolution. Our society and culture experience continual change now, change beyond our ability to project. But one thing is clear: We cannot expect an education concluded at age 18 or 21 to be still adequate at age 50. This fact coupled with the entrance of women to the work-force in greater numbers, underscores the need for extensive retraining and conversion of facilities to make them adequate to the needs of adult Americans. . . .

Perhaps most important of all, lifelong learning offers hope to those who are mired in stagnant or disadvantaged circumstances—the unemployed, the isolated elderly, women, minorities, youth, workers whose jobs are becoming obsolete. All of them can and should be brought into the mainstream of American life. Of course the lifelong learning movement will not by itself achieve this important goal. But it is a necessary step toward making the lives of all Americans more rewarding and productive. . . .

April 1981

Learning in the Workplace: Stronger Support from the Unions

Frances K. Barasch

In an era of higher education retrenchment, a new source of students with an estimated $2.5 billion in tuition funds has been attracting attention on the American scene. This new source comprises workers eligible for tuition aid plans that have been offered as incentives by major employers or negotiated by large blue- and white-

collar unions over the past two decades. At present, these resources remain largely untapped, but if the current national effort to promote worklife learning succeeds, it could bring about one of the most significant developments in postsecondary education in the last quarter of this century. . . .

Gregory Smith . . . directs the institute's project

for Worklife Education and Training Policies, an effort to extend education to adults of all ages and change America into a lifelong learning society.

What that learning society would be like may be foreseen in worker education programs already in effect at labor centers, on work sites, and in dozens of educational institutions across the country. One much publicized program is the education arrangement between the American Federation of State, County and Municipal Employee's District Council 37 in New York and the College of New Rochelle, which offers college credits to workers in degree programs conducted at union headquarters in lower Manhattan. Through its education fund, District Council 37 also provides support services: educational counseling, testing for placement, and information on internal and external education and training opportunities — all financed by employer contributions negotiated in District Council 37's contract. With negotiated tuition aid, easy access to the learning place, special course designs, and reportedly high participation and success rates the District Council 37 college may become a national model for workers' higher education programs. . . .

Nationally, about 22 percent of the negotiated worker education plans, identified by NIWL researchers, provide for a training and education "fund," defined in the report *An Untapped Resource* (May 1978) as a pool to which employers contribute certain monies to finance education and training opportunities for employees. "These funds," the report explains, "are usually administered by a board of trustees as part of an industry-wide or area-wide program." Much more restrictive than the electrical workers' programs, "the objectives of most training funds are to improve performance of employees on the job, to upgrade skills, to retain workers, and to reduce educational costs for employees." . . .

. . . [M]any go beyond basic skills and job training, providing the money for higher education efforts in unrelated as well as job-related fields. . . .

. . . Conservative estimates by NIWL are that "1.6 million workers (are) covered by 198 different (negotiated) plans." Another study by Richard E. Peterson and K. Patricia Cross reports 280 negotiated contracts offering tuition assistance to several millions (*Toward Lifelong Learning in America*, Berkeley, ETS, 1978). . . .

In spite of these provisions, workers' participation rates are extremely low. Only one to three in a hundred workers seem to use available plans, with white collar employees constituting the highest users. . . . Union officials . . . identify several different reasons for the low use; lack of interest is only one. Others are insufficient time off, lack of company incentives, insufficient management encouragement, and, most of all, restrictions in eligibility criteria.

According to research in *An Untapped Resource* and in *The Missing Link* by Patricia Cross (N.Y.: College Board, 1978), workers themselves usually believe that education is important but report many problems that deter them from it: the nature of the plans, financial or school conditions, personal circumstances, and company or union issues. There are also psychological barriers that prevent participation. Among blue and pink collar personnel, NIWL and College Board studies find, low participation rates often result from lack of information. Many workers eligible for tuition aid either do not know they are eligible, are not sure, or do not know how to apply. Others do not know what educational opportunities are available to them in their communities, and many are unfamiliar with admissions procedures in local education institutions. . . .

Providing information to workers is believed to be the key to rapid growth for worklife learning. . . .

In all of this, "unions are dead center of the effort to create a learning society," Gregory Smith told a conference of labor, management, and education leaders meeting in Boston to develop national policy for worklife learning. . . . One recommendation which grew out of the conferences was to invite leaders of national academic organizations into the dialogue and to encourage labor to negotiate for tuition plans in new contracts where they are lacking.

Ties That Do Not Bind

The High School/College Connection

Gene I. Maeroff

They show up for only two or three periods a day, spending the remainder of the schoolday as they wish—roaming the corridors, sitting in their cars in the school parking lot, loafing on nearby streetcorners. Some of the more ambitious ones hold part-time jobs during the hours they would normally be expected to attend classes. They are high school seniors, a group caught in the grip of ennui, watching a pause in their academic life lapse into an empty, time-serving experience. It is a purposelessness born of the leniency that enables students in many school districts to complete almost all of their graduation requirements by the end of the junior year or midway through the senior year.

The Elective Curriculum

A generation ago, when most high schools had a prescribed curriculum, each student had to take a full set of courses during the senior year. Now, students may satisfy requirements early and coast down the beginners' slope to a diploma. The introduction of more and more electives, one exchangeable for another, helped create the current situation in which a student can meet graduation requirements without a rigorous senior year. . . .

Colleges' Weaker Demands

Institutions of higher education, too, must bear some of the blame. Had they not erased requirements, it would not have been so simple for the high schools to collapse in their educational resolve.

An example of the influence of colleges and universities on the high school curriculum is seen in the study—or should one say the lack of study?—of foreign languages. Perhaps it was not for the best of reasons that secondary youngsters pursued foreign language instruction in large numbers. Their impetus was the entrance requirements of higher education. It was a bludgeon, but at least many a reluctant student was prodded into Spanish or French class. . . . But the nation's high schools lost this hold on their students during the 1960s, when . . . colleges [rushed] to rescind foreign language requirements, both for entrance and graduation. . . . By the middle of the 1970s, only 11 of the 148 large state universities mandated the study of a foreign language for a bachelor's degree.

As the 1980s began, the study of foreign and classical languages had almost disappeared from many high schools. . . .

The problem of foreign language study hints at the paradox of the curriculum reform movement under way in colleges and universities. Institutions of higher education blithely embark on their journey of change, often oblivious to the effects on the nation's high schools. It is an attitude fecund with arrogance, implying that college freshmen are born into this world with no previous schooling. Few institutions of higher education bother finding out whether their prescriptions for reform will make good medicine for the high schools. . . .

The cavalier approach of institutions of higher education permits no serious consideration of the concerns of high schools. Principals and teachers are seldom consulted, and students in the high schools are never asked for their opinions, though the impact of curriculum changes will influence their lives for at least the four years they spend in college. High school, however, is not the separate world that higher education would like to pretend it to be. If anything, interdependence is increasing. Fewer students will be graduated from the nation's high schools each successive year during the 1980s, and this will mean a smaller pool into which colleges and universities can cast their nets as they search for students. The imperative for forging bonds with high schools is no longer a matter of altruism. Colleges and universities will be especially affected by the manner in which incoming students have been prepared for postsecondary education. . . .

Only recently have some institutions of higher education begun acknowledging the possibility of such a responsibility. One indication of this awakening interest was the move in the spring of 1981 by the Association of American Colleges, an organization of hundreds of small liberal arts colleges, to start exploring avenues of cooperation with high schools. At about the same time, the California Roundtable on Educational Opportunity was established by leaders in higher education to give closer attention to the state's secondary schools.

College-School Cooperation

What would be helpful, whether initiated by organizations or by individual colleges, would be some integration of efforts with secondary schools in subjects like mathematics and science, where learning is sequential—a student who falls off the track finds it virtually impossible to climb back on at some point down the line. The planning ought to reach to the junior high school level and even lower to help provide the background essential for advanced studies. . . .

Remedial Education vs. Prevention

Testimony to this lack of cooperation was the birth during the 1970s of a new subject in the nation's colleges and universities. It is called "remedial education." . . .

The extent of the problem of inadequate preparation is enormous. Few colleges and universities have been able to escape it. In the 1980–81 academic year, the City University of New York spent $32 million of its $285 million instructional budget on remediation. . . . The need for such courses has altered the character of the university, giving it the role of high school as well as postsecondary institution, and making the teaching of basic skills almost as important a mission as the pursuit of advanced knowledge. . . .

Ohio State has not left student development totally to chance. . . . It began as a pilot project in 1976 and was extended to 100 high schools in central Ohio by 1980. A modified version of the mathematics placement test for freshmen was produced and administered to eleventh-graders at the participating high schools. Professors at Ohio State hoped that by telling students early enough of their weaknesses in mathematics there might be sufficient time for the youngsters to upgrade their skills and avoid remedial classes in college. . . .

. . . The Early Mathematics Placement Testing Program sponsored by Ohio State has helped boost the enrollment of seniors in high school math

classes. A student knows that if he can strengthen his background and get a high enough score on the placement test, he will not be assigned to remediation at the university. . . .

Blacks and Hispanics

While high school enrollments are dropping, another demographic change is also occurring in the form of an expanding black and Hispanic population. Inevitably, this will mean that these two minority groups will comprise a larger percentage of the nation's high school graduating class. . . .

In a state like California, where more than one of every five people are Hispanic, the issue of absorbing young Hispanics into higher education is of great significance. Recognizing this, the University of California started earlier than most institutions of higher education to enter into collaborative efforts with secondary schools. In 1976, the system's eight undergraduate campuses launched the Partnership Program with 104 junior high schools throughout the state. The program, now expanded to 250 junior and senior highs and 12,000 students, is aimed at students of all minority groups, trying to reach them while they have most of their secondary schooling ahead of them and there is still time to motivate them academically. The field workers sent into the secondary schools by the university are the key to the program. They work with students directly and through the school personnel to prod them to enroll in the courses they will need to get accepted by the university and to succeed in its highly competitive atmosphere.

Some Solutions

There is a kind of justice in the involvement of institutions of higher education in trying to build up the quality of schooling in the early years. Colleges and universities, after all, are culpable in the deficiencies of elementary and secondary schools, those lowly levels of education that professors sometimes hold in disdain. Did not the higher educational institutions train the teachers who contribute to the failings of the public schools? It is reasonable that colleges and universities should now be expected to turn whatever expertise they possess to the advantage of the nation's beleaguered public school systems.

One way that colleges and universities might do this is by "adopting" high schools. . . .

A major effort in this direction is being carried

out by the National Humanities Faculty, based in Concord, Massachusetts, which has enlisted some 800 professors from institutions throughout the country to accept brief assignments, mostly to secondary schools, but also in elementary schools and in community colleges. . . .

In Boston, it took a desegregation order by a federal district court to get colleges and high schools to talk to each other about teaching or about anything else. The outlines of cooperation were sketched into the desegregation plan by the court with the agreement of the colleges and universities, which could not actually be compelled to join the effort. Institutions of higher education were paired with individual schools to work together to find ways to lift the quality of education, which historically has been abysmally low in the Boston Public Schools. The idea of building the collaboration into the desegregation plan was an ingenious stroke aimed at combining school improvement with a more equitable racial mix. . . .

The citywide results of the effort have been uneven, but at its best it has produced pairings like that between the Massachusetts Institute of Technology and the Mario Umana Harbor School of Science and Technology. The school opened in 1976, giving MIT a stake in it from the beginning. The Harbor School owes its existence to the court, because the judge ordered the Boston School Department to create the school as a magnet to attract students from throughout the city, thereby promoting voluntary racial integration. . . .

. . . MIT has played an important role in developing the technical courses, helping also to train teachers and aiding in the acquisition of equipment and material. . . .

A basic problem addressed by the collaboration of high schools and colleges is . . . making certain that a youngster gets a proper grounding in math and science so that he does not cut off his career options early in life. . . . The Alfred P. Sloan Foundation has zeroed in on the problem through its Minority Engineering Program, which began in 1973 and will end in 1983 with a cumulative expenditure of $13.1 million. In its unspectacular way the program has been one of the nation's better attempts to help minority members in a specific academic area. The effort has also reinforced the notion of having to reach down into the junior and senior high levels if progress is to be made at the collegiate level.

No magic wand is going to enable minority students or any other kinds of students to cope with an engineering curriculum if they have not been adequately prepared in the early grades. What Sloan did was sponsor the creation of six regional consortia across the United States. Engineering colleges, public school systems, industrial corporations, and community organizations merged their efforts in each of the endeavors. Typically, the programs have included counseling, tutoring, field trips, clubs, and motivational activities, often involving parents and teachers along with the junior and senior high school students.

Another major phase of the Sloan project has been the development of curriculum materials aimed specifically at minority students. This has been achieved through the foundation's support of the National Coordinating Center for Curriculum Development at the State University of New York at Stony Brook, on Long Island. The materials are concentrated on the junior high school level, emphasizing once again the need for early intervention. A measure of the effectiveness of the Sloan program is the increase in the number of black and Hispanic youths going into engineering. . . .

An important educational lesson is being taught in . . . Middle College High School—an institution operating under the combined sponsorship of the New York City Board of Education and LaGuardia Community College of the City University of New York. Middle College admits its students directly from the ninth grade, providing them with a high school diploma and the option of continuing through the first two years of college and earning an associate's degree, all in one locale.

This is one of the best examples of a high school and a college merging their efforts in ways that cut to the core of each institution. . . . High school students are issued college identification cards and circulate freely through all the facilities. The populations of both institutions are served by the same library, cafeteria, and gymnasium, for example. Because of the sharing, the students at Middle College High School take their laboratory science and studio art courses in college classrooms, affording them sophisticated settings to which they would not otherwise have access.

The arrangement between the two institutions has also helped to get high school teachers and college professors to accept one another. . . .

All of the college level courses are open—with

academic credit—to those high school students who have advanced far enough in their own curriculum and are able to handle the work. This means that the high school, not having to mount a wide array of advanced offerings, is able to concentrate a large part of its resources on remedial education for those at the lowest end of the spectrum. Thus, students often fill in gaps faster than they would in an ordinary high school, where their weaknesses would not get as much attention. . . . [G]raduates of Middle College High School turn out to be far less likely than graduates of other city high schools to need remediation.

. . . [O]ther ventures . . . blend secondary and higher education for the benefit of the more academically inclined, students who might otherwise languish in the typical high school. One of them, Simon's Rock in Great Barrington, Massachusetts, began as an independent enterprise in 1966 and became a division of Bard College, across the state line in New York, in 1979. . . .

Students usually enter Simon's Rock directly from the tenth or eleventh grade, going right into college-level work and earning an associate's degree in two or three years, allowing them to reach the junior year of college a year or two early. In 1980, Simon's Rock began accepting students from the ninth grade into a Transitional Studies Program that strengthens their background before they embark on college-level work. Virtually all of the almost 300 students at Simon's Rock are early college entrants, making the institution profoundly different from a typical college or university that simply submerges a few youngsters in a sea of older students. Unlike such institutions, Simon's Rock is able to make early entrance its raison d'etre, addressing the special needs of the early entrance group. Counseling and advising, which usually get short shrift in higher education, have high priority at Simon's Rock, where members of the tiny faculty are accustomed to doing double duty as surrogate parents to youths living away from home at an age when most of their peers are still ensconced in the protective womb of the family. . . .

The nation's largest program offering college-level work to high school students is not affiliated with any particular institution of higher education and carries no guarantee of college credit. It is the Advanced Placement program of the College Entrance Examination Board and, in one way or another, most colleges and universities extend some sort of recognition to students who get high enough scores on the tests given at the end of the courses. . . . What won credibility for the program and ultimately made it successful was the use of nationally administered tests that imposed a single standard on all students. . . .

. . . What students of all levels of ability need is a willingness by policy makers to unclog the rivers of possibilities that ought to be opened to young people when they reach their middle teens. The waters should be stirred so that a natural flow connects high school, college, and the world of work, permitting youths to move back and forth as they progress into adulthood. . . .

September 1982

Education's Quiet Revolution—Changes and Challenges

D. J. Guzzetta

A quiet revolution is underway in education and, given its implicit and potential challenges, it must be heeded by all who have an interest in and a responsibility for social and educational foresight and leadership. . . .

This quiet revolution is embodied in the movement of traditionally nonteaching organizations into the arena of education. Companies, government agencies, consultants, the military, social agencies, professional societies, and commercial training groups all are moving into education, developing their own training and learning programs, often—but not always—supporting theories with current relevant experience, and using seasoned thoughtful practitioners for teachers. This movement has come as society demands more learning opportunities from traditional educational institutions that have been reticent in responding. The cost is lost potential for progress for all of us as a society.

One result of this lost potential will be even less control by those of us in education than we have today of quality and certainty of cooperative planning in combining social and educational needs. What we must hope for is an awakening to the need for higher education to recognize and exploit the potential of cooperative educational entrepreneurship by once again exerting leadership. . . .

. . . As a first step, we can identify some of the causes of this quiet revolution. The primary cause is the response of formal education to the public needs. For many years, we in higher education have been fond of saying that education is a lifelong process. There is no question of the growing trend toward continuous education and re-education in the professions, industry, and commerce. Rapidly advancing technologies are requiring regular learning, re-learning and un-learning updates for the practitioners. At the same time, an increased sensitivity to the importance of human interaction has given rise to an unprecedented number of human relations learning programs. Also, the growing numbers of individuals who find themselves changing careers or re-entering the labor market after a prolonged absence have required special educational offerings. And, the expansion of the concept of an active, fulfilling life beyond our eight-to-five workdays and our eighteen-to-sixty-five workyears has brought a similar expansion of educational offerings ranging through the humanities, the fine and applied arts, professional programs, and skilled crafts.

Almost any publication, speech, or interview concerning higher education over the last decade will tell you with almost patronizing pride, that we in higher education truly thought that we had been responding all of these years to the perceived public needs. We have been sincere about it, but we have not met the challenge. We have interpreted all needs in our own image: more courses, credit hours, campus classes and classical curricula. Those responses to needs that dared to stray off campus or into noncredit programming, for example, were usually regarded with serious skepticism by campus colleagues and treated as second-class efforts. Further, if any dared to tamper with the traditional methods of instruction by ex-perimenting with electronic learning technology or new forms of interaction, the "hue" became more "colorful" and the cry became more strident. Learning was educational only when the learner fit the traditional academic convenience.

A second cause of the quiet revolution is higher education's reluctance to recognize that the need for continuous education must also be applied within, to administrators and faculty on the campus. We have become so accustomed to thinking of change only in terms of knowledge and others, that it is generally outside of our reality to look to ourselves for the need to change. But, speaking for education especially, change we must. Otherwise, the only part of us that will be a cross section of society will be what we teach and not what we are. And, it is difficult to teach very well that which we are not.

A third fundamental source in the growth of the quiet revolution has been higher education's inability to work closely with other segments of society in developing new dimensions of formal learning in a world of rapid change. For example, *if* people will be changing jobs or even career paths more frequently, *if* a more comprehensive view of a fulfilling lifestyle is permeating our social fabric, *if* we are moving into a rapid-change culture, then what learning opportunities are required to help individuals examine and prepare for necessary changes in attitudes, public policies, social and economic trends, and the like? How can those of us responsible for the teaching and learning process become orchestrators and brokers, balancing a combined involvement of first, classroom and experience, and campus and community? *That* is our changing leadership challenge. . . .

Possibilities for the Future

What is the positive side of the picture? . . .

Already begun, I see a steady influx of first-time and returning older adults entering higher education, to restore, recycle, and recreate their knowledge, skills and talents, whether it be for career-entry, career-enhancement, career-change, to maintain professional currency, to obtain professional certification, or simply to enrich their quality of life. More companies will include educational benefits in their fringe packages and even unions are beginning to experiment successfully with providing combined apprentice/associate degree programs. We are already moving away from classifying our clientele in higher education by age groups. We will increasingly group them by purpose, previous preparation, and potential.

In addition, higher education also will turn its attention inward toward developing faculty capabilities to work with a broader age group, more flexible offerings, and better accountability of results, both in terms of significant learning and applicability to the combined needs of the individual and society. As part of this active introspection and reform, we will face the reality that we really do not know how people learn best. We will commit a larger part of our resources to identifying which learning approaches work best for what sort of learner. Until some gains are made here, we will be hard pressed to convince ourselves and others of the utility of our different educational techniques.

We will also develop more insights and more sophistication in looking outward as we establish learning networks within the community. Specifically, we will involve colleges or universities, public school systems, museums, social agencies, training divisions of local governments, unions, industry, and broadcast facilities. The result will be an exchange of resources, classroom learning, internships, students, teaching and research professionals, and some support services such as counselors, computers, and recreation. It will be possible to enroll not just in the university, but in a *communiversity*. We will have learned how to extend the town and gown concept to involve virtually all facets of higher education beyond the offering of programs and into cooperating with programs. . . .

November/December 1982

Educating Head & Hands

Berea College's Labor Program

Emily Ann Smith

. . . Eighty percent of Berea's students come from Kentucky and south Appalachia. At the core of the college's program is a commitment to help students with financial need receive a quality education and prepare for later life skills. A strong academic program is coupled with a unique labor program on the Berea campus. Berea's work-study program may be the most successful of its kind in the country. . . .

At Berea College all students work in the Labor Program. If there are 1,514 students enrolled, as was true in 1980, there are 1,514 jobs, with a margin for those who need to carry more than the minimum. Each student works a minimum of ten hours a week, two hours a day. . . . In the first year all new students, freshmen and transfers, are assigned by the Labor Office to their labor positions. Most do the work created by the presence of students themselves, work necessary to the basic maintenance of the College. . . .

Berea students pay no tuition except through

their labor, for which they receive hourly wages at special rates. Berea College could not operate as a low-cost quality institution without student labor. By their work, students help the College to keep costs down and the College is thus able to help them educate themselves and achieve their degrees.

Berea students, though they traditionally grumble about the first-year labor requirement, seem to recognize its fairness. . . .

In 1955 there were sixty-seven labor departments in the Berea Labor Program . . . and in 1979 there were 110. Students have a variety of experiences to choose from—five general categories of jobs: basic services, academic offices, College offices, the Student Industries, community services. . . .

Traditional Skills

The public often knows Berea College first through the Berea College Student Industries, which not only provide creative work in the crafts but encourage the interest of students and customers in some of the traditional skills of the Appalachian region.

. . . The primary purpose of the Student Industries is to give work to the students which will help to support the cost of their education and to provide them with educational work experience — all this at a minimum cost to the College. . . .

. . . Dean Albert Weidler, Berea's second Dean of Labor, once said that it is as important for a Berea student to have a good foreman as it is to have a good teacher in the classroom. Though double-duty supervisors, who can both produce and teach, are hard to find at any time, there have been through the years many excellent supervisors in the Labor Program. They have influenced students, not only by instruction in specific work procedures but by personal advocacy and example of ethical values. If labor supervisors do what the College hopes they will do, they will teach more than work procedures. Often the result for the student is an established preference for quality work of any kind and sometimes for quality living. . . .

The Berea Labor Program, at its best, can add power to a college degree. It provides a controlled apprenticeship in work. It asks for much, but not too much, and it gives much. It is carefully fitted to the academic curriculum, is subject to adjustments, but it is firm and is as purposeful as scheduled classes. The program has many benefits. The obvious one is that it allows students to get a quality education at a low cost. They study, they work in the labor system, and they receive wages for their work. A portion of their wages is an in-kind payment in the form of a tuition-free education. . . .

But aside from economics, Berea students value the independence of helping to put themselves through college. They often discover their own unrealized strengths and weaknesses in the labor discipline and in the competition with other students. Most take pride in personal accomplishment. In addition to opportunities for success in academic work, in athletics, in campus leadership, the Labor Program offers students another route to personal achievement in which courage and confidence are bolstered. Students especially like the fact that on the Berea campus everybody works, that everybody has the same chance to develop. For four years a student is a part of a democratic community in which social and economic distinctions are minimal. . . .

A Realistic Approach

Berea is realistic in the operation of its Labor Program. There are many difficulties in such a complex project. By accumulated experience, the College knows the variety of undergraduate abilities and limitations — of the wise and the diligent, the slow, the shy, the reluctant, the immature, the eager, also the sluggish. But it has years of success with the program and many methods of instruction and persuasion. Its classroom faculty who frequently supervise academic labor, and its supervisors in the industries and other labor assignments generally believe in what the system can do for a student. They also believe in the potentiality of most Berea undergraduates. One highly effective supervisor, whose discipline is firm and who consistently gets good results from the students she trains says: "The funny thing is that when you expect people to amount to something, they usually do." . . .

125 Years Later

One walks the Berea campus in its 125th year and thinks of those early students in 1859 shoving saws and those swinging hammers, coupled with Latin and Greek, higher mathematics, history, philosophy, English literature and rhetoric. . . . Berea still aims for the old union of head and hand, for the educational concept that the Ph.D. may well have callused hands, that the blue collar worker may well enjoy Shakespeare and know the text of the Constitution of the United States. It is a high aim but surely a worthy one for a democratic society whose destiny depends on the ability of its self-governing people both to know and to do.

A Remedy for Overeducation—A Year of Required National Service

Amitai Etzioni

If one looks at American schooling as a whole, one sees that it is top-heavy. A very high proportion of the young stay much longer in the educational sector, especially in colleges, than in most other societies. For instance, as many as 50 percent of Americans in the relevant age cohorts attend college, compared to about 10 percent in countries such as West Germany or France. (This is not to suggest that the United States should have as few of its young in college as these countries, but just as 10 percent may be much too restrictive, 50 percent may be too expansive.)

This overeducation is slowly being recognized as college graduates no longer find that a college degree is a secure ticket for a job, let alone a good job. Unemployment rates for college graduates under age twenty-five, though nowhere near those for inner-city youth, run quite high (5 percent to 8.3 percent between 1974 and 1977); more important, an estimated one fourth to one half of graduates hold jobs that do not require a college education. In the view of the Carnegie Commission on Higher Education, overeducation on the college level is both a misuse of scarce resources and a political time-bomb. . . .

Work-Study Opportunities

A more radical reform would start schooling at age four and continue it until age sixteen, to be followed by two years of mixed work and study. Schools could either recognize certain kinds of work as providing educational experiences equivalent to classroom-time (e.g., work as an apprentice instead of in the school's carpentry shop) or provide internships in voluntary or government agencies on a part-time basis. This is one of the recommendations of the National Commission on Youth, whose report has the telling title *The Transition of Youth to Adulthood: A Bridge Too Long*. The Commission would also lower the age of mandatory school attendance to fourteen. Taking a different approach, a Carnegie study, *Giving Youth a Better Chance*, suggests that school could be cut back to three days a week—in effect leaving half time for regular (rather than "educational") employment, without necessarily any loss to education.

The work-study years should be aimed at easing the transition from the school to the work world, and at adapting the last years of schooling to a large variety of needs, e.g., allowing some pupils a more vocational and less academic mix. This would work best if the work were meaningful and properly supervised, i.e., more educational, which is certainly now not always the case. Social psychologists Ellen Greenberger and Laurence Steinberg found that young people receive little on-the-job training in many of the jobs they typically hold. Few develop relationships with adults (potential role-models) on the job, and students who work use more alcohol and marijuana than those who do not. On the other hand, when Northwestern High School of Baltimore sent six hundred students to work one day a week as volunteers at hospitals, offices, and primary schools, the pupils gained in maturity, insight, and reality of expectations, as well as involvement.

A Year of National Service

A year spent serving the country, interrupting the "lockstep" march from grade to grade, right into and through college, has been widely recommended. While the suggested programs vary in detail, many favor a year of voluntary service, with options including the armed forces, Peace Corps, VISTA, and Conservation Corps. Some would make it the senior year of high school; I prefer for it to follow high school, replacing the first years of college for those who wish to continue, or providing a year between school and work for those not college-bound.

The merits of a year of national service range from primarily pragmatic to normative ones. . . . High unemployment among teenagers and young adults is creating a demoralized youth population and undermining the rest of society, since young unemployed persons make up a sizable part of the criminal population. A year of meaningful national service might well help many unemployed youths avoid enticement into crime. Much of the potential impact lies in psychic development, in enhancing the individual's self-respect, sense of worth, and providing a positive, constructive experience with which to start one's post-school life.

In terms of future employment, a year of national service could furnish young people with an opportunity to try their hands at a skill they might later want to develop. For those planning to go on to college, service after high school would provide a break between "work" in two institutions, and time out to consider their goals in a setting that is largely noncompetitive.

On the normative side, national service would provide a strong antidote to any ego-centered mentality as youth become involved in vital services shared by all. Thus, an important criterion for including a particular form of service in the program should be its societal usefulness; that is, promotion of values that transcend the mere advancement of self-interest. This could encompass myriad possibilities, from improving the environment and beautifying the land to tutoring youngsters having difficulty in school or visiting nursing homes, schools for the retarded, and other such institutions to check on the quality of services. At the same time, forms of service that infringe on the rights of others would be excluded; for example, volunteers would not be given responsibilities that would, in effect, take away jobs by providing a pool of cheap labor.

Rebuilding the Community

Finally, one of the most promising payoffs is that the program could serve as the "great sociological mixer" America needs if a stronger national consensus on fundamental values is to evolve. That is, national service could fill a role somewhat similar to that once served by the march toward the western frontier. At present, America has few structural opportunities for shared experience to develop shared values that are essential if the polity is to reach agreement on courses of action with sufficient speed and without disruptive conflict. . . .

. . . A year of national service, especially if it were designed to enable people from different geographical and sociological backgrounds to work and live together, could be an effective way for boys and girls, whites and nonwhites, people from parochial and public schools, North and South, big city and country, to get to know one another as equals while working together at a common task. The "total" nature of the situation — being away from home, peers, and "background" communities, and spending time together around the clock — is what promises the sociological impact. . . .

The single most important intraschool factor affecting education is not curriculum or teaching style, at least not as these terms are normally used, but the experiences the school generates. In many schools, perhaps as many as half, these experiences are not supportive of sound character formation, mutuality, and civility. While many factors combine to account for this weakened condition of many American schools, the ego-centered mentality is probably the easiest to reverse; it is almost certainly a good place to start the reconstruction of the schools, by providing legitimation for a structure under which self-organization will be more likely to evolve. Reconstruction must also draw upon other factors, many external to the schools, ranging from greater parental support for the schools' primary educational mission to a reduction in the number of other missions, which currently dissipate their resources and blur their focus.

Students in Public Service

Honoring Those Who Care

Frank Newman

At a time when college students are being depicted as careerist and apathetic, students from more than 120 campuses nationwide were recently nominated by the presidents of their institutions to receive the Robinson Student Humanitarian Achievement Award honoring their commitment to community service. The award, sponsored by Campus Compact, a project of the Education Commission of the States (ECS), was presented to the four students featured in the following interview conducted by Frank Newman, *Change* executive editor and president of ECS. . . .

George Arnold Cuevas Antillón, *of San Jose, California, and a student at Stanford University, is a tutor and coordinator of the Barrio Assistance program, a student-run tutorial and skills development program for primary school students from East Palo Alto in California. The Barrio Assistance group meets every Saturday morning for four hours of tutoring sessions. Cuevas designed the educational curriculum for the program and is responsible for maintaining the yearly budget of $13,700. He raised $8,000 by writing proposals to corporations and educational foundations and streamlined costs by working with the Ecumenical Hunger Program and the Migrant Education Program. Barrio Assistance also sponsors an annual food drive that provides food baskets to about 175 families. As a senator in the Stanford student government, Cuevas initiated a Community Service Fund that provides $60,000 for student-initiated public service projects. He also is the coordinator for Project Motivation, a voluntary student organization that encourages minority students to seek higher education. He is editor of the Chicano student newspaper,* Estos Tiempos, *and is active in the Stanford Students for Deaf Awareness.*

Eileen Doyle, *of Demarest, New Jersey, and a student at the University of Pennsylvania, is also vice president of the University City Hospitality Coalition, a group of students, community residents, and homeless individuals who work together to feed and befriend the homeless of Philadelphia. Doyle and her coworkers will soon establish a daytime "Survival Center" that will provide shower and laundry facilities, a clothing distribution room, a food pantry, tutoring for those seeking to return to school, and a reference file of shelters, housing, health care, and job training. The University City Hospitality Center originally offered one meal a week but has grown to provide five meals weekly, feeding 75 to 100 homeless at every meal. She is also a member of the West Philadelphia Improvement Corps, a research team devoted to improving the living conditions of the homeless, as well as giving them some control over their lives and their community.*

Diane Koucky *of Decatur, Illinois, concerned about the large numbers of disadvantaged children that live in the north side of Urbana-Champaign— a run-down, poverty-stricken area near the University of Illinois campus—initiated a project called "Hope for the Children" to expand the space and programs offered through Matthew House, a community house serving more than 250 underprivileged children. Her goal is to provide more meals for these children and to renovate the Matthew House building in order to create a safe house for children. In order to finance the renovations, she organized a group of students who created a coupon book, which they estimate will raise from $7,000 to $10,000. Through her leadership, various campus groups, such as the Residence Hall Association, the Independent Student Organization, the Interfraternity Council, and the Pan Hellenic Association, have agreed to help build the addition to Matthew House. Members of the Urbana-Champaign community have also volunteered their skilled labor for the project.*

Joseph O'Brien *from Worchester, Massachusetts was initially shocked at the poverty surrounding the Bronx campus of Fordham University and* decided to help by joining an all-volunteer campus organization called P.O.T.S.—Part of the Solution. Seeing a shortage of volunteers, he actively recruited students and eventually helped form the official volunteer group of P.O.T.S., of which he became the first president. His volunteer duties have included working in the P.O.T.S. soup kitchen, counseling, fundraising, and supervising construction on a newly acquired building. His fundraising activities on campus grossed $4,000; plus he solicited $1,000 from campus organizations, and a $2,500 donation from the university. With these funds, he purchased a three-story building next to the Fordham campus, where he oversees the renovation of the building into a kitchen that will feed 150 homeless a day and provide shelter for about 20 people a night. He wants to open a Community Empowerment Center at the P.O.T.S. soup kitchen and shelter, which would provide information on government programs, such as welfare and veterans' benefits, as well as listings of jobs and educational opportunities. He also hopes to implement adult education and basic job skills programs and provide assistance in the application and interviewing process.

NEWMAN: . . . One of the issues that comes up frequently about community service is that it takes students away from the formal centerpoint of their college experience, namely, their classroom studies. Did you find that as each of you became involved in these time-consuming activities it hindered you? . . .

O'BRIEN: . . . I found when I first came to school, that even though education has always been important to me, once I got involved in Part of the Solution in my freshman year, my grades went down a little bit. But it was so important to me because I felt there was a relationship between my community service work and the philosophy and history I came to college to study. I found that many of my professors were very negative about my outside involvements when I couldn't be in class because I had to go to an important meeting, for instance. Their attitude was 'you should be here to study and that's all.' But I think that's really wrong. I believe they should coincide—especially schools located in New York City. Your education should be related to some outer reality.

NEWMAN: You raise two interesting points: One, the reaction of the faculty, and two, whether it gave you the sense of relevance to the things all of you were studying. . . .

DOYLE: I don't know how much you can measure by grades, but my grades are fine. . . . What I've learned from the coalition, you can't even measure by academic standards.

NEWMAN: What, for example?

DOYLE: How to work with different kinds of people who have different visions. How to put some of the statistics into practice. An understanding of how powerless people feel and how you can make them feel like they have some power. And mostly, that once you start doing something, then you *know* you can do it. Two years ago I was really an unlikely candidate to be doing some of the things I'm doing now. . . .

NEWMAN: So, basically, what you're saying—in different words—is that whereas you can learn much in the classroom, there are certain things you can only learn by going out in person and putting yourself to the test. And the second point is that if you do go out and put yourself to the test, you begin to realize you can do far more than you ever thought you could. But it's a matter of getting yourself past a certain point.

DOYLE: Right. And I think a third point is that it's one thing to learn statistics, but they don't exist in a document; you can't just sit on campus and have all these nice theories about how the world could work and how you could do your things. Because people in the communities have their own ideas and their own goals, and it's not for people inside universities to just decide to superimpose their ideas on the outside environment. I think it's each of our responsibility to get out there and find out what people want and help them to do it. . . .

NEWMAN: What's the first step?

CUEVAS: First I started with the university itself—departments that would be willing to give us money. And then I wrote to corporations and foundations that usually give to charitable projects and asked them to send me information. I sorted through the information to find ones applicable to our program, and sent them a letter about our intended project. There's a whole process you may have to go through for fundraising that's really crucial. But I felt more confident about it after a while, and eventually I was able to talk to the heads of the foundations or corporations without being so intimidated anymore. I think there's a real sense of self-confidence in knowing that you can really make some positive change in the community by using research that's available to anyone. I also think you learn about the real world from being involved in these projects because I've noticed that most of the students involved in community service at the university level don't really perceive what's going on outside the university boundaries. Stanford happens to be located near a low-income area. And yet most of us never get a glimpse of that. Some students come from middle class or upper-middle class backgrounds and they grow up without actually witnessing what goes on in slums, ghettos, or poor neighborhoods. . . .

NEWMAN: There is a widespread feeling in the United States at the moment that college students are whatever the next phase beyond yuppy is—that they are very self-focused, not concerned about broader problems of the public or the poor. And yet you're saying that when you get people involved, they do respond. Is it that you're only dealing with a narrow group, or would you say that most college students you see are interested if you can give them an opportunity?

KOUCKY: It's exactly that. I think it's a big misconception that college students are apathetic or self-centered. We had a campus drive to raise money and to increase campus awareness for our project and we had volunteers galore. It's often that people don't understand or don't know. And I know that for myself, I really didn't have the background to pull me in, so I think that's a lot of the problem and that we're representative of it. I'm not unique or an incredibly wonderful person filled with noble ideas. I just had some good ideas and got some really good breaks and chances, and that's what everyone's looking for. We had our fundraiser out in the middle of the quad—and students would come out and say, 'let me give you my phone number. I didn't even know there were poor people in Champaign or Urbana,' or 'oh, my gosh, how could this go on?' The majority of them really had such a lack of knowledge about what's going on in the outside world. It was ignorance, not self-centeredness that kept them uninvolved. . . .

CUEVAS: In fact, I think most college students come from that kind of background. That's the problem. I think that again I would re-emphasize that most of us are just unaware in a lot of areas, especially urban areas, of what people are going through. But given the chance to have some sort of project available to them, they will be involved. . . .

September/October 1989

Learning By Doing Through Public Service

For Students and Professors Alike

Arthur Levine

This past summer, when President Bush was proclaiming national service as part of his mission and nine bills on the service issue were pending in Congress, Change *Executive Editor Arthur Levine conducted the following interview with Robert Coles about the role and meaning service can have*

in the lives of the nation's college students—and faculty. Coles, who is the author of the five-volume Children of Crisis *series as well as* The Moral Life of Children *and* The Political Life of Children, *is a professor of psychiatry and medical humanities at Harvard and has been actively involved in com-*

munity service as a teacher and a volunteer since the 1960s.

LEVINE: . . . [W]hy is service important?

COLES: Service is important for many reasons. Educationally, because I think it is a tremendous way for students to learn sociology and anthropology, psychology and social ethics, and, in a sense, to learn about others and about themselves in the most effective way I know. One does learn by doing as well as by reading. Education is not only a function of books, but a function of experience and connecting what one reads with ongoing observations and experiences.

Service is also important, I think, morally and ethically, which, after all, is part of what I think universities are about. Harvard in the nineteenth century, for instance, used to say its mission was to develop the character of its students. One of its primary missions. I am just old fashioned and conservative enough to believe that's important, and that part of the mission of a university can be to help develop the character of its students. And, by the way, the character of its professors, because community service is important, not only for the students. It would be tremendous to have us professors doing this kind of work alongside our students, learning with them and being part of that world of learning by seeing and doing and hearing. We, too, could benefit from the kind of soul searching that goes on when one is in a particular set of circumstances with others—finding out about their lives, maybe trying to make a difference in those lives, and also, maybe, perhaps having one's own life thereby changed. . . .

LEVINE: If you could design a service program for the nation, what would it look like?

COLES: I would like to see students of all backgrounds with their teachers involved in the projects where we are all needed—with the elderly, with children who desperately lack educational opportunities, on projects that would help the country ecologically and environmentally, in prisons—wherever there is a need for the kind of energy and intelligence that I hope both students and their teachers have.

I would like to see college students teaching in some of the schools. I teach, for instance, at a college and a medical school, but I also teach in a fourth-grade class in Cambridge. Those elementary school classrooms desperately need the kind of skills that college students have. Moreover, it would not hurt to have an occasional professor come in and help out. That professor might even learn something from these children, who are pretty sharp about what they see, including what they see about university life, because some of them walk right through the Harvard Yard on their way to school.

I would also like to see the range of activities be matched by the range of participation. I would like to see rich students as well as poor and middle class students doing community service. But this is a major problem. I would hate to see community service limited to minority students, for instance, who work out of their own sensitivity to their own personal experience. I would hate to see legislation written in such a way that only the poor students are being prompted into doing the service because it offers financial benefit.

Some of the students who need community service the most, I think, come from well-to-do backgrounds, students who are so geared to competitiveness and greedy self-assertion that we really are in serious moral jeopardy. Community service is a means for us, perhaps, to get some kind of moral assistance. That is just as much our need as, say, psychological assistance. . . .

LEVINE: In a lot of ways the universities and colleges are much more important actors than the federal government would be in the scenarios we have been talking about.

COLES: I wish our universities were more connected to this. The initiatives ought to be coming from them. They ought to be running down this road saying, "We not only want to be parties because we smell money around the corner, but we really believe that this is an urgent need of ours, an urgent intellectual need, an urgent moral need, an urgent educational responsibility that we, perhaps, have not taken as seriously as we might have over the decades and generations."

LEVINE: If a college were to come to you next week and say, "Yes, you are right. We think there is a moral requirement. Our students have got to

do some of that. An intellectual requirement."
What would you tell them to do? . . .

COLES: I would immediately go to some of the nearby schools and find out what kind of help they need from reasonably educated people. I would go to nursing homes. I would go to hospitals. I would go to places where the homeless are fed or find out whether there are homeless who are not being taken care of. I would then pull together my colleagues on the faculty and the students who are interested and see whether we could not respond to those needs.

It is terribly important—and I want to emphasize this as strongly as I know how—it is terribly important for more of us teachers to participate, to do the tutoring, to work in the soup kitchens, to visit the nursing homes or the jails; to bring our intellectual skills to these people and whatever nurturance and moral, intellectual, and emotional support we can offer to other people. In so doing, we have a lot to learn that will help us to become better teachers. So, I would begin to talk to the faculty as well as the students and, pretty soon, I think we would have a cadre of people, both teachers and students, out there helping others—being helped as we help others because service is a mutual thing. It is not only helping others; it is being helped. Because we learn, we affirm ourselves in certain important ways, I think, psychologically and morally. We have everything to gain by doing this as human beings and as citizens and as people who are trying to learn about the world. . . .

September/October 1989

Broadening Community Service to Include Low-Income Students

Karen Bojar

This past year I taught a course at the Community College of Philadelphia that offered students credit for community-service work and that introduced them to the non-profit, service sector. That experience taught me the value of the course for community college students—for a host of reasons, some not apparent when I began teaching it.

What was apparent to me before I began was that George Bush's model of privileged students going out to serve less privileged communities was not appropriate for community colleges or other institutions that serve students from low-income backgrounds. There is an unspoken assumption in the current debate that community-service experiences are most needed by privileged students, to deepen their sense of social responsibility. Low-income students are thought not to need such experiences; they enter the debate only when the topic turns to financial aid.

But community-service work can be of great value for low-income students. For many of my students, the less privileged communities are their own neighborhoods, and volunteer experiences can provide them with the skills they need to become leaders in their communities.

Contrary to stereotypes, many of my minority and low-income students are *not* interested solely in getting out of the communities, of moving upward and onward and leaving others behind. There really are students who want to work to transform their neighborhoods into viable communities. Actively involved, well-organized citizens can have an impact on a community's schools, physical environment, and safety. Citizen involvement in the community—whether called volunteerism or social activism—can have quick payoffs and lasting benefits. But to make that happen, students need to learn something about setting up and maintaining effective organizations.

Many low-income students cannot afford to put altruism at the very top of their list. Under tremendous economic pressures, they must think first of themselves and their families. Nonetheless, the desire to give to the community is a powerful one with many of my students, and consequently one of the themes of my course—"learn how to do good for yourself at the same time as you are doing good for your community"—rings true to them.

Beyond its benefits to the community, service work can have real payoffs for individual students. Through volunteer work, students can acquire skills and experience useful as an employment credential. This holds true for older students who've been out of the labor market caring for children and for younger students with no history of paid employment. Middle class students tend to be more savvy about marketing their volunteer experience; my students greatly appreciate advice on how to translate volunteer experiences into credentials for work.

My students also come to understand that community service can become an outlet for talents and energies under-used on the job. Students from non-elite schools are the ones most likely to wind up in jobs that do not offer a high degree of autonomy or opportunities for creativity. The range of skills and the humanist perspective I want my students to acquire will find little outlet in the kinds of jobs most are likely to get. An education in critical thinking, in social awareness—in short, our goals for general education—will for many students be of more use in their role as involved citizens than in their capacity as workers.

My students, like all others, want meaningful work. They come to see that volunteerism can be a powerful way of compensating for what's missing on the job. Caseworkers and counselors, for example, who work in direct service to distressed individuals, often turn to public policy or advocacy organizations for their volunteer work, finding there an outlet for the organizational or writing/public speaking skills underutilized at their jobs. A systems analyst or data processing clerk, her working hours spent in front of a terminal, might turn to direct service—counseling or tutoring—to find an outlet for the nurturing or interpersonal skills not used at work. An important point is that in volunteer activities people find a measure of choice and control that's not available in their jobs.

As I tell my students, you may get stuck in a job, there may be—through no fault of your own—limited opportunities for upward mobility, you may for a variety of reasons have to stay in your town or city, and you may in your work see little possibility for change or innovation. But the possibilities for change and discovery are endless in your volunteer work.

Students also come to understand that a lifetime of fascinating "career" changes awaits them in volunteer work. The issues that may attract them at one stage of life are not necessarily those that will interest them at another. . . .

For all these reasons, I hope that community service is taken not as a fad but as an occasion to rethink the collegiate experience. Already I see "programs" that relegate service to an extracurricular option. My experience teaches me that we should aim to integrate service into the academic program to make the experience itself a subject for serious reflection and study for which credit should be awarded.

Moreover, colleges need to take a broader view of what constitutes "service." Most programs focus exclusively on direct aid to individuals in need—for example, teaching an illiterate adult to read or providing companionship to a homebound elderly person. But community service can also include working to raise public consciousness of social problems, advocating for changes in public policy, helping people organize effective neighborhood groups that will enable them to take control of their communities and their lives.

Each of these options is indeed "service," and gives rise to occasions for learning. Students involved in all forms of community-service work need opportunities to share experiences and insights with other students and teachers engaged in similar activity. . . .

In addition to historical and philosophical frameworks, many students (and low-income students especially) need to learn how voluntary organizations work and are funded. Most know very little about the nonprofit sector—about boards of directors, foundation grants, and so on—but very much need that knowledge for effective work in their communities. If we want our students to view volunteer experiences as a lifelong endeavor, we must do more than simply provide opportunities for short-term service. We must help our students to develop the range of skills necessary to become leaders in their communities and to develop the vision and commitment necessary to sustain their efforts over the long haul.

EDITORIAL: **Service on Campus**

Arthur Levine

It's no secret that voluntarism is booming on college campuses. Yet a national survey of 9,000 undergraduates conducted in 1993 suggests several important and unexpected facts about the boom.

First, undergraduates are participating in community service in record numbers. Today nearly two out of three students (64 percent) are involved in volunteer activities. This is true at all types of colleges and universities—community colleges (59 percent), four-year colleges (67 percent), and universities (68 percent). It is happening in every region of the country—in the Northeast (61 percent), Midwest (65 percent), South (64 percent), and West (67 percent). It is a fact for both males (62 percent) and females (66 percent). Older (63 percent) and younger (65 percent) students are equally involved. So are whites (65 percent) and students of color (62 percent).

Second, students are taking on a broad range of volunteer activities. You name it; they're trying it. The largest proportion are active in fund raising (27 percent), working with children (24 percent), and church-sponsored projects (24 percent). But they are also working with charitable organizations (10 percent), environmental causes (9 percent), the elderly (9 percent), the homeless and hungry (7 percent), hospitals (7 percent), the handicapped (6 percent), the mentally ill (4 percent), and almost anything else one can imagine.

Third, student participation in service is not driven by idealism or love of country. Four out of five undergraduates surveyed think Congress does not have the interest of the people at heart, that the American family is breaking down, that media accounts of the news are biased, and that most people only look out for number one. Students also distrust the nation's social institutions and think they are more likely to worsen the country's problems than help to solve them.

Today's undergraduates believe they have been unfairly forced to assume the burden of festering social problems created by previous generations, problems ranging from the deficit and environ- mental pollution to poverty and racism. Because these problems are deemed large and growing worse, undergraduates feel they haven't the luxury of turning away from them and focusing on themselves as the students of the 1980s did. As a generation, they think they are compelled to confront the problems, indeed that they have been forced into service.

Students reject quick fixes. They reject large-scale institutional solutions. Instead they have chosen to focus on problems local to their communities, those that they see in their neighborhoods and on their blocks.

Fourth, the student commitment to service is low. For most undergraduates, their volunteer activities are separate and unrelated to their coursework and college life, so service tends to be marginal to their everyday worlds.

When student leaders were asked why, given these realities, participation levels are so high, they joked, "Service is PC [politically correct]. It fits the time."

Fifth, most students would like to make a stronger commitment to service. A majority work while attending college and have less time to give their volunteer activities than they would like. They often find the social problems they are confronting to be intractable, the solutions to be complex and illusive, and the pace of progress to be agonizingly slow and frustrating. Nonetheless, three out of five undergraduates (57 percent) say they would participate in a government program that reduced college costs in exchange for a year or two of full-time service.

In his inaugural address, President Clinton challenged the nation's youth to embrace service. Toward that end, last fall he signed into law an act establishing the Corporation for National and Community Service. The purpose of the new organization is to develop service opportunities for Americans of all ages and backgrounds and to harness their efforts toward solving the nation's most urgent social problems—education, human services, public safety, and the environment. Undergraduate participation is a key goal.

If student efforts are to be truly harnessed for the national good, the most pressing need now is to sustain those college students already involved in service, not to expand the participant pool. The historical reality is that student volunteer movements tend to be a passing phenomenon in higher education, rising and falling on campuses roughly every 30 years.

If the present movement is to be more than a passing fad, its student participants need the help both of the Corporation and their campuses. The Corporation can aid them best by departing from the traditional federal approach to service, approaches focused principally on providing full-time opportunities via programs such as the Civilian Conservation Corps in the '30s and VISTA and the Peace Corps in the '60s. The need today is to sustain the millions of students currently engaged *part time* in service, a need that will entail support for faculty and staff training programs, varied campus initiatives, research and dissemination projects, an information clearinghouse, and experiments in using federal financial aid to encourage service. The Corporation is already moving in several of these directions. It should also mount a publicity campaign designed to highlight both the importance of service and the accom-plishments of participants. Students very much need assurance that their service makes a difference and is valued by the nation.

For the campuses, service needs to be better integrated into student lives. Today, campus programs vary widely, from student-led extracurricular activities to administratively staffed centers to initiatives that embed service into the curriculum. When service is largely a co-curricular activity, as it is on many campuses, there is a tendency for it to be a peripheral part of many students' lives. As one student in our study said, "Service isn't important. If it were, it would be part of the curriculum."

Under the banner of service learning, a growing number of faculty and institutions are reaching a similar conclusion. More and more campuses are building courses around service, or are including service as an element in major and general education programs and in a variety of elective courses. Some are using service itself as a method of pedagogy, emphasizing active learning, which is the preferred learning style of a quickly growing proportion of undergraduates.

In colleges whose curricula provide undergraduates with meaningful service activities, students report that service has become a more central part of their lives. The quicker more colleges act to provide service learning, the brighter are chances that, this time, voluntarism will be more than a fad.

January/February 1996

Linking Service-Learning and the Academy
A New Voice at the Table?

Edward Zlotkowski

. . . [T]he survival of service as an important component of contemporary higher education is by no means assured. Whether recent attacks on the Corporation herald the end of still another short-lived period of service or—this time around—the service movement succeeds in establishing itself as an influential new voice in the ongoing debate on educational reform largely depends on how it further develops, how it focuses and utilizes the resources it now has available. And once again, the single most important variable is faculty participation.

Over the past two years, I have visited dozens of colleges and universities around the country to talk to faculty about service-learning. I have also spent countless hours talking to service-learning activists—faculty and non-faculty—at conferences, meetings, and special events. What I have seen and heard fills me both with great hope *and* with considerable concern. On the positive side,

I have repeatedly encountered a high degree of faculty interest in linking higher education with community concerns, as well as in linking students' cognitive skills with social awareness and moral development. This interest has transcended discipline, rank, and institutional type. On the negative side, however, these overt manifestations of interest have often seemed to float, as it were, in a kind of professional vacuum, unconnected to the defining constructs of academic life. . . .

How, then, are we to interpret these seemingly contradictory phenomena? How is it possible for service-related activities to be enjoying record levels of acceptance on campuses across the country—acceptance among faculty and administrators as well as students—and at the same time, for the service movement to have made relatively little impact on the culture and consciousness of the academy in general, on the way in which its members define themselves and their work? Are we to conclude that the strategy of reaching out to faculty has succeeded—only to prove inadequate to the task of winning for service-learning a secure place at the academic table? Or is the problem simply a matter of time—a natural gap between initial acceptance and full assimilation—so that all service-learning proponents need to do is to continue doing what they've been doing so far?

I believe the movement's future will be even brighter than its past, that it will succeed in escaping from the cycles of death and reincarnation that have so far marked its fate. I also believe, however, it will only succeed in achieving a permanent and influential place at the academic table if it makes some important strategic adjustments. Not surprisingly, those adjustments center on the faculty, for they all involve paying far more serious attention than has previously been the case, not to latent faculty idealism, but to the factors that shape faculty professional activity and faculty self-identity. Without these adjustments, the movement will either quickly exhaust its natural constituency (faculty already ideologically sympathetic) or lose many of its best practitioners through the failure of the academy as a whole to recognize and reward their work. In either case, the movement will not succeed in achieving the critical mass it needs to survive as a respected and influential voice for educational reform.

When reviewing the dialogue that has thus far developed around service-learning, one may be surprised to discover how few contributions disclose two qualities fundamental to the professional value system of most academicians: a) fluency in the language and perspective of a particular discipline, and b) critical depth and conceptual sophistication. . . .

. . . As a phenomenon with roots in the social and political upheavals of the late 1960s and early 1970s, the movement has, quite often, evidenced a fundamentally—if not determinantly—"ideological" focus. By this I mean a primary concern with the sociopolitical content of the word "service." . . .

Given this tendency, a distinction made by Thomas Ehrlich, board member of the Corporation for National and Community Service and former chair of the Campus Compact executive committee, takes on special significance. In his keynote address at last January's Colloquium on National and Community Service, Ehrlich articulated a point that, while not new, bears frequent repetition:

> Community service in the context of academic courses and seminars—often termed "service-learning"—is valuable for two fundamental and interrelated reasons: 1) service as a form of *practical experience enhances learning* in all areas of a university's curriculum; and 2) the experience of community service *reinforces moral and civic values* inherent in serving others [original emphases].

Ehrlich's clear and explicit recognition that there are two distinct, if also "interrelated," ways of assessing the value of service-learning, as well as his willingness (in his subsequent comments) to focus particularly on its educational value, should send an important signal to the service-learning community. Unless service-learning advocates become far more comfortable seeing "enhanced learning" as the horse pulling the cart of "moral and civic values," and not vice versa, service-learning will continue to remain less visible—and less important—to the higher education community as a whole than is good for its own survival. . . .

. . . [I]n their enthusiasm for the pedagogy's other benefits, proponents too often underestimate the importance of adjusting the message to the audience. No wonder so many faculty express an attitude of general approval (moral and civic virtue are indeed important) but personal disinterest (that's just not what I teach).

If such a critique is at all accurate, the strategy of forestalling another decline in campus-based service — by linking that service to the faculty's teaching mission — will not succeed unless faculty outreach is understood in a new, much more comprehensive way. Without abandoning the moral and civic concerns fundamental to the very concept of service-learning, advocates must begin investing more serious intellectual capital in moving not just from student-led community service to institutionally sanctioned service-learning, but also from one-size-fits-all service-learning to service-learning as a pedagogy carefully modulated to specific disciplinary and interdisciplinary goals. Only in this way, I believe, will the movement achieve that critical mass necessary to make its significance felt throughout higher education.

Fortunately, several recent developments suggest support for such a move. In December of 1993, a meeting was held at the Johnson Foundation's Wingspread facility in Racine, Wisconsin, to lay the foundations for the country's first faculty-based service-learning association. Since then, the "Invisible College," as this association has come to be called, has grown to over 60 members — a core of educators nationwide "who envision and model teaching linked to service and create sustained support for those who share this vision."

Among the first projects the college endorsed was the development of a monograph series on service-learning and the disciplines — a project now co-sponsored by Campus Compact and the American Association for Higher Education. . . .

. . . As collaboration grows among individual practitioners, service-learning must win increasing legitimacy within both disciplinary associations and individual departments. Indeed, wherever faculty interests are discussed, its voice must be heard. . . .

First, . . . respect for service-learning as a discipline-specific pedagogy must be much more deeply and widely established. Such an imperative carries both political and intellectual dimensions. Not only does it imply getting service-learning presentations and panels onto national and regional conference agendas, it also implies making

sure those presentations and panels demonstrate real vigor and sophistication of thought. . . .

Similarly, service-learning educators need to begin writing not just for service-learning publications, but also for professional journals in their fields. . . .

A second set of strategic initiatives should seek to link service-learning to other reform-related efforts in higher education. I refer here, first and foremost, to current attempts to rethink and expand our understanding of faculty work — from roles and rewards (Eugene Rice) to professional outreach (Ernest Lynton), from "scholarship reconsidered" (Ernest Boyer) to the teaching portfolio (Peter Seldin). Not only does service-learning have much to learn from — and offer to — those active in these areas, it also needs to position itself to make sure its concerns are reflected in the ways in which the academy redefines itself for the 21st century.

Two contemporary "interest groups" whose concerns and values comport especially well with those of the service-learning movement are 1) those whose primary concern is increasing pedagogical effectiveness (active learning, collaborative learning, critical thinking), and 2) those who focus their energies on issues of diversity and multiculturalism. Since both groups are active on a local as well as a national level, teaming up with them often requires little more than an awareness of the benefits of doing so. Unfortunately, our educational thinking has become so compartmentalized that we often miss what is right in front of us. . . .

With some justification, the thesis of this article could be reduced to the proposition that, with the curtailment of support for a federally sponsored national service movement, service-learning proponents must more than ever face two fundamental decisions:

■ Do they represent a movement of socially and morally concerned activists operating from an academic base or a movement of socially, morally, and pedagogically concerned academicians?

■ What ultimately takes priority in their discussions and writings: the suitability of moral and civic concepts such as "charity," "citizenship," and "justice," or the pedagogical rationales that allow engineers and dancers as well as sociologists and political scientists to see service-learning as directly relevant to their work? . . .

In a much-discussed opinion piece published

in *The Chronicle of Higher Education* in March 1994, Ernest Boyer eloquently summarized his vision of necessary and fundamental change in contemporary higher education:

> What I'm describing might be called the "New American College," an institution that celebrates teaching and selectively supports research, while also taking special pride in its capacity to connect thought to action, theory to practice. This New American College would organize cross-disciplinary institutes around pressing social issues. Undergraduates at the college would participate in field projects, relating ideas to real life. Classrooms and laboratories would be extended to include clinics, youth centers, schools, and government offices. Faculty members would build partnerships with practitioners who would, in turn, come to campus as lecturers and student advisers.

> The New American College, as a connected institution, would be committed to improving, in a very intentional way, the human condition. As clusters of such colleges formed, a new model of excellence in higher education would emerge, one that would enrich the campus, renew communities, and give new dignity and status to the scholarship of service.

Nowhere in this description does Boyer use the term "service-learning." But can there be any doubt that, of the various movements in contemporary higher education, none is more relevant to what he here envisions? . . .

May/June 1996

Lives of Commitment
Higher Education in the Life of the New Commons

Laurent A. Parks Daloz, Cheryl H. Keen, James P. Keen, and Sharon Daloz Parks

. . . Mainstream higher education has always placed the cultivation of citizenship among its central purposes, and many on campus are concerned about this tendency toward intensified individualism and tribalism. Yet caught in the riptide of postmodernism, and struggling to relocate our own culture on the global commons, we have foundered as we seek to discern a more adequate form of citizenship for the 21st century. What does it mean to educate people for citizenship on the new commons? How do people form and sustain commitment to a common good that includes the whole earth community? What is the role of higher education in the formation of the people we need for citizenship on the new commons of the 21st century?

. . . We have conducted detailed interviews with a representative sample of over 100 people who have demonstrated commitment to the *common* good through sustained work in such areas as education, economic development, social change, science and medicine, and a host of other fields. We have sought to learn what kinds of experiences encouraged them to understand themselves as part of a wider world. . . .

We have identified many factors that appear to be significant during the first three decades of a person's life. Not all appear in every life, and no single one is determinative, but in a variety of combinations they appear to increase the probability of living a life of commitment to a larger whole. They include publicly active parents, hospitable homes, safe and diverse neighborhoods, active participation in religious life, community adults who model commitment, youth group service opportunities, mentors, and for almost all of those we interviewed, critical experiences in college or graduate school.

The Importance of Higher Education
Higher education is not essential for commitment to the common good, nor does it guarantee it, but a good college education can play a crucial role. At their best, colleges and universities provide a place where students may move from ways of understanding that rest upon tacit, conventional

assumptions to more critical, systemic thought that can take many perspectives into account; make discernments among them; and envision new possibilities.

The deep purpose of higher education is to steward this transformation so that students and faculty together continually move from naiveté through skepticism to commitment rather than becoming trapped in simplistic relativism crusted over with cynicism. This movement toward a mature capacity to hold firm commitments in a world that is both legitimately tentative and irreducibly interdependent is crucial to the formation of citizens for a complex and changing future.

In our study, we found that this capacity for what William Perry calls "commitment in a tentative world" is characterized by a cluster of "habits of mind":

- *Dialogue*—grounded in an implicit understanding that meaning is constructed through an ongoing conversation between oneself and others;
- *Interpersonal perspective-taking*—the ability to imagine with reasonable accuracy how the world might look and feel to the other;
- *Critical, systemic thought*—the capacity to identify parts and the connections among them as coherent patterns, and to reflect evaluatively on them; and
- *Holistic thought*—a nascent form of multisystemic thinking that intuits life as a whole.

These habits grow only slowly during the college years and do not mature until later when, for many of our interviewees, they evolve into *dialectical* and *integrative-paradoxical* thought. But a good higher education lays essential groundwork for them. What sort of college environments foster this kind of learning?

A Mentoring Environment

Together, students, faculty, staff, administration, and the wider community constitute the complex ecology of higher education as a *mentoring environment* that can provide knowledge, challenge, support, and inspiration for both students and younger faculty. In conducting our interviews, we heard about courses that crossed disciplinary bounds, teachers who challenged old and partial ways of thinking, mentors who inspired students to do important work and coached them along the way, guest speakers who brought the world

onto the campus, vigorous dialogue among people who differed but were expected to respect one another, and key experiences of service, internships, and travel that enabled them to step out of the classroom into the world and bridge the gap between campus and commons. . . .

Constructive Engagement With Otherness

The single most salient pattern that we found in our study, however, was what we have come to call a *constructive engagement with otherness*. At some point in their formative years virtually everyone in our sample had come to know someone who was significantly different from themselves. This was not simply an encounter but rather a *constructive engagement* by means of which they could empathetically recognize a shared humanity with the other that undercut old tribal boundaries and created a new "we" from a former "they."

By this measure, cultural diversity on campus becomes a marked asset. Of her alma mater, one woman of Irish-Italian descent told us, "I had a wonderful education at the university. It had 26,000 people; I mean it was really one of the big innovations in urban university education." When we asked her what made it so wonderful she replied,

> It was the mix of people. Political persuasions all over the board, faculty from all over the world, students from all over. But I think what I treasured most was the fact that I had African-American and Hispanic teachers that were my professors—they weren't just students, they were my teachers. Leaders from the community that we were going to serve were teaching us. . . .

Beyond Mere Political Correctness

. . . Vital as it may be, simply putting people together on campus or providing opportunities for service learning, internships, and travel/study is not sufficient. There must be dialogue across real differences about things that matter, and that cannot take place if people are unable to speak about their experiences, questions, and insights, or to communicate what matters. A mentoring environment for citizenship in the 21st century must foster a constructive dialogue that imparts at least three sets of skills.

1. Critical, systemic thinking. It is difficult for constructive dialogue to take place if we can't move beyond simplistic thinking and unexamined assumptions. Effective dialogue in which each party in the dialogue frames a context that is large, robust, and differentiated enough to provide for *common* ground enables the conversants to recognize the complexity of an issue and to surface its underlying assumptions.

2. Perspective-taking and withholding judgment. This entails a set of reflective skills, some attuned to listening to the other and to reconstructing the other's perspective with reasonable accuracy, and some devoted to assessing one's own thoughts, claims, and responses. This implies not only a search for intersecting and resonant values and perspectives but also a capacity to honor difference by holding some contradictions and conflicts open as one proceeds forward, rather than trying to force them into premature, unwarranted, or demeaning resolutions.

3. Creating a safe and civil space. The skills of appreciation and civility need to be cultivated and protected. Treating each other decently, especially when we disagree and when difference challenges values we hold dear, is essential to the best work of the academy. As the academy now secures its most profound legitimacy in relationship to the new commons, hospitality needs to be extended to voices that were previously marginal. The act of setting norms, tone, and boundaries that can hold conflicted discourse creates a shared culture with a teaching power of its own.

The Current Challenge

These skills of dialogue undergird the habits of mind now needed in a diverse and complex world, but they are not inevitably absorbed or easily learned—on campus or elsewhere. To activate and cultivate them, we need to develop contexts in which genuine dialogue about real issues will be pursued. In the classroom, this means going beyond simply providing answers, or merely exchanging opinions, or focusing exclusively on technical disciplinary expertise; it points toward a deeper quality of listening and collaborative learning, to the small class or tutorial that links disciplinary knowledge with the search for practical wisdom. It encourages continual reconsideration of both the implicit and explicit curriculum through a re-examination of the relationships among the disciplines; the teaching functions of the professions; the commitments undergirding research; and the role of service learning, internships, and travel/study in fostering engagement with the contemporary world. . . .

Most specifically, faculty in the classroom as well as those who sponsor extracurricular work should consider ways to promote constructive engagement with otherness in those contexts. As we go about the vital business of transforming our campuses into a positive force for the formation of the kind of citizenship that is called for in the new global commons, we will increasingly recognize that diversity is not a problem to be solved but a strategic asset to be developed. Affirmative action is an important, but only an initial step; political correctness is the awkward beginning of a new and critical conversation. We are still learning how to go beyond simply trying to avoid stepping on each other's toes to participating in real dialogue in which the integrity of the particular is honored and simultaneously held accountable to the whole. . . .

. . . When this happens, the possibility is born for the growth of a larger commitment honoring and transcending the politics of identity and tribe: the possibility of commitment to a *common* good. . . .

January/February 1997

Higher Education and Rebuilding Civic Life

Zelda F. Gamson

. . . What would have to change for higher education to become a serious participant in rebuilding civic life in the United States?

We would need, first, to rebuild the social capital of higher education itself, which Ansley and Gaventa describe as "impoverished." What would this mean? It means, first of all, establishing or reestablishing relationships with communities and community groups—and not just businesses—and to do so in a way that takes them seriously. As Arches and her coauthors argue in this issue, the "new voices" in the civic chorus have their ways of "doing" civic life according to their ethnic, racial, and class cultures. We must recognize that communities are not voids to be organized and filled by the more knowledgeable; they are well-developed, complex, and sophisticated organisms that demand to be understood on their own terms—or they will not cooperate.

Second, our ways of handling power differences and diverse points of view and cultures should be models of the civic life we wish to encourage in our communities. Collaboration among groups—students, faculty, administration—should be the norm, not the exception that it is now. This means that we must expect and embrace conflict, not as a sign of disease but as a sign of health. As Mark Twain has Pudd'nhead Wilson say, "It were not best that we should all think alike; it is difference of opinion that makes horse-races."

Third, as Bensimon and Soto argue in their article, rebuilding the social capital of higher education will mean little unless we fight for maintaining and expanding the representation of the underserved populations of this nation in our colleges and universities. Only with these populations fully present on campus can we work on building the kind of diverse communities that exist in the larger society. If colleges and universities were truly to "internalize" diversity, they would more quickly learn how to work with external communities.

Fourth, as Gabelnick tells us, colleges and universities should be doing more to integrate the contemporary world into the curriculum, especially general education courses. In the tradition of John Dewey, they should, as Halliburton reminds us in his article, overcome the split between "skills" and "content," between liberal arts and professional preparation. Arches and her colleagues point out that ethnic studies programs have yet to be integrated with service learning, let alone with the general education curriculum. Preparation for engagement in civic life absolutely requires that we overcome these splits.

Fifth, we must devise ways of teaching and learning for civic life. It is not enough to define and structure the knowledge necessary for engagement in civic involvement. We have to pay close attention to how we teach and how students learn that knowledge. Fortunately, we know what to do and have living examples, as Gabelnick and Arches and her colleagues show in their articles.

Applicable here are active learning, such as the use of learning communities, collaborative learning, and reflective experiential projects; perspective-taking and intercultural communication; cooperation among students and between students and faculty; respect for the diversity of student capacities and learning styles; indeed, most of the seven principles of good practice in undergraduate education that Arthur Chickering and I have been promoting for the last 10 years.

Sixth—and perhaps most important—we need to get over the traditional research culture that has sapped the vitality of most of our colleges and universities by drawing faculty away from commitment to their institutions and communities. The denigration of applied research and problem-solving has further eroded higher education's connection to the world. The fetishism of much academic writing has contributed to the unintelligibility of academic discourse and depleted the ranks of public intellectuals.

Finally, the domination of research and publications in tenure and promotion decisions has had a chilling effect even on those faculty members who wish to engage as citizens outside of their institutions.

As Ansley and Gaventa put it, "a young, untenured professor does not have to be a heartless or craven careerist to find herself cut off from the very social problems and people that initially drew her to her discipline. She finds in her everyday academic life no existing conduits through which to receive information about or build relationships with those people and those problems. She is functioning in an environment starved for social capital."

Higher education, in short, needs to rebuild its own civic life. In doing so, it will learn from communities that are doing just that.

January/February 1997

New Voices in University-Community Transformation

Joan Arches, Marian Darlington-Hope, Jeffrey Gerson, Joyce Gibson, Sally Habana-Hafner, and Peter Kiang

. . . Community Service Learning with Newcomer Students

Traditional Western notions of democracy and citizenship participation undergird the rationale for mainstream community service-learning programs in the university. As the population of immigrant students and students of color from different ethnic cultures grows on our campuses today, however, these notions of civic consciousness and democratic values may take on different meanings for service-learning programs, depending on students' adaptations to the norms and institutions of the dominant culture and students' evolving relationships with their own ethnic communities. . . .

Community service-learning activities provide immigrant students with opportunities to transform their identities, especially if participation is grounded in the sociocultural realities of their lives. Redesigning a service-learning program or course to be relevant and appropriate to immigrant students requires an alternative model that educates and empowers them to become active citizens and *builders of their own communities* as well as the larger society. From her involvement with a program of this type, one student reflected: "I learned that there is so much that needs to be done to lift ourselves and our communities out of the chaos of contemporary American life. . . . I found that I had a role in my community to be a leader."

An ethnocultural perspective — exploring ethnic identity, cultural values, and beliefs in the context of self, family, social groups, and community — defines an alternative approach to community service learning. This approach makes use of newcomers' multiple identities as they explore ways to best serve their own ethnic communities as both cultural insiders and bicultural mediators with the mainstream society.

Through this increased awareness and understanding of culture and cross-cultural adaptation, newcomers gain adaptive mechanisms and skills with which to retain and reject traditions. At the same time, they create and synthesize new forms of identity, voice, and space for themselves and their communities. The Giving SEED (Students for Education, Empowerment, and Development) is an experimental initiative to create an alternative model of community service learning for newcomer students based on this ethnocultural perspective, evolving from a philosophy of empowerment and transformation that guides the work of CIRCLE at UMass Amherst.

The Giving SEED is a collective leadership and mentorship program that links immigrant college students with ethnic community youth to cultivate initiatives for change that affirm individuals' cultural identities and indigenous knowledge while strengthening community development capacity. Through the shared vision and action of community-building, students and youth gain not only an increased sense of responsibility, pride, and cultural identity, but valuable experience and skills in working together as collective leaders. As a Cambodian American undergraduate notes, "We want the youth to know that we decide to work with them not for the credits, but because we are their community and we want to help our younger generation get what they need for their future." . . .

Connections to Ethnic Studies

The Giving SEED model—with its roots both in the methods of critical pedagogy related to teaching, learning, and service and in recognizing the centrality of ethnocultural perspectives and sociocultural contexts—articulates with the principles and practices of Ethnic Studies programs (Asian American Studies, Black Studies, Latino Studies, Native American Studies), which have been committed to empowering students and communities through outreach projects and the curriculum for the past 25 years. It is no surprise, therefore, that the faculty and students who designed the Giving SEED model are also core activists in a concerted effort to expand Asian American Studies and Ethnic Studies at UMass Amherst.

Ironically, however, at the national level, references to lessons and models from Ethnic Studies programs are completely absent from the formal literature of service learning, just as Ethnic Studies practitioners (students, faculty, staff, community members) are absent from the gatherings of the community service-learning movement. This is unfortunate and unnecessary. If service-learning initiatives have largely ignored or been ineffective in influencing the *academic culture* of the university, as Deborah Hirsch and Edward Zlotkowski each suggest, then collaboration and alliances with Ethnic Studies programs and personnel seem all the more strategic to nurture. . . .

When we draw on these holistic, philosophical, and ethnocultural approaches that are central to Ethnic Studies and apply them through strategies of critical pedagogy, transcultural collaboration, and shared, comparative learning, the service-learning model that emerges is transformative for both individuals and communities, and, if sustained, will be for the university as well.

PHILOSOPHY, PSYCHOLOGY, AND METHODS OF TEACHING

Wilbert J. McKeachie

I suspect that each section editor found, as I did, that choosing the very best articles from *Change* for this volume was difficult. There were many that I would have liked to include. The rationale for selecting those that appear in the following section was essentially that they seemed to me to represent well the current *zeitgeist* and to form a sequence moving from broader issues to specific teaching methods. Accordingly, I began with John Dewey and end with cooperative learning.

David Halliburton's (1997) discussion in "John Dewey: A Voice That Still Speaks To Us" of Dewey's concern about the effort of powerful interests to control education and the media seems particularly timely. Today we decry the efforts of wealthy campaign contributors to influence legislators to cut taxes and thus reduce support of public higher education so that the costs are paid by students—reducing access for students from lower income families. John Dewey's emphasis upon participation in society; the significance of the environmental context; and the importance of service, cooperation, and community also presaged major aspects of contemporary education, as will be evident in other articles in this section.

Terenzini and Pascarella's (1994) article, "Living with Myths: Undergraduate Education in America," grew out of the wisdom gained in reviewing over 2,000 books and articles for their classic volume, *How College Affects Students*. The five myths they discussed suggest that many faculty members, administrators, and critics of higher education have neither read Dewey nor kept up with research on higher education. Like Dewey, Terenzini and Pascarella emphasized the importance of the environment, in and out of the classroom, as the determinant of an institution's effectiveness. They decried the myth that "Institutional prestige and reputation reflect educational quality" (p. 29).

Alexander Astin's (1987) article, "Competition or Cooperation? Teaching Teamwork as a Basic Skill," began on the same theme. Rather than thinking that educational quality is associated with the reputation of an institution in some sort of national ranking or with the resources represented by size of endowment or size of library, we should evaluate institutional excellence in terms of the education of students—the ability of an institution to contribute to students' intellectual development.

Astin's point leads into Barr and Tagg's (1995) "From Teaching to Learning: A New Paradigm for Undergraduate Education," which is almost certainly one of the most widely cited articles in the history of *Change* magazine. The idea of a shift from teacher-centered to learner-centered higher education struck a responsive chord not only among those familiar with the research on teaching and learning in higher education but also among administrators, faculty developers, and faculty members. Three of Terenzini and Pascarella's five debunked myths supported Barr and Tagg's point:

"Myth 2: Traditional methods of instruction provide proven, effective ways of teaching undergraduate students" (p. 29).

"Myth 4: Faculty members influence student learning only in the classroom" (p. 31).

"Myth 5: Students' academic and non-academic experiences are separate and unrelated areas of influence on learning" (p. 31).

Clearly Terenzini and Pascarella's demolition of these myths resonated with Barr and Tagg's proclamation, "A college is an institution that exists to produce learning" (p. 13).

Of course, few would ever have denied that colleges exist to produce learning. Nonetheless, not many educators took seriously John Dewey's famous saying, "Teaching is like selling. If no one has bought, you haven't made a sale. And if no one has learned, you haven't taught."

Higher education, like business, goes through cycles in which certain approaches or phrases direct much communication and thought. One recalls, for example, "management by objectives," "quality standards," "benchmarking," "planned program budgeting," and "zero-based budgeting" as business fads. These, like "educational technology," "behavioral objectives," and "independent study" in higher education had valuable features, but each dimmed from consciousness as a new catch-phrase emerged.

In higher education, "student-centered teaching" engaged teachers in the post-World War II decade. Research demonstrated that student-centered teaching was more effective for many educational objectives than teacher-centered instruction. Yet, as educational technology in the form of television, teaching machines, and computers became dominant in the 1950s and 1960s, the term "student-centered teaching" gradually faded from view. Let us hope that "learner-centered" has greater impact and a longer life than its progenitor.

Parker Palmer's (1997) "Community, Conflict, and Ways of Knowing" warned against the view that "learner-centered" means focused only on individual learners. He said, "Knowing and learning are communal acts. . . . They require a continual cycle of discussion, disagreement, and consensus over what has been and what it all means" (p. 25). He used words that do not easily roll off the tongues of academicians—words like "spiritual" and "love"—"love of learning" and "love of learners"—words that strike at the core of our values and selfhood.

In "Taking Learning Seriously" (included in the section on Promoting a Culture of Teaching), Lee Shulman (1999) also suggested that words like "faith," "hope," and "love" are at the heart of teaching. As President of The Carnegie Foundation for the Advancement of Teaching, he is in a position not only to facilitate the creation of a scholarship of teaching but also to promote community among committed teachers. The Carnegie Academy for the Scholarship of Teaching and Learning (CASTL), co-directed by Lee Shulman and Pat Hutchings, has been designed to support both of these goals.

Shulman pointed out that, if we are going to take learning seriously, we must recognize that students construct meaning out of their prior knowledge and their interactions with teachers and fellow students. ". . .[O]ne of the most important remedies for combating the illusion of understanding and the persistence of misconceptions is to support learners in the active, collaborative, reflective reexamination of ideas in a social context" (Shulman, 1999, p. 12). This provides a beautiful lead-in to William Welty's (1989) "Discussion Method Teaching: How to Make It Work."

Welty described his use of discussion—the preparation for class, the physical setting, the beginning of the class, questioning, listening, group work, ending the class, and "after class." I like his statement, "Successful college teaching demands that the teacher have available a number of techniques to use at the proper time and in the proper situation to maximize learning" (p. 42).

Even though the research indicated that discussion methods typically result in better thinking and retention of learning than lecture, positive results are not inevitable. Carol Trosset's (1998) "Obstacles to Open Discussion and Critical Thinking: The Grinnell College Study" described student views about discussion. Some students see discussion as an opportunity to convert other students to their own point of view; many see discussion as a method for reaching consensus. Too often, personal experience is favored over research evidence.

In "Cooperative Learning Returns to College: What Evidence Is There That It Works?" David Johnson, Roger Johnson, and Karl Smith (1998) summarized the extensive research demonstrating the effectiveness of cooperative learning and describe ways of using cooperative learning. We are reminded of the earlier article by Astin on the importance of teamwork and cooperation in contemporary society and the essential role of trust in fostering cooperation. This, in turn, re-integrated the theme of community that also ran through the work of John Dewey, Robert Barr and John Tagg, Parker Palmer, and Lee Shulman.

"Community," "cooperation," "trust," "joy," "faith," "hope," "love"—not the usual words for discussions of learning, but nonetheless at the core of our teaching-learning endeavor.

References

Astin, A. W. (1987, September/October). Competition or cooperation? Teaching teamwork as a basic skill. *Change, 19,* 12–19.

Barr, R. B., & Tagg, J. (1995, November/December). From teaching to learning: A new paradigm for undergraduate education. *Change, 27,* 13–25.

Halliburton, D. (1997, January/February). John Dewey: A voice that still speaks to us. *Change, 29,* 24–29.

Johnson, D. W., Johnson, R. T., & Smith, K. A. (1998, July/August). Cooperative learning returns to college: What evidence is there that it works? *Change, 30,* 27–35.

Palmer, P. (1997, September/October). Community, conflict and ways of knowing: Ways to deepen our educational agenda. *Change, 29,* 20–25.

Shulman, L. S. (1999, July/August). Taking learning seriously. *Change, 31,* 11–17.

Terenzini, P. T., & Pascarella, E. T. (1994, January/February). Living with myths: Undergraduate education in America. *Change, 26,* 28–32.

Trosset, C. (1998, September/October). Obstacles to open discussion and critical thinking: The Grinnell College study. *Change, 30,* 44–49.

Welty, W. (1989, July/August). Discussion method teaching: How to make it work. *Change* 41–49.

Competition or Cooperation?

Teaching Teamwork as a Basic Skill

Alexander W. Astin

During the past three years, those of us who work in higher education have been subjected to a spate of reports aimed at reforming higher education. Yet, when it comes to *implementing* the seemingly logical reforms of these reports, we often find ourselves unable to make much progress.

I suggest that at the heart of our difficulties in reforming higher education lies a fundamental conflict in *values*: That is, the values underlying our reports' recommendations are basically inconsistent with those that govern time-honored practices in higher education. Because those conflicting values are *implicit* rather than explicit, we are confounded when our attempts at reform fail.

I'd like first to discuss the values and beliefs that govern our educational practices, and then suggest an alternative value perspective more consistent with the spirit of reform suggested by the national reports. Prospects for reform will be much improved if we first understand these underlying value issues. . . .

For several years now I've argued that we tend to look at higher education "excellence" in two ways. For simplicity, I label these the reputational and resource approaches. The *reputational* view equates excellence with an institution's position in the hierarchical pecking order that is so much a part of our folklore in American higher education, a folklore we quantify by doing reputational surveys. The *resource* view equates excellence with such things as the test scores of entering students, the endowment, the student-faculty ratio, and the size of the library. Since the reputational and resource views are mutually reinforcing—having more resources enhances reputation, and a good reputation helps to bring in more resources—it is not surprising that both approaches yield similar rankings of institutions. . . .

But the reputational and resource approaches to excellence are flawed because they fail to address directly the central mission of most colleges and universities—the *education* of the student, or,

to put it more concretely, the fullest development of the student's abilities and talents. If talent development is indeed their principal *raison d'être*, why not define the "excellence" of institutions in terms of their ability to develop the talents of students?

A talent development view of excellence emphasizes the educational impact of the institution on its students. Its premise is that excellence lies in the institution's ability to affect its students favorably, to enhance their intellectual and scholarly development, and to make a positive difference in their lives. The "most excellent" institutions are, in this view, those that have the greatest impact—"add the most value," as economists would say, to students' knowledge and personal development.

What accounts for the persistence of the resource and reputational approaches to excellence? Why has the talent-development approach not been more widely accepted? I think the ultimate answers lie in the larger society, in the particular philosophical or value perspective that holds sway at any moment in time, and in our concept of the fundamental nature of human beings and of societies. The more I think about these issues, the more I conclude that there are two fundamentally different world views that one can adopt in looking at educational as well as societal issues. For simplicity, I characterize these as the *competitive* view and the *cooperative* view of human nature and of society.

In the first of these two views, America's greatest achievements as a society are attributed to our intense competitiveness; it is through "competitive spirit" that we've been able to achieve greatness as a society. Our free enterprise system certainly implies a competitive view: Individuals are given the maximum opportunity to compete with each other for the largest possible share of the resources and rewards in the society. . . .

A cooperative world view provides quite a different frame of reference. Under it, human progress and the development of society are seen as depending upon the ability of individuals and groups to cooperate with each other. Human progress is seen not as a victory in the struggle with other species or as a conquest of the environment, but as a manifestation of our ability to work cooperatively with each other toward common goals and to live in harmony with that environment.

Many of the issues that plague higher education these days can be better understood when viewed within this cooperative-competitive framework. Take, for example, the different conceptions of excellence. The reputational approach is inherently competitive: It fosters competition among institutions for higher and higher places in the pecking order. The same is implied by a resources approach: Institutions compete with each other for the largest possible share of the resource pool. . . .

The talent-development approach to excellence symbolizes a very different value perspective. To this view, all institutions share a common purpose in trying to maximize the educational and personal development of students. . . .

At a more basic level, the talent-development view symbolizes a cooperative value system by emphasizing the need to focus institutional energies on the task of helping students develop to their maximum potential. The institution, then, exists fundamentally to serve and help the student, rather than merely to amass resources or enhance its reputation.

For talent development to occur, the *student* has a role to play in the process, too: There must be a commitment and involvement on his or her part for effective learning to happen. Thus, in an ideal educational environment, we have an *institution* with a talent-development conception of its own excellence, and a highly involved *student* who is exerting significant effort in the learning process. This combination of student involvement and institutional commitment represents for me the kind of cooperation we need to achieve excellence of result. . . .

The key ingredient for a cooperative work environment, of course, is a sense of trust among employees at all levels of the organization. This understanding is supported by a fascinating new book by Alfie Kohn, *No Contest* (1986). Kohn's view of the research shows that an environment that encourages trust and cooperation (as opposed to competition) produces better results, not only in business, but in such fields as education, journalism, and the arts. Kohn provides a sociopsychological explanation for why cooperation seems to work better than competition, pointing out that people usually do better at tasks they enjoy; that is, at tasks where the motivation is *intrinsic* rather than extrinsic.

In my judgment, the capacity to be a good team member and to work cooperatively with coworkers should be one of the "basic skills" we try to develop in our general education programs.

Beyond this specific example, once one is open to cooperation as an ideal, it's possible to come up with a number of ideas about how curricular content should be modified.

For example, we hear a lot these days about developing student "communication skills." But how shall we define those skills? If we gave more attention to the social and value implications of the concept, I think we'd move beyond a focus on writing and speaking to look at the art of good *listening*. This neglected skill is not only of great practical importance, it also emphasizes the essence of cooperative spirit. Being able to listen, to understand the thoughts and feelings of others, is vitally important to the trust and empathy so necessary for cooperative living. (Those interested in how the curriculum can be structured to develop better listening skills might want to take a look at a program developed at St. Edward's University in Austin, Texas.)

On a more symbolic level, the development of interdisciplinary and transdisciplinary courses represents still another way to demonstrate the advantages of cooperation for students (and for us as faculty, I might add).

Curricular content represents only a small portion of the "values education" that goes on in academe: Our most important "teaching" may be independent of course content. This "implicit curriculum," as I like to call it, includes the process of establishing a curriculum, the teaching methods we use, how we grade and test our students, and our faculty personnel policies.

What I will do now is consider the extent to which this implicit curriculum fosters the development of cooperation and trust. Does it teach students the value and necessity of teamwork and cooperation? Does it show them how to cooperate? To what extent may it foster the development of contrary values, such as individualism and competitiveness? I think it is safe to assert that few liberal arts programs are consciously designed to encourage the development of values such as empathy and cooperativeness. Many such programs, in fact, seem, at least implicitly, to exemplify contrary values.

Establishing the Curriculum: In an effort to give students "broad exposure" to the liberal arts and sciences, general education requirements typically treat academic disciplines as discrete, autonomous fields of knowledge and inquiry: a little of this and a little of that. With the rapidly expanding knowledge base and proliferation of fields and subfields, the process of setting these general education requirements is often highly confrontational, with final decisions representing a kind of political compromise among competing disciplines. These strong interdepartmental rivalries are frequently acted out in the classroom, with the hard scientists disparaging the social scientists, the humanists disparaging the engineers, and so on. Even within departments, subspecialties often criticize and compete openly with each other (the clinicians and experimentalists within my own field of psychology being one striking example of such competition). . . .

Teaching, Grading, and Testing: Teaching can be viewed as a metaphor for cooperation: two people working together toward a common goal. But in many respects, our capacity for "teaching" cooperation in the classroom is compromised by traditional methods of testing, grading, and instruction.

Let's first consider pedagogical technique. Most lower-division teaching, especially in larger universities, still uses the lecture format. Several national reports have criticized this traditional model of instruction on the grounds that it assigns students too passive a role, thereby reducing involvement and inhibiting the learning process. It has one other serious deficiency as well: It leads students to view learning as a solitary process, where each student works independently of every other. Indeed, not only do students work independently of one another, they are encouraged to compete with one another.

This competitive emphasis is reinforced by the grading system, which is basically comparative or relativistic. The practice of grading "on the curve" does not say much about what a student has actually learned in a class; it merely ranks students

relative to one another. Under these conditions, one student's success signifies failure for some other student. Students are almost never encouraged, much less rewarded, for helping each other learn. In a recent article in *American Psychologist* (1985), Morton Deutsch has eloquently summarized the consequences:

> Through the repeated and pervasive experience of competitive struggle for scarce goods in the classroom, students are socialized into believing that this is not only the just way but also the natural and inevitable way of allocating scarce values in the larger, impersonal, nonfamiliar world. They also learn that there are winners and losers in such competitions and that, although it is possible for them to win, they are more likely to lose.

What is most regrettable about this heavy dependence on traditional arrangements is that it ignores a growing body of research that suggests that "collaborative learning" models — where students teach each other or work together on joint projects — are superior to competitive approaches. At the Higher Education Research Institute, we recently reviewed this literature and found that collaborative approaches produce better learning in the vast majority of studies; the method is highly cost-effective and helps solve two of our most vexing pedagogical problems: large class size and gross differences in educational preparation.

For my purpose here, however, the most important thing about collaborative learning is that it facilitates the development of teamwork skills and encourages the individual student to view each classmate as a potential helper rather than as a competitor. Under it, students learn to work together toward common goals.

The limitations of competitive classroom learning are compounded by the fact that professors must grade students as well as teach them. Any cooperative relationship between teacher and student is compromised because the teacher also passes final judgment on the student, and these judgments (grades) can have significant practical consequences for the student's subsequent opportunities. Thus, more than a few students come to see their professors less as teachers or mentors than as people to be manipulated, which hinders both parties from developing any real sense of trust in each other.

In my own classroom teaching, I continually

encounter this problem, even at the graduate level. The examining process has so conditioned students to "disguise their ignorance," so to speak, that I routinely tell my students that I cannot help them learn as long as they try to hide from me what they don't know or understand. It sometimes takes months before students can develop enough trust to believe that they will not be punished for exposing themselves in this manner.

The conflict of interest generated by the professor's dual role as mentor and judge was recognized many years ago by Robert Hutchins, who believed that the learning process should be separated from the testing and grading process. As president of the University of Chicago, Hutchins established the Examiner's Office, where students could go when they felt ready to be tested on a subject. Long since abandoned at Chicago, the Examiner's Office remains a largely untested concept that offers real potential for building a greater sense of trust and cooperation between professor and student.

In short, our favored methods of teaching and assessing undergraduates fail to enhance the educational process and reinforce feelings of competitiveness among students. They make it difficult for students and faculty to develop a sense of mutual trust and to view the teaching-learning process as a cooperative effort.

Faculty Personnel Policies: Faculty personnel practices have inadvertent effects on undergraduate students' beliefs, constituting a subtle form of "modeling." Students seldom participate directly in faculty personnel actions, but they are usually aware of the criteria used in hiring, promoting, and tenuring faculty. . . .

. . . We are all familiar with the "publish or perish" syndrome. This dictum gives the greatest weight to a candidate's research and scholarship; it relegates the functions of teaching, advising, colleagueship, and public service to second-class status. The most valued research and scholarship, of course, reflect highly competitive, individualistic activity. While some articles and books have multiple authors (signifying a cooperative or joint effort), such publications generally get *less* credit in the review process than do single-authored pieces. In other words, the process does not encourage scholarly collaboration. . . .

In summary, faculty personnel policies present students with a model of peer relationships that is far from ideal. Under it, institutional rewards accrue to those who are most successful in promoting their own professional status and visibility. Those who contribute to the welfare of their students, their colleagues, or their institution receive little or no recognition. Moreover, performance assessments of colleagues are done to judge rather than facilitate performance; the review process itself tends to foster competitiveness, anxiety, and a lack of trust among colleagues.

Current pedagogical techniques and faculty personnel practices do not encourage the development of such qualities as trust, empathy, and cooperation. Nor does the implicit curriculum give students an opportunity to learn effective leadership and teamwork skills. How are students being influenced by all of this?

Our research over the last two decades shows that the values and attitudes of college students are changing in both dramatic and unsettling ways. Several years ago at an American Association for Higher Education (AAHE) meeting, I reported some of these trends, which continue to this day. Students have become markedly more interested in power, status, and money. Conversely, they are much less concerned about helping others and contributing to their communities. It's almost as if students were aping their professors and their institutions by emphasizing competition and individualism over cooperation and teamwork.

While I've emphasized up to now the widespread competitiveness that permeates so much of higher education, there are promising signs of trends in the opposite direction. In his address to the annual meeting of the American Council on Education last fall, American Council on Education President Robert Atwell called on the membership to reconsider "the conflicting values of competition and the commonweal." Frank Newman and the Education Commission of the States have for some time now been promoting the idea of national service for all young people, and recently Terrell Bell's AASCU Commission on the Future of State Colleges and Universities called on institutions to incorporate some form of public or community service as a regular part of their undergraduate programs. Similarly, Ernest Boyer, in his recent book, *College*, advocates a renewal of commitment to the idea of community in higher education. And in my own state, the legislature recently passed a bill requiring the University of

California to establish a "Human Corps" program on its campuses.

The most important thing is for each of us to recognize that there is much that we as individuals can do on our campuses, in spite of our tendency to believe that trying to change an institution is much like trying to move Mount Everest. We can, for example, examine the way we teach our classes, treat our students, and treat our colleagues. And when we have an opportunity to participate in curriculum decisions, long-range planning, and similar kinds of group activities, we can take the initiative to introduce value questions such as "cooperation versus competition" into the deliberations. . . .

July/August 1989

Discussion Method Teaching
How to Make it Work

William M. Welty

. . . Most faculty in American colleges teach what they were taught in the limited ways they were taught. They value content and theory, and they feel the most efficient way to communicate that is by content-laden, theoretically based lectures. Even when they feel uneasy about students who "aren't getting it," there seems no other way. Attempts at discussions degenerate into directionless bull sessions or meaningless debates in which the facts are all wrong and the logic nonexistent. Ideally, we'd all love to teach graduate seminars but face a daily reality of mixed classes of many dozens of "average" undergraduates. So we lecture. What's the alternative?

There *is* a way to energize your classrooms, to excite a much higher percentage of your students, and to add more value to their education. You can get out from behind your lectern and still communicate content and theory—do so better, in fact. But to do this you will have to pay far more attention than you have in the past to teaching *process* questions, to the teaching *methods* you are using.

Most faculty don't know how to begin this activity. What follows here will help you understand discussion based teaching and, perhaps, get you started doing it. . . .

I do not, of course, contend that discussion teaching is the only, or even the best, pedagogical method available to college teachers. Successful college teaching demands that the teacher have available a number of techniques to use at the proper time and in the proper situation to maximize learning. One of those techniques—underused because most faculty do not understand its dynamics—is the discussion.

The particular technique described here is really a first step away from the lecture method of teaching. It is a method for leading a discussion in which a good deal of authority and control remains in the hands of the faculty member and in which a good deal of content and theory is still imparted by him or her as discussion leader.

The authority issue is an important one. Many advocates of discussion method teaching argue that for true learning to take place, the faculty member must relinquish authority and control and seek to empower students so that they are able on a continuing basis to learn for themselves. I do not dispute that goal as an ultimate one, but for the new convert, the approach must provide an orderly transition from the lecture method. Once the process becomes second nature, he or she may then be willing to consider methods that relinquish greater authority to students. This authority issue is an important one—keep it in mind as you grapple with the suggestions that follow.

Preparation before Class . . .

■ **Read the assigned material**—It goes without saying that the teacher must be *very* familiar with the reading assigned for discussion. She must be ready for almost any nuance to be discovered, for almost any connection to be made. The more thinking and reading she does about the assigned material, the better prepared she will be for the discussion about it. . . .

■ **Decide important concepts and outline**— Once you are sure you have a good grasp of the assigned material and its many nuances, . . . decide what important concepts you want to be sure are understood by every student in your class. Ask yourself, "Why did I assign this material?" Important concepts usually have somewhat important subconcepts, and before long we content-theoretical types are several layers deep in important concepts. Such thoughts usually lead to an outline, and soon there emerges a logical pattern that we can hope the discussion will take. Such an outline should make you more comfortable, but be sure the outline reflects in layers or levels what is most important and what is less, for in the heat of a good discussion you will have to discard getting at some of the less important concepts for the sake of making sure the more important ones are really understood.

At this point you should, as well, make notes about specific facts—important people and their relationships, chronology, sets of figures, any particulars that bear on the matters you feel are important. Nothing destroys the attempt to communicate the necessity of reasoning from the facts more than if the discussion leader can't keep the details straight. It is important to communicate this message to your students early in the discussion process, for the euphoria of the free-wheeling exchange of ideas is sometimes so overwhelming that even the best students forget to deal with the concrete aspects of the material.

■ **A question outline**—Once you are sure of your grasp of the facts, prepare a question outline to match your concept outline. It is important at this stage that you carefully think out questions that will promote *discussion*, not answers, about the concepts you want understood. If you are having trouble promoting discussion in your classes now, examine the kinds of questions you are asking. Do they signal that you know the answer and are asking to see if the students do? Such questions are the kind that promote participation from only those students anxious to show they know exactly what the teacher is looking for. The idea of a discussion is to encourage contributions that aren't necessarily the "right" answer, but that can be used to work toward a better understanding of the topic discussed. Most students are programmed to think that there is only one right answer, that the teacher knows it, and that he or she will reward those who know it and punish those who do not. Such thinking spells doom for a discussion class. Serious discussion teachers must work at overcoming this mindset; they must encourage creative and critical thinking, not memorization. Careful, well thought-out questioning is the first step in this process.

Build your question outline at least as many layers deep as your concept outline—one group of very general questions that covers the whole assignment and serves as a macro-outline for the class, then groups of more specific questions about different aspects of the outline that will serve to expose important points. Try to anticipate possible responses to the questions and think through what can be done with them—how they can be used positively—to move the class toward more understanding. Ask smaller questions, action questions, first; work up slowly to more global, thought-provoking questions.

With a general as well as a specific outline of questions to guide your discussion, you must think carefully about the really important questions— beginning, transition, conclusion—and highlight them in your outline. You should know *exactly* what question, word for word, you are going to use at these important times, and perhaps even who you are going to ask. Thinking ahead in such careful detail allows the leader more control over the discussion, something the beginning discussion teacher will probably welcome.

Ask questions, and more questions, and still more questions. If you hear yourself making too many declarative statements, the discussion is not going well. In class, instead of talking, you should be listening and formulating your next question. Think of your lecture as a series of interrogative statements.

■ **A board outline**—A good discussion leader should make use of the blackboard to help organize the discussion, which at times will seem to be going off in all directions. The board, in fact, is another very powerful control mechanism for the discussion leader. You choose what to write on the board and where to write it. . . .

Whatever you write on the board—it can't include everything said in a discussion class—you must think ahead of time just how you want the board to look at various times in the class. Therefore, make a board outline to help guide just what to write down and where. . . .

■ **Knowing your students**—You lead a discussion because you want *students* to learn something—*they* are the important ones in the process. To maximize that learning, you must know each of them as more than a number on your roster. Each learns individually and responds differently to the various stimuli of the discussion class. What are their strengths and weaknesses? What kind of participation will build on their strengths or improve their weaknesses? Think about who to ask certain questions, who to turn to during certain times in the discussion; for that, you need to know what to expect in response. . . .

■ **Looking at the whole semester and the whole institution**—Any single class outline cannot stand alone; it must fit with the plan for the entire semester. Part of this plan must be not only what content to cover, but how the discussion process can be enhanced as the semester progresses. Most of the institutions in which we teach encourage students to be passive in class, and students have been conditioned to model this behavior. Therefore, in planning the semester, remember that you are probably struggling with an institutional culture that discourages active participation. Work up to it slowly and schedule topics and discussions that keep in mind you are reorienting behavior patterns and that this will take more than one class. If you seek to encourage true discussion, you cannot do it by having a discussion here and a discussion there—it has to be a regular and substantial part of the course.

I would suggest a syllabus for a discussion course that errs on the side of complexity and length. I prefer a class-by-class outline that includes several study questions and background readings for each reading assignment to be discussed. The better prepared the participants are, the better the discussion; if the course outline helps this, you have sent the right message.

Physical Setting

. . . Know ahead of time what will be there and what you need to do to improve it.

■ **The ideal**—Let's describe the ideal room for a discussion course: tables and executive-type swivel chairs for the students, arranged in a U-shape; a small table in the front for the instructor; board space on at least two walls; room enough for the instructor to roam around the room.

The U-shape is the single most important environmental factor for the discussion class. It allows all the participants to see each other and promote interchange; it provides space for the leader to use, thus enhancing his authority and control in a situation where many instructors feel powerless. Tables provide the students with a natural protection against the terror of the discussion process. . . . The discussion leader needs enough space to move about the room in order to energize the discussion when it needs it—ideally, enough room to be able to contact physically every student in the room. The discussion leader must also be able to get to the board whenever he wants without stumbling over students and interfering with the discussion flow. . . . I would add to this utopia a name card for each student (tent cards made out of oaktag) so that you can refer to each student by name and so that students can refer to each other by name. For ten cents a student, it does wonders for group cohesion and mutual respect.

■ **Usual situation**— . . .

A discussion class cannot work in a room in which the students are seated in rows all facing an instructor who is barricaded behind a lectern. *The participants must be able to see and to talk to each other; the leader must be able to move quickly to any part of the room and to any student.* In a traditional classroom, all discussion comes at the instructor; *you* want to encourage straight-line communication, from student to student.

If you are confronted with the typical physical environment, come early and move the furniture to approach the ideal described above. If you can't come close to the ideal, be ready to compensate in other ways. If you get stuck in a room with fixed seating, get the room changed someway—the end will justify the means. . . .

The Class

. . . Arrive early enough to get yourself organized in the classroom—chairs moved, boards erased, lecterns moved out of the way, and notes spread on your table.

■ **Beginning the class**—. . . As a transition into the discussion, a short introduction by the instructor—essentially where the assignment fits in with the overall scheme of the course and some general opening remarks about it—usually is in order; but the shorter, the better.

Presumably, you have thought through carefully in your preparation just exactly what question you are going to ask. Your choice at this point is an important process question. Do you want to ask for volunteers or do you want to call on someone? If you decide on calling, you have yet another choice—giving the student some time to think about the question or requiring an answer immediately—cool calls or cold calls, as the jargon goes.

The choice of volunteering versus calling is an important one for the mood of the class. I prefer to stay with volunteers, hoping to play down the sort of recitation syndrome that you get when you have set up a cold or cool call environment. All things being equal, I would want to think that those students who participated wanted to do so because they had something to contribute at the time of the participation, not because I wanted them to participate.

You have to work hard to make the volunteering environment one in which a large number actually do volunteer. Usually the same hands shoot up in response to your first question. In an environment in which everybody expects to be called on, it is easier to encourage the shy and those who need more help in verbalizing their ideas. Also, the larger the class, the more likely you are going to have to force participation, and the earlier you start this in the semester, the easier it is for all concerned.

Cool calling at the beginning of class, therefore, seems a good compromise. Before you do anything else, state your first question, ask a particular student to think about an answer, and ask another student to serve as a backstop. Then go on to your introductory business, and when you get to the discussion, the student has had five or so minutes to think about an answer.

Early in the semester, I begin the class with a question that has accompanied the assignment in the syllabus. As students gain experience in the discussion method, I like to ask a different question, one they haven't specifically thought about in their preparation. The discussion proceeds differently, depending on which of these choices you make.

■ **Questioning, listening, responding**—Now begins the guts of the discussion class. The student, however she got recognized, is talking, and she isn't answering the question in any of the many ways you so painstakingly thought out the night before. How do you respond? Do you write on the board? Do you try to silence her? Do you

correct her? There are no sure answers; expect to feel existential uncertainty.

The key skills at this point are listening skills, a set of behaviors that college faculty probably haven't practiced since graduate school. You will get plenty of practice if you stick with discussion teaching. Make sure at the first level that you are hearing exactly what the speaker is saying. In order to test your hearing, you need to give the speaker some feedback—writing what she says on the board or repeating what she said. Beyond that, one needs to listen to the subtext of the student's words—what she means by what she is saying, what it reveals about what is important to her.

Discussion teachers can learn much from the counseling profession, especially the process called active listening. In that process, you as teacher must communicate back to the speaker that you understand what was said—text and subtext. But beyond that you must communicate what is important to you, the teacher, so that the student and the teacher can work together to take some action—to learn, in this context. The tricky part in the discussion classroom is that you have forty other people who have to be listened to and communicated with, and who must learn as well to practice active listening skills. The better you listen and the better you get all your students to listen, the better by the square of that your discussion will go.

What goes on in the discussion class is a very involved, complex process in which you use questioning, listening, and response activities to shape the discussion toward ends you have chosen. You must intervene at times with a question or a summary or a bridge from an earlier remark to help move the discussion toward your goals. At other times, you must allow discussion to take place without any obvious control on your part. In this sense, this questioning, listening, responding process is your ultimate source of power in the discussion classroom, more important than blackboards, U-shapes, tables, and room to roam. Like a double-edged sword, the power here cuts both ways; it can frighten you enough to make you long for the lectern. But resist temptation! You have thought lots of questions out ahead of time. You have an outline and a board outline on the table near you. You have a good idea where you want the discussion to go and the questions to get it there.

As you use questions and active listening to move the class toward the goal you have set, you have some other objectives to meet as well—which students are understanding, which are not; who needs to be helped, who needs some stroking, who some quieting. In addition, in the concern for keeping the discussion on track, don't force the outline so much that you discourage the free flow of ideas. A good discussion leader in this sense encourages a kind of "controlled spontaneity"—maintaining the right balance between freewheeling discussion and control. I like to think of the discussion process as a set of concepts that the discussion circles around, gets an understanding of from one angle, moves away from for a while, and then returns to from another angle—certainly not a linear process.

The objective, as much as covering your outline, is to engage true discussion, getting the students to talk to each other in a meaningful way. When that begins to happen, back away and let it go: you've created an important moment for learning.

In the final analysis, you've made whatever happens happen, by your use of the questioning, listening, and responding skills. These skills are not going to come overnight. They take practice, in the classroom and out. Find a trusted colleague who will watch you teach and give you some honest feedback. Better yet, have your class videotaped and review it with that trusted colleague.

■ **Body language**—To teach successfully by the discussion method, especially in the physical environment I have suggested, you must learn to make yourself aware of the message your body is communicating. Nothing conveys more clearly to students the boredom and irrelevance of education than a lecturer leaning on his lectern. On the other hand, the successful discussion class is led by a person constantly in motion. With the right space, the discussion leader moves toward a speaker or away; places himself between disagreeing parties or behind one party or the other; rushes to the board to write a telling comment; roams the aisles in search of new participants, or to stir excitement among the alienated, or to see how the board looks from the point of view of the back row. The leader can turn up the intensity by excited movement or calm a class into serious reflection by sitting and letting discussion proceed by itself.

Keep in mind, though, that each movement—each stance you take, where you put your hands, how your face reacts—in short, everything your body does—communicates something to your audience. You must be aware at all times (like an actor on the stage) of what your body is saying. . . .

■ **The board**—As I have suggested, the blackboard is helpful to the discussion process in a number of ways. It can serve to bring order into what seems a disordered discussion. It can be used to reward meaningful contributions. It is an effective summary of the discussion. It forces the leader to move to use it.

You need to have a very good idea before the class just how you want the board to look at various times during the discussion. Do not write on the board haphazardly. Do not make "chicken tracks" on the board. Consider carefully what you want on it before you grab the chalk.

Some examples: you might wish to use the board to symbolize the logic of the discussion by writing things in neat columns from left to right, drawing vertical lines to indicate when to move on to a new topic. Or you might want to take comments on many different ideas early in the discussion, using several boards to record them, allowing more reflective thought later in the discussion to highlight relationships. You might even want the board to communicate disorder. . . . Or, if you want to build a group's confidence that it can understand a difficult subject, fill the board with well-organized detail.

■ **Sense of time**—One of the most difficult things to control in a discussion is time—nothing seems to disappear so quickly in a good discussion and to last so long in a poor one.

Every discussion plan should have a beginning, a middle, and an end, with time targets for each thought out ahead of time. You have a given amount of time at your disposal. How much will you spend on each major part of your outline? . . .

If the period allotted is more than two hours, think seriously of planning a break, keeping in mind that unless planned for, a break often destroys a discussion, making it very difficult to pick up again. If you have a long period scheduled for one topic, think about a group activity as a more natural kind of break.

■ **Group work**—There is a natural hierarchy in discussion classes, from individual preparation, to small group, to class. At each stage, insights are added that were not apparent at the earlier stage. Class discussions improve if preceded by leaderless small-group sessions. Scheduling those is a problem, but if the subject matter or particular issue seems to lend itself, it is often worth the trouble. If students are having trouble with the discussion format, organize smaller study-group discussions before class. Small groups are a place where strong students can help weak students and shy students can more comfortably contribute — behaviors you want to encourage.

■ **Ending the class** — Discussion classes generally require that the leader formally end the class by summing up the discussion and stating its larger meaning, in terms of theory and relationship to the rest of the course. Sometimes, however, you might want the discussion to end without this, sending the participants away frustrated or with a sense of confusion, hoping that out of that might spring some independent work to clear up the confusion.

Like other aspects of discussion pedagogy, the end-of-class summary has costs and benefits. You want to give some direction to the discussion, but not so much as to drive out individual creativity and risk taking. You want to convey some theory, but not so much as to suggest that every question has a right answer that can be derived from that theory. Our classes should be rich and full of excitement and content learning, but in the final analysis we want to empower our students to learn on a continuous basis, and much of that activity has to be self-directed. Therefore, think carefully ahead of time whether you want to sum up and how you want to do it.

If you decide on a mini-lecture, make it a good one. If you decide the topic lends itself to more reading, this is the time for suggested bibliography. In business cases, students always want to know "what happened?" Sensing long ago that they were really searching for the "right answer," I usually resist revealing it, suggesting instead that they go to the sources and find out, and allowing for time to be reserved at the beginning of the next class if any want to report their findings. There are usually several reports. You need also to allow yourself time at the end of class to say a few things about the next discussion assignment. Perhaps it needs added emphasis on a certain preparation or hints as to where to go for help in making sense out of it. Certainly, words need to be said as to how the class just ending will relate to the next.

After Class

The after-class press of students looking for individual help, and your rush to get to another class or meeting, sometimes prevents the very important debriefing activity necessary for every discussion class. Before you get out of the room, take a good look at the board to see what the final result looks like and how it compares to your outline. Ask yourself what was covered well, what not so well, and what was missed. What questions worked and which ones failed? Make notes for yourself as to how you might revise the next time.

Shortly after the class ends, too, you need to go over each of the students in class and note how they did in the discussion. This needs to be done for several reasons — to help in your judgment of them, to help get to know them better, and, most importantly, to help you think about strategies that will help them get more out of future classes.

Grading classroom participation is another of those very sticky problems for the discussion teacher. To encourage participation you probably have to do it, but be aware of its costs. Trained as we are to grade written work, most of us have no idea how to judge verbal. Do you reward a student who talks a lot but says little? Do you penalize a student for trying out new ideas that are badly off-track? What about the student who just won't or just can't seem to make any contribution? These are tough issues that go to the heart of the discussion-class dilemma.

I grade participation, but I can't quantify it very well. I try to reward continuous, informed participation throughout the semester. I try to talk individually with those who do not seem to be participating, either to encourage some participation or to understand why there is none. In the final analysis, grading is one of those issues that needs to be discussed with peers. . . .

How to Start . . .

In the work I do with faculty, I stress that we all should get help from several different sources. First, watch an experienced discussion teacher teach. Sit in on *several* of her classes. Be sure you have read the assigned material before you sit in. Talk with her after class, emphasizing the methodological questions. Second, get somebody you trust to sit in on your classes and give you some honest feedback. To enrich this discussion, have the class videotaped so that both of you can see what is happening while you are discussing it. Third, form a discussion group with other interested faculty to share ideas and to talk out the important teaching issues that are highlighted by the discussion method and by your thinking about the process of teaching. I have used a series of cases about teachers in discussion classes to organize this process. Fourth, seek the feedback of your students, either in formal or informal discussion, or with some well-formulated written mechanism. Find out from them whether they think they are really learning more and enjoying it more.

Finally, practice, practice, practice. And become your own best critic.

January/February 1994

Living With Myths
Undergraduate Education in America

Patrick T. Terenzini and Ernest T. Pascarella

In early civilizations, myths played important roles in people's lives, bringing order to what would otherwise have been a chaotic and uninterpretable world. The Greeks *had* to have *some* plausible explanation for the passage of the sun across the heavens. But when myths continue to guide thought and action, despite evidence that they are without empirical foundation, they become dysfunctional and counterproductive. Persistence in the belief that the sun is actually Apollo's chariot passing across the heavens forecloses geocentric and heliocentric explanations of the movements of the sun and other heavenly bodies.

Does higher education have its own dysfunctional myths? From 1985 to 1990, we reviewed some 2,600 books, book chapters, monographs, journal articles, technical reports, conference papers, and research reports produced over the past two decades describing the effects of college on students (Pascarella and Terenzini, 1991). Based on that literature, we can identify at least five myths about undergraduate education in America. Faculty members and administrators alike embrace these myths, which structure how we think about and design undergraduate educational programs. The evidence also suggests these myths may impede the improvement of teaching and learning in our colleges and universities.

Myth Number 1: Institutional prestige and reputation reflect educational quality.

Most people believe that, for any given student, going to an institution with all (or most) of the conventionally accepted earmarks of "quality" will lead to greater learning and development. The fact of the matter is that it probably won't.

The evidence on this point is strikingly clear and cuts across a wide array of educational outcomes, including gains in verbal, quantitative, and subject-matter competence; growth in cognitive complexity and the development of intellectual skills; educationally desirable changes in a wide range of psychosocial traits, attitudes, and values; and the emergence of principled moral reasoning. Across all these outcomes, the net impact of attending (versus not attending) college tends to be substantially more pronounced than the impact attributable to attending one kind of institution rather than another.

After taking into account the characteristics, abilities, and backgrounds students bring with them to college, we found that how much students grow or change has only inconsistent and, perhaps in a practical sense, trivial relationships with such traditional measures of institutional "quality" as educational expenditures per student, student/faculty ratios, faculty salaries, percentage of faculty with the highest degree in their field, faculty research productivity, size of the library, admissions selectivity, or prestige rankings. Even when taking into account several methodological considerations that might partially explain this finding, the evidence is still persuasive: similarities across kinds of colleges substantially outnumber and outweigh their differences in terms of their effects on student learning and other educational outcomes.

It is important to be clear about two things we are *not* saying. First, we are not suggesting that graduates of all colleges have reached the same level of academic achievement or psychosocial development. The evidence suggests nothing of the kind. Indeed, after four years, the graduates of some colleges reach a level of achievement or development approximately equal to that of freshmen entering some other institutions. The point to remember is that differences across institutions in levels of student performance on outcomes measures (e.g., Graduate Record Examination scores) are attributable not so much to the institutions attended as to the kinds of students who enroll at those institutions in the first place. Most schools that *graduate* high-performing students also *admit* high-performing students.

Second, we are not saying that *any given institution* has no greater educational impact than any other. Indeed, certain individual institutions probably combine many or most of the things that *are* related to student learning and development (see below) into particularly potent educational programs and environments. Our point is that it is hardly possible to identify the most educationally effective institutions by relying simply on the resource dimensions traditionally used to judge or rank institutions for "educational quality." These widely used indicators of college quality are, more appropriately, measures of institutional advantage. They may look good and have intuitive appeal, but they reveal little of substance in terms of educational impact.

The evidence we reviewed strongly suggests that *real* quality in undergraduate education resides more in an institution's educational climate and in what it does programmatically than in its stock of human, financial, and educational resources. That is not to say that resources are irrelevant, but that to understand educational quality one must look beyond the obvious and easy measures of institutional wealth, resource availability, and advantage. One must look at factors such as

1) the nature and cohesiveness of students' curricular experiences;

2) their course-taking patterns;

3) the quality of teaching they receive and the extent to which faculty members involve students actively in the teaching-learning process;

4) the frequency, purpose, and quality of students' non-classroom interactions with faculty members;

5) the nature of their peer group interactions and extracurricular activities; and

6) the extent to which institutional structures promote cohesive environments that value the life of the mind and high degrees of student academic and social involvement.

What happens to a student *after* arrival on campus makes a markedly greater difference in what and how much students learn than the prestige, reputations, or resources of the institution. The questionable relevance of the characteristics we conventionally use to differentiate among institutions leads us to ask more about what our colleges do that *does* make a difference. That brings us to a second myth.

Myth Number 2: Traditional methods of instruction provide proven, effective ways of teaching undergraduate students.

Lecturing is the overwhelming method of choice for teaching undergraduates in most institutions. One study (Pollio, 1984), for example, found that teachers in the typical classroom spent about 80 percent of their time lecturing to students who were attentive to what was being said about 50 percent of the time. The evidence we reviewed is clear that the lecture/discussion mode of instruction is not *in*effective (indeed, we estimate average freshman-senior gains of 20–35 percentile points across a range of content and academic/cognitive skill areas). But the evidence is equally clear that these conventional methods are *not* as effective as some other, far less frequently used methods.

Long trails of research suggest that certain individualized instructional approaches are consistently more effective in enhancing subject-matter learning than are the more traditional approaches. These more effective approaches emphasize small, modularized units of content, student mastery of one unit before moving to the next, immediate and frequent feedback to students on their progress, and active student involvement in the learning process.

Of the five individualized instructional approaches we reviewed, four of them (audio-tutorial, computer-based, programmed, and visual-based instruction) showed statistically significant learning advantages of 6–10 percentile points over traditional approaches. The fifth method, the Personalized System of Instruction (PSI, or "Keller

Plan") approach, produced an average learning advantage of 19 percentile points, approximately twice as large as any of the other forms of individualized instruction. (PSI involves small, modularized units of instruction, study guides, mastery orientation and immediate feedback on unit tests, self-pacing through the material, student proctors to help with individual problems, and occasional lectures for motivation.)

The differences in effectiveness between individualized and conventional methods of instruction probably have multiple sources, but two are prominent. First, the lecture/discussion format rests on several assumptions:

1) that all students are equally prepared for the course;

2) that all students learn at the same rate;

3) that all students learn in the same way and through the same set of activities; and

4) that differences in performance are more likely due to differences in student effort or ability than to the faultiness of any of the foregoing assumptions.

If these assumptions are valid, why *not* deliver course material at the same pace and in the same fashion to all students?

Despite the fact that the research evidence, personal experience, and common sense all suggest these assumptions are untenable, most faculty members persist in teaching (and academic administrators encourage it) as if they were true. Individualized and collaborative approaches to instruction are more effective because they respond better to differences in students' levels of preparation, learning styles, and rates.

Second, in contrast to the passive roles students are encouraged to play in most lecture/discussion classes, individualized and collaborative teaching approaches require active student involvement and participation in the teaching-learning process. Such methods encourage students to take greater responsibility for their own learning; they learn from one another, as well as from the instructor. The research literature indicates active learning produces greater gains in academic content and skills; it clearly supports efforts to employ various forms of "collaborative learning."

Myth Number 3: The good teachers are good researchers.

One of the most frequent criticisms of undergraduate education today is that faculty members spend too much time on research at the expense of their teaching. The typical defense against this charge is that faculty members must do research in order to be good teachers. Faculty members who are researchers, so the argument goes, are more likely to be "on the cutting edge" in their disciplines; they pass their enthusiasm for learning on to their students. This faith in the instructional benefits of research is, of course, reflected in our faculty reward structures.

Proponents of the good-researchers-make-good-teachers point of view usually argue by anecdote; they cite faculty members who are noted scholars and who bring their research to the classroom, there (presumably) intellectually energizing their students. We do not doubt the existence of such faculty members. Indeed, most of us can think of individuals who are both outstanding scholars and extraordinary teachers. But such people are probably outstanding in most every academic thing they do, and the reason they come to mind is precisely because they *are* extraordinary. And one wonders: is exposure to these exceptional individuals a part of the experience of most undergraduates in today's universities?

The available empirical evidence calls the "good-researcher = good-teacher" argument sharply into question. Our review indicates that, at best, the association between ratings of undergraduate instruction and scholarly productivity is a small, positive one, with correlations in the .10 to .16 range.

In the most comprehensive literature review on this issue, Feldman (1987) reviewed more than 40 studies of the relation between faculty productivity or scholarly accomplishment and instructional effectiveness (as perceived by students). He found the average correlation between scholarly productivity or accomplishment and instructional effectiveness to be +.12. Put another way, scholarly productivity and instructional effectiveness have less than 2 percent of their variance in common. That means that about 98 percent of the variability in measures of instructional effectiveness is due to something *other* than research productivity or accomplishment. Feldman concluded that "in general, the likelihood that research productivity actually benefits teaching is extremely small or [alternatively] that the two, for all practical purposes, are essentially unrelated." It is worth noting, however, as Feldman points out, that if the evidence does not support the good-researcher = good-teacher argument, neither does it support claims that doing research *detracts* from being an effective teacher.

So long as the myth that research and teaching are closely and positively related persists, promotion and tenure decisions will continue to be made on the presumption that an institution can have the best of both worlds by allowing research productivity to dominate the faculty reward structure. Why bother to scrutinize *both* the teaching and research abilities of candidates for appointment, promotion, and tenure if looking mostly at the one will do? Find and reward good researchers, the logic goes, and chances are high you'll find and reward a good teacher.

Where the belief persists that research and teaching effectiveness are opposed to one another, proposed "reforms" of teaching will focus on quantitative solutions, on how *much* faculty members are required to teach rather than on how *well* they do it. Many statehouses and coordinating agencies are busy passing faculty workload policies that will require all full-time faculty members to teach a minimum number of credit hours. Such policies are likely to be counterproductive. There's no reason to believe that teaching more courses will result in better instruction. Moreover, since time is a finite commodity, such policies are likely to reduce the amount of research being done, in many cases by the country's best researchers.

In neither case is the teaching of undergraduates likely to improve. Teaching and research appear to be more or less independent activities. Each is essential to the mission of most of our colleges and universities, and each deserves recognition and reward. Until the good-researcher = good-teacher myth is put to rest, however, the research on effective teaching methods will continue to be ignored, reward structures will continue to go unexamined, good researchers will be excused for marginally competent teaching, and good teachers who do not publish will continue to be denied tenure. As for undergraduate instruction, it will be business as usual.

Somehow, as college and university faculty and academic administrators, we must get beyond the smoke of this long-standing myth and turn our energies to what *really* makes a difference in helping students learn. That leads to a fourth myth.

Myth Number 4: Faculty members influence student learning only in the classroom.

Many faculty members and more than a few administrators appear to believe that faculty obligations to contribute to the education of undergraduate students begin and end at the classroom or laboratory door. If these obligations extend beyond the classroom at all, it is only to the faculty member's office, to class-related questions or academic advising. Faculty workload policies and reward systems implicitly support this narrow conception of the faculty member's sphere of influence. The research literature does not.

What a host of studies demonstrate is that faculty exert much influence in their out-of-class (as well as in-class) contacts with students. "Instruction," therefore, must be understood more broadly to include the important teaching that faculty members do both inside and outside their classrooms.

As a backdrop, remember that as much as 85 percent of a student's waking hours are spent *outside* a classroom. Common sense should tell us that educational programs and activities that address only 15 percent of students' time are needlessly myopic. What the research tells us is that a large part of the impact of college is determined by the extent and content of students' interactions with the major agents of socialization on campus: faculty members and student peers. Further, faculty members' educational influence appears to be significantly enhanced when their contacts with students extend *beyond* the formal classroom to informal non-classroom settings.

More particularly, controlling for student background characteristics, the extent of students' informal contact with faculty is positively linked with a wide array of outcomes. These include perceptions of intellectual growth during college, increases in intellectual orientation and curiosity, liberalization of social and political values, growth in autonomy and independence, increases in interpersonal skills, gains in general maturity and personal development, orientation toward a scholarly career, educational aspirations, persistence, educational attainment, and women's interest in, and choice of, a sex-atypical (male-dominated) career field. It also appears that the impact of student-faculty informal contact is determined by its content as well as by its frequency; the most influential forms of interaction appear to be those that focus on ideas or intellectual matters, thereby extending and reinforcing academic goals.

Some faculty members consider informal, out-of-class contact with students to be "coddling" or (worse) irrelevant or inappropriate to the role of a faculty member. Such views reflect, at best, little knowledge of effective educational practices and of how students learn, and, at worst, a callous disregard. "Talk with students as persons outside of class? That's the dean of students' job": behind this attitude lies still another myth.

Myth Number 5: Students' academic and non-academic experiences are separate and unrelated areas of influence on learning.

Most theoretical models of student learning and development in no way suggest, much less guarantee, that any *single* experience—or class of experiences—will be a crucial determinant of change for students. Our review of the evidence indicates that the impact of particular within-college experiences (e.g., academic major, interactions with faculty, living on- or off-campus, interactions with peers) tends to be smaller than the overall net effect of attending (versus not attending) college. That same evidence suggests that a majority of the important changes that occur during college are probably the *cumulative* result of a set of interrelated and mutually supporting experiences, in class and out, sustained over an extended period of time.

To break this out further, the evidence shows that, compared to freshmen, seniors have a greater capacity for abstract or symbolic reasoning, solving puzzles within a scientific paradigm, intellectual flexibility, organizing and manipulating cognitive complexity, and using reason and evidence to address issues for which there are no verifiably correct answers (e.g., dealing with toxic waste, capital punishment, abortion, or even buying a used car). Students, however, not only become more cognitively advanced (i.e., become better learners), they also demonstrate *concurrent* changes in values, attitudes, and psychosocial development that are consistent with and probably reciprocally related to cognitive change. While there is insufficient evidence to conclude that changes in some areas actually *cause* changes in other areas, it is nonetheless abundantly clear that documented change in

nearly every outcome area appears to be embedded within an interconnected and perhaps mutually reinforcing network of cognitive, value, attitudinal, and psychosocial changes—all of which develop during the student's college experience. In short, the student changes as a *whole, integrated* person during college. (All these changes *may* be independent of one another, but we doubt it.)

Moreover, while intellectual growth may be primarily a function of the student's academic involvement and effort, the content and focus of that same student's interpersonal and extracurricular involvements can have a mediating influence on that growth, either promoting or inhibiting it. In some areas of intellectual development (such as critical thinking), for example, the evidence suggests it is the *breadth* of student involvement in the intellectual *and* social experiences of college, and not any particular type of involvement, that counts most. Thus, although the weight of evidence indicates that the links between involvement and change tend to be specific, the greatest impact may stem from the student's *total* level of campus engagement, particularly when academic, interpersonal, and extracurricular involvements are mutually supporting and relevant to a particular educational outcome.

The Campus' Role

What we've just said stresses the importance of individual student effort and involvement as a determinant of college impact, but it in *no* way means that particular campus policies or programs are unimportant. Quite the contrary. If individual effort or involvement is the linchpin for college impact, then a key matter becomes how a campus can shape its intellectual and interpersonal environments in ways that do indeed encourage student involvement.

The research on within-college effects suggests programmatic and policy levers. For example, we have long known that students living on-campus enjoy larger and more varied benefits of college attendance than do commuting students. A college might usefully ask, how can the most educationally potent characteristics of the residential experience (e.g., frequent academic and social interaction among students, contact with faculty members, more opportunities for academic and social involvement with the institution) be made more readily available to students who commute?

Research on the impacts of student residence

offers more clues. Considerable evidence suggests discernible differences in the social and intellectual climates of different residence halls on the same campus; halls with the strongest impacts on cognitive development and persistence are typically the result of *purposeful, programmatic* efforts to integrate students' intellectual and social lives during college—living-learning centers are not only a neat idea, they actually work! On relatively few campuses, however, are such programs available to students today.

Plenty of other ways exist for integrating students' classroom and non-classroom experiences in ways that reasonably reflect how students learn. While a discussion of those ways is beyond the scope of this article, it is useful here to return to our first finding, that the impact of college is more general than specific, more cumulative and catalytic. *Real* college impact is likely to come not from pulling any grand, specific (and probably expensive) policy or programmatic lever, but rather from pulling a number of smaller, *interrelated* academic and social levers more often. If a college's effects are varied and cumulative, then its approaches to enhancing those effects must be varied and cumulative, too, and coordinated.

Academic Affairs/Student Affairs

There is an organizational analog to Myth Number 5, that students' academic and non-academic experiences are separate and independent sources of influence on student learning. Since 1870, when Harvard's Charles William Eliot appointed Ephraim Gurney "to take the burden of discipline off President Eliot's shoulders" (Brubacher and Rudy, 1968), the academic affairs and student affairs functions of most institutions have been running essentially on parallel but separate tracks: academic affairs tends to students' cognitive development while student affairs ministers to their affective growth.

This bureaucratization of collegiate structures is a creature of administrative convenience and budgetary expedience. It surely has not evolved from any conception of how students learn, nor is it supported by research evidence. Organizationally and operationally, we've lost sight of the forest.

If undergraduate education is to be enhanced, faculty members, joined by academic and student affairs administrators, must devise ways to deliver undergraduate education that are as comprehensive and integrated as the ways students actually learn. A whole new mindset is needed to capitalize on the interrelatedness of the in- and out-of-class influences on student learning and the functional interconnectedness of academic and student affairs divisions.

In describing her efforts to bring together the activities of inner-city schools, social agencies, and neighborhoods to meet the basic physical, developmental, and educational needs of inner-city children, Cicely Tyson cites a suggestive African proverb: "It takes a whole village to raise a child."

John F. Kennedy stated that "the great enemy of truth is very often not the lie—deliberate, contrived and dishonest—but the myth, persistent, persuasive and unrealistic" (Schlesinger, 1965). It is time we put to use what we know with some confidence about what constitutes effective teaching and learning and put to rest educational myths that have outlived their usefulness.

Works Cited

Brubacher, J. S., and W. Rudy. *Higher Education in Transition: A History of American Colleges and Universities, 1636–1968* (Rev. Ed.), New York: Harper & Row, 1968.

Feldman, K. A. "Research Productivity and Scholarly Accomplishment of College Teachers as Related to Their Instructional Effectiveness: A Review and Exploration," *Research in Higher Education*, Vol. 27, 1987, pages 227–298.

Pascarella, Ernest T. and Patrick T. Terenzini. *How College Affects Students: Findings and Insights from Twenty Years of Research*, San Francisco: Jossey-Bass, 1991.

Pollio, H. *What Students Think About and Do in College Lecture Classes*, Teaching-Learning Issues, No. 53, Knoxville, TN: University of Tennessee, Learning Research Center, 1984.

Schlesinger, A. M., Jr. *A Thousand Days: John F. Kennedy in the White House*, Boston: Houghton Mifflin, 1965.

From Teaching to Learning

A New Paradigm for Undergraduate Education

Robert B. Barr and John Tagg

... A paradigm shift is taking hold in American higher education. In its briefest form, the paradigm that has governed our colleges is this: A college is an institution that exists *to provide instruction*. Subtly but profoundly we are shifting to a new paradigm: A college is an institution that exists *to produce learning*. This shift changes everything. It is both needed and wanted.

We call the traditional dominant paradigm the "Instruction Paradigm." Under it, colleges have created complex structures to provide for the activity of teaching conceived primarily as delivering 50-minute lectures—the mission of a college is to deliver instruction.

Now, however, we are beginning to recognize that our dominant paradigm mistakes a means for

Chart 1 **Comparing Educational Paradigms**

The Instruction Paradigm	The Learning Paradigm
Mission and Purposes	
• Provide/deliver instruction	• Produce learning
• Transfer knowledge from faculty to students	• Elicit student discovery and construction of knowledge
• Offer courses and programs	• Create powerful learning environments
• Improve the quality of instruction	• Improve the quality of learning
• Achieve access for diverse students	• Achieve success for diverse students
Criteria for Success	
• Inputs, resources	• Learning and student-success outcomes
• Quality of entering students	• Quality of exiting students
• Curriculum development, expansion	• Learning technologies development, expansion
• Quantity and quality of resources	• Quantity and quality of outcomes
• Enrollment, revenue growth	• Aggregate learning growth, efficiency
• Quality of faculty, instruction	• Quality of students, learning
Teaching/Learning Structures	
• Atomistic; parts prior to whole	• Holistic; whole prior to parts
• Time held constant, learning varies	• Learning held constant, time varies
• 50-minute lecture, 3-unit course	• Learning environments
• Classes start/end at same time	• Environment ready when student is
• One teacher, one classroom	• Whatever learning experience works
• Independent disciplines, departments	• Cross discipline/department collaboration
• Covering material	• Specified learning results
• End-of-course assessment	• Pre/during/post assessments
• Grading within classes by instructors	• External evaluations of learning
• Private assessment	• Public assessment
• Degree equals accumulated credit hours	• Degree equals demonstrated knowledge and skills

an end. It takes the means or method—called "instruction" or "teaching"—and makes it the college's end or purpose. To say that the purpose of colleges is to provide instruction is like saying that General Motors' business is to operate assembly lines or that the purpose of medical care is to fill hospital beds. We now see that our mission is not instruction but rather that of producing *learning* with every student by *whatever* means work best. . . .

Just as importantly, the Instruction Paradigm rests on conceptions of teaching that are increasingly recognized as ineffective. As Alan Guskin pointed out in a September/October 1994 *Change* article premised on the shift from teaching to learning, "the primary learning environment for undergraduate students, the fairly passive lecture-discussion format where faculty talk and most students listen, is contrary to almost every principle of optimal settings for student learning." The Learning Paradigm ends the lecture's privileged position, honoring in its place whatever approaches serve best to prompt learning of particular knowledge by particular students.

The Learning Paradigm also opens up the truly inspiring goal that each graduating class learns more than the previous graduating class. In other words, the Learning Paradigm envisions the institution itself as a learner—over time, it continuously learns how to produce more learning with each graduating class, each entering student. . . .

Chart 1 **continued**

The Instruction Paradigm	The Learning Paradigm
Learning Theory	
• Knowledge exists "out there"	• Knowledge exists in each person's mind and is shaped by individual experience
• Knowledge comes in "chunks" and "bits" delivered by instructors	• Knowledge is constructed, created, and "gotten"
• Learning is cumulative and linear	• Learning is a nesting and interacting of frameworks
• Fits the storehouse of knowledge metaphor	• Fits learning how to ride a bicycle metaphor
• Learning is teacher centered and controlled	• Learning is student centered and controlled
• "Live" teacher, "live" students required	• "Active" learner required, but not "live" teacher
• The classroom and learning are competitive and individualistic	• Learning environments and learning are cooperative, collaborative, and supportive
• Talent and ability are rare	• Talent and ability are abundant
Productivity/Funding	
• Definition of productivity: cost per hour of instruction per student	• Definition of productivity: cost per unit of learning per student
• Funding for hours of instruction	• Funding for learning outcomes
Nature of Roles	
• Faculty are primarily lecturers	• Faculty are primarily designers of learning methods and environments
• Faculty and students act independently and in isolation	• Faculty and students work in teams with each other and other staff
• Teachers classify and sort students	• Teachers develop every student's competencies and talents
• Staff serve/support faculty and the process of instruction	• All staff are educators who produce student learning and success
• Any expert can teach	• Empowering learning is challenging and complex
• Line governance; independent actors	• Shared governance; teamwork

... [F]or two decades the response to calls for reform from national commissions and task forces generally has been an attempt to address the issues *within the framework of the Instruction Paradigm*. The movements thus generated have most often failed, undone by the contradictions within the traditional paradigm. For example, if students are not learning to solve problems or think critically, the old logic says we must teach a class in thinking and make it a general education requirement. The logic is all too circular: What students are learning in the classroom doesn't address their needs or ours; therefore, we must bring them back into another classroom and instruct them some more. The result is never what we hope for because, as Richard Paul, director of the Center for Critical Thinking observes glumly, "critical thinking is taught in the same way that other courses have traditionally been taught, with an excess of lecture and insufficient time for practice."

To see what the Instruction Paradigm is we need only look at the structures and behaviors of our colleges and infer the governing principles and beliefs they reflect. But it is much more difficult to see the Learning Paradigm, which has yet to find complete expression in the structures and processes of any college. So we must imagine it. (See Chart I, above.) ...

That such a restructuring is needed is beyond question: the gap between what we *say* we want of higher education and what its structures *provide* has never been wider. To use a distinction made by Chris Argyris and Donald Schön, the difference between our espoused theory and our theory-in-use is becoming distressingly noticeable. An "espoused theory," readers will recall, is the set of principles people offer to explain their behavior; the principles we can infer from how people or their organizations actually behave is their "theory-in-use." Right now, the Instruction Paradigm is our theory-in-use, yet the *espoused* theories of most educators more closely resemble components of the Learning Paradigm. The more we discover about how the mind works and how students learn, the greater the disparity between what we say and what we do. Thus so many of us feel increasingly constrained by a system increasingly at variance with what we believe. To build the colleges we need for the 21st century—to put our minds where our hearts are, and rejoin acts with beliefs—we must consciously reject the Instruction Paradigm and restructure what we do on the basis of the Learning Paradigm. ...

January/February 1997

John Dewey
A Voice That Still Speaks to Us

David Halliburton

In a recent *AAHE Bulletin* article, a university administrator echoed John Dewey by calling for closer ties between the academy and the larger community, while on the same page a senior professor uttered a Deweyan call "to create ways of reconnecting with one another that fit the way we now live." In these as in many other instances, Dewey's still-timely voice is reaching listeners who are either new to his ideas or newly receptive to them.

A surge of scholarly interest, beginning in the 1980s, has led major presses to publish several ambitious studies of Dewey; this decade, his *Democracy and Education* is being read in 25 languages. The similarity between our 1990s and his 1890s is another factor in our growing sense of Dewey's timeliness. Now, as then, the hungry and the homeless challenge social resources; crime, drugs, and poverty plague overcrowded cities; and school systems struggle to provide immigrant children with the education they need to survive. In that period and ever since, Dewey, speaking as our most public and intellectual of public intellectuals, has left us a host of ideas on which to reflect.

The Public Intellectual

. . . Speaking to an American Federation of Labor local that he helped to launch, Dewey worried "about the effort of the big power trusts to control education both in public and private schools. We know that the instructions that went out to the publicity agents were to get hold of two things specially, the press and the schools." . . .

As a sort of publicist himself, Dewey took an interest in the rise of public opinion. The modern state, he observed, "rests upon . . . that impalpable thing called public opinion," the control of which "is the greatest weapon of anti-social forces" and which only an "informed publicity" could effectively resist. Unfortunately, informed public opinion is often in short supply, and "where there is not public opinion . . . our affairs remain very largely in the hands of bosses. . . ."

Informed public opinion presupposes, in turn, success in public education; but the image of education that Dewey envisaged when these remarks were made was largely negative. To illustrate bad teaching, he told the true story of a man who taught swimming without letting any pupils into the pool. One maverick plunged in anyway, and when asked what had happened, the teacher replied that the student had sunk. In the majority of schools things weren't necessarily better. Reliance on rote learning, recitation, and discipline—in these and other ways education had gone so wrong that Dewey imagined students suing their schools for educational malpractice.

By 1916, Dewey felt that the country had reached "a turning point . . . where we need a more carefully thought out constructive policy regarding public education and the duties and responsibilities that fall upon it in connection with our national life." . . .

Educating for Democracy

In a celebrated essay called "My Pedagogic Creed," Dewey held forth on these and related issues.

Participation. Dewey believed "that all education proceeds by the participation of the individual in the social consciousness of the race." In addition to reinforcing the concept of participation, this statement underlines the connection between civil society and the individual, a connection that Herbert Hoover's "rugged individualism," for example, endeavors to erase or hide. Dewey's individual is, to borrow from his colleague G. H. Mead, an essentially social individual.

Environment. "I believe that the only true education comes through the stimulation of the child's powers by the demands of the social situations in which he finds himself," wrote Dewey. Situation is a synonym for milieu or environment, the social medium by means of which education takes place—its background, or surroundings. But it is much more: "Human nature exists and operates in an environment. And it is not 'in' that environment as coins are in a box, but as a plant is in the sunlight and soil. It is of them, continuous with their energies, dependent upon their support, capable of increase only as it utilizes them, and as it gradually rebuilds from their crude indifference an environment genially civilized."

In a sense, this environment is like the air we breathe. Thus, Dewey speaks of it as "circumambient atmosphere" to which we become unconsciously habituated, as residents of a city become habituated to their neighborhood. It is "that underlying intangible thing which we call atmosphere and spirit," something in which we become "saturated."

Service. Sounding a contemporary note, Dewey suggested civic education, "the art of thus giving shape to human powers and adapting them to social service, is the supreme art. . . ." Further, he believed "that every teacher . . . is a social servant set apart for the maintenance of proper social order and the securing of the right social growth." Reverting to the sermon mode, Dewey avowed "that in this way the teacher always is the prophet of the true God and the usherer in of the true Kingdom of God."

In a more down-to-earth vein, Dewey argued during World War I that American youngsters could help the national effort more by working on farms than by military training. Farm work "enables the teacher to help evolve in the growing generation the idea of universal service in the great battle of man against nature. . . . It gives a chance for the expression of the idea of service to one's country which is not of the destructive kind."

Experience. In 1897, the year of the pedagogic creed, Dewey was more explicit about action than experience, but the importance of experience is everywhere assumed in this and many other texts. By the time of *Democracy and Education* (1916), experience is rarely, if ever, out of sight. It is crucial to the learning process, as Dewey explained, because "the initial stage of that developing experience which is called thinking is experience." Experience brings people together in civic association and participation to the degree that when we speak of the life of a community we are speaking of its experience: "The continuity of any experience, through renewing of the social group, is a literal fact. Education . . . is the means of this social continuity of life."

Community. The school, the family, the political party, and the general public all constitute communities. The particular job of the educational community, as Dewey saw it, was to overcome ever-competitive individualism with interactive cooperation, and this presupposed participation. "Mere instruction that is not accompanied with direct participation in school affairs upon a genuine community basis will not go far . . . ," wrote Dewey. "This participation should extend beyond the school and include an active part in some phases of the larger community life."

Cooperative learning in a school environment might involve working with your hands, interpreting experiences, or teaming up on a class project. But in-school activities represented only one part of the picture, since education owes much to the larger community: "the level and style of the arts of literature, poetry, ceremony, amusement, and recreation which obtain in a community . . . do more than all else to determine the current direction of ideas and endeavors in the community."

Dewey omitted reference to religious implications, presumably because community no longer fell clearly within the spiritual domain: "the office of religion as sense of community and one's place in it has been lost." In the broadest sense, community is ultimately what religion is, namely, a sense of a meaningful whole, and belief in such a whole is not without its compensations: "Within the flickering inconsequential acts of separate selves dwells a sense of the whole which claims and dignifies them. In its presence we put off mortality and live in the universal. The life of the community in which we live and have our being is the fit symbol of this relationship."

Activity. Since "only action really unifies," Dewey once observed that "expressive or constructive activities" should integrate various educational functions. More plainly, "every educative process should begin with doing something," that is, cooking, sewing, manual training. . . ." Educational activity is a hands-on affair and happens interactively, face to face.

Communication. "Of all affairs," Dewey declared, "communication is the most wonderful. That things should be able to pass from the plane of external pushing and pulling to that of revealing themselves to man, and thereby to themselves; and that the fruit of communication should be participation, sharing, is a wonder by the side of which transubstantiation pales."

Communication is the medium through which our words work in formative ways on today's agenda of needs. Communicating enables us to reconstruct: "When communication occurs, all natural events are subject to reconsideration and revision; they are re-adapted to meet the requirements of conversation, whether it be public discourse or that preliminary discourse termed thinking."

Character. In educational terms, how you learn is who you are, and vice versa. For Dewey, character is "that body of active tendencies and interests in the individual which make him open, ready, warm to certain aims, and callous, cold, blind to others, and which accordingly tend to make him acutely aware of and favorable to certain sorts of consequences, and ignorant of or hostile to other consequences."

Of the three types of character traits a student must have, as examined by Dewey, the first is force, or "efficiency in education," meaning roughly the right stuff to get the job done. The second, more intellectual trait is the capacity to judge; although force may be efficient willy nilly, if it is to achieve anything really worthwhile, the person exercising it must have good sense. Besides force and execution, a third, more affective trait is responsiveness: "there must also be a delicate personal responsiveness—there must be an emotional reaction. Indeed, good judgment is impossible without this susceptibility."

Complementing the psychological with the social, Dewey noted that any educational approach worthy of the name must develop "a love of active doing and effective executive capacity. The social aspect of character training is exhibited in the demand that education shall prepare students for an intelligent choice of a calling in which they may be most serviceable to the community."

Equilibrium and Integration. In *Art as Experience*, Dewey argued the need to maintain equilibrium or balance while attempting to integrate the issues listed above. In living together within an environment, human beings, like other organic entities, keep adjusting themselves to their surroundings as a way of adjusting their surroundings to themselves. When this tension is resolved, a state of equilibrium obtains unless or until some desire or need supervenes, whereupon the organism makes new adjustments to close the gap between itself and its surroundings, and so on. But the result is now an *active* equilibrium. In nature, form is arrived at whenever a stable, even though moving, equilibrium is reached. Changes interlock and sustain one another. . . . Because it is active . . . order itself develops."

The entire process, in which Dewey saw a parallel with artistic creativity, is one of participation: "For only when an organism shares in the ordered relations of its environment does it secure the stability essential to living. And when the participation comes after a phase of disruption and conflict, it bears within itself the germs of a consummation akin to the esthetic."

Higher Education. . . . Dewey believed the university to be a kind of organic whole. Indeed, the term *university* derives from *universe* — literally a turning into one. Fittingly, the first universities were cooperative, participatory ventures in which faculty and students effectively acted as one. Dewey carried the sense of wholeness over into his thinking about the relation of his experimental school to the university: "The problem is to unify, to organize, education, to bring all its various factors together, through putting it as a whole into organic union with everyday life."

Dewey sought, though he never managed to supply, a working model of the ways in which learners from the age of four right up to the college and university years could be brought together. As he put it, "We want to bring all things educational together . . . so that it shall be demonstrated to the eye that there is no lower and higher, but simply education."

The Democratic Ideal. James Marsh, a founder of American philosophy, convinced Dewey that American pioneering was not an achievement of loners but a stage in advancement toward a more nearly ideal civil society and democratic community. Noting how Marsh referred continually to the *community* of individuals, Dewey argued that "the essence of our earlier pioneer individualism was not non-social, much less anti-social; it involved no indifference to the claims of society, its working ideal was neighborliness, and mutual service."

Hazarding a working definition of the ideal, Dewey stipulated two essential elements, the first being that democracy should entail "not only more numerous and more varied points of shared common interest, but greater reliance upon the recognition of mutual interest as a factor in social control." The second element of the ideal, he reasoned, required "not only freer interaction between social groups . . . but change in social habit — its continuous readjustment through meeting the new situations produced by varied intercourse. And these two traits are precisely what characterize the democratically constituted society." . . .

. . . In the words of Dewey, "Democracy has to be born anew every generation, and education is its midwife." That is, each generation must regenerate. Education alone provides the necessary conditions for understanding and sympathizing with others; in a complex industrial civilization like ours, people "will not see across and through the walls which separate them, unless they have been trained to do so."

Diversity. Dewey's common faith was in part a faith in cultural pluralism. For Dewey, any democracy worthy of the name must not only embrace all comers, it must help them to participate in its processes and institutions. Dewey rejected outright the proposition that immigrants should abandon their traditions. Rather than serve as a melting pot, he contended that the nation should welcome and even nurture diversity. Rather than drill the population into faceless conformity — the likely consequence of a proposal for universal military service — he advocated a viable institution of national service that should "see to it that all get from one another the best that each strain has to offer from its own tradition and culture."

In a word, Dewey's credo was that everyone

should be free to be democratic in his or her own way; and if that means, in civic terms, the right to speak and to vote as one sees fit, it also means, in educational terms, the right to freedom of thought and inquiry. Putting the matter in even more general terms, Dewey observed that "a progressive society counts individual variations as precious since it finds in them the means of its own growth. Hence a democratic society must, in consistency with its ideal, allow intellectual freedom and the play of diverse gifts and interests in its educational measures."

A final reason for more active participation in educational development is that education, like democracy, is greatly in need of reform, and is thereby an opportunity for "present-day pioneering." . . .

September/October 1997

Community, Conflict, and Ways of Knowing

Ways to Deepen Our Educational Agenda

Parker J. Palmer

. . . Community must become a central concept in ways we teach and learn.

Many communal experiments in pedagogy have been tried in the history of American higher education, and many have fallen by the wayside. And the reason, I think, is simple: The underlying mode of knowing remained the same. You cannot derive communal ways of teaching and learning from an essentially anticommunal mode of knowing. The pedagogy falls apart if the epistemology isn't there to support and sustain it.

The root fallacy in the pedagogy of most of our institutions is that the individual is the agent of knowing and therefore the focus for teaching and learning. We all know that if we draw the lines of instruction in most classrooms, they run singularly from teacher to each individual student. These lines are there for the convenience of the instructor, not for their corporate reality. They do not reveal a complex web of relationships between teacher and students and subject that would look like true community.

Given this focus on the individual in the classroom, competition between individuals for knowledge becomes inevitable. The competitive individualism of the classroom is not simply the function of a social ethic; it reflects a pedagogy that stresses the individual as the prime agent of knowing. But to say the obvious, knowing and learning are *communal* acts. They require many eyes and ears, many observations and experiences. They require a continual cycle of discussion, dis-agreement, and consensus over what has been seen and what it all means. This is the essence of the "community of scholars," and it should be the essence of the classroom as well.

At the core of this communal way of knowing is a primary virtue, one too seldom named when we discuss community or set community against competition. This primary virtue is capacity for creative conflict. It troubles me when we frame the issue as community vs competition, because too often we link competition with conflict, as if conflict were what needed to be eliminated. But there is no knowing without conflict.

Community in the classroom is often advocated as an affective or emotional supplement to cognitive education; the debate often poses the "hard" virtues of cognition against the "soft" virtues of community. My point is that there is very little conflict in American classrooms, and the reason is that the soft virtues of community are lacking there. Without the soft virtues of community, the hard virtues of cognitive teaching and learning will be absent as well. Our ability to confront each other critically and honestly over alleged facts, imputed meanings, or personal biases and prejudices—*that* is the ability impaired by the absence of community. The ethos of competitive individualism breeds silent, *sub rosa*, private combat for personal reward—it's all under the table, it never comes out in the open—that's what competitive individualism is all about. Competitive individualism squelches the kind of conflict I am trying to name. Conflict is open, public, and often very noisy. Competition is a secret, zero-sum game played by individuals for private gain. *Communal conflict* is a public encounter in which the whole group can win by growing. Those of you who have participated in consensus decision making know something of what I mean.

A healthy community, while it may exclude this one-up, one-down thing called competition, includes conflict at its very heart, checking and correcting and enlarging the knowledge of individuals by drawing on the knowledge of the group. Healthy conflict is possible only in the context of supportive community. What prevents conflicts in our classrooms is a simple emotion called fear. It is fear that is in the hearts of teachers as well as students. It is fear of exposure, of appearing ignorant, of being ridiculed. And the only antidote to that fear is a hospitable environment created, for example, by a teacher who knows how to use every remark, no matter how mistaken or seemingly stupid, to upbuild both the individual and the group. When people in a classroom begin to learn that every attempt at truth, no matter how off the mark, is a contribution to the larger search for corporate and consensual truth, they are soon emboldened and empowered to say what they need to say, to expose their ignorance, to do, in short, those things without which learning can't happen.

Community is not opposed to conflict. On the contrary, community is precisely that place where an arena for creative conflict is protected by the compassionate fabric of human caring itself.

If you ask what holds community together, what makes this capacity for relatedness possible, the only honest answer I can give brings me to that dangerous realm called the spiritual. The only answer I can give is that what makes community possible is love.

I would like to think that love is not an entirely alien word in the academy today, because I know that in the great tradition of intellectual life it is not. It is a word very much at home in the academy. The kind of community I am calling for is a community that exists at the heart of knowing, of epistemology, of teaching and learning, of pedagogy; that kind of community depends centrally on two ancient and honorable kinds of love.

The first is love of learning itself. The simple ability to take sheer joy in having a new idea, reaffirming or discarding an old one, connecting two or more notions that had hitherto seemed alien to each other, sheer joy in building images of reality with mere words that now suddenly seem more like mirrors of truth—this is love of learning.

And the second kind of love on which this community depends is love of learners, of those we see every day, who stumble and crumble, who wax hot and cold, who sometimes want truth and sometimes evade it at all costs, but who are in our care, and who—for their sake, ours, and the world's—deserve all the love that the community of teaching and learning has to offer.

July/August 1998

Cooperative Learning Returns to College
What Evidence Is There That It Works?

David W. Johnson, Roger T. Johnson, and Karl A. Smith

. . . There can now be little doubt that cooperative learning is appropriate to higher education; it works. While it is never easy to implement, when all the critical elements are in place, it is very powerful. In this article, we review the theory underlying the use of cooperative learning, the research on it conducted at the college level, and the ways it may be used appropriately in college classes.

What Is Cooperative Learning? . . .

There are still colleges today in which faculty are required to grade on the curve. This norm-referenced approach to student evaluation requires students to *compete* with each other for grades, which has many unfortunate consequences for academic life. Many professors seek to avoid the pitfalls of such competition by using an *individualistic* approach to instruction. Each student's efforts are evaluated on a criterion-referenced basis. Yet students are expected to work individually to accomplish learning goals unrelated to those of the other students.

In contrast to competitive and individualistic learning, students can work together *cooperatively* to accomplish shared learning goals. Each student achieves his or her learning goal if and only if the other group members achieve theirs. Students work together in small groups to ensure that all group members achieve up to a preset criterion. When all group members reach criteria, each member may receive bonus points.

Cooperative learning is the heart of problem-based learning. It is related to collaborative learning, which emphasizes the "natural learning" (as opposed to training resulting from highly structured learning situations) that occurs as an effect of community in which students work together in unstructured groups and create their own learning situation.

Not all that glitters is gold, of course, and not all group efforts are cooperative. Simply assigning students to groups and telling them to work together does not in and of itself result in cooperative efforts. There are many ways in which group efforts may go wrong. Seating students together can result in competition at close quarters (pseudo-groups) or individualistic efforts with talking (traditional learning groups). The complexity of cooperative learning may partially explain why it tends to be used less than competitive and individualistic learning in college classes, even though it is by far the most effective of the three alternatives.

Cooperative learning is also underused because many students do not understand how to work cooperatively with others. The prevailing culture and reward systems of our society (and our colleges) are oriented toward competitive and individualistic work; the schools students came from emphasized class rank and required teachers to evaluate students on norm-referenced bases.

In addition, in most colleges, few resources are allocated for faculty development, meaning that most faculty have to learn how to use cooperative learning on their own. In large classes, underpre-

pared faculty assign students to groups and sometimes find the outcome chaotic. Finally, students may resist changes in instruction and pressure faculty to continue to lecture. Some, when first exposed to cooperative learning, may say, "I paid to hear you, not my classmates!"

As more experienced practitioners have found, none of these barriers is insurmountable. They weaken as knowledge increases of the theory, research, and practical procedures underlying cooperative learning.

The Theoretical Roots of Cooperative Learning

. . . The use of cooperative learning in college classes has its roots in the creation of social interdependence, cognitive-developmental, and behavioral learning theories.

■ **Social interdependence theory** views cooperation as resulting from positive interdependence among individuals' goals. Kurt Koffka (one of the founders of the Gestalt School of Psychology) proposed in the early 1900s that groups were dynamic wholes in which the interdependence among members could vary. Kurt Lewin stated that the essence of a group lies in the interdependence of its members (created by common goals); groups are "dynamic wholes" in which a change in the state of any member or subgroup changes the state of the other members or subgroups. Morton Deutsch (one of Lewin's students) first formulated social interdependence theory in the 1940s, noting that interdependence can be positive (cooperation), negative (competition), or nonexistent (individualistic efforts).

We (David was one of Deutsch's students) published a comprehensive formulation of the theory in the 1980s. The basic premise of *social interdependence theory* is that the way social interdependence is structured determines how individuals interact, which in turn determines outcomes. Positive interdependence (cooperation) results in *promotive interaction* as individuals encourage and facilitate each other's efforts to learn. Negative interdependence (competition) typically results in *oppositional interaction* as individuals discourage and obstruct each other's efforts to achieve. In the absence of a functional interdependence (that is, individualism) there is *no interaction* as individuals work independently without interchange with each other.

■ **Cognitive-developmental theory** views co-operation as an essential prerequisite for cognitive growth. It flows from the coordination of perspectives as individuals work to attain common goals. Jean Piaget taught that when individuals co-operate on the environment, healthy socio-cognitive conflict occurs that creates cognitive disequilibrium, which in turn stimulates perspective-taking ability and cognitive development. Lev Vygotsky believed that cooperative efforts to learn, understand, and solve problems are essential for constructing knowledge and transforming the joint perspectives into internal mental functioning. For both Piaget and Vygotsky, working cooperatively with more capable peers and instructors results in cognitive development and intellectual growth.

From the *cognitive science* viewpoint, cooperative learning involves modeling, coaching, and scaffolding (conceptual frameworks that provide for understanding what is being learned). Cooperative learners cognitively rehearse and restructure information to retain it in memory and incorporate it into existing cognitive structures.

More recently, we (the authors) have developed *controversy theory*, which posits that when students are confronted with opposing points of view, uncertainty or conceptual conflict results, which creates a reconceptualization and an information search, which in turn results in a more refined and thoughtful conclusion. The key steps for the student are to organize what is known into a position; to advocate that position to someone who advocates an opposing position; to attempt to refute the opposing position while rebutting attacks on one's own; to reverse perspectives so that the issue is seen from both points of view simultaneously; and, finally, to create a synthesis to which all sides can agree.

■ **The behavioral learning theory** assumes that students will work hard on those tasks for which they secure a reward of some sort and will fail to work on tasks that yield no reward or yield punishment. Cooperative learning is designed to provide incentives for the members of a group to participate in the group's effort. Skinner focused on group contingencies, Bandura focused on imitation, and Homans as well as Thibaut and Kelley focused on the balance of rewards and costs in social exchange among interdependent individuals.

Differences Among Theories

These three arenas of theory provide rich soil for cooperative learning. They all predict that cooperative learning will promote higher achievement than will competitive or individualistic learning. Each theory has generated a research base. There are, however, basic differences among them.

Social interdependence theory assumes that cooperative efforts are based on intrinsic motivation generated by interpersonal factors and a joint aspiration to achieve a significant goal. Behavioral learning theory assumes that cooperative efforts are powered by extrinsic motivation to achieve rewards. Social interdependence theory focuses on relational concepts dealing with what happens among individuals (for example, cooperation is something that exists only among individuals, not within them), whereas the cognitive-developmental perspective focuses on what happens within a single person (for example, disequilibrium, cognitive reorganization). The differences across these theoretical assumptions have yet to be fully explored or solved.

The Internal Dynamics That Make Cooperation Work

. . . Whenever two individuals interact, the *potential* for cooperation exists. But it is only under certain conditions that cooperation will *actually* exist.

As the research on cooperative efforts has evolved over the past four decades, five key elements have emerged as critical to actual cooperation: positive interdependence, individual accountability, promotive interaction, social skills, and group processing. Here is what each of these has come to mean for faculty members.

■ **First, you (the instructor) ensure that each student perceives that he or she is linked with others in such a way that the student cannot succeed unless the others do.** In every lesson, you structure *positive interdependence* so every student embraces a responsibility for learning the assigned material and for making sure that all members of the group learn it, too. You may supplement this positive interdependence by adding *joint rewards* (if all members of a group score 90 percent correct or better on the test, each receives five bonus points), *divided resources* (giving each group member a part of the total information required to complete an assignment), and *complementary roles* (reader, checker, encourager, elaborator). For a learning situation to be cooperative, students must believe that they sink or swim together.

■ Second, you structure *individual accountability* so that the performance of each student is assessed by a) giving an individual test to each student, b) having each student explain what he or she has learned to a classmate, or c) observing each group and documenting the contributions of each member. The purpose of cooperative learning is to make each member a stronger individual in his or her own right. Students learn together so that they can subsequently perform better as individuals.

■ Third, you ensure that students promote one another's success (helping, assisting, supporting, encouraging, and praising one another's efforts to learn) face to face. Doing so entails cognitive processes such as verbally explaining how to solve problems, teaching one's knowledge to classmates, and connecting present with past learning. It also leads to such interpersonal processes as challenging one another's reasoning and conclusions, modeling, and facilitating efforts to learn. The verbal and nonverbal responses of other group members provide important feedback as to a student's performance. Students also get to know each other on a personal as well as a professional level. To obtain meaningful face-to-face interaction, the size of groups needs to be small (two to four members).

■ Fourth, you teach students the needed social skills and ensure that they are used appropriately. The success of a cooperative effort requires interpersonal and small-group skills. Asking unskilled individuals to cooperate tends to be futile. Leadership, decision-making, trust-building, communication, and conflict-management skills have to be taught, just as purposefully and precisely as academic skills. Procedures and strategies for such skills may be found in David Johnson's *Reaching Out* (1997), David and F. Johnson's *Joining Together* (1997), and David and Roger Johnson's *Learning to Lead Teams* (1997).

■ Fifth, you ensure that students take the time to engage in *group processing*—the identification of ways to improve the processes members have been using to maximize their own and each other's learning. Students focus on the continuous improvement of these processes by a) describing what member actions were helpful and less helpful in ensuring effective working relationships and that all group members achieved learning goals, and b) making decisions about what behaviors to continue or change. Group processing may result in a) streamlining the learning process to make it simpler (reducing complexity), b) eliminating unskilled and inappropriate actions (error-proofing the process), c) continuously improving students' skills in working as part of a team, and d) giving group members an opportunity to celebrate their hard work and successes. . . .

. . . [U]nderstanding how to implement the five essential elements enables instructors to a) structure any lesson in any subject area cooperatively, b) adapt cooperative learning to their specific circumstances, needs, and students, and c) intervene to improve the effectiveness of any group that is malfunctioning.

The Research . . .

Meta-Analysis of College Studies

Since the 1960s, we have been developing a comprehensive library of all the research conducted on cooperative learning. We've found over 305 studies that compare the relative efficacy of cooperative, competitive, and individualistic learning on individual achievement in college and adult settings. The first study was conducted in 1924; 68 percent of the studies have been conducted since 1970. Sixty percent randomly assigned subjects to conditions, 49 percent consisted of only one session, and 82 percent were published in journals.

We classified the results of the research comparing cooperative, competitive, and individualistic efforts into three broad categories relating to quality of the college experience: academic success, quality of relationships, and psychological adjustment to college life. In addition, there are a number of studies on students' attitudes toward the college experience.

Academic Success. One of the most important influences on the college experience is whether students achieve academically. Academic success is, above all, the college's aim and the student's aim. It also, as Tinto documents, has numerous effects on college attrition: the higher the achievement of students, the more committed they tend to be to completing college. Academic success is also tied to eligibility for financial aid. For these and many other reasons, it is important to turn to instructional methods that maximize student achievement.

Between 1924 and 1997, over 168 studies were conducted comparing the relative efficacy of cooperative, competitive, and individualistic learning on the achievement of individuals 18 years or older. These studies indicate that cooperative learning promotes higher individual achievement than do competitive approaches (effect size = 0.49) or individualistic ones (effect size = 0.53). Effect sizes of this order describe significant, substantial increases in achievement. They mean, for example, that college students who would score at the 50th percentile level when learning *competitively* will score in the 69th percentile when learning cooperatively; students who would score at the 53rd percentile level when learning *individualistically* will score at the 70th percentile when learning cooperatively.

The relevant measures here include knowledge acquisition, retention, accuracy, creativity in problem-solving, and higher-level reasoning. The results hold for verbal tasks (such as reading, writing, and oral presentations), mathematical tasks, and procedural tasks (such as swimming, golf, and tennis). There are also studies finding advantages for cooperative learning in promoting meta-cognitive thought, willingness to take on difficult tasks, persistence (despite difficulties) in working toward goal accomplishment, intrinsic motivation, transfer of learning from one situation to another, and greater time on task. These results were recently corroborated in a meta-analysis focused on college level-one science, math, engineering, and technology courses.

Outcomes such as these have multiple, far-reaching impacts on students' experiences of college. Astin (1993), for example, concludes that cooperative student-student interaction and student-faculty interaction are the two major influences on college effectiveness (academic development, personal development, and satisfaction with the college experience). McKeachie and his associates (1986) find that learning how to engage in critical thinking depends on student participation in class, teacher encouragement, and cooperative student-student interaction.

Quality of Relationships. A host of researchers have investigated the quality of the relationships among students and between students and faculty. Our meta-analysis of the research using students 18 years or older found that cooperative effort promotes greater liking among students than does competing with others (effect size = 0.68) or working on one's own (effect size = 0.55); this finding holds even among students from different ethnic, cultural, language, social class, ability, and gender groups. The relevant studies include measures of interpersonal attraction, esprit de corps, cohesiveness, and trust. College students learning cooperatively perceive greater social support (both academically and personally) from peers and instructors than do students working competitively (effect size = 0.60) or individualistically (effect size = 0.51).

The positive interpersonal relationships promoted by cooperative learning are crucial to today's learning communities. They increase the quality of social adjustment to college life, add social goals for continued attendance, reduce uncertainty about attending college, increase commitment to stay in college, increase integration into college life, reduce incongruencies between students' interests and college curricula, and heighten social membership in college (see Tinto, 1993).

Psychological Adjustment. Attending college requires considerable personal adjustment for many students. In reviewing the research, we found cooperativeness to be highly correlated with a wide variety of indices of psychological health; individualistic attitudes are related to a wide variety of indices of psychological pathology; competitiveness seems related to a complex mixture of indices of health and pathology. One important aspect of psychological health is self-esteem. College-level studies indicate that cooperation tends to promote higher self-esteem than competitive (effect size = 0.47) or individualistic (effect size = 0.29) efforts. Members of cooperative groups also become more socially skilled than do students working competitively or individualistically.

Attitudes Toward the College Experience

The more positive a student's attitude toward his or her college, the more likely he or she is to stay in that college and participate fully in its life. A number of studies find that cooperative learning promotes more positive attitudes toward learning, the subject area, and the college than does competitive or individualistic learning. There are numerous social psychological theories, furthermore, that predict that students' values, attitudes, and behavioral patterns are most effectively developed and changed in cooperative groups.

Reciprocal Relationships Among Outcomes

There tends to be a reciprocal relationship among these outcomes. The more effort students expend in working together, the more they tend to like each other. The more they like each other, the harder they tend to work to learn. The more individuals work together, the greater their social competence, self-esteem, and general psychological health. The healthier individuals are psychologically, the more effectively they tend to work together. The greater the number of committed relationships individuals are involved in, the healthier they will be psychologically; healthier individuals, in turn, are abler to form caring and committed relationships. These multiple outcomes form a gestalt central to a high-quality college experience.

The Research Is Even More Impressive Than It Looks

The research on cooperative learning is like a diamond. The more light you focus on it, the brighter and more multifaceted it becomes. The power of cooperative learning is brightened by the magnitude of its effect sizes, but the more you read the research and examine the studies, the better cooperative learning looks. Here are some of the reasons.

■ **Cooperative learning is a very cost-effective instructional procedure.** It affects many different instructional outcomes simultaneously.

■ **The research studies are a combination of theoretical and demonstration studies conducted in labs, classrooms, and colleges as a whole.** While the lab studies may have lasted for only one session, some of the demonstration studies lasted for an entire semester or academic year. The combination of scientific and demonstration studies strengthens the confidence college instructors can have in the effectiveness of cooperative-learning procedures.

■ **The research on cooperative learning has** a validity and generalizability rarely found in the educational literature. This research has been conducted over eight decades by numerous researchers with markedly different orientations working in a variety of different colleges and countries. Research participants have varied with respect to economic class, age, sex, nationality, and cultural background. The researchers have employed a wide variety of tasks, subject areas, ways of structuring cooperative learning, and ways of measuring dependent variables. Vastly different methodologies have been used. This combination of research *volume* and *diversity* is almost unparalleled.

Ways To Use Cooperative Learning . . .

Using Cooperative Learning in College Classes

. . . In time, we developed three interrelated ways to use cooperative learning: formal cooperative learning, informal cooperative learning, and cooperative base groups.

Formal cooperative learning is students working together, for one period to several weeks, to achieve shared learning goals aimed at joint completion of specific tasks and assignments. Any course requirement or assignment may be structured for formal cooperative learning. Groups formed on this basis provide the foundation for all other cooperative-learning procedures. In formal cooperative-learning groups, instructors

■ *make a number of preinstructional decisions.* An instructor has to decide on the academic and social-skill objectives, the size of groups, the method of assigning students to groups, the roles students will be assigned, the materials needed to conduct the lesson, and the way the room will be arranged.

■ *explain to students the task and the concept of positive interdependence.* An instructor defines the assignment, teaches the required concepts and strategies, explains positive interdependence and individual accountability, gives the criteria for success, and specifies the expected social skills.

■ *monitor students' learning and intervene to assist students with tasks or with interpersonal and group skills.* An instructor systematically observes and collects data on each group as it works. When needed, the instructor intervenes to assist students in completing the task accurately and in working together effectively.

- *assess and evaluate students' learning and help students process how well their groups functioned.* Students' learning is carefully assessed and the performance of each is evaluated. Members of the learning groups then process how effectively they worked together.

Informal cooperative learning groups are used primarily to enhance direct instruction (presentations, demonstrations, films, videos); they are typically temporary and ad hoc, formed for a brief period of time (such as intermittent two- to four-minute discussions during a class session). Instructors may use informal cooperative-learning groups during a class by having students turn to a classmate near them to discuss briefly a question posed by the instructor or to summarize what their instructor has just presented. Doing so focuses student attention on the material and ensures that students process it cognitively.

Cooperative base groups are longer-term groups (lasting for at least a semester) with stable membership whose primary responsibility is to provide each student the support and encouragement he or she needs to make academic progress and to complete the course(s) successfully. . . .

Conclusion . . .

Faculty who use cooperative learning are on safe ground. There is a rich theoretical base for cooperative learning. As the research has evolved over the past 35 years, five basic elements have emerged as critical to cooperative work in classrooms: positive interdependence, individual accountability, face-to-face promotive interaction, social skills, and group processing. The research evidence itself indicates that a) the theories underlying cooperative learning are valid and b) cooperative learning does indeed work in college classrooms.

Three interrelated types of cooperative learning have been developed—formal cooperative learning, informal cooperative learning, and cooperative base groups. Used together, they provide a framework for effective teaching at the college level.

In many college classes, however, more attention is paid to developing Lone Rangers than to creating learning communities within which the achievement of all students is enhanced. The power of cooperative efforts is widely ignored. The whole instructional system aims to pluck out and nurture solitary individual genius—to find the next Michelangelo, for example.

As academic myth would no doubt have it, the great Michelangelo painted the ceiling of the Sistine Chapel, laboring alone on scaffolding high above the chapel floor. In fact, 13 people helped Michelangelo paint the work. As biographer William E. Wallace notes, Michelangelo was the head of a good-sized entrepreneurial enterprise that collaboratively made art that bore his name.

The powerful blend of individual and collective effort found in Michelangelo's cooperative team can be harnessed in any college class.

Resources

Astin, A. *What Matters in College: Four Critical Years Revisited,* San Francisco: Jossey-Bass, 1993.

Bruffee, K. "Sharing Our Toys: Cooperative Learning Versus Collaborative Learning," *Change,* Vol. 27, No. 1, 1995.

Deutsch, M. "Cooperation and Trust: Some Theoretical Notes," in M.R. Jones, ed., *Nebraska Symposium on Motivation,* Lincoln, NE: University of Nebraska Press, 1962, pp. 275–319.

Gamson, Zelda F. "Collaborative Learning Comes of Age," *Change,* Vol. 26, No. 5.

Johnson, D.W. *Reaching Out: Interpersonal Effectiveness and Self-Actualization,* sixth ed., Boston: Allyn & Bacon, 1997.

Johnson, D.W. and F. Johnson. *Joining Together: Group Theory and Group Skills,* 6th ed., Allyn & Bacon, 1997.

Johnson, D.W. and R. Johnson. *Cooperation and Competition: Theory and Research,* Edina, MN: Interaction Book Company, 1989.

———. *Learning to Lead Teams: Developing Leadership Skills,* Edina, MN: Interaction Book Company, 1997.

Johnson, D.W., R. Johnson, and K. Smith. *Active Learning: Cooperation in the College Classroom,* second ed., Edina, MN: Interaction Book Company, 1998.

———. *Cooperative Learning: Increasing College Faculty Instructional Productivity,* ASHE-ERIC Higher Education Report, Vol. 20, No. 4, Washington, DC: The George Washington

University, Graduate School of Education and Human Development, 1991.

———. *Academic Controversy: Enriching College Instruction Through Intellectual Conflict,* ASHE-ERIC Higher Education Report, Vol. 25, No. 3, Washington, DC: The George Washington University, Graduate School of Education and Human Development, 1996.

MacGregor, J. *Intellectual Development of Students in Learning Community Programs, 1986–1987,* Evergreen State College, Washington Center Occasional Paper No. 1, 1987.

Matthews, Roberta S., James L. Cooper, Neil Davidson, and Peter Hawkes. "Building Bridges Between Cooperative and Collaborative Learning," *Change,* Vol. 27, No. 4, p. 34.

McKeachie, W., P. Pintrich, L. Yi-Guang, and D. Smith. *Teaching and Learning in the College Classroom: A Review of the Research Literature,* Ann Arbor, MI: The Regents of the University of Michigan, 1986.

Smith, K. "Cooperative vs. Collaborative Learning Redux," Letter response to Bruffee article, *Change,* Vol. 27, No. 3, 1995.

———. "Cooperative Learning: Effective Teamwork for Engineering Classes," *IEEE Education Society Newsletter,* Vol. 17, No. 4, 1995, pp. 1–6.

Springer, L., M. Stanne, and S. Donovan. *Meta-analysis of Small Group Learning in Science, Math, Engineering, and Technology Disciplines,* Madison, WI: National Institute for Science Education, 1997.

Tinto, V. *Leaving College: Rethinking the Causes and Cures of Student Attrition,* second ed., Chicago: University of Chicago Press, 1993.

Wilkerson, L. and W. Gijselaers, eds. *Bringing Problem-Based Learning to Higher Education: Theory and Practice,* San Francisco: Jossey-Bass, 1996.

September/October 1998

Obstacles to Open Discussion and Critical Thinking

The Grinnell College Study

Carol Trosset

Like many institutions, Grinnell College hopes that one benefit of an increasingly diverse student body will be that students talk about their differences with each other. It sees open discussion of sensitive issues as an important part of the learning process—both in and out of the classroom. Since the college has made many attempts to foster a good climate for these discussions, recent reports that a number of students feel silenced have been disturbing news.

In an attempt to understand this problem, I undertook several semesters of ethnographic research, focusing on student assumptions about the purposes of discussion. The attitudes revealed by this study have far-reaching implications, not just for the discussion of diversity issues but for our educational mission of fostering critical-thinking skills.

Discussion as Advocacy

We presented approximately 200 students with a list of sensitive diversity-related issues (such as "whether race is an important difference between people"); for each, we asked whether it was possible to have a balanced discussion of that issue (involving more than one perspective, with each perspective receiving about equal support and with people being civil to each other). We also asked them to explain why they did or did not want to discuss the issue. The majority of students not only thought that balanced discussion of these issues was impossible but feared that a single viewpoint would dominate—and feared reprisal if one spoke against that perspective.

The main reason students gave for wanting to discuss a particular topic was that they held strong views on the subject and wished to convince others. Likewise, not having a strong view—or finding an issue difficult—was often given as a reason for not wanting to discuss a subject. This conflict is reflected in the following student responses:

- "I want to discuss the causes of sexual orientation because I have strong views on this issue."
- "I want to discuss affirmative action because I want to educate people."
- "I like discussing gender issues because I feel knowledgeable about them."
- "I'm not sure what multiculturalism is; I don't know much about it, so I don't want to discuss it."
- "I don't want to discuss race because I never know how to approach the subject."
- "In a few cases, people cry sexual misconduct when it isn't, so I don't want to talk about it in those few cases."

Some students are so convinced of advocacy as the point of discussion that they see silence as the only way to avoid it: "I wouldn't want to discuss religion as I don't want to impose my views on others."

A few explicitly generalized this model beyond the treatment of diversity issues, saying, "Ideally, you should talk in order to make the other person realize that what they said was wrong," or, "I don't want to talk about things I'm unsure of."

Only five out of the 200 students in our sample volunteered a different, more exploratory, view of discussion, such as "I want to talk about multicultural education because I'm not sure I know enough about it," and "I want to discuss race, as it would open my mind to things I don't experience myself."

In exploratory discussion, people who are seeking more information and other viewpoints speak in order to learn about things. This is very different from the advocacy model, in which people who have already made up their minds about an issue speak in order to express their views and convince others.

One of our annual surveys of first-year students found 54 percent preferred to discuss a topic on which they held strong views (over a topic about which they were undecided).

Another survey, with a differently worded question, found the same preference increasing over time, rising from 25 percent of freshmen to over 50 percent of juniors. (The preference declined slightly among seniors, but the sample of seniors was not representative.) There were no ethnic or gender differences correlating with this preference in either survey.

The Search for Consensus

When we asked students why people should talk about their differences, we quite often heard about the desire to reach a consensus:

- "The best thing is when opposing views find some point of agreement."
- "Ideally, people should talk in order to mold all opinions together in a compromise."
- "People should talk in order to achieve a unified world view, the dissolution of the idea of the other, and an awareness of the oneness of all things."

Some students also told us that there's no point talking about something unless people can agree: "Discussing these things is futile; it wears you out. It seems you can never reach a consensus." Despite the discouraged tone of this last comment, many interviewees expressed great optimism about the possibility that people with different views can find common ground.

Some students spoke about issues as if a consensus already existed:

- "I don't want to discuss race because it's not an important difference between people."
- "I don't want to discuss the causes of sexual orientation because this topic is irrelevant to the nature of homosexuality."

Sometimes this assumption was combined with a preference for advocacy. One woman wants to be an advocate representing a consensus she assumes to exist: "I want to discuss sexism due to a personal interest in stating the female experience."

When we asked how likely people were to listen to and think about what someone else said under various conditions, most students said, predictably, that they would be likely to listen to someone with whom they already agreed. A majority also said that they would be unlikely to listen to someone with whom they disagreed. Their reasons included the following:

- "I have a set opinion about the causes of sexual orientation—I wouldn't want to participate in a conversation when other people have disagreeable views, but I would talk with people who have similar opinions."
- "I have strong ideas about what constitutes a multicultural education—I would have difficulty listening to those who disagree."

- "A discussion of abortion wouldn't be balanced—I would have a hard time listening to the opposite view."

Most often, it seems, students created artificial consensus groups by only discussing difficult issues when they knew it to be "safe"—that is, in carefully selected groups with homogeneous opinions, as reflected in the following comments:

- "People don't talk about race on this campus—carefully selected company might mean opposing views are not present."

- "It appears that people prefer to interact with others who verify their own views, instead of actively pursuing alternative points of view. This could cause individuals to believe there is widespread support for their own views, when in fact there may not be."

Seventy-five percent of the students we asked said that they would discuss diversity issues with people of the same views or background as themselves, but only 40 percent said they would discuss the same issues with people whose views were unknown to them.

Personal Experience as the (Only) Source of Legitimate Knowledge

As with cases in which they already agreed with a speaker, most students we surveyed said they were very likely to listen to someone they perceived as knowledgeable. Before we interpret this as traditional academic respect for expertise, however, we must examine where students think knowledge comes from.

When we asked 47 students in interviews, "How knowledgeable are you about diversity issues?" most said they were fairly to very knowledgeable. When asked where their knowledge came from, most mentioned more than one source. Forty-three percent of the respondents attributed knowledge to personal experience, and another 35 percent said knowledge came from talking to others about their experiences.

This bias in favor of personalized knowledge (as opposed to knowledge accessible to all comers, such as that contained in scholarly writings—a kind of knowledge stressed by only six of the 47) is also visible in the distribution of which groups claimed knowledge of which issues. Thus, students of color were more likely than whites to claim to be knowledgeable about race, women were more likely than men to claim knowledge about gender, and homosexuals more likely than heterosexuals to claim knowledge about sexual orientation.

White males in their first two years were the only group likely to say that they had little knowledge of diversity generally. Their claim to know little about gender, "because I have no personal experience," shows that these claims attribute expertise not only to experience, but to a particular kind of experience (that of belonging to a typically less powerful group).

This valuing of one kind of experience helps to limit what can be said in discussions. For example, the following comments on sexism came from two men and two women:

- "Guys are not able to challenge women's sexist remarks."

- "Women are unlikely to be labeled sexist no matter what they say."

- "I want to discuss gender—it's easy to say, I'm a woman; as a woman . . ."

- "Not being a woman, I don't feel my comments would be seen as valid."

This bias both forces members of less powerful groups into the role of peer instructors, and supports the impression that members of more powerful groups have nothing legitimate to say.

The Right Not to be Challenged

Not only do people participate in discussion for the purpose of advocating views they already hold, but some of them expect to do so without anyone questioning or challenging their statements. In our most representative interview study, when asked, "As a member of a diverse community, what are your rights?" 15 percent of the sample volunteered the idea that they had the right to think or say whatever they liked without having their views challenged.

Some of the phrases used to express this position include

- "I have the right to present my views without being criticized";

- ". . . to not have people judge my views";

- ". . . to say what I believe and not have anyone tell me I'm wrong";

- ". . . to feel and think anything and not be looked down on";

- ". . . to hold my own beliefs and not feel attacked because of them"; and

- ". . . to speak my mind and not feel inhibited."

The students who claimed the right not to be

challenged were nearly all women. Twenty-five percent of the women we interviewed made this claim, compared to only 6 percent of the men. (Other statements in their interviews suggest that most Grinnell men expect their views to be challenged by others.) Equal proportions of whites and students of color made this claim (which was rarely made by international students). Particularly disturbing is the fact that this claim was made evenly across the four class years, suggesting that students who arrive with this assumption do not alter it as a result of what they learn.

Implications

We hear a great deal these days about the pedagogical benefits of discussion. But the assumptions we uncovered—such as the belief that advocacy is the purpose of discussion—illustrate why this method is often not as effective as we'd hope. Cultural attitudes of this sort have a pervasive impact on behavior. These attitudes affect not only how students discuss things among themselves, but how they hear what professors say and how they read course materials.

Many of us as academics share a number of expectations about the dispositions of educated people. These include exploring ideas from a variety of perspectives, learning about things outside one's own experience, evaluating the quality of evidence and arguments, and the capacity to be persuaded of new perspectives when presented with high-quality evidence and argument. In line with this, the fostering of critical-thinking skills appears in the mission statements of our institutions. But our students often do not share this common faculty agenda. . . .

Some students to whom I presented this research told me, quite articulately, that "your identity comes from what, not how, you think." One, apparently struggling with the need to change his views on certain subjects, said he resolved this by realizing that at his age his identity was still changing. These statements were strikingly different from the typical scholar's identification with how one uses evidence and argument—something that has nothing to do with one's conclusions of the moment, since these will always change in the face of new evidence and better arguments.

Radical Relativism

Developmental and learning-style theorists may take issue with my concerns; it's all a "stage" or just their "style," they say. Their challenges, however, beg the question of how we as teachers are going to accomplish our educational missions, which are centered around the development of critical-thinking skills and which require our students to grow analytically.

What should we do, for example, with a student who says, after reading Malinowski (whose publications were based on four years of detailed field research), we still can't say anything about the Trobrianders because "it's just his opinion"? Traditional relativism, of course, is an important part of anthropology; it is based on the idea that any statement is made from a particular perspective, which must be taken into account when considering its meaning. The radical relativism of students carries this perspective beyond its original intention and argues that, therefore, everything is "just" an opinion and that no comparisons can be made between ideas or perspectives. (Indeed, people taking this position usually argue that any perspective claiming the ability to make comparative judgments is inferior.)

This orientation among students supports their claim that there is no way to learn about something outside one's own experience. This assertion, in effect, denies the methodological basis of most disciplines. It also supports students' idea that people have the right not to have their views challenged. Critical thinking itself is devalued here, since the assessment of evidence and logic is seen as just another way of doing things.

Given these orientations, we need to recognize that when we recommend "tolerance" to students, they may not hear the same message we're trying to send. Many of us think of tolerance in terms of civility, of behaving in well-mannered ways toward all members of the community, whether or not we approve of their views or behavior. Many students, on the other hand, think that being tolerant means approving of all ways of being, and believing that all ways are equally valid (except, of course, any position that openly makes value judgments and does not extend equal approval to all).

Being Comfortable

Eighty-four percent of the first-year class we surveyed chose the statement "It is important for the college community to make sure all its members feel comfortable" over the statement "People have to learn to deal with being uncomfortable."

Across the student body, it is a common demand that the college as a whole, as well as its individual members, must act to ensure the comfort of all students, especially those who are members of traditionally underrepresented groups. At the same time, people insist that members of traditionally powerful groups (such as heterosexuals) should get comfortable, quickly, with previously unfamiliar groups and lifestyles.

"People are not interested in the sources of discomfort. They just want everyone to get comfortable," one student said. Of course, people should not be made to feel excluded because they belong to a minority group. But the demand for comfort often reaches much farther than this, sometimes to the point of claiming that no person should have to learn new behaviors or ways of thinking, or indeed do anything that might make him or her uneasy.

These e-mail messages were sent to colleagues of mine; the students clearly expect that they will be accepted as legitimate excuses:

■ "You haven't received my paper because I'm not comfortable with it yet."

■ "I'm not coming to class today because I haven't done the reading, and I'm not comfortable asking any of the other students if I can borrow their books."

Exploring new ideas, encountering people with different values, learning a new discipline's way of thinking, and having someone point out a flaw in one's argument—these can be *uncomfortable* experiences. For some people, simply finding themselves disagreeing with someone else is uncomfortable. Promising our students that we will make them comfortable may simply confirm them in their view that they have the right not to be challenged.

Ironically, typical suggestions for how to foster discussion feed into this attitude. Stressing the importance of making everyone feel "safe" often seems to result in making many people afraid to disagree with anyone, for fear of intimidating or offending them. Perhaps the teacher's solution is not ever-more safety and respect (words that can be variously interpreted), but cultivating a more careful distinction between the idea and the person.

Speakers need to remember this distinction when they issue challenges, but those on the receiving end also need to remember it, so as not to overinterpret any conceptual or factual challenge as a threat to identity. With respect to sensitive issues, it might help to encourage everyone to think less, rather than more, about identity; to focus students' attention not on their differences, but on some shared interest or problem-solving task that has the potential to bring them together.

Clearly, many students hold assumptions about discussion that present difficulties for teaching critical thinking. Deeply personal issues are, of course, among the most difficult places for anyone to apply such skills. But the ability to hold just such discussions would be an acid test of whether we have indeed fostered critical thinking in our students.

VISITING ACROSS THE DISCIPLINES: *Change* and the National Teaching Project

James Wilkinson

Classrooms are often closed worlds. What transpires between teacher and students within their four walls remains invisible and largely secret—known only to the participants. Innovations, discoveries, transformative experiences of all kinds may occur without so much as a whisper to the teaching community outside.

One of the consistent aims of *Change* has been to open classroom doors to readers and to create what we would now term a "virtual community" of pioneers committed to improving classroom practice. Its role in publicizing the American Association of Higher Education's (AAHE) National Teaching Project, funded by a three-year FIPSE grant in 1975–1978, provides the most striking example of this commitment. Vignettes of teachers, courses, and students appearing under the general title "Reports on Teaching" covered a variety of practices and personalities. Their professed goal was to rescue faculty members who cared about teaching from their isolation by demonstrating that they were not alone. Brave souls on other campuses shared their view that teaching mattered—teachers with names, department addresses, and syllabi. *Change* presented their experiments as worthy of emulation. The message was: Come into my classroom, see what I do, see if you like it, try it if you dare. These classroom visits were, of course, organized by discipline—the faculty selected by their respective professional organizations, in groupings inspired by Lee Shulman's observation that teaching occurs within a departmental or disciplinary framework.

However, the breadth of the samples presented in repeated issues of *Change*, from anthropology to romance languages, also had the perhaps unintended consequence of documenting the striking similarities that cut across disciplinary boundaries. Many of the problems described in these pieces were not unique to a single discipline. Once the secrecy of the classroom was breached, what emerged was how alike these innovative classes seemed. Encouraging student motivation, teaching indepth rather than superficially, creating new methods of grading to reflect the more varied student projects all typify common concerns. Most important, perhaps, was the effort to blur the distinction between student and teacher in a creative way, to encourage students' responsibility for their own learning by engaging them in innovative ways.

Kenneth Eble is quoted in a July 1976 article as follows: "One of the legacies of the sixties that shouldn't be forgotten is that experience and learning can often proceed side by side" (Miller, 1976, p. 43). Faculty members in disciplines as disparate as English and engineering came to the same pedagogical conclusion: students learn best when presented with real-life problems that resemble the research and problem-solving in which faculty themselves engage. Field studies abounded. We read of history students working in local museums, fledgling ethnographers interviewing subjects with tape recorders in the surrounding community, psychology students trained as paraprofessionals.

Other aspects of these explorations now seem dated. "Relevance," for instance — a concern inherited from the turbulent 1960s that greatly preoccupied faculty in the succeeding decade — is no longer a pressing issue. Many classroom innovations with evocative acronyms like SOAR, ADAPT, STAR, and EXPER SIM have passed from the scene without a trace. Language that combines organic metaphors with the terminology of social engineering, such as "creating projects" and "shaping plans," reflects the convergence of neo-romanticism and social science three decades ago.

Many of these pieces were written by journalists — writers whose chief professional focus was print or broadcast media such as *The New York Times*, *The Philadelphia Bulletin*, *The Progressive*, *Time*, and KQED in San Francisco. Journalists learn to personalize their stories. We learned about Robert De Guevara, a graduate student in sociology at the Social Systems Research Center at California State College, or James Maas, an associate professor of psychology at Williams College, and we followed them as they explored new approaches to learning and teaching. From there, it was a short step to the "teaching cases" that *Change* published in the 1990s. Because these pieces were written by nonspecialists, they remained accessible to faculty outside of the discipline. This journalistic pedigree also may explain one signal omission. Few of the pieces mentioned research or theory; results were most often anecdotal. Of course, for faculty it is the practical applicability of innovations that counts. Who cares what Piaget *would* have thought if it works. The pieces were exercises in induction — filled with specific facts about place and person that could counteract airy generalizations concerning contemporary practice.

The vignettes from the AAHE National Teaching Project serve as a reminder that educational innovation in the college classroom is at least three decades old. While we often deride the "traditional paradigm" of teaching — the "sage on the stage" dispensing wisdom to a captive (if not attentive) audience of undergraduates — that tradition had its detractors 30 years ago. How much progress have we made? The more recent survey reported in "Continuity and Change in the Study of Literature" (Franklin, Huber, & Laurence, 1992) suggested that the pace of change has been slower than often realized. Rereading the accounts of experiments now a quarter of a century old, it seems that much of what has characterized the movement to reform higher education during the intervening years has been to systematize, evaluate, and disseminate rather than to create something radically new. Still, *Change* deserves our thanks for having opened so many classroom doors to its readers, and reminding us how much — both problems and solutions — we continue to share.

References

Franklin, H., Huber, B., & Laurence D. (1992, January/February). Continuity and change in the study of literature. *Change, 24*, 42–53.

Miller, J. (1976, July). In the footsteps of Thoreau. *Change, 8*, 42–45.

Joseph Brodsky in Exile

Susan Jacoby

In most academic settings, a teacher defines poetry. For Joseph Brodsky's students, a poet defines teaching.

"I am really trying to show my students not *how* poetry is written but *why*," says Brodsky, poet in residence at the University of Michigan and a poet in exile from his native Russian land.

At 33, Brodsky is now regarded by many as the finest living Russian poet, a man who may some day rank alongside the most brilliant figures in Russian literature. . . .

One year ago, Brodsky was forced to leave the Soviet Union under pressure from the secret police. . . .

And thus he came to Ann Arbor—worlds apart from his own—and settled in to a new life of teaching young American students about life as viewed through the universal language of poetry. Brodsky sees academic life in America through new prisms that are worth more than a fleeting glance.

He taught two courses during the 1972–73 academic year: a graduate seminar in Russian poetry and a larger class described by a student as "Brodsky's Favorite Poems 101." He teaches in Russian and in English, English being one of the languages he learned by himself after he dropped out of Soviet high school at the age of fifteen. . . .

He is clearly more interested in his students' understanding of poetic value than in their adeptness at academic criticism of poetic techniques. Assigning a two-page paper on Pasternak, he told his graduate students: "When you write about a poet, I think the poet is watching you. It makes absolutely no difference to me what you write; I don't care about great displays of knowledge or brilliance. Your writing must be a personal act done for your own sake. Writing a paper is simply a chance for you to explore your real thoughts about a poet and your responses to his work. Don't reject this chance to think while you write because you're trying to figure out what the reader—in this case, me—will think of it. By the way, no one will get less than a 'B' in the course."

Brodsky is entirely truthful in saying he does not know how to lecture; his classes depend in large measure on whether his students are able to engage in an intellectual dialog that stimulates his thinking as well as theirs.

One student, for example, volunteered the opinion that "Garden of Gethsemane" was a failure. "How do you translate faith into art?" he asked.

"I can tell you exactly," Brodsky replied with a snap of his fingers. "It isn't so difficult to depict both God and a man, as Pasternak does in this poem. You simply combine physical details with certain devices—words, intonations—that don't belong to man. It's a blending of concrete flesh and, I would say, ecstatic devices. This is the work of the poet, because he combines both things in himself.

"About this matter of whether art can replace or displace faith—for a poet, his art is an act of faith. Embodying faith in art is not a matter of craftsmanship; the longer you work, the less of a problem this becomes. If your feelings are strong enough, you have the ability to put faith into words. If your own faith isn't strong enough, then your art becomes a diabolical business."

Even Brodsky's best students say they had considerable trouble becoming accustomed to his style of teaching. "He's the greatest teacher I ever had," said one graduate student, "even though I know teaching isn't his real work. It's absolutely astonishing for a graduate student to be asked, 'What did you think of this poem?' and 'Why?' The scientific school of literary criticism still holds sway; most of our classes are dissections of form, as though a poem were something you could take apart like a nuclear reactor. I know that most students simply aren't prepared to take opinions and defend them critically."

Brodsky says: "At first I was shocked when students were unable to respond to a 'why?' I keep trying to push them beyond these meaningless words they're accustomed to using. 'It's beautiful, it's profound, it's depressing'—all idiotic, meaningless terms. My students are not accustomed to precision in language, and this affects their entire thought processes. I think some of them are afraid of me because I attack them when they are wrong. Not personally, but I attack what they have said." One of his graduate students put it another way: "There's none of this bullshit with him that you get in a lot of courses when a student says something stupid and the professor drones on, 'Yes, that's a very interesting point.' You know the professor doesn't really have any respect for the student, but he's trying to 'relate' to him. Brodsky doesn't 'relate'—he throws out great big ideas for you to think about. He's not an American, so he didn't get hit with all of this junk about relevance in the sixties."

Brodsky is appalled by what he calls the "formlessness" of American education, particularly by his students' ignorance of history and classical literature. One trait he shares with many other recent Russian émigrés is a sense of shock at the relative lack of respect for literature in a society where every kind of book is readily available.

"I wasn't completely surprised," he told me, "because certain kinds of freedom are always taken for granted when the freedom is the result of previous generations' work. But it is still a sad thing to see. Books are taken much more seriously in Russia than they are here, because they're so difficult to get.

"I think my students' minds have been distorted—deformed is a better word—by the lack of standards in their education. For many of them, their education has meant the freedom to be ignorant—ignorant of the classics, ignorant of history. The Soviets have a good device when they insist on the teaching of history throughout their educational system. They distort history, of course, but that's not the point. It's the idea of studying history that's so important. I think history is the only source of moral education in a world where few people receive any formal religious training. Everyone in a university should be required to study history, and not just history in general but also the history of medicine, technology, science."

Brodsky uses the Russian word "vospitaniye" when he talks about moral education; it is a nearly untranslatable concept that takes in strength of character and spiritual values as well as formal knowledge. (In Soviet parlance, it also means instilling the official version of Marxism-Leninism in young people.) He feels that many of his American students lack a framework of values—any framework of values—to support them in their development. . . .

March 1976

Psychology: With a Little Help From Their Friends

Peter Janssen

It was hardly a traditional psychology seminar. For one, the 11 students in a section of Cornell University's Psychology 101 course were meeting at 7:30 one cold, winter night in the basement lounge of a coed dorm. For another, Cal Cohen, the soft-spoken, bearded teaching assistant (TA) leading the section was only a senior. And then there was the class itself.

"We're going to be physical tonight," Cohen began, asking everyone to push the plastic, over-stuffed chairs to the outer limits of the lounge.

He then asked two volunteers to lie on the floor. He told the rest of the class to kneel down and hold the volunteers' arms and legs. The volunteers were supposed to try to get up, as the students holding them down chanted "Get up, get up." After a few minutes of general confusion, Cohen called a halt and explained the moral of the lesson: "It is often the people who tell you to get up who hold you down." Everyone groaned good-naturedly, but Cohen warned: "Think about it; that's heavy."

What makes the class even more unusual than Cohen's teaching method is the fact that he is one of 21 undergraduate TAs in Cornell's Psych 101 (Introduction to Psychology) class who lead small sections at least once a week. Cornell has been using undergraduates as TAs in the course for the past 10 years—with increasingly good results. Says James B. Maas, the associate professor who teaches the course and set up the undergraduate TA program: "Everybody seems to benefit. The TAs say it is the highlight of their undergraduate career, while the students seem to like it too."

Maas is the likely proponent of such a system. He started teaching as a senior at Williams College in 1960; when a professor became suddenly sick, Maas took over the class. "They said I did a good job," Maas recalls, "and it was so stimulating that I decided to stay in teaching." He began teaching at Cornell in 1964 and acquired a reputation as an excellent teacher.

The recipient of Cornell's . . . Distinguished Teaching Award in 1972, he received the Distinguished Teaching Award of the American Psychological Association (APA) a year later. Maas served as the first director of Cornell's Center for Improvement of Undergraduate Education and as the president of the APA's teaching division.

When Maas started teaching Psych 101 it was then considered a huge crowd—400 students. In fall 1975, the class had 1,200 and was so big that it had to meet for lectures on Monday, Wednesday, and Friday in the university's concert hall. (Cornell's second largest single lecture class is about a third the size.) Officially, Psych 101 is designed to probe "the basic psychological processes such as brain functioning, perception, learning, and motivation; students are also introduced to more complex processes such as frustration, conflict, and behavior pathology." To keep things moving, Maas uses film and slides extensively, frequently showing 80 to 90 slides per lecture. In addition to attending three lectures, Psych 101 students must also attend one section meeting a week. The sections are supposed to hold 15 students each, but some are a bit larger.

Other psychology professors were dubious, to say the least, when Maas first used undergraduate TAs for the sections in 1965. "We were waiting for him to fall on his face," says one. "We were certain that the students would complain. After all, they're paying all this money for tuition, and what do they get for a teacher but somebody who's only a year or so older who may or may not be a personal friend. We also were pretty certain that undergraduates did not know enough or have the experience to lead a section. But the way Jim has carried this off, we've changed our minds." Maas admits that "the department was very skeptical at first. But now they're convinced. At least three other psychology courses are using undergraduate TAs, and other departments—chemistry, physics, mathematics, and biology—are using them too."

A major key to the success of the program, of course, is the selection of the teaching assistants. Until last spring, Maas selected and trained all the TAs himself. He now has the help of Gregory Carroll, who has almost completed work on his doctorate. Many prospective TAs know of the program because of their own experiences as students in Psych 101. To cast as wide a recruiting net as possible, however, Maas places an ad in the Cornell *Daily Sun*, the student paper, each spring. (Psych 101 is taught only during the fall semester.)

Applicants must have earned an A– or better in Psych 101 and hold at least a B+ cumulative average at Cornell. They must list all psychology courses they have taken (and grades), and include recommendations from faculty members. They also outline the topics they would like to teach in their sections. The job is prestigious—and popular; 15 students apply for every one accepted. . . .

. . . Basically we want TAs with sincerity, liveliness, and who are enthusiastic about the idea of teaching. Next to knowledge of content, the enthusiasm and motivation are probably the most important."

Once the TAs are chosen Maas invites them over to his house for an organizing session before summer vacation. "We talk business for about an hour—and then socialize for two," he says. The relationship between Maas and all of his students seems relaxed. He tells everyone—TAs, advisees, visitors—to call him Jim, and he tries to overcome the massive impersonality of his lecture class by showing up at 12:30 every Friday in a small conference room outside his office with a sandwich. He stays there for two hours, meeting with anyone who cares to drop in.

The TAs meet with Maas and Carroll just before school starts again in the fall to make sure they are prepared for their sections. Once actually teaching, they are videotaped at the beginning of the semester and often again toward the end. After the first taping Carroll meets with them individually to offer hints and advice. . . .

. . . They all . . . seemed to gather around the psychology department lounge to gossip, relax, and exchange ideas. They also seemed to have a good relationship with Maas. "My rapport with them has been very good," says Maas, "but they have some hesitation about coming to me with their dirty laundry. After all, I write their letters of recommendation to graduate school, so they always want to look as if they're on top of things when I'm around." . . .

July 1977

Sociology: More Than Techniques—A Research Center with Heart and Soul

James Benet

The Social Systems Research Center at California State College, Dominguez Hills, is described officially as "a training laboratory within the department of sociology." It occupies a big, informally arranged classroom in the social and behavioral sciences building, where it offers a number of undergraduate and graduate courses for regular credit. But the Center does much more for its students than offer academic courses. Its other dimension was vividly described by Robert De Guevara, a telephone company communications consultant who discovered the Center while advising the College on phone use. He is now a graduate student.

"I had it in the back of my mind to come back for a master's degree," De Guevara said. "Finding the Center and the help it gives people convinced me it could help me reach my goal or any goal in the field of education. One of the magnets is that the people here believe education is important, a means to success. And the group is attractive—multiethnic, many ages. The whole thing revolves around needs, with camaraderie and the excitement people thrive on. You can always find a willing ear."

It is striking that De Guevara's account does not mention sociology at all. However, in its way his description is quite as valid as the official one. Jeanne Curran, one of the founders, says that the original function of the Center was to do sociological research but more than that to develop a climate for learning that would produce a shared community with "peak thought experiences" involving the excitement and pain of learning. . . .

In its earliest conception, Curran says frankly, the Center was simply a means for keeping together a small group of women who had worked successfully to bring about the establishment of a child care center on the campus. In the course of that effort, they had done a survey of campus needs as perceived by the students—the maiden project of what became the Center. Why not, they asked themselves, do more research together? And why not even self-sustaining research for off-campus clients? And so the Center began with an instructor and two undergraduate students.

From the start the research was conducted by students with Curran acting only as advisor. Herman Loether, a member of the department . . . consulted and lent enthusiastic support . . . and between Curran and Loether a comfortably shared responsibility grew for the Center's activities. . . .

The sociology department, which has a unique history of support for new approaches to community and student needs, agreed to give credit for the work on a trial-run basis, and the Center quickly solicited and obtained projects. One was an assessment of employment needs for the neighboring city of Compton. Another, supported by a grant from the Women's Equity Action League, surveyed employment conditions for women in the Los Angeles area. But not all projects have had outside financial support. In the spring of 1973, the sociology department agreed to formal establishment of the Center.

Faculty and students have fashioned the Center's policies as they go along. Today each research project is carried out by a student director and student staff working with a client—along the lines of the think tanks that have sprung up across the country in the past few decades. Two of the most experienced students . . . serve as overall directors of the Center. Faculty are listed only as advisors on the research projects. They are still the teachers of the courses for academic credit that the Center offers (Workshop in Social Research, Graduate Workshop in Research and Theory, Action Research in Institutional Settings, to name some), but on the research projects it's the student directors who sign the final reports.

The Center is still evolving. After several years it became clear to faculty and student leaders alike that some way had to be found to quickly teach new students the principles of collecting, coding, and analyzing data. Four of the student directors set up workshop sessions, generally taught by experienced students but in some cases by faculty. This year, for the first time, these were incorporated as a requirement for new students in the workshop courses. Required sessions represent a modification of a basic Center principle that it's good to experience the pain of creation but "nobody should lay it on you. It's a Zen saying that everyone should choose his pain."

The structure of student progress is unusual but clear cut. By signing a bulletin board list, students join an available research project. Those capable of becoming project directors are informally identified by their good work and formally rewarded by a letter of recommendation from the student directors. Curran says, "We know people are close to being promoted to director when they never have time to comb their hair."

Directors take on teaching responsibilities under faculty supervision and lead a research project, posting working hours and maintaining a project work-flow chart. Ultimately, the director prepares a paper suitable for professional publication and presents it at a professional meeting. So quickly did the students push past faculty expectations in writing their professional papers that now the department of this small, 7,000-student college is one of the principal contributors to the annual professional meeting of the Pacific Sociological Association. (The professors do not appear as coauthors.)

In addition to its academic function, the Center strongly cultivates psychological understanding, leaning on "rap sessions" to talk out personnel problems. Posters decorating the Center's walls are inspirational rather than merely amusing or wittily rebellious: A picture of a rowboat carries the legend, "If there's no wind, row!"

January 1978

These Reports on Teaching

Progress and Prospects

Joan L. Stableski

Three years have passed since the Reports [on Teaching] were but an idea, and it has been a learning experience for the *Change* staff. With each new discipline, we've increased our understanding of the diversity—and commonality—of views and approaches encompassed in the fields covered. . . .

In deciding to feature, whenever possible, one social science, one hard science, and one humanistic discipline in each Report, we hoped to encourage an interest by all professors in the efforts of their colleagues in other fields toward this very common goal: the improvement of teaching and the increase in student learning in every subject.

The roadblocks to improving students' education don't really differ all that much from discipline to discipline. After acknowledging that each field has its unique characteristics which translate into special needs in the classroom, we are still struck by the similarities of the concerns. Though the historians and the chemists, the political scientists and the physicists may be worlds apart in the subject matter they teach, they are much closer than many are willing to admit in the difficulties each confronts when faced with a class of 15 or 50 or 500 undergraduates.

The introductory course, for one, is the migraine of every department in every discipline. Yet many teachers have been able to approach the problem with resourcefulness and creativity. Using media or self-paced instruction, peer teachers or computers, each discipline has its variation on the theme; but the challenge is the same everywhere and much can be learned from listening to the fresh ideas of others who see it from a different perspective. . . .

How important is . . . endorsement [of the disciplinary associations]? This leads to the somewhat worn argument that runs: Until the gatekeepers of professional prestige stand behind good teaching as an activity as worthy of recognition as research, all efforts to bring it into the limelight will be wasted. Yet this series of Reports stands in part as witness to the concern of the directors and education officers of the disciplinary associations, without which it never would have succeeded. And individual articles throughout the Reports attest to the willingness of many college and university administrators to underscore that concern.

It might be worth considering the possibility that some of these leaders are ahead of a pack that's unwilling to follow. There is a tremendous support system within the professoriat—exclusive of administrators or associations—that can choose for itself how to award the informal kind of prestige that often is much more powerful than any outside awards or titles. And only when more professors are willing to be outspokenly supportive of good teaching not only by colleagues within their own disciplines but by those outside them as well can the kind of environment be created where this program and similar efforts matter.

Hans Mauksch and Lawrence Rhoades said it well in the overview article for the sociology section of Report on Teaching #4: "One of the perplexing problems confronting any attempt to improve undergraduate teaching is the absence within academic disciplines of collegial communities based primarily on teaching." To carry that to its next logical step—and one that is not beyond the reach of concerned educators—perhaps it is entirely possible to create such communities that extend *beyond* academic disciplines, to the point where it's not the prestige of the individual professor or the total allegiance to the subject that matters as much as the education of every student.

January/February 1992

Continuity and Change in the Study of Literature

Phyllis Franklin, Bettina J. Huber, and David Laurence

EDITOR'S NOTE: A Change *survey of chief academic officers reports that English as a discipline has changed the most in response to multiculturalism.*

It's common knowledge that major changes have taken place in the college literature classroom. We hear that English departments across the nation have remade their curricula. The English faculty, which until recently concentrated on the well-known works and authors of the literary canon, now focuses on works by women and minorities, and also on products of popular culture and the mass media. Old distinctions of aesthetic quality have given way. The investigations of critical theory, deconstruction, feminism, and Marxism dominate the field. Educational goals for the classroom, which once centered on aesthetic appreciation, have altered accordingly. . . .

But how true, really, is this common knowledge? For some time, many close to the field have wondered about this picture of the English literature classroom—now so widely accepted—particularly about how solid a basis it has in fact. Beyond a handful of anecdotes, little evidence for the supposed state of affairs has been offered. Nor have questions been asked about the appropriateness of using anecdotes to generalize about curricula and teaching nationally. There are, after all, over 1,300 English departments in . . . the United States . . . . How much does anyone really know about what most of these teachers do in their classrooms?

Public controversy about the college study of literature is said to surface every 20 years, which is just long enough for most people to forget what the earlier arguments were about (see Thomas W.

Wilcox, *The Anatomy of College English*, Jossey-Bass, 1973, page 163). A century ago, the charge of intellectual slackness brought James Russell Lowell, who was then president of the Modern Language Association, to the defense of a curriculum revision that exchanged the classics of ancient Greece and Rome in their original languages for such educationally dubious moderns as Dante, Machiavelli, Montaigne, Bacon, and Shakespeare. "And shall we say," Lowell rabble-roused, "that the literature of the past three centuries is incompetent to put a healthy strain upon the more strenuous faculties of the mind? . . . that none of these (modern authors) set our thinking gear in motion to as good a purpose as any ancient of them all?" ("Address," *PMLA* 5 [1890], page 16).

A generation later, in the 1920s and '30s, the dispute repeated itself in a new guise when efforts to make American literature part of academic study in English were resisted by, as one scholar recalls, "academic elders who viewed the study of English literature later than the era of John Dryden as too easy to warrant serious effort, or considered research in American literature as no more than intellectual slumming" (Clarence Gohdes, editor, *Essays on American Literature in Honor of Jay B. Hubbell*, Duke University Press, 1967, i). . . .

We began by questioning the validity of recent, widely circulated assertions of dramatic change in the teaching of literature. Our findings indicate these assertions are overstated. The major authors and works of literature remain pre-eminent in the courses we surveyed, and almost all the literature teachers we queried endorse the traditional goals of the literature classroom.

But there have also been changes. For example, feminist approaches to the study of literature represent a new dimension in the literature classroom, and attention to the effects of race, class, and gender on the creation and interpretation of literature is also new. These innovations, however, have not displaced traditional classroom goals or approaches to literary study. Almost all of the respondents who want their students to understand the effects of race, class, and gender also support established goals: 95 percent want students to learn the intellectual, historical, and biographical backgrounds of the period; 88 percent want students to understand the formal qualities of literature and derive pleasure from their reading; and 86 percent want students to read closely and explicate texts.

That this is so will not surprise people familiar with the history of English studies, which has long included a variety of methodologies and a range of intellectual interests. Accretion is characteristic. For decades the New Critics fought the philologists until the New Criticism came to dominate the field. But the philologists never disappeared, and there are signs that philology is staging a comeback.

Experience suggests that change is rarely viewed dispassionately. Undoubtedly, some will object to the innovations we identify here. Others will welcome them, and still others will complain that so much remains unchanged. All are entitled to their views. Our hope is that future discussions of these views will be based on more than anecdotes.

SCIENCE EDUCATION REFORM:
Getting Out the Word

Daniel L. Goroff

A magazine whose goals include helping to solve the problems of postsecondary science education directly would have to look more like *Scientific American, Quantum*, or *The American Mathematical Monthly* than like *Change*. The restless, reformist, and exhorting spirit of this magazine's title and content is directed instead at changing the way we *talk about and understand* educational challenges like teaching college-level science.

Few vehicles besides *Change*, in print or otherwise, have been capable of building shared vocabulary and understanding about academic work. This is no small task, and it is particularly important if reaching scientists is a priority. In contrast to their humanist colleagues who easily negotiate and often revel in subjectivity, scientists expect to share references, concepts, and terminology easily when it comes to professional matters. Learning a science is like learning to speak a foreign language; studies show that typical biology textbooks introduce students to even more new vocabulary than foreign-language textbooks do!

Standardization of technical terms facilitates the communication among scientists, past and present, that makes it possible to build on one another's work so effectively. The cumulative way that science progresses compared with other disciplines implies, in turn, that how and what an instructor can successfully teach depends more critically on what other instructors do in their courses. A stronger sense of communal responsibility is required among teachers of mathematics than among teachers of English, for example. In trying to exercise their responsibilities together, scientists are quick to notice that consensus about words and concepts, let alone principles, is hard won when discussing educational matters. This makes sharing and coordinating pedagogical practices or reforms surprisingly difficult for scientists. There is much reinventing of the wheel, and that, as the saying goes, is when you are lucky enough not to reinvent the flat tire.

In sum, the communal nature of scientific vocabulary helps make science cumulative. For science *education* to be cumulative, too, teaching needs to be a collective responsibility. However, this is difficult without a shared vocabulary for exchanging educational ideas, and it is especially difficult for scientists since they take common terminology so much for granted when exchanging technical ideas.

Change has served as a forum that helps alleviate this vocabulary problem. Its readers can more quickly invoke shared meanings for such phrases as "teaching by inquiry," "stalking the second tier," "case studies," "peer instruction," "Perry stages," or "pedagogical content knowledge." The *Change* articles selected for this section illustrate both the need for and the development of ways like these to talk about the improvement of post-secondary science education.

The first article in this collection, "Science: The Art of Inquiry," (Arons) appeared in 1969. Spurred by Sputnik, many science and mathematics professors spent the 1960s working on large curriculum reform projects, mainly at the pre-college level. Most focused their attention on *what* was taught, to the exclusion of other factors that might have helped with the implementation of their work. The *Change* article by Arnold Arons, a pioneering reformer and investigator of physics education, introduced some concern about *how* the curriculum was taught. Arons worried about an overemphasis on scientific facts and an underemphasis on the scientific processes that produced them. Rather than talking much about teaching, though, he made his point in a way scientists can readily grasp by recalling stories about how Galileo, Faraday, and Dalton made their discoveries. He communicates almost nothing directly about the pedagogical implications of his observations. Though cogent and well-presented, such an approach may seem unsatisfying to those who have grown accustomed to more normative analyses of classroom practice that might have been hard to articulate or appreciate in 1969.

During the 1970s, the editors of *Change* seem to have felt the need to address how, as opposed to what, subjects were being taught in college classrooms. In part, this may have been a response to public curiosity about campus activities following the student uprisings. Perhaps there was also a desire to re-focus on education rather than politics. Regardless of their motivations, Joan Stableski and Richard Meeth directed an ambitious "National Teaching Project" with support from the Fund for the Improvement of Postsecondary Education. From 1976 to 1981, the project's "Reports on Teaching" appeared in *Change* issues as groups of several articles about a given discipline, each describing how a professor was conducting his or her course. Three points about this remarkable series are worth noting.

First, as routine as reports on teaching might seem today, this undertaking was clearly considered quite radical at the time. Concerned that their audience might not know how to read, understand, or put into context such accounts, the editors included long explanations of the project in introductions to each publication. They also solicited and printed various endorsements, including letters from senators and public figures, college and university leaders, disciplinary associations, and prominent faculty members. (One of the few critical comments came from Michael Scriven, who found it irresponsible that reports never mentioned the cost or sustainability of innovations.) In addition, an unusually strong and independent evaluation component was built into the project from the beginning, including a commitment to publish the findings in *Change*. The 24-page evaluation written by J. Bruce Francis that appeared in the August 1978 issue began with the following paragraphs that highlight the courage and insight involved:

> *Change* magazine has sometimes been called a maverick in higher education. Often taking a critical line against the sacred cows of academe, and using a journalistic rather than scholarly style, it has nonetheless built itself into a major force that helps shape the attitudes and practices of educational policymakers. With its National Teaching Project, *Change* once again has challenged entrenched attitudes, this time by undertaking, with the help of its first federal grant, two formidable tasks: to publicly elevate the stature of college teaching, and to evaluate fully and openly its efforts to do so.
>
> Teaching is at once the most noble and least rewarded of faculty activities. Honored more with lip service than concrete gain, it has become a secondary activity for many faculty and often produces less pride than the completion of even the most abstruse and arcane of scholarly studies. For *Change* to employ its editorial talents and prestige to make teaching more important is a noble though possibly quixotic undertaking. (p. 49)

The second point to note about the "Reports on Teaching" is that the very same pedagogical techniques, rationales, and policies identified as innovative in the

1970s are the ones that still count as innovative today. Case studies, computer-related procedures, internships, modular instruction, multimedia, peer teaching, practica, role-playing, self-paced instruction, simulation and games, team teaching, interdisciplinary courses, and unprepared students are among the headings published in an index of the project's output. That lexicon remains very much intact and useful today. Granting that self-paced and modular instruction had a low profile for a while, the distance-learning craze has nevertheless brought these topics back to the fore, too. In fact, nearly every report contains paragraphs that could be cut and pasted seamlessly into documents written yesterday rather than a quarter of a century ago. Even the discussions about computing and multimedia seem astonishingly current since they tend to concentrate more on enduring pedagogical issues rather than on transient technological ones. Names, categories, and ways of talking about pedagogy codified by the National Teaching Project have remained robust in the face of many other changes over the years.

Though it predates the National Teaching Project, the article excerpted here on "Zacharias' Latest Experiment" (Van Dyne, 1971) was in most ways typical of many of the reports that followed. Jerrold Zacharias was a more influential figure than many of the other faculty later profiled, and the experiment described has more of the free-wheeling spirit of the 1960s than is apparent later. However, the account follows a journalistic template suitable for Madlibs. In its mature form, the pattern for "Reports on Teaching" began with sentences of the form: "Dr. X has been teaching Subject Y for four years as an assistant professor at Proper Name Z College, a picturesque institution located on the banks of the W River. Tall, energetic, and somewhat shaggy, Dr. X has always been well-liked by his students. Yet for some time, he has felt restless about his teaching and how passive his classes are. So last year, in Dr. X's words, he 'finally worked up the courage to do something about it.'" The next paragraph contained a description of some innovation, accompanied by more quotes from the good doctor about his good intentions. There followed an account of what actually happened expressed in terms of the lexicon mentioned above, together with enough remarks from students and colleagues to hint that all did not go according to plan. Dr. X then sketched what he would do differently next time, concluding that everyone has learned a great deal, himself included.

As may be obvious from this caricature, the stylized reports generated by the National Teaching Project were written by journalists rather than faculty members. This is the third point to note: few professors were considered able or willing to provide useful accounts of teaching. Hardly any rhetorical tradition for doing so existed at the beginning of the project, but it was beginning to take hold by the end in the early 1980s. Professional societies play an increasingly important role, especially in the sciences. Included below are excerpts from three surveys authored by executive directors of mathematics, chemistry, and biology associations to introduce the "Reports on Teaching" in their fields. Willcox (1977), Dodge (1976), and Haight (1976) did not write as active faculty, but they were all well-informed, frank, influential, very supportive of the project's goals, and somewhat at a loss to provide specifics beyond mentioning the innovations of a few isolated professors. Through the 1980s, many of the professional societies began actively encouraging their members to present conference talks and newsletter articles about teaching in ways that would have been unimaginable a decade earlier when these groups were first approached by the National Teaching Project. By the early 1990s, Lee Shulman and Pat Hutchings were effectively describing and encouraging this process—in the pages of *Change* and elsewhere—as part of "making teaching community property." (See also Wagener's 1991 study of mathematics departments, "Changing the Culture of Teaching," excerpted in the section on "Promoting a Culture of Teaching and Learning.")

The 1991 article by Priscilla Laws on "Workshop Physics" marked a turning point in this trend. Here finally was a piece written by a physics professor reporting on her own tireless and inspiring experiments in physics education. The treatment was neither as breezy nor as easy to read as what the journalists produced, but it was worth the effort. The first section recounted how Halloun and Hestenes at Arizona State obtained disturbing results with the unusual test they devised to measure students' understanding of the concepts of physics and how their findings were replicated at Dickinson College by Wolf and Laws. The next sections described the steps then taken to develop, implement, and test the "Workshop Physics" course at Dickinson against these and other criteria. The final headings spoke of preliminary outcomes, interpretations based on other literature, unexpected results, applications to other courses, and conclusions.

Clearly, Laws structured her article more like the presentation of research findings in a scientific journal rather than the presentation of anecdotal reporting in a news magazine. Use of this academic template, in marked contrast to the style of the earlier "Reports on Teaching," tended to attract the attention and approval of advocates for what Ernest Boyer dubbed "the scholarship of teaching" in his landmark book of 1990, *Scholarship Reconsidered*. A few scientific journals had, by then, begun publishing papers by professors about pedagogy that closely resembled other papers in the discipline. Foregoing the numerical data, footnotes, and other technical trappings, *Change* helped present this kind of literature to a broader audience.

Priscilla Laws not only presented a mature account of *how* she teaches, but the first-person sentences of her opening paragraph also evidenced concern about *who* she teaches. A discipline-independent and politically-minded focus on the question of who scientists successfully reach was developed further in articles by Lynn Arthur Steen (1991) on scientific literacy and by Sheila Tobias (1990) on the second tier of the talent pool for science. The issues turned toward equity and access, challenging the traditional elitism of big science from a policy perspective. Indeed, both Steen and Laws originally developed their pieces for Project Kaleidoscope, a vital movement dedicated to improving science education for all students that Jeanne Narum began in 1989 as a coalition of four-year colleges.

To reach her memorable conclusion about the second tier of science talent ("they are not dumb, they are different," p. 11), Tobias (1990) employed the methodology of a social scientist. There was quite a punch to the observations, interviews, and journal entries gleaned by enlisting bright nonscientists to take science courses. This work, like Steen's, was still reminiscent of a genre that is particularly American and especially Washingtonian. The pattern is for "policy experts" to first identify an unusual formulation of some problem that may or may not be grounded in reality and then, believing that every problem has a clever solution, propose a fix that also may or may not be realistic. Tobias (1992) herself eventually offered such a critique of the process of science reform in a provocative article based on her book "Revitalizing Undergraduate Science: Why Some Things Work and Most Don't." Her sophisticated plea for "strategies rather than solutions" explicitly addressed deans and provosts, too, reflecting a gradual change in the *Change* readership as items for faculty about pedagogy become more commonplace within disciplinary channels.

The article by Kenneth Bruffee (1992) on "Science in a Postmodern World" was a direct response to the earlier work of Tobias. He pits quotes from her against the way Bruno Latour and Steve Woolgar expose science as "not a methodological evidentiary process but a process of interpretive construction" (p. 20). Also enlisted by Bruffee to challenge the traditional view of science he saw Tobias promulgating were Ferdinand de Saussure, Ludwig Wittgenstein, Clifford Geertz, Richard Rorty, and other thinkers that scientists may not have realized were relevant to their teaching if not for *Change*. Where else but *Change* could a spirited and public philosophical debate like this about pedagogy have erupted in 1992?

In ways that eventually facilitate collective progress, such clashes of ideas help words and concepts become more narrowly specified in meaning and, at the same time, more broadly shared throughout a community. Immediate dialogue for this purpose cannot take place in a magazine, of course, but Pat Hutchings did shepherd the publication in *Change* of case studies in the form of short stories about college teaching specifically designed to provoke organized discussions among faculty. The science incident included here (Goroff & Wilkinson, "Case," 1993a) was accompanied by an edited transcript of professors debating and analyzing, agreeing and disagreeing, about compelling issues raised by the case (Goroff & Wilkinson, "Response," 1993b).

Today, as technology poses questions about *where* we teach that challenge basic premises of higher education, it is good to know that there are still magazines like *Change* to which we can turn, not necessarily to solve the problems, but to help set the terms of debate in powerful, thoughtful, and enduring ways.

References

Arons, A. (1969, May/June). Science: The art of Inquiry. *Change, 1*, 31–35.

Boyer, E. (1990). *Scholarship reconsidered: Priorities of the professoriate*. Princeton, NJ: Carnegie Foundation for the Advancement of Teaching.

Bruffee, K. (1992, September/October). Science in a postmodern world. *Change, 24*, 18–25.

Dodge. R. A. (1976, July). The anachronisms of biology education. *Change, 8*, 6–7.

Francis, J. B., & Associates. (1978, August). An evaluation of *Change*'s National Teaching Project. *Change, 10*, 49–63.

Goroff, D. L., & Wilkinson, J. (1993a, November/December). Case number one: Force and inertia—A case about teaching introductory physics. *Change, 25*, 22–23.

Goroff, D. L., & Wilkinson, J. (1993b, November/December). Response to case number one: Hockey pucks, monkeys, and misconceptions—Four faculty talk about "force and inertia." *Change, 25*, 24–29.

Haight, G. P. (1976, July). Balancing chemistry's priorities. *Change, 8*, 4–5.

Laws, P. (1991, July/August). Workshop physics: Learning introductory physics by doing it. *Change, 23*, 20–27.

Steen, L. A. (1991, July/August). Reaching for science literacy. *Change, 23*, 11–19.

Tobias, S. (1990, July/August). They're not dumb. They're different: A new "tier of talent" for science. *Change, 22*, 11–30.

Tobias, S. (1992, May/June). Science education reform: What's wrong with the process? *Change, 24*, 13–19.

Van Dyne, L. (1971, September). Zacharias' latest experiment. *Change, 3*, 16–18.

Wagener, U. E. (1991, July/August). Changing the culture of teaching: Mathematics at Indiana, Chicago, and Harvard. *Change, 23*, 29–37.

Willcox, A. B. (1977, January). Mathematics: To know is not to teach. *Change, 9*, 26–27.

Science: The Art of Inquiry

Arnold Arons

Twenty-five years ago, the discontinuous impact on society of wartime scientific developments sensitized many educators to the need of imparting to an educated citizenry a heightened literacy in matters of science, and in the nature, essence and limitations of scientific thought. Since then, much has been written and said about teaching science as a part of liberal education, and a few moderately successful programs have come and gone.

Despite the sporadic activity and unabating discussion, however, it is remarkable how little of what I would call the "intellectual component" of the study of science has penetrated the textbooks and other course materials used in general education programs. With few exceptions, the new textbooks are little more than updated surveys that add new vocabulary to the old lists. They allow even less breathing space than their predecessors for the mastering of insights that lie behind the vocabulary; and they do little or nothing to help students stand back and view the impact of scientific knowledge in the perspective of intellectual history, to question the evidence from which their knowledge derives, or to question its mutability and limitations.

If one wishes eighteen- or nineteen-year-old students to acquire some perspective toward the intellectual content of science, to be able to articulate intelligent statements about its methods, processes, successes and limitations, it is not enough to teach them a few of the end results of successful scientific inquiry, to show them how to calculate how high a stone will rise when thrown into the air or how rapidly molecules move in a gas, and then blithely assume that the intellectual insights will develop automatically by some process of osmosis or spontaneous generation. Mature intellectual insights can indeed be developed, but they most definitely do not arise easily and spontaneously in the great majority of students — either prospective scientists or nonscientists. It is necessary to lead students deliberately into these perceptions, to give them time to absorb the impact, to

help them articulate statements, arguments, and analyses. . . .

Whether they have studied much physical science or not, students arrive at college having heard endless clichés about "exact science." They take this terminology literally, and implicitly ascribe to science an aseptic kind of infallibility that is a profound distortion of the actual facts. If from the earliest starting points one calls their attention to the idealizations and approximations that constitute the art of scientific inquiry . . . and which are present in *every* quantitative application of a scientific theory to prediction of physical effects, students can readily be brought to see that no quantitative prediction is ever exact in a literal sense, and that perhaps what most accurately distinguishes the so-called "exact science" from other human disciplines is the ability to assess in numerical terms how inexact one's predictions are, and to what extent, therefore, one's analysis should be regarded as *un*reliable.

From the didactic manner in which scientific concepts are forced on students in early schooling, it is understandable that they acquire the notion that scientific terms are rigid, unchanging entities with only one absolute significance that the initiated automatically "know" and that the uninitiated must acquire in one breathless, brain-twisting gulp. It comes as a revelation and a profound relief to many young people if one introduces them very explicitly to the fact that scientific terms go through a sequence of evolution, re-definition, sharpening and refinement, and that scientists start at a crude, initial, intuitive level and, profiting from insights gained in successive applications, develop concepts to sophistication. At each stage the original word stands for a new and more sophisticated idea; its meaning has been changed in significant, intrinsic ways; it no longer denotes only the first intuitive idea to which it was applied. This modest self-consciousness about the process of definition and re-definition enormously increases the confidence of students in their own grasp of sequence of thought, opens their eyes to similar shifts and extensions in the generation of other concepts, and alerts them to watch for similar semantic shifts that are rarely pointed out to them in the social sciences and humanities. . . .

Each teacher can readily satisfy his own tastes and predilections, provide his own emphasis and orientation. There are the aspects that James Conant referred to as the "tactics and strategy of science"; there is the dramatic interplay of inductive and deductive thought in the Newtonian Synthesis; there is the fascinating, partly scientific, partly sociological question of the validation and acceptance of scientific theories; there is the question of the "reality" of entities that transcend our senses — atoms, molecules, electrons; there is the conventionalist suggestion by Poincaré that we would always preserve the law of conservation of energy by inventing a new form of energy for every new phenomenon that did not fit into our previous scheme.

But regardless of what specific illustrations one elects to use, it is essential to give students time to relive and absorb the intellectual experience involved, to allow them to set it into a broad frame of personal reference so that they can begin to raise at least some questions of their own and articulate a few ideas from within themselves rather than parrot questions and ideas that are handed to them *ex cathedra*.

To achieve this immersion it is necessary to give students an adequate frame of reference, and that means it is essential to study enough of the relevant substantive scientific subject matter to make such discourse and discussion meaningful. This does not mean it is necessary to follow every historical dead end in exhausting detail, nor is it necessary to become involved in mathematical analysis that is excessively formidable and time-consuming, especially for nonscience students. Each teacher must seek an optimum balance that will vary with the particular group of students; they should be exposed to enough scientific subject matter to make their involvement genuine but not so much as to bury them.

The essential criterion is that they should not end up regurgitating secondhand pronouncements about the nature and processes of the scientific enterprise without ever having articulated any such insights out of their own intellectual experience. Without at least some participation in comprehension and interpretation of scientific concepts, theories and philosophy, secondhand statements about science have no more educational value than a commentary on poetry without a reading of the poetry, or a dissertation on the philosophy of history barren of any knowledge of the history of anything.

Rather than step into a classroom and beat our breast about the quandaries into which the release of nuclear energy has precipitated mankind, rather than pontificate about the still undefined ethical and moral problems that will descend on us with the synthesis of living matter and the control of genetic mechanisms, it seems to me far more effective and rational to get students to confront science through more modest insights and experiences. I am convinced that such studies contribute to the development of better educated men and more intelligent citizens in exactly the same way as do an awareness of history and a sensibility to literature. As educated men they must then, together with the rest of us, confront the grave problems that are not yet material for the classroom.

Zacharias' Latest Experiment

Larry Van Dyne

MIT's Dr. Jerrold Zacharias has a zest for experimentation that has kept him on one frontier after another for nearly four decades. . . . Now, at 66, he is director of MIT's Education Research Center and father figure for one of the more prominent entries in the country's growing parade of free style college learning experiments.

Although the experiment, called the Unified Science Study Program (USSP), is run by other people on a day-to-day basis, it was essentially Zacharias' conception. USSP students—freshmen and sophomores—are allowed to spend all their time on "projects" that interest them; the faith is that as they go about their work they will double back and pick up whatever skills—calculus, physics and the like—appear to them necessary or useful. "It was perfectly obvious," Zacharias says of the beginnings of the program, "that the ideal way for somebody to learn is for him to work on things he wants to work on. We simply needed a mechanism that would allow a student to jump into his own briar patch, where faculty members could make sure he didn't jump into too deep a thicket and could help him when he tried to hack his way out." The major requirement for USSP students, he says, is that they be "interested in and working on something." . . .

USSP started in the fall of 1969 when MIT told incoming freshmen they could enroll full-time in USSP instead of the usual first year fare of calculus, physics, chemistry and humanities courses. Many of the newcomers were skeptical about their ability to handle the promised freedom. . . .

For a few of MIT's bright, self-confident students the new-found freedom seemed perfect. They quickly started their own projects and became deeply involved. One boy was simply given space in a biology lab and went to work immediately on cell association in chicks. Other students, however, found the freedom tough going. One decided after three weeks to leave the program and take regular course work. . . .

But as the first year progressed an ill-defined anxiety about the program spread among the USSP staff. . . .

. . . "Although nobody said so, I think we all realized that sooner or later something would have to be required of the students," says one staff member. And what would be required was a kind of "contract" between a student and the staff member who was his adviser. The student would put down in writing what he wanted to do, why, how, and to whom he would report his activities. It was also clear that written documentation—journals, solved problems, lab data, computer programs and so on—would be required at the end of projects and that deadlines would be enforced.

The new policy did not rule out considerable contract negotiation and re-negotiation; but it did, it was hoped, mean less nonsense and sloppiness. . . .

Judah Schwartz, a 37-year-old physicist who had handled the operations of USSP from the beginning, believes the process of drawing contracts is crucial to USSP because it forces students to formulate problems carefully, a skill he believes many people have lost. "A young person formulates problems for himself and solves them until he gets to school," he says, "then he spends some longish period of time in school solving somebody's else's problems. He loses whatever facility he ever had for formulating his own problems. There is something wrong when a PhD candidate walks into a professor's office and says, 'I want to do a PhD. Do you have a problem?' And that happens over and over again."

Some considered the new policy an infringement on their original understanding of the program. But before it had been fully tested that spring, the rush of events at Kent State, Jackson State and in Cambodia led to a campus-wide student strike, and many students ended up finishing their projects during the summer or in the fall when they returned to Cambridge.

The first year reaction to the program was mixed. One student wrote afterwards:

"I will always consider my study at USSP as

important in my life, for if nothing else, it has given me the uninterrupted opportunity to define my life's goal. It is too easy in the established course mode of high school and college to drift aimlessly through the system . . ."

Another student was not so enthusiastic:

"The quality of what I learned this year has left much to be desired in my mind. I wrote very little; my journal is pitiful indeed. By the regular program's standards I have lost a full year. I still have all degree requirements ahead and a quarter of my time gone.

"I cannot blame USSP entirely. Much of this lack of success is my fault; doubtless, it was I who wrote nothing; it was I who was inefficient about projects; it was I who failed to pursue topics of interest to any depth . . . Yet, USSP is an experiment, and I am a guinea pig. Must not the experi-menter watch to see that no harm comes to his guinea pigs? I have gotten an education this year, but it has been an education in retrospect. I have learned . . . that I must be much more wary of my freedom." . . .

Zacharias himself . . . is convinced that his basic notion—that students should become more responsible for their own education as they become more mature—is still sound. "Many of our students, like many adults, want to be led around in every way," he says. "Most want complete lectures, complete textbooks, complete specifications of what to learn . . . It's very difficult to transfer the responsibility to them . . . Of course, I'm not satisfied. I'm never satisfied with a static situation. But we're learning fast and the rate at which we're learning is increasing."

July 1976

Balancing Chemistry's Priorities

G. P. Haight

While chemistry curricula have proven themselves one of the more successful devices for training professional practitioners, they remain one of the greatest sources of academic frustration. Teaching at the upper levels has not, as yet, been particularly troubled. While individual problems do arise, often due to the gradual obsolescence of teachers and equipment in a continually evolving science, by and large teachers of upper-level courses are dealing with a well-selected group of students. A recent study at the University of Illinois, for example, found no junior-level chemistry majors who ranked below the ninety-fifth percentile in their high school classes. The roots of this selectivity lie in both the difficulty of introductory chemistry courses, and in natural limits to the numbers of those who have talent for and take pleasure in the solution of chemical problems.

Chemistry teaching at the introductory level, however, is deeply troubled, largely as a result of the increasing volume and sophistication of knowledge in the field. The principal problem here involves the selection of the material to be taught. Pressures to include a descriptive body of basic factual knowledge, along with principles governing chemical structures and processes, experimental techniques, and theoretical frameworks, all compete for a slice of the introductory pie. One consequence has been the excision of much factual material in favor of principles, theory, and sophisticated, modern laboratory techniques. (Recently, however, environmental concerns have appeared on the chemical scene, and the application of chemistry to the environment has encouraged a revival of descriptive material, especially in courses designed for nonmajors.)

The other side of the coin is the sheer volume of information that often seems to defy selectivity. Chemistry has shared the excitement of the rapid development of science, and chemistry teachers have in many cases been involved in this development. They have thus been generally sympathetic to a tendency to include the latest developments in their introductory courses. This has led to expansion of texts, terser summaries of information, and continued complaints from students about too much material, too rapidly covered. A year of organic chemistry in 1900 required a 200-

page text. In 1975, 1,500 pages are covered in the same time.

A second problem in chemistry teaching is the expansion of the student population. This demographic expansion occurred during the post-Sputnik era when high school courses were upgraded through such projects as Chem Study and the Chemical Bond Approach. Thermodynamics, kinetics, and molecular orbital theory followed. Courses became more abstract and more sophisticated, at the same time as a large, new student population, less well-prepared and less sophisticated intellectually, appeared in chemistry classes. This led to a rash of efforts to design special chemistry courses for special people, *viz*, chemistry for poets, chemistry for liberal arts, chemistry for nurses, and chemistry for underprepared students. There may, of course, very well be suitable ways of teaching descriptive material without mathematics, chemical processes without physics, and so on, to students with limited backgrounds in such supporting subjects. But heated and divisive arguments regularly occur over whether introductory chemistry can or should be different things to different people — whether courses for nonspecialists are or can be different courses, or just watered down courses for the less competent. While experience shows that many casual students, especially in required chemistry courses, are less competent and less motivated than majors, many competent nonmajors take chemistry with genuine interest and are capable of outstanding achievement even in a course designed for chemistry majors. Which students to aim for and what spread of abilities and motivation to consider in planning courses for nonmajors probably troubles chemistry teachers as much as or more than any other single question.

A third source of trouble in chemistry teaching is the development of technical aids to teaching, learning, and communication. Technology holds great promise in many respects. It can display visual phenomena with film and easily edited videotape, and provide individual self-paced instruction through computers. But the time required both to review and create these teaching and learning materials is hard to impose on a teaching schedule. Moreover, ability to perform well on tests generally seems to be independent of the method of teaching. And in any case, well-written textbooks with carefully planned study exercises have provided individualized, self-paced study systems for two centuries, prompting one to wonder if the time and expense of developing new techniques is worth the effort. The problem, then, is twofold, requiring first the development of an array of technological teaching techniques, and second, effective incorporation of these techniques into existing curricula.

A fourth source of difficulty concerns the growing interest among some chemistry teachers in learning theory and educational psychology. Perhaps 50 percent of all students in introductory chemistry courses cannot operate at the Piagetian formal operational level essential to the attainment of chemical insight. Educators are seeking to define student goals and limited objectives, a development many think may discourage independent thinking on the part of students.

Most of these problems will be with us until and unless teachers of introductory courses can settle on a cohesive body of descriptive material to provide a basic chemical vocabulary; the levels of theory, explanation, and abstract thinking accessible to the students admitted to each course; and adequate systems either for selecting students for chemistry courses or for selection of courses by students themselves despite variations in their preparation, ability, and motivation.

The selection of material, in terms both of quantity and quality, is ultimately the governing concern. How best to deliver the material is an aggravating but secondary problem. In the words of one of my colleagues: "What can we leave out of what we must cover in order to get to that which is interesting? And why do we consider it most important to include that material we least understand ourselves?"

The Anachronisms of Biology Education

Richard A. Dodge

"Traditional biology programs are rapidly becoming anachronisms for too large a segment of the constituency of higher education." This recent statement from the education committee of the American Institute of Biological Sciences (AIBS) reflects a growing concern that biology education has neither kept pace with realistic career training developments nor provided for the public's need to understand the discipline. Many studies and reports have pointed to an overproduction of conventionally trained biologists, and they question society's ability to absorb ever increasing numbers of them. While biological educators are currently enjoying slightly improved employment prospects, the increase in teaching positions may reflect recent concern for environment, energy, and health-related topics, rather than for biology in the traditional sense. Students appear to be pursuing the subject as preparation for what they perceive as more idealistic careers.

A recent editorial in *BioScience* suggests that these students are seeking the "other biology." The other biology is seen as an application of broad biological understanding to fields that once neither required nor expected such knowledge. The emergence of environmental legislation, for instance, has stimulated a need for practitioners to conduct the necessary studies for impact statements. While placement announcements for these positions more often indicate a preference for legal or economic backgrounds, some training in the biological sciences is certainly perceived as germane.

Social scientists, too, are recognizing the need for more biological emphasis. A recent National Science Foundation (NSF) reorganization placed biology and the social sciences under the same directorate. Still the emerging marriage of the social and life sciences has not been well received by more traditional biological educators, and as a result, social science departments are teaching more and more biology while biology departments often teach little of a social nature.

Cognizant of this trend, however, some two-year and small four-year institutions are beginning to effect a merger of the disciplines. Such courses as biology and ethics; the social concerns of biology; or biology, man, and society now compete for undergraduate enrollment. For as society becomes increasingly aware of the influence of biological knowledge on population control, disease, food production, environmental protection, genetic regulation, and so on, more and more nonbiologists will be involved in what must be considered at least "semibiological" fields. How will traditional academic biology departments respond to this changing application of biological knowledge? Unfortunately, many programs are ill-equipped to provide flexible and adaptable training for these students. On the other hand, the programs . . . at Purdue, South Dakota State University, Antelope Valley College, San Diego State University, Tulane and elsewhere — have in fact focused on the need for a broader outlook on biology education and for more flexibility in the teaching of the subject matter.

The AIBS education committee believes that the needs of biology students are more far-reaching and expansive than many academic departments realize. In discussing the problem of anachronisms, the committee concluded that a desirable program of biological education must improve the ability of individuals and society to adjust to rapid change brought about by advances in biological knowledge; emphasize the potential role of biology education in social, political, and economic decisions; recognize and endorse the need in higher education for alternative programs of study in biology and for pedagogical alternatives in its instruction that will address themselves specifically to the first two goals mentioned; encourage the development, testing, and implementation of alternatives in biology education in prestigious institutions across the nation; and perform continuous evaluation of the impact of these programs and revise them accordingly.

The concern is that conventional biology instruction tends to serve the field's several subdisciplines rather more than those areas of interest or concern outside the discipline's traditional purview. All too often, it serves an elite clientele with little regard for the needs of the larger society. The old-school biologist may look with scorn on the applied aspects of the discipline, and the attendant concern that erosion of academic rigor results from the teaching of applied subjects may help to explain the banishment of many related and dependent studies from the biology department. Thus, in contrast to chemistry, applied biology must often now be taught in schools or departments other than biology—in the school of agriculture, for example, or of natural resources.

This escape of satellite subjects from biology's orbit has occurred largely because biology programs are not flexible or open enough to provide the specialized training required in applied fields. There have been efforts to design individualized, modular, or minicourse biology programs … — but they have emerged in response to the special needs of students in such fields as agriculture, health, social biology, wildlife management, and other areas.

By contrast, the usual introductory course in biology may reflect the biological subdiscipline studied by the instructor, who has probably had little training in, or exposure to, law, politics, economics, and the social and psychological sciences. Frequently, he is ill-equipped to explain the subtleties of a continually evolving career market. Development of open-ended and multiple-track individualized instruction, however, allows for varied learning experiences, and the recent work of Volpe and others is beginning to fill the need for a more synoptic approach to the subject.

A great deal of evidence indicates that most people will follow a single career during their lifetime. However, the notion of "career" itself has expanded, and NSF projections indicate that by 1985, a large proportion of science and engineering graduates will have found employment outside the academic and research fields as currently defined. The present system usually does not provide an education that permits the learner career mobility, flexibility, and adaptability. Traditional training prepares the graduate for narrow career choices. Once a biologist, traditionally trained for research, enters the teaching field (at least 70 percent of all biologists have primary responsibilities to teaching), there is little opportunity to bring his or her expertise to focus on the educational enterprise. The pedagogical aspects of the biologist's training and opportunities to explore alternative fields have been neglected in favor of research. And so the cycle repeats itself, and biology education drifts further from the needs and concerns both of its students and of society.

Generally, the first and only exposure to biology a nonmajor receives is in a required freshman course. Because many introductory courses are designed for the potential major, a typical freshman botany, zoology, or general biology program has little practical value for the nonmajor. The last thing a nonmajor needs is to understand molecular biology, microscopy, or the life cycle of a liverwort. Yet the discipline persists in promoting the myth of the necessity of traditional biology in general education. The time has come to devise programs that explore biology as it pertains to every citizen's life, environment, mental and physical health, and political decisions.

The *BioScience* editorial referred to before suggests "such a program would be directed toward what have been called the parabiological professions, such as the social worker who must know enough physiology, anatomy, and nutrition to be able to organize effective outpatient programs for the aged; the staff officer for a regional environmental board who must combine ecology, soil science, chemistry, psychology, political science, and aesthetics in implementing a generalized land-use program." Instruction should provide multidisciplinary training programs designed to provide students with the resources to meet changing career goals. A few such programs—the minicourse and BIO-TECH project, Mulligan's zoo experiences, and Jordan's BioCO-TIE program—have already met with some success. And certainly Avila's work with disadvantaged students has demonstrated that nonbiology students can and will profit from meaningful biological experiences. But more is needed.

If NSF and Bureau of Labor Statistics data are to be believed, the system will be full of life science PhDs within a decade. Many will be underemployed or employed outside the field of biology. The teaching and research opportunities for these developing biologists will not be met by programs now found in traditional departments. What about the "other biology"?

Mathematics

To Know Is Not to Teach

A. B. Willcox

When I emerged from graduate school in the fifties I entered the college teaching community reasonably well trained in the scholarship of mathematics. I knew about as much as a college teacher needs to know about mathematics and about the experiences of learning and creating it. Perhaps because mathematics is closer to pure thought than almost any other discipline, I and most of my fellow graduates began teaching careers with the idea that the essence of good teaching was a lucid and concise exposition of the structure of mathematics. My calling was to lay before the student as clearly as I could the logical chain of ideas that constitutes mathematics, stepping aside at appropriate moments to allow the student to forge links of his or her own. The real thrill of learning mathematics, after all, was a sudden recognition of "the pattern," the discovery of the solution to a puzzle. If one knew mathematics, had experienced the unique thrill of seeing order where there had been disorder, and possessed a reasonably logical mind, then he could teach mathematics.

I must openly acknowledge the widespread reputation of mathematicians as, shall we say, casual teachers. The reputation is largely undeserved. There are outstanding exceptions, and the overall average is better than the myth and rising. But we cannot point altogether with pride. I am convinced that as a PhD of the fifties, I was about average in my concept and technique of teaching. Graduate training in mathematics completely ignored the technique of teaching except insofar as a teaching assistant received positive or negative feedback from his largely unsupervised classroom experience. The graduate learning experience was itself so far removed from the undergraduate educational scene that its contributions to classroom technique were probably negative in the balance. The graduate professor successfully focused his knowledge for an audience of dedicated apprentice scholars. Understandably, his students emerged as teachers with the same focus.

Fortunately, the mathematical community is coming to recognize that good teaching, the art of transmitting knowledge in such a way that it will soak into young minds, is as important as possessing the knowledge itself. Naturally, the first responsibility of the teacher is to be authentic, to be competent in his or her field, but knowledge must be transmitted to live. Mathematics teachers are working harder at their teaching. It is beginning to show. And I am convinced that almost anything they try will work.

Is this heresy? Perhaps, though I hasten to add that not all educational experiments are successful, whatever "success" means in this laboratory. Not all teaching innovations endure and many that do are not transportable. But I find it hard to imagine any serious and carefully planned teaching innovation that will not contribute ultimately to better teaching. Even a teaching experience that is largely negative usually points toward a promising alternative, and I have yet to learn of a teacher who has taught students less during an innovative classroom experience than he or she usually taught in the traditional mode.

The direction of teaching improvements in mathematics in the past few years, as I see it, is primarily toward increasing our students' understanding of the role of mathematics in society. This is a loaded phrase of course, and I am using it broadly. Mathematics closely related to the mainstreams of thought. It is vital to man's efforts to understand his physical, intellectual, and social environment and it receives stimulation and direction from these efforts. In the headlong rush of the fifties and sixties to teach our students more and better mathematics, we probably neglected the relationships between mathematics and the real world. Mathematics students and the field as a whole suffered. There is a growing awareness of this blind spot, and teachers are rushing to add "relevance" to their repertoire. The teaching projects in this report reflect this trend, but many of the changes are taking place quietly in classrooms where the teaching is still generally considered to be traditional.

There is also a great deal of experimentation with various modes of self-paced instruction as teachers strive for an antidote to the mass marketing of the expansionist sixties. Experimentation with the use of various media in large group instruction is still going on, but these projects too are searching for more personalized instruction.

Mathematics has several important instructional assets that we should not fail to use in our efforts to improve undergraduate teaching. For example, there are few if any strong cultural factors to influence the content and methods of undergraduate mathematics. Mathematics has strong cultural ties but it does not itself espouse controversial theories. The mathematics teacher is therefore free of many of the constraints felt by teachers of, for example, history, sociology, or even biology. We are also fortunate in that mathematicians do not generally specialize at the level of undergraduate study. Almost any reasonably well-trained mathematics teacher is scientifically qualified to teach any undergraduate course; certainly any PhD should be so qualified. For this reason, it is easier to assemble a team of mathematics teachers to experiment with new teaching techniques in a particular subject than it is to assemble such a team in another field. We have a responsibility to use such special assets wisely.

In searching for teaching projects to nominate for this report, we wrote to the directors of several innovative projects that were widely discussed in the late sixties and early seventies. The response might be considered discouraging. A typical reply included the statement, "In spite of initial successes, I notice that many such programs eventually regress toward the old-fashioned prototypes — perhaps for very good reasons." Another person, who has been extremely active and influential in the leadership of the Mathematical Association of America, the organization most directly concerned with undergraduate mathematics teaching in the United States, advised that our efforts to improve the quality of teaching be restricted largely to improving the ability of new PhDs to teach in the traditional mode. He reasoned that most of the innovative teaching projects have very little influence on 95 percent of the teaching. In the end, none of these vintage teaching projects turned out to be suitable for discussion in this report. Discouraging? I think not. This is the normal life cycle of teaching innovation. One might as well be discouraged by the fact that even the great eventually die. The teaching innovation that evolves back to the traditional prototype leaves tradition changed in some way. Few innovative teaching experiences have profound influence on the vast majority, but even the least has some influence. The most radical experiment can teach even the strict traditionalist something useful. Only by continually trying out new ideas can we grow, and if we do not grow, we gradually die.

Good teaching is hard work, and improving teaching even a little takes real effort. Any college teacher who fails to realize this is not fully equipped for our profession. Any college teacher who does not work hard to improve his or her teaching technique neglects one of our primary professional responsibilities. Any college teacher with a vision for better teaching who does not dare to experiment, for fear of failure or out of reluctance to break rank, is wasting one of our most precious natural resources. I congratulate the editors of *Change* and the directors of the Undergraduate Teaching Program for providing reports of some of the attempts of our colleagues to grow in their teaching. We will all grow a little from their efforts.

They're Not Dumb. They're Different.

A *New "Tier of Talent" for Science*

Sheila Tobias

. . . Who will do science? That depends on who is included in the talent pool. The old rules do not work in the new reality. It's time for a different game plan that brings new players in off the bench.

— Shirley M. Malcom, AAAS

Everybody says it in one fashion or another: we need to teach more students more science. To me, a policy-oriented social scientist, this means we have to identify the able students who are choosing not to do science; find out why they are put off by science and attracted to other occupations; and, if necessary, change the recruitment, rewards, and opportunity structures to match their temperament and needs.

But "recruitment," "rewards," and "opportunity structures" are not the usual stuff of educational reform, at least in science. So it should not be too surprising that science educators are promoting, instead, a massive restructuring of the nation's elementary and secondary science curriculum and the training or retraining of virtually everyone who teaches science from kindergarten through twelfth grade. . . .

The fact is, a very large number of American high school graduates survive their less-than-perfect precollege education with their taste and even some talent for science intact. As many as half a million students are probably taking introductory college science at some level each year. The problem is that between 1966 and 1988 the proportion of college freshmen planning to *major* in science and mathematics fell by half. Even after the introductory course, the flow out of science continues seemingly unchecked: a third to a half of those who initially indicate an interest in science leave science well into the major, some even after completing a science degree.

The "hemorrhaging" of would-be science workers at the *college* level is a fact too long ig-nored; understanding and stemming it become matters of urgent strategy. . . .

But scientists are not likely to rethink recruitment, rewards, and retention so long as they continue to expect the next generation of science workers to rise, as they did, like cream to the top. This is why introductory college courses remain unapologetically competitive, selective, and intimidating, designed to winnow out all but the "top tier"; it explains why there is little attempt to create a sense of "community" among average students of science and why good students are often given the wrong message that there is no room in science for people like themselves. . . .

To solve the science shortfall we are obliged to think and think hard not just about who does science and why, but who doesn't do science, and why not. To this end, we should examine, as a beginning construct, the student on the "second tier." . . .

Stalking the Second Tier

The second tier is a loose hypothetical construct, which includes a *variety* of types of students not pursuing science in college for a *variety* of reasons. They may have different learning styles, different expectations, different degrees of discipline, different "kinds of minds" from students who traditionally like and do well at science.

But then again they may not. It is important in thinking about the second tier *not* to populate it with people or even types we already know. We simply cannot predict who would be attracted by differently configured science instruction any more than we can imagine how recruitment, reward-structures, and instruction in science should be changed. Hence, the initial strategy was simply to locate a group of students who have not taken science in college and to find out what happens when they do.

I and my colleagues began the study by recruiting a small and diverse sample of postgraduates to stand in for the second tier. With one exception . . . all had been science avoiders in college, but had demonstrated ability in other fields. Each of them was then asked to "seriously audit" a semester-long introductory course in calculus-based physics or chemistry. They were expected to perform as well as they could in their courses, and they did. In addition, they were asked to focus their attention on what might make introductory science "hard" or even "alienating" for students like themselves. . . .

The study began with at least one assumption: The second tier is not the second rate. . . .

Final Speculations . . .

. . . The second tier project, of which only two examples are included here, involved only introductory courses in physics and chemistry and not biology, because physical science is where the shortfall is expected to occur and where attrition at the college (and graduate) level is highest. Our auditors were students who might have done science in college, but chose not to. As more mature learners, they found the subjects "fascinating," the teaching adequate (even "good," given the goals of the introductory courses), but not designed to *woo* them or people like them into science.

In a postscript to the project, [one] professor made his assumptions quite explicit: he fully expected his introductory physics students to be already committed to the subject and to want to improve their problem-solving skills. For our auditors, that focus produced a certain *tyranny of technique*. They hungered — all of them — for information about *how* the various methods they were learning had come to be, *why* physicists and chemists understand nature the way they do, and *what* were the *connections* between what they were learning and the larger world.

They also suffered mightily from the absence of community. This was exacerbated both by the large class size common in introductory science and by the lack of a contagious enthusiasm for the subject matter, even among those of their fellow students who were doing well. To be sure, we have no evidence that those whom we are calling "first tier" (students whom even poor teaching might not dissuade from science) were alienated

or disappointed by these courses. Our students, however, needed more attention, more depth, and more excitement.

For some years now, the four-year liberal arts colleges have been producing a larger *share* of physical science majors than the research universities. One reason is that they do not, as a rule, offer engineering, agriculture, nursing, or the like, so their introductory science courses need not function as "service factories" for other degree programs. Another reason is that class size, even at the introductory level, is relatively small and professors are readily accessible. But surely another factor must be the science departments' need to populate their programs: either they prime the demand for science or they have too few students to teach. Recruitment has to be intentional at colleges like these, and from their institutions' output data, it appears that it is.

Why, in the face of a much-touted shortfall, have the large research universities not adopted a similar strategy? . . .

I have already offered one of my speculations: the prejudice among faculty members that "true" science students will not need to be appealed or pandered to, but will rise like cream to the top irrespective of what happens in their introductory courses. Other pressures are also at work. 1) It is easier to teach the standard course in the standard way; 2) it is necessary to pack in as much material as possible to prepare students for the next course in the sequence; 3) it is "cost-effective" to gather 300-plus students in a single classroom for one presentation; and 4) since there are no outside teaching funds with which to pay skilled native English speakers to lead the laboratories and recitation sections, it is necessary to employ graduate students who have been selected on criteria very different from teaching, however impoverished their instructional skills . . . and so on. This "prejudice" and these "pressures" are very real, and should inform our thinking about how to stalk a next cohort of talent for science.

Recommendations

"Science education policy is not made by government; it is made by college science departments."

Shirley Malcom, AAAS

. . . The first step is a moral and strategic imperative: no college student should be permitted to say "no" to science without a struggle. This will involve forays into the comfortable, prejudice-laden views of the science professoriate, many of whom believe that one has to have a "mathematical mind" or a "scientific bent" to do science. No longer can we afford binary classifications of students into those who can do science and those who can't and *never will*.

■ Recruitment and especially ongoing support for any student who crosses the classroom threshold into science should be a conscious goal of introductory courses in science. . . .

■ As part of this pursuit, the issue of class size has to be addressed anew. There is conflicting literature on the effects of class size, but one finding is indisputable: that class size and teaching methods are inextricably linked. . . .

. . . [S]maller classes that allow just such "interaction," and/or the formation of small study groups, are exactly what we need to reach next-tier students.

■ All students who decide to leave science should be given "exit interviews" conducted by someone within the department. . . .

■ If the science professoriate cannot find the time or expertise to undertake these added duties, a new cadre of professionals, trained in both science and counseling, should be recruited to act as "science advisers." . . .

■ Resident advisers and other college support staff should be recruited from among science majors to be the role models, to teach "survival strategies," and to advise beginning students interested in science. . . .

■ Most importantly, the science faculty must find a way to provide the welcome and success nontraditional science students require *in the classroom*. Freshman science should become again what it once was: the most exciting, mind-expanding course in the curriculum. Studies show that science-intenders who change majors, like our second tier stand-ins, had a need to *enjoy* their science courses.

This does not mean those courses should be made easy or watered-down. Our stand-ins wanted *more* challenge, not less, but of a different kind. For them, their courses—particularly their exams—were diminished in scope and value by what they called the *tyranny of technique*. Baldly stated, course exercises were of insufficient *intellectual* content to appeal to their wide-ranging minds and interests.

As K. Patricia Cross reminds us, any reform of college science education, if it is to take place at all, must happen *in the classroom*, where the professor comes to teach and the students come to learn.

Not all students prepared to do science can be recruited to science no matter how much we do for them. It would be foolish to claim that they could. . . . But there still remain, I believe, a good number of students who could be recruited and retained if they were made to feel, as Stephanie put it so well, that there is something science could give to them and something they could give back to science.

And, until we know who they are, we dare not decide in advance who they are not.

July/August 1991

Reaching for Science Literacy

Lynn Arthur Steen

. . . Jon Miller at the Public Opinion Laboratory at Northern Illinois University . . . has sampled scientific literacy for over 20 years along three dimensions—content, process, and impact on society. . . .

According to this three-dimensional criterion, only 6 percent of adults are "scientifically literate."

Among college graduates, the percentage is higher, but nothing to be proud of—it is about 17 percent. What's worse, only one in four college graduates who major in science and engineering qualify as scientifically literate, and only one in ten of those who major in education do so.

The data on mathematical or quantitative

literacy—numeracy, for short—are equally dismal. . . .

Scientists and mathematicians worry a lot about the scientific pipeline—especially about the severe under-representation of blacks, Hispanics, and many other minority populations. Until recently, few worried about students' scientific or mathematical literacy. But attitudes are changing on this issue as scientists and educators begin to realize the potential for policy disasters when a scientifically illiterate electorate confronts challenges of unprecedented significance posed by issues of energy, environment, and health. It's clear to virtually everyone that the present system of science education works well only for those *already* committed to science; it fails almost totally in the broader task of educating citizens.

What Works

Volumes have been written about the crisis in science and mathematics education. . . . [S]everal themes emerge that provide guidelines rooted in persuasive research and effective practice. . . .

Community: Students learn best in circumstances that provide not only intellectual stimulation, but also the social, emotional, and ethical contexts necessary for sustained motivation. Learning science is hard, and although some students have the tenacity to persevere in spite of external hurdles, most do not. Students need to be invited to participate in the shared values and common culture of science; they need to be socialized into the scientific community even as they struggle to learn the methods and results of science itself.

Construction: Students do not simply learn what is taught. Rather, their experiences modify prior beliefs, yielding a scientific knowledge that is uniquely personal. Learning takes place when students construct their own representation of knowledge. Facts and formulas will not become part of deep intuition if they are only committed to memory. They must be explored, used, revised, tested, modified, and finally accepted through a process of active investigation, argument, and participation. Science instruction that does not provide these types of opportunities rarely achieves its objectives.

Connections: To make sense of science and mathematics, students must be encouraged to make connections—whether to social, historical,

or personal contexts, to scientific and social phenomena, or to elegant argument and compelling logic. Science and mathematics provide distinctive windows through which students can view the world and see connections to other things they value. Good teaching constantly reveals these connections, both within the sciences and in other areas of life and knowledge.

Continuity: Science and mathematics form a seamless fabric of learning from pre-school years through graduate study and research. The essence of science can be heard in the two-year-old's incessant question: "Why?" College science and mathematics departments both receive students from schools and also prepare teachers for schools. Since teachers tend to teach as they were taught (and not as they were taught to teach), it is vitally important that college science and mathematics instruction exemplify the best standards for teaching.

Programs that work in undergraduate science and mathematics exhibit many of the characteristics of community and connections. The evidence from around the country in all types of institutions is remarkably clear:

- The success of undergraduate research experiences in drawing students into scientific careers is based, to a great extent, on the opportunities such experiences provide students in making connections and constructing knowledge within a community of faculty and student colleagues.
- The remarkable record of the historically black institutions in educating students in science and mathematics—these institutions produce black undergraduate majors in the mathematical and physical sciences at rates 50 percent higher than the proportion of students they enroll—is due in large measure to the strong role that community plays in setting and supporting high expectations for students.
- The programs pioneered by Uri Treisman at the University of California enabling black and Hispanic students to succeed with calculus are centered on special efforts to establish an effective learning community among these students, to enrich the curriculum in ways that maintain continuity with students' personal development, and to make connections with things students value. . . .

Active Learning

Science and mathematics learning thrives in vigorous communities that help students make connections with issues of importance to them. It thrives when students experience a continuity in their studies that helps them construct their personal knowledge-map of science and mathematics. Despite unmistakable, very real disputes about the content and organization of science education, it is important to note the widespread *agreement* about these and several other fundamental principles of instruction:

■ *Raise expectations*. If more is expected in science and mathematics education, more will be achieved. Students can succeed in science and mathematics, and they will succeed if we expect them to. Colleges must expect all students to become conversant in science and mathematics.

■ *Increase breadth*. Most students would benefit from a curriculum that reflects the power and richness of the sciences. Each introductory course should be designed as if it were the last science or mathematics course the students will take—since, for the majority of students, it will be.

■ *Use computers*. Just as computers have changed the practice of science and mathematics, so they must also change what we teach and how we teach it. Some topics are just no longer as important as they used to be; others are more important. Scientific computing adds an important new paradigm—computer simulation—to the empirical and theoretical methodologies of science.

■ *Engage students*. Students are not empty receptacles waiting for knowledge to be poured into them. Rather, their experiences modify prior beliefs, yielding a scientific knowledge that is uniquely personal. To ensure effective learning, science and mathematics faculty must employ strategies that make students active participants in their own learning, not passive receivers of knowledge.

■ *Encourage teamwork*. Employers repeatedly stress the importance of being able to work with a team on common objectives. Most complex problems demand the talents of many different people. Yet science is too often taught in a competitive manner that encourages isolated student work. Science students must learn how to work with others to achieve a common goal: to plan, discuss, compromise, question, and organize.

■ *Stimulate creativity*. Students often complain that science is "dull" because instruction stresses problems that are to be solved by one proper method yielding a single correct answer. Nothing could be further from the practice of science or mathematics. Exploration, conjecture, dead-ends, "what-if" analysis, strategizing, and—most important—vigorous argument are the norm in scientific practice. Students need to see this face of science from the very first moment.

■ *Reduce fragmentation*. In an effort to organize scientific knowledge into easy-to-learn pieces, courses have been fragmented into chunks selected to illustrate textbook methods. Real problems don't come in compartmentalized form. Fragmentation destroys the methodological unity of science that is its primary source of power.

■ *Require writing*. Nothing helps a student learn a subject better than the discipline of writing about it. Writing advances the goal of learning to communicate about science and mathematics; it helps students clarify their own understanding as they try to put ideas into coherent written form; and it provides an opportunity for students who like writing better than abstraction to grow in science or mathematics with a vehicle more suited to their abilities. Writing enhances learning by involving students in the expression of meaning.

■ *Encourage discussion*. Most talk in a science or mathematics class comes from the teacher, not the students. In typical courses, students serve as scribes, taking notes and asking occasional questions for clarification. None of this engages the student's mind as effectively as does vigorous argument and discussion. The role of evidence in science and of proof in mathematics can be learned only by doing, not by listening.

Instructions rooted in these practices can energize students and faculty in a special type of shared enterprise—a natural science community. Students enmeshed in such a community will learn not only the knowledge of science, but also its culture, enterprise, and motivation.

Scientific Literacy . . .

But the value to society of scientifically literate leaders goes well beyond the traditional benefits of informed public policy and well-founded decisions. The culture of science has much to teach the men and women who are to be tomorrow's leaders—to learn from mistakes, to share ideas freely, and to rely on data. These and other features of the scientific method are important lessons that all students should learn.

Effective introductory courses will raise the water table for all who study science, thus also helping to build strong majors. . . . What is said of calculus in fact applies to *all* first-year courses in science or mathematics: each introductory course should be a pump rather than a filter in the scientific pipeline.

The shift in metaphor from a filter to a pump conveys subtle implications for faculty responsibility. If first-year science and mathematics courses are designed to filter out weak students, the responsibility of faculty is to set standards sufficiently high so that only the "very best" students pass on to the next tier of courses. If such courses are supposed, instead, to pump as many students as possible into further study of science, then their primary goal must be to provide the motivation and self-assurance necessary for effective learning.

Challenges

With few exceptions, introductory college courses in science and mathematics are total failures. Since the vast majority of students who enroll in them never go on to further study in either science or mathematics, they serve no introductory purpose. Neither do they instruct students effectively in the nature of science or mathematics. At their best, they offer the two-dimensional shadow of a rich, multi-dimensional world; at their worst—which is all too often—they dash motivation and produce another wave of science avoiders ready to convey their attitudes about science to their children.

To be fair, the challenges facing college faculties in this area are virtually overwhelming. Students enter college spread out over approximately five years of schooling in their mathematical and scientific preparation. Although some students are prepared and eager to move ahead with advanced study in specific subjects (e.g., physics, calculus), the large majority would probably be better served by courses that provide legitimate introductions to science and mathematics. Such courses must:

- Engage students in the process of scientific discovery and mathematical practice—actively, regularly, and relentlessly. Passive learning should be taboo.
- Challenge students in a manner appropriate to their preparation. The goal must be to build well-founded self-confidence so that each student leaves the course as a science enthusiast rather than as a science avoider.
- Introduce the power and breadth of science or mathematics, including methodology, fundamental principles, and impact on society.
- Serve as a legitimate and effective transition from high school study to higher courses in science and mathematics.
- Provide future teachers with experience in the excitement of scientific discovery.

It is possible to accomplish goals such as these, but not within the confines of the traditional first-year science or mathematics courses. . . .

Workshop Physics

Learning Introductory Physics by Doing It

Priscilla Laws

I n 1985, after 20 years of teaching at Dickinson College, I began to question the way introductory physics is taught in college. . . .

. . . Robert Boyle, John Luetzelschwa [and I] . . . came to the idea of abandoning lectures in favor of a computer-enhanced workshop format for introductory physics.

In 1986, the federal Fund for the Improvement of Postsecondary Education (FIPSE) awarded us a three-year grant of several hundred thousand dollars to develop the Workshop Physics program. . . .

Implementing the Program

In . . . 1987, we plunged headlong into using the new workshop format to teach our first classes of 75 students. Each section of Workshop Physics meets for three two-hour sessions a week with up to 24 students, an instructor, and two undergraduate assistants. Each pair of students shares the use of a Macintosh computer and an extensive collection of scientific apparatus and other gadgets. Student assistants staff the Workshop labs during evening and weekend hours to facilitate out-of-class collaboration. With a total enrollment of about 75 students, the allocation of faculty contact hours is essentially the same as it had been under the lecture system. However, we hire additional student help for classroom assisting and equipment management.

The structure of the courses is based on a program of guided inquiry embodied in a Student Activity Guide. With topics keyed to standard textbooks, each unit occupies about a week. Students usually begin a unit by exploring preconceptions about physical phenomena and then making qualitative observations. After some reflection and discussion, the instructor helps students develop definitions and mathematical theories. The week usually ends with quantitative experimentation centered around verifying mathematical theories.

Between class sessions, students are asked to read the textbook and work the requisite number of sacrosanct problems.

Every few weeks a two-hour written examination is given. Besides being twice as long as the exams in more traditional courses, these exams have sections on concepts, data analysis, and experimental design as well as conventional textbook-style problems. Course grades are based on examinations, written and oral problem solutions, activity guide entries, formal lab reports, and class participation. Surveys indicate that a typical student in the calculus-based courses spends about six hours out of class each week on coursework.

The Role of the Computer

The unique computer activities center around the use of Microcomputer-Based Laboratory, or MBL, tools for collecting and displaying data. Dickinson and Tufts collaborated in developing an MBL computer interface, software and sensors for use with Macintosh computers. MBL software is used in two ways: First, the microcomputer is particularly powerful when it is set up to display a real-time graph of changes in a physical variable such as position or temperature. Seeing a time trace of the position of one's own body or the temperature of a rapidly cooling liquid reveals a way of learning about how the abstraction known as a graph can represent the time evolution of a parameter. . . .

Second, students enter data directly into a computer spreadsheet for analysis and eventual graphing or transfer data to the spreadsheet from an MBL data file. . . . Spreadsheet calculations are also used as a tool for numerical problem-solving and mathematical modeling. In select cases where taking real data is not feasible, we have used simulations.

Last, but not least, the computer is used for the creation of formal laboratory reports that include prose along with computer-logged data tables, graphs, and diagrams. Students can perform and write up an entire experiment without picking up a pencil or pen.

Preliminary Outcomes

. . . [O]ver 250 Dickinson students have worked under the guidance of six instructors to complete Workshop Physics courses. A summary of our findings looks like this:

1) Student attitudes toward the study of physics have improved dramatically.

2) A greater percentage of students have mastered concepts considered difficult to teach because the course requires students to confront and overcome classic misconceptions.

3) Student performance in upper-level physics courses and in solving traditional textbook problems is as good as or better than that of students taking our traditional lecture courses.

4) We know by observation that students who complete Workshop Physics are considerably more comfortable working in a laboratory setting and working with computers.

5) Some students seem to have an expanded vision of the observational basis of physics, and the connections between concepts.

In addition to positive outcomes, we have encountered two significant problems: some students complain that Workshop Physics courses are too complex and demand too much time, and a small percentage of students thoroughly dislikes the active approach. . . .

Unexpected Outcomes

Our Workshop Physics program realized several unanticipated benefits. One is the rapid assimilation of our freshmen into the physics learning community at Dickinson. . . .

A second phenomenon is the sense of pride and belonging that our upper-class majors acquire when they serve as classroom assistants. We now consider classroom assisting an essential ingredient in our undergraduate physics program. Assistants are re-exposed to introductory topics, and the teaching role helps these students improve their communication skills.

A third such outcome is that the Workshop Physics program is guiding reform in upper-level courses. . . .

Finally, a few prospective students interested in physics are actually choosing to come to Dickinson as a result of the reputation the program enjoys.

Application to Other Courses

Sometimes, when we present our program to science faculties, we hear remarks like, "Workshop teaching methods sound great, but I have too many (or too few) students," or "That should work in physics where experiments are easy to do, but I don't think it will work in my field." But introductory science courses in which active learning is promoted through direct experience and guided inquiry are being developed at every type of institution and in every one of the major science disciplines.

Conclusions

The idea that learners should be active constructors of their own knowledge is a theme running through many studies in science education and cognitive psychology. The principles of active learning are being adapted and applied in hundreds of new educational environments. Curricular materials, computer software, and a wealth of new experiences are rapidly becoming available to others who want to join the enterprise of discovery-based science teaching.

The time has come! We should help undergraduates move from being passive receivers of truths revealed in the canonical introductory science texts, to being disciplined solvers of problems, and finally to becoming constructors of their own knowledge. For those few who study science at the advanced level, they should aspire to create new knowledge that is worthy of being re-constructed by future students. We should help our students ask and answer the questions posed by Arnold Arons: "How do we know? What is the evidence for . . . ?" (A *Guide to Introductory Physics Teaching*, NY: John Wiley, 1990). We must, as teachers, transform ourselves from authorities who reveal truth, to facilitators who design creative learning environments for our students in which they can use the full range of talents and intelligences that they bring to the study of science. We must inspire ordinary people to become extraordinary.

Our enterprise is both exhilarating and exhausting. It requires a partnership among students, faculty, administrators, professional organizations, private foundations, legislators, and government agencies. It represents a blending of new and old ideas about learning with new laboratory tools. A new philosophy of science education is emerging. It is epitomized by a proverb serving as the Workshop Physics motto:

I hear, I forget.
I see, I remember.
I do, I understand.

May/June 1992

Science Education Reform
What's Wrong with the Process?

Sheila Tobias

... There are not yet any agreed-upon strategies for change within undergraduate programs. What is to guarantee that science education reform at the undergraduate level—despite renewed attention and some outside funding—will be any more successful and long-lasting than pre-college science education reform has been in the past?

It was with this question in mind that I began a two-year quest for undergraduate science programs that "work." My purpose was to locate them, study them, and try to tease out, by means of narrative case studies, what works (and what doesn't work as well as hoped) in a variety of undergraduate settings. ... My criteria for "what works" were the obvious: recruitment of students to physical science, a high rate of retention of those students once they crossed the introductory threshold, and a hard-to-measure outcome I thought of as "high morale" among students and faculty engaged in discovering and teaching science.

While there is much diversity in the case studies included in my resulting book, *Revising Undergraduate Science: Why Some Things Work and Most Don't*, several things are clear: Nowhere is quality or reform the product of some "quick fix." Nowhere is an outside idea—not even an outside expert—as significant in achieving high-quality instruction as continuous local initiative and control. And except for certain programs that are helped by outside funding for instrumentation and to support undergraduate research, much of the best of what is underway is internally prompted and internally paid for.

All this flies in the face of the model for change that has traditionally dominated the science education reform process. Which leads me to two

conclusions: First, that we need to find new ways to nurture departments and faculty who know how and are willing to make change. Second, that we need some new thinking about science education reform more generally.

The "Culture" of Science Education Reform

New thinking begins with a critique of old thinking. Since the launching of Sputnik 35 years ago, Americans have been obsessed with the reform of science education. Task forces meet and commissions recommend, but little makes it way from the edge to the center of the educational process. What is new and different—New Math, PSI, writing across the curriculum—is initially embraced but hard to locate only a few years after promulgation. In education there appears to be a strong default mechanism—an inertia in the system—that educational reform, as currently practiced, rarely diverts from its course.

At the rate of about one per week, some 300 reports on the problem of American science and mathematics education have been issued since 1983. ... Yet, with certain notable exceptions, such as *A Nation at Risk: The Imperative for Educational Reform* and *Everybody Counts: A Report to the Nation on the Future of Mathematics Education*, it is hard to show that these reports have had much impact. ...

Some few provide insight into the problems of reform itself in a nation that cherishes local autonomy at the school and college levels. But when the authors finally come around to solutions, they reach for a laundry list that ranges from the difficult (improving teacher education) to the near impossible (changing public perceptions of mathematics and science).

Nor are the reports consistent. . . .

Science education reform at the college level is at risk of becoming mired in the kind of "culture of reform" that has tied pre-college science in knots for decades. I use the term "culture" here in the way it is defined by anthropologists David Schneider and Clifford Geertz, to refer to a group's shared meanings, its patterns of explanation and action, its intellectual *ecology*. What is striking about this "culture of reform" is how ardent and energetic reformers seem to be in inventing the new—yet how difficult reform is to implement, to propagate, and to sustain. They shake, one might say, but nothing much moves.

"Problems" and "Solutions"

One aspect of the culture of science education reform reflects the problem-solution approach dominant in experimental science. Trained in problem defining and problem solving, those who would reform science education tend to frame extremely complex issues in terms they are familiar with—namely, "problems" and "solutions." But reform may not be a "problem" to be "solved." What problem hunting and problem solving may lead to instead is reductionism. And, indeed, looking closely at various proposals for change, one finds they oversimplify extremely complex processes and favor theoretical, universal solutions over more modest, incremental change. Moreover, having found, or at least identified, some solution, scientist-reformers are not inclined to compromise. In this way, a problem-solving orientation can lead to rigidity in practice. Since their thinking is in terms of solutions rather than strategies, their recommendations are rarely expressed in terms of options or cost-benefit ratios. Nor are they rooted in the pragmatic, the real, the here and now. They do not offer practitioners, as one person I interviewed put it, any suggestions as to "what we can do tomorrow."

Another aspect of the science reform culture is that recommended changes are often out of context, both in terms of institutional constraints and in terms of the needs and abilities of the students (or faculty) they are supposed to serve. This indifference to context may also reflect the problem orientation of the reformers because it rests on an unexamined belief that, once articulated, the "right way" will be self-evident, teacher-

proof, and appropriate for a wide variety of institutions. In the course of my research, I met so many scientist-science educators motivated by just such a vision that I constructed my own version of their composite *Weltanschauung*.

First, they believe there is one best curriculum or set of pedagogies waiting to be discovered, like the laws of nature, like quarks. If they haven't been discovered so far, they believe, it's because researchers haven't worked hard enough. This idealized curriculum or set of pedagogies is not only "right," it is universal—and will work best irrespective of teacher, content, and place. Second, by pursuing abstract studies of the nature of knowledge and cognition, researchers can find this curriculum or best set of pedagogies, and, more important, prove these to be the best, experimentally. And third, such experimental evidence will persuade instructors everywhere to adopt a particular program.

Yet history proves the contrary. . . .

The "grand reform" of college and pre-college physics . . . met with similar disappointment. In his history of physics curricular reform between 1955–1985, appropriately entitled "Uses of the Past," the physicist Arnold Arons summarizes decades of reform as having produced few innovations that have had lasting impact on physics teaching. "Curricular devices and instructional formats have been invented and reinvented by succeeding generations," he writes, "and, in each reincarnation, are seized upon in the hope that a panacea has been found for instructional problems that fail to go away" ("Uses of the Past: Physics Curricular Reform 1955–1985," *Journal of Educational Thought*, Alberta, Canada: University of Calgary, Winter issue, 1992).

Arons' work is unusual in its attention to the past, and he chides the physics community—though the same criticism could be extended to education reformers more generally—for indifference to what has gone before. "One traverses a steady stream of committee studies and reports," he writes, "which assess and reassess the same problems and make similar recommendations for improvement in almost identical phraseology without reference to the preceding reports and without inquiry into why so little change has taken place." This is not to say that nothing was achieved in the post-Sputnik era. The infusion of material resources and cultural support substantially strengthened the scientific community and contributed to scientific innovation. The problem is that educational reform in science and mathematics was neither mainstreamed nor sustained. (See Philip W. Jackson, "The Reform of Science Education: A Cautionary Tale," *Daedelus*, 1983, Vol. 112, No. 2, pages 143–166. See also James Duderstadt's review of these matters in his keynote address as reprinted in *The Freshman Year in Science and Engineering*, Report of the Alliance for Undergraduate Education, 1991, page 3.)

Materials and Techniques

The great preponderance of efforts to reform science education has been concentrated on course materials and teaching techniques — what Arons calls "delivery systems." . . . What hinders them are the pace, the conflicted purposes of these courses (i.e., to provide an introduction to the field, to lay a foundation for a research career, to weed out the "unfit"), the attitudes of professors and fellow students, the implicit conventions of particular sciences, exam design and grading practices, class size, the exclusive presentation of new material by means of lecture, and the absence of community — a host of variables that are not specifically addressed by most reforms. . . .

Innovation versus Managing Change

The quest for a solution by means of short-term innovation is a case in point. Innovation and change are presumed to operate in tandem. Innovation is considered, indeed, to be the *parent* of change. Yet, in some instances (and science education reform may be one of these), innovation and change are in competition for reformers' energies and dollars. In any such competition, innovation wins because innovation is more interesting than change — more experimental, less troublesome, and less political. But what if innovations have little effect on things as they are? No one wants to believe this, yet it may be true. . . .

Perhaps educators could learn something from what business and industry call "innovation" but understand, operationally, to be "managing change." Business has produced a large body of literature about change. Rosabeth Moss Kanter's *The Change Masters*, a much-quoted study of innovative companies, documents again and again that innovation in large organizations (and physics departments, science divisions, and school districts certainly qualify as large organizations) requires "bargaining and negotiation" to accumu-

late the information, support, and resources necessary to create change (*The Change Masters*, New York: Simon and Schuster, 1983). . . .

The process of transforming innovation into change — even, we are told, of getting teachers to accept the findings of educational research (see Virginia Richardson, "Significant and Worthwhile Change in Teaching Practice," *Educational Researcher*, October 1990, pages 10–17) — is essentially a political process. And so, it is necessary to ask political questions: Who wants change and reform? Who is going to feel insecure as a result of what is being proposed? Who profits from the status quo? How can the necessary players be gathered to counter institutional inertia? And, most important: How can the innovation be modified, even if this means it is less than "perfect," so that it can serve other needs of the organization? Many educational reformers — scientists in particular — fail to acknowledge how *political* this process is and — even when they do — don't have the diplomatic skills (or the stomach) to see it through.

The "Burden" of Intermittent Funding

Another factor in the failure of innovative programs to result in permanent change is the expectation among innovators and administrators alike that anything new and good will have to be funded from the outside. What actually happens when interventions are funded is very often the reverse of what was intended. In many colleges, someone seeking an improvement — perhaps a modest one — is told by the department chair that it will require "outside funding." But an outside agency is not interested in backing a modest improvement, only an "innovation" that will have a distinctive ring. To get funding, the reform-minded faculty member refashions a modest improvement into a sometimes overblown innovation, complete with plans for formal evaluation and dissemination. With a little luck, the innovation will be funded. But when funding runs out or the innovator burns out — or the outcome (by some measure) is less than significant, funders may lose patience with the reform. Worse yet, a message is conveyed that is just the opposite of what was intended — that reform is a dubious undertaking and that reformers have to get their own money while standard programs have first dibs on mainstream funds. . . .

Apart from the burden on innovators of writing

proposals and the postponement of difficult political battles that are inevitable if mainstream privileges and resources are ever going to be redirected, innovation through outside funding has other disadvantages. Funding for individual projects is usually short-term and painfully intermittent—exactly what is counterindicated for long-term change. So, even though such proposals include plans to evaluate and to disseminate, innovations tend, in fact, to disappear when either the innovator moves on to another project or the funding cycle ends. Many are the exemplary college programs so dependent on outside funding that, as a department chairman told me bluntly, "when our funding stops, we're dead."

Strategies versus Solutions

My conclusion is that the search for a single universal solution to the problems of teaching and learning science at college will inevitably be disappointing. The reason change is pursued at the level of instructional materials and teaching techniques, I believe, is not because anyone really expects a "perfect course" or a universally applicable set of pedagogies to be devised, but rather because of a habit of doing reform in this manner. The temptation is to solve a problem with a product . . . because, for innovators and funders alike, the messy, intensely local alternatives are harder to conceptualize. If there is no universal solution, then the experimental model may not lead the way. And if hypothesis generating and hypothesis testing is of limited use, then what are we to do? The one answer college administrators fear most is that whatever we do, it will be harder, of longer duration, more ambitious, and more difficult politically and psychologically to sustain. This does not mean that some increase in our knowledge base is not useful, but it does mean we cannot expect change to occur either as an automatic result of increased knowledge, or as an outcome of almost randomly generated innovation. To rely on breakthrough experiments is to misunderstand the educational process and, ultimately, to mismanage its reform.

Scientists who undertake educational reform are still scientists who, inevitably, bring to their projects the training and the habits of doing science. But reform is not a scientific process, so it is not altogether surprising that past innovations, and even large-scale national curricular efforts, have foundered for reasons that are systemic to

the process: Practitioners' resistance to change; a dependence upon funding that is at best intermittent; the difficulty of mainstreaming nontraditional approaches; and, above all, the vain search for the "magic bullet" that will permanently solve the problem. The history of science education reform is littered with well-intentioned failures. What is to guarantee that even the programs that work today will still be around and still be working tomorrow?

Another Model: Cumulative Improvement

In his article, "A Nation At Risk, Revisited," written three years after A Nation at Risk was published, Gerald Holton makes the point that what we need is not more short-term programs, but "a device that encourages cumulative improvement over the long haul," a strategy that, at its core, involves close attention to things as they are and, in place of one-shot cure-alls, a commitment to ongoing change (Gerald Holton, "A Nation at Risk, Revisited," *The Advancement of Science and its Burdens*, Cambridge, England: The Press Syndicate of the University of Cambridge, 1986, page 277).

Unlike universal solutions produced by outside experts or innovations in the hands of creative loners, cumulative improvement challenges online managers (professors, department chairs, and deans) to determine what is possible in the near or mid-term. The cases described in *Revitalizing Undergraduate Science: Why Some Things Work and Most Don't* illustrate this approach. In each of these cases, the improvement is specific, the constituency well defined, and institutionalization is given high priority. While the jury may still be out on how well these projects achieve their aims in the very long term, a focus on do-able, high-leverage activities seems to me to be sound.

Programs That Work

What can we learn from programs that work, and from programs that don't work quite as well as they were intended? . . . First, that change, when it occurs at all, is not the result of top-down, expert-driven, product-oriented solution-hunting, but originates rather in local commitment and reallocation of resources at the midlevel of management—in the case of college and university science instruction, of the *department*. Second, that money, when it is spent, must find its way *directly* into instruction. One good use of money is to support faculty research that also supports and engages undergraduates. Another is for improved laboratory equipment and instrumentation. Yet a third might be using funds for what Luther Williams, NSF's Director of Education and Human Resources, calls "post-performance rewards" for instructional units that do continuously improve. . . .

. . . One most important lesson is that a true process of reform is all-engaging. In the places where programs work, ideas are solicited from faculty and implemented locally by the department. Where programs don't work, some "creative loner" is proceeding without internal support and commitment. Lasting change occurs, as far as I can identify it, when everyone wants it—when there is a near universal "buy-in" so that the commitment is collective. . . .

The places where programs work are very often four-year institutions—state and private—that have no graduate students to draw on and so are hungry for undergraduates to participate in faculty research. . . .

In places where programs work—even where classes are not small—grading is personal (not mechanistic). Hence, competition between students tends to be lessened. Where classes are small, there is of course more intimacy between the professor and his or her class. . . .

Taken together, one can draw a tentative conclusion: That the model for science education

reform is not the experimental model—not even the research model—but a *process model* that focuses attention continuously on every aspect of the teaching-learning enterprise, locally and in-depth. To improve cumulatively, there have to be feedback mechanisms in place so that one knows almost immediately—not just at the end of a course—that something is going wrong, that some of the students are losing confidence, that instruction is in trouble. Once a problem is identified, a solution is sought—locally, incrementally, quickly.

The Japanese call this process "Kai Zen" (meaning, quite literally, "change in the direction of the good"), as it is applied to continuous quality improvement in manufacturing. In programs that work, faculty pay continuous attention to "what we teach, whom we teach, and how we teach" (see James Duderstadt, "Keynote Address," *The Freshman Year in Science and Engineering*, The Alliance for Undergraduate Education, University of Michigan conference, 1990, page 6).

In places where programs work, faculty and department chairs are not waiting around for the traditional "reward system" to change, although there are some interesting moves afoot to redefine "scholarship" so as to create credible expectations for teaching. . . . Deans and department chairs have discovered the power of the "little 'r' " —the small reward for work well done—the enabling reward so that things can be done a little better each time. . . .

September/October 1992

Science in a Postmodern World

Kenneth A. Bruffee

The heart of the problem [in revitalizing . . . undergraduate science] is the tension between the way scientists do science and the way they tend to teach science. Scientists *as* scientists are bearers of a tradition of pragmatic thought that is central to Western culture, a tradition based on the interpretive ability, in collaboration with other scientists, to construct, manipulate, and calibrate models and symbol systems. As teachers, however,

scientists present themselves to their students as something quite different, something a little like museum curators, as if a scientist's main job were to accumulate, maintain, and display curious and useful facts about the natural world.

Of course these two roles . . . are not inherently contradictory. . . .

Nevertheless, it seems clear that the first priority of college and university science education should be to acquaint students with science as science is actually done, in order to help them become members of the pragmatic intellectual community that science teachers represent. It should not be to acquaint students, however attractively and accessibly, with the wonders of nature. . . .

. . . [S]cience is not a methodical evidentiary process but a process of interpretive construction. In their 1986 ethnographic study of research work at the Salk Institute, *Laboratory Life: The Social Construction of Scientific Facts*, Bruno Latour and Steve Woolgar show how interpretive construction plays out in the everyday working lives of scientists. They demonstrate that scientists do carry on a conversation, but not with nature. The conversation scientists carry on is with each other.

Scientific knowledge, according to Latour and Woolgar, is what the members of some scientific community say, or perhaps what they are able to say—directly and indirectly, in speech and, even more importantly, in writing—to other members of that community. "The construction of scientific facts" is largely "a process of generating *texts* whose fate (status, value, utility, facticity) depends on their subsequent interpretation" by other scientists. A scientific lab is "a hive of writing activity" where scientists "spend the greatest part of their day coding, marking, altering, correcting, reading, and writing."

Understanding science as interdependent, interpretive, and constructive does not necessarily imply that scientists never come up with anything that could be called "truth." It does imply a particular understanding of the truth that they come up with. The interpretive, constructive conversation involved in scientific inquiry is rigorously governed, as the British historian and philosopher of science Nicholas Jardine explains in *The Scenes of Inquiry*, by long-established, local, everyday details of research practice by which interpretation and construction proceed—practice such as "the use of particular types of instrument . . . , particular routines of observation and description" and the conventions of conversation, spoken and written, about scientific work.

The tectonic shift in our understanding of science that this constructive understanding of science represents is one that college and university science education can no longer ignore. And reading Tobias's evidence from this perspective suggests quite a different solution to the problems of science education from the one she offers. It suggests that college and university science students should be learning collaboratively how scientists confront the uncertainties and ambiguities of science by collaboratively constructing, interpreting, manipulating, and calibrating scientific models and symbol systems. In short, college and university science students should be learning how to "talk science" *with* each other and "write science" *to* each other.

Science education of this sort would benefit both teachers and students. It would help science teachers overcome the troubling difference between the way they conduct their professional lives as scientists and the way they try, as college and university science teachers, to induct new members into that professional life. It would help science students by reclaiming for introductory science courses the excitement inherent in the pragmatic, interpretive intellectual tradition that scientists represent.

In teaching science as an interpretive, constructive process, science teachers would of course continue sometimes to display what scientists believe they now know about the natural world and the changes it undergoes. But what they would emphasize is the uncertainties that scientists encounter in the interpretive process by which they build models of the natural world and calibrate those models and symbol systems against precedents and standards so as to establish them as "actual reality."

Chemistry teachers, for example, would continue to explain what electrolytes are and how they dissociate. But their primary task would be to create conditions in which students learn how and why chemists construct the model they call "electrolytes," how they construct and manipulate symbol systems that express changes in that model, and how they decide whether or not that model and those symbol systems are reliable by testing them against precedents and standards currently accepted by the community of chemists. . . .

Approaching science as a pragmatic interpretive tradition would contribute to liberal education by showing that, along with literature, philosophy, religion, music, history, and the arts, scientific knowledge comprises a set of beliefs. It would show how these beliefs are justified, how they become established, how they have been challenged in the past, and how they are being challenged today—both from within disciplinary communities and from without. . . .

CASE NUMBER ONE: **Force and Inertia**

A Case About Teaching Introductory Physics

Daniel L. Goroff and James Wilkinson

Alan Spence thought about the lecture for Physics 7 he was going to deliver the next morning and couldn't stop worrying. There it sat, eight pages of notes, all in that buff manila folder on his desk, ready to go. And yet Spence could not help feeling there was something wrong. Was he taking the right approach? He didn't want to talk down to his students in this introductory physics course, even though few of them had strong physics backgrounds. And yet he also needed to acknowledge that they were having trouble with the material. Two of his teaching assistants had phoned during the weekend, each saying that the discussion sections last Friday had been slow and the students had been unsure of themselves. "I don't know, Alan," John Fisher, one of the TAs, had remarked with graduate student cynicism, "I think we've got a bunch of losers this semester. And it's not going to get any better."

Tomorrow's lecture would mark the start of the third week of the course. In the first two—after some introductory propaganda—Spence had run through a quick review of velocity, acceleration, and the rest of the math needed for kinematics even though, in theory, students were supposed to have had all this already. Now he felt it was time to get down to business and start talking about the concepts of force and inertia in Newton's Laws.

But were the students even ready for Newton's First Law? What evidence of inertia could he draw from his students' own experience that would seem real? Physics demonstrations alone were not enough, he had to admit. Many had been added to the course when its laboratory component was abolished a few years earlier. Spence felt particularly proud of his last performance: an electromagnet released a toy monkey from the ceiling at precisely the moment he fired a heavy ball straight at it from the other side of the lecture hall. After arching slowly across the room, the ball precisely struck the falling monkey in midair, and the class broke into spontaneous applause. The Teaching Assistant reported that, while students vividly recalled "the monkey shoot" in the weekly discussion section that followed, none could give him a coherent explanation of it in their own words. "They could not even say what we were trying to show," Fisher told Spence with disgust.

But that was all about vectors and formulas and math, Spence now told himself. Tomorrow he was going to talk about real physics. Newton's Laws seemed so intuitive to him, and he wanted mechanics to seem that way to his students, too. He tried to remember the freshman physics class he had taken at Halcyon, an idyllic liberal arts college. It was not so different from the course he was teaching now. He had fallen in love with the subject then and had never wavered since.

Nor had he wavered in his view that students could be brought to love physics as he did. As a graduate student at Midwest University, he had volunteered to tutor undergraduates having difficulties with introductory physics, and had achieved some modest successes. His conviction was that many more students could do real science than believed they could. Since physics dealt with everyday events—bouncing balls and accelerating automobiles—students, Spence argued, had merely to overcome their fear of representing these events in mathematical terms in order to move forward in the field.

Thus the opportunity to teach just this sort of introductory course was one Alan Spence jumped at when he was appointed an assistant professor at Ivy University, an elite research institution on the East Coast. It was no secret in the department that most faculty felt Physics 7 to be a chore and preferred teaching more advanced material. But Spence saw it as a chance to introduce students to science the way he thought it should be taught. For him, Physics 7 seemed ideal.

Ideal but not without rough spots. Still thinking of tomorrow's class, Spence looked again at the manila folder he kept for Physics 7, then at the one lying next to it containing the journal article he was working on. Hesitating for an instant, he toyed with the idea of setting aside altogether the lecture notes he had inherited from the senior member of the department who had originally developed the course. "Turning tomorrow's class into a question-and-answer session instead of a lecture might give me a chance to nudge the students in the right direction," Spence speculated to himself. "After all," he concluded, "how can I expect them to follow all these new concepts if I don't understand what *mis*conceptions they already have?" His cat, Kepler, appeared out of nowhere and jumped up into his lap. "Kepler," Spence murmured, "I bet you understand force and inertia better than *they* do." It was not a comforting thought.

The next morning, Alan Spence walked into Lecture Hall C at exactly 10 o'clock, as usual. By this point in the semester, he had little setting up to do, and he was eager to get started right away. Unfortunately, students had gotten into the habit of straggling in, then waiting until the last possible moment to take their seats. Spence watched them diffuse down the precipitously steep stairs leading to the demonstration table and projection screens at the front of the room. It reminded him of an opera house, or perhaps an operating theater in a teaching hospital. On occasion like this, however, Spence was never quite sure whether he was the surgeon or the patient.

The clock at the front of the lecture hall now read 10:10. Spence blew into the lapel microphone which an attendant had placed on the desk, made sure it was working and clipped it to his tie. He cleared his throat and began with the question he hoped would get the class into Newton's First Law and thinking about that subtle concept, inertia.

"Why," Spence asked his 200 students, now poised over their notebooks and ready to write, "do objects stay in one place?" For a split second he wondered if someone would volunteer an answer. But they were used to rhetorical questions and so he quickly continued: "We might think it's natural. Aristotle, after all, believed that objects all had a 'natural place' to which they returned and where they remained by virtue of their intrinsic nature. But a great deal of classical physics has to do with the real explanations of why and how objects move." He made the point visually by placing the toy monkey, this time wearing a scarf with the school colors, on the table facing the class. "Is this monkey going to move?" he asked.

"No," someone shouted from the back of the class, "it's monkey see, monkey do." There was scattered laughter from the other students.

"OK, we can take for granted that the monkey likes it just where he is. Perhaps Aristotle was right. Now, in order for the monkey to move, we have to apply force. What will happen if we do that? Newton's First Law of Motion states: '*A body remains at rest or, if already in motion, remains in uniform motion with constant speed in a straight line, unless it is acted upon by an unbalanced external force,*'" Spence said as he wrote this sentence on the board. Just as they had learned to do in high school, the students dutifully copied each word down into their notebooks.

"Now for the moment we'll just pass over what we mean by 'unbalanced,'" Spence continued. "We know that if we give something a push across the table, it will move. But then its motion slows, and it will stop." Spence gently pushed the monkey. "What kind of 'outside force' is involved here?" he asked.

No one raised a hand.

"Let me try another example," Spence went on after the silence had become painfully long. "Let's suppose we have a hockey puck—just a circular piece of hard rubber that's flat on two sides. Now, if I give the puck a push on this table top, it will behave pretty much like the toy monkey. That is, it will come to rest very soon. But if I apply the same force to a hockey puck on an ice rink, it will go much farther. How do you explain that?"

"Friction!" came five or six voices.

"Yes, friction," Spence answered, relieved. Maybe things were going to go all right after all, and Fisher had just been exaggerating. He continued, "Now as some of you may remember from your high school physics, there is something called the coefficient of friction that tells us just how much friction an object will encounter on a specific surface. Rubber has a much higher coefficient of friction on the table than it does on ice, so the puck slides much farther in the rink than it does here. If the coefficient were zero, then, according to Newton's First Law, the puck would continue indefinitely—right?"

Looking around, Spence noticed an arm in a

gray sweatshirt slowly rising out of the middle of a group of large young men. "When I take a slapshot," the student said, "I always thought it's the force of my stick that keeps the puck going in a straight line. Your law seems to say it would do that without any force at all?"

"Yes," replied Spence, "once it's going. And it would keep going forever. If there were no friction, of course. Which is impossible in practice."

"How about in a game?" Spence thought he heard someone next to the original questioner say. But before he could make sense out of the remark, he noticed the hand of a young woman on the other side of the hall that had been raised for some time.

"I may be missing something," she began, "but are you saying that friction is a force?"

"Yes, precisely. An unbalanced external force that keeps things from following the uniform motion they would otherwise," Spence replied. This was getting frustrating. Spence could see the class wasn't following, and he was both eager and afraid to keep moving. Finally, a student he recognized from office hours blurted out, "Isn't there just some formula for the First Law you can tell us?"

"We'll see soon that the First Law does follow from $F = ma$, which is Newton's Second Law, but I wanted us to try to understand it conceptually first." The groans that came from the back of the room should not have surprised Spence. He knew that even most of his departmental colleagues would say that the real test of physics learning was whether students could do the problems, not whether they understood the underlying concepts or the nature of the field—whatever that might mean. Will they ever get to the Second Law at this rate? Spence wondered. This was not going at all as he had imagined.

"But Professor Spence . . . ," he heard as he looked down at his notes. It was the hockey player again. "Professor Spence," the student repeated, "you've said that physics is about the real world. And now we suddenly have a world with no friction, which is impossible. Are we talking about the real world here or about make-believe?"

"That's a good question, one that physicists and philosophers have had to wrestle with," Spence responded, stopping to take a deep breath. It *was* a good question. Talking about models came to mind, but perhaps that was too obvious and too time-consuming. Spence straightened out his arms to either side and grasped the table as if to steady himself, then started to speak. . . .

November/December 1993

Response to Case Number One: Hockey Pucks, Monkeys, and Misconceptions

Four Faculty Talk about "Force and Inertia"

Daniel Goroff and James Wilkinson

On August 5, 1993, four experienced teachers met over lunch at the Derek Bok Center for Teaching and Learning at Harvard University to talk about the case "Force and Inertia," reprinted on the previous pages. Participants in the discussion were Paul G. Bamberg, director of science instruction in continuing education and senior lecturer in the Department of Physics, Harvard University; Andrew M. Gleason, Hollis Professor of Mathematics and Natural Philosophy, Emeritus, Harvard University; Daniel L. Goroff, associate director of the Derek Bok Center for Teaching and Learning and senior lecturer in the Department of Mathematics, Harvard University; and Judah L. Schwartz, professor of education, Harvard University, and professor of engineering science and education, MIT.

First Reactions to the Case

BAMBERG: There are at least two important questions raised for me as I read the case. First, did Alan Spence intend for the discussion to take the turn it takes? That is, was it his aim to provoke a discussion of natural philosophy or did he let himself get sidetracked into it when students latched onto something that he meant as a brief introduction? Second, how appropriate to Physics 7 is the discussion that Spence gets into? I would say in a general discussion course for non-scientists, it would be highly appropriate; but in an engineering physics course, some people might say that if you get sidetracked into half an hour of philosophy in every lecture, our bridges will be falling down.

GLEASON: My first analysis is that Spence was quite wrong to tell students that physics is about the real world. He should have said, "Physics is an effort to understand the real world in terms of models of the real world." And then he could say, "You see it's hard to push the toy animal and easier to push the hockey puck. And we can extrapolate from that to imagine a situation in which it doesn't take any force at all to keep the puck going."

SCHWARTZ: That's right. I tell my freshman physics students that $20,000 a year isn't enough to buy truth. What you learn in Intro Physics, I tell them, are the stories people make up to describe the world around them. And some stories are better than others.

GOROFF: But can't you also sympathize with somebody who is teaching a core course in begin-

ning physics who wants to make it sound relevant and important and helpful? A short way of saying that is to say that physics is about the real world.

GLEASON: Yes, but there's a price to that shorthand — the price of not spelling it out.

GOROFF: Do you lose the students' interest if you spell it out?

GLEASON: No, I don't think so.

SCHWARTZ: I would argue that the enticement that results from telling students that physics is about the real world — and thus the promise that it may help them to understand and possibly control the world they live in — comes from the fact that students know enough about the various successes of technology to realize that physics is not an idle exercise, that you really *can* get to something potent by going down this road.

GOROFF: But if it's not about the real world, if we say it's about models and such, doesn't that run the risk of encouraging a purely mechanical approach to the course, as if all students have to do is learn how to manipulate these models?

GLEASON: That *is* all they have to do!

SCHWARTZ: As soon as you say "model," though, there's an implied caveat because models break. Part of learning to work a model is learning where it breaks down. And that's fine. . . .

PROFESSIONAL, GRADUATE, AND TEACHER EDUCATION:
Criticism and Reform

Joan S. Stark and Malcolm A. Lowther

Professional education and graduate education often have been considered synonymous in educational literature. Nothing could be further from the truth. In fact, much professional education takes place at the undergraduate level, and much graduate education is not professional in the sense of preparing a student for entry to a specific career. Over 50 percent of students taking baccalaureate degrees are enrolled in programs to prepare them for specific professional roles, for example, in agriculture, architecture, interior design, engineering, nursing, teaching, or physical therapy. At the graduate level, students may pursue any of the above fields or one of the uniquely graduate fields such as medicine, veterinary medicine, dentistry, or law. They may be studying an arts or science discipline at an advanced level. Because so many students pursuing doctoral study in arts or sciences potentially will seek positions as college teachers, such study is increasingly referred to as professional in intent. Hybrids of undergraduate and graduate programs also exist. For example, students in a six-year pharmacy curriculum may begin as undergraduates, but even initially they direct their work toward a doctor's degree. Some universities may offer such specialties as social work, library science, or teacher education as undergraduate majors, while others allow students to enroll in such fields only at the graduate level.

Clearly, graduate and professional education are not synonymous. However, they overlap in ways that make it confusing to discuss them together and nearly as confusing to discuss them separately. Despite this confusion, we will address professional and graduate education together, a strategy that allows us to stress some important similarities and differences. We will also pay special attention, as did *Change* magazine during the past 30 years, to teacher education, which traditionally has been one of the most commonly selected undergraduate professional fields.

Professional preparation includes learning academic concepts, acquiring necessary professional skills, integrating those concepts and skills in practice, and becoming socialized into the profession. In short, since the educational program is usually undertaken to obtain a reasonably well-defined occupational entry position, the students must achieve both competencies and attitudes. For faculty members teaching in professional programs, a key goal is to develop a multifaceted but intellectually coherent program that will help students become competent practitioners. Since faculty members are obliged to relate theory and new knowledge to the world of professional practice, they must stay abreast of and are often strongly influenced by the community of practitioners and other external interests in society.

Beginning with a flurry of reports about the deficiencies of undergraduate education in the mid-1980s (National Institute of Education, *Involvement in Learning*, 1984; Association of American Colleges, *Integrity in the College Curriculum*, 1985), undergraduate professional education has been a target of criticism by some segments of the public. In comparison with specific propositions about what and how students should learn in the general portion of their education, the criticisms of professional education seem vague indeed. Without specific details or context, professional majors often are accused of being "narrow" and "over-specialized." At the same time, some segments of the public endorse professional education as being "relevant," practical, and necessary to the economy of the states and nation. In the context of this general debate, faculty members in most professional fields have been in a mode of self-assessment since about 1980, questioning the efficacy of traditional ideas and practices. Because of their discipline-specific nature, major reports commissioned by the professional field associations and accrediting agencies are seldom read by those outside of the field. Nevertheless, such diverse fields as pharmacy, social work, medicine, accounting, and journalism have been under reexamination and embroiled in change. (See, for example, the changes in accounting education described by Wyer, 1993.)

One change in nearly all professional preparation programs has been an increased emphasis on developing students' communication skills. This includes written communication in all fields, but it also includes interpersonal communication important to effective client relationships in the human services or "helping" professions such as nursing and social work, and effective teamwork in such "enterprising" fields as business and engineering. Another common change is increased emphasis on understanding the context in which the profession is practiced. For example, physicians in training are being sensitized to patient diversity in religious and cultural backgrounds that strongly affects their treatment. Architecture students must design buildings tailored to the aesthetic and economic preferences of today's society, but they study their craft from a historical context. Less frequently, professional fields have experimented with including more emphasis about professionally related ethical dilemmas (Bok, 1976; Weisberg & Duffin, 1995) and with finding techniques to ensure that students develop the flexibility required to adapt to rapid technological advances. (See Stark, Lowther & Hagerty, 1986, for a more complete discussion of these trends in several fields).

The wide-ranging critiques of higher education in the mid-1980s stressed the importance of active learning and involvement of students in their education. For many professional fields, however, pedagogical techniques that include active learning are not new. Professional students have long been engaged and involved in their learning through the use of case studies and practical projects. They learn collaboratively through the use of clinical teams and problem-based learning. Furthermore, internships in many professional fields help students connect classroom learning with the real world. As another response to the critiques, educators in some professional fields rejuvenated an old idea (McGrath, 1974) and examined how they might better help students integrate learning from liberal education courses with that of professional courses so that contextual knowledge would be more easily applied in practice. At the instigation of professional faculty groups and some interested colleges, several projects funded by the Fund for the Improvement of Postsecondary Education made progress in raising consciousness and beginning implementation of such interdisciplinary ideas. (See, for example, Stark & Lowther, 1988.)

Recently critics have demanded that colleges demonstrate accountability and credibility, especially by showing how much students are learning. The ways in which professional disciplines demonstrate their credibility to the public has changed over the 30-year period. Many professional fields support specialized accrediting agencies which, since the Serviceman's Readjustment Act of 1945 (GI Bill), have been subject to review and recognition by the U.S. Department of Education (USDE or its predecessor agencies). Only in recent years has the USDE allowed more than one accrediting agency to be recognized. Thus, multiple agencies may now compete for the loyalties of a single type of program. Business schools that were discontent with their traditional accreditor (American Assembly of Collegiate Schools of Business [AACSB]) now have created an alternative accrediting agency. Similarly, the National Council on Accreditation of Teacher Education (NCATE), which formerly held a monopoly in approving teacher education programs, is facing rivalry from the Teacher Education Accrediting Council (TEAC). Debates about the role and scope of such accrediting agencies, which can be extremely influential in some fields, encompass many philosophical and pedagogical debates. Like regional accreditors who examine an entire college or university, specialized accrediting agencies are now required by USDE to emphasize demonstrable outcomes of student learning and must ask departments to show plans to assess educational results. For some fields, such as nursing, where skills and understandings have long been emphasized and documented, the transition to the assessment era has been relatively easy. For other fields, such as the performing arts, where judgments of quality and competence are more subjective, the new demands have met more resistance. For fields that typically require licensing or certification by public entities, there also have been changes in requirements for increased continuing education (for example, in medicine), for additional advanced education prior to licensing (for example, in certified public accounting), and for disclosure of passing rates on nationally standardized or state-level examinations of candidates (for example, in teacher education).

Because of their close connection with the marketplace, professional education programs are influenced by supply and demand cycles. In the last 30 years, the demand for graduates with business degrees (and thus business enrollments) rose sharply, then fell slightly. Between 1973 and 1983 alone, undergraduate business and engineering enrollments each increased about 75 percent. In contrast, during the same decade undergraduate education and library science enrollments decreased 50 percent and 78 percent, respectively, as the demand for new teachers at first fell sharply only to rise again in the 1990s. The supply of scientists, engineers, and physicians has been of considerable concern to economic analysts and policymakers over the entire period. After the Soviets launched Sputnik in the 1950s, increased emphasis on the production of scientific manpower resulted in an excess of trained personnel by the 1970s. Another shortfall, predicted for the late 1980s, had not materialized by the 1990s; rather, a surplus continued, especially since many Ph.D.-prepared scientists seek jobs in colleges and universities (Tobias, 1995). Beginning in the late 1970s, discussions of high unemployment for doctoral graduates in arts and science fields joined those concerning the oversupply of lawyers, doctors, and scientists. Virtually every issue of the *Chronicle of Higher Education* contains a lament from highly educated individuals who are unemployed. Acknowledging the tendency of graduate and professional schools to adjust slowly to the labor market (whether due to indifference or self-interest), policy makers have encouraged universities to cut enrollments, provide more realistic career counseling, and help students adjust their expectations. In medicine, the combination of reduced federal grants, the effects of the managed care revolution, and the influx of international medical students have made predictions and appropriate responses especially difficult (Hartle & Galloway, 1996).

Nearly all professional fields have experienced a content overload in the last 30 years. The conceptual knowledge base in each field has expanded, new technology has changed the nature of practice, and obligations to serve new clients and markets have expanded. After much deliberation, some professional fields have expanded their first degree programs from the typical undergraduate four years to five years in architecture and six years in pharmacy. Teacher education is but one of the many undergraduate professional fields in which the credit hours required have increased gradually so that students in some colleges take well over four years to finish a baccalaureate program. Because of its importance in the future of the nation, however, the debate over appropriate program length for teacher education has received more public attention than similar discussions in many other fields. Especially in the mid-1980s, proposals for reforming teacher education abounded. They ran the spectrum from suggestions for lengthening and strengthening the period of professional training to proposed legislation that would allow any college graduate to teach without special training. The discussions, which often involved representatives of teachers' unions and state policy makers as well as faculty members, often grew contentious and caused strained relations within the profession.

The Holmes Group, a self-constituted group of education deans from large universities, issued a report, *Tomorrow's Teachers*, that suggested requiring a graduate degree for initial entry to teaching in K-12 schools. Proponents argued that effective teaching should be founded on: (1) intensive knowledge of the subject area gained through a solid course of study in the arts and sciences; (2) knowledge about the learning sciences; (3) sufficient time to master both of the aforementioned areas of knowledge; (4) the ability to attract academically able students, including post-graduates belatedly interested in teaching; and (5) increasing the responsibility of arts and sciences departments for teacher preparation (Gifford, 1986). The concept of master's level entry to the field also was endorsed by the Carnegie Forum's task force on teaching in its report, *A Nation Prepared: Teachers for the 21st Century*. The Carnegie group suggested additional measures that it believed would transform teaching to a true profession, including creation of a National Board for Professional Teaching Standards (Murray, 1986; Shanker, 1986). A substantial portion of the teacher education community, however, not only opposed these ideas but was also threatened by them. State colleges and small private institutions currently producing about 80 percent of the nation's new teachers felt that such proposals would thrust the nation into a severe teacher shortage, destroy the colleges that now serve their states and regions in the substantial production of teachers, exclude capable individuals from minority groups, and place control of teacher education squarely in the hands of the research universities that produce few teachers and traditionally have shown the least interest in teacher training (Gifford and King, 1986). The American Association of Colleges of Teacher Education, representing many of the state colleges, issued *A Call for Change in Teacher Education* that presented alternative suggestions for reform. As the century closes, reactions to this debate have led professional programs in diverse directions. In some cases, teacher education has become a five-year program; in other cases (for example, Iowa) state legislators have passed laws to curb such initiatives by barring colleges from requiring more credits than the standard four-year degree for prospective teachers. The National Board for Professional Teaching Standards has been created and is attempting to provide recognition for teachers who excel professionally. Its future influence on teacher education is still unclear.

What is interesting about the teacher education discussion is the length of time the controversy has been sustained with minor variations on the same criticisms. The content of articles in *Change* in the mid-1980s advocating teacher education reform is hard to distinguish from that appearing in the late 1990s (Murray, 1986; Haycock, 1996; Tucker, 1986). Some progress may be on the horizon, however, as reflected in the recent *Change* article by John Goodlad (1999). Yet additional critical reports continue to argue the case for reform in teacher education. For example, a group of college presidents convened by the American Council on Education issued a proclamation in 1999. The report, entitled *To Touch the Future: Transforming the Way Teachers are Taught*, once again urged committed presidential involvement, stronger coordination of teacher education with the arts and sciences, strengthened clinical training, and support for continued professional development of employed teachers. If teacher education is undergoing significant change, it apparently has not been successful in documenting improvements to convince a skeptical public that things are different. Perhaps this is because the recommendations and subsequent changes have focused more on program logistics and power relationships than on actual teaching and learning in the classroom.

The debates about preparing teachers for K-12 education, as well as reforms in higher education more generally, have helped to stimulate increased discussion about the role of graduate education in the preparation of college teachers. Most professions attempt to prepare graduates with concept knowledge, practice skills, and the ability to integrate the two. The consistent exception to this has been preparation for college teaching. In Ph.D.-level training, the primary skills learned are those of researcher, while the primary role of the occupation entered is teaching. In the last two decades of the twentieth century, national concern about preparing college teachers has escalated. Several research studies and action projects, including a major effort undertaken jointly by the Carnegie Foundation and the American Association for Higher Education, are addressing the problem and now involve the research universities that prepare the majority of college teachers. Recent efforts were described in *Change* articles by Gaff and Lambert (1996) and by Nyquist et al. (1999), but the main story of success or failure remains to be written. A desirable outcome would be for universities to adopt the stance that college teaching is itself a profession requiring entry-level preparation and continued professional development. If so, the education of college teachers could well adopt the model used by many of the other professional preparation fields. It would include study of the learning sciences and supervised field experience, as well as firm grounding in the conceptual bases of the discipline. Insofar as it is the only source of future professors, graduate education in any field is intricately linked with other types and levels of professional education. As many recent critiques argue, the connection between graduate education and K-12 education is especially close. One can imagine that if college professors in arts and sciences were prepared to teach according to the best and latest practices, students preparing for K-12 teaching would have stronger appropriate role models as well as stronger content knowledge.

References

Association of American Colleges. (1985). *Integrity in the college curriculum: A report to the academic community*. Washington, DC: Association of American Colleges.

Bok, D. C. (1976, October). Can ethics be taught? *Change, 8,* 26–30.

Gaff, J. G., & Lambert, L. M. (1996, July/August). Socializing future faculty to the values of undergraduate education. *Change, 28,* 38–45.

Gifford, B. R., & King, J. E. (1986, September/October). Should we abolish the bachelors degree in education? Absolutely. *Change, 18,* 31–36.

Goodlad, J. I. (1999, September/October). Rediscovering teacher education: School renewal and educating educators. *Change, 31,* 29–33.

Hartle, T. W., & Galloway, F. J. (1996, September/October). Too many PhDs? Too many MDs? *Change, 28,* 27–33.

Haycock, K. (1996, January/February). Thinking differently about school reform: College and university leadership for the big changes we need. *Change, 28,* 13–18.

McGrath, E. J. (1974, Summer). The time bomb of technocratic education. *Change, 6,* 24–29.

Murray, F. B. (1986, September/October). Teacher education: Words of caution about popular reforms. *Change, 18,* 18–25.

National Institute of Education. (1984, October). Involvement in learning: Realizing the potential of American higher education. Report of the NIE Study Group on the Condition of Excellence in American Higher Education. Washington, DC: U.S. Government Printing Office.

Nyquist, J. D., Manning, L., Wulff, D. H., Austin, A. E., Sprague, J., Fraser, P. K., Calcagno, C., & Woodford, B. (1999, May/June). The road to becoming a professor: The graduate student experience. *Change, 31,* 18–27.

Shanker, A. (1986, September/October). The Carnegie report: An endorsement for teacher education. *Change, 18,* 8–9.

Stark, J. S., & Lowther, M. A. (1988). Strengthening the ties that bind: Integrating undergraduate liberal and professional study. Ann Arbor: University of Michigan, Professional Preparation Network.

Stark, J. S., Lowther, M. A., & Hagerty, B. M. K. (1986). *Responsive professional education: Balancing outcomes and opportunities. ASHE-ERIC Higher Education Report No. 3.* Washington, DC: The George Washington University and Association for the Study of Higher Education.

Tobias, S. (1995, July/August). Science education in a post-shortfall environment: Restructuring supply, restructuring demand. *Change, 27,* 22–25.

Tucker, M. (1986, September/October). Better teachers: The arts and sciences connection. *Change, 18,* 1–17.

Weisberg, M., & Duffin, J. (1995, January/February). Evoking the moral imagination: Using stories to teach ethics and professionalism to nursing, medical, and law students. *Change, 27,* 21–27.

Wyer, J. C. (1993, January/February). Change where you might least expect it: Accounting education. *Change, 25,* 12–17.

I. CRITICISM AND REFORM IN PROFESSIONAL EDUCATION: SOME ILLUSTRATIONS

January/February 1969

Zacharias on Professional Education

Jerrold Zacharias

For the past several years I have been very much involved in the professional education of scientists, engineers, physicians and teachers, and I have become intensely aware of the problems and the need for improvement in how we educate these professional people. Equally important, but less close to home, is the education of non-professionals — skilled technicians, nurses' aides, dental assistants, mechanics, and so on. One might think that these professions and vocations are vastly different from one another. To be sure, in specific skills and subject matter, they frequently are. But no matter how, when or for how long I study their problems, I inevitably arrive at the same general conclusions for all of them.

First, I believe that both professional and non-professional education begin in early childhood. I believe someone might start to become a physicist with, for example, a Meccano set, a radio or a Model T Ford. An engineer might start with the same "tools," and so might the skilled mechanic. A biologist might start with a frog, and so might a nurse. These highly motivated young people receive similar general education in elementary and secondary schools, but when they reach college they believe that they will begin to move closer to their professions. What our colleges generally do, however, is to put these students through a series of courses which are designed to improve their ability to do something, but which do not come close to the actual work or profession that they want to pursue.

This process is much like beginning a detective story, not with the crime, but with a long discussion of the nature of legal systems — how the law came down from the Romans, through the Germans, through the British Common Law, and finally to the form that the law now takes in the United States. There would be side paragraphs or chapters, laboratory exercises on the Bertillon system of fingerprinting and various other scholarly approaches to the detection of criminals. To be ultra-modern, there would certainly be an exercise in the use of computers in collating criminology data. In addition, there would be a pro and con discussion of felony-proneness tests. After all of this, the last chapter would state that a murder was in fact committed, and the reader would be given a précis of how the various, described mechanisms were used to effect detection of the murder.

This is not a joke. This is in fact what we do. And we do it in the education of scientists, engineers, physicians and teachers.

What can we do that is different? For one thing, I would like to see us find a means of telescoping professional training from twelve years (four years of secondary school, four years of college and four, sometimes five, years of professional school) into a maximum of six for some, eight or ten for others. But most importantly, I would like to see us learn how to start engaging the attention of students on subjects in which they have already evinced some interest.

Western Reserve Medical School has a system which bears on this point. Every entering student is assigned to the case of a family in which the wife is pregnant. He stays with the case at least two years, following the expectant mother to the obstetrician, to the hospital and through post-natal care. At the same time, he is assigned to a group of eight or nine students and a physician-discussion leader. The group discusses the cases which the students have been following. When the students meet with difficulties in areas in which their discussion leader is not an expert, appropriate physicians are called in. The students also frequently meet in groups larger than nine to permit inter-group comparisons and exchanges.

In any event, the freshman medical student at

Western Reserve learns early what it means to be a doctor, and he learns why he should know something about blood chemistry, microbiology and neurophysiology. Contrast this with students regimented in groups of four, carving a cadaver which bears only a slight resemblance to an intact, live human being.

In another example, freshman physics students at M.I.T. are allowed to choose project laboratories where they start to work on either an experimental or a theoretical topic. The work is just barely manageable by them, but it forces them to face the need for learning much subject matter that they otherwise would just "take in" because somebody said they should. The students, after discussions with advisors, select topics that their instructors think are possible for the students to handle. The work has to fit the students' needs. In theory and in experiment, this program is conducted in biology, chemistry and mathematics, as well as in physics.

These examples also have to do with the preparation of teachers. Clearly, the "crime" of the detective story in this case is the act of teaching, the "patient" is the pupil and the "project laboratory" is the classroom. Generally, education students in colleges are given courses which are *about* teaching, but which are not teaching itself. Most professors in education schools are not themselves teaching children, and their courses are peripheral — the philosophy, the methodology and the psychology of education. But they do not ordinarily have the student start to learn about teaching by *doing* some teaching.

At present, a prospective teacher is likely to learn "about" education in the early years of his college career, while actual teaching experience comes later. I believe that the two programs could be combined, with advantages to both. Not only would the student get a feel for teaching and learn the problems, possibilities and pitfalls of the classroom, but he would also learn a great deal about his subject matter. As a matter of fact, I would like to see both prospective teachers and non-teaching professionals do some learning by teaching.

There are two important notions here. One is extensive and intensive interaction with at least one and possibly several faculty members for guidance — guidance in substance, taste, style and judgment. I say "at least" one, because it is so easy for a student to be entrapped by someone who is interested in only a very small part of a discipline and does not provide enough scope for the student to stretch his intellectual muscle.

Secondly, there should be a rapid transfer of responsibility and authority for learning from the faculty to the student. I would like to see all students considered as if they had their minds made up. They would then start working — with guidance, apprenticeship arrangements, and so on — in the professions which seem most likely to them. I believe very much in an apprentice system. In the old days the system had the great drawback that the apprentice had no easy mechanism for transcending the disciplinarian. This is no longer true. There are people, books, films, guides, programs, magazines, journals, newspapers — on and on — which allow a student to go as far as he wants to go.

Obviously, a great many students in college do not know what they want to do. One has to help them find out, and the way to help them is to have them make a commitment of some sort to a profession which they might enter. Let them tackle it as if they were going to be in that profession. If they do not like it, then they can change and study something else.

I see no reason why a student who has chosen one path at a certain point should not be able to take a different path later. Education should permit him to decide to do anything at any time, and it should permit him to change his mind many times if necessary. He should not be forced by the system or the curriculum to prepare for one thing when he is, say, thirteen, and find that the next four, six, eight or ten years are irreversibly fixed — whether he has decided to become a teacher, doctor, scientist, writer, artist, salesman, clerk, mechanic, fireman, or whatever. This is the danger of education, that it be so tightly planned that it becomes terminal — terminal in number of years and courses of study, and, even more dangerously, terminal in the limits on the student's freedom of choice.

Naturally, if a student has made up his mind, he's that much further ahead and he might just as well take advantage of it. But there is no way under heaven that some general set of prescribed courses can prepare a student to do "anything he chooses." This is a myth of many broad liberal arts programs. Most especially what this does not do is help a student make up his mind, which in my view is the most important thing.

September 1974

The Time Bomb of Technocratic Education

Earl J. McGrath

. . . The most generous inference about education one can draw from the present infractions of the law and the indecent disregard for the public good is that it is deficient and lopsided. And we now travel on a road fraught with social disaster. To restore a proper balance between preparation for careers and the cultivation of values, these two functions of the academy *must* be associated with a more pervasive educational element. General and liberal education is the thread that ought to weave a pattern of meaning into the total learning experience, particularly in the liberal arts colleges. Unless such a balance is restored, career training will be ephemeral in applicability and delusive in worth; and value education will be casual, shifting, and relativistic.

The country, and its schools, now seem hell-bent on preparing the young for whatever slots society manages to provide. The current vogue of career education, of intense but narrow-gauged preprofessional study, now finds its advocates among many of the most influential groups in America today, including the federal government, legislators, parents, and some leading academics. Carl Kaysen, for example, the director of the prestigious Institute for Advanced Studies in Princeton, recently wrote in a paper for the American Council on Education that college is "primarily training in a profession. This should become the norm; it need not be the universal practice any more than liberal education is now. Such a goal appears to me to be more consistent . . . than the liberal arts education we presently proclaim."

The inclusion of more professional training courses within the ideological framework of the liberal arts college, to be sure, need in no way threaten its integrity. There are, however, three dangers in a further vocationalization of the curriculum. The first arises out of the short-sighted attitude of students that the more instruction they have in their future calling, the faster they will rise in the echelons of responsibility and compensation. A proper equilibrium can be maintained simply by limiting the amount of subject matter in career majors to the same proportions as those in the established academic disciplines. Thirty or forty hours of journalism, accounting, or computer science need not narrow or professionalize an undergraduate education any more than an equivalent amount of instruction in chemistry, psychology, or music. Even with this amount of concentration, a four-year program of some 120 hours should leave ample opportunity for a broad general education and the election of nonprofessional courses according to the student's own particular intellectual preferences.

If the integrity and the standards of a proper liberal arts college are to be preserved, career preparation must be of a character and level appropriate to an institution of higher education. Learning exercises consisting of repetitive how-to-do-it techniques and memorized facts hardly meet this standard. Instruction ought to be so grounded in theory as to achieve two indispensable goals of higher learning: first, it ought to provide sufficient general knowledge even in a technical field to enable the student to apply what he or she learns to the wide variety of circumstances in which it will later be needed; second, it ought to prepare students to extend their competence as new knowledge and skills emerge, and inculcate the habit of doing so. No matter how adequately the learner is prepared to apply what has been learned to the current demands of an occupation, unless he understands the general principles involved and has acquired the ability to master new techniques and knowledge, he will soon become incapable of dealing with the swiftly changing occupational demands.

The old doctrine of transfer of training from one task to another may now be partly discredited, but certain common intellectual processes are involved in the practice of any vocation. The processes of abstract reasoning and generalization from a body of data, and the differential application of relevant principles are essential to all continued intellectual growth. Instruction which does not cultivate these abilities, regardless of its current value, is not worthy of a liberal arts college. Those who fear, however, that career education will inevitably function at lower intellectual levels than those maintained in the more academic disciplines ought to examine existing practices. Some instruction in the traditional liberal arts disciplines is no more demanding of the higher mental processes, and no less dependent on rote learning, than occupation-related instruction. . . .

. . . In the midst of the present social malaise, what steps have our universities consciously taken to help shape human events in other directions? What have they done to help students even to understand the causes of social malaise, or to consider various means for its cure? The large, complex universities with dozens of specialized schools and departments, with their single-minded dedication to the advancement of knowledge, with their wide diversity of goals and services, have largely abandoned any serious effort to deal with value problems. This is not to deny that occasional professors exhibit in their teaching or personal relationships with students a lively concern for the implications of their subjects for the amelioration of the human condition.

As the distinguished philosopher Abraham Kaplan observed in *Change* some years ago, even the company of scholars, presumably concerned with the nature and destiny of man, has of late not helped students come to grips with matters which were the primary concern of the teachers of philosophy in an earlier day. Kaplan exhibits in his own professional work the primacy of scholarship. Yet, he admonished his colleagues:

> . . . That philosophy has been set apart from our basic concerns is a mark of this new failure of philosophic nerve. . . . When we turn away from the things that are important on the face of it, we are not necessarily approaching fundamental matters; it might be that we are coming to occupy ourselves with trivialities.

In some measure Kaplan's censure of colleagues in his own discipline applies to the activities and dominant interest of scholars in the other humanistic fields and in the social sciences as well. Indeed, it has been the students' recognition of the remoteness of learning from living that has caused them to raise questions about relevance with persistent vigor. Even if their concern has at

times seemed misguided and polemic, it is hard to dispute the general validity of their criticisms.

Reorienting the academic enterprise toward a concern with the problems now afflicting humanity will require a major effort. A probing reexamination of American education's purposes and dedication to the task of moral readjustment will be hard to achieve under prevailing professional preoccupations, the social stratification of the society of learning, and the glacial movement of academic change. In the universities the needed redirection may be impossible to achieve. Indeed, a sound argument could be made for a division of labor between the work of the universities and that of the undergraduate colleges. The former might assume primary responsibility for the advancement of knowledge and the training of the workers needed to continue these scholarly activities. Primary responsibility for the dissemination of knowledge among the members of the body politic could be placed in the colleges. The politics, as well as the rigid structure of the academic society, make any such specialization of labor highly improbable.

Today's hard-pressed independent colleges, should they have the nerve, can accomplish a rearrangement of priorities more easily than most other institutions. Unlike the universities, they are less dominated by the graduate and professional faculties whose purposes, if not alien to their own, are at least diversionary. Even our smaller church-related colleges with an expressed commitment to goals broader than cognitive learning have aped the professional activities of the university guilds. To be sure, their statements of purpose typically exhibit concern for the affective, aesthetic, and spiritual life of the individual, but the realities in their classrooms often do not reflect these objectives. . . .

The choices we make between war and peace, between freedom and restraint, between personal greed and public dedication, material and spiritual satisfactions, should be determined by the character and quality of our education. But are they now?

Regardless of the individual student's commitment to a particular vocation, he must acquire an understanding of the fateful decisions he and his contemporaries will have to make in the years ahead. To set its house in order the academic family must scrutinize the value commitments in its own profession. For centuries, persons of learning who valued truth, and fought for the right to pursue it, suffered suppression, abuse, professional ostracism, and occasionally martyrdom. At no other time in our national existence has the preservation of freedom of speech been of such imperative urgency. Any impairment of the particular type of freedom which guarantees members of the profession the right to express opinions in accordance with the dictates of their consciences will surely undermine the academic establishment. . . .

Interrelating career preparation, value considerations, and broad, liberal education in college education will require readjustments of seismic proportions. Under a variety of names, the effort to broaden higher education has been a recurring matter of discussion among members of the academy and intellectuals, practically since the corporate organization of universities in Europe. For a quarter of a century the faculties diligently recast the goals and reorganized the curriculum to provide a more comprehensive common education for undergraduate students. Some residual benefits of these efforts of the thirties and forties can still be found in some courses in some colleges, but in the main the old veneer of the distribution system only covers up a return to specialism. Is it sheer Micawberism to expect a general education effort today to be any more successful than earlier attempts?

What evidence now exists that a similar effort would be any less abortive today than it was earlier in this century? There are indications that conditions are much more propitious today than at any time since the elective principle with its equivalency of knowledge destroyed the concept of an undergraduate education for intelligent and informed living. The most significant factor in the substantial change in circumstances is that an American institution that annually is inhabited by nine million sons and daughters of our citizenry is simply too visible, too consumptive of the public monies, and too central to the soul of the culture to have a nation remain oblivious to its failings.

If a renewed effort to extend the scope and substance of education beyond sheer acquisition of facts and skills is to be more successful today, the earlier objections of superficiality and irrelevancy must be squarely met. The human preference to concentrate at once in a field of intellectual interest can be offset by showing students that lasting success in a vocation in the seventies and eighties may be as much a result of the breadth of knowledge and the intellectual flexibility brought to it as the temporary advantage or the specialized knowledge and expert skills. The criticism of irrelevancy can be met by showing a vital connection between the program of general studies in the various fields of knowledge and the problems of our times.

To meet the charge of superficiality, the whole concept of the function of higher education needs rethinking. The idea that dominates the purposes of elementary courses, namely, that they must lay the foundation for a lifetime of study in a given discipline, must be abandoned. To be pedagogically sound and to have any abiding usefulness to the student, a completely different organization of material is required. The mistake made a generation ago was in beginning with the idea that a general education course in the social sciences should be a construction of a maximum amount of knowledge drawn from a number of disciplines. This procedure led to a hurried skimming of topics, little consideration of the interrelationship of knowledge, and too much reliance on rote learning.

Instead of beginning with a consideration of the amount and kind of material to be contributed by the various disciplines and organizing it in reference to the internal logic and the sequence of ideas in each, the methodology of organization today ought to begin with an analysis of the problems, issues, and activities in which all citizens become involved and need to deal with. The relevant material from a variety of disciplines' materials should then be focused on life situations and interrelated to show that the unity of knowledge can be made to correspond with the unity of life.

The attitudes among students today suggest that a reorganization of the contents and the procedures of teaching on this basis would make a broader program of education more acceptable than it was in the thirties. Moreover, today the serious concern of younger members of the profession centers on Herbert Spencer's question raised a century ago, "What education is of most worth?" Faculty members, especially those with recent Doctor of Philosophy degrees, are increasingly critical of the purposes, programs, and remoteness of higher education from life. They criticize the detachment of scholars, the reductionistic objectivity of scholarly investigation, and the failure of the learned to utilize their existing riches of knowledge to ameliorate the conditions of life and to shape public policy.

The tight labor market in the academic profession may also have a positive influence on the attitudes of both the younger and the more firmly established faculty members. In an earlier day, whole departments, especially those of the natural sciences, opposed the general education movement. Institutions which consider the feasibility of reviving such an effort will now find either within the present teaching staff or in the pool of new PhDs a large company of highly competent scholars who are willing, and because of revised conceptions of the purposes of college education, eager to join in cooperative efforts to design a program of general studies relevant to the needs of the individual and of society at large. . . .

. . . We can no longer go on pretending that our pursuit of professional competence, of pure vocationalism, of sheer technocratic efficiency, can ensure our culture's survival, when the values which are the mortar of every civilization are slipping through our fingers before our eyes.

October 1976

Can Ethics Be Taught?

Derek C. Bok

Americans have few rivals in their willingness to talk openly about ethical standards. They are preached in our churches, proclaimed by public officials, debated in the press, and discussed by professional societies to a degree that arouses wonder abroad. Yet there has rarely been a time when we have been so dissatisfied with our moral behavior or so beset by ethical dilemmas of every kind. Some of these problems have arisen in the backwash of the scandals that have recently occurred in government, business, and other areas of national life. Others are the product of an age when many new groups are pressing claims of a distinctly moral nature — racial minorities, women, patients, consumers, environmentalists, and many more.

It will be difficult to make headway against these problems without a determined effort by the leaders of our national institutions. But the public is scarcely optimistic over the prospects, for society's faith in its leaders has declined precipitously in recent years. From 1966 to 1975, the proportion of the public professing confidence in Congress dropped from 42 to 13 percent; in major corporate presidents from 55 to 19 percent; in doctors from 72 to 43 percent; and in leaders of the bar from 46 to 16 percent. Worse yet, 69 percent of the public agreed in 1975 that "over the past 10 years, this country's leaders have consistently lied to the people."

It is also widely believed that most of the sources that transmit moral standards have declined in importance. Churches, families, and local communities no longer seem to have the influence they once enjoyed in a simpler, more rural society. While no one can be certain that ethical standards have declined as a result, most people seem to think that they have, and this belief in itself can erode trust and spread suspicion in ways that sap the willingness to behave morally toward others.

In struggling to overcome these problems, we will surely need help from many quarters. Business organizations and professional associations will have to take more initiative in establishing stricter codes of ethics and providing for their enforcement. Public officials will need to use imagination in seeking ways of altering incentives in our legal and regulatory structure to encourage moral behavior.

But it is also important to look to our colleges and universities and consider what role they can play. Professors are often reluctant even to talk about this subject because it is so easy to seem censorious or banal. Nevertheless, the issue should not be ignored if only because higher education occupies such strategic ground from which to make a contribution. Every businessman and lawyer, every public servant and doctor will pass through our colleges, and most will attend our professional schools as well. If other sources of ethical values have declined in influence, educators have a responsibility to contribute in any way they can to the moral development of their students.

Unfortunately, most colleges and universities are doing very little to meet this challenge. In several respects, they have done even less in recent decades than they did a hundred years ago. In the nineteenth century, it was commonplace for college presidents to present a series of lectures to the senior class expounding the accepted moral principles of the time. This practice may seem quaint today, but in its time it served reasonably well as a method of moral education. In 1850, it was easier to discern a common moral code that could be passed along from one generation to the next. Partly because of their positions of authority, and partly because of the force of their personalities, many presidents seem to have left a deep impression on the minds and characters of their students.

In the intervening years, society changed in ways that eventually discredited these lectures. Students became less inclined to fear authority or to be greatly impressed by those who held it. More serious still, the sense of a prevailing moral code broke down. As early as the 1850s, the president of Oberlin College could declare with certitude that slavery was immoral, even as his counterpart at Mercer College was vigorously upholding the practice on biblical and pragmatic grounds. As social change led to new sources of conflict, college presidents seemed increasingly arbitrary and doctrinaire when they attempted to convey a set of proper ethical precepts. And since their lectures were didactic in style, they failed to prepare students to think for themselves in applying their moral principles to the new controversies and new ethical issues that an industrializing society seemed constantly to create. By World War I, the tradition had all but ended.

In its place, many colleges introduced survey courses on moral philosophy. These offerings have acquainted students with a great intellectual tradition in a manner that could scarcely be called doctrinaire. But they have rarely attempted to make more than a limited contribution to moral education. Since the classes usually consist of lectures, they do not develop the power of moral reasoning. To the extent that these courses are simply surveys of ethical theory, they likewise do little to help the student cope with the practical moral dilemmas he may encounter in his own life.

Professional schools have never shown much interest in providing lectures on moral conduct or surveys of ethical theory. Many of them have simply ignored moral education altogether. But others have tried to approach the subject in another way by attempting to weave moral issues throughout a variety of courses and problems in the regular curriculum. This method has the advantage of suggesting to students that ethical questions are not isolated problems but an integral part of the daily life and experience of the profession. As such, the efforts are valuable and should be encouraged. But it is doubtful whether this approach by itself can have more than limited success in bringing students to reason more carefully about moral issues. Most professors have so much ground to cover that they will rarely take the time to acquaint their students with the writings of moral philosophers on the ethical issues under discussion.

Still more important, if a professional school divides the responsibility for moral education among a large number of faculty members, most instructors will not have a knowledge of ethics that is equal to the task. Many of them will give short shrift to the moral problems and concentrate on other aspects of the course materials that they feel more equipped to teach. The difficulties are clearly illustrated by the findings of a recent report from a prominent business school. After listing a wide variety of moral issues distributed throughout the curriculum, the report described the reactions of a sample of students and faculty: "Almost without exception, the faculty members indicated that they touch on one or more of these issues frequently . . . but while they were certain they covered the issues, they often had second thoughts about how explicit they had been. Almost equally without exception, students felt the issues are seldom touched on, and when they are, are treated as afterthoughts or digressions."

In view of the disadvantages of the traditional approaches, more attention is being given today to developing problem-oriented courses in ethics. These classes are built around a series of contemporary moral dilemmas. In colleges, the courses tend to emphasize issues of deception, breach of promise, and other moral dilemmas that commonly arise in everyday life. In schools of law, public affairs, business, and medicine, the emphasis is on professional ethics. Medical students will grapple with abortion, euthanasia, and human experimentation, while students of public administration will discuss whether government officials are ever justified in lying to the public, or leaking confidential information, or refusing to carry out the orders of their superiors. In schools of business, such courses may take up any number of problems — corporate bribes abroad, deceptive advertising, use of potentially hazardous products and methods of production, or employment practices in South Africa.

Whatever the problem may be, the classes generally proceed by discussion rather than lecturing. Instructors may present their own views, if only to demonstrate that it is possible to make carefully reasoned choices about ethical dilemmas. But they will be less concerned with presenting solutions than with carrying on an active discussion in an effort to encourage students to perceive ethical issues, wrestle with the competing arguments, discover the weaknesses in their own position, and ultimately reach thoughtfully reasoned conclusions.

What can these courses accomplish? One objective is to help students become more alert in discovering the moral issues that arise in their own lives. Formal education will rarely improve the character of a scoundrel. But many individuals who are disposed to act morally will often fail to do so because they are simply unaware of the ethical problems that lie hidden in the situations they confront. Others will not discover a moral problem until they have gotten too deeply enmeshed to extricate themselves. By repeatedly asking students to identify moral problems and define the issues at stake, courses in applied ethics can sharpen and refine the moral perception of students so that they can avoid these pitfalls.

Another major objective is to teach students to reason carefully about ethical issues. Many people feel that moral problems are matters of personal opinion and that it is pointless even to argue about them since each person's views will turn on values that cannot be established or refuted on logical grounds. A well-taught course can demonstrate that this is simply not true, and that moral issues can be discussed as rigorously as many other problems considered in the classroom. With the help of carefully selected readings, students can then develop their capacity for moral reasoning by learning to sort out all of the arguments that bear upon moral problems and apply them to concrete situations.

A final objective of these courses is to help students clarify their moral aspirations. Whether in college or professional school, many students will be trying to define their identity and to establish the level of integrity at which they will lead their professional lives. By considering a series of ethical problems, they can be encouraged to consider these questions more fully. In making this effort, students will benefit from the opportunity to grapple with moral issues in a setting where no serious personal consequences are at stake. Prospective lawyers, doctors, or businessmen may set higher ethical standards for themselves if they first encounter the moral problems of their calling in the classroom instead of waiting to confront them at a point in their careers when they are short of time and feel great pressure to act in morally questionable ways.

Despite these apparent virtues, the problem-oriented courses in ethics have hardly taken the curriculum by storm. A few experimental offerings have been introduced, but they are still regarded with indifference or outright skepticism by many members of the faculty. What accounts for these attitudes? To begin with, many skeptics question the value of trying to teach students to reason about moral issues. According to these critics, such courses may bring students to perceive more of the arguments and complexities that arise in moral issues, but this newfound sophistication will simply leave them more confused than ever and quite unable to reach any satisfactory moral conclusions.

This attitude is puzzling. It may be impossible to arrive at answers to certain ethical questions through analysis alone. Even so, it is surely better for students to be aware of the nuance and complexity of important human problems than to act on simplistic generalizations or unexamined premises. Moreover, many ethical problems are not all that complicated if students can only be taught to recognize them and reason about them carefully. However complex the issue, analysis does have important uses, as the following illustrations make clear:

- In one Harvard class, a majority of the students thought it proper for a government official to lie to a congressman in order to forestall a regressive piece of legislation. According to the instructor, "The students seem to see things essentially in cost-benefit terms. Will the lie serve a good policy? What are the chances of getting caught? If you get caught, how much will it hurt you?" This is a very narrow view of deception. Surely these students might revise their position if they were asked to consider seriously what would happen in a society that invited everyone to lie whenever they believed that it would help to avoid a result which they believed to be wrong. . . .

- Courses in moral reasoning can also help students to avoid moral difficulties by devising alternate methods of achieving their ends. This is a simple point, but it is often overlooked. For example, many researchers commonly mislead their human subjects in order to conduct an important experiment. Careful study can often bring these investigators to understand the dangers of deception more fully and exert more imagination in devising ways of conducting their experiments which do not require such questionable methods.

- Even in the most difficult cases — such as deciding who will have access to some scarce, life-sustaining medical technique — progress can be made by learning to pay attention not only to the ultimate problem of who shall live, but to devising procedures for making such decisions in a manner that seems reasonable and fair to all concerned.

There are other skeptics who concede that courses can help students reason more carefully about ethical problems. But these critics argue that moral development has less to do with reasoning than with acquiring proper moral values and achieving the strength of character to put these values into practice. Since such matters are not easily taught in a classroom, they question whether a course on ethics can accomplish anything of real importance. It is this point of view that accounts for the statement of one business school spokesman in explaining why there were no courses on ethics in the curriculum: "On the subject of ethics, we feel that either you have them or you don't."

There is clearly some force to this argument.

Professors who teach the problem-oriented courses do not seek to persuade students to accept some preferred set of moral values. In fact, we would be uneasy if they did, since such an effort would have overtones of indoctrination that conflict with our notions of intellectual freedom. As for building character, universities can only make a limited contribution, and what they accomplish will probably depend more on what goes on outside the classroom than on the curriculum itself. For example, the moral aspirations of Harvard students undoubtedly profited more from the example of Archibald Cox than from any regular course in ethics. Moreover, if a university expects to overcome the sense of moral cynicism among its students, it must not merely offer courses; it will have to demonstrate its own commitment to principled behavior by making a serious effort to deal with the ethical aspects of its investment policies, its employment practices, and the other moral dilemmas that inevitably confront every educational institution.

But it is one thing to acknowledge the limitations of formal learning and quite another to deny that reading and discussion can have any effect in developing ethical principles and moral character. As I have already pointed out, problem-oriented courses encourage students to define their moral values more carefully and to understand more fully the reasons that underlie and justify these precepts. Unless one is prepared to argue that ethical values have no intellectual basis whatsoever, it seems likely that this process of thought will play a useful role in helping students develop a clearer, more consistent set of ethical principles that takes more careful account of the needs and interests of others. And it is also probable that students who fully understand the reasons that support their ethical principles will be more inclined to put their principles into practice and more uncomfortable at the thought of sacrificing principle to serve their own private ends.

To be sure, no one would deny that ethical values and moral character are profoundly dependent on many forces beyond the university — on family influences, religious experience, and the personal example of friends and public figures. But this is true of all of education. Everyone knows that outstanding lawyers, businessmen, and public servants succeed not only because of the instruction they received as students but because of qualities of leadership, integrity, judgment, and imagination that formal education cannot hope to supply. Nevertheless, we still have faith in the value of professional schools because we believe that most students possess these personal qualities in sufficient measure to benefit from professional training and thereby become more effective practitioners. In the same way, we should be willing to assume that most students have sufficient desire to live a moral life that they will profit from instruction that helps them to become more alert to ethical issues, and to apply their moral values more carefully and rigorously to the ethical dilemmas they encounter in their professional lives.

Even if we are prepared to agree that these problem-oriented courses on ethics have a valuable contribution to make, there is a final, practical objection to consider. To put it bluntly, much of the skepticism about these courses probably arises not from doubts about their potential value but from deeper reservations as to whether those who teach the courses are really qualified to do so. Unfortunately, it is simply a fact that many courses in applied ethics have been taught by persons with little qualification beyond a strongly developed social conscience. Of all the problems that have been considered, this is the most substantial. Poor instruction can harm any class. But it is devastating to a course on ethics, for it confirms the prejudices of those students and faculty who suspect that moral reasoning is inherently inconclusive and that courses on moral issues will soon become vehicles for transmitting the private prejudices of the instructor.

What does a competent professor need to know to offer a course of this type? To begin with, instructors must have an adequate knowledge of moral philosophy so that they can select the most useful readings for their students and bring forth the most illuminating theories and arguments that have been devised to deal with recurrent ethical dilemmas. In addition, teachers must have an adequate knowledge of the field of human affairs to which their course is addressed. Otherwise, they will neither be credible to students nor succeed in bringing students to understand all of the practical implications and consequences of choosing one course of action over another. Finally, instructors must know how to conduct a rigorous class discussion that will elicit a full consideration of the issues without degenerating into a windy exchange of student opinion.

These requirements are not insuperable, but they present real difficulties because in most universities there is no single department or program that is equipped to train a fully qualified instructor. Professors of law or business may understand judicial procedures and corporate finance — they may even be masters of the Socratic method — but they will rarely have much background in moral philosophy. Philosophers in turn will usually know virtually nothing about any of the professions and may even lack experience in teaching problem-oriented classes. If moral education is ever to prosper, we will have to find ways of overcoming these deficiencies by creating serious interdisciplinary programs for students seeking careers of teaching and scholarship in this field. Fortunately, the time is ripe for developing such programs, since professional schools are beginning to recognize the moral demands being made on their professions while philosophy departments are finding it more and more difficult to place their PhDs in traditional teaching posts.

But is the effort worth making? I firmly believe that it is. Even if courses in applied ethics turned out to have no effect whatsoever on the moral development of our students, they would still make a contribution. There is value to be gained from any course that forces students to think carefully and rigorously about complex human problems. The growth of such courses will also encourage professors to give more systematic study and thought to a wide range of contemporary moral issues. Now that society is expressing greater concern about ethics in the professions and in public life, work of this kind is badly needed, for it is surprising how little serious, informed writing has been devoted even to such pervasive moral issues as lying and deception. But beyond these advantages, one must certainly hope that courses on ethical problems will affect the lives and thought of students. We cannot be certain of the impact these courses will have. But certainty has never been the criterion for educational decisions. Every professor knows that much of the information conveyed in the classroom will soon be forgotten. The willingness to continue teaching rests on an act of faith that students will retain a useful conceptual framework, a helpful approach to the subject, a valuable method of analysis, or some other intangible residue of intellectual value. Much the same is true of courses on ethical problems. Although the point is still unproved, it does seem plausible to suppose that the students in these courses will become more alert in perceiving ethical issues, more aware of the reasons underlying moral principles, and more equipped to reason carefully in applying these principles to concrete cases. Will they behave more ethically? We may never know. But surely the experiment is worth trying for the goal has never been more important to the quality of the society in which we live.

January/February 1993

Accounting Education

Change Where You Might Least Expect It

Jean C. Wyer

Everyone knows what classes in the first accounting course are like: endless replications of "number crunches" based on rules that have little to do with any reality other than the course grade. The class is highly subscribed because accounting graduates get good jobs, because it is a prerequisite for other courses, or because parents think it is a good idea. It is rarely described by students as interesting or fun. Right?

Not for the students in Dick Dietrich's Accountancy 201 class at the University of Illinois. Instead of getting a syllabus with strings of exercise numbers, they are introduced to Sandy, a recent graduate who has a sudden opportunity to promote a rock concert. Working in groups, the participants take Sandy's place planning the concert. They grapple with selecting performers, negotiating contracts, and reporting on their progress to Sandy's very generous grandparents. From the other side of the instructional divide, Professor Dietrich and his colleagues Anita Feller and Larry Tomassini portray the agents for the bands, arena management, and ticket sellers in simulated negotiations with the student groups.

The U of I experiment is part of Project Discovery, a joint effort with the University of Notre Dame. This pilot program is one of many experiments fundamentally challenging the way accountants are educated. Curricula that were once described in content-based credit-hour lumps (e.g., 6 hours of Intermediate or 3 hours of tax) are newly defined in terms of desired skills and abilities. At an increasing number of institutions, the old lecture and textbook-based courses that focused on learning computational rules are being scrapped in favor of completely new approaches that include concern for critical thinking and interpersonal skills.

On the first day of class at the University of Southern California, students found modeling clay, sticks, and bowls on the tables in their classrooms. Students are formed into teams, which are asked to assume that they have been transported back to ancient Mesopotamia to develop a system for communicating trade transactions without writing or numbers. Course leader Karen Pincus says that the exercise "bonds students into their groups" and creates some very interesting answers (including, in one case, models of anatomically correct sheep!).

The first redesigned course at USC, Core Concepts of Accounting Information, is already in its fourth term and is now followed by a completely new second-year course. A third course, for the senior year, will follow this spring. The work at USC is supported by direct funding from one of the large accounting firms, Coopers & Lybrand, and from the Fund for the Improvement of Postsecondary Education.

Widespread Change

Change is bubbling up all over the accounting education landscape. The themes that reach across many of the current experiments are common to other innovations in higher education curricula: providing more active learning experiences, improving communications and teamwork skills, and exercising a broader range of cognitive abilities. The goal is to help students learn to reason from context instead of practicing the application of rules to narrow, stilted fact patterns.

What is surprising is that these changes are

taking root in a discipline that does not seem a likely candidate for innovation. The momentum from swelling enrollments and from educating almost 5 percent of all undergraduates each year has given rise to a large, complacent discipline. Its traditional curriculum has been so prescribed and consistent across institutions that one can often accurately guess what a student is studying just by knowing what semester she is in.

Arts and sciences faculty often look at their colleagues in accounting with envy. In addition to high salaries, the discipline seems to have many desirable characteristics:

- a problem-solving focus;
- a national testing program;
- recent increases in enrollments;
- highly sought-after graduates;
- a curriculum that is easily filled with seemingly important content; and
- a natural, supportive external constituency.

Also, because of its technical nature, the discipline is largely untroubled by issues of political correctness and multiculturalism.

Despite these apparent assets, the forces for change in accountancy education gained strength in the late 1980s. A number of stakeholders realized that the conditions under which accountants practice required a broader education. There were concerns about the quality and number of accounting graduates available to enter the profession. Changes in technology, regulations, and the complexity of business transactions made the accountant's tasks much more difficult. A rapid increase in the use of computers to perform repetitive tasks made the existing focus on "debits and credits" seem to serve academic tradition more than the needs of the profession. Classroom problems in "problem solving" were too narrow; professional exams trapped the curriculum in triviality.

Finally, because of very active regulatory agencies, the academic impulse to teach *all* the pronouncements had stretched the curriculum beyond its limits. In the mid-'70s, there were 15 Statements on Auditing Standards; now there are 71. Intermediate accounting texts suddenly began to have over a thousand pages and weigh several pounds. Faculty began to notice that accounting texts would soon need handles and wheels.

In 1986, the largest organization for accounting faculty, the American Accounting Association (AAA), issued a report on the state of the discipline.

Most commonly known by the name of its chairman, the Bedford Report warned that "The current state of most professional accounting education programs is inadequate to meet the needs of this expanded profession." Its clear call for change was followed by the appointment of additional study groups to chart a course for change.

Soon thereafter, the membership of the American Institute of Certified Public Accountants (AICPA), an organization representing over 300,000 individuals, voted to require 150 credit hours of education for membership by the year 2000. This action stimulated efforts to include similar requirements in state licensing laws. The development left accounting educators with the problem of what to *do* with all this required educational time.

One response—it is now a virtual movement—has been to require a "fifth year" of collegiate accountancy studies. The move in this direction never settled on a single model. Depending on the exact wording of the applicable law or statute (accountants are licensed separately by each state), the 150 hours may lead to graduate or undergraduate degrees or to a certificate. The array of possible models sounds a little like curricular flashcards: four plus one, two plus three, three plus two, etc. Critical and unanswered curricular questions include whether the additional hours should focus on more specialized training or on broader general education.

The requirement for additional hours of collegiate study has the potential for disenfranchising smaller, independent colleges that will not have the faculty resources to offer additional course work. While articulation agreements or consortial arrangements may help these colleges provide access to fifth-year work, the loss of prestige and identity from being unable to provide complete preparation may be significant.

The "Big Six"

To this point, the story of change in accounting education is much like that in many other disciplines, but there is one major difference. Many accounting graduates hope for and find initial employment in the "Big Six"—the large, international public accounting firms. These partnerships hire 10,000 graduates each year and donate more than $20 million to support higher education. Internally, each firm operates its own education division to provide continuing graduate-level training to its professional employees. It is not uncommon for a firm to manage over a million contact hours of training each year.

The firms' recruiting activities are part of the system for determining institutional prestige. Placing graduates with the Big Six is an important quality indicator for most universities. It is a connection to significant external resources, plus opportunities for faculty experience and access to research subjects and data.

This concentration of employers made it possible for them to take advantage of their implicit power to give force to a systematic statement of their needs. In 1989, the CEOs of the top international accounting firms jointly issued a paper detailing what they felt the profession needed from educators. (While the understanding of quality relationships with suppliers was not well developed then, in retrospect the CEOs were acting as good customers in making an explicit statement of their needs to their suppliers.) The paper described in some detail the desired knowledge and skills they wanted to see in the graduates they hired (see below).

The CEOs' report, *Perspectives on Education: Capabilities for Success in the Accounting Profession*, stated further that "Passing the CPA Examination should not be the goal of accounting education. The focus should be on developing analytical and conceptual thinking—versus memorizing rapidly expanding professional standards." The CEOs felt that the CPA Examination rewarded the memorization of standards and pulled education away from developing analytical and conceptual thinking. This statement represented a major shift for both institutions and firms. Many accounting educators had adopted CPA-exam pass rates as the sword by which they would live or die. Recruiters, likewise, were accustomed to the simplicity of rating schools by their pass rates.

Funding for Change

The design of new courses and materials takes significant incremental resources. In their white paper, the large firms pledged $4 million over five years to help create the changes they sought in the curriculum. The major portion of the money was for grants to universities and colleges for course-development activities. The CEOs were clear that they wanted to create change: "The commitment of these funds is contingent on the condition that they be used effectively and in a timely way for the design and implementation of innovative curricula, new teaching methods, and supporting materials that will equip graduates with the capabilities for success in our profession."

To provide a vehicle for creating the change described in the *Perspectives* paper, the Accounting Education Change Commission (AECC) was founded in 1989. Its membership has included professors, deans, practitioners from public firms and industry, a college president, and a professor of higher education. Funded by large firms, the AECC's most visible, largest activity is a grant program that has provided over $2 million to postsecondary institutions to fund specific experiments in accounting education (see below). It has also issued formal pronouncements on the first course in accounting, the objectives of accounting education, and on the importance of teaching.

Stimulating and maintaining a dialogue among the over 6,000 faculty in the discipline requires a lot of contact. In 1991–92, members of the AECC gave 50 speeches and published 15 articles. Statewide, regional, and national meetings of accounting educators have devoted countless sessions to discussing issues and examples. Faculty from pioneering schools are often on the road, describing their new programs. Meetings on educational topics, such as the AICPA's Accounting Educators Mini-conference, are routinely over-booked.

Not all of this new discussion has been supportive of the kinds of change the AECC wants. Traditional university tensions between teaching and research have been heightened by the industry's demand for an increased focus on teaching. Much of the talk about changing traditional evaluation mechanisms and the raising of pedagogical and curricular topics at academic meetings has threatened faculty who are used to a system where prestige is based on research performance. Accusations that the change proponents are "research bashing" are not uncommon. Some faculty dismiss the whole effort as misguided.

Change in the Classroom

The current wave of accounting education change is not far enough along to show whether it meets the needs of the profession, but its impact on students and faculty in the learning process is apparent.

Students—Say what one might about the traditional curriculum, for students it was predictable. At USC, students express uncertainty about the changes underway. Mike Diamond, dean of USC's School of Accounting, observes that students are risk-averse; they worry about the effect that the different courses will have on their grades and on their prospects for getting a job. They ask, "Why do this to me? If the program was good before, why do we have to change?" Diamond also notes that he "never realized how much students rely on the invisible support system of word of mouth, war stories, and exam files." When they undercut the traditional safety net of intelligence supplied by the student grapevine, administrators need to pay special attention to rumor control.

Students are also concerned at the University of Illinois. Participants in the new curriculum are not getting the rote practice on problems that students in the traditional sections do; some of them worry that they are "not learning." As Dick Dietrich notes, "With an exercise in class and a case for homework, they *do* know the material. But they don't feel that they know it unless it is pounded into their heads."

Despite these uncertainties, many students really like the new courses. After four semesters and 2,500 students, USC has seen a sharp decrease in the rate of withdrawals. In its traditional curriculum, the drop rate was in double digits; for the new Core Concepts course, it is 3 percent. Karen Pincus feels that the increased persistence is caused by motivation. "There's something going on every day. There's something to pay attention to and get involved in."

The experimental group at Illinois has lost only one student. The low drop rate is an unexpected event. Under the traditional curriculum, Professor Dietrich notes, "We thought many students were ill-suited for what we were trying to do at Illinois and for the profession. We wanted more creativity and more intuitive behavior. [The new] curriculum may not appeal to some of the students who were attracted to the old curriculum."

Faculty—The hard effort of actually making a new course work is carried forward by faculty members, often into the wee hours of the morning. At USC, where both the content and the pedagogy changed, the additional effort is high in the initial semester that a faculty member teaches the new course. By the third term, however, faculty members have adjusted to the new design and material.

Professor Pincus reports that the primary difficulty for faculty is "not knowing whether the new

plan will work at all or whether it will work as well for other faculty." Individuals often respond to this uncertainty by proposing changes in the materials and methodology. Once professors have survived a term, they are much less likely to seek modifications. Despite their anxiety, most faculty are successful in making the transition to more active learning and less structure in the classroom.

The cooperation required to design and implement these changes has the added advantage of bringing faculty together. The shift to teamwork is not always easy for faculty who may be more used to the role of independent contractor. Professor Pincus observes, "We're as bad at working in teams as our students."

Beyond the obvious changes in the classroom, the work of implementation can have other benefits. Curricular innovation can excite mid-career faculty. The energy it creates often fuels a renewal that spreads beyond teaching to research and service activities.

The Future

Change in accounting education is very much a work in progress. Whether faculty and students will "live happily ever after" with new course designs is not yet clear. There are many uncertainties to be faced in the change process:

- Will accounting firms have the constancy of purpose needed to hire, train, and advance the new graduates?
- Will the discipline be able to maintain the cohesion it needs throughout the change process?
- Will much larger numbers of institutions and faculty members be able to make the change to a new epistemology and classroom style?

Despite the trials of the change process, most of its participants remain strong proponents of sustained attention to the curriculum. Mike Diamond reflects this attitude: "I don't want to come back in a wheelchair in 50 years and find that no one has made more changes."

Excerpts from *Perspectives on Education: Capabilities for Success in the Accounting Profession*

Skills for Public Accounting

- Communication skills: . . . practitioners must be able to transfer and receive information with ease. Practitioners must be able to present and defend their views through formal and informal, written and oral, presentations.

- Intellectual skills: Individuals . . . must be able to use creative problem-solving skills in a consultative process.
- Interpersonal skills: Working effectively in groups with diverse members to accomplish a task is essential. . . . The practitioner must be able to influence others; organize and delegate tasks; and withstand and resolve conflict.

Knowledge for Public Accounting

- General knowledge: . . . education for accounting must include a sufficiently large, broad and

deep general education component to yield a level of knowledge that is characteristic of a broadly educated person.

- Organizational and business knowledge: . . . public accountants must have an understanding of the economic, social, cultural and psychological forces that affect organizations.
- Accounting and auditing knowledge: Accounting knowledge cannot focus solely on the construction of data. . . . Accountants must be able to use the data, exercise judgments, evaluate risks and solve real-work problems.

II. Criticism and Reform in Graduate Education to Prepare Professors as Teachers

October 1980

Beyond the Relativism Myth

Donald E. Miller and John B. Orr

The scene was the conference room of the Graduate School. A thick oval table dominated most of the floor space. Around the perimeter sat five faculty members. At one end was a slightly nervous graduate student who several weeks prior had completed his written qualifying examinations for the Ph.D. degree. Now the oral examination was about to begin. During this two hour ritual, one thing became blatantly clear. Here was a student who, like several other students we had examined in recent years, was bright and articulate. He knew a great deal about his specialization: the history of Western ethics. What he could not do when questioned, however, was tell us about his own ethical views. He seemed perfectly capable of arguing both sides of the same issue. He had joined what Philip Rieff has identi-

fied as an emergent class of intellectuals who have learned "to think without assent."

He was a typical student in that he had entered his graduate studies career as a person who was full of moral passion and half-baked views on a variety of ethical issues. Then he began the "educational process." The more he read, the more seminars he took, the more he realized that there are at least two sides to every issue and usually a half dozen or more. He started to learn the fundamental humanistic insight that all is not as simple as first meets the eye. He learned that moral views are conditioned by time, circumstances, and geographical location. He began to gain a scholarly distance on his religious and political commitments. He grew cynical about the moral passion of those who express their concerns in overly simple terms. He had developed a full-blown case of an occupational disease that is becoming all too frequent—"thinking without assent."

In 1966 Peter Berger and Thomas Luckmann published *The Social Construction of Reality*, which was an instant success. As with any best seller, it did not break new ground. It merely summarized in readable form various currents which many individuals were feeling but were stumbling to articulate. The root assumption was that all perceptions of reality are conditioned by social circumstances. The belief systems of individuals are products of their social situations. The value commitments of the members of a society reflect the self-interest of persons who wield power.

Berger and Luckmann were impressed by the pluralism of modern society. They offered a rationale for Max Weber's voluntarist view of society as a place where opposing factions struggle for control—a kind of "war of all against all." In Weber's terms, we in modern society witness about us the "war of the gods"; the only available alternative, thought Weber, is to choose the "demon" which we wish to light our way.

The unfortunate plight of many graduate students, and not a few of their professors, is that they never feel capable of choosing their demons. Instead, they experience a moral paralysis born of knowing all the options, of being able to explain the logic of each, and of understanding that the outcome depends upon one's starting point. They have learned too well the insight of the social construction of reality. The transcendent base of the moral order is excluded by their phenomenological bracketing of all but the empirical world. From the detachment of their scholarly perspective, the world indeed does seem like a sea of relativism.

The experience of "thinking without assent" is not an option that academics self-consciously choose for themselves. It is not the choice to drink a sweet nectar. To the contrary, "thinking without assent" *happens* to you and often is accompanied by nostalgia for the former purity of heart. Something important and beautiful is lost: the power to choose and to act with a singleness of vision; the exhilaration of knowing that one's life counts in a cause that transcends private interests and limited perspectives.

To Peter Berger's credit is the fact that after enunciating the methodology of the sociology of knowledge, he elected to apply the paradigm to the very system that he had articulated. Which is to say, if the discipline of sociology is inherently engaged in the art of debunking—that is, of revealing the socially constructed character of all knowledge—then it is also possible to debunk the debunkers, i.e., those who have defined the world as a social construction. Stated differently, if relativism is the end-product of sociological wisdom, it is possible to relativize the relativizers. The result of this approach is that one may start to see the social conditionedness of the sociological perspective; the question of truth, says Berger, emerges with a pristine forcefulness. Relativism is just another myth. It is as vulnerable to debunking as any other myth, however useful it may be in providing paradigms for understanding and analyzing social experience.

Thus stated, what are the options open for persons who must attempt to work out moral beliefs in a pluralistic society? One possibility, of course, is simply to accept the fact of pluralism, to affirm it as an advance in human culture, and to embody it as a refreshing model for directing one's life. A person can become "a pluralist society writ small." That is, a person can disavow coherence or integration as a virtue, and, pursuing a vision of enriched experience, can seek meaning in a variety of places and under the tutelage of a variety of disparate gurus. In 1970, Orr and Nichelson's *Radical Suburb* suggested that such an expansive style of life was in fact developing as a socially legitimate choice. Following Philip Rieff's discussion of Psychological Man and Robert Jay Lifton's descriptions of Protean Man, they argued that the expansive style relocated one's sense of moral groundedness in the aesthetic, i.e., in judgments that a pluralist life could be validated in terms of its beauty or its ability to generate feelings of satisfaction.

Frankly, however, although this "pluralist society writ small" appears to be a livable alternative for large numbers of people, it is so suicidal for the maintenance of institutional life that it is not really socially viable over the long term. The related self-fulfillment ethic, narcissism, or whatever one wants to call it, is certainly dominant in today's culture, but its limitations as a universal ethic seem clear indeed. The world is filled with too much pain and too many problems to allow oneself to endorse an ethic that fails to address the good of the human community as a whole or that allows the luxury of avoiding the universal implications even of one's own multiple commitments.

Another way of dealing with the enticement of "thinking without assent" is to endorse the tunnel vision of one of the available competing dogmas. In spite of the fact that this alternative appears to be a pathologically self-deceptive mode of handling the frustrations of pluralism, it actually may represent a creative choice. Surprisingly, Robert Jay Lifton argued that the currently emerging protean style of life is not so much the embodiment within single individuals of various perspectives and possibilities as much as it is a propensity in individuals faddishly to adopt dogmatisms—to be conversion-prone. Although he wrote earlier than Lifton, the sociologist Pitirim Sorokin extended the point. Writing in his 1941 *Crisis of Our Age,* Sorokin observed that when a sensate society (with its cult of experience and its exhaltation of cynicism) enters its final period, the agents of change are certainly not the cynics who "think without assent." Instead, they are the true believers who turn against jadedness and sophistication and who find a belief-ful place to stand. They will be agents of the new "ideational" or "idealistic" eras that will renew cultural energies.

The problem for many persons caught in the myth of relativism, however, is that they cannot will themselves into conversions, even if they desire to find secure places to stand. Conversions happen. They are not available on demand. Furthermore, many who "know all the options" feel silly in the presence of naive dogmatism. Secretly, they cannot understand how anybody can live in the modern world and not "see through" or at least relativize any and every belief system.

There is a way to deal with the myth of relativism, however, which does not seem to require one to hide one's head in the sand or to sacrifice intellectual integrity. This is the way finally taken by Ernst Troeltsch when, in the face of his own carefully considered conclusions about relativism, he affirmed his own membership in the Christian community. The decision did not represent a denial of relativity. Clearly, Troeltsch knew that had he

been born in another time or place that he might have been a Buddhist or a Jew. The point was that he had *not* been born in another time or place, and that he could *not* imagine his own identity apart from the Christian traditions of Europe. For Troeltsch, then, handling relativism required acts of commitment to traditions embodied in communities. The experience was dialectic; it involved consulting the tendencies of one's own spirit, while acknowledging that this spirit is nurtured in an array of voluntary and virtually genetic communities.

Those who follow Troeltsch believe that it is better to work within the framework of some prioritizing structure—admittedly it may not be that of Christianity—than to be blown about by every passing fad. Value systems do not exist as abstract philosophies. Those that have beneficially impacted the world have always been embodied in a community of individuals for whom the system gives direction to their goals and projects, to the way they relate to each other and to their neighbors, and to the role they play as individuals in institutional life. This alternative is finally the alternative of choosing a community to which one can commit oneself, i.e., a community enough in tune with one's dispositions that commitment, however tentative, is made possible.

It is through participation in a community that the myth of relativism begins, at least experientially, to erode. Communities are not abstract entities. They are not bodies of pure cognition. Quite the contrary, communities are concerned with nurturing members—meeting the concrete problems which always fill the lives of individuals. And they are also faced with the question of how to relate to the larger community of which they are a part. In the concreteness of everyday decisions, all does not seem relative. Some choices are clearly superior to others. Furthermore, within the context of communal life one does not have the luxury of forever postponing decisions while one waits for a clearer vision. The exigencies of the moment call for decision, and when one makes a mistake, the membership of the community is faced with the task of offering absolution, or in the case of a misjudgment of the collective membership, of offering restitution to those who have been faulted. The very dynamic of communal life spawns prophets and priests, sages and organizers.

There are many types of communities to which

one may entrust one's loyalties, political and religious communities being, perhaps, the two most distinctively voluntary. But whatever the nature of the community, communities unlike individuals cannot survive on a relativistic platform. The community which stands for nothing has no membership. Consequently, those who lead communities seek ways to renew the collective sentiments which bind members to the group. They create rituals and tell stories; they involve the membership in collective acts of moral affirmation. For the anomic relativist who joins a community, the option of detached cognitive deliberation is not possible. In community, one cannot "think without assent."

Indeed, the choice to join a community is the self-derived invitation to seduction—that is, seduction into the corporate vision. To work, to celebrate, and even to argue together is to be transformed by the collectivity. As Durkheim clearly saw, it is within the experience of collective effervescence—for example, of a religious community worshiping or of a political group chanting, marching, or protesting—that the individual transcends himself. Self-transcendence is a byproduct of gaining a sense of collective identity. And on an experiential level, self-transcending experiences are often paired with the professed experience of *the* transcendent. What begins as a gathering of a human collectivity may end, for the individual, as an experience in which communal goals are granted a virtually unconditional status.

People who are engaged actively in a community—whether it be a political cause, a club, a "university tradition," a religious movement, or whatever—are literally forced to make decisions about transcendent principles. They cannot escape. As John Rawls correctly points out, the necessities of everyday group life require decisions at least about the principles in terms of which conflicts will be adjudicated. Theories of justice, whether acknowledged or not, shape even our most informal arrangements for ensuring due process, for protecting our group rights, and keeping group conflicts relatively humane. When people are involved in a cause that inspires their loyalties, they cannot "think without assent" about the transcendent principles that govern their very actions in espousing that cause.

In some ways, what is being proposed is a reversal of the "moral man, immoral society" argument of Reinhold Niebuhr. What is being asserted is that individuals, devoid of community, are often immoral, for they see no way beyond the pluralism of modern culture so long as they remain detached from the power of communal persuasion. It is precisely in community that they gain a sense of moral identity. Addressing the other side of Niebuhr's statement, collectivities do characteristically seek their own interests. But the function of prophets—of persons crying out for greater justice and mercy—is always exercised within a communal context. It is the role of the prophet to challenge the morality of communal life and the collective vision—to remind people that they should justify their public actions before the bar of some transcendent principle. A prophet without a community is a madman raving in the desert.

The moral vision of the collectivity is internalized as individuals are persuaded by the rhetoric which issues from the scholar, priest, or politician, depending upon the nature of the community. The effective promulgator is one who speaks in images, metaphors, and symbols, because these are the stuff from which life-plans are structured. Within a community, rational propositions inform life-style choices, but so do images which can be visualized and which can thus serve as goals to be actualized. It is not only in systematic ethical argument, political addresses, and sermons that moral images are enunciated. Moral images are also manifested in the lives of individuals who populate communities, whether religious or academic. Indeed, such role models are surely as persuasive as pictorial images or moral propositions.

Higher education constitutes a kind of moral community within which people are related to transcendence. Although the university operates differently from a church or political organization, it also has its rituals—its gatherings of faculties, its ceremonies of examination and degree conferment (listen sometime to the moral rhetoric of a commencement address). Even in its architecture—in statues and quotations etched in stone—there is often witness given to this as a community whose members gather to celebrate and to discover "truth." The assumptions of the university are strongly normative, involving a network of traditions, roles, images, propositions, rights, myths, and values—all supported by an incredible matrix of committtees—in terms of which faculty and students live and work together.

This fact is crucially important for anyone who reflects on the myth of relativism, particularly on the increased incidence of persons who are learning to "think without assent." This pathology may be spawned by the very ethos of pluralism. But it is being experienced as an especially painful problem in higher education, because one of the very bases of community in higher education has been the resistance against allowing disciplinary theories to become thinly veiled expressions of sectarian commitments. With all the qualifications academics must make concerning their ideal of objectivity, something like dispassionate inquiry and criticism has historically been at the heart of the enterprise. "Thinking without assent," then, has been a sacred value, at least in some sense. And when "thinking without assent" is identified as a *pathology* with serious moral consequences, the university necessarily must experience a crisis of confidence concerning its own foundations as a community.

We do not believe that higher education should withdraw from its passion for critical reflection. Inherent in the very meaning of the phrase "academic freedom" is a non-relativistic assumption—namely, that there are truths which transcend personal and political bias. Members of the academic community possess an historic role definition which requires them to surmount political pressures, personal self-interest, and even institutional loyalty in search of objective analysis and judgment. The university is a type of moral community in which independence of mind is honored as people gather together—albeit in separate disciplines and schools—in pursuit of objective knowledge and visions of a better society. The contribution of the university to the larger society of which it is a part rests on the presumption that scholars who are unfettered by self-interested loyalties are free to describe, analyze, and investigate that to which they elect to direct their attention. Indeed, implied in the scholarly task is the idea that one's commission involves going beyond a survey of alternative theories or paradigms. Unfortunately, too many contemporary academics have lost the sense of scholarly passion of which Max Weber

spoke so eloquently in his famous address, "Science as a Vocation." They see themselves as organizers, catalogers, and promulgators of their discipline's stock of information.

We believe, however, that increasing numbers of academics are nervously wondering whether they want to nurture a generation of students and colleagues who *morally* "think without assent." We suspect that at least a prophetic minority of academics want instead to distinguish between *critical thinking* and "thinking without assent" and that they want to find the institutional patterns for encouraging persons to make their way beyond the myth of relativity. For these people, the stakes appear to be high. Not only does the myth of relativity train people to "think without assent" (and thereby to distance themselves from communal obligations), but also it ultimately drains from the university the motivations or affections that give energy to the academic enterprise. Academics, after all, simply have a need to justify their activities as making a difference, as somehow being important to the social fabric. And scholarship, at its best, is indeed associated with obligations to decide about the good, the beautiful, the efficient, and the just. Apart from accepting such obligations, academics can only (albeit sometimes secretly) feel guilty about accepting the elaborate system of support and protection provided for their enterprise by the civic society.

In this regard, one witness that prophetic academics can make is to show in their own communal commitments the necessity of entering the battle of the war of the gods. By their own involvement in voluntary communities they can image the unauthenticity of detached pontification. It is as role models that professors show that there is a way out of relativism. Professors should not turn reflection into dogmatism because, after all, the classroom is for critical thinking, rational discourse, and surveying of alternative positions. Still, the academic and other spheres of public life should not be entirely separated, as Max Weber suggested. Weber's belief that somehow the university cannot be the servant of private or collective interests should of course prevail. But the political involvements of Max Weber should also not be forgotten. Nor should our students forget ours. Passion, while not the god of the classroom, should be close at hand—all the while balanced by critical thinking.

"Thinking without assent" is a *moral pathology* within our pluralistic society. To deal with it as such clearly ought to be on higher education's agenda, and the passionate association of the academy's citizens in the communal life of our culture can provide a milieu in which new convictional possibilities for the pluralistic society can be explored.

May/June 1995

Another Century's End, Another Revolution for Higher Education

Donald Kennedy

. . . We are entering another time of great change in American higher education; just what the results will be is uncertain, because colleges and universities are so well structured to resist change. But I think it may bring us to a closing of the circle first opened a century ago with the innovation of graduate study. At that time, the research university was an entirely novel product of its era—the likes of which had never been seen before on this continent. And now, 100 years later, the research university stands at the very center of a challenge and an opportunity. That is because, although it does not provide higher education for most of the Americans who receive an education, it *does* train most of those who provide that education. If I am right about the prospect of another century-closing revolution in higher education, it will happen in—and because of—the research universities. . . .

The corporate values that academic institutions are being urged to adopt—frequently by trustees who come by them quite naturally—often fit uncomfortably into the university environment. The traditions of the academy strongly favor individuality, creativity, even heterodoxy. Freedom of action is highly valued. Accountability is viewed as much less important than independence. The introduction of norms that emphasize hierarchy, team loyalty, and discipline is difficult, not because they are not worthwhile values, but because these values are not those deemed especially important for scholarship or teaching. They create a dissonant kind of bewilderment, if not outright hostility. . . .

A second trend, barely begun and bearing some relationship to the first, is the assertion of somewhat more control over the work that goes on, particularly the work of faculty. The present situation in the research universities—especially the most prestigious—is one in which there are few firm customs with respect to duties and hours, and even fewer rules. In the farewell address following his second term as Dean of the Faculty of Arts and Sciences at Harvard, Henry Rosovsky took note of the "secular decline of professorial civic virtue" in that distinguished faculty. But he also made clear that it had taken place in an environment almost devoid of clear requirements. In the most distinguished research universities, faculty members often have few prescribed teaching obligations, no regulations governing their availability to students, no requirements with respect to advertising, and no enforced limits on the time they spend away. . . .

. . . Academic freedom means a great deal, but it should not mean freedom from responsibility to students.

Can the academic "center"—that is, administrative leadership—move us out of this vacuum? That will be difficult, because the action is all peripheral: it takes place at the level of departmental faculties. To expect change to come easily would represent yet another triumph of hope over experience. . . . [T]here is a powerful tradition of local control over most of the things that matter: disciplinary direction, exercised through the choice of new faculty; curriculum; appointment and promotion criteria; and above all, the character of graduate study, about which I'll say more later. Departments are the units in which the institution's strategy for academic development is formulated in practice. They are managed by consensus, and their chairs are temporary stewards who seldom lead and are thus likely to maintain the status quo. Change led from the center is equally problematic. University leaders have become hesitant about attempting major initiatives. The politics of academic life make faculty support critical, and efforts to create major shifts in direction are always risky . . .

Envisioning the Future

It is impossible to talk about the future without recognizing that it may be very different for different kinds of institutions. Indeed, one of the new directions may involve major changes in the roles and importance of these different institutions. For example, I see emerging now an increasing respect for the special things that can be accomplished in the environment of small liberal arts colleges — although that has not yet been revealed in such hard statistics as yield rates. In addition to the strengths these institutions have always had — including manageable scale and a focus on the individual student — they are now benefiting from a good private funding environment and from the collateral effects of overproduction of excellent scholars.

But the most important changes will involve the research university. These will be important not only because research universities are highly visible — both heavily influenced by political trends and heavily influential on other institutions — but also because of the special and pivotal role they play with respect to the rest of the enterprise. Research universities are where three-quarters of the PhDs are trained to staff the faculties in the other 3,900 higher education institutions.

Yet, strangely, we do almost nothing to prepare these students for the roles they will fill.

In the professional schools of our research universities, deliberate efforts are made to ensure some kind of readiness for the world of practice. These efforts often include, for example, required courses that deal with some of the ethical challenges of the profession. Thus, law schools offer courses in professional responsibility, medical schools in medical ethics, business schools in business ethics. Nothing of the sort is made available to PhD candidates in the academic disciplines. And our efforts to improve teaching ability tend to be handed out from the administrative center. Although the responsible units are often rather

effective, they encounter quiet opposition in many departmental locations, where graduate students are told that teaching doesn't really matter — at least not in comparison with research.

Instead, it is assumed that apprentices will learn what they need to know from watching journeymen — the mentors under whom they study as graduate students. This assumption suffers from two serious weaknesses. First, the mentors after whose abilities, ideals, and styles students are modeling their own have little or no experience with the kinds of institutions in which the latter will teach. Their own histories are primarily in research universities, and their ideas of what is important come mainly from that culture. Second, they often show little or no interest in encouraging those parts of their students' development that relate to activities other than the particular research project at hand. Discussions of pedagogy, or the appropriate limits on personal relationships between faculty and students, or the need for objectivity in reviewing the scholarship of others — to cite only a few examples — are rare in the environments in which most graduate training takes place.

The most unfortunate consequences of this lack of preparation, sadly, often show up in the president's office as unresolved disputes between faculty members and students about intellectual property, as complaints about teaching, as sexual harassment charges, or as grievances about authorship. Our inattention to these dimensions of academic life — call them ethics for the professoriate — produces an unfortunate and unnecessary harvest of later difficulty.

Armed with my own experiences with such outcomes, I decided to offer a seminar course for dissertation-level PhD students intent on pursuing academic careers. It attempts to deal with a wide range of personal and professional challenges in academic life: improving one's teaching, dealing with grading disputes, objectivity in the classroom, managing personal relationships with students, sharing credit for academic work, the responsibility of reviewers, conflicts of interest, and so on. I have given it for two years now, and the experience has been both rewarding and fascinating.

Among the things I've learned so far, the following seem most significant. First, most graduate students are being told little or nothing about these matters — they simply aren't part of the conversations most doctoral candidates have with their mentors. Second, the expectations and behavioral norms they are absorbing vary enormously among the disciplines, leading to a restrictive pattern of propagation of highly specific subcultures. Third, students have a real eagerness to deal with such issues, and express interest in and astonishment at these differences as they emerge in discussion. Fourth, the students are (of course) both bright and committed, so they become deeply engaged and are willing to change their own (and one another's) views.

My experience convinces me that graduate education can be changed to reflect the real needs of the profession, and that the changes would not even have to be far-reaching. But we will have to be prepared to give up the idea that departments and schools have only minimum collective responsibility for the outcome. As long as doctoral training emphasizes the kind of guild preparation we have now, it will not change. More mixing of the disciplines and sub-disciplines, as well as more experiences that entail professional preparation, will be required. And even that modest centralization of the process will, we may be sure, meet resistance.

As things stand, we are in the odd position of preparing faculty for their roles as scholars and giving little attention to their roles as professors. Indeed, almost no recognition at all is given— either by professional description or by organization—to the fact that all academic scholars belong to the same calling. (For example, "John is a biochemist" is a familiar introduction; "Margaret is a professor" is not. Likewise, there are literally hundreds of "professional" scholarly societies, and only one that recognizes teaching.) This larger calling is to a real, if non-functional, community—one that has an important but unacknowledged status above the research guilds. We need to give it a substantive professional identification.

The next generation of faculty will have to be better prepared for membership in that community, for the roles they will play in places like the ones in which they were trained, as well as for those they may have to play in different places. But in addition to different roles, they will have to be prepared for a different time.

A technological revolution has taken place, coupled with a demographic and occupational one. In the workforce, increasingly unstable employment patterns are already leading to a wave of involuntary early retirement—and those who remain employed are more likely to be in shifting service occupations that require the repeated re-injection of educational experiences. These forces will reshape the demand for education across the life cycle. At the same time, new technologies will make possible forms of distance learning that were previously unheard of. These technologies will reorder the values we attach to different kinds of institutions. As one observer inquired, "If every student in America can take colonial history from Bernard Bailyn, what will differentiate Harvard from Local State?" If the incubators of the professoriate cannot prepare students for the personal and professional challenges they now face in the rest of the system, how will they get students ready for a new world?

So far I have drawn a fairly discouraging picture of the capacity of the higher education system— and particularly the research universities, where the heart of the problem lies—to change in the necessary ways.

But fortunately there is good news, and much of it comes from a developing revolution within the profession itself. It is best indicated by a new enthusiasm for teaching and mentoring—what one might call the nurturing parts of the academic life. Serious experiments at reforming the way teaching is evaluated and rewarded are under way in many institutions, stimulated significantly by efforts made by AAHE and organizations it has helped start. It will not be long before "teaching portfolios"—summaries of materials and accomplishments—will be used regularly in appointment and promotion procedures. Even more important, peer review of teaching will become just as much a custom as peer review of research. How to do it is no mystery; the problem is getting people to accept that level of accountability for the quality of their own work.

This trend is even more remarkable because of where it is happening. Perhaps because of the intensity and the instrumental character of the research there, the science departments have always been especially resistant to changes of the kind I have been discussing. But young scientists are suddenly being heard from, and their message is quite different. At a symposium at Stanford late in 1994, about 500 graduate students and postdoctoral fellows gathered to hear a discussion of alternative careers for PhDs in the biomedical sciences. Following a panel in which teaching received a lot of attention, a very distinguished senior scientist (himself a superb teacher) rose to say that in his view there is little point in trying to teach people how to teach; if one knows the subject matter, the rest simply follows. That is not the good news. The good news is that the audience actually booed.

Earlier that year, the national group of Presidential Young Investigators gathered at the behest of the National Science Board for a meeting. These include the very best and most accomplished young researchers in the universities, and one might have expected them to display the norms of their discipline. Asked to select the topic for the meeting, they chose undergraduate science education, and after several days of hard-working sessions produced a document with serious recommendations on how to put new emphasis behind the teaching function (*America's Academic Future: A Report of the Presidential Young Investigator Colloquium on U.S. Engineering, Mathematics and Science Education for the Year 2010 and Beyond*).

The National Academy of Sciences, the home of the senior elite of American science, is now a firm advocate for attention to teaching under its new president, Bruce Alberts—who actually takes time from federal science policy (the preferred domain of past NAS leadership) to advocate education reform at the K–12 level. With his encouragement, the academy sponsored a major convocation this spring devoted to undergraduate education in science, mathematics, engineering, and technology. For the first time in my memory, the legion of senior researchers is being mobilized to support teaching improvement. It is a significant watershed.

Conclusion

My message is one of hope. A hundred years ago, the transformation of American higher educa-

tion brought us the graduate school and made research universities out of a group of English colleges. The benefits have been enormous. But the people who support these institutions now believe that something was lost in the process—and I think they rightly suspect that it is their focus on students.

Now reform is in the air, and I think it will result in a new kind of institution. Its features will include a balanced respect for teaching, including teaching as scholarship; a sense of responsibility for undergraduate students that includes more than just their intellectual development; and a special understanding that in training their own graduate students, research universities are preparing people for careers full of complex challenges in a variety of places.

This last is a point of exceptional leverage. Reform of graduate education is the key to accelerating change, because it is the vital node through which the academic culture is transmitted. If we can make significant improvements there, it may lead to a remarkable event: the closing of a century-long circle, through which we remarry the best of the old college values with the best of the newer scholarly tradition. The graft that was accomplished 100 years ago put the graduate seminar and original research onto the rootstock of the English college. Judging by its success, one has to say that the graft has been a good idea. But have the two elements yet achieved real compatibility? I think not—and in that respect, the highest achievements of American higher education are still ahead of us. If I am right and we are lucky, we all may be able to participate in that final closure.

September/October 1986

Teacher Education

Words of Caution About Popular Reforms

Frank B. Murray

... Reform in the fundamental way we prepare teachers simply won't be possible without reform of the non-professional components of a student's course of study, of the liberal and general education plus the academic major and minor that constitute the bulk of the teacher's university-level preparation. The day's wisdom, backed by the national reports, properly insists that the teacher not only know subject matter thoroughly but have the mark of an educated, thoughtful, and well-informed person as well. To assure that teachers are well educated, teacher-education programs are therefore critically dependent upon the larger and particular efforts of arts and sciences faculty.

It is here that matters become more complicated; one cannot call for "more arts and sciences coursework" without inquiring about the character and effect of that expanded study. In all too many colleges and universities, there has been a failure of the faculty to assume a corporate responsibility for the entire undergraduate program. Higher education's recent national reports have laid it out for all to see: baccalaureate goals are fuzzy, general education is in disarray, there is no core of learning deemed fundamental, important skills are left to chance, expectations are low, and students disengage.

Without belaboring the point or seeming to suggest that the problems are all over on the arts and sciences side, let me say that the concrete recommendations of higher education's national reports are absolutely critical to the preparation of better teachers. In *all* undergraduate classrooms we need clarity of purpose, effective teaching, high expectations, and student involvement to bring about the educational result we want. The mastery of a core of fundamental and enduring ideas, to cite another undergraduate need, is important for all students, but it is more important for teachers, especially elementary school teachers, than it is for any other professional group.

And curriculum is only part of the problem. The nature of teaching is equally a barrier to the kind of understanding the teacher must have. There is little in the contemporary university to encourage the faculty to go beyond the firmly held, but naively limited, view of teaching as merely presenting or telling correctly. The prospective teacher's active involvement in genuine problem solving, especially during the critical first two years of the baccalaureate curriculum, is required for teachers to develop a mastery of knowledge at a level that guarantees their authoritative and confident response to the inevitable and legitimate requests they will have from their pupils to "do" or "perform" subject matter and not just talk about it.

In sum it is entirely too easy for critics to say that prospective teachers need to take more courses outside the colleges of education. Of course they should, but they must undertake programs of study very different from those found in the modern university.

Everyone argues (and I would agree in principle) that prospective teachers need to know in depth that which they will teach about. Most critics overlook, though, what the research has to say on the matter. A recent report by the U.S. General Accounting Office reviewed the most rigorous and recent research on the relationship between teachers' effectiveness and their mastery of subject matter in college. It failed to find any consistent relationship between teachers' subject-matter knowledge and their pupils' understanding of it, except in the most advanced high school courses.

The finding shouldn't surprise anyone familiar with university organization. We leave matters of subject-matter competence and the major to disciplinary departments; they concentrate on preparation for graduate study or entry-level employment. That limited focus almost never contemplates a student-major carrying the discipline into a K–12 classroom or, indeed, what that student might need to understand to do so effectively.

We do know what a teacher must understand to teach subject matter effectively, but it is far removed from what he or she will find in most departments. The teacher's role is to find and present the most powerful and generative ideas of a discipline in a way that preserves its integrity and leads to student understanding. This implies that a teacher comprehends the structure of the discipline, its key points and their origins, and the criteria by which one distinguishes the important from the trivial. This kind of understanding, slighted in traditional programs, is of fundamental importance to the teacher—and must have a central place in the teacher's education.

Novice teachers must inevitably reformulate their college majors into a teachable secondary or elementary school subject. Even those with relatively strong backgrounds often struggle with the diversity of high school content and consequently rely upon rule-based explanations, rather than conceptual ones, in responses to pupils. The traditional major often does not confer a level of understanding that empowers the teacher (or even the typical college graduate) to understand, for example, why magnetic force is not a good analogy for gravitational force, why some light objects sink while some very heavy ones float, why Fifth Amendment protections are vital, why the invention of the number zero was critical, why scientific laws are not ever proved but only disproved, how the sun "burns" in an outer space vacuum of no oxygen, why non-representational art is still art, and so on. Few college graduates, in fact, can give a coherent response to the inevitable child's question of why people in the southern hemisphere do not fall off the earth.

To recapitulate: the "reform" is that all teachers, at secondary and elementary levels alike, shall understand the subject matter they teach in depth, with those understandings based both on the integ-

rity of disciplinary knowledge and the needs of classroom professionals to prompt pupil learning. This ever-so-necessary reform cannot go forward without the full commitment of all university departments whose majors go on to teach.

Virtually every evaluation of teacher-education programs finds that graduates attribute their success as teachers to their student teaching course or to their first years in the classroom as teachers. Indeed, the grade a student receives in practice teaching is one of the few academic predictors of teaching success. Many reformers thus believe that an extension of student-teaching opportunities into other parts of the teacher education program is worthwhile.

There are reasons for skepticism about the widely held claims for the benefits of the traditional clinical experience, not least because it is so uniformly praised by its participants. Almost no person fails these courses and almost all earn top marks for their efforts; yet almost all student-teachers quickly conform to the practices of their supervising teaching and rarely put into practice a novel technique or risk failure. The student-teacher's success is so swift because he or she invariably conforms to the norms of the school and gives up the norms of the college of education.

By its very nature, student teaching is a stressful experience, constituting as it does a kind of final examination of all that might have been mastered in the teacher education program. It is a tested axiom that organisms under stress regress to levels of behavior that are lower than their true competence; newly acquired behaviors are driven out under stress by older, more primitive and better established behaviors.

Student-teachers are no exception to this general principle and, under the stress of teaching on their own for the first time, they invariably fall back on a set of naive or novice teaching behaviors possessed long before they entered teaching training. Like many teachers, parents, and children, they teach exclusively by telling and showing the correct behavior or answer. The problem is that the student-teacher "succeeds" too easily by relying on fairly primitive techniques and does not risk the experimentation that would provide a basis for reflection and analysis of teaching. The typical student teaching experience is not a genuine laboratory experience, because the possibilities of failure and risk are minimal. The emphasis is upon limitation and subservience to the supervising teacher, not upon investigation and the solving of novel problems.

The classic defense against regression under stress is overlearning, or practice well beyond what is needed for simple mastery of the skill. The reform of teacher education through increased clinical experience must therefore make two provisions: a provision for overlearning and a provision for an experimental environment in which innovative and risky teaching styles can be tested and thought about.

Until the last two decades, what served for scholarship in education relied heavily upon findings from other disciplines, particularly the behavioral sciences. The transfer of those findings, collected in non-school settings, to issues of educational practice was generally unsatisfying to everyone. It was unsatisfying because it was unconvincing and rarely provided unambiguous guidance about educational policy.

Within the last twenty years, however, the science of education, promised by Dewey, Thorndike, and others at the turn of the century, has become more tangible because the powerful methodologies of the behavioral sciences have been turned on the schools themselves, not just on distant laboratory simulations of instructional situations. Life in classrooms, in other words, has been studied in such a way that fairly convincing and counter-intuitive conclusions about schooling and pupil achievement are now possible.

The irony is now that the promise of a science of education is finally about to be fulfilled, the current reform tendencies, based upon older tales and literature, call for a decrease of the time allocated to the study of these emerging findings.

Basically, the new literature demonstrates that bright, well-meaning, and well-educated persons will make a number of predictable pedagogical mistakes, mistakes that will have disproportionately negative consequences for pupils who traditionally do not do well in school—or who are quite unlike their teachers in background and temperament. We can expect these well-meaning adults to teach as they have been taught by their own teachers and parents. They will be novice teachers and they will in fact teach the way young children teach each other—by direct telling and demonstration of the correct information. There will be a general failure to employ the more indirect, but very powerful, teaching strategies, like maieutic methods, role playing, and the social interaction and cooperation strategies.

The use of such strategies requires a disciplined practice that typically exceeds that provided even in the ordinary teacher education program. It takes a trained level of practice for a teacher to wait more than a few seconds, for example, for pupils to answer a question before filling in the silence with elaborative comments and thereby disrupting the pupil's thinking. It takes a trained level of practice, beyond that provided in the usual program, to increase the number of higher order questions the teacher asks, to decrease the portion of teacher talk, to provide advanced organizers, plans, and clear directions, to increase academic learning time, to give teachers the cognitive resources to make the ten non-trivial pedagogical decisions they make each hour and manage productively the 1,500 distinct interactions they have with pupils each day.

The ordinary person, and even many licensed teachers, treat pupils for whom they have low expectations in a damaging fashion—they may even do so out of a well-meaning, but professionally misplaced, sense of kindness. They, will, for example, seat these pupils farther away, treat them as a group and not as individuals, smile at them less, have less eye contact with them, call on them less, give them less time to answer when they do call on them, give them fewer hints, give them less "answer follow-up," give them less praise overall but more for marginal answers, ask them about more rote and routine matters, and interrupt them more often. Typically, low-achieving pupils, minorities, boys in the lower grades, and girls thereafter receive this kind of treatment, treatment that upon reflection can only be seen as educationally limiting and may one day be seen as educational malpractice.

Because adults and many practicing teachers are largely unaware that they consistently treat some of their pupils in these ways, teacher education programs will undoubtedly have to devote *more* time to instruction in pedagogy, not less. The untrained—or undertrained—person will make these and other costly mistakes without any awareness of the nature of and consequences of their actions.

In addition, those who have avoided the study

of educational research will advocate wrong-headed policies, like the failure to accelerate gifted pupils. They will give their pupils bad advice, like "don't change answers to multiple-choice questions because the first guess is best." They will not know how to decide whether an educational innovation, like a reformed spelling alphabet, will facilitate or harm initial reading. They would not know whether the grades they give their pupils should show a normal distribution or have some other form, or by what criteria to decide the matter for themselves. They would not know whether it was better to hold an underachieving pupil back to repeat a grade or to give that pupil a "social" promotion—nor, again, on what basis to make such a decision.

Teacher errors of judgment, like those of pedagogy, can be overcome by ordinary persons through deliberate, disciplined study and developed habits of reflection. Rather than "less time on methods," the goal of better classroom practice will inevitably require more time for relevant instruction and practice during the university years.

The "reform" of imposing standardized tests as a new hurdle to teacher-preparation entry, certification, and continued licensure comes more from state boards and legislatures than it does from campus sources. Even so, in some campus quarters there is a disinclination to object, in the name of "tightening standards."

A reasonable case can be made that the principal achievement of psychology has been the invention of the psychometrically sound standardized intelligence and aptitude tests. The best of these are remarkably reliable and meet significant empirical and theoretical tests for validity. Even so, there are severe limitations upon what can be had from these tests, particularly when one asks for a prediction of who will do well in a teacher education program and, more problematically, who will succeed as a teacher.

On the whole, what these tests predict best is a person's performance on another standardized test; the more similar the test the better the prediction (i.e., the higher the correlation coefficient). After that, the next thing the test predicts best is a person's grades in school, especially the grades that were earned nearest to the time the test was given. But even here, the person's performance on the very best tests accounts for only about 25 percent of the variance in their school performance, the remaining 75 percent being due to other factors.

The percentage of the variability in teachers' performance that can be attributed to their performance on any standardized test of intellectual or academic accomplishment is so low (about 10 percent at best) as to make it nearly ridiculous to give performance on these tests a central place in the decision about who should teach or be retained as a teacher. It has proved impossible, with our existing measurement techniques, to establish any meaningful connection between standardized test scores—or even school grades—and later performance in any of the professions, including teaching.

There are good reasons for this lack of a strong connection and thus no responsible investigator advocates giving these scores a central place in any decision about the potential of a prospective teacher. Used as supplemental information, test scores confer a marginal increase in the accuracy of prediction about eventual teaching proficiency; but no competent psychometrician would supplant this other information.

The rule, confirmed repeatedly, is that the best predictor of performance in a situation is the most recent past performance in that situation or a similar situation. Thus, high school grades, not SAT scores, are the best predictor of college grades; the best predictor of teaching performance is past teaching performance, and no other factor or combination of factors will yield a better prediction. Often that is why performance in the student-teaching course, as limited as it is, is a predictor, however weak, of later teaching success.

The point is simply that the skills needed to do well on a standardized test seem only remotely connected to the skills needed to teach well, if only because the two situations—the testing setting and the classroom—have so little in common. Existing tests cannot bear the burden that current reforms place on them. Bright people, high scorers on these tests, do most things better than low scorers, but that is not the issue, because many bright people are poor teachers, and many persons of modest intellectual endowment are very good teachers. The very best available tests simply do not tell us who is which.

Even if they could, there is little indication that predictions of teacher success from a standardized test will rise much beyond where they currently rest because it is now generally agreed that it makes no sense to think of teaching as a set of generic skills that cut uniformly across various subject matters, school and classroom settings, and pupil characteristics. Besides, even the most optimistic researchers never attribute more than 20 to 25 percent of the variation in pupil achievement to anything the teacher does or can do.

My point has been that many of the common "reforms" one hears talked about across campus are not, by themselves or together, likely to improve teacher education. This is so because either they focus on factors that are largely irrelevant to the education of teachers or because they do not realistically take into account demographic constraints and the need for larger changes in undergraduate education and disciplinary programs.

Of course I do not believe, after having expressed doubts about several "reforms," that no reform should occur. Any reform probably won't amount to much, though, if it simply reshuffles existing arrangements. . . .

September/October 1999

Rediscovering Teacher Education
School Renewal and Educating Educators

John I. Goodlad

Teacher education—the professional preparation of elementary and secondary school teachers—has been a neglected enterprise, long suffering from status deprivation. As the field's host institutions made the transition from normal schools to teachers colleges to state colleges to state universities, some colleges of education found it prudent to downplay their teacher-education role and sought status through identification with the research criteria of the arts and sciences. Many dropped preservice, undergraduate teacher preparation entirely and moved exclusively to graduate status.

Most of the top-ranked schools of education—from their mention in the Cartter Report of 1977 to their inclusion in the *U.S. News & World Report* rankings of today—prepare only a handful of beginning teachers or none at all. Since each of these schools is housed in a major, research-oriented university, an observer might conclude that there is no dwelling place for teacher education in the most prestigious mansions of higher education.

My assumption in what follows is that higher education has a moral responsibility to provide leadership in ensuring well-educated teachers for the nation's schools. In my book, deliberately eschewing teacher education rather than elevating it to a position of high priority confers shame, not prestige. The unavailability of teaching as a career

choice for freshmen in our most distinguished universities accounts for only a blip in the supply-side statistics, but the message to institutions not in the top research and doctoral categories of the Carnegie Classification is akin to a blast of cold Arctic air: If teacher education is not good enough for flagship universities, why is it good enough for us?

Suddenly, however, teacher education has been rediscovered in policy circles and linked significantly to school reform. Fifteen years of public attention to school reform has now expanded to include higher education and the teacher education function traditionally attached to it. The stances institutions can take in the domain of teacher education are narrowing down to just three, the first of which probably is untenable: opt out, comply with state regulations, or assume moral and programmatic leadership.

In what follows, I first describe the work to date of a national network of school-university partnerships embracing virtually all the types of colleges and universities in the Carnegie Classification, all of which chose the third option. I then expand on the sea change taking place in expectations for institutions sponsoring teacher education and the available options of "compliance" or "leadership," with special attention to leadership. In concluding, I return to the network of renewal and some of the lessons learned that might be useful in making the inescapable institutional decisions that lie ahead.

There exists today in the United States an unusual educational improvement initiative called the National Network for Educational Renewal (NNER). The NNER's agenda—the Agenda for Education in a Democracy—guides the efforts of educators in 33 colleges and universities, over 100 school districts, and more than 500 schools joined in partnership for the simultaneous renewal of schooling *and* the education of educators. Three of these school-college partnerships educate more than half of the teachers produced in their respective states, in programs quite different from those in place just a few years ago.

One of the remarkable features of NNER is that key leaders at all levels made a voluntary choice. The impetus for change was not from state mandates with their carrots and sticks; the NNER participants are doing what they are doing for the best of reasons: they want to. . . .

The Agenda for Education in a Democracy grew out of my inquiry into the nature of schooling and school change. . . . The agenda's three parts—mission, conditions necessary to the mission, and strategies for implementation—present a daunting challenge.

A four-part *mission* is set for teachers and teacher-educators: enculturation of the school-age population in a social and political democracy, comprehensive introduction of the young to the human conversation, the exercise of caring pedagogy, and the moral stewardship of schools and teacher education programs. The necessary *conditions* to be established for the conduct of this mission number at least 60, contained in 19 reasoned propositions or postulates. The *strategies* call for symbiotic partnerships between schools and institutions of higher education, the latter, in turn, bringing to the collaboration professors from both colleges of education and departments of the arts and sciences.

Intensive immersion of key actors in the agenda through a yearlong leadership program, an annual meeting of participants, setting-to-setting networking, and the wonders of modern electronic communications has produced the psychic energy and synergy necessary to individual and institutional renewal. Evaluations provide testimony to the power of an agenda that apparently resonates because of its connections to both the world of work and the larger ethos inhabited by those drawn to and involved with it. Lacking the common agenda, it is unlikely that the three long-separated cultures—teacher education, the arts and sciences, and the schools—each with a piece of the curriculum, would have come together in partnership to put the programmatic pieces together in a reasonably coherent, mission-driven whole. . . .

Once upon a time, not long ago, colleges and universities routinely received from the state a set of mandates regarding the preparation of teachers. These typically were rewritten every few years, and added to each year as the legislature mandated additional requirements—a course in audiovisual education or substance abuse, for example. Accreditation by the National Council for Accreditation of Teacher Education (NCATE) was an option. The state requirements were so prescriptive—even intrusive—that there would be periodic roilings within the campus committees responsible for compliance. However, with the school, college, or department of education as the designated unit for accountability, broader campus life was little affected.

Except in those institutions, mostly smaller, where the education of teachers represented the major curricular and budgetary commitment, neither the chief academic officer nor the arts and sciences departments were very much involved in any of this. The faculty generally was in the enviable role of being able to gripe about both the impositions and the "Mickey Mouse" courses perceived to come with them. But since these were the exclusive responsibility of the teacher-educators, even the weakest of the arts and sciences departments had someone to look down upon.

A profound sea change is becoming apparent. . . . When public officials and the press connected teacher education to their dissatisfaction with schooling, many faculty tried to put the blame on their institution's teacher-education program one more time. But now such scapegoating is unlikely to deflect blame: the disappointing performance of prospective teachers—university graduates—on tests addressed primarily to wider aspects of college-level learning imply a deeper problem and a much wider faculty responsibility.

Troublesome questions arise. Assuming that we

want all teachers to be both well-educated citizens and well-prepared in the subject matters of their teaching, do present curricular offerings and student advisement ensure such outcomes? Assuming that teachers require grounding in certain subject matters in order to advance the public mission of schooling in our democracy, how is that outcome to be ensured? Assuming that future teachers need to learn certain subject matters twice—once for themselves and once more for the teaching of children or youths—are the provisions for such deep learning adequate? Assuming that some students should be directed away from teaching because of academic and other shortcomings, are there policies that need to be changed, like that of allowing free access to all undergraduate programs once admitted to the institution?

Given our increased understanding of the pedagogy required to deal with the diversity of the school population, is it reasonable to assume that a well-educated teacher versed in the relevant subject matters and pedagogy requires only four years of higher education? Since teachers, future teachers, and teacher-educators all agree that field experiences, student teaching, and internships are the most impactful determinants of teaching behavior, does it make sense to continue the present, rather casual arrangements for where these components are provided and by whom?

Given the relevance of these questions (and many more of like importance), the blinders and earplugs of denial and scapegoating must be quickly removed. Unlike the days of simple compliance and of responsibility narrowly assigned, a campus-wide response has to be made by any college or university that wants to prepare teachers for elementary and secondary schools today. Accreditation, too, may well disappear as an option.

The old order changeth, yielding place to new. The new is an order that involves decision-making presidents, academic vice presidents, deans and faculty members in the arts and sciences, and their counterparts in teacher-education units.

For most public colleges and universities, opting out of teacher education is not a choice. It might be reasonable for the regents of a state system such as the California State University or the State University of New York to allocate responsibility to most but not all of their campuses, given a nearby availability of alternatives in heavily served regions. Given the fact that aspiring teachers come predominantly from local constituencies, however, such decisions are sensitive. A legacy handed down from generation to generation that seriously interferes with quality in teacher education is the idea that becoming a teacher is virtually a right and that preparation programs should be handily nearby and minimally demanding.

Putting aside the option of not offering a program, the available paths are simple compliance with state regulators or vigorous acts of self-determination. It is not difficult to envision the consequences of the former. What remains today of institutional autonomy in teacher education will be given up to a system of "standards" and testing as accountability all built around this year's school reform model. It is wishful thinking to assume that this model can be confined to the realm of teacher education and not sift into wider elements of the curriculum as well.

Only some of the consequences of the alternative—vigorous, self-determined acts of leadership—are predictable. One that is predictable pertains to the hard work of comprehensive renewal. What is not predictable is the degree to which there can emerge a productive balance between the carnivorous appetite for chewing on academic meat sometimes exhibited by policy-makers and the oversensitivity to curricular autonomy sometimes displayed by faculty members. Recent growth in the former activity has caused me to feel uneasy with the accolade "education governor."

For institutions of higher education that decide to take the high road of leadership, there is some good news. There is now a sizable domain of fundamental agreement on what needs to be done if teacher education is to become a robust enterprise, sufficient to call in question the wisdom of the attractively simple panaceas for the "reform" of teacher education that surface routinely. The 1996 report of the National Commission on Teaching & America's Future mapped this terrain, drawing from the work of the Holmes Group, our NNER, other improvement ventures, and a body of research sufficient to rule out the need for a new comprehensive study. This report carries with it a rare commodity: the clout of the policy-makers in agreement with specialists in the field.

The major elements of this agreement are rapidly becoming conventional wisdom about the improvement of teacher education (although they are far from realized in practice). These include the necessity for school-university partnering, for the regular involvement of faculty members in the arts and sciences, for partner or professional schools serving as "teaching" schools, and for these schools and university-based teacher education to renew *together* — hence the concept of "simultaneous renewal" guiding the change strategy introduced by the NNER in 1986 and subsequently adopted by the American Association of Colleges for Teacher Education and the Holmes Partnership.

Not quite as widely articulated is the considerable agreement about the need for top-level leadership in both higher education and the K–12 school system to elevate teacher education as a priority. In addition, there is a growing commitment to increasing field experiences in the curriculum and to integrating university- and school-based activities into a coherent whole. Some partnerships on the forefront of renewal are restructuring the faculty reward system to recognize the human-intensive nature of this combined work.

The relatively modest implementation of these agreements so far is testimony to the reality that they are fraught with difficulties little envisioned in the commissioned reports. The cultural differences between schools and universities are such that merely *talking* together about common problems often is taken as a mark of success. When such conversations then lead to serious partnering, the time and effort required to plan and effect simultaneous renewal begin to separate the truly committed from those individuals who merely like to talk.

School principals and teachers are under increasing pressures these days from parents responding anxiously to calls for school reform and from dealing with the reform proposals themselves; greater involvement in teacher education is readily perceived as one more burden. It is not easy for university personnel to be participant-cheerleaders when they themselves are uneasy about glacier-like changes in the reward structure and about the prospect that state interventions will wipe out their efforts one more time. For many professors in the arts and sciences, the preferred course is to regard participation in the schools and in teacher education as a short-term service contribution and as time away from the teaching

and research that really matter. All these factors pose challenges to institutional leaders, for whom simple compliance with state schemes ever beckons.

The National Commission on Teaching & America's Future set as a goal a qualified, caring, competent teacher for every child by 2006. Given the Commission's membership, it is difficult to comprehend collective naïveté of such magnitude that its members talked themselves into believing in the attainability of that goal. Rather, it should be taken as a challenge to be worked toward.

There are two reasons, both familiar, for institutions of higher education to join with partner schools in picking up that challenge. The first is practical to the point of being efficient: token compliance is likely to be viewed negatively by state policy-makers — and in state appropriations. The second reason is a moral one: exerting leadership in designing programs that will attract and produce superb teachers for the nation's schools is simply the right thing to do.

In the minds of many would-be reformers, teacher education is in the quick-fix category. At a conference of educational leaders, I once heard a state superintendent of public instruction give the back of his hand to complexity with the proposal that "several of us sit down together over a weekend and come up with a plan for taking care of this teacher-education thing." There are now many others in positions of power who come close to sharing such a view. Like it or not, higher education does not enjoy a long time frame for determining its stance, for "taking care of this teacher-education thing." Prudence now calls for shedding the institutional proclivities both for "going it alone" and for not appearing to be in a copying mode. There is now hard-won experience from which lessons can be learned and time saved without any loss of institutional identity and prerogative.

For example, it is now possible to see firsthand in the NNER exemplary demonstrations of virtually everything recommended by the National Commission on Teaching & America's Future. No single setting illustrates the full array. But a carefully planned trip to five or six sites would provide a quite comprehensive picture. To ensure a productive journey, however, there should be an underpinning of preliminary reading and accompanying conversation among representatives of those three critical groups of potential actors—from nearby schools likely to become partners, from the teacher-education faculty, and from the arts and sciences departments.

It would be useful, too, to tap into the experiences of the 100 or so teacher-preparation sites claiming to be following parts of the NNER agenda but without the help of the NNER and its two supporting agencies in Seattle. The interesting observation likely to emerge during this period of study and observation is the degree to which the settings of the NNER are committed to a common agenda and yet are markedly varied in their implementation.

Thoughtful inquiry into the history of teacher education, its neglect in the emergence of the American university, and the recommendations for change now gaining attention provides some potentially useful lessons to guide institutions committed to improvement.

First, continuation of the myopic tendency of colleges and universities to look at only their own role in teacher preparation will spell doom. The power of the student teaching and beginning experience will ensure teachers cloned in the present (ineffective) ways. Consequently, there must be a symbiotic partnership between the two institutions pursuing a common mission—the preparing university and the receiving school—with *both* engaged in renewal.

Second, the time and effort involved in creating and maintaining such partnerships for simultaneous renewal necessitates a *continuous relationship* somewhat akin to that between a medical school and a hospital, except that several "teaching" schools are needed. The investment in each partner school will grow over time and must not be abandoned. Schools other than those designated "partner schools" can be helpful in providing various field experiences without becoming part of the symbiosis.

Third, the more schools and universities collaborate and the more they embrace a need for one another in producing better teachers and schools, the more troublesome the mechanics of management will become. Imaginative leadership is needed to create new organizational arrangements and perhaps entirely new settings (such as the recommended center of pedagogy), and perhaps to handle a budget for the whole of teacher education, deal with government, select partner schools, ensure curricular renewal, and much more.

When, for example, a professor in the mathematics department who is also a necessary member of the teacher-education faculty retires, there should be no resulting squabble over the availability of resources for his or her replacement.

Fourth, whether it is adapted from elsewhere or created anew, there must be a clear and common agenda of mission, conditions to be put in place, and designated roles for the three groups of major participants. Given these necessary components, the agenda will be complex and, consequently, a continuing source of conversation. But it must be reasonably figured out in advance. Belief that one will emerge as a natural corollary of initiating and carrying out tasks is misguided and potentially fatal to progress.

Fifth, the tenure of designated leaders in schools, school districts, colleges, and universities is markedly shorter than it was even a dozen years ago. School principals move on to larger schools or to superintendencies, just as academic vice presidents move on to presidencies. Consequently, any change that depends on just a few such designated leaders is hazardous. The message: Leadership must be widely shared, which in turn means that preparation for leadership must be a built-in, continuing activity.

Early on in the history of the NNER, senior staff members of the two supporting agencies, the Center for Educational Renewal at the University of Washington and the independent Institute for Educational Inquiry nearby in Seattle, launched a leadership program of readings, seminars, and special projects. Most settings now have a cadre of individuals sufficiently immersed in the agenda to qualify them for cloning the program and for deepening understanding among their own colleagues. Our data suggest a correlation between the success of this effort and steady penetration of the agenda, even in the face of a complete or near-complete turnover of designated leaders.

The sixth lesson is directed specifically to the top leadership of colleges and universities. From the late 1950s to the present, education faculty have responded, often reluctantly, to the call for increased research productivity and publications. In our evaluations, referred to earlier, we found professors with a dozen or so years remaining in their careers struggling to cope. Many thought they had prepared for and been employed for careers in teaching and teacher education. They watched young colleagues, perceived to be better prepared for research, moving up the academic ladder while these veterans saw themselves stalled. They told us that the only apparent recourse was to give less attention to time-consuming, unrewarded chores such as supervising student teachers in order to try to meet the changing expectations—for which many felt unprepared.

Many presidents, academic vice presidents, and provosts are now becoming impatient with their education faculty, which appears not to be moving fast enough to meet the sea change in expectations for higher education. These campus units could easily become the scapegoats one more time. What some of those administrators don't fully comprehend is that their education unit may now be staffed with professors who adapted successfully to the research expectations of centralized promotion and tenure committees. The dean of education finds herself or himself in a delicate, if not hazardous, position—of persuading a faculty just recently praised for its grant-getting and research productivity that greater attention to outreach, with special attention to teacher education and school improvement, is now the name of the game. Not surprisingly, that faculty will be skeptical, even annoyed. And a dean has only so many chips to use up in seeking to balance the pressures of another sea change in expectations with sufficient faculty approval to stay in office.

In my view, top-level campus administrators share responsibility for sustaining this balance. They must take the lead in articulating the changed expectations. Furthermore, given the degree to which external pressures call for responses that embrace the arts and sciences, the leadership responsibility can hardly be delegated solely to the dean of education. Nor can leadership be assumed successfully by the central administration without serious effort on its part to learn enough about teacher education to make wise decisions.

A longer perspective on higher education reveals the extent to which progress across professional schools has come in spurts. Rarely have there been sufficient resources to develop the whole university at once; consequently, in one era, the primary effort was directed toward medicine, in another, toward law; more recently, we redid engineering, then business. Now the time has come—in fact, it's long overdue—to launch an era of concentrated attention to teacher education. The reasons are both practical and moral: practical because the university's very standing is at stake; moral because it is the right thing to do.

ASSESSING STUDENT LEARNING

Barbara D. Wright

Since 1985, *Change*'s articles on assessment have provided neatly placed points of reference for major events in the post-secondary assessment movement. At the same time, they reflect our own evolving perceptions of the movement, what has caused it, where it is going, and how long-lived it would be. When we connect these dots, we do not get a detailed chronicle, but we do find that *Change* has given us a remarkably accurate profile of this 15-year phenomenon.

At the same time, *Change*'s picture, like the movement itself, is more nuanced than the connect-the-dots metaphor suggests. These articles take us from early calls for attention to the first diagnoses of why assessment was a tough sell or doomed to failure. They portray ongoing struggles to harmonize improvement and accountability, the vagaries of politics, and the shortcomings of traditional testing and grading. More recently, they have challenged us to reconsider our aversion to national standards, and they suggest a transformed role for accreditation. In short, the history of the assessment movement since 1985 is here—not in exhaustive detail, but rather in colorful, suggestive strokes.

When Pat Hutchings' and Ted Marchese's review of the assessment movement appeared in fall 1990, it marked what many thought would be the halfway point in its trajectory. The expectation was that assessment as an "issue" would have a shelf life of perhaps 10 years, from its beginnings in 1985, after which it would either be so thoroughly institutionalized—or so thoroughly overtaken by other "fads"—that it would become a non-issue. Russ Edgerton, then president of the American Association of Higher Education (AAHE), made the implicit explicit when he introduced the Hutchings and Marchese article with his pep talk, "Assessment at Half Time" (1990). In reality, however, the career of assessment has proven to be more complex, more marked by fits and starts, and—most surprisingly, given the difficulties involved—far more long-lived than most of us expected.

Hutchings and Marchese offered an array of assessment case studies. These examples were framed by a history lesson, observations about contemporary context, and cautious optimism about the benefits, if assessment was undertaken with a focus on student learning and with the goal of improvement, rather than compliance or data collection. The cautions and advice have stood the test of time; the assessment programs cited, meanwhile, have met mixed fates. We have learned in the intervening years that getting started really is just the beginning. Assessment demands sustained commitment, from top administrators on down. Otherwise, what is launched with great fanfare can disappear again in less time than it takes to say "face validity."

A gradual convergence of many factors had taken us to this apparent mid-point. In the 1970s, influenced by competency-based education, faculty members in many disciplines began to ask the kinds of questions destined to become the stock in trade of the assessment movement, for example, "What should our students know?" "What skills should they command?" and trickiest of all, "How will we know?" An excellent example of this thinking was the article by Nancy Pirsig, "What a Historian Should Know" (1976). It was, of course, competency-based education, reinforced by continuous individual student assessment, that became the basis for Alverno College's current, unrivaled status as the mother of all assessing institutions.

The early to mid-1980s saw growing dissatisfaction with the quality of higher education, both inside and outside of the academy. In 1985, Peter Ewell's "Assessment—What's It All About?" introduced *Change* readers to the combination of pressures that was beginning to drive prescriptive state mandates to assess. In the same issue, William Turnbull asked the question at the heart of national unease: "Are They Learning Anything in College?" (1985) Turnbull called upon stakeholders—the higher education community, but also K-12 educators, state officials, students, and the public—to forge new partnerships, focus on teaching and learning, assess effectiveness, and do so with respect for diversity among institutions. We are still working on that agenda. In early 1987, Ted Marchese weighed in with the official birth announcement of the assessment movement ("Assessment: Fact or Fad?"); a few months later, AAHE sponsored the second in a continuing series of assessment conferences. AAHE had been stunned by the strong attendance and sense of urgency in the air at its first conference in fall of 1985. Realizing that the movement needed a broker between policymaking and educational communities if both accountability and educational improvement were to be served, AAHE took that role upon itself and the AAHE Assessment Forum was the result. Its primary goal was to provide an open forum for debate, one where many voices could be heard: policy makers as well as administrators; producers of standardized tests as well as faculty, students, employers, accreditors, funders, and others. The Assessment Forum also functioned as a clearinghouse for ideas and information about model institutions; it began to provide much-needed literature on assessment for the "happy amateurs"—campus faculty and administrators with little or no formal training in assessment—who found themselves getting involved. Since then, the literature gap has been filled, assessment workshops and conferences have proliferated, and the learned societies now routinely offer support for assessment in their disciplines. Yet demand for the Forum's annual conference and information services continues unabated.

In 1987 ("Assessment—Where Are We?"), Peter Ewell described an important policy shift. The "second generation" of assessment mandates was proving more flexible, more tolerant of diverse institutional missions and local approaches. At the same time, Ewell issued several warnings—warnings that are still on the mark today. First, institutions needed to hold up their end of this new bargain and assess in good faith. Second, both policy makers and institutions needed to focus on using assessment findings for improvement, not merely reporting or archiving them; otherwise neither accountability nor improvement would be served. The same issue of *Change* offered a counterpoint full of reasons for campus resistance and questions about the meaningfulness of the whole enterprise (see Steven Spangehl's "The Push to Assess," 1987). Though assessment practitioners have repeatedly addressed such concerns, their responses have not always registered, either on campus or beyond.

1991 was the year Total Quality Management (TQM), a.k.a. Continuous Quality Improvement (CQI), hit the assessment scene, comet-like. Every workshop and session on the subject at that year's Assessment Forum conference was filled to overflowing, and the seemingly insatiable demand continued the following year. In 1993, CQI became an official part of the assessment effort at AAHE (see Marchese's "TQM: A Time for Ideas" or Ewell's "Total Quality and Academic Practice—The

Idea We've Been Waiting For?"). By May 1996 (see Marchese's "Bye, Bye, CQI"), however, the phenomenon had burned itself out, except for pockets of enthusiasm in business schools and administrative units. Despite great compatibility between the two approaches, CQI, with its jargon and alien cultural origins, could not compete against the greater robustness and palatability of assessment.

In late 1991, Ewell detected yet another policy shift, expressed in "Back to the Future," with a return to greater prescriptiveness and stronger stress on accountability in state mandates. Behind these new policy initiatives lay several factors: impatience at the lack of progress on campuses; the budget stresses of the recession; and a changed view of post-secondary education as private good rather than "public utility." His advice to institutions, still relevant today: shape up and do this thing right, before it is done to you. In a witty complement to Ewell, Roger Peters (1994) interpreted the rising tension between accountability and improvement, decried the effects of ham-fisted bureaucracies, and challenged institutions to muster the courage to search diligently for bad news, then do something about it.

Other facets of the assessment debate also appear at regular intervals in *Change*. There is, for example, the problem of improving the fit between what students learn in college and what is required of them on the job. In late 1992, Peter Cappelli critiqued traditional grading and argued for more innovative assessments of student performance that would align better with the needs of the workplace. At the height of the culture wars, Alexander Astin (1993) asked how students are affected by multiculturalism on campus, described ways to assess those effects, and concluded that there are widespread and beneficial effects on students' cognitive and affective development.

Peter Sacks (1997) took on standardized testing in "Standardized Testing: Meritocracy's Crooked Yardstick," in the context not only of state mandates but also of attacks on affirmative action, noting that commercially available, multiple-choice tests are a peculiarly American way of determining educational progress that is virtually unknown in the rest of the world. Robert Holyer (1998) asked us to reexamine our reflexive rejection of national standards for post-secondary education, pointing out that we already accept many implicit forms of national standards, such as standardized testing. In part, Holyer's piece is a rebuttal of Sacks; yet he also argues that most educators are wise enough not to place undue faith in test results or use them to the exclusion of other evidence. Alas, that restraint is not generally shared by U.S. policymakers or the public.

Most recently (1999), *Change* reported findings of the National Center for Post-secondary Improvement (NCPI), which surveyed institutions to determine "the nature, extent, and impact of student assessment strategies." The NCPI found little collection of data on more complex educational outcomes and even less use of information for educational improvement. Is it fair to conclude, then, that after 15 years the assessment movement has had little or no impact? Or is it more accurate to speak, as the NCPI report does, not of "revolution" but of "evolution"? My money is on the latter interpretation.

Granted, some of the pressures that initially drove assessment have lessened. As the economy has improved, state budgets are under less stress and appropriations to higher education less contested. While performance funding initiatives remain popular (see Burke, Modarresi, & Serban, "Performance—Shouldn't It Count for Something in State Budgeting?" 1999), they have lost their edge, and attention at the state level has shifted to other matters, for example, building to accommodate the baby boomlet or providing information technology. As stock portfolios have grown in value, as campuses have gotten their annual tuition increases under control, and as the availability of federal support for colleges has increased, the general public has become less angry, less anxious. As the labor market has improved, graduates are getting jobs—even if employers are not entirely happy with their preparation, particularly in the area of higher-order skills.

At the same time, interest in assessment remains intense, particularly on campuses. In fact, one of the curious things about the Assessment Forum's annual conference is the virtually inexhaustible supply of novices who attend it and their hunger for guidance. What is going on here, and how do we explain assessment's staying power? Arguably the single most important reason why assessment has persisted is its championing by regional and professional accreditors. Though mandated to require assessment by the federal government in 1987, accreditors' response has been far more than perfunctory. Stung by earlier criticism that they were failing to safeguard the public interest, accreditors today are doing some of the most important work in the field. By shifting from an inputs- and process-based definition of institutional effectiveness to a focus on student learning outcomes, accreditors are challenging institutions to rethink their reliance on inputs as indicators of quality. Two *Change* articles, "Accreditation and Academic Quality Assurance" (Dill, Massy, Williams, & Cook, 1996) and "Guard Dogs or Guide Dogs? Adequacy vs. Quality in the Accreditation of Teacher Education" (Dill, 1998), suggested the tack that accreditation is taking.

At first glance, the powerful influence of accreditation may seem counter-intuitive. After all, accreditation standards tend to be so generic as to allow all sorts of wiggle room, self-studies and visiting teams vary greatly in quality, and the rhythm of fifth-year reports and decennial reaccreditation seems so sluggish as to be utterly ineffectual. However, while administrators, legislators, or state boards may become distracted by other issues, accreditors keep coming back, even if it does take five or 10 years. There are schools that have been asked repeatedly what they are doing about assessment and why it is taking them so long. They are starting to get the idea that assessment matters—and is not going away. Given the magnitude of the sea change in campus culture that we expect institutions to undertake, perhaps this epic pace is exactly what is required. After all, it is the deep ocean wave we want to affect, not the ripples on its surface.

It helps the staying power of the movement that assessment stands at the point of confluence for a whole series of ideas and issues in education, some with a long history and deep roots. These range from questions about campus structures or faculty roles and rewards to new understandings of teaching and learning, from critiques of traditional methods and instruments to new definitions of the disciplines and the rise of interdisciplinarity, from a fixation on canons of content to a focus on more generic intellectual skills, from the rise of new educational technologies to the impending retirement of an entire generation of faculty, from specific legislative measures to diffuse public dissatisfaction. This powerful convergence comes at a teachable moment for the academy, a moment occasioned by self-doubt and necessity as well as by exciting new ideas.

The messages are both internal and external to the academy. Campuses may debate endlessly whether they represent ignorant meddling or a welcome widening of the dialogue. My own bias is toward the latter view, uncomfortable as some of those messages may be. I see a democratization of higher education in progress. Democratization means several things. It means, for example, respecting and including the voices of those who have traditionally been excluded. In the case of higher education, this has meant, almost as a point of pride, the voices of students as well as voices from beyond the campus: everyone from K-12 educators or employers or policymakers to parents and the general public. Assessment provides these voices with a vehicle for input.

At the same time, the democratic process requires a sense of civic responsibility and community effort. The democratization of education on campus has meant pulling faculty back from anarchic individualism or from a survivalist focus on departmental turf. It has meant creating new communities of interest across boundaries seldom traversed in the past, for example, among disciplines, between the major and general education, between academic and student affairs, and between academics and administration. The best assessment is intensely participatory and decentralized down to the lowest viable level, even as it operates within a larger framework of goals and expectations widely discussed and broadly accepted. Assessment represents a new way to mesh education on campus with the requirements of the society that both supports it and depends on it. That is a challenge likely to keep us busy for decades to come.

Will assessment become a permanent fixture on campus? While nothing is forever, assessment has already outlived the prophecies of naysayers several times over. It has good and powerful forces behind it. It may well prove to be the single most powerful tool we have, the shovel that will help us move that proverbial graveyard into the new century.

References

Astin, A. W. (1993, March/April). Diversity and multiculturalism on the campus: How are students affected? *Change, 25,* 44–49.

Burke, J. C., Modarresi, S. I., & Serban., A. M. (1999, November/December). Performance: Shouldn't it count for something in state budgeting? *Change, 31,* 16–23.

Cappelli, P. (1982, November/December). Colleges, students and the workplace: Assessing performance to improve the fit. *Change, 14,* 55–61.

Dill, D. D., Massy, W. F., Williams, P. R., & Cook, C. M. (1996, September/October). Accreditation & academic quality assurance: Can we get there from here? *Change, 28,* 17–24.

Dill, W. R. (1998, November/December). Guard dogs or guide dogs? Adequacy vs. quality in the accreditation of teacher education. *Change, 30,* 13–17.

Edgerton, R. (1990, September/October). Editorial: Assessment at half time. *Change, 22,* 4–5.

Ewell, P. T. (1985, November/December). Assessment: What's it all about? *Change, 17,* 32–36.

Ewell, P. T. (1987, January/February). Assessment: Where are we? The implications of new state mandates. *Change, 19,* 23–28.

Ewell, P. T. (1991, November/December). Assessment and public accountability: Back to the future. *Change, 23,* 12–17.

Ewell, P. T. (1993, March). Total quality and academic practice: The idea we've been waiting for? *Change, 25,* 49–55.

Holyer, R. (1998, September/October). The road not taken. *Change, 30,* 41–43.

Hutchings, P., & Marchese, T. (1990, September/October). Special report: Watching assessment—Questions, stories, prospects. *Change, 22,* 12–38.

Marchese, T. (1987, January/February). Editorial: Assessment: Fad or fact? *Change, 19,* 4.

Marchese, T. (1993, May/June). TQM: A time for ideas. *Change, 25,* 10–13.

Marchese, T. (1996, May/June). Editorial: Bye, bye CQI. *Change, 28,* 4.

National Center for Postsecondary Improvement. (1999, September/October). Revolution or evolution? Gauging the effect of institutional assessment. *Change, 31,* 53–56.

Peters, R. (1994, November/December). A faculty view: Some snarks are boojums—Accountability and the end(s) of higher education. *Change, 26,* 16–23.

Pirsig, N. (1976, March). What a historian should know. *Change, 8,* 33–36.

Sacks, P. (1997, March/April). Standardized testing: Meritocracy's crooked yardstick. *Change, 29,* 25–31.

Spangehl, S. (1987, January/February). The push to assess: Why it's feared and how to respond. *Change, 19,* 35–39.

Turnbull, W. W. (1985, November/December). Are they learning anything in college? *Change, 17,* 23–26.

What a Historian Should Know

Nancy Pirsig

The history competency project at Sangamon State University started with one basic question: What should a person be able to do with a bachelor's degree in history? Phrased another way: What should history graduates be competent to do? For example, should they be equipped not only to read but also to critically analyze news stories that appear in the daily papers? As many faculty at Sangamon State can attest, the answers to questions like these lead to further questions, such as: What, really, is history? Why should anyone study it? And how do you define an educated person? . . .

"I think we really started this whole thing from a gnawing sense of the inadequacy of our own education, including graduate education," says Christopher Breiseth. "It was sobering to some of us holding PhDs from very traditional universities [Breiseth's doctorate is from Cornell] to realize we had never systematically analyzed our profession or attempted to define, with any degree of precision, what an undergraduate should gain from a liberal arts education focused on the study of history. And as we searched the literature, no one around the country seemed to be asking questions quite as presumptuous."

As faculty wrestled with what the study of history should be for the general student, one thing became very clear to Breiseth. "In everyday life situations—like reading a newspaper or listening to a political candidate—we want our graduates to be able to think analytically, recognize assumptions, investigate a complex situation, separate it into its discrete parts, and draw these together into a coherent synthesis, demonstrating an ability to recognize and defend their own assumptions in terms of the evidence."

One task, then, has been to develop an approach to history that will help students integrate their learning and develop the real-life skills Breiseth mentions. To this end, the faculty have settled on three broad, yet intersecting, "historical understandings" or competencies which the student is expected to master: an understanding of the major forces shaping the contemporary world; an understanding of oneself in the contemporary world, as a means to understanding others in a historical perspective; and an understanding of the functions of culture in our own and other societies as they affect institutions, values, and behavior. A fourth competency serves as a necessary tool for the others—the ability to identify, locate, and interpret primary and secondary historical materials.

Students work toward these competencies in a program that requires no specific number of credit hours for graduation but is rather an alternative path toward a BA in history. In an initial semester-long colloquium, students are introduced to faculty members available to help them in planning a self-paced program. Each student chooses from among them a mentor/adviser with whom he or she will work closely. Together they select two or three areas that interest the student most for historical study, and go on to develop specific projects leading to the competencies. . . .

. . . Students can pursue projects through independent study or field work or through traditional courses, provided their course work leads to the stated understandings. . . .

Current events orientation is not the only departure from tradition. Students help make up tests to deepen their understanding of what they are supposed to learn and why. During the course they are introduced to the idea of what a historian does and what a competency-based program is. Their skills are assessed and those who choose to enter the history project at Sangamon agree to work on their weaknesses. . . .

. . . It became necessary to think about restructuring the history curriculum, or using existing courses to meet competencies; providing learning experiences outside the classroom, including independent study and field work; finding ways to assess competencies; defining "competency credits" and basing a degree on those definitions; deciding what the student's transcript would look like; and grappling with the implications of a time-variable degree which is awarded on the basis of something other than credit hours. . . .

. . . "We care about themes, issues, learning to think rather than strict content memorization," says Nina Adams, assistant professor of history at Sangamon State and last year's codirector of the program. "None of the history courses come on strong with, 'Do you remember the date of such-and-so?' but rather, 'What is the connection between . . .?' or, 'Compare this to that and give your reasons.'"

According to Adams, the project was conceived to meet the specific needs of students who come to Sangamon State from the community college. "With open admissions for all community college graduates, we found more and more students who did not . . . know the meaning of, 'Organize. Synthesize. Analyze.' When students have no library experience, it's useless to say, 'Go look up. . . .' We were letting them take a drib of a course here and a drab of a course there and were assuming they had the skill and background to put the whole thing together into some sort of coherent experience that would help them in some way through life. And it just wasn't happening.

"The great attraction for us now," she is quick to point out, "is that it works for all different kinds of students. If you have some who are highly sophisticated and skilled, it gives them a layout of what they can do, what all the possibilities are, right away, and then they just take off like rockets, and that's great." . . .

Larry Shiner, dean of academic programs, explains, "The real key to competency education is achieving competency in the faculty; getting them to develop the kind of skills they need to help the student achieve competency. We are working on a faculty development plan in which there are two key elements: one, concern with the faculty member as a facilitator of learning who must be able to do things like state objectives—not only for a course but for individual students; and two,

[concern with his or her] ability to assess where students are and where they've got to go. Faculty aren't really trained in assessment. They've only learned to give certain kinds of tests and grade certain kinds of papers."

What Shiner singles out as special about a genuine competency project is that "heretofore what we've done is say, 'Put together enough courses in which all these things are going on and you'll get a BA degree, and that in itself says you're competent.' We've never said too clearly what that meant. It could just mean that you're competent at conning professors, or after X hours of courses you're sufficiently socialized to know how to operate in the system. Now if this project or any other really comes up with new ways of assessing competencies without credit collecting, and means it, then we could really have something."

Indeed, one of the knottiest aspects of the program has been setting up a fair procedure for assessment. In the latest plan, the student directs a committee consisting of the mentor, at least one other historian, another student, and additional faculty, if appropriate, to review periodically and approve the student's program and progress and to assign competency credits according to the type of experiences and projects the student wishes to undertake.

In addition, the committee later serves as an evaluator in each of the three broad areas of competency, when a student decides to demonstrate his or her grasp of, for example, "the major forces shaping the contemporary world." The important thing is that the assessment procedure is not simply a transfer of course credits into competency credits, and the degree is not automatically granted in four years (or two years at Sangamon, which is an upper-division school). . . .

. . . We decided to stop counting hours and instead to focus on what the student must learn in college, how well, and which evaluative instruments to use in measuring proficiency." . . .

Are They Learning Anything in College?

William W. Turnbull

. . . Observer-participants convened recently by the Association of American Colleges, taking a hard look at recent trends, concluded that we have

> . . . a crisis in American education as it is revealed in the decay in the college course of study. . . . Evidence of decline and devaluation is everywhere. The business community complains of difficulty in recruiting literate college graduates. Remedial programs, designed to compensate for lack of skill in using the English language, abound in the colleges and in the corporate world. . . . Foreign language incompetence is now not only a national embarrassment, but in a rapidly changing world it threatens to be an enfeebling disadvantage in the conduct of business and diplomacy. Scientific and technological developments have so outpaced the understanding of science provided by most college programs that we have become a people unable to comprehend the technology that we invent and unable to bring under control our capacity to violate the natural world.

In the recent past, those who point with pride have been outnumbered considerably by those who view with alarm.

Expressions of discontent with the colleges follow hard on the heels of widespread criticism of the schools. . . .

. . . [P]eople keep asking the deceptively simple question, "Are they learning anything in college these days?"

Many people, besides state administrators, see as much reason to ask the question about colleges as about the schools. Others who would like to know the answer include: the state legislators; the students and their parents, as direct participants and consumers; employers, as recipients of the "product"; the press; and the taxpaying public concerned with the soundness of investment in education for the future of the country.

The colleges themselves, as responsible institutions interested in their own quality and in self-improvement, have of course had a long-standing interest in assessment. The appraisal of student accomplishment, expressed in course grades, is integral to the procedures of every college. Traditionally, the faculty has exercised the grading responsibility, but left the monitoring of other indicators, such as scores on external exams and dropout rates, to the administration or the office of institutional research.

Grades mean a great deal to students and parents, but vary so widely among institutions as to be virtually meaningless to anyone outside the walls of a single college. . . .

The consequent lack of data about student performance and a college's leaves the stakeholders in higher education—people at the state and national levels—with little information about the learning outcomes of a single college or of a system of colleges. . . .

These conditions lead public officials to ponder instituting some broader form of assessment in higher education, transcending the single campus. As they ponder, institutional anxiety rises. Faculty and administrators fear that any assessment across institutions will be simplistic, incomplete, and insensitive to differences of mission; the results could be misinterpreted and lead to inappropriate prescriptions; bad information could be used to infringe upon institutional autonomy. . . .

It is easy, in focusing on the internal-external tensions, to miss important points of agreement. Both institutions and external groups would like to have more and better assessment information. No one is sure how or where to get it, how to use it, or even whether or not a reasonably good system can be put in place. Most people see the lack of good evaluation instruments as a major impediment to moving ahead, although they may disagree as to the likelihood that such instruments and techniques can be devised.

The problem is to envision a set of circumstances in which the several parties involved could meet at least their principal needs for information, preferably through cooperative effort.

Any assessment program designed to be effective across institutions calls for hammering out agreements on value choices and operating principles. These might well be codified through a cooperative effort among the people with the most direct roles to play in creating the assessment system: e.g., a group of faculty, institutional administrators, and state agency representatives.

An example of a value choice might be agreement that the overriding purpose in gathering data is to provide a basis for improving instruction, rather than keeping score or allocating blame. From such a choice would flow several operating principles designed to maximize the utility of the information for instructional feedback to teachers and students. Statements such as those listed below would follow:

- As much as possible, the assessment system should be made integral to the teaching within an institution. It should yield information useful to the individual student and teacher.
- Leadership in assessment should be provided by faculty.
- The results of assessment should be expressed in ways that provide a maximum of information, useful for instruction and guidance, to the student and the teacher. Secondary uses of assessment should be for institutionwide and statewide planning and improvement.
- While the priority should be on instructional feedback, it should be possible to aggregate those same data usefully for other purposes.
- From the outset, the assessment instrument should be planned cooperatively to serve multiple uses. Similarly, the methods of expressing and applying the results should be jointly planned.
- Some indicators useful in institutional and system wide planning, such as data on persistence or success after graduation, should come from sources other than classroom instruction. Faculty, institutional administrators, and state-agency representatives should participate in the development of these indicators.

Agreement about principles provides a basis for an assessment system built cooperatively from the ground up. I think the cooperative approach is appropriate: faculty, institutional administrators, and state agencies have mutual interests in any assessment system put in place.

A cooperatively designed assessment program might take an infinite variety of forms. . . . Let us assume that a hypothetical statewide program includes many or all of the following elements: . . .

Assessment Near Graduation. The senior examinations, like those given earlier, would include both objective and faculty-graded essay material. They would include measures of higher-order skills and exams of some breadth in the central academic subjects. Scores in these skills and broad area exams would be calibrated to their counterparts at the freshman and sophomore levels to yield measures of development or "value added." Finally, the assessment program would include major field examinations in the curricular areas offered in the college.

The foregoing measures would yield individual results that could be incorporated into a college's ongoing work with students. Some of the scores could also be included in data aggregated at institutional and state levels for assessment purposes.

Institutional Surveys. A set of institutional surveys would also be devised for monitoring aspects of student development and opinion about the institution that do not call for records specific to the individual student but yield aggregate data useful for policy decisions. . . . Such surveys, using efficient sampling procedures, would provide a maximum of planning data for a minimum investment of the time. . . .

Indicators of Institutional Functioning. Some of the most important indicators of institutional functioning come . . . from such "unobtrusive measures" as dropout rates . . . or success rate in entering the next higher level of education after graduation. Such indicators are especially useful if maintained systematically by an institution over a period of years. . . . [T]hey can also be aggregated across . . . a system . . .

None of these elements is particularly novel. . . . What would be unusual is to find all of them designed and used by a *group* of institutions working in concert within a state to yield comprehensive pictures of educational performance and trends. . . .

An unusual and important feature of a comprehensive system of information spanning the undergraduate years is that it allows for the measurement of change. If student gains are to be a focus of assessment, the measures must be designed from the beginning to be linked across educational levels. The emphasis on change or "value added," which is basic to the recent report, *Involvement in Learning*, is an important idea that requires both careful definition and a system of assessment that exhibits continuity from beginning to end. With such a continuous design, it becomes meaningful to focus on performance at graduation in relation to performance at entrance. The potential to do so is critical in comparisons across institutions that vary enormously in selectivity. Developing colleges and open-door institutions quite properly resent being compared with others on the basis of the scores of their graduating seniors without reference to how far the students have come in their learning since they entered the institution. . . .

A comprehensive, cooperative approach of the kind outlined here is unlikely to be developed quickly. It may, however, be possible to create conditions under which an assessment system could evolve as a cooperative enterprise not only within a single state, but on a multi-state basis. . . .

The creative talents of faculty members are needed to solve the issues of quality assessment in higher education. But the efforts of scattered individuals working with inadequate resources are unlikely to move us forward very rapidly. To create, try out, evaluate, and improve further new approaches to assessment will entail a great deal of time and large amounts of money.

The alternative is to organize a mutually reinforcing set of consortia, interest groups, cooperatively arranged workshops, and labor-sharing arrangements that can speed up the invention, development, and diffusion of improvements and cut costs at the same time. Only through concerted, cooperative effort will we quickly and surely develop solutions responsive to important questions about higher education—questions that are being raised more insistently both inside and outside the ivied walls. More importantly, such an approach could help ground our assessments firmly where they belong: in the effort to improve teaching and learning.

January/February 1987

Assessment: Where Are We?

The Implications of New State Mandates

Peter T. Ewell

Calls for explicit assessment of the results of higher education became increasingly insistent throughout 1986. Some of these calls were prompted by a number of recent critical reports on the undergraduate experience, but more and more they come from *outside* the academy—from state authorities, from accrediting bodies, and from the public at large.

Observing this development, two consequences seem apparent. First, assessment is here to stay. . . . But at the same time, the character of "assessment" is shifting. . . .

Evidence of assessment's growing prominence is abundant. Some eleven states have now offi-cially addressed assessment as a matter of policy or statute. . . .

The most notable development of the past twelve months has been seizure of the "high ground" of assessment by external agencies and authorities, mostly by state government—either through direct legislation or indirectly through the action of a statewide governing or coordinating board. . . .

. . . But what actually has been mandated? Here, the past year's acts provide relative reassurance. In general, states have avoided many of the pitfalls of standardized measurement and are undertaking programs that reveal both a sensitivity for differences among institutions and a sense that meaningful assessment efforts take time to develop. . . .

. . . Indeed, the primary thrust of most current state initiatives is to encourage institutions to undertake their own appropriate local assessment efforts. Two themes are apparent here, and they often work parallel to each other.

First, states are establishing programs—generally through their coordinating boards—that will require institutions to report performance on a number of identified outcomes criteria. . . . Nothing is said about how such assessments are to be accomplished; institutions may select their own appropriate methods. . . .

A second emerging theme is state encouragement and support of selected "lead institutions" to experiment with assessment. . . . Support for these demonstration programs is often substantial and multiyear and comes in the form of a categorical grant awarded as part of an established quality improvement or "centers of excellence" program. . . .

. . . [R]egional accreditors have taken a similar tack. SACS guidelines, for example, do not specify how assessment of "institutional effectiveness" is to be undertaken (though a list of possible data-gathering methods is suggested). Like the newer state programs, the choice is left to each institution. Also, like the states, regional accreditors want to assist institutions in undertaking appropriate assessment efforts. . . .

Given these external initiatives, what have institutions been doing in the name of assessment?

Most institutional assessment efforts are only just getting started. . . .

Some of these new examples are the "lead institutions" funded under state categorical grant programs; some are institutions undergoing self-study according to the new SACS criterion. Still others have undertaken assessment on their own—to demonstrate the credibility of their educational product, to evaluate and improve their curricula, or to get a "head start" on what they expect will ultimately be a requirement. Among all these institutions, several patterns are notable.

First, these are *institutionwide* efforts, intended to produce an integrated multifaceted program of activities. For public institutions particularly, this implies creating assessment as a separate, visible activity, focused primarily on developing a database for curricular and program evaluation. . . .

These efforts also typically involve "pilot" projects across a range of cooperating departments. . . .

Finally, most such efforts provide central coordination and support for assessment. . . .

For private institutions, assessment efforts have tended to emanate from existing curriculum committees and are more often seen as an integral part of the curriculum. . . .

In contrast to most public university efforts, private college assessment initiatives often go far beyond the giving of a standardized test. King's College (PA) is developing a "rising junior essay" to assess writing and critical thinking; it will be graded by faculty teams using ETS holistic grading techniques. A number of private colleges are developing senior "capstone" examinations that involve oral presentation before external examiners.

Despite the differences, both public and private institutions exhibited growing sophistication about assessment. One manifestation is a willingness to experiment with assessment techniques that go beyond standardized tests. . . . [O]ne finds new attention to investigating noncognitive as well as cognitive development: a task force at James Madison is weighing how to assess student development along a number of Chickering's "vectors of identity" and Kohlberg's stages of moral development.

. . . [I]nstitutions are attempting to document student course-taking patterns, students' "quality of effort," and other "input" factors in an attempt to understand and improve outcomes. . . .

Looking over patterns of external initiative and institutional response, I see cause for both satisfaction and concern.

The primary cause for satisfaction is that most assessment initiatives—albeit externally mandated—are being undertaken sensitively, deliberately, and with appropriate attention to differences across institutions and student groups. . . . [F]or the most part, externally mandated assessment requirements have not exhibited the Neanderthal measurement mentality that many initially feared. A second cause for satisfaction is the creativity with which some institutions—often on their own initiative — have moved forward on the assessment issue. Their experience demonstrates that faculty, once convinced of its utility, will not only actively endorse assessment but will use and sustain it as a vital part of academic discourse.

But the past year has also raised disturbing issues. First, there is a growing tendency for institutions to react to what they think external agencies want, rather than to what those agencies actually say they want. . . .

A second issue is related. Because assessment is increasingly a mandated activity, there is a subtle but growing tendency for institutions to view it as a reporting requirement rather than as an active mechanism for instructional improvement — an external rather than an internal imperative. Thus they will often assign responsibility for assessment to a distinct office, committee, or individual outside the regular structure of institutional decision making. . . .

What can be done to lessen these tendencies? A first answer is simply a plea for greater communication. . . .

A more satisfactory answer is for external authorities to place as much evaluative weight upon the actual improvements and changes made as a result of assessment as they currently place on collecting such information. So long as it is only information that is required, the clear message of externally mandated assessment is accountability.

If, as states and accrediting bodies claim, the name of the game is improvement, then incentives should be structured around what is done rather than what is counted. . . .

. . . [W]e need to find much better ways of using assessment information in institutional and curricular decision making. . . . [T]he answer lies in forging more explicit links between assessment and the planning/budgeting process; a base of experience on this issue does exist, but most institutions will need to learn by doing. . . .

What we need to assure is that the action takes place. If there is cause for concern about assessment in the coming year it is not, I think, that external initiatives will inappropriately dictate academic policy. It is that in their scramble to discover the *what* and *how* of assessment, institutions will forget *why* they are engaging in the process in the first place.

September/October 1990

EDITORIAL: **Asssessment at Half Time**

Russell Edgerton

In 1986, the National Governors' Association issued a blunt report on education titled *Time for Results*; . . . [which] urged states in their dealings with higher education to go beyond "resource measures" . . . and insist that colleges and universities develop programs that would measure what their undergraduates were really learning.

In less than five years, assessment has traveled from being an item in a reform report to a condition of doing business. The Education Commission of the States reports that more than three-quarters of all states have a student assessment effort planned or in place. And, according to the American Council on Education, the majority of all colleges and universities is in some stage or other of developing assessment programs.

There is a cycle to public issues — from early awareness, to confrontation, to a "working through" process, and finally to a new consensus. We seem to be approximately halfway through the cycle on assessment. After lots of heat and controversy, campuses are in various stages of working through their responses. By 1995 it's likely that assessment will decline as a public issue — not because it's gone away, but because it has become so routine. Thus, it seems a propitious time to catch our breath and see what lessons we should learn from the early campus encounters with assessment. . . .

. . . [T]here are now well-developed, attractive models that other campuses can look to for guidance.

The majority of campus leaders, however, has approached assessment with an attitude of reluctant compliance. Consciously or unconsciously, they have signaled the message: let's do just enough so as not to *appear* to be at odds with the governor's office or the next accreditation team to visit campus.

Five years ago, when assessment arose from the mists of state capitals like some shapeless apparition, such reluctance was excusable, perhaps in some states even justified. But no longer. Now we know what the thing is and what, in the right hands, it *can become*.

So my message is this: toss out all those *Chronicle* clippings complaining about how stupid, unfair, and simplistic it is to try and assess student learning. Call your cabinet together. And give them a pep talk—in the great tradition of Knute Rockne and Vince Lombardi—about how your campus team should play in assessment's second half. Here are some talking points:

Point 1. State pressure will continue. . . .

. . . When governors and legislators think about us in higher education, all too often they see us as privileged people caught up in obscure research projects, no longer serving our students' or society's larger needs. . . . We can send a strong message to the contrary by taking assessment seriously.

Point 2. The people pushing assessment are our allies! . . .

. . . Political leaders in nine states recently reported in a survey sponsored by the AAHE and the Education Commission of the States that they saw assessment as a way to *strengthen* the case for budgetary expansion. Many legislators are amazed that college and university leaders don't themselves initiate assessment so they can bring better arguments to the table!

Point 3. We're in charge of how assessment is done. . . .

. . . The states, by and large, have left it to each individual campus to determine how assessment can best be done. Most of us have been given lots of running room to come up with forms of assessment that fit our unique missions.

Point 4. If we define assessment in worthy terms, the faculty will find it worth their time. . . .

. . . [A]ssessment, properly understood, isn't about tests and other modes of measurement. It's about what's behind these. It's a mindset that asks questions—good questions, hard questions, *legitimate* questions—about what and how much our students are learning.

Rather than being "someone else's answers to someone else's questions," assessment can give us a way to answer our own questions. . . .

Point 5. Let's play to win, and be clear what we mean by winning.

Winning isn't just getting the score, or keeping score, but improving the score. . . .

The deal we want to make with our funders is this: If we do assessment in good faith, you in good faith have to help us address the results of assessment. If we find that our students require more remedial help than anyone thought, then we want the resources to address this task. If the math deficiencies of our students begin with eighth-grade algebra or before, then let's cooperatively tackle that problem from the beginning.

OK, let's go out there and play with heart—as if we *really* do care to know what our students are learning.

Watching Assessment

Questions, Stories, Prospects

Pat Hutchings and Ted Marchese

For the past four years, the two of us have been watching assessment—as observers and critics, as collectors of stories and documents, and through campus visits, fifty in all. Here, we set forth our sense of what this complex, often puzzling movement is about; how it plays out on campuses . . . ; and what its prospects may be for lasting effect on undergraduate education.

Our view of assessment is mixed. As a phenomenon, it is at once powerful, scary in the wrong hands, increasingly a matter of law, and home to the day's most provocative discussions of teaching and learning. As a movement, it tilts at the deepest structures and habits of academic culture; its practice on campus is marked by tricky beginnings and important accomplishments. The one sure thing is that assessment warrants close attention. Here's how we see it.

1. Hard Questions . . .

. . . [A]ssessment is best understood as *a set of questions*—questions that are not, in fact, entirely new, but that now come at us with greater insistence. At bottom they're questions about *student learning*:

- What is the college's contribution to student learning? How and what do we know of that contribution?
- Do our graduates know and can they do what our degrees imply? How do we ensure that?
- What do the courses and instruction we provide add up to for students? Are they learning what we're teaching?
- What knowledge and abilities do we intend that students acquire? Do they have opportunities to do so? Are they successful? At what level? Is that level good enough?
- How can the quantity and quality of student learning be improved? What combination of college and student effort would it take to achieve higher levels of performance?

These are good, important questions; we need to be able to answer them. They're also hard questions, not the least because they bring to the surface fundamental issues of institutional purpose.

They are questions, we've found, that faculty understand—questions good teachers ask about their own students. Is this student getting it? How do I know? What constitutes acceptable work? What can I do to help my students succeed? "What I understand by assessment," a community college faculty member wrote to us, "is asking, 'Are my students learning what I think I'm teaching?'" Faculty ask assessment's questions because they need answers to do their daily work with students. Assessment, for faculty, means a habit of looking at teaching in terms of its effects: learning.

Individual faculty are not alone in asking such questions. Departments and programs, even entire institutions, are learning to ask about their cumulative impact on student learning—about "what it adds up to." What knowledge and abilities should (and do) our accounting majors have when they graduate? In what ways do all of the teaching and course-taking in biology come together—or not—for students? What are the outcomes of our general education program? Do the recipients of our degrees in fact possess the traits of intellect and character the college promises in its catalog?

Not surprisingly, assessment's questions ring loud bells for higher education's outside constituencies. The public at large retains a faith that higher education is a good thing, something it wants for its children. But there's a sense, too, that things aren't quite right on campuses, that a great deal of money is being spent to uncertain effect.

Policymakers have questions particularly about undergraduate teaching and learning, which they see as neglected. At a recent meeting of state leaders in Santa Fe, New Mexico, Joyce Holmberg, an Illinois legislator, noted, "I get constituent complaints all the time that the best professors are off doing research, not teaching at the lower division.

The quality of teaching in our universities is a real problem. Tell me how to fix it." To Holmberg and others—in all but about 10 states now—assessment looks like part of the answer; its questions are their questions.

It need hardly be said that legislators' rendition of those questions—often embodied in mandates—differs in tone from the versions asked by campus administrators, whose versions differ yet from those of faculty members. There have been hard feelings, tension, and lots of frustration on all sides. Getting the various levels of questions to connect rather than collide has proven a major stumbling block.

But with the noise turned down it's possible to hear a common note as well: that when it comes to higher education, we *all* need to ask not just about the funding, facilities, credentials, and curricula but about *results*. Assessment's questions raise that issue; they make *student learning* the result that counts in gauging institutional performance.

II. A Tradition of Questions Lost . . .

Assessment's questions are far from new; indeed, in asking about the cumulative effects of college and a given student's readiness for a degree, assessment points back to earlier ways of thinking about educational quality. . . .

In the closing decades of last century . . . the American college became today's university. Along came an elective system and a great expansion of subjects for study, huge increases in student numbers, the ascendancy of research and graduate study, faculty authority and autonomy. . . .

. . . In the 1880s, . . . instruction and evaluation (grading) were combined within individual courses, each course was assigned a credit-hour value, and when the credits (C average or better) totaled 120 the degree would be issued. Not without protest did this all happen. As late as 1911 Harvard president A.L. Lowell addressed the Association of American Universities on the topic, "Disadvantages of the Current American Practice of Conferring Degrees (With the Exception of the Ph.D.) on the Accumulation of Credits in Individual Courses, Rather Than As The Result of Comprehensive Examinations upon Broad Subjects." . . .

It has been many decades since the comprehensive examining of seniors played a significant role in the award of degrees. In losing that practice, we lost as well a tradition of asking questions about our graduates' competence and about the cumulative effects of our teaching and curricula.

III. . . . and Questions Found

Now, thanks to assessment, these questions are with us once again. Why now? . . .

. . . Ten years ago UCLA's Alexander Astin recast debate with an argument that traditional ways of thinking about quality in higher education—quality as a function of *resources* (high student SATs, faculty Ph.D.s, endowment, library holdings) . . . —told too little, misled even; that the real measure of quality was found in a college's results, its contribution to student learning, the "value added" from the experiences it provided. Outcomes mattered in this view, as did attainments over time, and *evidence* of the two—an agenda for assessment—was advanced as a necessity.

By the mid-'80s, Astin's views had taken hold in an undergraduate reform movement growing within the academy, spearheaded by two influential reports. In late 1984, a National Institute of Education study panel (on which Astin sat) issued "Involvement in Learning," which argued that to strengthen learning one needed to a) involve students in their studies, b) set high expectations, and c) assess and provide feedback. In early 1985, the Association of American Colleges' "Integrity in the College Curriculum" also made this learning-assessment link, calling it "scandalous" that colleges failed to assess the impacts of their teaching. Behind both reports lies a view that quality is indeed a function of student learning.

A subtle but important development over the next two years was the way this view of quality gained currency within the academy. It came to permeate convention speeches, journal articles, faculty debates, and, late in 1986, a book by the president of Harvard, Derek Bok's *Higher Learning*. In varying tones, William Bennett, Ernest Boyer, and a host of others gave further voice to "the need to assess."

It was in part from educators themselves, then, that state policymakers took their interest in assessment. Spurred by concerns about "economic competitiveness" and "workforce capability," the education-minded governors of the mid-'80s began asking now-familiar questions about student learning and undergraduate performance. Missouri Governor John Ashcroft, in his capacity as chair of the National Governors' Association Task Force on College Quality, put it bluntly in 1986:

> The public has a right to know and understand the quality of undergraduate education that young people receive from publicly funded colleges. ... They have a right to know that their resources are being wisely invested and committed. ... We need not just more money for education, we need more education for the money.

Many governors (and legislators) turned to assessment because it was a "solution" they recognized from the K–12 level. ...

Adding to their interest was the visibility of several successful assessment programs in higher education. Alverno College and Northeast Missouri State University, both of which had used assessment ... to improve student learning, were glowingly profiled in Ashcroft's NGA report, suggestively titled "Time for Results."

A combination of ideas, then—that quality was a function of learning, that learning should be demonstrated, and that assessment could be a lever for improvement—undergirded state interest in postsecondary assessment.

That interest has now moved assessment ... to a "condition for doing business." ...

Judging by recent surveys of governmental activity on the issue (it is higher than ever), public interest in assessment will endure. That's likely, too, because the civic and economic imperatives behind the demands for educational performance are worldwide and can only grow. If you talk with legislators and lay trustees, you know they *like* assessment's questions, and want them answered; they see them as questions about quality improvement, not unlike those they pose to other state agencies and services or back in their own businesses. Indeed, they seem surprised that colleges haven't *routinely* sought evidence about impacts and effectiveness, and see the absence of assessment as self-serving protectiveness.

As late as 1987 one could still hear assessment called a fad; but no more. To many observers—certainly to us—assessment's questions seem sure to be with us in a big way for a long time. ...

V. Against the Grain

Assessment has had a difficult start on *many* of the campuses we've visited in the last four years.

What we've come to understand is that the questions it poses run up against some of the deepest structures and habits of academic life. Four factors in particular make assessment "against the grain."

First, assessment runs against the grain in asserting faculty and institutional responsibility for student learning. On many campuses the tradition is otherwise: Teaching is understood to require mastery of subject matter, clear delivery, prompt and fair grading, the keeping of office hours; as for learning, "the good students will get it." Assessment, on the other hand, assumes that the point, indeed the test, of good teaching is student learning—and that there's a shared responsibility (with the student) to make that learning happen. ...

Second, for many faculty, the tasks and processes assessment would evoke threaten sacred territory. One of the reasons people choose faculty careers is because they prize autonomy: the freedom to pursue one's own research agenda, to teach what one wants... it's critical to scholarly inquiry and to the special relationship between teacher and student that is rightly guarded.

It is against this high regard for individual autonomy that assessment interposes questions about a *collective* faculty responsibility for student learning. ... Nowhere is this expectancy more against the grain than in respect to general education, where the absence of collective attention to coherence and outcome has so often resulted in what Ernest Boyer years ago labeled a curricular "disaster area."

Within departments and majors, too, assessment calls for faculty to get a lot clearer among themselves (and with students) about collective aims for cumulative learning. The language here—of "goals," "objectives," and "outcomes"—is enough to put off many faculty. Even more problematic for them is that assessment doesn't stop with goals; it wants to ask about the connectedness of goals to particular courses and instruction. Pretty soon, as one faculty member told us, "It looks a lot like assessment will be telling me how to teach my course. Whatever happened to academic freedom?"

Marching everyone to the same music is *not* what assessment's advocates have in mind; we've not found anyone arguing in its name for the lockstep, teacher-proof curriculum of the high school. Nor is academic freedom, except in its mushiest and most sweeping sense (allowing anything to go forward in any classroom), at issue here. Assessment does, however, pose a counter to faculty autonomy by calling for work together toward common goals for which *some* shared responsibility is assumed. . . .

Third, . . . is that prevailing reward structures make it difficult to take assessment and its aims seriously.

For faculty on many campuses, assessment's questions arrive at a time of rising pressure for research productivity and publication. Insofar as assessment is about better teaching, the climate for it is distinctly uncongenial. . . .

. . . But even on the larger number of campuses where teaching is the primary mission, it's often not clear that work on *assessment* will be rewarded. . . . Faculty naturally ask themselves: If I do this difficult thing, will anybody care? . . . Will it ever make a difference? . . . Are the costs . . . worth it?

These questions become especially problematic in that assessment presumes collective activity. Where and how does *that* get rewarded? . . . [R]eward structures in higher education almost universally run to the individual, and therefore counter to the aims of assessment.

Rewards for assessment (and for student learning) are problematic not only for individual faculty but for institutions. Where assessment is mandated, it's often unclear exactly what the state wants, even what priority it attaches to assessment. . . .

Assessment in many states, in fact, comes as the latest item on an already crowded "quality control" docket — program review, special audits, accreditation, certifying exams — none of which will be eliminated to make room for assessment . . . raising concerns that assessment will go down a similar road, lost in a continuing din of state "initiatives," with no tangible reward for the institution that resolves to do assessment well. . . .

Public institutions have come to know well the bases on which they will be rewarded — for sponsored research, victories on the football field, and sheer enrollment. But as Missouri's higher education commissioner Charles McClain observed last fall at a meeting in Santa Fe, "How often has an institution been rewarded because its students *learned* more?"

Fourth, the assessment movement itself seems to embody a growing tension between campus and statehouse, raising questions about "whose agenda" higher education will serve.

On the one hand the states complain about their colleges and universities: that they pay too little heed to public agendas (like school reform); that academics are off on their own agendas of institutional and personal aggrandizement; that tuitions keep going up but that student attainment and performance levels do not; that faculty are coddled, teach too few hours, are never in their offices, and leave the important work of educating undergraduates to foreign TAs; that higher education has been off the hook too long when it comes to providing evidence of effectiveness. . . .

On the other hand, institutions look around and see signs of threat and intrusion on all sides: states lurching from agenda to agenda; mandates rolled out one after another, hastily enacted and poorly understood; unreal timelines for "results"; expectations that colleges will overcome, with no increment of resources, years of public neglect of elementary and secondary education; and, more generally, that not much new money stands behind all the talk about the new importance of education. . . .

. . . [S]uch tensions are an essential backdrop to much of what's going on today in the name of assessment. They explain in part why there are mandates, and why those mandates are not always eagerly embraced. . . .

VII. So What? . . .

. . . Five years into this movement, what do we know about the acid question: Does assessment improve student learning? . . .

The two of us have also been trying to answer the "so what" question — mostly by asking it of the dozens of campuses that are now three-to-five years down the road. What we've heard by way of response are a hundred stories — stories about the redesign of courses in a nursing sequence, the repair of an advising system, increased retention of minority students, a new goals statement for an engineering program, the more systematic use of student study groups in large science courses . . .

. . . [Q]uestions about assessment's impact — its power to improve things — are still premature on lots of campuses. . . .

Leaving aside questions of strict cause and effect, one can nevertheless point to institutions that are active in assessment *and* have improvements to report. One such is Alverno College, where a highly sophisticated longitudinal study follows

Alverno College

Assessment at Alverno College dates back to 1973, when faculty and administrators reshaped the curriculum around eight cross-cutting abilities, a transformation that led in turn to a search for new ways to elicit demonstration of those abilities from the student. The faculty developed a set of principles and practices that would constitute a framework for performance assessment; those in turn led them to the assessment-center method of business and industry, which faculty adapted to educational purposes by focusing not on selection but on diagnosis and development.

Today Alverno's assessment program encompasses scores of different activities used to monitor and foster on-going, individual student learning. It's best understood not in terms of methods (there are many) but as a set of educational principles:

■ assessment puts the focus on the student's progress toward publicly identified learning outcomes, with explicit criteria for success.

■ assessment calls for the student to integrate what she knows with what she can do — the concept of performance.

■ assessment is not an "add-on" but an on-going, integral part of the learning process.

■ assessment entails feedback to the student: detailed, behavioral diagnoses of strengths and weaknesses through which she eventually develops the skills of self-assessment necessary for independent learning.

■ assessment entails externality; student performances are evaluated not only by their teachers but by external assessors.

■ assessment samples student performance in a variety of settings (the major, support area, off-campus experiential learning, etc.) and in multiple modes (writing, speaking, group interactions, etc.).

Assessment at Alverno focuses on the individual student. But to pursue larger questions about impact and effectiveness, the college also employs sophisticated program evaluation. In Alverno's Office of Research and Evaluation, funded out of the college budget and in place since 1976, researchers examine the impact, value, validity, and effectiveness of Alverno's educational assumptions and programs, and work with faculty to refine the links between teaching, assessment practice, and long-term learning outcomes.

students through college and beyond. Nowhere, perhaps, are there better, more complete data about gains in student learning over time — data that would seem to document the impact of assessment. But behind those gains lies not only assessment (as most people use the word) but Alverno's powerful learning culture: consistency and clarity of purpose, teaching aimed at those purposes, a sense of responsibility to students, a sophisticated, institution-wide conversation about learning, and a view of teaching as a valued professional activity. Assessment at Alverno is essential to all of the above, but it's also part of a bigger picture, and separating out its effects is not possible — or particularly useful.

What one sees at Alverno and on other assessment-minded campuses — at King's, UTK, Miami-Dade Community College, Northeast Missouri State — is that assessment is but one of three or five or eight major things going on that add up to high-impact undergraduate education. It's not only that assessment's effects can't be separated

out, then; multiple, linked lines of work have to be in place for significant gains in learning to occur . . .

. . . [S]o if the question is whether assessment fixes things, the answer is no. But what if you ask, Are things more likely to improve with assessment than without it? Does assessment contribute to a set of conditions where improvement is more likely? Our answer is yes. . . . [T]he dozens of other campus stories we've studied show that assessment can a) raise questions and prompt processes that help clarify collective goals and expectations; b) identify problems and put them "on the table" in ways that force attention; c) build habits of inquiry and a culture of evidence about student learning.

With the right leadership and sense of purpose, assessment can do these things even where it *is* "against the grain" — indeed, over time, it can help change the deeper institutional values and shape cultures more conducive to teaching and learning. . . .

In sum, where assessment is working, it's almost

impossible to pull out the causes and effects. Where it works, it works because it's integral, not as a separate function off by itself but as a process woven into daily activity. Seen this way, assessment becomes a powerful, if insufficient, condition for change.

VIII. Assessment and Change: Prospects for the Long Term

Barbara Wright recalls the moment in her work as director of UConn's assessment project when her FIPSE program officer wondered whether assessment in Storrs would be a mere "blip on the screen" or lead to "real change in campus culture." "My God," Wright panicked, "is *that* what we're supposed to do? Change the campus culture?"

Our answer—the answer implied by the story of assessment as it's told here—is yes; assessment *is* a story about institutional change. As such, it invites a final question: What, over the long term, are the prospects here for deeper, lasting change?

The answer to *that* question, we've come to believe, may have only a little to do with assessment itself. Institutions, given the day's pressures and mandates, will *do* assessment; the issue is, to what effect? And effect, as we think the stories in this piece suggest, has less to do with a technically correct doing of assessment than with a larger

mindset that undergraduate improvement is possible, necessary, and a priority. . . .

. . . Assessment is powerful in such places because there's a larger principle of *integrity* at work. . . .

Institutions that are taking assessment seriously have a different slant on accountability. While recognizing obligations to external publics, they want to look inside to deeper-running responsibilities.

They think, for example, of the institution's obligation to its students. . . . Some campuses are beginning to think, as well, of students' accountability for their own learning, and are teaching students to "self-assess," to take responsibility, to ask the "what-it-adds-up-to" question of *themselves* as learners.

Most important to the quality mindset behind assessment is the accountability that educators have as professionals to each other . . . to deliver, in their teaching and related work, on mutually agreed upon purposes (this, the professional obligation that goes with the autonomy that faculty have traditionally enjoyed). . . .

With these deeper forms of accountability understood and in place, institutional aims find expression in the work of all members of the campus community. Where that's the case, you want questions about those aims—and evidence of their accomplishment. You want assessment.

November/December 1991

Back to the Future

Assessment and Public Accountability

Peter T. Ewell

State assessment mandates, since the time they came into vogue some six years ago, have always harbored a contradiction: is their primary intent to prompt instructional change within the academy or to inform the wider public about results?

For a time, it appeared these ends were compatible—that the public and academic agendas for assessment could be made broadly coincident. After an early (sometimes acrimonious) debate about common statewide testing, most states set-

tled on a decentralized path that allowed institutions considerable latitude in developing their own approach to assessment. So long as each public institution assessed its students' learning, and thereby showed its care for undergraduate improvement, the public charge would be met.

But in the past year, this bargain has started to come apart. New state proposals for common outcomes testing are coming forward again. On top of them, a *national* assessment effort has unfolded with astonishing consensus, force, and speed. These developments, I believe, return us to some old, basic issues about the role of assessment in public accountability. In the immortal words of Yogi Berra, "it looks like déjà vu all over again." . . .

Is there a pattern in this turbulence? From its midst, I believe, three themes emerge.

First, accountability is back, more strongly than at any time since assessment's inception. A new note of insistence is pervading public rhetoric. . . .

Second, in current hard times, neither states nor institutions feel they can afford assessment as a stand-alone activity, funded and disconnected from clear decisional consequences. This means that assessment must more fully "enter the institutional bloodstream" to be effective; equally certainly, to stretch the anatomical metaphor, the funds for it will increasingly "come out of our hides."

Third, as the federal government ponderously enters the assessment arena, it seems destined to repeat, at considerable cost, the rocky history of state assessment initiatives. Consistent with that history, though our natural inclination may be to hide and watch, higher education must involve itself in this important development from the start.

A New Look

If accountability is indeed back as the major driver of state assessment policy, what's responsible? . . .

. . . Traditionally, public colleges and universities were seen as a kind of "public utility" — providing needed services that enabled citizens of the state to advance in their careers and enhance their quality of life. As a "public service," the accountability demands placed on higher education thus centered on issues of "access" and "efficiency": How equitable was the system in conferring its presumed benefits to citizens of the state, and how careful were higher education's managers in husbanding the public's resources?

Recently, in contrast, public officials have come to see higher education as a strategic investment, enabling the state to build its economy and infrastructure by developing manpower and attracting new industry. From this perspective, accountability becomes less a question of equitable and efficient operations than documenting a concrete return on investment. . . .

But state officials also recognized at an early point that the best way to achieve lasting change

in an enterprise as creative and complicated as higher education was through processes that were decentralized and institutionally owned. . . .

Finally, it's important to remember that we in higher education actively *convinced* many governors, legislatures, and lay boards that this was a good idea. . . . [M]ost state officials were happy to endorse an approach based on institutional initiative.

Notions of educational "investment" and decentralized management combined, then, to yield today's pattern of institution-centered assessment, best exemplified by Virginia. The approach provided a window of opportunity for institutions, time within which they could develop "authentic" assessments that best fit their circumstances. But the approach also represented a policy gamble for state officials, who recognized that "ownership" might for some institutions provide a smokescreen for doing nothing. Sooner or later, state officials knew, they would be forced to ask for an accounting.

Part of what I believe has happened in the past year is that they've started to do so — and sometimes they haven't liked what they've heard in response. Some are voicing simple impatience at the length of time that the process is taking without showing tangible results. Others note a visible lack of action on assessment on more than a few campuses, and take that as a sign of higher education's unwillingness to make undergraduate improvement a priority. . . .

. . . [W]e need to examine dispassionately our own performance as institutions — both in making assessment happen and in helping state leaders address some real policy dilemmas. . . .

One is a problem of closure — in particular, the inability of a rich and diverse body of local, institution-level assessment activity to produce straightforward summary evidence that higher education overall is doing its job. . . . This continuing inability to document effectiveness and improvement hurts higher education's cause, especially in hard times; legislators are increasingly reluctant to support higher education spending without such evidence. . . .

This leads to a second, more direct difficulty: uneven institutional response. From the beginning, state leaders recognized that adopting a decentralized approach entailed the risk that some institutions would wholeheartedly embrace the effort while others lagged behind. . . .

... [A] particular resulting dilemma is how to handle a single "problem institution" of this kind without negatively affecting the others. A prime recent illustration is the University of Missouri, where the perceived resistance of the Columbia campus to *any* kind of assessment eventually led the regents to mandate sophomore testing—even though the system's three other campuses had healthy local initiatives in place.

A final difficulty, arising out of the vastly different conceptual worlds of state and institution, is the inability of leaders at each level to effectively see each other's problems. In Missouri, for instance, state leaders were astonished that university officials didn't recognize a connection between cooperation with the regents' testing mandate and political support ... to increase appropriated funds for higher education. ...

An Emerging Agenda

While state-level developments such as these suggest a future assessment agenda more focused on accountability, the now rapidly escalating federal interest in assessment is a wild card. ...

... [N]ew federal assessment initiatives appear largely uninformed by state experience. If advantage were taken of that experience, what might be usefully learned?

First, effective assessment requires *clear purposes*. The current National Goals process has fashioned an unprecedented consensus with respect to the substance of the six goals, several of which indeed have already served as a useful point of reference for coordinated action. Less obvious are the reasons why these goals ought to be *assessed*, and the uses to which the resulting information will be put. Is the assessment process intended simply to provide broad public benchmarks, or should it be capable of informing future action? If the latter, what kind of action, at what levels, and by whom? ...

Second, meaningful assessment is dependent upon *long-term commitment* and requires *unusually long timelines* for development. While the technical dimension of this injunction appears well-recognized at the national level, its political and organizational dimensions do not. ...

Third, sustained assessment requires a *constituency*, and "information" alone provides an insufficient basis on which to sustain one. As many state policymakers have realized, assessment can easily become a "train on its own track," unconnected to other policy levers that really matter, like institutional funding mechanisms, program review or approval procedures, or faculty reward systems. ...

But the biggest lesson from state-level experience is directed less at national policymakers than at ourselves: once started, assessment in some form is *going to happen*. Early, proactive institutional efforts to help shape the process in many states proved both welcome to state leaders and beneficial to the quality and utility of the resulting effort.

But this kind of involvement has *not* so far occurred at the national level. In the short run, higher education's strategy of avoidance may well seem effective—by not participating, we may well have prevented greater scrutiny and goals directed at our own performance. But we also run the dangerous risk of being left out of the first truly national effort to shape education policy in decades, and the consequent danger at a later point of a far greater intrusion based on protocols we had no hand in shaping.

A "Fork in the Road"?

Taken together, recent state and national developments suggest that we are rapidly approaching a decisive point for assessment policy. Today's rhetoric in campus-based assessment emphasizes creativity, authenticity, and utility; for the moment, current national assessment proposals (based on authentic, performance-based methods) echo those emphases, and have integrity and promise if implemented as designed. But without active, consistent support from the academy, the vagaries of the political process may well substitute something quite different.

At both the state and national levels, too many higher education leaders remain on the sidelines, waiting for the political winds to shift. Not only does this appear to me unlikely, but it also risks isolating higher education further from the publics whose support we badly need. ...

College, Students, and the Workplace

Assessing Performance to Improve the Fit

Peter Cappelli

The concern that national economic competitiveness is suffering because students are inadequately prepared for employment has helped focus attention on the relationship between education and the workplace. Recommendations for improving the fit between graduates and jobs range from new curricula, such as that proposed by the Secretary's Commission on Achieving Necessary Skills (SCANS), to national tests of student competencies, advocated by the National Education Goals Panel.

Yet the best mechanism for improving the fit between students and jobs may be simpler than any national test or mandated curricula. Employers are willing to extend good job offers to students who have the skills needed to be effective at work, and students are increasingly desperate for those offers. The problem is a lack of information about what those skills are and who has them.

Employers know, as they select personnel, about the competencies most clearly associated with good job performance. They also know that existing assessments of college student performance cannot effectively measure those competencies. The challenge, therefore, is to provide information about student performance in college programs in ways that highlight the competencies most relevant for success in employment. With that information, the labor market can perform its traditional task of rewarding students who possess the credentials that employers need. And the changes in student behavior that will be driven by these incentives will help push changes in curricula and pedagogy far more effectively than any attempts at mandated reforms. . . .

Reviewers of all categories of selection procedures, such as Reilly and Chao (1982) and Hunter and Hunter (1984), assert that grades are well toward the bottom of any ranking of selection devices in terms of their predictive power. Grades may help determine one's occupation and income, largely through facilitating admission to graduate schools, and graduates receiving a college degree earn significantly more than those simply taking college courses, but grades as a measure of performance in college are poorly related to actual job performance. Richard Klitgard, in *Selecting Elites* (Boston: Basic Books, 1985), reviews the literature mainly in sociology, which finds that student performance explains how students get sorted into occupations but that such performance explains little about the success within occupations. . . .

Whatever the reason, the fact that grades do not predict performance means that employers will not rely on them when making hiring decisions. . . .

Colleges and KSAs [Job-Relevant Knowledge, Skills and Attitudes]

It should come as a great relief to those concerned about the potential dominance of education by business to learn that the KSAs identified here as necessary for most jobs are *not* narrow sets of job-specific skills. Indeed, they represent basic educational competencies necessary for citizenship and are compatible with most of the other objectives of education. Just as importantly, most of these KSAs are *already* taught in college, albeit some indirectly.

The relevant math skills are developed in math classes and in courses that use applied math; critical thinking is taught explicitly in logic courses and implicitly in a broad array of courses across the social and behavioral sciences; students learn to work with data in statistics courses and in all branches of the sciences that use applied statistics; communications should be a part of every course that requires discussion and writing; interpersonal skills are often taught directly in courses (e.g., negotiations and group dynamics), or are developed in courses that require team projects and in extracurricular programs such as team sports and organizations. Motivation and personal characteristics such as integrity are no doubt the least likely to be taught in a classroom context, although military and religious schools do make explicit attempts to develop these characteristics; extracurricular activities, including athletics, may develop them as well.

Suggestions about how the KSAs relevant to employment could be developed more thoroughly in college classrooms usually involve only changes in pedagogy, not in content. Courses in any subject that require students to write papers, discuss material, and work in groups go a long way toward developing many of the listed KSAs. And when such courses challenge students to analyze problems and think critically about them, we are more than halfway toward completing the list. Courses that make use of math concepts and data deepen the list further, especially when they teach students to *apply* math and data analysis to specific problems.

Given our discussion to this point, it's easy to see why grades are seldom good predictors of job performance, even for courses in which the subject matter may seem relevant to jobs. Consider a course in human behavior—its material is directly relevant to employment—that is taught in a large lecture format, with students talking neither with the instructor nor with each other, and with a syllabus built around the memorization of results from prior research. Few job-related skills are developed in the process of presenting such course material. Multiple choice tests, which are typically used for grading courses like these, could not reveal relevant skills even if they had been developed.

Now consider the same course taught in a small-group discussion format with students doing at least some of their work in teams; with the material requiring students to apply theories and statistical methods to real-life problems; and with grades based on class participation and critical, written engagements with the subject matter. In such a class, the education process develops many useful skills, and the grading procedure can evaluate them. . . .

Improving College Assessments

The fact that grades—the main, present method for representing student performance—fail to capture many of the skills most relevant to jobs contributes to a discontinuity between the worlds of education and work. Employers waste time and effort in the recruitment and hiring process. . . . Market mechanisms cannot work without information; the absence of information-rich assessments of skills obtained in education means that the market system that should take students from college to jobs works poorly.

Fortunately, experiments in alternative assessment methods are underway. The University of Massachusetts at Boston, for example, requires students to complete an essay exercise at the end of their four-year program in order to judge their critical-thinking abilities. Alverno College may have the most elaborate alternative system, evaluating the KSAs of their students and validating these against studies of successful alumnae practitioners. The University of Michigan, the College of William and Mary, and other colleges have experimented with compiling representative portfolios of student work produced over their college careers; admittedly, such portfolios right now can be difficult for a non-expert—such as an employer—to assess.

Encouraging as these experiments are, great improvements could be made by *all* colleges if they were to assemble existing information about student performance in more innovative ways. To its own and its students' advantage, a college might, for example, construct an overall measure of performance on written material—such as an average "grade" for all research papers produced by a student during college—that would reveal a great deal about written communication abilities and, by inference, problem-solving abilities and creativity. A summary class-participation "grade" across all courses would reveal something similar about verbal communication skills. Such indicators require no new data to construct, only changes in record-keeping.

Significant student projects, such as semester-long laboratory experiments or group projects, are work samples with direct relevance to job performance, and the assessment of these efforts could be included as part of a student's overall record. Employers already solicit bio-data from students in the form of job applications (although the accuracy of this self-reported information is often questionable). Colleges could help ensure the accuracy of information about school-related extracurricular activities by reporting it as part of a student's record, all the better if they add details (positions held, duties performed, etc.) to highlight its significance. Several colleges and universities, such as Penn State, already produce a separate "activities transcript" that presents information about student leadership activities in a single form accessible to employers.

There is every reason for believing that employers would jump at the chance to make use of this repackaged assessment information; any school providing more job-relevant assessments would have a great competitive advantage in securing jobs for its students (at least for those students who perform well!). . . .

Washington observers tell us we may be headed toward the development of a national system for assessing college student performance, toward a standardized test of college outcomes. . . . Whatever the merits of such tests, it is unlikely that they will provide as much information about a student's job-relevant skills as a simple repackaging of existing assessments and experiences could. The benefits of more job-relevant assessments — as a signal to employers that provides incentives for students to achieve, as a reduction in the selection costs for employers, and as a way of strengthening relations between colleges and employers — are important enough for smart colleges to begin making changes now.

March/April 1993

Diversity and Multiculturalism on the Campus

How Are Students Affected?

Alexander W. Astin

. . . [D]ebates over . . . the dangers and benefits of multiculturalism have abounded, but so far little hard evidence has been produced to support any of these claims. . . .

. . . [A]s an educator and a researcher, my most important question about multiculturalism and diversity is how *students* are affected by campus policies and practices. I recently . . . examine[d] this question empirically in a major national study of undergraduates attending 217 four-year colleges and universities. . . .

. . . The findings present a clear-cut pattern: emphasizing diversity either as a matter of institutional policy or in faculty research and teaching, as well as providing students with curricular and extracurricular opportunities to confront racial and multicultural issues, are all associated with widespread beneficial effects on a student's cognitive and affective development. In particular, such policies and experiences are associated with greater self-reported gains in cognitive and affective development (especially increased cultural awareness), with increased satisfaction in most areas of the college experience, and with increased commitment to promoting racial understanding. Emphasizing diversity and multiculturalism is also associated with increased commitment to environ-mental issues and with several other positive outcomes: leadership, participation in cultural activities, citizenship, commitment to developing a meaningful philosophy of life, and reduced materialistic values. If we confine our analyses just to outcomes that are relevant to the goals of most general education programs, the effects of emphasizing multiculturalism and diversity appear to be uniformly positive.

Perhaps the only outcome consistently associated with diversity variables that might be considered "negative" is the positive effect on participation in student protests. While protest activities are often seen by some faculty, and especially by campus administrators, as a nuisance or possibly even as detrimental to campus order and tranquility, engaging in such protests seems to be associated with generally positive outcomes for the individual student participant. It is also true that an emphasis on multiculturalism is associated with increases in the student's political liberalism, but how one chooses to value such an effect would depend on one's political orientation. . . .

One thing that we tend to forget about academic freedom is that it is not merely an end in itself but that it has a larger purpose: the pursuit of truth. The link between academic freedom and the pursuit of knowledge is often overlooked in the PC debate, but the underlying logic is really very simple: the quickest and surest way to the truth is to encourage the expression of diverse points of view and to promote active discussion and debate of these different views. This is really what academic freedom is all about.

May/June 1993

TQM

A Time for Ideas

Ted Marchese

I t's fascinating to watch the arrival of Total Quality Management (TQM)—or Continuous Quality Improvement (CQI), as it is called by its health care practitioners—in higher education. A few campus pioneers began their TQM effort in the eighties; the big wave of interest kicked in during the 1991–92 academic year; by now, it's hard to find a campus without a knot of people trying to implement the thing.

On almost any campus, thin as the knowledge may yet be, people are already stoutly for Total Quality or deeply skeptical of it. What the quick-to-judge miss— . . . is that Total Quality is complicated, important, difficult to implement, and far from figured out. . . .

. . . [I]t's a code word for a big tentful of ideas aimed at the transformation of the modern corporate enterprise. In the eyes of the quality movement, the late-20th century corporation is bureaucratic, oversized, sluggish, self-absorbed, unresponsive, and repressive of initiative and talent; worse, it is uncompetitive. To achieve its desired transformation, the Total Quality movement over time has gathered in loose union ideas from systems theory, humanistic and industrial psychology, management theory, human-resource and organizational development, statistical process control, plus lessons from earlier attempts at quality improvement like quality circles. All of these ideas, in many guises and combinations, aim to remake organizations so they become more focused, disciplined, quick-footed, humane, and competitive. . . .

. . . The danger is that we'll be put off by the fervor, the formulas, or the smell of fad and miss the fact that a very important set of ideas about the organizations we work in . . . is now at our doorstep. The issue, then, is less TQM itself than the appropriateness of the set of ideas behind it to problems we know we face.

What are those ideas? . . . [H]ere are six important ones, with reflections on their applicability in higher education.

The first idea is *customer focus.* In earlier days, quality was defined as what the craftsman or the professional said it was. . . . The new dispensation is that quality is what the *customer* says it is. . . .

A customer focus impels organizations to be specific about the parties they serve. Who *are* your customers? . . . The external customers of a college, for example, would likely include funders and donors, employers, and graduate schools; internally, customers would include students (in their academic roles, "learners"), but also, for any employee of the college, "the people down the hall who receive my work." Must you *do* everything the customer wants? No, good judgment applies as ever.

Writ large, the doctrine of customer focus is a call to everybody in the organization to get out of the cubbyholes they work in and talk with the real people they're serving. . . .

The focus on customers offers another advantage, that of demystifying quality. . . . The assessment movement broke through these closed-end ways of thinking with the insight that an institution's quality was a function of its contributions to student learning—contributions that are knowable and trackable. In the same spirit, the quality movement enters its own, new way of judging quality: the degree to which customer needs or expectations are met. . . .

The second idea is *continuous improvement.* This is a simple idea, clear enough in its stating, sprung from the intensely competitive world of automotive, computer, and similar industries. . . .

Simple as the concept seems, the embrace of "continuous improvement" as an organizational imperative has profound consequences: to reach ever higher performance levels every year out, an organization needs to think systemically about the constant improvement of all processes that deliver value to its customers. . . .

Continuous improvement, as idea and as imperative, is probably *the* stranger for the academy among Total Quality's tentful of ideas, especially when it comes to the daily tasks of undergraduate education. A community sense or ethic that teaching and learning need continuously to be improved—and all that would follow from that, notably assessment—is absent from our discourse. . . . The missing ethic is less personal than corporate: somehow, despite all the good will, talent, and effort of individual faculty, there's seldom a collective . . .

The third emphasis is *management by fact*. The notion of continuously improving the quality of an organization's goods or services implies that "quality" has to be specified and monitored. If you're serious about quality, corporate managers say, you have to be as specific as possible about what you *mean* by quality *and* systematically keep track of how you are doing. . . .

TQM's statistical armamentarium includes dozens of relatively simple ways of tracking organizational or unit performance. Most of these tools—indeed, the habit of looking for and preferring data—would be entirely new to the informal, loosely coupled, problem-chasing world of academic administration.

These "be clear, keep track, use data to improve" injunctions are close in spirit to what higher education has come to learn from assessment. Assessment, of course, has been an uphill battle these last eight years; even now it's little more than an episodic veneer in most institutions. . . .

A fourth idea is that of *benchmarking*. The word itself can be confusing—people think it implies a statistic or norm. In today's corporation, benchmarking means the "systematic search for best practice." . . . It searches out that "best practice," studies it, adapts it, and tries to do as well or better. . . .

In undergraduate education, the same absence of ethic that constrains continuous improvement

makes searching for "best practice" almost a non-existent practice. One consequence is that even our best innovations don't spread. Over the past years, well-conceived, cost-effective approaches have been developed for scores of academic processes: . . . [M]ost of these innovations have gone nowhere. There must be 500 "successful" FIPSE projects that have never been replicated. . . .

A fifth, very important emphasis in the quality movement is *people*. An organization avid for improvement sees people as its greatest resource. It does everything possible to give every employee the preparation, tools, and initiative to contribute to corporate goals. . . . For employees, the watchwords become training, teamwork, responsibility-taking, and mutual accountability; for leaders, the call is to provide vision and strategy, to coach, mentor, and be a team player, and to tend to what Peter Senge and others label "organizational learning." In TQM, 85 percent of the problems that arise in the course of work are attributable to the organization's systems, just 15 percent to the shortcomings of individual employees. The manager's job, then, is to improve constantly the work systems of the organization, to drive out blaming and fear, to remove obstacles in the system that prevent persons or teams from doing their best work.

A lot of powerful ideas are packed into the preceding paragraph; many of them contradict prevailing norms on campuses where blaming and fear infect relationships, teamwork is rare, and managers know best. . . .

In companies like Motorola, . . . a remarkable 5 percent of the company's expenditures are devoted to employee education, training, and development; Motorola, which has realized 15 percent or greater productivity gains for eight years running, thinks its return on investment for employee training is 30–1. Question: Why is it that in almost any university or college—organizations devoted to learning—the comparable expenditure will be a fraction of one percent?

The sixth insight has to do with organizational *structures*. Quality champions argue that, to assure the delivery of value in the marketplace, work has to be organized around the needs and preferences of *customers*, not those of the corporation or its employees.

In the bureaucratic world of old, the particulars of most work processes tended to be clustered within neatly tiered departments or disciplines ("silos"), each with its own turf and norms. . . .

From a quality perspective, American colleges and universities seem incredibly vertical and compartmentalized—like a corporation of 10 years ago. Indeed, we practice "over the wall teaching" as students traipse across loose collections of freestanding courses on the way to degrees of unspecified outcome. Anything that requires cross-unit collaboration, like student advertisement or general education, never seems to be done well. . . .

. . . I return to the ideas that TQM has put in the air. One of those ideas is that organizations should be driven by the intrinsic motivation in all of us to do our best work. Might it be that a fine sense of our own possibilities—and of our obligations to students, knowledge, our publics, and to one another—could serve as impulse for a homegrown push for higher quality?

What vision might drive such a push? What is it we hope for from our work? Last winter in *Change*, Jane Tompkins listed what she wanted from her university work: a common enterprise; belonging; good feelings in the workplace; a community of hope; an integrated life. Here's another answer, from Max DePree's "Leadership is an Art"—a little book written by the CEO of a quality-oriented furniture company:

> We would like to find the most effective, most productive, most rewarding way of working together. We would like to know that our work process uses all the appropriate and pertinent resources: human, physical, financial. We would like a work process and relationships that meet our personal needs for belonging, for contributing, for meaningful work, for the opportunity to make a commitment, for the opportunity to grow and be at least reasonably in control of our own destinies. Finally, we'd like someone to say "thank you."

November/December 1994

Accountability and the End(s) of Higher Education

Some Snarks are Boojums

Roger Peters

Most public colleges combine assessment (systematic inquiry into learning in order to improve it) with accountability (demonstrating results in order to justify funding). This twofold quest resembles Lewis Carroll's "Hunting of the Snark" (1876/1960):

> *If your Snark be a Snark, that is right:*
> *Fetch it home by all means—*
> *You may serve it with greens,*
> *And it's handy for striking a light.*

Like the Snark, assessment is ambitious, and promises both to nourish and to illuminate. Indeed, assessment has led many professors to ponder, discuss, and modify their instructional goals, some for the first time. A few have discovered that specifying goals concretely enough to appraise their achievement brings the joy of inquiry to teaching, especially when those inquiries spring from ideas and methods of their own disciplines. Assessment has a niche in the academic ecosystem.

Accountability, on the other hand, chills further a regulatory climate that already threatens higher education with extinction. . . .

> *But if your Snark be a Boojum . . .*
> *You will softly and suddenly vanish away,*
> *And never be met with again!*

Accountability is a Boojum, and widespread faculty resistance to it is not merely self-serving. . . .

An Elusive Creature

Since the mid-1980s we have pursued accountability with standardized and home-grown tests, surveys of alumni and student satisfaction, performance and portfolio ratings, and other measures.

This evidence confirms the results of decades of quantitative research showing that though many graduates lack important knowledge and skills, most colleges do a pretty good job. After analyzing two decades of outcomes research, Pascarella and Terenzini (1991) conclude that even with confounding variables controlled, graduates "make statistically significant gains in factual knowledge and in a range of general cognitive and intellectual skills." . . .

But neither sophisticated quantitative research nor voluminous accountability reports have mellowed public or legislative attitudes toward professors. . . .

If accountability has failed to persuade the public and its officials that their money is well spent, it has failed even more dismally to persuade faculty to shred their dog-eared lecture notes or learn new tricks. Claiming that the effects of college are a) self-evident, b) ineffable, and/or c) already measured by grades, most faculty continue to reject demands for accountability as picayune and counterproductive if not spiteful, and go about their business as usual.

In fact, accountability hasn't helped us address our major problems. Demonstrating graduates' low levels of scientific understanding and quantitative skills has, at most schools, had little effect on the structure or practice of general education. Nor has accountability done much to raise the low status of teaching. . . .

No Consensus

There are several reasons behind accountability's failure to provide information that convinces constituents that the overall effects of college are worth the cost. Above all, the validity and utility of testing schemes depend on some agreement about what should be taught and learned, and on all sides that condition is routinely not met.

We faculty rarely specify general education outcomes concretely because we have no consensus on general goals—and no consensus that there should be a consensus. The acrimony of faculty reactions to assessments of general education, the failure of many attempts to integrate curricula around real problems or practical skills, the proliferation of majors that use general education courses mainly to recruit students, even the debates about the canon, are all signs of deep differences about the ends of higher education. . . .

There is no greater consensus on goals in the government than on campus. According to John Folger and Dennis Jones (1993) of the National Center for Higher Education Management Systems (NCHEMS), "Attempts to bring [faculty] priorities into line through accountability requirements have seldom been successful, largely because state governments have failed to specify expectations regarding priority outcomes in sufficiently discrete and concrete terms." Governments don't specify outcomes concretely because there is no consensus on educational goals or how to measure their achievement. Like faculty members, officials trained in different disciplinary epistemologies find it even harder to agree on assessments than on the goals themselves. . . .

Educational Goals Are Political

Discussion is unlikely to generate consensus on general goals beyond the campus because educational goals are deeply political. The history of educational experimentation and assessment—including the recent skirmishes over so-called "outcomes-based education" in K–12—demonstrates that even basic goals such as literacy (verbal, cultural, and other competitors) are subject to wildly different interpretations by citizens with different views about what should be read and how it should be understood. The "higher" the goals get the more political they become. . . .

External Measures Deprofessionalize Faculty

Faculty in many disciplines (including the hard sciences) reject the notion that objective measurement is the best way to inquire about learning. As a result, few faculty have been willing to take time from teaching or research to do assessment, or to use its results to modify their methods. Finding forms of accountability that will satisfy them will not be easy, for faculties' preference for clinical judgments is not merely self-serving; in some cases it reflects a deeply held epistemology that will be very difficult to change. . . .

Like the intuitive understanding of other experts, that of the master teacher is difficult to translate into the objective evidence required by accountability regulations. Jerome Bruner (1986) calls these two views of what constitutes good evidence "narrative" (literary, intuitive, and interpretive) versus "paradigmatic" (scientific, objective, and logical):

> The two (though complementary) are irreducible to one another. . . . Each . . . has operating principles of its own and its own criteria of well-formedness. They differ radically in their procedures for verification . . . arguments convince one of their truth, stories of their lifelikeness. . . .

The consequences of centralized control of education by external examinations show how micromanagement of complex enterprises can put workers in double binds. In effect, faculty are being asked to admit, retain, and speedily graduate remedial students (many of whom hate college and will do just fine without it) while they a) maintain high standards for grades and b) ensure that seniors get good scores on standardized exams. As legislators micromanage higher education in the name of "efficiency" and "productivity," businesspeople are moving in exactly the opposite direction: toward decentralized control, autonomy for those closest to the customer, and toward intuitive, holistic modes of assessment. . . .

Even as we congratulate ourselves over the attractiveness of U.S. higher education to students from around the world, we eagerly deprofessionalize and regulate away what makes it unique: its accommodation of diverse students and goals. As the last generation of broadly educated professors plans retirement, this downward spiral is about to accelerate. External examination in the form of a national baccalaureate exam or similar requirements by states is likely to complete a vicious cycle in which deprofessionalized disciplinary specialists teach bored and cynical students to take tests designed by specialists in testing. . . .

To satisfy legitimate demands for convincing evidence that we are worth our keep, we must transform not only colleges but the universities that train their faculties. If we don't we are likely to meet the fate of Carroll's Baker:

> *In the midst of the words he was trying to say,*
> *In the midst of his laughter and glee,*
> *He had softly and suddenly vanished away—*
> *For the Snark was a Boojum you see. . . .*

Connoisseurship

One possible solution is accountability based on what Eisner (1991) calls "connoisseurship": the ability of well-educated people to recognize good writing and thinking when they see them — whether or not they can agree on an objective definition. Such intuitive, holistic, expert judgments can be rendered reliable and convincing. At my college, an autonomous panel consisting mainly of faculty, but including employers, K–12 teachers, and other constituents rates samples of students' work using a holistic scoring system that they developed. . . . Rather than measuring achievements of analytically defined goals, panels develop a holistic consensus on standards by rating the same "anchor" essays then discussing, negotiating, and (usually) resolving — by compromise if not by persuasion — differences in ratings.

Our experience suggests that such discussion can resolve differences in evaluations of concrete examples of high-level academic performances, even among faculty and community members of different disciplines and backgrounds. This system of assessment provides feedback that we can "own" because it honors our professional judgments. Rotating panel membership spreads this ownership to an increasing proportion of the faculty. When samples are senior theses or other work produced as part of programs, this system combines the authenticity of performance-based assessment with the reliability and easily communicated standards of tests. It provides students with evidence of achievement — or need for improvement — employers and other community representatives with concrete evidence of what graduates can do, and participating K–12 teachers with concrete examples of what college professors expect. . . .

September/October 1996

Accreditation & Academic Quality Assurance

Can We Get There From Here?

David D. Dill, William F. Massy, Peter R. Williams, and Charles M. Cook

In the following discussion, we . . . suggest . . . that the real challenge to voluntary accreditation—the inadequacy of collegial mechanisms of educational quality assurance—has not been effectively addressed in the contemporary debate. . . . [W]e offer some concrete suggestions about how the U.S. voluntary quality-assurance system could be reformed for the better. . . .

We believe, along with the authors of the Accountability Study, that the most needed reform is the renewal of *internal* mechanisms for quality assurance in colleges and universities, and that the concept of an academic audit conducted by regional accreditation agencies could be a necessary component of this reform. . . .

We believe this situation can change only if there is a structural alteration in higher education as a whole. What is needed is a coordinated program of self-regulation that would require all postsecondary institutions to allocate faculty time and other resources to academic quality-assurance activities as a fundamental business requirement. We suggest that this coordinated effort should be the primary focus of any future reforms in accreditation. The established quality-assurance mechanisms in several European nations suggest how such a reform might be implemented. . . .

Within the international quality-assurance community, . . . accreditation is generally not perceived as sufficient to assure the quality of teaching and learning. For these purposes, the additional processes of assessment and academic audit have been developed.

Assessment

1. The assessment process evaluates the quality of specific activities—such as educational or research quality—within academic units. Assessment goes beyond accreditation to make graded judgments about academic quality levels rather than binary judgments relative to threshold standards.
2. Assessments generally are directed at the subject or program level, evaluating their delivered performance.
3. Assessment uses a combination of performance indicators, self-study, and external peer review.
4. Assessment can be organized by an external agency (such as an independent or quasi-independent government body), an institutional consortium, or by institutions themselves.
5. Assessment results generally are public and often are published in a way that permits comparison of institutions.
6. Assessment defines quality relative to an institution's mission, not according to some universal standard of academic excellence to which only elite institutions can aspire.
7. Assessment cycle times tend to be in the range of 5 to 10 years.

This international definition of the term assessment differs from its use in the United States, where it generally describes the procedures used for evaluating what has been learned by individuals or groups of students. The international concept of assessment is closer to what Americans might describe as systematic program review, save that assessments in other countries generally address either teaching quality, or in separate exercises, research quality. Our use of the term in the following discussion focuses on assessments of teaching quality—the evaluation of the quality of student study programs and the campus provision of teaching and learning. . . .

Lessons for the United States

What can we learn from other countries' implementation of teaching assessments and academic audits . . .?

Any academic quality-assurance system must attempt to balance the seemingly polar goals of accountability and improvement. The ideal system would select a portfolio of quality-assurance elements that, when combined, best balance the advantages and risks associated with each goal. In the United States, where today only the process of accreditation exists to assure the public of the quality of campus teaching and learning, the goals of accountability and improvement both appear to receive insufficient weight, particularly when compared to academic quality-assurance systems in other countries.

As we argued earlier, it is imperative that effective steps be taken now to restore public faith in the capacity of the higher education community to assure and improve the quality of teaching and learning in U.S. higher education. This can be done in two ways—first, by encouraging quality assessments of teaching and learning at the institutional level as a new means for strengthening the internal performance of colleges and universities, and second, by promoting academic audits at the regional level as a means of external accountability. In the arguments that follow, we suggest how such a system might work.

The experience of other countries suggests that an essential first component of any balanced quality-assurance system is a systematic process for assessing the quality of teaching and learning at the level of individual academic programs. Abroad, such assessments have encouraged increased attention to teaching and learning within universities, promoted communication and coordination among faculty members in subject fields, and measurably improved departmental mechanisms of quality assurance. . . .

. . . [I]n a country the size of the United States the sheer scale of the enterprise makes systematic external assessment of all the varied academic programs prohibitively complex and expensive, we would argue that, at the subject level, quality assessments of teaching and learning are best made by individual institutions.

The superficial similarity of such quality assessments to institutional-level program reviews—reportedly carried out by two-thirds of public institutions and one-third of private institutions in the United States—may lead some to believe that the necessary mechanisms for internal accountability are already in place. Existing program-review procedures, however, fall well short of the idea. Program reviews tend to focus on program productivity and on external reputation as measured by research and scholarship. Very few such reviews explicitly focus on the quality of teaching and learning, much less lead to observable improvements in student learning. . . .

The lessons learned from the implementation of academic audits in . . . Europe, suggest several critical components that are essential to an effective audit. First, the purpose of the academic audit is not to assess academic performance; it is to evaluate the rigor and reliability of each institution's system for assessing the quality of teaching and learning, as well as its overall academic quality-assurance procedures and the effectiveness of their implementation. Academic audits should be clearly focused on evaluating the institution's own quality-assurance processes and its efforts at internal improvement. In contrast, the broad range of issues covered by the traditional U.S. accreditation process—and the consequent demands upon accreditation review-team members during their campus visits—prevent the type of in-depth investigative procedures characteristic of academic quality audits. . . .

Second, external audits should be conducted by trained teams of academic peers and other professionals knowledgeable about and experienced in the process of institutional-level quality assurance. Because audit teams evaluate the process of academic quality assurance rather than academic standards themselves, audit teams (in the Netherlands, for example) often include foreign academics, as well as individuals experienced in quality assurance in business and government. . . .

Third, while the quality-assurance process for an institution must be determined by the institution itself, audit teams should ascertain whether academic staff have given careful thought to quality assurance and can articulate and defend the choices made. . . .

Fourth, effective academic audits avoid focusing on the formalities of quality assurance—policy statements, rules and procedures, meeting minutes—and instead follow "audit trails" leading to selected academic programs, which involves conducting interviews with faculty members and students to determine whether the staff have internalized the institution's quality improvement and assurance process.

Finally, academic audits must be made available publicly. . . .

For all these reasons, . . . we . . . believe that the well-established system of regional, voluntary self-regulation offers the best potential vehicle for correcting the imbalance in the current U.S. quality-assurance system. We suggest that a critical role for the newly emerging Council for Higher Education Accreditation would be to restore public faith in voluntary self-regulation by encouraging the development of institutionally based teaching and learning quality assessments and experimentation with academic audits. . . .

Which way to quality assurance in higher education? We believe that a known route exists: a new, mutually reinforcing system of institution-based quality assessments of teaching and learning and a coordinated regional system of external academic audits.

March/April 1997

Standardized Testing
Meritocracy's Crooked Yardstick

Peter Sacks

Most Americans have taken standardized mental tests from the day they entered kindergarten. Test scores have told the gatekeepers of America's meritocracy—educators, academic institutions, and employers—that one student is bright, the other is not bright, that one is worthy academically, the other less so. Some, with luck, are able to overcome the stigma of poor performance on mental tests. But others will not.

Indeed, not only is it a stigma, but one that is largely unrecognized in our culture. Meritocracy's gatekeepers brand those who score poorly on standardized tests as somehow deficient, incapable. Psychometricians and educators use quasi-clinical terms for such people: remember the teacher or counselor who patronized an ambitious, competent child as an "overachiever" because her academic performance exceeded what tests predicted? Or recall the hand-wringing over the "underachiever," the student whose brilliant test scores predicted greater things than what he actually accomplished?

These terms have largely disappeared from public discussion, one result of a revolt against standardized testing over the past 10 or 15 years in the United States. Influential scholars like Harvard's Howard Gardner and Yale's Robert Sternberg have argued forcefully against the narrow views of ability measured by traditional tests. Many educators now sing the praises of new, "authentic" alternatives to standardized testing, such as "performance assessment." Advocates of performance assessment say schools ought to focus on what people can do and less on how well kindergartners,

high school students, and prospective teachers can take tests. . . .

. . . With roots in intelligence testing that go back generations, the mental measurement establishment continues to define merit largely in terms of test-taking and potential rather than actual performance. The case against standardized mental testing may be as intellectually and ethically rigorous as any argument made about social policy in the past 20 years, but such testing continues to dominate the education system, carving further inroads into the employment arena as well, having been bolstered in recent years by a conservative backlash advocating advancement by "merit."

How has the standardized-testing paradigm managed to remain entrenched, despite the many criticisms leveled against it? . . .

The revolt against testing became most aggressive in the late 1970s and early 1980s, culminating in a string of successes for the movement, particularly against aptitude testing for university admissions. There were influential books and reports, such as Stephen Jay Gould's *The Mismeasure of Man*, David Owen's *None of the Above*, James Crouse and Dale Trusheim's *The Case Against the SAT*, and the 1980 Ralph Nader report, *The Reign of ETS*. New York's 1979 "Truth in Testing" law gave takers of standardized mental tests a new floor of protection. Activists and educators launched the National Center for Fair & Open Testing (FairTest), the nation's first organization devoted to protecting the interests of millions of consumers of standardized tests.

These attacks on standardized testing were

backed up by a mounting body of evidence that such tests played a key role in a rigged game, one that favored society's well-positioned elites under the guise of "merit." . . .

The Evidence

A long line of independent academic research bolsters the claims of the anti-testing movement. Much of the research confirms suspicions that such tests thwart rather than help educational reform and that they continue to produce inaccurate—if not biased—assessments of the abilities of many Americans. From this recent work, we know that:

■ *Standardized tests generally have questionable ability to predict one's academic success, especially for certain subgroups. . . .*

■ *Standardized test scores tend to be highly correlated with socioeconomic class. . . .*

■ *Standardized tests can reward superficial learning, drive instruction in undesirable directions, and thwart meaningful educational reform. . . .*

The Shifting Policy Landscape Since 1980 . . .

. . . [A]nti-testing trends have been counterbalanced by a conservative backlash that promises to reinforce standardized testing's continued domination of the educational system.

On the anti-testing side of the policy balance sheet, some of the more significant events of the last few years include the recent elimination of a standardized-testing requirement from the federal Elementary and Secondary Education Act. . . .

The rising popularity of performance-based assessment in schools and colleges has contributed to the anti-testing side of the policy ledger, too. . . .

The OTA [Office of Technology Assessment] reported earlier this decade that almost half the states (21) had launched performance assessment programs. But it would be an overstatement to conclude that states are embracing the new and abandoning traditional tests. Indeed, most states continue to use traditional standardized tests, supplemented by forays into performance assessment. Only a tiny handful of states, such as Kentucky, Massachusetts, and Vermont, have taken steps to eliminate traditional multiple-choice tests.

On the anti-testing side of the ledger, too, a small but growing number of undergraduate colleges have made standardized admissions tests optional. . . .

Entrenched or on the Wane?

What, then, are we to conclude from recent developments? Is standardized testing on the wane? Some observers say so. But it would be naive to underestimate the hold that mental measurement has on the American mind. Recent events running opposite to the anti-testing movement suggest that standardized testing remains entrenched and is ready to dig itself in deeper in coming years. . . .

. . . Critics of affirmative action argue that people ought to be judged on "merit," not gender or race; to them, the indisputable, "unbiased" criteria for admission are grades and (especially) standardized tests. Abolishing affirmative action means that test scores, regardless of their limits or what educators may think of them, become far more decisive a factor in admissions decisions. This has already happened at the University of California. . . .

Similarly, under the banner of higher academic standards, recent moves by the NCAA have given new prominence to the already huge role standardized test scores play in determining which athletes get scholarships to attend college. Despite strong opposition from FairTest and other groups, the NCAA recently *raised* the standardized test scores required for athletic eligibility. . . .

"We're seeing a lot of this," says Bob Schaeffer, FairTest's public education director. "People keep believing that to show you're tough or to raise standards means you increase test score requirements, when in fact you're doing neither. You're increasing the potency of severely flawed assessments. In the wake of *The Bell Curve*, there is a revival of the notion that merit equals test scores. . . .

Indeed, in the name of "higher academic standards," a conservative backlash in recent years has resulted in several states shelving efforts at alternative forms of assessment in public schools. . . .

When you add up these shifting, often contradictory trends in policy, the net result doesn't look like a standardized-testing establishment that is withering under the heat of popular revolt. Indeed, in many respects, the standardized testing industry has even greater dominance over American lives than it did at the time of the Nader report in 1980. Indeed, just 26 states in 1980 had mandated testing programs for public schools; in 1990, 46 states did so, according to OTA. . . .

What Are the True Costs of Standardized Testing? . . .

. . . [T]he educational institutions that continue to buy the tests—the costs of which are born by test-takers or taxpayers—would argue that standardized tests are a cost-effective way to evaluate people. It's obvious; standardized testing is cheap.

But how cheap is it, really? Research findings about the utility of test scores raise profound questions about the social and economic costs of a de facto national policy that has institutionalized the use of standardized tests for college admissions and as the gauge of local and national educational progress. While the tests might be cheap to individual institutions, in many cases these institutions bear neither the direct costs of the tests nor the indirect social costs of testing.

It seems reasonable to question whether the marginal benefits of standardized tests in terms of their predictive validity are worth the hundreds of millions of dollars test-takers and taxpayers spend annually on the exams. Also, a true economic analysis of the nation's de facto testing policy would have to factor the "opportunity cost" of testing: what is foregone when teachers spend inordinate amounts of time teaching to tests that might have minimal connection to what students really need to learn? In one typical urban school district, the OTA valued such lost opportunities at as high as $15 million per test, or $110 per pupil. Compare these estimates to the apparently cheap $6 per student in direct outlays the district normally reports as the "cost" of the test.

Moreover, a cost-benefit analysis would need to account for the social and economic costs of erroneous decisions about people. What are the true economic costs to a nation of wrong decisions about its people's talents? . . .

"American Tests"

First, Americans are fascinated with mental measurement to a degree that is rare in other countries. In contrast to what Europeans call "American tests," the examinations for college or university admission in other industrial countries are typically essay tests, in which students demonstrate knowledge of various subjects they've learned in the classroom. These tests are not unlike what American educators are now calling "performance assessment." Compared to other countries, Americans appear to be far more obsessed with IQ, the notion that intelligence—most often defined narrowly as logical-analytical ability—is both inborn and representable as a single numerical score. . . .

Similarly, our culture places an exceedingly high value on the notion of potential to achieve, rather than achievement itself. For most Americans, a "gifted" student is one who scores off the charts on aptitude tests, not one who demonstrates advanced practical knowledge on worthwhile endeavors. "We are one of the few societies that place so much emphasis on intelligence tests," Yale psychologist Robert Sternberg told *Skeptic* magazine. "In most societies there is more emphasis on what people accomplish." . . .

Indeed, the notion that merit and achievement equal high test scores, or that higher "standards" means requiring higher test scores, is repeated constantly in the popular culture. This reinforces the widely accepted legitimacy of standardized tests to rate students, teachers, schools, and colleges. . . .

In addition, standardized tests serve the economic interests of colleges and universities, particularly their need for prestige, which is often the main asset they have to market to potential "customers." . . .

But perhaps most responsible for the grip that mental testing has on America is that it is a highly effective means of social control, predominantly serving the interests of the nation's elites. Most people would agree that, in a democracy, merit is a good basis for deciding who gets ahead. The rub is how you define merit. We've settled on a system that defines merit in large part as the potential to achieve according to test results. It turns out that the lion's share of the "potential" in our society goes to those with well-to-do, highly educated parents. Aristocracies used to perpetuate themselves on the basis of birth and parentage. But America's elites now perpetuate themselves with gatekeeping rules of their own making, rules legitimated by scientific objectivity. . . .

. . . Americans largely buy into the rules of this

rigged game. With the small exception of FairTest, there is little organized opposition to the mental measurement establishment. Besides a few studies over the years, the federal government, which is the only entity with sufficient power to regulate the testing business, has been quiet on the subject, preferring to let private enterprise have its way. . . .

September/October 1998

The Road Not Taken

Robert Holyer

. . . It is time to recognize that assessment makes good sense not just as a political expedient but as a permanent educational policy.

In affirming the central idea of outcomes assessment, we need to realize that we have a variety of options, some of which are better than others. The approach adopted by the accrediting agencies is to require institutions to assess their own distinctive goals and commitments.

The virtues of this approach are many. It requires the assessment of something broader than the individual course. It brings faculty together to develop common goals and means of assessment. It will produce results that will help institutions improve their performance—or at least modify their claims. And it preserves institutional uniqueness and educational diversity. . . .

However, assessment of this sort cannot address the issues of common standards. We will still have no clear idea about what a bachelor's degree means, no clear idea of what graduating with a certain major means, and no common gauge of student and institutional achievement. Consequently, there is good reason that the public will not and should not be satisfied with this approach. There is also good reason for the academic profession not to be satisfied with it. . . .

For this and other reasons, it is wise to give far more sympathetic attention to the alternative: national standards.

I am often surprised by the level of hostility that greets this suggestion. It is assumed that national standards would have to be imposed by the federal government and would produce an unhealthy degree of institutional uniformity. Federal involvement in turn raises the specter of government regulation, which faculty from both ends of the political spectrum easily unite to oppose. What is so often absent is the recognition that there are alternatives to this understanding of national standards.

It is instructive to be reminded of the many cases in which we already use national measures, successfully and voluntarily. The ACT and SAT, of course, are forms of national assessment, as are the GRE, LSAT, MCAT, and the host of other admissions tests currently in use. It is also instructive to recall that the ACT and the GRE have *subject* area tests, the latter now widely accepted, and that there is a flourishing industry in AP courses and tests, covering a growing number of subjects.

Many disciplinary and professional societies have devised national standards and tests to go with them. . . . [T]he American Chemical Society has constructed national exams for the standard chemistry courses; teachers, nurses, architects, and the like prepare for common licensing exams; and there are parallel efforts under way in many other disciplines.

What is instructive about these efforts is to realize, first, that when we ourselves have had a self-interest in assessing students educated at different institutions—for example, for college or graduate-school selection—we've had no difficulty embracing national standards. Second, the common assessments we use have not been developed by the federal government but within the disciplines or broader educational community. Third, so far there is little indication that the use of these common measures has diminished the distinctiveness of our institutions or produced an unhealthy kind or degree of uniformity.

Fourth, even as we use these instruments, there

is little indication that we place undue faith in them or use them to the exclusion of other reliable indicators. . . .

In short, the irony is that, while we seem to fear national standards, we've made great strides in developing them voluntarily and using them wisely.

The wise course, then, will be to spend our collective time and energy bringing order and coordination to our current situation and working toward a universally recognized set of national standards. Our collective integrity as a profession is, to a degree, tied to the faithful execution of this task. To be sure, its successful completion will require uncommon degrees of imagination and good will, but it is a better long-term road to travel than the one the accrediting agencies have chosen for us.

November/December 1998

Guard Dogs or Guide Dogs?

Adequacy vs. Quality in the Accreditation of Teacher Education

William R. Dill

. . . [T]he public has little sense of accreditation as *either* a guard for quality or a guide toward excellence.

Specialized accreditors historically started as guard dogs to distinguish acceptable from inferior programs and, more than agencies advertise, to boost the privileges and status of professions. What we need today is more of a guide dog model— less to evaluate, more to help schools diagnose what the world needs, and especially to find ways of turning the slow-moving wheels of academe toward higher levels of performance.

Suppose accreditors left off vetting program characteristics and really worked with schools of education on the difficult challenge of assessing what graduates do with their educations? Suppose they recast themselves as conveners of academics, practitioners, and related publics to stimulate institutional efforts to improve programs? Suppose they preened less as advocates for their specialties and became better guides to the world at large about how to be discerning customers, partners, and critics?

Agencies do try to perform both roles. But playing the guard gets in the way of being a guide. . . .

. . . [I]t is not clear what NCATE recognition guarantees. It tells more about a program's features and funding than its outcomes. The public is looking at results from California to Massachusetts— at appallingly low pass rates on entry-level teacher certification examinations. In three states where comparisons of examination results have been made, graduates of NCATE-accredited programs did no better than graduates of non-accredited ones. . . .

Reasons for a "guide dog" model. Agencies that have tried to help schools in non-evaluative ways to focus on the future, broaden their perspectives, improve programs, and build capacity for planning and self-assessment can point to some real successes. AACSB has been party to a welcome shift of emphasis in business education. NCATE's study of needs and opportunities related to information technologies was a very helpful effort. AAHE's initiatives to establish Teaching, Learning, and Technology Roundtables; to share experience about service learning; and to explore student, teacher, and course portfolios are cases in point. . . .

. . . It makes sense for all of us who want to assure the public that schools are doing a quality job to limit as far as possible the investments we ask campuses to make simply to document and justify how things *are* and to unleash as many resources as we can for tangible efforts to see how good we can make them *become*.

Clearly, in the "guard dog" to "guide dog" shift, I am slighting some areas in which it is important to the public welfare to assure that an educational program is covering some bases. For those areas, focused, periodic reviews may still be essential. But much that agencies now include under their umbrella of evaluative ambitions is neither urgent nor, if important, effective as a protective assurance. Even in essential areas—like whether a fledgling architect can size a beam—knowing that something is covered by a program does not diminish the need to test individuals by licensing examinations or carefully supervised early work assignments.

In business, music, journalism, and art, professionally focused curricula are only one route to careers in the field. . . . In these fields, accreditation status means little. The best programs have ratings and reputations that come from other sources. . . . many programs have built strong reputations without ever seeking accreditation.

In converting from evaluators to facilitators of improvement, suppose we no longer had labels that say Babson College is AACSB-approved. . . . We could survive. After all, no such labels adorn liberal arts programs or many of the hundreds of specialties that colleges and universities offer.

State licensing boards would have to retreat from dogmatic cut-offs that require graduation from accredited institutions toward broader advisories about the preparation someone planning to take an examination or apply for a license should receive. We would be back where we ought to be: judging individuals on the basis of what each can do (rather than rough-screening them on where they are from) and focusing institutions on making a case for the achievements of the graduates they have produced. . . .

. . . What matters is how well each agency helps accelerate efforts by institutions to find ways to do a better job and how much each can take a societal as well as a specialist's view of its efforts. We should be able to find ways, short of awarding accredited status, to signify publicly whether or not different schools have commitments to maintain and improve quality. . . .

By focusing on tomorrow, with incentives to innovate, rather than on yesterday with penalties for non-compliance, we should be in a better position to achieve positive reforms. The better we guide, the fewer guard dogs we will need.

September/October 1999

Gauging the Impact of Institutional Student-Assessment Strategies

Revolution or Evolution?

National Center for Postsecondary Improvement

. . . [A] new National Center for Postsecondary Improvement (NCPI) national survey [is] the first of its kind to examine the nature, extent, and impact of student-assessment strategies. Although these efforts hold great promise, what the survey suggests is that student assessment does not yet constitute a revolution. Instead, the assessment movement represents an important evolution in how institutions go about the business of improving their educational processes and outcomes.

Measuring National Momentum

NCPI researcher Marvin Peterson of the University of Michigan, and colleagues Marne Einar-

son, Catherine Augustine, and Derek Vaughan, worked together to . . . design a survey examining how colleges and universities support, promote, and use student-assessment data to improve student learning and institutional performance. . . .

Assessing Student Assessment

[T]he survey indicated fairly substantial institutional activity in collecting student-assessment data. Institutions in the sample most often collected objective information on students' academic progress (96 percent), basic college-readiness skills (88 percent), and their academic intentions (80 percent). A fairly high proportion

... (74 percent) also queried students about satisfaction with their undergraduate experience.

However, far fewer institutions indicated engaging in more complex assessment activity, such as collecting information on current students' higher-order skills (34 percent), affective development (35 percent), or professional skills (34 percent). ... Most ... emphasize the use of easily quantifiable indicators of student progress and pay less attention to more complex measures of student development.

The methods for collecting student data are similarly traditional—primarily an emphasis on quantitative instruments. Institutions make limited use of ... more qualitative—assessment methods such as portfolios, capstone projects, observations of student performance, and interviews or focus groups with current students, employers, or alumni. ...

... The overriding motivation [for conducting assessment] is to prepare self-studies for accreditation purposes (69 percent), followed by internal improvement efforts, which include bolstering student achievement and academic programs. ...

One problem is that assessment practice does not necessarily match an institution's motivation for collecting the data. ... Despite the intention to improve student achievement ... 38 percent do not engage in studies connecting student experiences to student outcomes. ...

... Considering the extensive research on the impact of student-faculty interaction on student performance and the growing use of educational technology, a lack of attention in these areas is one of the surprises the survey uncovers.

Apparently, administrators are not using assessment to inform their budgetary decisions, either. ...

Focusing on Faculty

The inconsistency inherent in what campuses report as the motivations for and uses of student assessment may have its roots in the role that faculty members play in many of these initiatives. Assessment is oriented toward improving academic outcomes, but there remain relatively few links between measures of student assessment, on the one hand, and the faculty's classroom responsibilities on the other. Too many campuses avoid linking these strategies to the faculty members who implement them or to activities in the classroom. ...

On many campuses, the use of assessment data to guide academic planning is undermined by a lack of corresponding commitment to faculty accountability for student performance. ... [F]ew departments tie faculty evaluation, promotion, and rewards to improved student performance.

Uses and Impacts of Assessment Information

Perhaps the most disappointing finding was that institutions reported they are not using student-assessment data very extensively in academic decision-making and they believe this information has little or no impact on institutional performance—either internally on faculty, student, or educational patterns or externally on relationships with constituencies. Indeed, campuses reported almost no efforts to even monitor these impacts. While the general finding is that student-assessment data are seldom used to make decisions, when an institution did engage in research on student performance, provided professional development, and practiced academic planning, it was more likely to use student-assessment data in decision-making.

Perspective

State agencies and institutional accrediting bodies may have stimulated the adoption of assessment activities by many postsecondary institutions, but these initiatives appear to have had little impact on how institutions have supported or used student assessment to improve their academic performance. Overall, the picture of institutional support for student assessment is an evolutionary one: considerable adoption of some types of student-assessment measures and some effort to support and promote assessment are both evident. Still missing is a sustained commitment to using student-assessment data to make academic decisions, to link goals to educational improvement, and to monitor the impact of assessment—internally and externally—on institutional performance. ...

EVALUATING COLLEGE TEACHING:
Myth and Reality

Peter Seldin

No group is more full of myths about teaching and its evaluation, more reluctant to admit that there are good and bad teachers, and more resistant to the idea that teaching skills can be acquired than teachers themselves.

This mythology is often grounded in dubious assumptions about the nature of teaching and learning and about the characteristics of teachers and students. Rarely are these myths confronted by practical experience, thoughtful observation, or careful reasoning. For that reason, this chapter examines five common assumptions— touched on in one way or another by the *Change* articles in this section—that help create or dispel a mythology of teaching and its evaluation.

1. There is no way to identify good teaching. Meeth (1976) took this position in his *Change* article, suggesting that since we do not know what effective teaching is, we are unable to evaluate it properly. Cross (1989, p. 12) saw it differently. She said, "We cannot continue to hide behind the excuse that we . . . can't tell a good teacher from a poor one. The sentiment defies our common sense and is contrary to most research on the question." Carson (1996) identified effective teachers as those remembered by their students decades later for their special ability to: (1) link students to their discipline; (2) use stories, examples, anecdotes to explain tough concepts; and (3) truly care about their students and their learning.

Eble (1986) agreed, pointing out that faculty singled out for making a difference are also heavily involved in assisting student learning by providing extra help, working closely with teaching assistants, and setting up mentoring programs.

The critical characteristics of effective teaching have been identified in the more than 10,000 studies on teaching effectiveness published in the last 20 years. Those studies are in general agreement. In addition to the characteristics mentioned above, the important teacher qualities include professional competence, the ability to motivate students and effectively communicate at their level, fairness, and positive attitude. These points of important teaching traits are not far removed from those employed by Socrates.

2. Good teachers are born not made. The marginal truth in this belief applies no more to teachers than it does to those in any other profession. Hence, there are born dentists, born accountants, born physical therapists. In truth, though, born anythings spend an enormous amount of time conditioning their minds, acquiring skills, and endlessly practicing. Potentially great teachers become great teachers by the same route: through conditioning mind and spirit, acquiring skills, and through endlessly practicing in the classroom.

It is true, of course, that some teachers have certain natural advantages—charm, verbal fluency, an ability to communicate well with students, a warm smile, patience—but the skills are as likely to be acquired as inborn. Perhaps that is why Kunz (1978) said that teacher evaluation must be linked to specific strategies for improvement, and why Carson (1996) argued that teachers can increase their effectiveness by learning how to communicate their love for their academic field, to be attentive to their words and action so their respect and concern for students is apparent, and to find strategies for signaling their availability.

Tobias (1986) described an innovative teaching improvement approach: non-science professors are taught science by their colleagues for the express purpose of providing feedback to the instructor. As part of the process, the non-science professors respond to two questions: what is making this subject difficult for me? What could be done differently to make it more clear?

Too often, professors look upon evaluation of teaching and professional development as unrelated processes. The fact is that they are a single process and make most sense as such. While administrative evaluation can be helpful in making tenure, promotion, or retention decisions, its core purpose is to identify areas of needed or desired improvement and to point the way to professional development.

The movement to improve teaching has been adopted, in various forms, by a rapidly increasing number of institutions. Although reliable numbers are hard to come by, it is estimated that today as many as 1,000 colleges and universities have centers devoted to improving teaching—a stunning jump from the 80 centers cited by Meeth (1976) some 24 years ago in *Change*.

3. There are no differences in effectiveness of different methods of instruction. This may be the case if the criterion used is student performance on final examinations, certainly an important outcome of higher education. However, there are others. As McKeachie (1969) correctly pointed out, other important goals include problem-solving and critical thinking skills, interest in the field, motivation, and attitudinal or value changes. It is in these areas, rather than student performance on final examinations, that differences in teaching methods appear.

In truth, there is no one best way of teaching. What is best for one teacher may be quite different from what is best for another (McKeachie, 1999), and no one method is best for all goals, students, or teachers. Perhaps that is why Whitfield (1982), in his *Change* review of a book by Epstein on preeminent professors, reported that some were fluent lecturers and delivered histrionic performances while others used the Socratic method. Some took a personal interest in their students; others did not. While most were mentors, some had a coherent set of doctrines, while others did not.

4. Student ratings are the only source of information needed to determine teaching effectiveness. It has become as common for students to grade teachers as for teachers to grade students. In fact, student ratings have become the most widely used—and, in many cases, the only—source of information on teaching effectiveness (Seldin, 1993). Tapping just one source of information is a dangerous approach, however. In her article, Carson worried that many will confuse such simplistic assessment outcomes with quality of teaching. Frey said that even properly developed student ratings that provide reliable and valid data about teaching should be considered with other evidence.

Cashin (1989) argued that students are unqualified to provide valid reports on a number of important matters of teaching effectiveness. These include an array of factors related to subject matter mastery, course design, and curriculum development. Seldin (1999) agreed, saying that no single source of evaluative information can capture the individuality and complexity of teaching.

5. The evaluation of teaching has not changed much over the years. In truth, both the conversation and the process have changed significantly.

How has the conversation changed? Perhaps the best way to see it is to compare the table of contents of two well-received books by the same author on the topic of evaluating teaching, one published in 1980, the other in 1999.

The table of contents in the 1980 book listed only the following chapters:

- Student ratings
- Colleague evaluation
- Self-evaluation
- Other ways to evaluate teaching.

By comparison, the table of contents in the 1999 book contained the following chapters:

- Student ratings
- Using student feedback to improve teaching
- Peer observation
- Self-evaluation
- Post-tenure review: evaluating teaching
- Evaluating teaching through classroom assessment
- Using the World Wide Web to improve teaching
- Teaching portfolios
- Administrative courage to evaluate the complexities of teaching
- Building a climate conducive to effective evaluation
- Building successful teaching evaluation programs

Without doubt, the conversation about evaluating teaching has changed, becoming broader and deeper. New approaches, such as the teaching portfolio, have been developed. The technology movement is in full swing. There is greater concern for creating an environment conducive to meaningful evaluation. Beyond that, however, there is now a keen awareness that evaluation data can and should be used to improve teaching performance, not just for personnel decisions.

Clearly, the conversation has changed. More significantly, so has the process used to evaluate teaching performance. In his *Change* article, Seldin (1984) documented those changes over the five-year period from 1978 to 1983. Since then, Seldin (1999) has extended his study and now has documented the changes over the 20-year period between 1978 and 1998. (See below.)

Information Sources Cited as "Always Used" in Evaluating Teaching, 1978, 1988, and 1998

Information Source*	1978	1988	1998
Systematic student ratings	54.8%	80.3%	88.1%
Evaluation by department chair	80.3%	80.9%	70.4%
Evaluation by dean	76.9%	72.6%	64.9%
Self-evaluation	36.6%	49.8%	58.7%
Committee evaluation	46.6%	49.3%	46.0%
Colleagues' opinions	42.7%	44.3%	44.0%
Classroom visits	14.3%	27.4%	40.3%
Course syllabi and examinations	13.9%	29.0%	38.6%
Scholarly research/publication	19.9%	29.0%	26.9%
Alumni opinions	3.4%	3.0%	9.0%
Grade distribution	2.1%	4.2%	6.7%

*In descending order by 1998 scores
Source: Seldin (1999)

Seldin (p. 21) cites the following key changes in the evaluation of teaching in this period:

- Systematic student ratings have become the most widely used source of information.
- The department chair and dean are still important sources of information but with sharply diluted power.
- Self-evaluation, classroom visits, and course syllabi and exams are far more widely used.
- Committee evaluation and colleagues' opinions continue to play major roles.
- In altering their evaluation practices, colleges are gathering more information from more sources and doing so more systematically.

Why has the evaluation of teaching been so dramatically transformed? Some of the answer is found in administrative displeasure with the inadequacies of systems used in the past. Another part is a response to competition from Internet-based providers like the University of Phoenix and University Access that offer academic modules, courses, and entire degree programs. The movements to promote peer review and more recently the scholarship of teaching also contribute to these changes.

More of the answer likely lies in the burgeoning teaching portfolio movement. Portfolios are factual descriptions of a professor's teaching strengths and accomplishments. They often include student ratings, classroom observation reports, syllabi and other teaching materials, and a reflective statement addressing teaching philosophy, objectives, and strategies (Seldin, 1997).

It is clear that teaching evaluation methods are changing. Some factors are getting more weight and others less. What is unresolved is which of the shifts will turn out to be improvements and which will be short-lived fads. More certain is the likelihood that a direct outgrowth of improved teaching evaluation practices will be improvements in teaching performance.

References

Cashin, W. E. (1989). Defining and evaluating college teaching. *IDEA Paper* no. 32, IDEA Center, Kansas State University.

Carson, B. H. (1996, November/December). Thirty years of stories: The professor's place in student memories. *Change, 28,* 11–17.

Cross, K. P. (1989). A proposal to improve teaching or what "taking teaching seriously" should mean. *AAHE Bulletin, 39,* 9–15.

Eble, K. E. (1986, July/August). A group portrait. *Change, 18,* 21–47.

Kunz, D. (1978, February). Viewpoint 2: Learning to live with evaluation. *Change, 10,* 10–11.

McKeachie, W. J. (1969, November/December). Letters: Effects of teaching. *Change, 1,* 4.

McKeachie, W. J. (1999). *Teaching tips* (10th ed.). Boston, MA: Houghton Mifflin.

Meeth, L. R. (1976, June). An overview: The stateless art of teaching evaluation. *Change, 8,* 3–5.

Seldin, P. (1984, April). Faculty evaluation: Surveying policy and practices. *Change, 16,* 28–33.

Seldin, P. (1993, July 21). The use and abuse of student ratings of professors. *The Chronicle of Higher Education*, p. A-40.

Seldin, P. (1997). *The teaching portfolio* (2nd ed.). Bolton, MA: Anker.

Seldin, P. (1999). *Changing practices in evaluating teaching*. Bolton, MA: Anker.

Tobias, S. (1986, March/April). Peer perspectives on the teaching of science. *Change, 18,* 36–51.

Whitfield, S. J. (1982, March). Review: Masters: Portraits of great teachers. *Change, 14,* 53–54.

LETTERS: **Effects of Teaching**

Wilbert J. McKeachie

I read your report of the analysis of research on college teaching methods, *The Teaching-Learning Paradox*, by Robert Dubin and Thomas Taveggia ["Happenings," July–August 1969] with much interest, albeit with some dismay at their conclusions. Your report said Dubin and Taveggia "concluded that there are no measurable differences in effectiveness among various methods of instruction." In the original study the sentence concludes, ". . . when evaluated by student performance on final examinations." While my own reviews (1968, 1969) and that of Wilbur Schramm (1962) do find some differences that are relatively consistent, we would agree that on the whole differences in teaching methods produce relatively little effect on student performance on *final examinations*, particularly if the content evaluated by the examination is included in a textbook available to all students. We do *not*, however, agree that there are no measurable differences in effectiveness of different methods of instruction.

Dubin and Taveggia say, "To say that content learning, as measured by course examinations, is not relevant to the reasons why students are in college is simply to fly in the face of reality" and "transmission of knowledge is a primary function of college training." This implies that most college educators would say that content learning is not important, but I suspect that the more common view is that while knowledge is an important outcome of higher education, there are other important goals, such as the retention and application of knowledge to new problems, problem-solving and critical thinking skills, interest, motivation, skill for further learning, and attitudinal or value changes. It is in these areas that consistent differences between teaching methods do appear. Thus administrators may not assume that all teaching methods are equally effective so that they may choose the cheapest without concern.

RESEARCH: **The Ongoing Debate: Student Evaluation of Teaching**

Peter W. Frey

Teaching competence is not easily documented. The university teacher is one of the few professionals whose work is seldom observed by his peers. His teaching reputation is often based more on hearsay than on substantive evidence. For this reason, promotion committees frequently make final tenure decisions without seriously considering information about teaching. To counter this tendency, many campuses have recently instituted a system of student instructional ratings. Unfortunately, this approach has little more credibility with the faculty than the hearsay system.

Even though students are the only people who observe a teacher's course daily, many faculty seriously question the reliability and validity of student instructional ratings. My present purpose is to analyze these issues in light of recent research developments and to indicate what implications this work may have for the faculty evaluation process.

Although there are several acceptable procedures for assessing the reliability of a measuring instrument, the most meaningful index of reliability for student rating data is the extent to which students agree about the strengths and weaknesses of different teachers. In my *Science* report of October 5, 1973, 13 different instructors were rated by students in two multisection calculus courses. The ability of students to discriminate among teachers on several different traits was examined.

When asked to comment on the clarity of the teacher's presentations, the students were consistent in selecting the same teachers as the "best" and "worst" instructors on this trait. Statistical analysis of this outcome indicated that a difference as large as that observed would be expected on a chance basis less than one time in a million.

When students were asked to comment on the work load in their calculus classes, the differences in their mean ratings for each instructor were also extraordinarily reliable. These results suggest that students can clearly discriminate among the teaching performances of different instructors. . . .

In my own research, I have been particularly concerned with the questions of what information should we be interested in and how should it be collected. I believe that there is generally a positive relationship between student ratings and good teaching but that the strength of this relationship depends critically on the technical sophistication of the rating questionnaire. I have several biases in this regard which I would like to discuss. First, I believe it is useful to consider the student as an information source rather than as an evaluator. The rating items should be worded in terms of observables and statements of opinion or attitude should be avoided when possible. Secondly, I think it is necessary to treat the teaching situation as one having many dimensions that can be rated separately. The common habit of designing questionnaires which elicit overall opinions on a simple good-bad dimension completely defeats this objective. Thirdly, I believe that it is important to take into account the fact that students' perceptions are a product of their own personalities as well as of the teacher's behavior. Thus the impression that a teacher creates depends not only on his own behavior but also on the behavior and expectations of his audience. Any analysis which assumes that teacher ratings depend entirely on the target and are independent of their source will be woefully inadequate.

In order to use this approach, I have attempted to identify several attributes of teaching which are common to most classes and which can be described by students. By analyzing student response patterns on rating forms, my factor analysis research has indicated six relatively independent dimensions of teaching. These are presentation clarity, work load, personal attention, class discussion, organization-planning, and grading. In addition, I have found that students can provide a general estimate of how much they have learned in the course. The items which elicit this type of information I have listed under the heading "student accomplishment."

Evaluation for each individual, be he student, faculty, or administrator, consists of taking what the teacher said and did and considering these factors in terms of one's own value system and educational philosophy. Certainly, one student may value one aspect of the course more than a second student would. These considerations imply that any overall rating that a student makes will reflect two different types of factors: the events which the student observed during the course and his evaluation of these events within his own value system.

I believe that a student can provide information about his or her observations relatively uncontaminated by a value system if appropriate questions are asked. My research objective over the past several years has been to develop an instructional rating form which accomplished this end. The object was to collect and summarize student observations in such a way that each member of the academic community could use this information to make his own evaluation of each course.

My study reported in the October 5 issue of *Science* provides a good example of this approach. This study followed the same general design as those discussed previously except much greater emphasis was placed on the construction and administration of the rating form. The study involved calculus teachers who used a common syllabus, common text, and common final exam but in all other respects had complete responsibility for the conduct of their classes. The mean final exam performance of each instructor's students was used to validate the teacher's ratings. The results indicated that the several traits correlated differentially with the exam performances. The student accomplishment ratings, as might be expected, showed the strongest correlation with the amount actually learned ($r = .87$). Several of the specific traits also showed high correlations, e.g., presentation clarity ($r = .75$) and organization-planning ($r = .62$). The personal attention trait bore only a weak relationship with the mean exam scores (r = .31). This last observation is important because this trait usually is a major component (i.e., is heavily weighted) when students make an overall evaluation of a course.

The value of collecting separate information about each trait can be demonstrated by considering the predictive validity of two of these traits taken in combination. Although the presentation-clarity and work-load traits taken individually correlate .75 and .44 respectively with the external criterion, a simple linear combination of the two correlates .95 with this same criterion (i.e., the mean final exam performance of each instructor's students). This tremendously strong correlation not only reflects the high reliability of the measures being correlated (each is the mean of 30 to 40 raw scores) but also clearly indicates that student rating information, when collected and analyzed appropriately, can provide valuable data for administrative decisions.

The distinction between students as evaluators and students as information sources is essential. When a student makes evaluative judgments about his teacher, he is likely to weight the specific teaching traits somewhat differently than would a faculty member or an administrator. In my example from the calculus study, the presentation-clarity and work-load traits taken in combination were the best predictors of good teaching. It is probable that the student's value system would emphasize different traits, such as personal attention or grading. I believe that the low positive correlations (r = .30 to .40) which are commonly observed in validity studies reflect this student bias. The much stronger correlations observed by myself and Gessner reflect our emphasis on specific teaching traits which are more germane to the actual amount learned.

On the basis of the preceding discussion, it is fairly clear that an instructional rating system, when properly developed, can provide reliable and valid information about teaching. These kinds of data should be made a permanent part of each faculty member's record and should be available at promotion time for consideration in conjunction with the other evidence.

When care is taken to develop a technically sound measuring instrument, instructional ratings can provide a documented record of faculty performance which is valuable to all concerned. Systematic student ratings can provide the instructor with information to assess the effectiveness of his teaching procedures. Use of such information by promotion committees would encourage the instructor to devote the necessary time and effort to do his best teaching. Periodic instructional ratings can also be used to assess the relative strength or weakness of undergraduate teaching programs and thereby suggest directions for the development or improvement of these programs. Course ratings can aid the students in selecting courses. Judicious course selection by the consumer (i.e., the student) should eventually have a salutary effect on the product (i.e., the teaching).

Course ratings can also be useful to departmental chairmen in assigning instructors on the basis of their relative strengths in teaching different types of undergraduate courses. Finally, instructional ratings which focus on specific teaching traits can provide data concerning which teaching styles are most effective in different instructional settings. This information would be invaluable to those educators who are preparing graduate students for future teaching positions.

Because some form of a student instructional rating system seems inevitable in the faculty evaluation process, faculty should take an active role in its development in order to insure the university's future quality. It is clear that student instructional ratings can be reliable and valid; it is the obligation of faculty to insure that such is the case at their own institutions. This task will not be accomplished by imitating the cowardly ostrich.

The Stateless Art of Teaching Evaluation

An Overview

L. Richard Meeth

Systematic, comprehensive, and valid evaluation of teaching has been an educational problem for many years. It continues to evade educators, although most administrators and legislators desire it as a meaningful way to determine rewards and sanctions for faculty, and most serious teachers seek it as a way of improving their performance and more closely relating what they do to what students learn. Most evaluation of teaching has resulted instead in unfair and inconclusive distinctions among teachers without establishing reliable or valid relationships between what teachers do and what students learn.

The evaluation of teaching presumes consensus among educators about what constitutes effective teaching. But educators don't know what makes up effective teaching; they don't have a good research base, don't agree on the validity of what research they do have, don't believe the evidence that is presented in that research, and don't act on any of it in a broad systematic way throughout higher education.

More than 80 centers have been developed in colleges and universities in the last decade that focus on improving teaching. All have in common a lack of consensus about what is most important to improve. This problem springs from the dearth of research about the relationship of teaching to learning. If we better understood how students learn, we might better understand how and what teachers ought to teach. The many lists of teaching activities prepared over the years, while isolating both overt and covert behaviors, cannot be ranked very conclusively from most important to least important in terms of producing learning. Each college faculty that develops an evaluation form lists those items that they value as most important without knowing whether or not their items are significant, peripheral, or inconsequential in terms of learning.

The problem is not only deciding what should be improved about teaching, but also knowing when or if things have improved. In other words, there are few standards by which teaching can be judged. The *Change* Reports on Teaching, for example, focus on "improved" teaching primarily because improvement provides a comparative standard for evaluation, i.e., a behavior is more effective today than it was yesterday. When an absolute standard of good or best teaching is implied, it is hard to find agreement on what that might be. Some have settled simply for words like "innovative" or "different" as a standard, but these have no necessary correlation with quality or learning outcomes. Accepting what exists as a base and attempting to improve it by appropriate, responsible evaluation, while plodding along without an overall frame of reference, seems best in the absence of definitive research or agreed standards.

If there are few standards, there are even fewer criteria against which effectiveness or improvement can be evaluated. Robert Thorndike, writing in another context, suggested three categories of criteria—ultimate, intermediate, and immediate—that can be applied to teaching. Ultimate criteria have to do with learning outcomes, intermediate criteria with the process of teaching, and immediate criteria with the sense of experiences of teaching or learning. Obviously, immediate criteria are furthest removed from learning outcomes. Student evaluations of teaching fall into this category and, while better than nothing, are still a long way from relating teaching to learning. The sense of learning assessed during or immediately after the experience frequently has little to do with the long-term effect of the experience.

Many institutional programs of faculty evaluation center on methodology without much regard for criteria. It often appears more important to decide whether a colleague visits the classroom by invitation or by chance than to determine what will be observed during the hour. Very few peer observations of teaching are based on a predetermined set of criteria to be assessed. When these do exist, as often as not they have been borrowed from another list at another college. Even when

Defining Improved Teaching

I. Ultimate Criteria	II. Intermediate Criteria
The students learned what the instructor was trying to teach — in cognitive, affective, and/or psychomotor development — in rate and/or absolute achievement	Students were motivated to learn
	The structure of the learning experience was determined by the goals of the experience
Learning continued after the formal experience ended — rate and/or extent of later learning known	The content was well ordered, comprehensive, and appropriate to the abilities of the learner
Students retained what was learned	Teacher involvement in the learning experience was in harmony with the goals of the experience
Teacher goals and/or outcomes for the learning experience were met	Time was provided for students to contemplate and respond
Student goals and/or outcomes for the learning experience were met	Rewards and sanctions were appropriate to the goals of the learning experience
The learning experience related to other learning experiences students might have had (congruence, continuity, sequence): prior learning was capitalized upon; learning increased in other formal experiences the students had at the same time; learning improved in the rest of a sequential series the students had afterward	Students understood what they were doing, why they were doing it, and how they would be evaluated in the learning experience
	Goals and/or outcomes were clearly specified
	Evaluation criteria, standards, and methodologies were clear and appropriate to the goals of the experience
The learning experience positively affected the attitudes and/or behavior of the teacher, other faculty members, and administrators within the immediate learning community	Student products reflected the goals of the learning experience
The learning experience cost less than traditional ways of delivering the same experience: the same learning for less money; more learning for the same money; more learning for less money	The kind and variety of instructional resources were congruent with the goals of the experiences and abilities of the learners
Enrollment levels were sustained or increased in subsequent offerings of the learning experience	Methodology was appropriate to the goals of the experience and the abilities of the learners

inclusion of each item is hotly debated, the discussion is rarely grounded in a researched rationale of effectiveness. For example, educators know that immediate criteria (a sense of the experience of learning and teaching effectiveness) may have nothing to do with actual learning or teaching effectiveness, yet the primary criteria applied to postsecondary teaching relate to student perceptions at the time of the formal experience.

The criteria selected to apply to the teaching experiences described in these issues were developed by the editors interacting with the teaching project advisory board. Some of their ideas about the difficulty of developing criteria were reported

in the February 1976 issue of *Change*. In most cases intermediate criteria were used in selecting experiences for these Reports primarily because even the most improved teaching has not been well researched. These criteria are by no means an end; simply a point of departure and a way of classifying in the hope of seriously moving forward the evaluation of teaching. They are reprinted here because they are generally applicable to postsecondary teaching and may expand and focus the debate about what should be included in such a set of criteria. . . .

Another problem confronting serious evaluators is the lack of effective models. Barak Rosenshine of the University of Illinois wrote recently, "The number of studies which have looked at both teacher behavior and student outcomes is embarrassingly small. The quality of many of these studies is questionable and the results of these studies are not sufficiently strong or clear to direct . . . evaluation of teachers. What is lacking is research demonstrating an experimental or correlational connection between teaching skills and measures of change in student achievement and affect. The state of the art, then, is one of a lack of research." . . . It does seem strange that a profession as broadly practical and important to the society would continue so long on such a shallow base of evidence. It seems even stranger, however, that the society would not have insisted long ago on more evidence of what works and why, and, if empirical evidence is not appropriate as a base, would not have urged moving toward another perhaps more humanistic base of understanding of teaching effectiveness. . . .

Finally, evaluation of teaching has suffered from gross inattention. Quoting [Donald] O'Dowd, . . . "Higher education, by its very resistance or inattention to the study of its major activity, has denied itself the very means by which it can improve." In spite of the numerous teaching improvement centers, research on teaching is nominal and incidental in most colleges and universities. The privacy of teaching, the disinterest of some disciplines, and limited rewards for improvement have all contributed to this inattention. By failing to give serious thought to the evaluation of teaching before trying to improve it, faculty, in the sciences at least, deny themselves the essence of what they are attempting to provide their students—the knowledge of results. Thus, the standard for students is higher than it is for teachers.

And yet teaching goes on and learning continues. Failure to solve the problems of evaluation has not stopped the activity of teaching or its ultimate effect. There is ample evidence that students are learning and changing as a result of their college experiences. Nor is it appropriate to cease teaching until the problems of evaluation are solved. But it is fitting that more attention be paid by governments, disciplinary associations, professional associations, and campus faculties to finding ways of rewarding both the research on teaching and the evaluation of teaching based on that research. As one effort to increase this attention, *Change* is sponsoring a national meeting of the education officers of the major disciplinary associations to discuss further ways of evaluating and improving teaching.

The evaluation of teaching effectiveness is a stateless art. The problems are serious and difficult to overcome. Inattention to the development of evaluative standards and criteria will never produce researched models of effective teaching or methodologies for determining effectiveness. The effort to improve teaching will not be complete until there is a better base for evaluating that improvement. To this end, the Reports on Teaching are dedicated.

January 1977

What Is Improved Teaching?

L. Richard Meeth

When this project [the Change Project on Undergraduate Teaching] was launched, one of the first staff conferences centered on the question, What is improved teaching? The question continues to come up each time a teaching experience is reviewed. Then as now the choice of the word "improved" was intentional.

Other terms were discussed and rejected. . . .
. . . [G]ood teaching is rejected because it presumes an absolute standard, *innovative* because it emphasizes newness, and *unique* because it suggests a one-time-only experience. All three words are too limiting to cover the range of growth that is taking place among teachers in higher education.

Why talk about the outcome rather than the process, improved teaching rather than improving teaching? We have talked about the act of improving for a long time in American education without specifying where we wanted to come out. What is the purpose of a journey without a destination? Some description of the dimensions of improved teaching may provide goals against which concerned educators can assess their progress. . . .

There are some things that improved teaching is not. Improved teaching experiences do not necessarily have universal applicability. Some are limited in the ways in which others can adapt or adopt them, though most have dimensions — either principle, process, or product — that others can utilize. Readers of these Reports are occasionally disappointed to discover that all activities described in their disciplines cannot be reconstructed in whole or even in part. Unfortunately there is a human tendency to reject that which cannot be absorbed totally. . . .

Improved teaching does not mean, in the words of Jerry Gaff, director of the Project on Institutional Renewal Through the Improvement of Teaching, that all examples of it are "complete models of effectiveness." Most improved teaching, in fact, is not as effective or complete as those who direct it would like. But by unconsciously imposing absolute standards on others' attempts at bettering their teaching, observers frequently fail to recognize the extent of change that has taken place. All teachers are not at the same place on any continuum of improvement. This project has occasionally reported experiences that were at a simpler, more fundamental level than those of many faculty teaching in that field. If the context of a teaching experience does not exactly coincide with the perspective of an observer, he or she too often rejects the total improvement, failing to see the principles or the pieces that could fit his or her setting or, worse yet, failing to see that contexts can change as well. It is disheartening to see a faculty member visit a colleague and fail to grasp the significant changes in an improved teaching situation because of some imposed standard or expectation of completeness.

Improved teaching is not popularizing the obvious or mundane body of information normally communicated by pedestrian teachers. The popularizer has his place in the circus of education, but to mistake popular for improved teaching is to look only at superficial teaching techniques without regard for substance.

Improved teaching does mean, however, that the experience is better than the way the teacher taught it before, but not necessarily better than

anyone has ever taught the course or structured the experience. The distance a teacher moves in understanding how to make his or her teaching more appropriate, meaningful, effective, or whatever the word might be depending upon the criteria used to assess improvement, is one critical dimension of improved teaching. But all improved teaching does not change enough to make any difference. Some that is better than it was may still not be good enough in that students, in spite of the improvement, do not learn any more or at all from the teaching. So there must be other aspects as well.

Improved teaching must mean that students learn more from the experience than they learned before. The outcome or the product must be greater or better. To focus entirely on what the teacher did to structure the learning experience is to leave out a fundamental criterion. But even when students learn more from the improved teaching than they did from the previous experience, outcome cannot be the exclusive criterion of definition. Rate of improvement and change in students are only two parts of the larger whole.

So improved teaching means that the instructional process is less ambivalent, more pointed, more efficient. In an intermediate sense, the teaching process flows more directly out of its purposes. The learning activities that link purpose with product are more obviously and directly apparent. When there is congruence among purposes, activities, teacher, and learner, the participants tend to know it. At this point the art of teaching comes through most clearly.

As with any art form, when it is done well the whole is greater than the sum of the parts. There is a synergism about improved teaching that comes through in the way both teacher and student respond, though it frequently defies capture. When writers and photographers seek to report examples of improved teaching in these Reports, they often say that the writing fails to convey the spirit of the experience. Because teaching is both craft and art, there is a spirit about improved teaching that may not be replicable.

Finally, improved teaching means that a particular learning experience reflects the force of a professor who, in the words of Kenneth Eble, "has paid attention to teaching," made notable changes in the ways he or she directly or indirectly affects learning and attitudes about learning, and consciously helped others see some applicability to what they do elsewhere in their own teaching. There is a self-consciousness about improved teaching that comes after any pilgrimage, but because the activity is teaching, the pilgrim has the opportunity to reconstruct both the pain and the joy from the time and place when he did not know if his journey would be effective to the point when the whole is recognizably better. . . .

February 1978

VIEWPOINT 2: **Learning to Live With Evaluation**

Don Kunz

. . . The classroom has been a private place for a long time, and there are many reasons we are reluctant to embrace teacher evaluation. Some of our excuses sound melodramatically self-important; others seem trivial. But they all arise from fears that such schemes challenge much of what we profess to value as humanists. If unexamined, such fears can incapacitate us in bitterly defensive behavior. My position is that we should make them serve in developing worthwhile means for evaluating instruction. Our fears should be put to work.

The less significant forms of resistance that humanities professors offer arise from long-standing interdisciplinary warfare with the social scientists. In our contacts with them we are likely to be bewildered by their statistics and annoyed by their language. . . .

This humanist preoccupation may seem merely a matter of style, but it goes deeper. Humanities professors are likely to view the whole business of evaluation as the pseudoscientific posturing of sober-faced psychologists or educationists or zealous colleagues bent on a crusade. The evaluators promise a battery of questions anatomizing the significant facets of teaching, a variety of response scales categorizing the possible answers, computer printouts with detailed technical instructions for interpretation, and numerical accuracy to the third decimal point. . . .

All this may explain our reluctance to get involved with evaluation but does not justify it. Many professors' objections to evaluation simply arise from confusion over what it is. What is most commonly referred to as an instructional evaluation system is really an end-of-term measurement of student attitudes about the instruction they have received. This becomes an evaluation system only after people make value judgments about what it measures and how that relates to the instructor's intentions in his courses, his epistemology, and his metaphysics. And even at that point, evaluation isn't comprehensive: It taps only one source of information and does so only when it is too late to correct any problems. This means its use is judgmental rather than improvement oriented. Such a scheme elicits fear.

Because the response scale comes in four or five digits, the numerical printout resembles nothing so much as a tally of undergraduate cumulative grade point averages, and it encourages insecurity about being graded by students (especially if we are uncertain about the validity of the grades we assign them). From here we leap to the fear of revenge and the prospect of trading grades in a shameful inflationary spiral until all standards are lost and all authority eroded. Under such circumstances, our fears may be legitimate.

It makes good sense for faculty to object to an attitude measurement device being passed off as an instructional evaluation system designed to improve teaching. Such an instrument can tell reliably and validly how students feel about teachers and courses and may indicate how some attitudes affect their learning. But it provides little information about whether the professor knows his subject or has significantly affected student achievement.

Other measures, though, could offer insight into these critical dimensions of teaching. An evaluation system worth having would use some mixture of sources (self, colleagues, administrators or alumni, as well as students), methods of collection (visitation, video taping or student testing, as well as attitude measurement), and kinds of information (syllabi, assignments or graded examinations, as well as classroom behavior) to reach judgments about various forms of teaching (planning, testing, and interaction with students). This material would be read as carefully as a multiple narrative novel.

The principal obstacle to such an evaluation reform is our present defensiveness. Humanities professors must educate themselves about, and help to design, teacher evaluation systems or they will be justly victimized by them. A wealth of useful material about measurement and evaluation is available. . . .

But . . . with over 2,300 studies to examine, it would be useful to seek direct, personal guidance. Painful as it may seem, I suggest that humanities professors make friends with colleagues in an education or psychology department. Try to learn their jargon and to teach them English. They will be so grateful that they will steer you to the seminal information and help you translate it. If you ignore previous research, you will only be setting out to reinvent the wheel; and if you are part of a commit-

tee engaged in that enterprise, your wheel may become an iron maiden. . . .

Unfortunately, even the most valid, comprehensive, and humane evaluation system will not be worth the effort necessary to design and operate it unless other conditions are met. Teacher evaluation must be initiated by faculty, supported by administration and students, and administered by a neutral agency. Even then, it must be recognized that evaluation is just one part of the puzzle of improving teaching and learning.

In order to achieve that goal, evaluation must be tied to a voluntary, confidential agency of knowledgeable, sympathetic people who can help faculty interpret the information collected and devise strategies for improvement before the end of the term when a new class begins with quite different learners under changed circumstances. And finally, evaluation and systematic improvement must be undertaken in the context of a reward system which ensures that demonstrably good teaching is reinforced with security, money, and status as much as published research — which is, after all, a kind of teaching too.

March 1982

The Presence of Great Teachers, Verified by the Presence of Great Students

Stephen Whitfield

I magine thumbing through a college catalog and discovering the following listings:

ANTH201	Cultural Anthropology	Prof. Benedict	TTh 10
ENGL 270	Modern Poetry	Prof. Richards	MWF 11
GOVT 138	Political Theory Sec. 1	Prof. Arendt	MWF 10
PHYS 390	The Structure of the Universe	Prof. Oppenheimer	MWF 1

Such a curriculum might exist only as a Platonic idea, an ambitious dean's fantasy, had Joseph Epstein, the editor of *The American Scholar*, not arranged for former students of these and eight

other preeminent professors to assess the aims and methods that exerted such influence over them. The result is *Masters*, a collection of essays drawn mostly from that quarterly which, if nothing else, can help sustain the morale of a profession whose exertions are as necessary as they are problematic, whose skills are as decisive as they are undefinable.

No single standard of what constitutes great teaching has ever emerged — not even the Socratic. . . . A few of these distinguished teachers, like I. A. Richards, Yvor Winters and Frederick J. Teggart, were extremely fluent lecturers and delivered histrionic performances. But others . . . radiated intelligence most easily in seminars. . . .

. . . [T]he problem that is most systematically evaded in this anthology does not refer to the vagaries of method, nor to the link between personality and pedagogy, but to what seems a tautology. The presence of great teachers may be verified only by the existence of great students. Perhaps not even Socrates' reputation would have soared so high were Plato not sitting in the front taking notes. . . .

This book permits few other generalizations. Some of these teachers were downright hostile to the modern trends that their students embodied. Some tried to foster a coherent set of doctrines among their disciplines; most of them, however, were mentors without a precise or formulaic message. Tenacity of memory distinguished some of these lecturers, and others were vastly learned even outside their own subjects. Yet all of them distilled

within the limits of a semester such amplitude and activity of mind that the possibilities of civilized learning were felt for still another generation. All of these teachers exemplified human excellence, which takes many forms. For example, Whitehead "took a personal interest in those with whom he had to deal and knew both their strong and weak points," his ex-student Bertrand Russell once recalled. "He would elicit from a pupil the best of which a pupil was capable. He was never repressive, or sarcastic or superior." . . .

Reference

Epstein, J. (Ed.) (1981). *Masters: Portraits of great teachers*. New York: Basic Books.

April 1984

Surveying Policy and Practices
Faculty Evaluation

Peter Seldin

A diminishing number of professors are selected for promotion and tenure these days, and many professors are perplexed by the criteria by which they were judged. Decision makers, the chairpersons and academic deans, are also perplexed by the promotion-tenure procedures and question the validity and legality of their decisions.

The process whereby an institution appraises a professor's performance has taken on new importance since a professional career may depend on it. With faculty mobility mostly a thing of the past, the decision to promote or to grant tenure has major impact on the professor's career. For their part, colleges and universities are under growing pressure to render sound decisions in the face of higher operating costs, fund shortages, shrinking student enrollment, and the threat of genuine competition from giant corporations who are moving into higher education.

In an examination of policies and practices behind these institutional decisions, all the accredited, four-year, undergraduate, liberal arts colleges listed in the U.S. Department of Education's *Directory* were surveyed early in 1983. University-related liberal arts colleges were excluded to make the population more manageable. A questionnaire

went to 770 academic deans and 616 (80 percent) replied, an unusually high response, suggesting the seriousness with which the deans perceived the problems in evaluating faculty performance. The survey also sought to uncover changes in institutional policies and practices since 1978 when a similar survey was conducted. For comparative purpose, the base data for both surveys were identical.

First developed and used by the American Council on Education in 1967 and revised by the Educational Testing Service in 1977, the questionnaire was designed to gather information on institutional evaluation of faculty performance in connection with tenure, promotion in rank, salary increase, and retention.

For complete study findings, readers are referred to *Changing Practices in Faculty Evaluations*. This article is confined to the significant changes in the evaluation of faculty performance and of classroom teaching.

Evaluating Overall Faculty Performance

In considering a professor for promotion in rank, tenure, or retention, academic deans today select and weigh a wide range of factors. The questionnaire offered the deans thirteen criteria for consideration, and Table 1 summarizes the relative importance given by the deans to "major factors" in 1978 and 1983.

Deans continue to regard classroom teaching as the most important index of overall faculty performance. However, significant changes have occurred in other areas. The traditional measures of academic repute, research, publication, and professional society activity seem to have assumed new importance. The number of deans citing research as a major factor in overall faculty evaluation rose between 1978 and 1983 from 24.5 to 33.4 percent, and those citing publication from 19.0 to 29.2 percent in the same period. Consistent with that change, 17.0 percent of the deans perceived activity in professional societies as a major factor in 1978 and 24.5 percent in 1983.

It seems clear that the higher public visibility of published research and professional society activity so prized by deans is a product of the economic stress of many colleges. As a New York dean said: "High visibility of our faculty is the name of the game today. Professors doing research, publishing journal articles, and presenting papers at professional meetings are in the public eye." The remark lends credence to the often-heard observation that professors are paid to teach but are evaluated and rewarded for their research and publication.

Probably for similar reasons, public service was cited as a major factor by 17.4 percent of the deans in 1983, 3.7 percent more than in 1978. Colleges appear to be encouraging faculty members to get involved in community and civic affairs. At the same time, colleges expect faculty members to involve themselves in campus committee work. This is supported by a rise from 48.8 to 52.6 percent of deans citing committee work as a major factor in faculty evaluation. It also seems to reflect a trend toward decentralization and a broader sharing of the institutions' nonteaching load.

Student advising is still considered a major factor despite slippage from 66.7 to 61.7 percent during the five-year period. Deans recognize the value of student advising as an outreach effort to keep students content and in school.

Length of service in rank still merits high if somewhat declining importance (49.9 to 46.8 percent). Presumably, colleges relying on it as a major factor in evaluation would argue for a positive correlation between the number of years in rank and the overall contribution to the college. That argument may be destined for vigorous challenge by younger faculty members with fewer years of service in rank but rapidly expanding reputations. . . .

Table 1 **Frequency of Use of Factors Considered in Evaluating Overall Faculty Performance in Liberal Arts Colleges, 1978 and 1983**

Factors	1978 (N = 680) Major Factor %	1983 (N = 616) Major Factor %
Classroom Teaching	98.8	98.7
Supervision of Graduate Study	2.2	3.7
Supervision of Honors Program	2.5	1.9
Research	24.5	33.4
Publication	19.0	29.2
Public Service	13.7	17.4
Consultation (Gov't., Business)	1.2	2.4
Activity in Professional Societies	17.0	24.5
Student Advising	66.7	61.7
Campus Committee Work	48.8	52.6
Length of Service in Rank	49.9	46.8
Competing Job Offers	3.1	1.8
Personal Attributes	38.4	28.6

Table 2 *T-Tests of Differences in Mean Scores of Factors Considered in Liberal Arts Colleges in Evaluating Overall Faculty Performance, 1978 and 1983*

Factors	1978 (N = 680) Mean Score	1983 (N = 616) Mean Score	t
Classroom Teaching	1.01	1.01	−0.87
Supervision of Graduate Study	2.26	2.14	1.77
Supervision of Honors Program	2.36	2.36	0.06
Research	1.83	1.71	3.68**
Publication	1.89	1.76	4.30**
Public Service	1.96	1.92	1.40
Consultation (Gov't., Business)	2.41	2.36	1.58
Activity in Professional Societies	1.88	1.80	2.79**
Student Advising	1.34	1.40	−2.00*
Campus Committee Work	1.52	1.49	1.38
Length of Service in Rank	1.57	1.63	−1.62
Competing Job Offers	2.69	2.72	−0.81
Personal Attributes	1.74	1.86	−3.22**

The test was a *t*-test for differences in independent proportions.
*Significant at .05 level of confidence
**Significant at .01 level of confidence

Table 2 shows the *t*-tests of differences in mean scores of factors.

There are significant differences in the data at the .01 level of confidence between the mean scores of four factors in 1978 and 1983. They are research, publication, activity in professional societies, and personal attributes. . . .

Evaluating Teaching Performance

In general, liberal arts colleges have been proud of the high caliber of their teaching staffs, a fact borne out by the deans' almost unanimous citation of classroom teaching as a major factor in evaluating overall faculty performance. How is teaching effectiveness assessed? What sources of information are used by the colleges? Table 3 examines the sources of information and their frequency of use by deans in the 1978 and 1983 studies. Several significant changes emerge. For the five-year period, five of the fifteen sources of information changed by at least five percent. More important, all five changed in the same direction, with each in more prevalent use today. This indicates that the information-gathering process is becoming more structured and systematic, and that colleges are making a concerted effort to reexamine and shore up their evaluation systems.

Table 3 shows the predominant sources of information still to be the department chairperson and the academic dean, with the chairperson easily the front runner. In fact, the gap between them widened from 3.4 to 6.3 percent in the five years.

How sound is the chairperson's judgment and what is it based on? This is a question with no readily available answer. It has been argued long and loud by many that administrators probably make sound judgments. They point to the analogous situation of clinical medicine, where experienced physicians often respond to obscure symptoms with a correct diagnosis, but would be at a loss to explain the leap from symptoms to diagnosis.

While chairpersons and deans have ready access to a faculty member's teaching load and classroom enrollment data, they do not personally observe what goes on behind the closed classroom door unless they open that door. Without classroom observation and/or examination of instructional materials, chairpersons and deans must depend on other informational sources on which to base teaching performance judgments.

The key question is, therefore, on what or whom do administrators depend for information?

Table 3 Liberal Arts Colleges Citing Sources of Information as Always Used in Evaluating Teaching Performance, 1978 and 1983

Sources of Information	1978 (N = 680) % Always Used	1983 (N = 616) % Always Used
Systematic Student Ratings	54.8	67.5
Informal Student Opinions	15.2	11.5
Classroom Visits	14.3	19.8
Colleagues' Opinions	42.7	43.3
Scholarly Research & Publication	19.9	27.3
Student Examination Performance	2.7	3.6
Chairman Evaluation	80.3	81.3
Dean Evaluation	76.9	75.0
Course Syllabi and Exams	13.9	20.1
Long-term Follow-up of Students	2.2	3.4
Enrollment in Elective Courses	2.7	1.1
Alumni Opinions	3.4	3.9
Committee Evaluation	46.6	46.1
Grade Distribution	2.1	4.5
Self-Evaluation or Report	36.6	41.9

It appears they rely in part on faculty committees. In 1978 and again in the 1983 study, over 46 percent of the deans cited faculty committees as "always used" as a teaching evaluation source.

The question persists: how do faculty committees arrive at decisions? Are decisions based on solid, relevant information? It appears that the committees' impressions of a professor's classroom competence are partly based on the professor's record of research and publication. This record was a source of information "always used" by 19.9 percent of the deans in 1978, and 27.3 percent by 1983. How relevant are research and publication to classroom teaching?

Arguably, if they provide insights into the professor's teaching effectiveness, they can be useful measuring rods. Demonstrably, however, the number of textbooks, journal articles, and monographs offering such insights is quite modest.

Both administrators and faculty committees rely on student ratings to help shape their judgments. Indeed, the use of written student ratings has shown a dramatic rise between 1978 and 1983. Student ratings are now "always used" in personnel decisions by more than two-thirds of the colleges. Students have acquired a strong voice in

the appraisal of their teachers. This may very well be an outgrowth of the campus unrest of the sixties and student demands for a greater role in academic decision making. Clearly, they are achieving their goal, at least in the area of professional evaluation.

Table 4 shows the shifting importance of informational sources in connection with teaching evaluation in the five-year period, as well as t-tests of differences in mean scores of the sources of information. Analysis of the data indicates significant differences at the .01 level of confidence in mean scores of three informational sources: systematic student ratings, classroom visits and course syllabi and tests.

Classroom visits have not only expanded but they have also exacerbated the academic conflict over their value. "The only way to know how a professor teaches is to see him in action," writes a Massachusetts dean. "Classroom visitation is mandatory at this college." A contradictory judgment comes from an Illinois dean: "Classroom visitation has no value."

Increasingly, teaching appraisals are deduced from a rather careful analysis of course syllabi and examinations. Are the instructional materials

Table 4 *T*-Tests of Differences in Mean Scores of Sources of Information Considered in Liberal Arts Colleges in Evaluating Teaching Performance, 1978 and 1983

Sources of Information	1978 (N = 680) Mean Score	1983 (N = 616) Mean Score	*t*
Systematic Student Ratings	1.64	1.44	4.46**
Informal Student Opinions	2.31	2.41	−2.03*
Classroom Visits	2.67	2.43	4.60**
Colleagues' Opinions	1.73	1.71	0.47
Scholarly Research & Publication	2.34	2.23	1.90
Student Examination Performance	3.08	3.03	1.20
Chairman Evaluation	1.27	1.26	0.15
Dean Evaluation	1.32	1.36	−1.18
Course Syllabi and Examinations	2.41	2.22	4.23**
Long-term Follow-up of Students	3.16	3.15	0.48
Enrollment in Elective Courses	3.04	3.12	−2.02*
Alumni Opinions	3.06	3.08	−0.63
Committee Evaluations	2.06	2.06	−0.10
Grade Distributions	3.12	3.07	0.90
Self-Evaluation or Report	2.08	1.96	2.02*

The test used was a *t*-test for differences in independent proportions.

*Significant at .05 level of confidence

**Significant at .01 level of confidence

current, relevant, and suitable to the course? What can be gleaned from examination results? Although not widespread, there is greater use of handouts, reading lists, homework assignments, and student-learning experiences to help appraise the professor's teaching. All this is consistent with the trend to locate more sources for, and give more structure to, information gathering.

Table 4 also indicates significant differences at the .05 level of confidence between mean scores of three sources of information: informal student opinion, enrollment in elective courses, and self-evaluation or report.

It is no surprise, and no real loss, that reliance on informal student opinions has declined. Such opinions were picked up in the past in chance encounters with students. The scraps of information have largely been replaced by systematic student ratings.

Self-evaluation has won popularity as an assessment tool. The number of colleges accepting self-evaluation as an important component in the multisource evaluation process has grown. Many academics, administrators and professors alike, believe that self-evaluation may provide insights into course and instructional objectives and also classroom competency.

However, self-evaluation as an assessment tool also has no shortage of detractors. At best, it is controversial. One ardent supporter, an Oregon dean, writes: "Self-evaluation is the keystone in our appraisal system." An equally ardent opponent, a New Jersey dean, argues: "Any professor up for tenure or promotion is going to provide a self-appraisal that portrays him as the greatest thing since sliced bread." Opponents perceived self-evaluation largely as self-serving.

Faculty evaluation has been transformed in several vital areas in recent years and is still changing. The changes reflect administrative and professional displeasure with the inadequacies of evaluation systems used in past years. Included below are the most significant findings in the assessment of overall faculty performance and of classroom teaching that emerged between the 1978 and 1983 studies.

- Academic deans are still almost unanimous in finding classroom performance the most important index of overall faculty performance.

- Research, publication, and activity in professional societies have gained importance.
- Student advising is considered very important, but has lost ground.
- The department chairperson and academic dean still dominate the evaluation of teaching performance.
- The professor's research and publication record has gained importance as an index of teaching performance.

- Administrators rely much more on student ratings, which have enjoyed a dramatic rise, to help shape their judgments of teaching performance.
- Classroom visits, course syllabi and examinations, and self-evaluations have gained currency in the assessment of classroom teaching.
- Liberal arts colleges are gathering information from more sources, and doing so more systematically for professor evaluations.

March/April 1986

Peer Perspectives on the Teaching of Science

Sheila Tobias

I am neither a physicist nor a mathematician, but, rather, a feminist who, ten years ago, became interested in why otherwise intelligent college students, many of them women, underenroll in mathematics and science. . . .

What if, I began to speculate, other people like myself, i.e., teachers in the humanities, the social sciences, law, theology—even fine arts—were to attend classes in mathematics and science for the express purpose of providing feedback to the instructor? How better to find out what really makes physics difficult, for example, than to remove all barriers to learning physics—namely youth, lack of confidence, unsophistication, inability to concentrate—except for the one barrier, newness to the field.

My idea was to set up short-term learning experiences for nonscience *professors* during which they would be taught science by their colleagues. In addition to having them interrupt the proceedings with questions and comments, I would have them log their reactions—both their cognitive and emotional responses—on a page divided vertically down the middle, an exercise used in treating math anxiety. On one side of their pages of notes they would record the material, as well as they could. On the other, they would deal with the twin questions: What is making this subject difficult for me? What could I, or the instructor, do to make it come clear?

What I had in mind was a teacher/learner laboratory where the only difference between the teacher and the learner would be naivete about the subject. In all other respects—age, intelligence, confidence, maturity, and self-image—the students would be peers of the instructors.

I carried "Peer Perspectives" around for some time. . . . until Hellmut Fritzsche, chairman of the department of physics at the University of Chicago, called . . . and said, ". . . let's do it here."

Fritzsche took upon himself the selection of the instructors, in this case, two master teachers of physics, one an experimentalist, one a theoretician, and the selection, by way of personal invitation, of the nonscientists who would participate as learners. The time was set for March 1985, the location, Ryerson, Chicago's historic physics classroom building, and the time-frame, two days of intense lecture presentations with discussion. . . .

There were, as I have said, to be two levels of feedback. The first was during and immediately after the sessions and consisted of discussions about the style and clarity of the lectures, the usefulness of the demonstrations, and more philosophically, about the nature of "truth" and "understanding" in physics. The second level of feedback consisted of letters composed anywhere from two days to two months after the experiment and addressed to Hellmut Fritzsche and myself for purposes of analysis. What follows, then, might be considered a "textual analysis" of some of the more fulsome of the comments we received, together with notes and suggestions from the nonscientists as to what science teachers might do to better reach students who are, after all, but younger versions of their colleagues: verbally mature, curious, selectively confident, but woefully unsure of themselves in the science classroom.

Let's begin with some comments: . . .

> I had difficulty picturing the presumably familiar phenomena that were used to illustrate more abstract concepts such as oscillating springs and railroad cars moving in relation to one another and to stationary objects. And I had difficulty following the descriptions of apparatus used in various experiments.
>
> I could follow what was being described, but I could not grasp what was actually happening in what was being described. It was like seeing without any faculty of intelligent perception.

The observer has given us a good description of how it feels to be left behind. He describes his problem acutely: he is seeing without perceiving; following without grasping; viewing but not picturing; and is aware of how much is being missed.

Might the problem reside in the fact that students have to be taught to *see* physics demonstrations quite as systematically as they have to be taught to solve problems? If necessary, the demonstration needs to be reconstructed in another medium (flow chart at the blackboard, computer graphics, etc.) in order to come clear to the one who is just learning to see.

Another commentator needs to travel back and forth between the demonstration and the words used to describe the principle at stake. She writes:

> There were times when Isaac's demonstration just didn't make the point, but when he put it in words, I understood. And I wished he would do the demonstration one more time because I thought that then I would see what we were supposed to have seen.

"For some of us," she goes on, "words point the way. Verbal explanations, restated several times and in different ways provide clarity." For others, it is the demonstrations that bring the concepts to light. And for still others, it is the mathematical descriptions. "Perhaps," she concludes, "it would be wise to use all of these ways at once, each and every time." . . .

In fact, our instructor appeared not at all aware of how difficult and even off-putting some of his demonstrations were to an audience that, in the normal course, doesn't see material things happen before their eyes. Some students in our group couldn't really discern when a spring was being compressed or when it had expanded. While the wave traveling along the slinky made an indelible, indeed, permanent impression, the finer inferences were simply not noticed or grasped.

But back to verbal descriptions: these are a major issue for the liberal arts learner. Another member of the group noticed this at once:

> I think the problem of definitions is particularly important for physics. One starts out being aware that "ordinary" words will have special meanings and the meanings of some words may be quite different from what they are in other uses. When Mel Shochet started talking about "static measurement," without defining it, I was a bit nervous. Did he mean what I think "static measurement" means — measuring something that is still and not moving? I didn't know and still don't know. Does counterintuitive mean against everyday intuition? Or does "counter" mean "non" or "un" intuitive?
>
> I also needed, and would have found helpful, much more in the way of real world examples of the usefulness of what was described. Why is it important to know about waves? What difference does it make? At the end of his first lecture, Abella pointed out that two waves can interfere in time and he demonstrated the effect. He then said that this was a way of measuring unknown frequencies. If we have one that we know and one from a distant galaxy, then we can determine the distance of that galaxy. This could have been said earlier as an example of a potential usefulness of a known frequency and then repeated at the appropriate time.
>
> All this takes time and you may have to decide to cover less in each lecture and in each course. But complete coverage, with liberal arts students, may not be as important, in any case, as understanding. And to achieve understanding students need time, time to think about the ideas during the lecture itself. We got this kind of time when

one of our number asked a question. But if class size is large and if the students aren't brave enough to ask a question, then things just go on and on without a break. I noted, several times, how glad I was that one of us asked a question.

So, what did we learn from this experiment? First, that it is unusually rich in outcome, easy to mount, inexpensive to run, and, for participants on both sides of the lecture podium, fun. Second, that while it would be foolhardy to claim that sophisticated teachers of the arts, the humanities, law, and theology are exact replicas of liberal arts undergraduates, they *resemble* them in ways that reflect real differences in style and course expectations from those of students who feel more comfortable in mathematics and science.

With more time for deeper immersion in the various units of a physics course (proposed in an experiment to be conducted by professor Richard Hake and myself at the University of Indiana in the fall of 1986), our nonscience colleagues might have been able to articulate more specifically their substantive misunderstandings. But one overall complaint needs to be heeded even on the basis of just this one experiment:

> I had no sense that the lecturers had themselves any sense of the kind of misunderstandings that were going on. I think they need to pay less attention to their derivations and demonstrations and more attention to their students.

Without the insight and continuing feedback from those who might critique their courses, lecturers in science cannot improve their wares. Those students for whom the material doesn't make sense simply disappear from the rolls. They either fail or take the first opportunity to drop out. Thus, the typical science instructor does not have access to the very special problems that they experience; he just never finds out what went wrong. From colleagues, alike in every way except for their newness to the field, he can learn more precisely what facilitates understanding and what makes his subject hard.

Most importantly, the feedback from "Peer Perspectives" will permit what is so often lacking in science courses: the means by which the courses might self-correct.

July/August 1986

A Group Portrait

Kenneth E. Eble

. . . [R]eading the dossiers submitted to AAHE by presidents in support of faculty who are "making a difference" was not such a chore as it might seem. For these dossiers identify the faculty members helping to make their colleges or universities more than just collections of privately striving individuals working in widely separated departments. These individuals are, in Russell Edgerton's words, "committed, courageous, and creative members who inspire and serve the entire campus community."

These dossiers are revealing not only of individuals but also of the variety of institutions that comprise higher education. The institutions represent the full range from community colleges to major research universities, some known to everyone, others scarcely recognized outside their own localities. . . .

The dossiers submitted to AAHE give me some contrary hopes. I am cheered by the fact that the faculty selected are such a diverse lot and that they manifest excellence in such diverse ways. Their individual achievements are very often connected with special services to students or the curriculum, or to the community outside. They are effective leaders and innovators. Trying to identify the qualities they have in *common* has been a demanding and rewarding task.

What are these qualities? First, most of these leaders, as might be expected, have been at their institutions a long time and have neither worn out their welcome nor been worn out by it. . . .

All the dossiers are heavy with recordable achievements—papers delivered, consulting engaged in, work published, committees served on, conventions attended, offices held—the lists impress even the reader familiar with successful academic careers. Clearly, these outstanding citizens are outstanding even in view of the many expectations commonly placed upon college and university professors. . . .

Among those who began by doing and continue to do extensive scholarship, I think there is some shifting away in their later years from the highly specialized articles that appear in disciplinary journals. One nominee in the sciences developed what was virtually a second career as his interest in teaching led him to develop, from Piaget's insights, better methods of teaching science. . . . While being someone who "makes a difference" on a given campus does not exclude those who publish well and often, it includes many whose talents and energies do not find their principal outlets in published scholarship.

Second, for all those represented in this sampling, undergraduate teaching is not something disavowed or put behind them. Despite their senior positions and their academic distinctions, these professors are still heavily committed to undergraduate education. . . . These professors, even in the sciences, seem to be little inclined to limit their efforts to the bright students or even to students in their own disciplines. "Outreach" characterizes the activities of almost every nominee. They fit the description provided of one professor who "made a difference through educational service, fulfilling a crucial biblical and economic challenge: 'To feed the hungry.' "

These professors are heavily involved in assisting student learning in various ways: setting up tutorials and other means for students to get extra help, establishing in-service programs for teaching assistants, working in various kinds of mentoring programs, and being leaders in many kinds of educational innovations. About half have received awards for teaching excellence. Students, who furnished letters of support for most nominees, speak of personal attention given freely, of inspiration, even to the nearly impossible level described by one former student of "causing one to be simulta-

neously humble, inspired and resolved to do and be better."

A third common characteristic is that all are vital, active, energetic professors. "Dedicated" is an abused word, but it appears frequently in these dossiers and carriers more than common conviction. It is not a kind of hollow respect for their teaching these individuals are receiving, simply because that is the best that can be said of them. Their dedication to teaching has not kept them from gaining grants, starting new programs, winning fellowships, writing articles and books, and working with many groups inside and outside their disciplines. It probably can be inferred that the cost of their dedication is having to work hard and at a number of different commitments.

Fourth, these professors tend to be activists, seeing education in wider social contexts. They all are important in "shaping the social conscience and the very image of the university," to quote from a specific dossier. "Vision" is a word often attached to them, "a rare ability to look beyond the parochial and the present." . . .

Fifth, within the university, these individuals have been particularly successful at gaining commitment to their enterprises from other faculty. Many have been leaders in establishing or maintaining liberal or general education programs, or in gaining faculty cooperation for other important purposes. . . .

Sixth, these individuals have obviously found ways of working successfully with colleagues, both administrators and faculty. . . .

The strength of American higher education lies as much in the diversity and quality of its many post-secondary institutions as in the achievements of its great universities. And the strength of these diverse institutions owes much to the presence in some numbers of individual faculty who can be identified as responsible leaders and citizens. Ernest Boyer has identified them as "distinguished faculty who contribute to the quality of campus life beyond the lecture halls and labs." The measure of a college or university does not reside solely in degrees awarded and the magnitude of the research program or even in the reputation of its faculty. An equally important measure is the presence of numbers of faculty leaders who are perceived as "making a difference."

Thirty Years of Stories

The Professor's Place in Student Memories

Barbara Harrell Carson

Here Is A Memory:

"I remember especially one night—after 10 p.m.—working with my lab partner on a particularly involved experiment. We had run the experiment several times and were not getting good results. [The professor] suddenly appeared and himself stayed with us, teaching every step through until we understood what had been going wrong. That was one of the most important memories I have of this devoted teacher." (1966 graduate)

And Here's Another:

"I especially remember [one professor], who taught using notecards for his lecture notes. He'd say things like 'When I taught this poem in 1958, I thought it was too sentimental, but in 1960 I began to see how the poet was using that sentimentality for the purpose of. . . .' Sometimes he'd tell us three or four past opinions of a piece. That made it okay for us to disagree with him, even to dislike a poem he especially liked! If he could disagree with himself, then we didn't have to slavishly agree with his opinion of the year! But his general passion for his subject was contagious." (1964 graduate) . . .

What astonishes me about these vivid and specific narratives is that they were written from 29 to 31 years after the students left the college classroom. They came my way in response to a letter I sent to graduates of Rollins College asking for stories about their most effective professors. . . .

In their love of what they're teaching, successful professors turn passive students into academic activists. . . .

While they consider a professor's communication of his or her love of the subject matter one of the most important catalysts for their own involvement in the subject matter, graduates looking back on their college careers are also aware that this quality alone does not produce effective teachers. Illustrat-ing this, one alum spoke of a professor who "loved his topic and had been teaching it for ages. But he loved his topic too much and got caught up in [it], rather than noticing whether anyone was learning anything or gaining his love of the topic." What such a response illuminates is the second major characteristic of effective teachers: they unite love of subject with a deep concern for, and connection with, their students.

Indeed, the single quality the Rollins alumni most frequently associated with effective teachers—more often than brilliance and love of subject and even more often than enthusiasm in the classroom—was a special attitude toward and relationship with students. (Richard Light's recent studies in the Harvard Assessment Seminars underscores the typicality of the Rollins responses.) The message these professors gave to their students was, first of all, that they cared about them. While expressions of that caring took many forms, the constant behind the variety was the students' sense of specific, personal attention. Sometimes simple, attentive listening was enough to earn a professor's place in a student's memory. . . .

A more academic expression of her teacher's caring about her came from the student who remembered: "As a final project, I wrote a daily journal about my ideas on the [material] we were studying. When I received my journal from [the professor], instead of finding only a grade, I found as [many] written comments as I wrote. She read every sentence and it made the difference. At the next semester, I declared my major [in her field]."

For another student, evidence of the professor's caring came when he helped her salvage an apparently doomed senior independent study: "Part of my agreement with [the professor] was to write a research paper. Thousands of index cards (with, frankly, a lot of information I did not understand) accumulated and still the paper did not 'come.' Panic set in. . . . The semester was nearly over—the registrar waited. [The professor] convinced the librarian to allow the microfiche (a new research tool) to go to his office . . . and there, together, we talked through the paper and slowly it fell together. He even went and got deli food. Hours passed, midnight came and went. I got done—I think I even got a B."

That deli supper connects with many memories in these narratives of students and professors eating together—a frequently cited indicator of professors' caring and a vivid reminder of the psychology and symbolism of sharing food. Twenty or 30 years later, former students still recall spaghetti dinners and barbecues, class breakfasts and holiday meals at professors' homes. The connection between such encounters and their classroom performance wasn't lost on the graduates: an informal conversation at a professor's open house made it easier, one student wrote, to "see [my professor] as a person rather than a lecturer and also [made me] feel like she appreciated my opinions and insights. It made me, a relatively introverted person, feel more comfortable in expressing myself in the classroom. Although these classes were not my best as far as grades go, I learned a lot and remember a lot of what I learned nine years later."

Surprisingly, the single most frequently cited evidence of a professor's caring also seems the most mundane: accessibility. Most treasured of all were professors who backed up stated open-door policies with smiles that were genuinely welcoming rather than with perfunctory greetings, professors who "really enjoyed being with the students—in or out of class"; professors who "never made you feel like you were a bother"; professors who didn't think they were "above having an intellectual conversation with [students] even though [their] education and experience were obviously vastly superior."

For many, the availability that was remembered with gratitude took very practical forms: a phone number for students to use when a computer problem cropped up; the possibility of evening conferences; advising sessions for students considering graduate school. Thinking back to a professor who had accommodated her special need for late conference hours, one alum explained the connection between her professor's accessibility and her own classroom performance—and what she emphasized was not what she learned in those extra conferences concerning the subject matter. Instead,

she remembered, "it motivated me to perform well in his classes."

The depth of feeling accompanying descriptions of such out-of-class encounters initially seems disproportionate to the professor's actions. ("I shall never forget them," one alum wrote of two faculty members who counseled him about graduate school.) However, as the former students said again and again in various ways, they saw such occasions not just as a reflection of their teachers' geniality or as a source of practical help, but as signals of their own worthiness. People they respected considered them important enough to invite them to their homes, to discuss their future with them, and to devote extra time to them. What a powerful message for people just leaving behind the teen years, with all their accompanying doubts about self!

Other respondents read an acknowledgment of their individual worth into their professors' recognizing them and remembering their names. "He has an incredible memory for names, faces, and facts," one graduate recalled. "My first class with him . . . had about 60 students. We did not sit alphabetically. By our second class he was calling us by name. It showed me he really wanted to get to know all of us personally, not just lecture. The class was at Tuesday/Thursday 9:30. I missed a few Thursday classes and he noticed. He pulled me aside one day and said I was spending too much time at Rosie O'Grady's Wednesday night [for] nickel beer. It made a big impression on me that he 1) knew I was missing and 2) cared enough to say something. I straightened up pretty fast. . . ."

The link between a professor's expression of personal interest and a student's learning, intimated in these stories, becomes even clearer in stories the alums tell of events that I think can best be described as a personal "tapping" (to borrow a term from the selection process of fraternities and sororities). These are incidents in which the professor acknowledges the student's academic or intellectual potency and—sometimes overtly, sometimes implicitly—invites the student into active participation in the scholarly community or into a specific academic discipline. The professor's ability to see personal worth and academic ability—unrecognized by the students themselves—has transformative power. Students change majors; they grow in self-respect; they start working harder—or more effectively; and, even years later, remembering their professor's confidence in them, they see both their past and their future in a new light. . . .

. . . I have come, in fact, to believe that this "tapping" may be the single most influential act a professor can perform.

As the graduates' stories make clear, the invitation to become active in the academy can take many forms. . . .

. . . Another remembered: "One day, he called me into his office. . . . He told me that he liked the way I expressed myself. This was the first time a teacher had applauded me. I switched my major [into his field] immediately."

From the vantage point given by the passing years, many of the Rollins graduates have come to realize that one of the most telling signals of their professors' respectful caring lay in challenging them to higher levels of achievement than they had thought possible. . . .

As one former student observed, his professor's "ability to demand the best from students—not just let them slide through . . ." was an expression of "respect . . . for the student as a person questing for knowledge." Students responded with a caring of their own—a determination not to let their professors down: "He cared about me as a person, and as a student. I knew he wanted me to do my best, and so I did."

Sometimes that challenge to greater achievement came from a professor who cared enough to criticize. An editor of the campus newspaper in the 1970s recalled turning the paper into a highly successful "social rag"—students were reading it; advertising was selling; the paper even became financially self-supporting. Smug in that accomplishment, the student editor was surprised when a professor "challenged me weekly to improve the content of the paper by examining issues surrounding the school. . . ."

Pondering his own experience with the power of professorial criticism to communicate respect for student potential, another graduate described a professor who "scoff[ed] at me for telling someone how to vote in the upcoming national election for which I had not registered. . . ." The incident, the alum conceded, was "relatively minor," but it indicated his professor's "willingness to call me on my 'stuff.' I guess the key is that this professor didn't just grade my classroom performance and

ignore [everything] else, but treated me as a fellow member of a larger community—a community that we could make better by explaining to each other our values and by living according to those values."

Such stories suggest an answer to those who object that interpersonal relationships may be very nice, but really have nothing to do with teaching. One graduate confronted this challenge directly. Realizing that she had spent all her time writing about the atmosphere her "warm . . . caring and giving" professor had created in class and the relationship he developed with students outside of class, she added in the margin: "I haven't said anything yet about his effectiveness as a teacher. Telling you the type of person he is [is] very important. Once you understand that, you'll know why sometimes I did my homework not because I wanted to, but because he seemed to care so much, and I didn't want to let him down." Another declared: " . . . you wanted to perform well because you didn't want to disappoint the professor; in fact, we were always raising the bar for ourselves."

Studies of the relationship between emotions and cognition explain in another way the link between how students feel about their professors and how they perform in the classroom. In an article published in *American Psychologist* in 1980, Robert Zajonc explains that it is likely that the very first stages of both learning and remembering what was learned are affective. "When we try to recall, recognize, or retrieve an episode, a person, a piece of music, a story, a name, in fact anything at all," Zajonc writes, "the affective quality of the original input is the first element to emerge." More recent research has revealed the physiological basis for the connection: when we respond to something with emotional intensity, stress hormones excite the part of the brain that transforms impressions or short-term memories into long-term memories. The greater the affective intensity, the easier both the original imprinting and the recall.

"Students learn what they care about . . . ," Stanford Ericksen has said, but Goethe knew something else: "In all things we learn only from those we love." Add to that Emerson's declaration: "The secret of education lies in respecting the pupil," and we have a formula something like this: "Students learn what they care about, from people they care about and who, they know, care about them"—a proposition underscored by the narratives of the Rollins graduates.

The third characteristic of effective teachers—their skill at and commitment to connecting their subject matter and their students—received less explicit treatment by the Rollins alums, perhaps because the most important path to that connection lies in the engagement stimulated by the professors' passion for their subjects and by their personal interest in their students. Still, the graduates were emphatic in identifying the instructional techniques distinguishing effective from ineffective teachers.

The two charges most often leveled against ineffective teachers were that their presentation and purpose were muddled and that they "taught straight from the book and didn't make you think." While effective professors linked students and subject matter in a variety of ways, their classes were marked by clarity and organization and by lively exchanges among professor and students. Most respondents agreed with the graduate who declared: "The better teachers seem to be 'great' moderators of conversational/discussion type classes. Often students have much to offer but are not encouraged to share that info."

In the best of such classes, the professor posed questions that lead the students far beyond recitation-level responses, and the class discussions included student exchanges with each other as well as with the professor. Remembering a sociology class like that, a 1984 graduate described herself as "enthralled: I had never encountered a professor who turned class discussion back to the student." These classes "made me think, examine my own predisposed opinions. A professor who can challenge a student on that level can make a permanent impact."

Another, who graduated two decades before, described "the best teacher I ever had at any level. ... He believed that teaching was best done by helping his students to think out answers for themselves rather than telling them what to think. He asked thought-provoking questions and refused to accept glib answers; those just made him ask follow-up questions until it was clear that the student was actively engaged in teaching himself/herself."

Twenty-nine years after graduation, a biology major recalled the "active process" characterizing his favorite classes: "I remember a class-long discussion in Botany, relating to the meaning of a weed." On a field trip with an entomology class, he remembered, "our job was to ask intelligent questions to the persons in charge of the facility. Boy, did I learn a lot, not just about the subject, but how to communicate and think more deeply."

The other strategy for connecting students with subject matter most often associated with effective teachers was their capacity to tell stories, to introduce real-life examples, to exemplify tough concepts with anecdotes and illustrations. The Rollins alums distinguished this practice from the storytelling of ineffective professors, like the one who "talked a lot about himself in ways that did not relate to the course"—a trait repeatedly associated with arrogance and narcissism. When they referred to their own lives, the great storytellers did it to illuminate their subject matter and to enrich the learning of their students.

Through their specific illustrations, effective professors helped students see the connection between "the world's details" and "the 'Big Picture.'" Believing that the lessons taught by their disciplines were "relevant and timeless," they led students to "apply the lessons learned to life. ..." Such concrete stories "made you think about your own future," one alum declared. ...

For me, these stories about effective teachers have been a cause for celebration. Seeing how many of my colleagues are esteemed by their students—and how intensely and for how many different reasons—has magnified my pride in this profession. ...

... This plentitude emphasizes that none of us has to be—or can be—*the* teacher for all students. Instructively, one student praised a professor for teaching her "to think more broadly" and another for teaching her "to focus."

In addition, I believe that this multiplicity provides another cause for celebration: it makes me suspect that there are strategies we can all develop to increase our effectiveness as teachers. I believe we can discover ways, consistent with our own personalities and philosophies, to communicate our love of our academic fields; we can all be attentive to our words and actions, so that our respect and concern for students is apparent; we can find strategies for signaling our temporal and intellectual availability. We can all show students that, though they don't yet know it, they *can* dance.

But while these stories were a cause of celebration—and challenge—for me, they also brought continuing puzzles. For example, given their emphasis on the personal relationship between professor and student, I'm troubled by the movement in education today toward teacher-free "learning environments." As I think over the richness of interactions reflected in these students' stories, I am also saddened that such descriptions may seen foreign to many faculty and students. That many will think this a romanticized, Mr. Chips version of education may, indeed, be a marker of the loss of the personal in education today. The seriousness of this loss is underscored by Richard Light's studies at Harvard, which conclude that a personal connection between teacher and student may, in fact, be the single most important avenue to student growth and to students' satisfaction with their education.

And, of course, I'm troubled by what has sometimes become the focus of academic assessment today. Recognizing the contribution of assessment at its best, I yet worry about the tendency to easy reductionism, to a quantification that cannot possibly capture the complex and ambiguous—but lasting—education reflected in these students' memories of their college experience. I worry that many—in the general public, in state legislatures, and within the academy—may confuse simplistic assessment outcomes with quality of teaching. I worry that we as professors may think that the students who make the C's in our courses carry little away, when actually, from their perspectives, their lives may have been changed.

Beyond any grade or simple test of outcome, these graduates remind me that the college experience has just as much to do with the larger lessons they described: lessons about the rewards of persistence, about their own competence and potential, about the joy of learning about life's complexity. I suspect that those lessons beyond the subject matter are inextricably tied to the hard work of learning the academic discipline itself. Perhaps, really, what effective professors provide in their very toughness are situations of disequilibrium, challenges to old ideas and old behaviors that, in the presence of encouragement and direction, nudge students into significant developmental changes. Maybe, in the end, that's what students are acknowledging when they remember these teachers as the ones who changed their lives.

Still, the mystery remains: what will this professor do that will make a difference to that student? The unpredictability of that exchange is enough to add piquancy to every encounter with a student. . . .

TEACHER NARRATIVES

Diane Gillespie

Scattered throughout the issues of *Change* are faculty members' reflections about teaching drawn from their own experiences with students. As a highly personal form of inquiry, a teaching narrative focuses on actions taken over time and their significance. In the process of telling a story, the narrator extracts certain elements from an experience and interprets them to render the experience meaningful. Narratives, then, are not theories, nor are they a collection of empirical facts about an event. They exist in what might be called an epistemological middle ground. The storyteller reaches down into the concrete particulars for evidence and then up into abstract ideas for insight and understanding. Good teaching stories are well-grounded, their meanings supportable.

Gregory Marshall's (1999) story is an excellent example. A crystal bowl sat on top of his bookcase to remind him of "an important truth" about his life as a teacher. In his essay he described how Sister Mary, a correspondence school student whom he never saw while teaching her, subsequently brought him this bowl in appreciation for his written instruction and encouragement. In the process of telling, he discovered new meanings about *functioning* as a teacher and how carrying out those functions brings him joy (p. 36). Ellen Cantarow's (1972) story tells about her experiences teaching a radical text that her students found boring and irrelevant. In reflecting on their reactions, she discovered her own limitations as a radical teacher: "I was responsible not simply for raising critical questions but for working with some of my students and with others on campus to build a viable student movement" (p. 61). The meanings of teaching stories often ripple out, extending far beyond the actual event toward broader understandings of the multiple contexts implicated in the story.

In dancing between the meanings of events and the stubborn facts of experience, good storytellers can make the ordinary come alive for perceiving and conceiving anew. The process is iterative: once a meaning arises, it calls forth fresh material from the situation; such material evokes yet other possible meanings. It is this continual recasting of experiences that makes narrative a highly imaginative act. Without stories, our theories become reified and stiff, and the concrete details of teaching life become uninteresting, even burdensome. Indeed, all of the pieces in this section underscore the necessity of narrative for imaginative reconsideration of one's practices in the classroom, for bringing the past into the present in a way that re-informs and uplifts ongoing practices. What changes in these stories over time are the cultural meanings of teaching.

Most teaching stories concern teachers' struggles to close the gap between their students and their subject matter that is embodied in the teacher. Cognitive psychologists tell us that complex information cannot be reduced through linear procedures, no matter how rigorous the logic in the reduction process. Rather, expert knowledge is holistic and schematized; often its organic complexity takes on aesthetic dimensions that become the source of one's love for, even passion about, one's subject matter. Such knowledge does not easily decompose into basic parts for novices to take in or memorize. Experts work with and through gestalts and metaphors, more like weavers than stonemasons. In contrast, novices see only the factual parts, the rudimentary outline, often in disfigured form. Socrates stands out as a pedagogical hero because he recognized the delicacy and skillfulness needed to close the gap. He, like other pedagogical humanists, reminded us that our actions have moral dimensions: a teacher cannot close the distance by force, through an authoritarian act, or settle for inaccurate representations. Students need to appropriate their own understandings and evaluate their new knowledge, even when they do not have all the pieces. Their impartial reconstructions, misunderstandings, evasions, and circumlocutions inevitably set teachers on edge.

The earliest stories in *Change* document teachers' struggles with the new democratic mandates to largely white, male-dominated, middle- to upper-class institutions of higher education. Ellen Cantarow (1972), Peter Elbow (1971), Robby Fried (1973), Leonard Kriegel (1972), and Michael Mahon (1971) all told stories about opening up their classrooms to students as partners in—as opposed to objects of—an educational enterprise. Holding fast to the integrity of their subject matter, they narrated stories of trying to get students to appropriate knowledge for themselves—to become active and engaged in the classroom. In all of these pieces, teachers were exploring how to break out of an authoritarian, hierarchical mode, one that glorified the subject matter but neglected students and pedagogy. Most of them were teaching students who were entering the academy for the first time.

In his story "Teaching: My Classes Tell Me," Elbow told how, in eschewing the authoritarian role, he put the onus for learning on students. Tough-minded (at times vitriolic) about his students, he aimed to make them author their own learning. "Behind my ostensible openness lies an intense demandingness. If I didn't really want to be demanding, I could teach the old 'well-run' course that students let roll off their backs so easily" (p. 33). Kriegel chronicled the growing distance between himself and his students at City University in the late 1960s as the student body dramatically changed with open admissions. He lamented the attempt of some of his colleagues to stuff this gap by holding, for example, classroom rap sessions. Such capitulation, he argued, resulted in the classroom becoming "a circus ring, its inhabitants untrained monkeys" (p. 15-16). Sympathetic to the egalitarian thrusts of the student movements, though, he re-evaluated academic traditions through the eyes of radicals "to create the new kind of intellectual relationships that were needed" (p. 16).

Mahon told the story of Cuddie, a student who confronted him about the authoritarianism implicit in his "open" discussions. Mahon invited him to teach the class; surprisingly, Cuddie did use highly imaginative exercises in an attempt to release his classmates' intuitive energy. Mahon's reflections reinforced the student-centered view characteristic of these early pieces. He argued that a true education "open[s] up the student and the teacher to a dynamic, imaginative perception of the world they so incredibly inhabit" (p. 50). Up against such ideals of teaching and learning that characterized the thrust toward democratizing educational institutions, Kriegel confessed, "A teacher . . . had to learn to function with a minimum of guilt" (p. 16).

These authors also look critically at the larger institutional and cultural contexts of their teaching. Fried argued that classroom troubles are but a part of larger institutional ailments: "From the fragmentation of student movements to the often vicious infighting of faculty in departments, a dismal picture takes shape: Everyone is working for his or her own salvation, and there doesn't seem to be enough salvation to go around" (p. 53). These essays pointed to "the nearly absolute isolation in which we all teach" (Cantarow, p. 58). Indeed, as these titles illustrated (Fried's was "One Teacher's Quest for Liberation"), the struggle was lonely and individualistic.

Whatever effects the various movements had on democratizing educational institutions for students, throughout the 1970s and 1980s teaching itself remained unequal to research in consideration as a worthy endeavor. A fairly private enterprise, unrewarded by most universities, teaching was devalued. No matter how hard teachers toiled to educate an increasingly diverse student body, if their enterprise itself was devalued, the claims that higher education could realize democratic ideals or even provide equal opportunity were illusory. Teaching itself had to become "a first among equals" before institutions could realize democratic educational practices.

In 1989, the American Association of Higher Education created, as part of its national conference, a forum on exemplary teaching honoring those teachers recognized by their institutions as embodying the ideals of Jaime Escalante. A group of teachers came together to participate in a "public" discussion about good teaching. Without a fixed agenda, many participants started telling their teaching stories, an experience that led me to write "Claiming Ourselves As Teachers." During this time, Parker Palmer was conducting conversations about teaching with faculty groups across the country. He saw in the powerful stories told by faculty the energy for a new movement that valued good teaching—a way to end the isolation. His 1992 essay "Divided No More" offered teachers a way of thinking about themselves as part of a larger movement that itself might be the basis for institutional reform.

These pieces about the power of narrative to transform teachers and to create a new culture of teaching were part of a national effort to reconsider teaching as scholarly endeavor, an effort that reached fruition in Ernest Boyer's (1990) policy recommendations in *Scholarship Reconsidered*. Once teaching came to be seen as "community property," to use Shulman's (1993) terms, and not private act, assessment flourished and the emphasis on teaching shifted to student learning. This recent attention to teaching and learning, however, did not—like the shift to student-centered teaching in the early 1970s—spawn the publication of teacher stories in *Change*. After all, our larger public culture requires even less from us now in the way of storytelling, and our academic communities are more transient, usually task-bound committees or afternoon workshops. Teaching itself is becoming more complex with demands to use new technologies.

More than these, narrative lives on the outskirts of teacher inquiry because it uncovers vulnerabilities and pain. Fried found it in the stories he told: "Pain. You can brush it away, bury it inside, tell yourself the world's corrupt. Or you can let yourself feel it, feel the pain, the disparity between what you are and what you want to be, as a teacher and a human being" (p. 52). "I was not a great teacher," Gregory confessed in his story about Sister Mary, "and my notions of 'literary and writing instruction' were pretty much canned stuff taken straight out of my college and grad school courses" (p. 36). Such disclosures do not fit easily into accounting systems that reward formal representations of ourselves. Perhaps it is not surprising that the majority of teaching stories told in *Change* were those of white male faculty members who might have felt less risk in exposing themselves than women and people of color for whom such vulnerability could have meant loss of safety in a system that historically deemed them unprepared for the rigors of academic life.

Invitingly, the types of rich documentation that have resulted from more public attention to teaching practices and student learning will continue to make us long for teaching stories from the broadest possible range of teachers. In "Can We Talk? Interracial Dialogue in the University Classroom," for example, Lawrence Blum (1998) chronicled his students' dialogues as they studied materials in a course entitled "Race and Racism." Reading his journal entries, which described in detail the development of his students' critical thinking, we cannot help but wonder about Blum as a teacher and how he used these journal entries to tell this as a story about his teaching.

When I wrote "Claiming Ourselves As Teachers," I was worried about the resilience of narrative as a mode of inquiry for university faculty. I am not worried now. Echoing the theme of Elbow's 1971 essay, Mark Weisberg (1999) discussed in "Discerning the Gift" his search "to consider abandoning the authoritarian methods [he] had been using" (p. 30). A law professor, he veered from the typical law school course and discovered "a voice and an authority [he] didn't know [he] had"—a voice and authority he wanted his students to discover in themselves, too (p. 30). He told the story of how teaching a new textbook "opened a door, and walking through that door led [him] to reimagine [himself] and what [he] was doing" (p. 31).

Such stories as the ones included here probably will remain outside of formal accounting systems because they keep the deeply personal alive in them and thereby in our midst. As Weisberg concluded, "Now I think of [stories] as the primary medium of education" (p. 37). If we are lucky, we will continue to have good teaching stories calling to us from the pages of *Change*. They make us mindful about our practice, attentive to our situations, and hopeful that our own stories will transfigure our teaching into more than it otherwise would have been.

References

Blum, L. (1998, November/December). Can we talk? Interracial dialogue in the university classroom. *Change, 30*, 27–35.

Boyer, E. L. (1990). *Scholarship reconsidered: Priorities of the professoriate.* Princeton, NJ: Carnegie Foundation for the Advancement of Teaching.

Cantarow, E. (1972, May). The radicalizing of a teacher of literature. *Change, 4*, 50–61.

Elbow, P. (1971, January/February). Teaching: My classes tell me. *Change, 3*, 28–33.

Fried, R. (1973, May). One teacher's quest for liberation. *Change, 5*, 48–53.

Gillespie, D. (1989, July/August). Claiming ourselves as teachers. *Change, 21*, 56–58.

Gregory, M. (1999, January/February). Teaching narrative: Correspondence school and Waterford crystal. *Change, 31*, 32–37.

Kriegel, L. (1972, Summer). Surviving the apocalyse: Teaching at City College. *Change, 4*, 54–62.

Mahon, C. M. (1971, October). Pala at Dominguez Hills. *Change, 3*, 45–50.

Palmer, P. J. (1992, March/April). Divided no more: A movement approach to educational reform. *Change, 24*, 10–17.

Shulman, L. L. (1993). Teaching as community property: Putting an end to pedagogical solitude. *Change, 25*, 6–7.

Weisberg, M. (1999, May/June). Discerning the gift. *Change, 31*, 29–37.

Teaching: My Classes Tell Me

Peter Elbow

. . . [T]he main thing I've come to believe through the exploration described here—and the main thing I wish to stress—is that better teaching behavior comes primarily from exploring one's *own* teaching from an experiential point of view: "What did I actually do? What was I actually experiencing when I did it? Can I say what feelings, ideas, or experiences led me to do it?" This approach leads to very different teaching behaviors for different people and even different teaching behaviors for the same person at different times. All these behaviors will indeed be "right," I would say, so long as they rest upon a symmetrical premise: an equal affirmation of the *student's* experience, his right to ground his behaviors in his experience, and thus his right, like the teacher's, to embark on his own voyage of change, development, and growth as to what is right for him:

> I am not in this world to live up to your expectations
> And you are not in this world to live up to mine. (Fritz Perls)

After five years of regular college teaching—trying to be Socrates and a good guy at the same time—and after three years of nonteaching while I was finishing my Ph.D. but thinking a lot about teaching, I reentered the classroom to discover an unexpected set of reactions. I found I couldn't stand to tell students things they hadn't asked me to tell them. I knew I knew things that were both true and important, but that only made me feel all the more gagged and mute. I even found I couldn't stand to ask questions—except the question, "What is your question?" Nothing seemed worth saying in a classroom till a student had a question he took seriously. I was no longer willing to listen to the thud of my question lying dead on the classroom floor. I refused to coax interest. I also felt it as a refusal to pedal alone. If they won't pedal, neither will I. No source of energy seemed bearable except their motivation. And not only motivation but experience. If they are not talking from the experience of the text read—even the

felt experience of getting nothing from the text—then count me out.

These were troublesome feelings. Giving in to them seemed to mean abdicating my role as a teacher. But they wouldn't go away and I was feeling ornery. So with respect to most of the leadership activities of teachers, I'd become by Christmas a kind of dropout, a conscientious objector, a giver-in to repugnance.

I'm prepared to consider the hypothesis that these feelings are some kind of pathology: some kind of petulant backlash at having finally submitted to graduate school, or some kind of atrophy of the deep sexual hunger to tell people things. But on the other hand, perhaps the real pathology is the hunger to tell people things they didn't ask you to tell them. If this turns out to be true, if unsolicited telling turns out to hinder rather than help our goal of producing knowledge and understanding in students, then we will have to be honest enough to set up arenas where teachers can work off this appetite.

Perhaps my metaphor is too unsavory. But not too sexual. One thing sure is that teaching is sexual. What is uncertain is which practices are natural and which unnatural, which fruitful and which barren, which legal and which illegal. When the sexuality of teaching is more generally felt and admitted, we may finally draw the obvious moral: it is a practice that should only be performed upon the persons of consenting adults.

But since I am not sure which is pathology—unsolicited telling or holding back—and since I don't yet know the grounds for deciding the question, I am merely asserting that it is possible to have these feelings, act on them, and live to tell the tale. Not go blind and insane. It is not a trivial point since so many teachers share these feelings but scarcely entertain them because they feel unspeakable.

My present introductory literature course is the latest product of these feelings. It is a sophomore course, but comparable to freshman English since it is more or less required and is the first English course taken. Most courses are structured around a class hour, a set of books, and a teacher's perception of the content. If a student's goals, perceptions, and motivation can fit into that structure, fine; if not, too bad. I have tried to stand that model on its head. The core of my course is each student's goals, perceptions, and willingness to do something about it. The other ingredients—the class hour and the teacher's perception of the content—are invited to fit into that structure if and where they can; and if not, too bad.

The course has three rules. (1) The student must state on paper, for everyone to read: at the beginning, what he wants to get out of the course; at mid-term and end of term, what he thinks he is getting and not getting. Each student may pursue his own goals; read anything and go in any direction. The only constraints are those imposed by reality. For example, I make it clear I am not going to spend any more time on the course than if I taught it in a conventional way. (2) Each student must read something each week: either literature or about literature. I offer my services in helping people find things suitable to their goals. (3) Each student must put words on paper in some manner once a week and put it in a box in the reserve reading room where everyone can read everyone else's and make comments. (There are about 20 in the class.) The writing need not be on what was read that week, though I ask the student to jot his reading down somewhere on the paper. Attendance is not required. Anyone who follows these rules is guaranteed an A. If not, he is not taking the course and I ask him to drop it or flunk it. (I try not to be coercively nondirective: if a student's goals are to read what the teacher thinks most suitable for an introductory course and to get out of it what the teacher thinks he ought to get out of it, I try to help him with these goals.) . . .

In the end, I am led back to a new perception of those original pesky feelings: something has been motivating me all along which only now comes to awareness. I sense differently now those refusals to tell things unsolicited, to ask questions, and to pedal alone. I feel them now as more positive. Behind the reticence and sense of being gagged lies a need to be genuinely listened to, to carry some weight, to make a dent. I want a chance for my words to penetrate to a level of serious consciousness. And that need is great enough that I'll pay a large price. I'll settle for very few words

indeed. Behind my ostensible openness lies an intense demandingness. If I didn't really want to be demanding, I could teach the old "well-run" course that students let roll off their backs so easily. It's my desire to be heard that makes me insist that the students figure out what they want to know.

I am like the teacher of the noisy class who says, ever so sweetly, "Now boys and girls, I'm not going to say another thing until you are quiet enough for me to be heard." (Stifled cheers!) But my intuition had enough sense to take things into its own hands and insist that I didn't have a chance of being heard until they made *more* noise. I think this is true even at the literal level. In my few good classes, I have to fight to be heard, but my words carry more real weight—the weight of a person and not just a teacher. If I want to be heard at all, I've got to set up a situation in which the options of whether to hear me or tune me out—whether to take me seriously or dismiss me—are more genuine than in a normal classroom field of force. I'm refusing, therefore, to be shortcircuited by a role which students react to with the stereotyped responses to authority: either automatic, ungenuine acceptance or else automatic, ungenuine refusal.

I don't know whether this underlying need to be truly heard is a good thing or a bad thing—whether the ineffectual part of my teaching comes from not fully inhabiting this basic feeling, or from not having gotten over it. I imagine two different answers from students. I imagine them saying,

Well it's about time you had the guts to feel and admit your mere humanity—your desire to get through and your need to make a difference. There's no hope for you as a teacher as long as you come on with this self-delusion about being disinterested, nondirective, and seeking only the student's own goals and motivation. In that stance, you can never succeed in being anything for us but cold, indifferent, and a waste of our time—ultimately enraging.

But I also hear them saying,

For Christ's sake, get off our back! We've got enough to think about without your personal need to make a dent on us. What do you think we are? Objects laid on to gratify your need to feel your life makes a difference?

My teaching has benefitted in the past from searching more deeply the feelings which generate it. So I trust this new clarification of feeling must be progress, even if I don't yet know what to think of it.

October 1971

Pala at Dominguez Hills

C. Michael Mahon

Aldous Huxley's imagination, laboring against the fact of cancer, created in his last days a utopian island called Pala. Pala's inhabitants are freed from mind-forged manacles through a liberating education. Though the regents of this world eventually destroy the island, "the fact of enlightenment remained."

"You're probably the best authoritarian teacher I've ever had." This from Cuddie, a bearded, barefoot freshman, English 102, Intro. to Lit. He's bright and likable.

As we walk out of class, I beg his pardon and ask him to repeat. "I said, you're probably the best authoritarian teacher I've ever had."

A forced smile. While my spirit groans with pique, ego desecration and interest, I compassionately ask him to explain.

He explains. I *do* have much class discussion. I seemingly conduct an "open" classroom but, *merde*, I always neatly lead the students to a definite conclusion as the period ends. Did Beethoven actually write his string quartets to fit one or two sides of a shellacked disc?

"You think and we think we're thinking, but you're programming us. It's a lot more fun than a lecture, you're a nice guy, we often feel good; but, all the same, very little *real* learning is going on."

I'm irritated and interested because I know he's right. It's always been that way. I don't lecture because, one (a rationalization) — it's against my pedagogical philosophy; and two (the truth) — temperamentally I like to look at and listen to students, occasionally even listen *to* them and approve with winsome smiles their clicking into my superior sensibility.

Despite $3 in my wallet until the next paycheck three long days ahead (I *am* a typical Capricorn), I treat Cuddie to coffee and an egg salad sandwich, then listen to his munchings, animadversions and suggestions. To my surprise, he has it all neatly figured out. Condensed version:

"For one thing, you constantly ask 'Please explain that' or 'What do you mean?' Never ask a student to explain himself, at least not in the early stages of investigation. You'll shatter his preverbal, intuitive understanding, unless he already knows how to play the English major game. And then he'll probably only return to you what you want to hear. If you must ask questions, ask *dumb questions*. Also, you as teacher should disappear as much as possible in the classroom. Sit with the students. Have a student lead the discussion. If there's factual information which can't emerge out of the discussion then do it straight on — lecture. Then disappear."

All right, all this sounds fine, I've heard it dozens of times before, and, honestly, I thought that I was occasionally doing it. So I challenge him to lead a class. Show me, flower child, show me. And, by the way, have you ever done this before?

It seems he has. He's a member, a founding member, of some new quasi-religious, quasi-philosophical cult which turns out to be a not-too-clearly thought-out melange of cybernetics, Christ and Buddha, if that's possible. He's been using a method with initiates which he thinks defines Good Teaching.

He's delighted at the opportunity. No shyness here. Only he solemnly warns me that there's a risk: he may "take the class away from me." Not dispirited by this prospect, I graciously surrender Friday's class to him. We've been doing Ferlinghetti's *A Coney Island of the Mind*. He informs me that no preparation is necessary. Since inevitability, as Aristotle so cogently observes, is more dramatic than surprise, I'll confess he astonished me Friday. Though he failed to take the class away, he did blow my mind and forced me to think . . . even to write an article. Right on!

A good day for the Friday class. It is warm, sunny and smogless. The oil wells surrounding the campus, some satanically disguised as grasshoppers, pump away in a most lineal, logical, obedient manner, all bright and glittering in the clear air. The hour of eleven is always right: that gracious learning-teaching hour when breakfasts have been digested and just a slight edge of lunch hunger whets the students' minds to a fine pitch of receptivity. Cuddie has dressed up for class: he's wearing sandals. He sits calmly on a desk before the class, looking compassionately vacant. I sit in the back between Mary and Fred. Mary, a girl who has never spoken in class, but hands in sensitive papers whose endearing neologisms convince me that she writes them. Fred's a tanned, crewcut lad, usually saturnine and normally mildly stoned, one of the Silent Majority who secretly reads the *Free Press*, wonders what ever happened to Eugene McCarthy and will probably become, oh Lenny Bruce, a member of the Supreme Court.

As is his wont, Cuddie speaks quietly, a real cool McLuhanesque delivery. He first explains that with my permission we're going to play a game, that all are invited to play but no one need participate unless the spirit moves him.

"Is there any poem in *A Coney Island of the Mind* that you want to talk about?"

Not unexpectedly, silence—that obdurate classroom silence keelhauled by squeaking desks, rustling papers and scraping of boots, sandals and bare feet sliding along the floor. He waits. And waits. And waits. His benign, terminal expression does not change. I immediately sense he possesses that most rare and precious of teaching gifts—being able to endure silence without evoking tension, and that even rarer and more precious gift of not rushing in, in a mild panic, to fill the vacuum of silence. I sadly lack this gift. In this type of silence there is not the tension of apprehension but the tension of alert anticipation, in which the sense of mechanical time may reappear. (Bergson's definition of mechanical time = lapsed attention.) I squeak my desk, rustle papers and stretch my legs while Mary fingers her beads, and Fred groks upon the *ding and sig* of his right thumbnail. Finally—after ten seconds?—two minutes?—

throats are cleared and I hear scattered mumblings of "Poem 9" and "Poem 7."

"Let's turn to Poem 9." We turn.

"Would anyone like to read it aloud?"

Again, long silence. Unexpectedly, Mary begins.

> See
> > it was like this when
> > > we waltz into this place
> > a couple of Papish cats
> > > is doing an Aztec two-step
> And I says
> > Dad let's cut
> but then this dame
> > comes up behind me see
> > > and says
> > you and me could really exist
> Wow I says
> > Only the next day
> > she has bad teeth
> > > and really hates
> > > > poetry

Longish silence. Cuddie mildly requests another reading and without delay the class extrovert, a drama major, broadcasts the poem.

"Fine. Now we're not going to discuss this yet. I want you now to play a game with me. Don't get hassled if you can't do it; you may find that you'll want to join in as we go along.

"I want you to first wipe away any pictures in your mind. See in your mind a white, blank screen, alive and brightly white. Okay? Now throw onto this screen any image, I repeat *any* image, *any* picture which the poem evokes. I don't care how vague or clear it is, how related or unrelated to the poem it may seem to be. You may find it helpful to close your eyes but you don't have to. Just get an image there." Mary and I stare wide-eyed while Fred closes his eyes.

"Now, to the right of that picture, place any opaque container you wish to imagine. Take your time." We take our time. "Now take your image, place it inside the container and seal the container. Any problems?"

Some giggles. The class gusher, Sylvia, speaks up. "But how can I enclose my image in any *container*? It's boundless! It's infinite! It's —it's— LOVE!" She smiles maliciously.

Cuddie seems to be taking her objection seriously. "Sylvia, can you imagine the bathtub in your home?"

She pouts. She won't give in. "Yes, but the feeling is infinite!"

"But your bathtub isn't . . . or is it?"

"Yes, yes," she pants.

"Then I wouldn't want to take a bath with you," he mumbles. His Three Stooges sarcasm affronts Sylvia. "Well," she retorts, "I can't play this game."

"Cool, but just relax and maybe you'll want to join in later."

He looks away, his eyes moving slowly over the class, taking his time to regain the mood.

"Now you have your container with your image in it." (Both *yours* are lightly stressed.) "Now to the right of your container, picture a velvet black bag. Okay? Now place into the velvet black bag everything that you don't understand about the poem. Fine. Now tie a string tightly around the top of the bag, open your container again and place the bag inside the container along with your image. Shut it tight. Now just stare for awhile at your container which now holds your image and the black velvet bag." We stare.

"Now to the right of that container, imagine another just like it. To the left, imagine another just like it. So we now have three identical containers, each enclosing your image and bag. Let's try two more containers, one to the right and one to the left. We see, then, five containers all in a row."

He pauses and appears to be trying himself to see all five. Many smiles around the room but complete silence.

"Okay. Now push all five containers back into one container. There. Now in any manner you wish, reach out and pull that container within yourself so that all you have left is that blank white screen again. If you want to, sprinkle some magic water on it, reduce it to the size of a capsule and swallow it. However you do it, get that container off the screen and into yourself. Ingest it. Get it into your bloodstream."

In the silence I hear gulpings. I myself feel a peculiar internal reaction.

"Let's relax a moment." For a moment, papers, feet, desks, pencils clamor to life, then subside back into silence.

"Would anyone volunteer to read the poem aloud again?" This time five or six hands shoot up. Francine, a black girl, a sad, beat, black girl who never speaks up, reads the poem badly and beautifully.

"Now I want you to tell me about your image."

Words in the air. From all over the classroom the static of voices. What I hear are highly personalized interpretations, interpretations which gravitate around my interpretation but highly charged and colored by the student's own life.

Francine, with nervous giggles, almost breaks down into euphoric laughter. "I saw a white man waking up with a black chick and discovering that his romantic ideas about us, about her, aren't . . . well . . . what he thought they'd be. Only I feel sorry for the black girl because he wanted her to be something different from what she was. He shouldn't be disgusted. He should try to understand her." (Right, my categories: levels of reality, the imposition by force of one myth on another and, interestingly, perhaps a comment on some esthetic snobbery in the poem.)

Greg, the class intellectual, S.D.S., says, "I saw a vague Aztec relief in bright colors, a sort of handsome, stern Rouault-king face, confronting a white slave girl. Around them dance different races. The king is about to lead the slave girl to bed, but I know by the way his fingertips touch her shoulder that he'll be disgusted in the morning."

Caroline, fat, clever, braless, given to dresses that flaunt her obesity, says, "I saw only the vaguest patterns, crossing lines that intersected but did not touch. Right, Greg, like Mondrian."

Cuddie, sitting calmly on the top of a desk, simply nods his head as the responses grow. Students who seldom speak now speak out. The verbally smart, the assured, speak with greater clarity and spontaneity.

The bell rings. Suddenly the bell rings. I, too, caught up, want to have my academic way, to atone to the God of Precision for possible student lapses of sentimentality. I wave my hand. Cuddie cuts off the students.

"Yes, Mr. Mahon?"

"Look, Cuddie, I'm really impressed by much of what's been said"—damn that *much* qualification!—"but there are a couple of factual aspects of the poem not even mentioned which are pertinent. Why, for example, Papish cats and Aztec two-step? What does Papish mean and what's an Aztec two-step?"

Ah, hah! Only two students, to my disbelief,

know what "Papish" means and none knows "Aztec two-step."

"Do you think, Mr. Mahon, this knowledge is essential to understanding the poem?"

I see that I had thought it was essential but obviously not to an essential understanding. In my "discussion" of this poem, I would have begun investigation of these phrases before launching into an explication. "Well, they may not be essential, but they're decidedly pertinent and will aid us to reinforce our impressions."

"Good. Will you please tell us what they mean?" I do so. Papish = pejorative for Catholic. Aztec two step = "Montezuma's revenge" = diarrhea = the natural scatalogical revenge of a great, conquered culture on its "godly" Christian oppressors. And . . . Fred turns to me in his desk and says, "If you had told me this at the beginning of class, it would have been information. Now it's like talking to you over a cup of coffee. Since I've really experienced this poem, I can now take it and assimilate it into my own experience."

I want to continue with my incisive analysis, but Cuddie cuts me short. Students crowd around him to continue the discussion. I sit in the back of the room, impressed, elated, somewhat depressed, somewhat piqued.

"I cut you off because I saw that you were going to tie up the poem neatly in an academic ribbon. Because I did cut you off, students left the class still thinking and talking about it. They may be thinking about it for a long time. Leave it open-ended. Your facts were pertinent and helpful— but only *after* the experience of the poem. And, to answer your other question, this technique works beautifully with longer works. Try it with your next assignment, Lady Murasaki's *The Tale of Genji*. Yea, I know what I did today was a gimmick and you can't repeat it, but the principle behind the gimmick is valid for real teaching and learning. Also, the principle works well even in, and perhaps especially, with science. Take a formula or concept and instead of memorizing it, ingest it, *experience it*."

I did think out the principle and tried it on Murasaki's novel with some success mitigated by my old conditioning. Most teachers present novels first as structure, as form, whereas the teacher and most readers remember a novel as a series of images. I'm aware that I have to do most note reviewing on the formal aspects of a novel. In class this presentation of form appears as the teacher's spontaneous reaction to the work. It comes, of course, after the fact of experience. . . .

Cuddie's session emphasized the tenderness with which the teacher must treat the intuitive, nonverbal response. The teacher must also, at an appropriate point, guide the student to embody the response into words. This approach asks the teacher to let the experience bloom and radiate, cautions him not to violently force his concept upon the intuition of the student but rather let the student work out his own concept, for we best nurse our own children. At times, if the concept will not come or if the student simply does not see what lies before him, as in the fact of Shakespeare's punning in Sonnet 30, the teacher may be forced to intervene; but such intervention should be only a desperate measure. A classroom which creates the ambiance of welcoming and developing intuitive responses will provide the basis for true education . . . which is opening up the student and teacher to a dynamic, imaginative perception of the world they so incredibly inhabit.

Of a similar approach in *Island*, Huxley wrote:

What those children you saw here were being taught is a very simple technique—a technique that we'll develop later on into a method of liberation. Not complete liberation, of course. But half a loaf is a great deal better than no bread. This technique won't lead you to the discovery of your Buddha Nature, but it may help you to prepare for that discovery.

The Radicalizing of a Teacher of Literature

Ellen Cantarow

... Last year I taught a book that is relatively unknown by people in the field of literature; certainly it isn't one of those books you would consider "literary" in the usual sense of the term. This book is Bill Haywood's autobiography; I taught it in my English composition course at the University of Massachusetts, Boston, where the students are petty-bourgeois and working-class. Bill Haywood was the founder of the Industrial Workers of the World, sometimes known as the Wobblies. The IWW, active in America near the beginning of this century, galvanized the energies of thousands of workers. It represented the only *movement* I would consider revolutionary at that time. ...

My students' reactions to the book were mixed. Nearly all of them were shocked to learn that what their history books had told them about unions had simply ignored the struggles of the IWW. They were particularly surprised to find that Gompers, touted in their high-school textbooks as a great hero, had been instrumental in smearing the IWW and had worked in collusion with the government to help destroy the union. Again, nearly all the students were confused by the style of the book. A remark made in both of my classes was that the book didn't "seem like literature." I interpreted the remark to mean that the book didn't have a story line, and in particular didn't present a continuous record of individual development and self-involvement. But finding this out for sure was difficult, since it was nearly impossible for my students to discuss the book directly. I found that our discussions revolved around the questions raised by the book, but continually veered away from the book's specific content. Thus we spent several sessions in which some students heatedly debated the following questions: Should the miners own the mines? Should secretaries run offices? Should working people in general control and run their workplaces? What is the nature of work in the first place? Why is most work boring? What makes work different from your hobby? How could being on the job be like working at home on your hobby? I imagine it was

a feat in the first place to have raised the issue of workers' control and to have continued discussion of the issue over several class sessions. On the other hand, it was impossible to discuss the content of Haywood's descriptions of IWW struggles, of particular instances described in the book in which miners *had* attempted to control their workplaces. A simple explanation for my students' inability to talk about these things was that some of them simply didn't read much of the book. In conference with them I learned that many, in particular the women, had found the book boring. My private conclusion was that they found union struggles remote. Few of them had had any direct experience with unions. Those few whose parents belonged to unions said that their parents didn't attend union meetings. In the case of the women, I understood that union battles were even more abstract for them, the practice in unions being as sexist, and as exclusionary as in other American institutions. But then again I received a few really impassioned papers the sentiments of which could not have been feigned. One student, born in Lawrence, wanted to go back to that town to talk with old people who might have been involved in the great strike of 1912, in which Haywood was a leader.

I can draw few conclusions for certain from my experience in teaching Haywood's book, but one thing was sure: Haywood's politics made my students very nervous, and this was predictable, given the rampant anti-Communism of the neighborhoods in which they lived, the pervasiveness of cold-war ideas in their communities. The absence from the campus of radical activities that might arouse the sympathies of the mass of students and galvanize their energies ensured, moreover, that the Left would continue to be remote from their experience.

In general, life at U Mass Boston insistently raised the same questions. Was I a teacher of literature, or not? I a woman revolutionary socialist using literature as a means of groping through the paradoxes, compromises, and occasional exhilaration that constituted radical political work in the university? Was there, ideally, no split between being the one thing—"a teacher of literature"— and the other—"a woman revolutionary socialist"? I felt I should be able to say, "I teach literature because I am a socialist." But such an answer, though theoretically right, was too simple to describe the real circumstances. Again, what did political experience have to do with the experience of reading literature? I was unable fully to translate my own exhilaration about Bill Haywood's autobiography in a way that would make it meaningful for my students; indeed, in the absence of ongoing political work at U Mass there was no way to do that; the task could not be, and can never be, an individual one.

This last reflection raises an important problem—though many in the profession would consider it not a problem but a norm: that is, the nearly absolute isolation in which we all teach. In the English department at U Mass, team teaching by two of the junior faculty was attempted last year for the first time, and with success. But even in the atmosphere of a liberal department, it is hard to find that happy confluence of time, topic and well-matched people which is necessary for team teaching. For the structure of the prevailing situation—in which this is only an experiment— fosters professional individualism, competition, mutual distrust, isolation. . . .

Summer 1972

Teaching at City College
Surviving the Apocalypse

Leonard Kriegel

With a sense of impending apocalypse, I returned to the City College of New York in September 1969, after a sabbatical year abroad as a Fulbright lecturer at the University of Groningen in the Netherlands. . . . During the year when I was away, . . . letters from colleagues, along with the week-late copies of *The New York Times* which I religiously scanned, spoke of a rising tension between blacks and whites on campus. In April 1969, the tension exploded as black and Puerto Rican students barricaded themselves within the South Campus gates and renamed the college the University of Harlem. Stirred by the prospect of open racial warfare, the college administration closed the entire campus for two weeks. In the Netherlands, I felt as if I were in some surrealistic educationist's dream, as I sat before a television set in a small Dutch family hotel in the Hoge Veluwe, reading Thomas Pynchon's *V* while watching Finley Student Center burn.

When I first walked onto the campus the following September, I could still smell the tension in the air. The college paper portrayed a campus community that seemed on the verge of dissolving: "Badillo Declines Bid to Head the College"; "Urban, Ethnic Studies Dept. Created"; "College

Plans for Additional Facilities and Adoption of 3-Semester Year to Implement 'Open Admissions' Plan"; "Board Sets Guidelines on Campus Disruptions." There was an article in which the acting president of the college was quoted as telling the United States Senate Permanent Investigating Committee that student groups such as S.D.S. and the Du Bois Club were both "treasonous and anti-American." Interspersed were pieces on Open Admissions and its prospects for success, the growing drug problem on campus, the rising crime rate in the snack bar. I closed the paper and walked over to the South Campus cafeteria. New graffiti saluted me from the walls: "Big Pig is Watching as We Get High." Underneath, an ugly porcine face.

I didn't know what to expect when I first went to meet my classes. Perhaps I wanted to discover a "new breed" of students, purged of all destructive impulses by what everyone had begun to call "the events of last spring." But to hope for such a miracle was like believing that American problems could be solved by repeating pietistic formulas. All that I could bring myself to do was to try to redefine my own feelings about teaching at the City College. . . .

In 1969 it was obvious that City's spring explosion had crystallized several uncomfortable problems facing me and those who shared my politics. We were going to have to redefine our function; we were going to have to think about the kind of college we wanted and the kind of society that college reflected; above all, we were going to have to ask ourselves what prices had to be paid and who was going to be asked to pay them. During my first few weeks back, I spoke to many people with whom I had worked in the antiwar movement and in the faculty movement intended to redistribute administrative power at the college. Obviously, we had been unsuccessful. The war continued to rage in Vietnam and the acting president of the college was the conservative ex-chairman of the faculty senate. The faculty Left was scattered and disheartened, maintaining different points of view which seemed irreconcilable. Some dismissed all questions of class and maintained that skin color had become the true leaven of the harmonious university; others insisted that the college remain a school chiefly concerned with academic excellence (as if American universities had not long since taken leave of so narrow a view of academic goals—and for good reason). . . .

The task I faced in separating truth from rumor was formidable. Which professor, if any, had been knocked down in his classroom by a group of angry black and Puerto Rican students? A few colleagues admitted that they had been harassed in their offices or classrooms, but they inevitably sounded as if the fault was theirs. There were stories of classes conducted in homes or even in the venerable cloisters that Mr. Rockefeller had imported into Washington Heights' Fort Tryon Park. Paranoia had lunged to the surface. *They* had invaded our offices. Desks had been ransacked—it was difficult to discover anyone whose desk had been ransacked, but everyone knew someone in another department who, in turn, knew of a colleague whose desk had been ransacked—and notes destroyed. One colleague told me that his office had been left in seemingly meticulous condition after the strike had ended. "Except that they smashed the frame on the picture of my children on the desk. Then they burned the picture. I suppose it was intended to be symbolic. I think that was the only time I felt afraid". . . .

Students and faculty alike seemed to want little more than to put City College out of their minds, even in September. The sense of apocalypse soon gave way to a desire to get through the year. After

a week, no one expected a repetition of "events of last spring" yet few ventured opinions about the future.

In the college, as in the nation, we were in the process of drenching everything in the vat of the new Puritanism. Guilt was widespread, rampant, and indiscriminate. Never mind that the powers in this America still sent their sons and daughters to Harvard and Vassar and Yale rather than to City College. Never mind that institutions and their functions had relative merits and faults. Guilt was like margarine, a cheap substitute that looked like the real thing and could be spread over everyone's bread.

Radicalism became a question of how much virtue one could claim as he sought to keep from being "co-opted." (Not the least of our sins was our vocabulary.) No longer did there seem to be a faculty left at the college, not, at least, one that spoke out of any collective philosophical analysis. Perhaps this, too, was a greater reflection of American life than I was prepared to accept.

Educational experiment became its own justification. In a peculiar sense, no one on the faculty saw himself as primarily an intellectual. For the time being, intellect had to take second place to the task of restoring egos. Teaching seemed to have degenerated into a relentless pursuit of vindication. But the intellectual structure itself was being reduced to an amorphous state. A freewheeling cultural formlessness spread over the entire curriculum, able to promise everything because it did not have to deliver anything at all. The endless possibilities were a Chinese menu of intellectualism, created by changes in curriculum requirements adopted the year before.

As a profession, college teaching seemed to mock itself. During the winter of 1969–70, I was aware that most of my colleagues felt as I did: we were no longer sure of what we stood for or what we could achieve. So many of my friends at the college—in history, in physics, in English—had lost faith in the "relevance" of their disciplines, as if intellectualism had to be immediate or not exist at all. Talk about teaching became more abstract and theoretical as the mere attempt to hold the attention of a class became more difficult. Apparently no idea was too ludicrous to be incorporated into this self-mockery. If students weren't interested in physics anymore, then the fault lay not with the students or with the teaching but with the discipline. A way had to be found that would make physics more immediate, less difficult and, inevitably, more "relevant."

As our faith in what we had previously offered diminished, we now competed with our students to make a City College education more "relevant". . . . No demand, no slogan, no half-formed idea could be too far-fetched for consideration. But all discussion dissolved into political posturing. What Lukacs had written of Mann brought forth stifled yawns; spirits ran free only when the room echoed with the latest pronouncements of Jerry Rubin or whispers of immortality culled from the *Village Voice* or the revolutionary word from Eldridge Cleaver. In any case, why read *Dr. Faustus* when *Slaughterhouse Five* was so much more relevant? "Fascism is not *our* problem, Dr. Kriegel". . . .

Ultimately, I had to face the edges of my own mind threatening to burn out. When nothing could be held up as excessive, when everything could be reduced by one simple equation into an aspect of man's liberation, the classroom became a circus ring, its inhabitants untrained monkeys. A difficult time in which to be a teacher, an intellectual. Inevitably, one's memories were defensive. I could not deny that the record of intellectuals in our century left a great deal to be desired. Their ability to resist, as Orwell had so frequently reminded me, was not very great. And now there were different gods claiming different thrones. It was difficult to resist the temptations of "relevance," just as it had earlier been difficult to resist the temptations of one of those "smelly little orthodoxies" Orwell wrote about. "What shall we rap about today?" asked the young sociology instructor of his class, eyes vapid with anticipation, life kindled by that sea of faces before him, *his* students. . . .

By the fall 1970 semester, City College seemed to have weathered animosities and tensions for so long that they had become encrusted with age. The faculty had pulled up short, preparing itself for another holding action, one that might once again reveal how it could make itself useful.

As a teacher, as an intellectual, as a member of the college faculty, I was as glaring a series of contradictions as anyone else I knew. Although I believed in the necessity of new modes of education and experimentation in the classroom, I nonetheless found myself placing greater and greater reliance on the traditional cultural orientation to which I had been exposed as an undergraduate. It now had greater meaning for me than I had

been willing to grant in the past. I thought of myself as egalitarian, but I wanted to avoid the kind of faculty-student relationships which now patronized professors as the professors had once patronized students. I insisted on the educational rights of blacks, but I wanted assurance that the cost of that long-overdue equality would not be borne by those white students who needed "free" education and City College as much as blacks and Puerto Ricans did.

The problem that continued to disturb me was the question of my own ability to straddle radical and traditional education, to create the new kind of intellectual relationships that were needed. In part, I was not altogether convinced of their validity. I was not even certain about what was "new" in their offerings. Yet I eagerly accepted the opportunity to teach in an experimental program in humanistic studies when it was offered to me the following year. And I wanted to teach in the remedial programs that Open Admissions was to make necessary on a massive scale. The college's function was not to change, but the work it was being called upon to do had drastically changed. A teacher, it seemed, had to learn to function with a minimum of guilt. The younger people I met in the department seemed to me among the most hopeful signs of life I could observe at City. Many of them wanted to teach remedial writing and reading to our incoming students, not because of what the courses were but because of the necessity of behaving in a human manner. At the same time, a steady diet of such courses would be intolerable for most of them, as it would have been for me. . . .

By late 1970, there was a growing uneasiness about the future of college teaching as a meaningful profession. A faculty no longer capable of seeing its function was inevitably bound to be confused. The profession's loss of status corresponded to its loss of function, and this, in turn, reflected its growing lack of faith in the validity of intellect.

By late 1970, I felt less able to judge myself or my peers. I could only observe them, for their actions seemed as confused as my own. The more I saw of the college faculty, the more I realized that its problems could be found on almost any college campus in the country. At New Haven, at Berkeley, at Cambridge, men and women had decided to become teachers and scholars. Not, certainly, a momentous decision as the world measures such things. A profession, a way of working through, of existing in the world. They had not looked upon college teaching then as a form of self-abnegation, but somewhere along the line self-discipline had turned into self-abnegation. We all seemed to be beating our breasts over the blacks or the "hardhats" or the Middle Americans or any other abstraction close at hand.

By 1970, it was obvious that we needed to free ourselves from masochistic self-exploitation. We had come to the point where we were willing to consider any solution to America's educational ills, no matter how unrealistic it might sound; it was time now to take a step backward. Our indecisiveness had affected our students, too, just as their doubt and hesitation before the demands of intellect had been made our problem. Perhaps we were simply too tired by 1970. There had been too many crusades, too many demands, too much rhetoric, too many claims upon our allegiance. It was time to turn our attention once again to just what a college education was intended to do for the student. Perhaps it was time to look at our limitations, to scale down our conception of the academic landscape to where it served neither as

savior nor devil for this America. But we had to do this with the full awareness that our responsibilities were the responsibilities of democratic education, that they remained both intellectual and social. . . .

Whatever its faults and no matter how uncertain its prospects, City College seemed a natural part of the world again. And by September 1971, it was only part of New York, not all of it. I felt a fresh excitement about teaching, an excitement that focused on what was happening in the minds of my students. For one thing, despite the bulletin-board advertisements in the Finley Student Center offering term papers, students seemed to be reading once more. And learning seemed important again. Whether these were temporary signs or whether they signaled the beginning of different times was not clear. Perhaps it was no more than a brief reprieve from chaos or the hardening of political weariness into traditional American pragmatism. All I knew was that educating students was not only once again possible, it was once again central to my own life. It felt good to be a teacher. It hadn't felt as good for a long time.

One Teacher's Quest for Liberation

Robby Fried

. . . As teachers we face tough personal questions of commitment that have profound meaning in a human, ethical context: whether to work with our students, in every class, to reach mutual understanding about the learning goals and methods to be used; whether to raise at department meetings the really crucial issues about the learning and working environment we share; whether to work openly in support of a colleague who we feel is being treated badly by the institution—or whether, instead, to withdraw from these challenges and seek a comfortable identity as "good teacher," "fair grader" or "nice guy" and leave the rest up to "those who want to deal with all that political crap." Decisions on such questions say what kind of people we are.

However convenient it is to see others as the source of our predicament—apathetic students, conservative faculty, manipulating administrators or the philistines "out there" in society—our real sense of powerlessness comes from lack of vision. We cannot liberate ourselves because, frequently, we cannot *see* anything different. We know one way to teach a course, one way to advance ourselves professionally, one way to deal with situations that frustrate and confine us. Far from spurring us to try new approaches, our myopic condition consumes our energies in either trying to make unworkable methods work or in punishing (or consoling) ourselves for our poor performance.

Do these scenes seem familiar?

She sits in her office with a pile of term papers in front of her. The one in her hand is probably a forgery, but it would take considerable time and effort to prove it. Anyway she gave the final exam yesterday, the grades are due in forty-eight hours and most students have gone home for vacation. Still, she can't let cheating go unpunished, can she? Unless, of course, the student really *did* write that paper. . . .

His department voted to recommend John for promotion and tenure, but the dean has sent it back for "reconsideration," whatever that means. John had a talk with him two weeks ago. It was very cordial and gentlemanly. John mentioned his experimental sociology seminar; the dean had volunteered that "good teaching" was now being weighed "significantly" in all tenure decisions but lamented the lack of adequate measurements for teacher evaluation, and they left the matter at that. He then asked John how things were going on that research project they had talked about last year. John smiled, somewhat embarrassed, and said he'd been working on it (he really hadn't) but that it was slow going, what with the demands of his teaching schedule, and of course the new baby in the family.

The dean had nodded sympathetically but then said: "You know, John, how sad it is for some of these people with tenure who've done no really productive work in years. Someone once thought they were good teachers, but they just dried up." John wondered whether he had been told this because the dean was on his side or as a warning. He left the dean's office, ushered out with a firm handshake and an amusing anecdote. John was relieved that the dean hadn't said "no," yet he had felt slightly anesthetized by the whole encounter. And now that he thinks about it, John doesn't have the slightest idea *where* he stands. . . .

There is pain here, the pain of frustration, insecurity, paralysis. There is lack of essential human communication: the words she ought to share with her student, he with his dean, . . . somehow cannot be articulated. So each berates and consoles himself by turns.

There are moral issues involved that touch fundamental human chords within these people, but their situations compel them to treat these issues like tactical maneuvers: how to handle the student's paper, how to "psych out" the dean's true intentions. . . . When we allow ourselves to deal tactically with matters that vibrate genuinely within our moral core, we do some damage to ourselves.

Last, each of the . . . scenarios exposes the essential powerlessness of the people involved. There is nothing any of them can do about it! In the end, she will accept the student's paper, he his dean's decision, they their chairman's willfulness, because the alternatives seem exhausting, risky, futile.

Picture yourself in their place. There is nowhere to look for an answer, is there? No higher law of academic procedure, no all-seeing person to turn to. Nobody's going to bail you out because, after all, it was you who got yourself into this mess in the first place. Some teachers *don't* have a problem with plagiarism. Some teachers get their promotions. The chances are you tell yourself that you are to blame. You're no kid. You know the rules of the academic game. Are you asking for someone to stand there and hold your hand?

Pain. You can brush it away, bury it inside, tell yourself the world's corrupt. Or you can let yourself *feel it*, feel the pain, the disparity between what you are and what you want to be, as a teacher and a human being. Until the point comes when you find yourself saying: "There *must* be a better way of relating to my students, so that none feel it necessary to cheat to get through my course. . . . There *must* be a better way of pursuing my professional growth; there *must* be a better way of working things out with the members of my department. . . . There must be a better way, *because if there is not, it doesn't make sense for me to remain in the university!*"

It may be true that few people are either tough or lucky enough to resolve such dilemmas. Those who were drawn to the university in the first place may have real trouble finding jobs and ways of life that will prove more congenial and rewarding. And the knowledge that the work outside is no more hospitable reinforces our fears of confronting our situations. But I was lucky.

My crisis point came four years ago when, as an instructor who really loved teaching Freshman Comp, I found myself in a "Catch 22" situation. I was told that in order to remain in the English department, I would have to start working on a Ph.D. But once I got the degree, I would be "overqualified" for Freshman Comp.

This climaxed a period of intense frustration, during which I and other young instructors strug-gled against departmental priorities over which we had little influence. Much of that struggle was destructive. We sat around in our offices feeling angry, threatened, humiliated, powerless. We didn't face our dilemma squarely or develop strategies to protect our values and our jobs, but instead heaped sarcasm and scorn on senior professors who we felt were forcing their values on us.

Getting myself out of that paralysis was doubly difficult: I had to break out of the professional stranglehold and out of my own pessimism and cynicism as well. Almost by chance, I joined a group of faculty and students who were trying to develop an experimental college. Here were people who were not content to do their own thing in isolation but were ready to put their ideals into form and create an alternative environment for both faculty and students. And together we dreamed, conspired, hassled, sweated, fretted and fought our way into existence as an experimental program in basic education: in effect, an educational counterculture within the university.

This counterculture, while our program lasted, had for me all the attributes of freedom and incentive that my former situation had denied me: escape from the seniority system (I taught a seminar in Shakespeare, the subject of my master's thesis); freedom from being "owned" by any one department; tremendous opportunity for personal development through confronting genuine educational and political issues; and the rewards of working with students who were themselves free to determine their educational lives. The result was a liberation both personal and professional.

Students and faculty were available to one another when we needed help, encouragement, support and sometimes just a chance to relax and laugh at ourselves. I couldn't have made it alone, and I don't think most people could. That mutual support has grown into very warm friendships that have survived the demise of our experimental program and my own departure from the campus. But the experience has changed my life. Liberation, it turns out, is something you *can* take with you.

At the heart of what ails the university community is the great difficulty students and faculty have in collaborating among themselves. From the fragmentation of student movements to the often vicious infighting of faculty in departments, a dismal picture takes shape: everyone is working for his or her own salvation, and there doesn't seem to be enough salvation to go around.

Somewhere in our professional training they forgot to teach us the collaborative skills, the ones that allow us not only to compete or even coexist with our colleagues but to be creative with them. And we, in turn, urge students to broaden themselves cognitively—while we isolate them affectively—in pursuit of intellectual development.

But people just plain need each other, in education as in life. That need includes but goes beyond the availability of rational dialog and constructive criticism. Academic freedom has got to mean the freedom to involve, to affect, to influence each other in the crucial situations we face—not just the freedom to be left alone, however important that may be at times.

It is our isolation that must be overcome. Though for me the end of isolation and alienation was coincident with the creation of an experimental program, other teachers have begun liberating themselves by finding colleagues in their own departments or in other disciplines, with whom they have joined in creative, supportive association. Such relationships do not by themselves guarantee our liberation, but they are indispensable to it.

Once this "support level" exists in our personal and professional lives, we can move to confront our situations without constantly tripping over our anxieties. We can demand that academic freedom provide some cover for our searchings *within* the university, not just for those opinions which provoke attacks from without. Once we no longer have to swallow our frustration, anger or fear, we can cease blaming our students or making scapegoats of ourselves. We begin asking questions about everthing we do, and receive sympathy instead or sarcasm from our colleagues. We treat classroom "failures" not as confirmation of our inadequacy or our students' incompetence; they become the focus for self-examination and professional growth. And our educational "successes" prompt us to demand that all our teaching experiences be fulfilling.

What remains is to combine the truest educational philosophy we know with the people on our campuses we feel closest to, and work from there to improve our working-learning environment. We can focus on implementing a new major, or a reappraisal of the university itself. We can include students, other faculty, administrators and people from outside the campus in our efforts.

But it all begins with our ability to say where we stand educationally, and to work with others who share our vision. That's the hard part. Far easier, perhaps, to accept our respected identity as college professor, retreat into our disciplines and let the university take care of itself. There is plenty to keep us busy—classes to prepare, articles to write, committees to sit on, students to see. Far easier, perhaps; but then, liberation never is the easy choice.

July/August 1989

Claiming Ourselves as Teachers

Diane Gillespie

S trangers to each other, we sat around tables in small groups and self-consciously began speaking about our teaching. No one in my group had ever been called upon before to tell about himself or herself as a teacher. Embarrassed by the implication that we were "powerful teachers," and somewhat skeptical about our task, each of us began by telling a story about our teaching. During this exchange, the immediate circumstances of our coming together faded as we discovered personal meanings in each of our narratives.

The telling of the stories particularly caught my attention. I found myself transfixed by the storytellers' expressiveness. Each wanted to represent a student's experience, to recapture that student's struggle with a particular concept or assignment. We intended to tell a story about our students' transformations; yet, barely audible between the phrases and only momentarily visible on our faces, stories about our own development as teachers also emerged.

Lana, for example, told about the student who, after the first class meeting, felt insecure about her ability to complete the final class project. After thirty minutes of talk about the assignment, the student decided to stay in the class. Throughout the semester she sought Lana out to discuss her fear and uncertainty. "I was scared, too," Lana stated, "because I kept thinking about the possibility that she could fail, but I never let on, even though I constantly questioned myself." Throughout the semester, her interaction with the student exemplified what the authors of *Women's Ways of Knowing* identify as the confirmation-evocation-confirmation cycle in connected teaching: she encouraged her student and listened to her ideas, a process that created new responses and efforts from the student who stimulated Lana to respond in more complex ways.

In this case, the student completed her final project. Lana and her colleagues were so impressed that they submitted it to a national competition: it won a prize.

No one had asked Lana to tell this story before. In most faculty forums on university campuses such a story would have been dismissed by an oblique reference to its sentimentality. What goes on in one's classes is, really, a private matter; research and publication are the legitimate topics for public speech. If a professor wants or needs to talk about teaching, he or she can consult with the faculty development office—a place that further privatizes teaching. To talk publicly about one's teaching as if it were meaningful is to embarrass oneself; it's like discovering at a formal dinner that you're eating someone else's salad.

Such embarrassment characterized many of the early interchanges among the participants. Some felt suspicious about the purpose of a national forum that not only condoned but also welcomed public talk about teaching. "Something must be wrong here," one of the participants blurted out. Another proudly announced that he was chosen because his dean owed him a favor—no guilt by association there.

These attitudes may be related to the historical development of teaching as a private act. Teachers have been sequestered in their classrooms. As a result, they have found it difficult to find public forums where, in Madeleine Grumet's words, they could "serve the fruit of their inquiry to others." At universities, especially, legitimate "public" talk almost always concerns research—those are the stories worth telling.

Stories about teaching, in contrast, remain uncalled for and, when told, often seem illegitimate. Just as we have failed, as Grumet notes, to create "public" space to honor what would be the art of

teaching, so we lack language that would give us access to its forms.

Without telling her story to colleagues who can witness her instructional acts, Lana may not see her own transformation and growth. Interpreting the story as her sentimental attachment to a student's success negates her artistic performance. With this student, for example, she came to trust her own judgments and to manage a student's unease and insecurity. In *her* story she is learning as a teacher to create and sustain an attitude of benign firmness, a kind of holding pattern that teachers must sustain so students can experiment with new forms of behavior and paradigms of thought. One cannot take over the project; nor can one desert the student. The pressure is intense; as the student further invests her identity in the project, the instructor further invests her identity in the student's achievements.

Students succeeding against the odds often point to teachers such as Lana or Jaime Escalante, who take the time to "see" and "hold with" them; such students are often otherwise rendered invisible and voiceless in impersonal educational institutions. (Good teachers work hard. In our fatigue, who among us does not want to respond automatically to an insecure student—such as Lana's—by saying, "If you're not prepared to do the work, you're in the wrong class"?) The stories told in our small group focused initially on students who often had several strikes against them and who had been deemed the "wrong kind of students," in Lee Shulman's apt phrase at AAHE. I had expected to hear those stories; like Jaime Escalante's, they spilled out like jewels across our table.

I was unprepared, however, for what followed, the gradual discovery of our *own* stories, as university professors, told privately over the dinner table following the more formal meetings.

They were not traditional success stories. Even though each of us had gained considerable recognition for our teaching, we had often been made to feel fraudulent, even like "the wrong kind of faculty." One of the participants said that after he had won the outstanding teaching award at his university, another faculty member came up to him in the hall the next morning and pointed to a sentence in a book on teaching that read, "Popular teachers are never the truly great teachers."

As we probed more deeply our ambivalence

about being designated "good" teachers, our stories became more painful to tell.

Early in my career when I was a teaching assistant, for example, a dean tried to fire me for subversive classroom activity during the very week my fellow graduate students voted me the most outstanding teacher of composition. After awarding me all-university merit for outstanding teaching two years in a row, my then vice chancellor refused to give me tenure; instead, he found a loophole so that I could get a Ph.D. ("You see, Diane, you are the wrong kind of teacher without a Ph.D.," he stated. "But," I responded, "why the awards?" And I thought to myself, "What about this baby I'm seven months pregnant with?")

Into the evening, five of us told stories about the dark passages in our histories and our struggles to gain institutional legitimacy. Like our students, we had succeeded against the odds. But the telling unnerved us, caught us off guard. In a work environment that structurally prohibits certain narratives, all one can do is try to *pass* in public by telling the right kind of story. Minority psychologists have called this experience "dissembling." One acts "right" in public, "wrong" in private.

Perhaps in this dissembling (by both the institution and the teachers of "wrong" students) our experiences become relevant to other university faculty. In our stories of pedagogical disobedience (e.g., our willingness to teach the wrong students at the wrong place) lies an unspoken challenge for those who want to teach only the right kind of student in the right place.

Jerome Bruner describes a "canonical image of self-hood" as one produced by the institution (in this case the university) to ensure order, control, and (most important for university faculty) authority—a sense of rightness and propriety. "Once furnished with its canonical images and formulae for reckoning, (the academician) becomes a seasoned operator of the system and a seasoned deployer of self." Faculty learn early on how to institutionalize their story, to get it right, in their reappointment and tenure files and in their cases for merit.

But most faculty recognize at some deeper level that their vita is not their story and that the organizational structure against which they teach hears no stories—not about their teaching, not about their research, and not about their professional lives. In disillusion, many harken back to memories of what it must have been like when everything was right—the students, the faculty, and the place. I think about the professor who, over forty, still tells stories about his graduate school days at an ivy league school; like Allan Bloom, he was the right kind of student.

But the majority of faculty live uneasily with canonical images of self-hood, struggling privately against a public definition of the teaching self as marginal. "It is really my teaching that I want to remember," said a retiring business professor to me years ago in a private consultation about his teaching. "It's almost too late to recover that part of my life that I put on the back burner as I published for and served this university. I have two more semesters left. What can I do?" Much younger and unseasoned, I was stunned by his recognition of dissembling and frightened by the tears in his eyes. I had dismissed it then as the sentimental musings of a man about to retire. But his story haunted me as I returned from the AAHE conference. I finally realized that he had never had opportunities to tell his teaching stories, and thereby to renegotiate the meaning of his teaching and integrate his concrete experience into a teaching self.

In structuring the AAHE workshops on teaching around the concrete experiences of the faculty, the organizers helped us replicate that holding pattern Lana executed successfully with her student. They asked us to participate in a narrative mode and stood back while many of us wrestled with what sense we made of our teaching and our own history as teachers. Not all of us will win prizes as a result of that effort. At most, many of us will continue to renegotiate the meaning of our teaching, save our stories in their full detail, and encourage real talk about teaching among our colleagues.

As Bruner describes it, "What one seeks in story structure is precisely how plight, character, and consciousness are integrated." That kind of integration takes time, a sense of community, and public space, all of which may be unavailable to faculty working in increasingly bureaucratized schools. How, then, are teachers to claim their own experience? In what narrative forms and forums will their stories emerge?

Can We Talk?

Interracial Dialogue in the University Classroom

Lawrence Blum

In my experience, students of all races are hungering to be heard, to listen to others, and to have honest conversations about race and racism. I recently taught one course that brought out particularly clearly the challenges of teaching racially volatile material, of integrating personal experience and academic learning, and of negotiating the minefields of identity politics. It taught me the satisfactions of helping students cross racial barriers and of learning from one another.

The class—"Race and Racism"—met once a week. A master's-level course with a few doctoral students, it raised pedagogical issues similar to those I'd found teaching undergraduates. The class consisted of nine black students, of whom one was African (from Ethiopia), one Jamaican (but had spent most of her life in the United States), the rest African American; in addition, it included one Cuban American, one Filipino American, one Russian Jewish immigrant (seven years in this country), and one Japanese student who had only recently arrived in the United States. The remaining 13 students were white and non-Hispanic.

I addressed the issue of my own racial identity in the first class. I laid claim to being professionally competent in the area of "race studies" and affirmed that that field excluded members of no race. I was more qualified to teach the course than a black or Native American person who was not expert in that field, just as blacks or Native Americans who studied English history could teach that better than white Anglos untrained in that area.

At the same time, I said, race very much affected the quality of people's experience in our society, and that this experience would sometimes be relevant to the course. I acknowledged that there were forms of discrimination or devaluing that I as a white person would not have experienced, that we all needed to be willing to recognize these and other racially based experiential

differences and learn from them. People who did not have a certain experience could be helped by others to gain some understanding of what it was like to have it. The racial differences did not constitute insuperable barriers.

The first five weeks of the course explored the genesis of the idea of race. American slavery was non-racial in origin, and the choice of Africans (over Irish, Native Americans, or pauperized English persons) was based primarily on reasons of social control, agricultural skills, and economic benefit. However, once Africans had become the only slaves in the United States, a racial ideology that essentially created the very idea of "race" itself (in its American form) arose to rationalize it.

In addition, I emphasized that slavery had existed in virtually every society in the world, and that prior to the advent of New World slavery, slavery was not racial in nature. In small groups, the students discussed the question "How could Africans sell other Africans into slavery?" Some students already grasped that the idea of "Africa" as a politically and socially unified entity able to confer a morally meaningful identity did not exist in the 15th to 18th centuries; members of other tribes were not "fellow Africans" to the members of the tribes who captured and sold them to European slave traders. Some students do not like to focus on this question, since they want to see slavery as a uniquely American institution. (Some aspects of American slavery were indeed unique, but not the basic ownership of some human beings by others.)

About a third of the way through the course, I began to keep a diary of each class, in order to have a better record of student reactions. . . .

October 1 (Fifth Week of Class): Using Audrey Smedley's excellent synthesis, *Race in North America: Origin and Evolution of a Worldview* (Boulder, CO: Westview Press, 1993), I ended the historical portion of the course by discussing the way 19th-century natural science had attempted to legitimate the racial world view—alleging that human beings could be divided up into discrete groups, generally marked by certain sets of physical features (called "phenotypes"), and possessing distinct forms of human characteristics such as intelligence, industriousness, trustworthiness, and the like. We then discussed the almost total rejection by 20th-century social, behavioral, and biological sciences of "race" in anything like this sense.

The class reaction to scientific and philosophical arguments against "race" was instructive. For many students, the detailed rejection of the idea of race that forms so deep a part of the way we look at human beings was a revelation, or at least a firming up of directions their own thinking had been taking, and they embraced this view. There were racial differences, however, in the reaction to what we initially called the "no-race" view.

A few white students became so enamored of the intellectual and scientific rejection of "race" that they tended to lose sight of the social reality that blacks are still doing quite badly compared to whites, that blacks of all classes frequently suffer racial discrimination, racial insensitivity, and stereotyping, and that all endure a legacy of historical racism. For some of these white students, the "no-race" argument seemed to provide a way of thinking of themselves as being anti-racist, without either having to engage blacks on a personal level about their experiences or to come to grips with the actual plight of black people in our society.

Counterposed to this small group of white students was a small group of blacks who would not accept the argument against "race." It seemed to deny their own experience and the historical experience of peoples thought of as "black": "Of course there are races; I'm black and because of this I am treated as an inferior in this society, as blacks have always been. Blacks have very different experiences from whites. So how can there be no races?"

Yet several of the black students reacted entirely differently from both of these groups. They did not see the "no-race" view as denying the social and historical reality that particular groups—especially their own—have been treated very differently because of perceived differences in "race." (That is, *racism* can exist, even if there are no races.) What they did feel was that rejecting the *inherent* distinction between groups implied by the term "race" was liberating.

Two black students in particular, Ahmad and Randall (all names of students mentioned in this article are fictitious), brought to the surface the humanistic message underlying the no-race view—that human beings are akin to one another in ways that the notion of "race" denies. This message had gotten lost in my own presentation; in fact, I myself had become so focused on putting the argument against race on a firm *intellectual* foundation that I had lost sight of its moral and political significance. Randall, an idealistic member of the local police department, who struggled with the racism he saw in his fellow officers but was hopeful about racial progress, suggested that we change the name of the view to the "one-race (the human race)" view rather than the "no-race" view, to emphasize the common humanity revealed by the argument. . . .

As for my own closing thoughts, I wished I could have had another semester to continue the course. While I did not question the important task of integrating responsible academic learning with a venue for open interchange on charged racial topics, I wondered whether students were being provided with sufficient space in their lives—and particularly in other classes—for that interchange. A colleague suggested that too few courses at the institution provided space for the sort of conversations the course had allowed, so students tended to load expectations onto the racial dialogue aspect of this course at the expense of more traditional learning. If so, more teachers need to venture into the thicket of America's racial complexities within the framework of their various disciplines and courses.

Teaching Narrative

Correspondence School and Waterford Crystal

Marshall Gregory

As a teacher—and like every other teacher—I stand at the intersection of many more vectors, variables, forces, emotions, ideals, aspirations, and accidents than I can even track, much less control. The component of space and time I stand in now is only the forward crest of a wave that has been gradually shaped by a great many particular drops of experience, whose formative effects I was not vividly aware of at the time they happened.

Once I start thinking about it, however, I realize how different I am from the greener-than-grass, 27-year-old University of Chicago graduate student who, without five seconds' worth of teaching experience, suddenly found himself standing at 8 a.m. in front of a class of freshman writing students at the University of Wisconsin-Milwaukee—students who expected me to know something not only about reading and writing but about how to *teach* reading and writing.

It was a terrifying moment. Without even knowing how, I remember opening my mouth and beginning that mysterious projection of self, that ever-incomplete exploration of ideas, and that always uncertain social invitation to students—all very big-ticket items—that we somehow squeeze behind this small but significant word: "teaching."

As I look back on my teaching career, I am struck less by what I have (perhaps, perhaps not) learned about teaching problems or teaching principles than by the memory of student faces and student stories. My mind's eye brings to me students' faces like shadows from the dark: my mind's ear brings to me students' stories like voices from another world. I do not possess complete stories for all the students I have known. Constraints of time, inclination, and reticence have often blocked the stories, and with regard to some students, I possess only tantalizing but often sad and sometimes terrifying fragments. . . .

. . . [O]ne whose story has meant the most to me over the years is, curiously, a student whose face I saw only once. The relationship between me and Sister Mary Thecla is my favorite teaching story.

I first came into contact with Sister Mary while I was in graduate school at the University of Chicago. . . .

. . . I worked at high-paying, blue-collar, industrial jobs in the Chicago area during the summers—Youngstown Steel, Erie Lackawana Railroad, Rock Island Railroad, assorted construction jobs. During the school year, I taught school, which really meant only grading tests and essays, at the American Correspondence School (ACS), the world's largest correspondence school for high school students, located in Hyde Park right next to the University of Chicago.

Grading the essays and test papers of faceless high school students from around the world was not an ideal introduction to teaching. There was no eye contact, no body language, no questions and answers, no colleagues to consult, no talk in the hall, no consultations in the teacher's office. But I did write in the margins of my students' tests, and when they gave evidence of keen perception or good writing or intellectual aspiration, I tried to encourage their lonely dedication and isolated perseverance.

By far the most perceptive, eager, and thoughtful student I had was a young woman recently arrived in this country from Ireland—a nun. Sister Mary Thecla, assigned to a convent in White Springs, New York. Sister Mary was thrilled to be taking the high school survey course in American literature, and I was thrilled to have her as a student. She was fresh, intelligent, enthusiastic—nay, breathless—and I wrote notes of praise, encouragement, and literary and writing instruction in the margins of each of her tests and essays. On the last of her papers for the course, I attached a letter encouraging her to think about going to college and assuring her that she would certainly do well if she could only find a way to go.

I heard nothing from Sister Mary for several

weeks and did not expect to hear from her again at all. But finally I did hear, and in the unexpected form of a personal letter. The day my own letter to her had arrived, attached to her final exam, Sister Mary's mother superior had been inspecting the White Springs convent, and, somehow, Sister Mary found the courage not only to show mother superior my letter but to ask if she could—on the basis of my recommendation—be given permission to attend college. The mother superior said yes, and Sister Mary was writing to let me know that, wonder of wonders, she would be attending Loyola College in Chicago at the beginning of the fall term.

Since I left Chicago for the University of Wisconsin-Milwaukee a little before Sister Mary arrived, I never met her, but we did correspond—not frequently, but often enough to let me know that she was loving her work and doing well. As Sister Mary was approaching the end of her college career, however, I received a call from her one day: could she and a friend come by my house in Milwaukee next Sunday afternoon for an hour or so?

At the appointed time Sister Mary arrived, a smiling young woman with Ireland in her face. She said that she did not want to finish her college years without thanking me in person for writing the letter that had made all the difference in her life. She also said that she had a gift for me, at which point she pulled a beautiful, hand-cut, 1880s Waterford crystal bowl from her bag and presented it to me. The last time she had visited her parents in Dublin she had brought this bowl—a family heirloom—back with her. She had carried it in her lap to make sure that nothing happened to it while it crossed the Atlantic. Now she wanted me to have it as a remembrance of her affection and gratitude in return for my instruction and encouragement. In an hour she was gone.

Sister Mary and I continued to correspond once or twice a year after that for a few more years, but eventually she left her order, got married, moved to California, and had children, and our relationship died a quiet and I hope graceful death. I have not heard from her since, which is probably the right ending for this part of the story.

Having been grateful and having expressed her gratitude, Sister Mary was under no obligation to be grateful forever, and she and I never spent the kind or amount of time together that would have allowed us to become friends. I only met her on the one occasion when she came to Milwaukee. We were not friends; we were teacher and student, and, like most teacher/student relationships, it was quite appropriate for ours to end at that point in time when we had each played out our proper roles.

But surely the meaning of the story does not end with the relationship. Surely the story's larger meaning is not about Sister Mary and me as individuals but about teachers and students in general. I was not a great teacher. At the time I was correcting Sister Mary's high-school reading and writing, I had never taught a class in my life and my notions of "literary and writing instruction" were pretty much canned stuff taken straight out of my college and grad school courses.

The point to this story is that regardless of whether that person is greatly talented or not so talented, whether profoundly wise or not so wise, or whether deeply insightful or not so insightful, some things just cannot happen without a teacher being on the spot and acting like a teacher, doing the things that teachers do, and relating to students as only teachers can. The point to the story, in other words, is not about the *quality* of my teaching but about my *functioning* as a teacher.

With Sister Mary, I was simply performing the functions that teachers typically perform: encouraging, advising, instructing, "bringing along." You don't have to be the smartest person in the world to perform these functions, although intelligence is always an advantage; nor do you have to have every feature of your own life perfectly in order. But you do have to be observant of the student as a student, not so absorbed in your own disorders that you cannot see the other as represented in your students.

I take comfort from my Sister Mary story, not merely because Sister Mary honored me with her respect and gratitude, but because the story suggests to me that the career I have chosen and to which I have now devoted many years is one that can make a positive difference, not only in individual students' lives but also—indirectly and at a distance, to be sure (which is quite good enough to satisfy me)—for society as a whole.

My own ethic of personal duty tells me that I have three jobs to accomplish in this world. The first is to grow and develop, to attempt to make the most out of the gifts, talents, and opportunities that have been given to me. My second job is to make some kind of positive contribution to the world: to do *something* to make the world more sensible or more peaceful or more civil or more intelligent, or at least to help the people I come in contact with live lives of greater productivity, charity, and effectiveness. It is not my job to do this in some grand way, by affecting the lives of thousands or by leading the masses, but merely to make my contribution as I can and when I can.

My third duty is to enjoy performing the first two duties: to derive joy from tending to my own growth and development and from making my own contribution to the world. I cannot do any of my jobs properly if I am sour, bitter, grim, beleaguered, or persistently angry. Joy is not just the icing on life's cake; it's the yeast that transforms the flour and other ingredients into cake in the first place.

What I've found is that the various means by which I have tried to meet my ethic of responsibility get all entwined and connected. I have loved, for example, being a spouse and a parent. My wife and my children have taught me more about life and duty and responsibility — but most of all more about joy — than I could ever have learned on my own. In addition, I usually love being a home owner and a pet owner, and so on — but none of these, I find, is disconnected from my being a teacher, and my being a teacher is disconnected from none of these. "Spousing," parenting, teaching: these are all extensions of my duties to grow and develop, to make my contribution to the world, and to enjoy the life of performing the first two.

I can neither prescribe for others nor judge (most of the time) the choices that others make. I only know that I could not have grown and developed or made my contribution to the world as an insurance salesman or a stock broker (I hate trying to talk other people into buying things) or as a scientist (I am not good enough at math, although I am fascinated by astronomy and biology) or as a chef (not enough intellectual content), or as anything else besides a teacher.

The teaching life has been hard in many ways. It is, contrary to claims by the author of *Profscam*, both underpaid and overworked. It requires, like a lot of other professions, the greatest intensity of input during those years when many of its practitioners also need to devote great intensity to other endeavors like raising families; and the constant tightening of budgets and loss of public respect that have occurred simultaneously in the last 20 years or so create much anxiety and feelings of being underappreciated.

Yet, for me, the teaching life has been congenial to my tastes and talents. I am grateful to the profession that allows me to do things I have always loved doing — reading literature and talking with others about its beauty and significance — and that also allows me to grow, to develop, and to make my contribution to the world.

My contributions, like everyone else's, are more like investments than negative outlays. As Coleridge says in "Dejection: An Ode," "we receive but what we give." Sister Mary Thecla was every bit as important to me as I was to her. As a student, she helped me to do what as a teacher I needed to do, and as a teacher, I helped Sister Mary become what she needed to be.

More than other kinds of relationships, perhaps — such as ones based on getting people to do things they may not want to do, or, worse, things that may not be good for them — teaching offers a mutuality of tending, rewarding, and relating that moves in two directions at once: from the teacher to the student and back again. Thus, in addition to helping people get to places in the world they want to go to and helping them to do the things they want to do, teaching satisfies our deep craving for meaningful forms of social connection that are neither cynically exploitative nor personally intimate, but that nevertheless balance the personal with the professional and enrich the professional with the personal.

It is a way of life that is — at least most of the time — both civil and civilizing, a way of life that provides deep personal rewards and yet calls us out of ourselves toward important forms of service to and connection with others. Like any other mode of life, teaching can be abused or done poorly. There is no way of life that will protect us from the lapses of our own good will or the failures of our intelligence. But treated with respect for its power to shape and mold, and approached with the humility and modesty that such power requires, teaching can be a rich and rewarding life. Sister Mary's crystal bowl, refracting the light as it sits on top of one of my bookcases, reminds me of this important truth and helps make me content with the teaching life I have chosen.

Discerning the Gift

Mark Weisberg

That's what teaching should be about but isn't: discerning the gift. Too often, by contrast, the central activity of our discipline is judging. The major thing we have learned to do in life is to assign grades.
— Mary Rose O'Reilley, *The Peaceable Classroom*, (Boynton/Cook, 1993)

Twenty years ago, in June 1979, I was sitting in a large room in the Banff Centre awaiting the opening session of the inaugural Canadian Law Teachers' Clinic. Thirty law professors and six clinic faculty had gathered for a 10-day retreat to explore methods for improving teaching. I was there because after 10 years of teaching, I was feeling stale and was looking for new ideas.

None of us knew what to expect. We had been told that the 10 days would include demonstrations of teaching methods, small-group work, microteaching, and reflection. And we knew that the opening session would demonstrate the Socratic method. A colleague from another law school, an excellent practitioner of this method, would teach a case to us using it. As students, we would experience it firsthand and then could evaluate its strengths and weaknesses.

We had read the case the night before. Our colleague was introduced, and after a brief introduction to the case, he asked his first question. I thought I knew the answer; heart racing, I raised my hand.

I don't know why I raised my hand. In law school I had been mostly silent, afraid of being wrong and looking foolish. And that fear hadn't dissipated; I still felt it at conferences or during the question period after a visiting lecture or seminar. Yet here I was in a room with 35 colleagues, no less, with my hand in the air.

Our demonstrator recognized me, and I offered my answer. He countered with a question, deflecting me from my answer. I tried to explain. Another question. And another, pushing me further and further off the track I wanted to be on, the track I "knew" to be right. And by the end of

his 25-minute demonstration, it was clear I had been right. He ended where I had begun, although he never acknowledged that I had begun there.

I think even then I could empathize with him; after all, if someone was offering him the right answer in the first five minutes, what was he going to do in the remaining 20? But empathy wasn't my predominant feeling. I was angry; I had been manipulated, confused, made to look foolish. I had not been taken seriously.

After the demonstration, the clinic director invited our responses. Again I raised my hand, this time even more nervous. I described how I had felt when the demonstrator had not responded directly to my answer. That response generated an interesting discussion of the Socratic method and after the sessions, several positive comments by participants, thanking me for risking saying what they were feeling.

I felt affirmed, vindicated, even powerful. At the same time, I was horrified. I taught predominantly by the Socratic method. That demonstrator was me. And what I had felt in that room might be what many of my students felt in my classroom.

That day began my search for different approaches to teaching. It taught me what it could mean to put myself in someone else's shoes, how liberating that could be, and how much I could learn from doing it. And not just someone else's shoes; the experience of being a student again allowed me to revisit my own life as a law student who had felt voiceless and disempowered, and to discover a voice and an authority I didn't know I had.

That discovery encouraged me to consider abandoning the authoritarian methods I realized I had been using to mask deeper feelings of being inadequate and fraudulent. If I knew who I was, maybe I didn't have to work so hard to keep other people from finding out by confusing them about who they were and what they thought. And if I could discover a voice and an authority, maybe my students could, too.

Then, an opportunity. Returning from the clinic, I found in the mail a flyer from Little, Brown & Co. advertising several books and offering complimentary copies to law teachers. One of the books was *The Legal Imagination: Studies in the Nature of Legal Thought and Expression* by James Boyd White. The advertisement didn't indicate much about the book or the author, but it did say that as well as legal materials, the book contained fiction, poetry, and history. Curious, I ordered a copy.

Several weeks later, a thick yellow book arrived on my desk. Despite its unusual color (most law school book covers are black, dark blue, or maroon), the book had the format of a legal casebook: excerpts from "cases," followed by notes and questions designed to open lines of inquiry about the cases. But true to its color, the cases this book contained weren't judicial opinions; they were poems, short stories, excerpts from novels, historical documents.

These cases were grouped in chapters that purported to examine a lawyer's relationships to language and to people, to ask what it might mean to speak and think and act as a lawyer. And at the center of these chapters was a series of writing assignments, inviting students to explore differing dimensions of those questions. Typically they would ask the writer to describe a real or imagined experience (say, an occasion on which the law controlled what a speaker could say, or a time when the writer had judged someone, or a situation in which people had organized their social relations), and then to reflect on what it meant to have had that experience: what it suggested about legal language, about legal judgment, about legal rules, about the relationships between personal and professional lives.

This book appealed to me. I loved literature and always had enjoyed working with students on their writing. In fact, I had discovered I liked teaching in law school when I was offered a job teaching expository writing to first-year university students, and a co-teacher and I designed a writing course using fiction we wanted to read.

I decided to try using the book, and wrote a vague course proposal for an upper-year writing seminar based on it. The late 1970s/early 1980s was a boom period for new courses, and we didn't have any focused on writing, a skill everyone acknowledged all lawyers must possess. In that environment, the curriculum committee approved my proposal, and in 1981 I began teaching the seminar.

When I say a vague course proposal, that's what I mean. I knew I wanted people to write frequently, and I planned to respond regularly to what they wrote. I expected people stimulated by the readings to write interesting papers and make interesting conversation. I hoped to have fun, hoped that as my students had fun and wrote regularly, they would become better writers. But that was about it; I hadn't articulated more detailed objectives, hadn't developed a conception of how I wanted us to spend our classroom time, and I wasn't sure what people would learn. The clinic had disrupted my expectations, made me want to change, but I wasn't sure how or what to change.

And even if I had been able to know what I imagined for the class, the conception of teaching motivating my vision wouldn't have been the one from Mary Rose O'Reilley with which I began this article. I wasn't as interested in discerning each person's gift as I was in the more customary teacher's role of identifying the gifted.

The Legal Imagination changed that. The book and the course that took shape with it opened a door, and walking through that door led me to reimagine myself and what I was doing. Or to use a different metaphor, teaching the Legal Imagination course became a mirror in which I discovered who I was and what I believed as a teacher.

How did that happen? One important dimension was the writing assignments themselves. Taking a cue from the author's introduction, I decided to ask everyone to write 10 papers during the 13-week semester. Each week before class I'd reproduce and distribute several of them, without attribution, for everyone to read. Papers were due on Tuesday, and by Wednesday afternoon all the students had a collection of papers in their mailboxes to read for Thursday's class.

To ensure that everyone began and ended on the same footing, I made the first three assignments and the last two mandatory. Students could choose five from the remaining seven or eight, and for one of those five could rewrite an earlier assignment. Some weeks there was a choice of assignments, and any week, if they preferred, students could write on a topic of their choice.

Selecting papers to reproduce, I looked for pieces I thought were evocative, that expressed differing perspectives, and that modeled a variety of writing styles. But equally important, I wanted everyone to have at least one paper reproduced, particularly in the first weeks, and to have each writer represented substantially during the course. So each week I tried to select a different group of writers.

Knowing that what they wrote might be reproduced certainly helped people approach their papers seriously. And since to write is to commit, people came to class engaged. Although I could not have said it then, building on that engagement became the organizing motive for everything else I tried in the course, both with individuals and with the group.

The course became the forum for my own learning. After 10 years of teaching and the Law Teachers' Clinic, I was ready to learn. . . .

Conclusion

I've said that I began teaching Legal Imagination without a clearly articulated set of learning and teaching goals. That's no longer true. Teaching this course has helped me discover those goals and identify at least some of the conditions that make achieving them possible.

As my title suggests, I've come to think of discerning each person's gift as the most essential goal, for me and for my students. It's the one from which almost everything follows: good writing, honest communication, meaningful collaboration.

Our institutional arrangements often work against achieving this goal, as do our training and our personal resistances. So to achieve it I think we have to try to create conditions that help us along. Here are some I've discovered.

Writing is a form of making meaning; so are all forms of learning. Those forms are most authentic, most powerful, when we're centrally connected to them, when we feel as if what we're writing or learning somehow is ours. That's why I now understand one of my central teaching obligations as helping students become responsible for their own meanings.

Doing that takes time; too often students seem to understand their university and their professional education as focused on producing someone else's meanings. To turn them toward making their own meanings requires encouraging them to trust themselves to do it and to trust me to mean it. And at least in a writing course, it also means trusting their peers.

Trusting yourself entails coming to know who you are, or to use another metaphor, finding your voice(s). If you're not sure what that voice might be and in fact are used to keeping it out of what you write and what you say, finding a voice can seem risky, just as it did for me at the Canadian Law Teachers' Clinic. And just as the atmosphere at the clinic felt safe enough for me to risk reimagining myself as a student and as a teacher, I understand my job as trying to make the spaces in Legal Imagination safe enough for people to risk experimenting with voices, to risk bringing what they know and care about to what they're writing, to discover their gifts.

To know who you are, it helps to be able to listen to your self. I think that's a skill. Usually we're so busy reacting, our heads are so full of noise, that we can't listen or we've forgotten how. So I try to model listening and to create spaces that make listening possible by remaining silent, by trying to listen and respond to what people are writing, and to who they are in writing — by using strategies designed to encourage people to listen to each other.

Cutting across all of these conditions are stories. Stories are how we connect, how we understand our lives, and how we come to understand others. Stories are what we love to listen to. I now think of them as the primary medium of education. Certainly that's what they've been for me.

MEDIA AND TECHNOLOGY:
Plus ça change

Kenneth C. Green

In the era preceding the Internet, French quips often occupied the place now captured by technology metaphors. Both convey an acknowledged understanding, an accepted shorthand spanning context, conversation, and prose. If my memory of French classes long ago serves me correctly, *plus ça change* is the accepted shorthand for "the more things change, the more things stay the same."

A strong sense of *plus ça change* emerges from the more than 80 feature articles, editorials, commentaries, and other documents on media and technology published in the pages of *Change* between 1969 and 1999. Admittedly, the times and technologies have changed over three decades. However, the pages of *Change* offer some key insights on current issues that have stood the test of "time"—both the reflective, sometimes reactive, "academic time" as well as the faster moving, more pressing sense of "Internet time."

What makes a *Change* article on media and technology important? What makes some papers significant, while others simply provide a historical reminder of events, issues, and technologies long past and now forgotten? The articles cited as among "the best" of *Change* on media and technology offer information and insight that transcend the context of the time in which the article was first published. Allen Hershfield's 1980 essay, "Education's Technological Revolution: An Event in Search of Leaders" still speaks to the current information technology challenges confronting the campus community: "getting a new method of instruction adopted widely requires thousands of faculty members to make *individual* decisions to use the new method." (p. 48; original emphasis). Similarly, Harlan Cleveland's 1985 essay, "Educating for the Information Society" raised issues that continue to dominate campus conversations and curriculum discussions (included in the section on "Curriculum").

Not surprisingly, the chronological summary began with television and ends with the World Wide Web. Television—and the evolution of educational television into public television—is the primary focus of technology articles between 1969 and 1976. The first article on multimedia in teaching, emphasizing film and images but not computers, appeared in March 1976 (Trombley, 1976); the same issue also included the first *Change* articles on computer-based instruction (Jenkins, 1976; Miller, 1976; Sugnet, 1976).

Some technologies discussed in the pages of *Change* were short lived; other educational events and initiatives dependent on media and technology are with us today. For example, most of us would recognize the functional elements of the Electronic Video Recording device (EVR) described by Benjamin DeMott in his 1971 essay, "EVR: The Teacher in a Cartridge" as an early version of today's VCR or portable DVD. That technology never moved into the classroom and has since been surpassed by media on compact disks (CDs) and digital video disks (DVDs) as a step towards "broadband" over wires and airwaves.

Some of the earliest articles are laden with language and insight that seems strangely familiar and seemingly current. A 1969 article profiling "Miami-Dade's Encounter With Technology" could describe the instructional experience with various technology resources common to many campuses today:

> No one claims to have any objective test for effectiveness, and often what one man prefers to do with gadgets another will do with chalk and talk: "if the teacher feels it works, it's valid. . . . [W]e try to give the faculty choices." (Schrag, 1969, p. 26).

Similarly, Dwight Allen's 1971, "The Decline of the Textbook," the first of several *Change* articles on this topic, accurately captures the concerns many faculty express almost three decades later:

> Whatever happened to the once-beloved textbook? It's in failing health, I'm afraid, ailing from a recurrent modern illness call "obsolescence". . . . Why so preeminent for so many years and now so increasingly ignored? I for one continue to bid it well, but the textbook's near monopoly as a source of learning had to be broken, so that we can move on to new approaches to learning. (Allen, 1971, p. 37).

If references to the World Wide Web and the assertion that textbooks compartmentalize knowledge and impede interdisciplinary teaching are added, Allen's assessment that textbooks "are the very epitome of a pedagogy that outlived its limited usefulness" sounds contemporary.

A 1972 editorial by then-*Change* editor, George W. Bonham, considered the unfulfilled promise of television:

> For better or worse, television dominates much of American life and manners. . . . Part of [the] lackluster record of the educational uses of television is of course due to the heretofore merciless economies of the medium. But profound pedagogic mistrust of the medium also remains a fact of life. The proof of the pudding lies in the fact that on many campuses, fancy television equipment . . . now lies idle and often unused. . . . Academic indifference to this enormously powerful medium becomes doubly incomprehensible when one remembers that the present college generation is also the first television generation. Television has shaped much of their lives and attitudes, and taught them much of what they know. (Bonham, 1972, p. 11).

Substitute "computers" for "television," and Bonham's 1972 terse assessment speaks directly to many of the challenges that confront colleges in the Internet era. The recommendations Bonham offered almost 30 years ago—set national goals for the appropriate uses of television, cooperate with federal agencies to translate goals into public policy and practice, begin national pooling of instructional resources, and assess the economics of instruction with television—may seem strangely familiar when the newly formed Congressional Commission on Web-based Education releases a final report and supporting documents in November 2000.

Beyond the contextual clips and quips, the pages of *Change* also introduced readers to topics and raised issues that cast a current shadow over campus discussions about information technology, media, and distance learning. The several articles on the British Open University highlighted the role of infrastructure in fostering innovation (see Maclure, 1971). It is one of several lessons from the British

Open University that have not been easily transported to the United States as campuses here confront the challenges of technology implementation, user support, curriculum development, and distance learning.

These pages also provide a painful reminder that most in the campus community, including many self-proclaimed scholars of higher education, pay little attention to the history and the historical literature of higher education. Although technologies may be new and constantly changing, the implementation challenges seem structural: faculty engagement, infrastructure resources, unfulfilled expectations, and uncertain outcomes. *Plus ça change.* The more things change, the more they remain the same.

References

Allen, D. D. (1971, January/February). The decline of the textbook. *Change, 3*, 37–39.

Bonham, G. W. (1972, February). Editorial: Television—The unfulfilled promise. *Change, 4*, 11–13.

Cleveland, H. (1985, July/August). Educating for the information society. *Change, 17*, 13–21.

DeMott, B. (1971, January/February). EVR: Teacher in a cartridge. *Change, 3*, 40–43.

Hershfield, A. F. (1980, November/December). Education's technological revolution: An event in search of leaders. *Change, 12*, 51–52.

Jenkins, E. (1976, March). The potential of PLATO. *Change, 8*, 6–9.

Maclure, S. (1971, March/April). England's open university. *Change, 3*, 62–69.

Miller, J. (1976, March). Understanding the total process. *Change, 8*, 46–49.

Schrag, P. (1969, March/April). Miami-Dade's encounter with technology. *Change, 1*, 24–27.

Sugnet, C. J. (1976, March). Course management by computer. *Change, 8*, 20–23.

Trombley, W. (1976, March). The human dimension of history. *Change, 8*, 37–40.

EDITORIAL: **Educational Media: A Mixed Bag**

George W. Bonham

There are few neutrals in the debate over educational media. Each side garners its armies of aficionados and detractors. Emotions run high, more intense perhaps than any rational analysis would suggest. And it can be readily understood that people who sit astride high-cost, high-capacity technology cannot be asked to be diffident about their particular interest.

This much, at least, is clear: Reports to the effect that higher education is being revolutionized by technology are, to say the least, highly premature. One may not wish to dampen the McLuhanite message, but for the Academy, at least, the second electronic coming is still on the way. Nonetheless, there are now notable pockets of surprising resilience and venturesome projects, and they need to be discussed and encouraged.

Whatever the technological inroads in American pedagogy, the products have been, by any measure, a mixed bag. On the whole, the past few decades have remained for academics an Age of Tinkering. Tinkering, of course, is learning of a very special kind, and while costs have often been excessive and learning effectiveness has rarely been what the technologies had promised, the general lessons of how properly to harness educational media have stuck. . . .

. . . The ultimate success of instructional television projects, computer-aided learning, and multimedia learning is never known until the projects are finished. This makes for many a sleepless night—a discomfort academics would rather avoid.

This is not to say that educational technology may not in time play a central role. But that time has clearly not come. And the problem is not with technology per se, but with related matters, such as the often extraordinarily high costs relative to learner benefits, and relatively sparse proof that media-based learning is any more effective than traditional approaches. . . .

Media, for all the unnerving machinery, speak to the larger dimensions of learning and perceiving. Education, Margaret Mead said recently, "today oscillates uneasily between emphasizing mastery and freedom from restraint, discipline and spontaneity, conformity and originality of the kind usually associated with the arts and religious inspiration. These dichotomies are expressions of an older, culturally limited conception of the human person. What we need now is to develop systems of education that are consonant with human development—in which precision is cultivated in relation to spontaneous multisensory involvement and the disciplined use both of the mind in the usual sense and of the whole body."

Media, when creatively applied, can achieve those ends. Despite the more obvious frustrations, it is important that academics remain open to media's enormous potential.

England's Open University
Revolution at Milton Keynes

Stuart Maclure

In the midst of one of England's election campaigns Labor Party leader Harold Wilson— then seeking to create a Kennedy-type image . . . in September, 1963, made a dramatic bid for the expansion of British higher education, which subsequently was to challenge just about every traditional assumption of what British university life was supposed to be about.

Now, in 1971, Britain's much-heralded Open University—a mere gleam in Wilson's 1963 bid for the "intellectual" vote—in one fell swoop has upped Britain's college-going population by a good 40 percent, without adding a single campus in the process.

Founded on a myth—albeit politically necessary and potent—the Open University represents an historic mixture of hope and hokum. And its enthusiastic supporters and admirers are not confined to England alone, but now virtually span all five continents. From the start, the Open University has generated worldwide fascination among academics and national planners, with American and Japanese educators imminently ready to adapt Harold Wilson's hobby horse to their particular national patterns of education. . . .

The Open University's first term began on January 10, 1971—a Sunday morning—when those viewers who were watching the BBC's second channel instead of washing their cars saw the opening telecasts of Britain's newest institution of higher education.

With an initial enrollment of 25,000 it has become, overnight, second in size only to the University of London among British universities. Within the next four or five years it is almost certainly going to move into first place, with about 40,000 students.

None of the undergraduates, however, will live at the Open University's headquarters at Milton Keynes, a new town being developed fifty miles north of London. None of them will attend lectures or tutorials face to face with the 200 faculty or the 540 supporting personnel, or engage in

ritual sherry-drinking with the president, Dr. Walter Perry. All the teaching will take place outside the university by means of educational technology—some simple, some sophisticated.

The television component—half an hour a week for each course—is inevitably what has caught the public eye. But the essence of the Open University is variety in media and teaching techniques. Radio broadcasts will be used for half an hour a week for each course, for example. The main substance of the instruction will be carried out through correspondence courses sent regularly through the mail. The courses are to be augmented by one-week summer schools which the Open University will organize in existing universities and colleges. Students are expected to attend, but it is not suggested that someone who could not make it would automatically be penalized.

To back up all these teaching methods, some 250 local study centers have been set up throughout the United Kingdom. They will be open three or four nights a week so that students may consult the part-time staff of 3,000 tutors and counsellors. . . .

The original notion of the Open University was as a "university of the air" to combine educational television with a national correspondence college. Its progenitor was Dr. Michael Young, author of *The Rise of the Meritocracy*. A sociologist and social innovator, he had already achieved amazing success in mobilizing middle-class consumers into a Consumers' Association, with a large testing program for consumers' goods. He had been less successful in education, where he tried to mobilize opinion against the built-in social class biases reflected in the system. . . .

As for the TV contribution it will be important in all the courses, but especially vital in science. Students without access to a TV set are not being allowed to take the science course at all. Science raises the most obvious difficulties for any correspondence course and has called forth some of the most ingenious responses. . . .

Personal tutoring through the 250 local study centers to supplement the correspondence courses was one of the original ingredients of the Open University plan. A great deal depends on the quality of the part-time staff. Many acting as guides and counsellors may never have hitherto undertaken university work. Others will be teachers at conventional universities doing some moonlighting.

Most of the centers have been rented from local schools—rooms in technical colleges and similar institutions set aside for evening use by the Open University and equipped with all the necessary gadgetry to rerun TV programs. "Study Centers," according to the official guide, "provide facilities for watching and listening to programs, for group discussions and for personal interviews with counsellors. The larger study centers will in addition provide specialist class tutoring, access to computer terminals, space for private study and informal contact with fellow students and staff." . . .

In the first group of enrollees, the typical Open University student is between twenty-one and forty, middle-class, with a good standard of secondary education (sometimes including the necessary entrance qualification for a conventional university) and some professional or adult education after leaving school. . . .

Of the 40,000 who sent in completed applications to the Open University, only 2 percent of them were deemed "unsuitable." Some evidence was required of willingness and capacity to study which, in the case of those who had left school at fifteen or sixteen, meant being able to show that they had taken evening courses or professional studies in the meantime. About a fifth of the applicants were interviewed before being accepted, and the difficulties of part-time study were discussed. . . .

In one important respect the enrollment has been a disappointment to the University's founders. It had been intended to weight the recruitment in favor of those who had left school early and were in manual or semi-skilled occupations. . . . In practice the first 25,000 applications only brought in 601 from workers in manufacturing industry and 769 from shopkeepers and workers in sales and service industries. These compared with more than 10,000 teachers, 3,000 professional people, 2,500 housewives and 1,600 administrators and managers.

It is obviously much too soon to pass a judgment on this Open University. But it is already beginning to look as if its most important achievements will be indirect—influencing other universities and other colleges—rather than as the direct agent of social change which its political patrons believed they were founding.

Fortunately, there are important items on the other side—important enough to more than compensate for the ideological nonsense. In a real sense, the Open University offers the prospect of a breakthrough in educational technology—not just the hardware but the planning and coordination of different techniques. It is bound to have a revolutionary impact on existing methods in higher education. If the Open University techniques can work at all with hard-pressed part-time students, they must be infinitely more effective with students in conventional settings. The Open University will be a laboratory where teaching methods can be scientifically studied and radical innovation tested. This could be what Britain—and probably America as well—needs to achieve: an enormous increase in the productivity of education—at the secondary as well as the higher level—and to link this improvement of productivity with the individualization of learning . . . Until now universities have been incredibly conservative and uncurious about their teaching methods. When they have tried new techniques such as TV it has simply been to search for new ways of doing old things. The Open University will challenge their old orthodoxies. . . .

February 1972

EDITORIAL: **Television: The Unfulfilled Promise**

George W. Bonham

For better or for worse, television today dominates much of American life and manners. . . .

It is then all the more remarkable that this powerful new characteristic of American life continues to be ignored or rejected by so many of our intellectuals, and only to a smaller degree by academics as well. . . .

Academic indifference to this enormously powerful medium becomes doubly incomprehensible when one remembers that the present college generation is also the first television generation. Those in college today have never known a world without television since the day they were born. Television has shaped much of their lives and attitudes, and taught them much of what they know. It got to them a good fifteen years before Political Science 101, a fact still largely ignored by those who preside over the present shape of higher education. . . .

We would urge that . . . the university leadership of this country . . . form a national task force to accomplish the following objectives:

1. To investigate and set forth a series of national goals in terms of the appropriate educational uses of cable television in America.

2. To consult, lobby and cooperate with the Federal Communications Commission, the executive and legislative branches of the Federal government, with NASA (in terms of satellite interconnections for cable TV) and the various state education agencies, to translate such goals and objectives into practical public policy.

3. To begin a national pooling of instructional resources, where the best of Yale can be seen in San Bernardino, . . .

4. To begin determination of the economics of instruction by cable in terms of national investments in continuing and higher education, in which, to say the least, one percent of the total higher education outlay should in time be allocated to this national outreach program.

We believe that higher education has far too long laid down its mantle of social initiatives. . . . [T]he time has come to show the country that the universities are still capable of looking beyond their noses to grasp a vast if complex opportunity, which carries bold educational implications. . . .

November/December 1980

TECHNOLOGY & LEARNING:
Education's Technological Revolution: An Event in Search of Leaders

Allan F. Hershfield

How many times, over the past fifty years, have members of the academic community and the public at large read or heard forecasts of an impending educational millennium because of a particular technological innovation? Fifty years ago, radio broadcasting was supposed to revolutionize education. Soon thereafter, teaching machine aficionados predicted sweeping changes that would be brought about by their particular device. Then, television was touted as the medium that would bring about extraordinary changes in the educational process. Likewise, computers, lasers, videocassette and videodisc machines, and communications satellites have been pushed by one individual or another as innovations that would have a major impact on the educational process.

Although one can, indeed, identify creative uses of instructional television, computers, programmed instruction, and satellites by institutions of higher education, few of these innovations are part of the regular educational processes in most of our institutions of higher education. . . .

Systemic Barriers

Those outside the university, and, indeed, many people within it, do not understand the central role of the faculty, particularly in the field of instruction and curriculum development. In most instances, individual faculty have (and should continue to have) almost complete freedom to develop and use whatever methods of instruction they deem appropriate—within the broadly defined boundaries of professional responsibility. Thus, the decision to use a particular method of instruction is an individual one reserved to each faculty member, and getting a new method of instruction adopted widely requires thousands of faculty members to make *individual* decisions to use the new method.

Course Development

The course development process in a traditional college or university is basically labor intensive, involving a single faculty member in the development of a particular course. Usually, no major capital investment is required except that originally needed for buildings, laboratories, libraries, and so forth. Apart from an occasional summer grant . . . no major costs are associated with such an activity. Most new courses are developed *as they are taught* . . . Faculty are, in effect, being paid a single sum of money to develop and to deliver a course.

Courses or units developed to use new technology effectively, frequently involve recording an entire course or much of the material in advance, in one or more forms such as films, videotapes, computer programs, programmed texts, audiotapes, or slides. This course development process is quite different from the traditional one just described, and it is not consistent with common institutional practices and faculty and administrative values and behavior. . . .

Traditional administrative practices and values make it difficult even to think about funding course development in the high technology mode. Funds are divided into hundreds of small "pots" and allocated to departments. . . . [T]his "bits and pieces" resource allocation system [is] often excluded from consideration.

The full-scale, technologically based course development process is heavily capital intensive—with very large amounts of resources being required to develop a single course or unit. Capital is needed to produce and test the software, to set up and operate a system to deliver the course, and to provide funds to update 10 percent to 20 percent of the software on an annual basis. Few, if any, American states, colleges or universities have any regular mechanism for funding course development activities of this nature on a large scale. . . .

Technological Considerations

It is difficult to find, within most American universities and colleges, trained instructional technologists who can deal with a wide variety of technological and nontechnological approaches to education with equal competence, professionalism, and ease. One tends to find experts in instructional television, computer-based instruction, and audiovisual equipment such as film and overhead projectors. Each of these individuals is a devotee of his or her particular form of technology and recommends it vigorously to resolve *every* pedagogical problem. "Experts" such as these often lose sight of students as the beneficiaries of the educational process. Moreover, faculty, administrators, and students have all too often been frustrated by the failure or inadequacy of both the equipment and the software provided by these "experts," and this too contributes to the reinforcement of negative attitudes towards the use of technology. . . .

Other Higher Education Institutions

If one cannot expect a technological revolution in higher education to begin at prestigious universities, is it then possible that other, different types of American institutions of higher education will make the changes necessary to move in new directions? With the possible exception of some community colleges, the prospects for this sort of change are not good. . . .

. . . Most observers believe the coming reduction in the eighteen- to twenty-four-year-old cohort will have a differential effect on different types of universities and colleges. . . . A pending decline may provide an incentive to move in new directions—assuming this movement starts before the decline begins. . . .

Policies and Practices Intended to Facilitate the Use of Instructional Technology

A number of changes in institutional policies and procedures can activate faculty to become involved in the development and use of instructional technology and at the same time, protect their jobs, and reward them for their efforts.

Obtaining Development Capital

State and national government officials and individuals in the private sector, interested in stimulating the use of instructional technology, must create some regular funding mechanism to provide the capital necessary to develop and deliver instructional software, and they must be willing to re-examine and discard those measures of efficiency which prevent faculty and administrators from developing and using technologically based approaches to instruction.

Teamwork

As many faculty as possible should be involved in the development of the course.... [I]nvolving several faculty members as a group, preferably on a full-time basis for the development of the course, removes the members from a system that reinforces individualistic behavior.

An explicit orientation may help faculty members understand the differences between the normal pattern of faculty behavior and that required to develop packages of mediated materials successfully. The orientation must show that the effective development and use of instructional technology is basically a team effort requiring careful planning by and close cooperation of highly skilled professionals in several fields. First and foremost among these is, of course, the faculty member. The faculty member is the content expert responsible for ensuring that the course goals are current, accurate, and appropriate to the entry level knowledge of the students.

A second skilled member of the team might be a learning theorist who would help the faculty member determine sequence of content and the particular type of learning experiences most likely to help the students attain the goals set for particular units. One might also employ instructional technologists skilled in the design and production of instructional materials for a wide variety of media—computers, television, radio, programmed texts, simulation games, slides, tapes, charts, graphs, overheads, and photographs. The technologists' role is to know the basic characteristics of each medium, to recommend the most effective and efficient combination of media to help particular kinds of students attain course objectives, and to help the faculty member and the learning theorists produce materials for each medium....

Use of High Technology

Both students and faculty must come to understand the advantages they can derive from the effective use of instructional technology; what the limits of this technology are; and when it should not be used. The high technology, capital intensive mode of course development described earlier can best be used for those courses and parts of courses in which the content is relatively stable, and the teaching-learning objectives are fairly clear. Basic, introductory courses in almost any discipline other than performance courses in theater arts, music, and art are generally appropriate for this type of developmental work.

The professor's role would be changed, by use of the high technology mode, to that of tutor in a comparatively small group. This will allow face-to-face interaction rather than the presentation of material to hundreds of students assembled in massive lecture sections....

Conclusion

Although much university level instruction is not suited to the development of sophisticated packages of mediated materials, American and European colleges and universities are making little effort to develop and use instructional technology effectively in those areas that show great promise....

... If institutions of higher education do not move quickly to take advantage of this technology, private industry and new types of non-profit educational organizations will do so.

The Computer and Higher Education

A Change for the Better?

Michael S. McPherson

Everyone involved with higher education is being forced to think more seriously these days about the implications of the revolution in computer technology that is upon us. . . .

We can identify two kinds of technological change. One lets us do the same things more quickly or cheaply. The other allows us, or causes us, to do different things, and perhaps even to become in some way different people. The revolution in spinning and weaving technology around 1800, for example, brought great economic change in Europe and North America, but did not bring a comparable revolution in clothing. On the other hand, railroad networks did profoundly affect our notions of time, distance, and travel, and brought structural changes in the commercial and residential use of space. Telegraph services and typewriters made business communications more efficient; telephones brought new kinds of interactions, not simply greater speed.

In computer futurism, the lines are already drawn between those who see data processing as a tool that will let us do better what we are doing now and those who regard it as the basis of a new "information society." Interestingly, those who foresee the most far-reaching changes tend to be optimistic about them; those who are more conservative about the impact of computers are often more concerned about potential abuse. . . .

At least in science and education, no use is as significant as quantitative analysis. . . .

In . . . 1981 . . . , Stephen White of the Alfred P. Sloan Foundation in New York urged that the analytic skills of applied mathematics, along with technology and the elements of computer science, be made a central part of the undergraduate curriculum. "What the computer has done," he argued, ". . . is provide scope for analytic skills that has never before existed, and in so doing it has altered the world in which the student will live as well as the manner in which he will think about the world."

One of the responses to this paper came from Donald L. Kreider, chairman of the mathematics department at Dartmouth College. . . . He suggested that computers permit "a marriage of pragmatic skills and theoretical structure that has eluded teachers for generations." Some powerful procedures for solving equations were rarely used because they were impractical for paper and pencil methods; as computer algorithms they give students new insights into the fundamental concepts involved.

Ironically, there is still only scattered "hard" quantitative evidence that people learn mathematical ideas better with computers than they do conventionally—in fact, the evidence that they learn anything better is still disappointing. But they clearly feel better about learning, and at Dartmouth more students have chosen to concentrate in mathematics since the introduction of computers in the department's courses. As teaching methods are changed to take advantage of computer capabilities, educated people will be more sophisticated mathematically.

Different questions about the nature of education are raised by the computer's ability to retrieve information from a great variety of data bases. . . .

Recently, a Midwestern police chief complained that his officers were so busy checking license plates for overdue traffic tickets that they were neglecting to investigate the serious crimes against which computers still could help little. There is a lesson for education here. Once people see what computers can do, they need little persuasion to embrace them. But they sometimes need reminding that being educated means in large part dealing with questions that resist computer-based techniques. Computers have been better at making lots of small improvements than at tackling complex political decisions, moral issues, artistic creation, and aesthetic judgment. . . .

Let us turn back to the two "information revolutions." Writing endowed the word with a life independent of the speaker's. Printing eventually permitted the almost limitless multiplication of the word. One changed qualitatively, the other quantitatively, the ways of education and the educated.

Computing will fall somewhere between the two in its impact. But wherever it falls—and it will be much closer to printing—it will disappoint those who long for its powers.

May/June 1986

The New Computing in Higher Education

Steven W. Gilbert and Kenneth C. Green

Thousands of faculty members and administrators have decided that 1986 is the year they will have a personal relationship with computing. . . . Like their predecessors, most academics now getting started on computing are professionals who haven't been computer users before. . . . What they realize is that they are embarking on a journey they can no longer delay. . . .

For faculties as a whole and their academic leaders, the "microcomputer revolution" comes with forces that are hard to resist. The cost of technology has declined dramatically: students routinely use (and many own) desktop systems more powerful than the most costly mainframe systems of the 1960s and early 1970s. Dramatic changes in the design of software—away from complex, mathematical programming languages to problem-oriented application programs—have made computers more accessible and attractive. Then there is the increasing access to computing in elementary and secondary schools, which means that many students arrive more "computer competent" than some of the professors they meet in classrooms. . . .

Implementation Issues . . .

. . . [T]he "new computing" revolution in higher education would appear to be healthy and vibrant.

But is it? What will the educational consequences be of all this individual effort and institutional investment? Like many in the academic community, we have great hopes for and see great benefits from the "microcomputer revolution." Colleges may indeed be on the verge of realizing the much-discussed, long-awaited potential use of the computer to improve both instruction and

learning (qualitatively different activities). Yet we also share the sentiment expressed by Harvard's Derek Bok in his 1983–84 president's report, that "experience should make us wary of dramatic claims for the impact of new technology." . . .

Campus efforts to acquire and integrate technology raise complex issues at the heart of academic life. These efforts also involve significant costs. Given limited resources, most campuses opt for one-time, risk-aversive decisions—in part because they have no way to amortize the costs of these decisions over appropriate time periods. . . .

A Choice of Revolutions . . .

. . . [I]t makes sense for campus leaders to look at general classes of computing applications rather than to regard "computing" as a single phenomenon.

What are those "general classes"? In higher education, we believe there are three. First, computers are critical tools in academic research (particularly mathematical modeling and statistical analysis); they assist in the acquisition and generation of information. Second, and this has been a dream for computing for at least twenty-five years, they have a role in instruction, in class and out, to help people learn. Third, there is their role in enhancing personal productivity, both of faculty and staff in their professional work and of students in their academic work and subsequent careers. . . .

The conceptual model we propose is dynamic: the components continually change character to reflect changes in the underlying technology. For example, while the "information" dimension traditionally involved the generation of new knowledge, today's technology adds the component of affordable, local access to information via data banks and communications networks, access that can aid student learning and personal productivity. The trick for campuses in coming years, then, will be to integrate computing into the curriculum in ways that recognize all three dimensions and their interdependence, especially when it comes to the support of instruction and student learning. . . .

Toward "Perfect" Computing

We must beware of what Peter Keen of MIT has called the "counter-implementation strategy" of "Yes, but let's do it right." That is, one way to postpone indefinitely the widespread use of a new technology is to support it enthusiastically while insisting it must be embraced only when its every detail is complete as part of a comprehensive, integrated plan. Sometimes a new technology can become useful more quickly and practically through a less-than-perfect implementation at a lesser price.

If we are to wait for the "perfect system," we will wait forever. The horizon keeps moving farther away as we approach it. Our expectations will grow, machine capabilities will grow, but the price for the "full function," "state of the art" systems will decline only slowly. . . .

July/August 1990

Open Universities

Closing the Distances to Learning

Daniel Granger

From Britain to Thailand, Japan to South Africa, distance learning is an important part of national strategies to educate large numbers rapidly and efficiently. In the U.S., educators are finding distance learning not only efficient for outreach to new populations, but an effective medium for new instructional models.

The concept and practice of distance learning has thrived in the U.S. since before the turn of the century—as correspondence study, home study, and independent study. But "distance learning" as a term associated with new technologies offering a full-fledged alternative to classroom education got its biggest boost internationally with the founding of the British Open University (BOU) in 1969. The BOU gained rapid visibility and recognition by broadcasting its video course components weekly throughout the United Kingdom on the BBC network. (Films such as "Educating Rita" both reflect and add to that visibility.) Since then, new government-supported "open universities" in other countries have been established at the rate of about one every two years, with at least three more in the planning stages.

The impetus for this global development is both social and economic. Many nations, advanced as well as developing, have recognized the need for widespread access to education that is effective and efficient in order to participate and compete in the international community. Distance education, as demonstrated by the British Open University, offers an attractive model. . . .

Students Learning at a Distance

Students enrolled in distance learning programs abroad, for the most part, resemble those served by adult or continuing education programs in the U.S. Usually between 25 and 40 years old, they are adults coming to education with a purpose, career-oriented or personal. With many competing demands on their time and energy, conventional undergraduate education is an impossible luxury. . . .

Student-Centered Education

Probably the most significant characteristic of distance education as currently practiced internationally is not the use of technology, but the fact that its organizing principle is the needs of the learner—that whatever the inherent demands of the content, it must be made accessible to the learner, first across the distances of space and time, and secondly across the distances of knowing and learning. Virtually all distance learning programs began with a primarily geographical notion of providing access. As their faculty developed the best instructional materials possible, administrators established regional centers or other delivery mechanisms to make those courses available. Literature in the early 1970s spoke of distance learning as an "industrialized model" of education, designing and creating high-quality courses to be delivered to hundreds or even thousands of students.

Students, however, even—or perhaps especially—at a distance, have never been uniform learning machines. Distance educators came to recognize very quickly the importance of closing that last metaphorical "distance" to the individual learner—of learning skills, previous preparation, and personal context. The literature now speaks of distance courses involving a "guided didactic conversation" between course tutor and student in order to individualize the course to the student's knowledge, skills, and needs. . . .

. . . Recommendations of American educators for educational improvement merge with the ideas of distance educators for engaging students in ways that involve them actively in learning. These similarities are apparent in at least three areas:

■ Actively engaging students in the discourses of learning.

■ Establishing connections between learning and the students' experience.

■ Providing students with a range of learning modes.

1. *Engagement in the Discourses of Learning*— With the increasing recognition of the social nature of knowledge—that it does not exist apart from a community of knowers—educators now focus more deliberately on the student's engagement with a community of learners: through academic dialogue with a faculty, collaboration with fellow students, or some other communicative exchange. . . . The key is the autonomy with which students conduct their own studies—that they come to and integrate the shared knowledge with their own concerns and perspectives. Distance educators foster this sense of community through a very deliberate tutor-student relationship (the "guided didactic conversation") to establish firmly in the mind and imagination of each student a clear "idea of university." Distance itself can be an advantage here in focusing and concentrating the exchange with faculty or peers (e.g., by mail,

phone, or electronic mail) on the academic matter at hand—rather than being deflected by environmental circumstances.

2. *Connections between Learning and Students' Experiences*—These connections are encouraged both because they enable the student's learning to begin with and build on his or her existing knowledge and because they can provide vital reinforcement to the learning process. Linking studies to as much of students' full context as possible enhances, intensifies, and integrates new learning and skills within the texture of their lives. Campus-based efforts like problem-solving projects and simulations are attempts to create a realistic experience, although these often are necessarily limited and controlled. Distance education, by its nature, functions within the context of students' lives. Rather than experiencing this as an unfortunate distraction, distance educators can build from and with students' experience to reinforce learning. This is true not only in practical or professional areas, but in the liberal arts as well. Direct experience of ethical dilemmas, life and death situations, and the varieties of human behavior provide a firm foundation for studies in philosophy, literature, history, and the social sciences.

3. *Range of Learning Modes*—Increasingly, educators agree that there are many roads to learning and that the diversity among learning styles and learners themselves should be reflected in the learning modes available. There is a common interest in individualizing instruction and shaping both content and pedagogy to the needs of individual students. One reflection of this is the wider use of the "learning contract," which individualizes content, pedagogy, time, and resources. Distance educators are revising concepts of course structure and development in order to provide greater flexibility in course use. The classroom, both in structure and format, is seen by more educators as only one of a number of instructional options. In learning technology, researchers in both conventional and distance modes are experimenting with various interactive media (such as Apple's hypertext) to explore greater possibilities of individualization.

Students themselves are already discovering alternatives to a four-year campus-based undergraduate experience. Their motives are quite practical, both in terms of efficiency and effectiveness. They will frequently combine two years of classroom experience (often at a community college) with two years in a variety of distance learning modes, including structured distance courses, independent study, work/study projects, and other forms of experiential learning. Not only is this less costly than a four-year residential education, but working students can test and reinforce their learning through practical experience. . . .

January/February 1991

The Technological Revolution Comes to the Classroom

Robert B. Kozma and Jerome Johnston

In a 1986 keynote address to a national conference on computing in higher education, Nobel Laureate Herbert Simon discussed the "second industrial revolution" ushered in by the invention of the computer. . . . Simon suggested that for the computer to bring about a revolution in higher education its introduction must be accompanied by improvements in our understanding of learning and teaching, and by changes in the organizational structure of our colleges and universities.

Harvard President Derek Bok shares Simon's cautious optimism. Writing in . . . 1986, he speculates that at the very least, new technologies can engage students in a more active process of thinking and problem solving, and at best they may help us develop new insights into human cognition and new ways of helping students learn. However, Bok doubts that computers can contribute much to the learning of open-ended subjects such as moral philosophy, . . . literary criticism, or social theory — fields that cannot be reduced to formal rules and procedures.

Such cautious optimism reflects an excitement about recent developments, but uncertainty about their larger effects. . . .

It is our belief that we have crested a hill since 1986 when Simon and Bok expressed their views. . . . We believe that the computer *has* launched a revolution in learning and teaching in higher education. . . .

This article is a status report on the computer revolution in the classroom: what the revolution's impact has been so far, what direction it is taking, and what challenges lie ahead. . . .

We base this report on our four years of experience with the EDUCOM/NCRIPTAL Higher Education Software Awards Program, on our research conducted at the National Center for Research to Improve Postsecondary Teaching and Learning (NCRIPTAL), and on the research of others.

The Computer's Evolving Capabilities
. . .

The characteristics of the computer that most immediately account for its growing ubiquity are its ability to employ a wide range of symbols and to operate on symbolic expressions in powerful ways, for these are the capabilities that most closely correspond to human cognitive and social behavior. Though the computer's capability to manipulate numerical symbol systems was the reason that the more quantitatively inclined disciplines were first to adopt this technology, most of us have become interested in the computer because of its facility in handling words. But numbers and words are no longer the only symbol systems that we can use with computers. It is becoming increasingly easy to create, access, and manipulate a range of sounds and graphic images. This capability has been expanded further by the marriage of computer and television in the interactive videodisc and by the development of digitized video that can be stored inside the computer. The computer now has instant access to high resolution pictures of artifacts, maps, buildings, works of art, authentic sound and voice, and full motion video. . . .

. . . [T]hese symbolic expressions are all present at one time, in one place, for easy access. Pictures, sounds, graphs, words, and numbers can be presented side-by-side, and integrated to show the multiplicity of ways an idea can be expressed.

More importantly, the computer can be used to transform information from one symbol system to another. A musical score can be entered into the computer and the computer can transform the score into a musical performance. Numeric data from the natural and social sciences can be converted to graphs or coded map displays. Thus, students can use their skills in one symbol system to gain understanding in another and they can learn to express their knowledge in a variety of forms.

But computers not only employ a range of symbol systems, they differ from other media in the ways they can be used to structure and apply this information. The computer can be used to connect information based on the ways ideas are related to each other. Words can be linked to their definitions or to referent pictures; concepts can be connected to their examples; principles can be linked to animated or video demonstrations. The computer's processing capability can be used to create procedural systems in which information provided by the user determines what happens next. Such explicit representations of the relationships among information and symbolic expressions can serve as models for how knowledge can be related, structured, and used internally in human memory.

As Simon pointed out, the success of a major innovation is preconditioned on the occurrence of a variety of corollary events and conditions. Consequently, the impact of the computer on higher education cannot be assessed, or even discussed, in isolation. We cannot disentangle it from the cognitive requirements of the curricular goals and instructional tasks we set for our students; from the interests, skills, capabilities, and deficiencies that students bring to the classroom; and from the physical and social demands placed on students by the classroom, dormitory, and home environments. Understanding the impact of computers in higher education means understanding this complex net of reciprocal relationships between people and situations; it means examining the use and impact of technology in context. . . .

Advancing the Revolution

. . . Over the past four years, we have examined over 700 software packages and instructional innovations. Using a process that involves instructional psychologists and faculty experts from 18 disciplin-

ary associations, we have identified 91 outstanding examples of how the computer is making a difference in higher education. . . .

From reception to engagement. The dominant model of learning in higher education has the student passively absorbing knowledge disseminated by professors and textbooks, what Simon calls the "infection theory" of learning. With technology, students are moving away from the passive reception of information to active engagement in the construction of knowledge. . . .

Social Power is a game designed to give students a sense of how abstract sociological principles work in the real world. As a member of the board of directors of a large multinational corporation, students learn skills in the analysis of power relationships, coalitions, social networks, and power strategies. As one of five board members with equal power, the players must use a variety of techniques to obtain more power. They do this by managing personal resources and making deals with other board members (Robert Leik, et al., University of Minnesota, Distinguished Social Science Software, 1987). . . .

From the classroom to the real world. Too often our students walk out of class ill-equipped to apply their new knowledge to real-world situations and contexts. Conversely, too frequently the classroom examines ideas out of the context of gritty real-world considerations. Technology, however, is breaking down the walls between the classroom and the real world.

CompuGraph v. Chang is a videodisc simulation of a legal case in which law students make decisions about how to handle an entire court case from client interviews to courtroom defense. Students interrupt realistically portrayed events when they feel the lawyer's behavior is inappropriate. Feedback is multifaceted and includes legal doctrine, litigation techniques and strategy, and even courtroom etiquette (Daniel Burnstein and Jacquelyn Camp, Harvard Law School, Weston Vernon Jr. NCAIR Award for Best Educational Software in Law, 1990). . . .

From text to multiple representations. Linguistic expression, whether text or speech, has a reserved place in the academy. Technology is expanding our ability to express, understand, and use ideas in other symbol systems. . . .

Crystal is a tool for constructing, visualizing, and analyzing crystal lattices. Students can view the three-dimensional crystal from any angle and then calculate parameters for the model, such as distances and directions between atoms. The three-dimensional viewing capability enhances the understanding of the scientific principles for students who have difficulty visualizing three-dimensional objects (Mark Franklin, et al., Dartmouth, Distinguished Engineering Software, 1990). . . .

From coverage to mastery. Expanding on their classic instructional use, computers can teach and drill students on a variety of rules and concepts essential to performance in a disciplinary area. . . .

Spanish Microtutor covers all the basic topics of Spanish grammar. Each lesson includes a tutorial, exercises, and tests. The students control the pace of the lesson, have access to the glossary and help functions, and receive detailed feedback about their performance. When students have ready access to such a program, grammar instruction can be relegated to homework, freeing up class time to practice language production and receive corrective feedback from the instructor—a resource that cannot be duplicated by the computer (Frank Dominguez, University of North Carolina, Distinguished Foreign Language Software, 1989).

From isolation to interconnection. Technology has helped us move from a view of learning as an individual act done in isolation toward learning as a collaborative activity. And we have moved from the consideration of ideas in isolation to an examination of their meaning in the context of other ideas and events.

The Electronic Dialectical Notebook uses a classroom of networked computers to support classroom writing activities in a college core course designed to develop critical thinking skills. Each student reads a short on-screen text and a focus question posed by the instructor. After the students compose a response, the notebooks are exchanged electronically between randomly selected pairs of students who then comment on each other's ideas. The *Notebook* challenges students to conceive of reading, writing, and thinking as social acts (Susan Kirschner, et al., Lewis and Clark College, Best Curriculum Innovation [Writing] 1988). . . .

From products to processes. With technology, we are moving past a concern with the products of academic work to the processes that create knowledge. Students learn what it is that scholars do: how historians, mathematicians, and authors

write, think, and solve problems. They learn how to use tools that facilitate the process of scholarly work. . . .

MacScope converts a Macintosh computer into an oscilloscope. It goes beyond the oscilloscope in guiding students to analyze the displayed data. It transforms collected data into visual representations and tables that the student can analyze while the data are still present on the screen (Elisha Huggins, Dartmouth College, Best Physics Software, 1989).

From mechanics to understanding in the laboratory. The scientific laboratory is one of the most expensive instructional arenas in the academy. It is costly to maintain the proper equipment and supplies, and to provide supervision to student scientists. It is also limited as a learning experience. So much time is required to replicate classic experiments in the discipline that there is little time left for students to explore alternative hypotheses as real scientists do.

Chemical Reactions is a videodisc chemistry laboratory with 14 lessons that are dangerous and expensive to perform in a real lab. The program is designed to foster use of the investigatory methods used by professional chemists. Students choose a combination of equipment and strategies and see the results in an authentic video sequence. The interactive nature of the medium allows the students to be active participants in the experiments even though they are not really "mixing" chemicals (Loretta Jones and Stanley Smith, University of Illinois, Best Chemistry Software, 1989). . . .

Teaching in the Classroom

Most of the award-winning computer innovations are designed to give students a more active role in constructing knowledge, with an implicit change in the role of the teacher. The teacher becomes more of a coach or mentor, helping students solve problems presented by the software. . . .

. . . To incorporate computer technology into a course, teachers must give a great deal of attention to designing (or redesigning) activities for students. They must explore the possibilities afforded by the computer and find or develop suitable software. In the early stages of innovating, a great deal of attention is given to the technical requirements: hardware, software, room design, and fund raising. Even after several years early adopters report that the technical demands continue. Evolution of computer capabilities and campus computer standards leads to continual demands for change — e.g., demands to adapt software to run on a different computer, to incorporate new technical capabilities into the software, . . .

Facilitating Change

What factors affect the pace of change in the academy? If we look across the array of early adopters in our case studies, it is striking how many developed their innovation from personal conviction and resourcefulness instead of in response to institutional support. . . .

When the tools of academic research and productivity can be used in an identical fashion in the classroom, then change comes faster. For example, statistical packages that served scholarly work of social scientists were easily moved to the classroom as it became accepted among sociologists to train students to conduct real studies, or to use an existing data set to learn how to do research and interpret data.

Can institutional support increase the pace of change? . . .

We can get better insight on this issue by looking at a large-scale adoption study we did 10 years earlier. . . . In this study we found that most instructional innovations were "individual adoptions." The innovation represents a personal decision by an individual faculty member. . . . Because of the personal nature of these innovations, they were rarely disseminated to others and were frequently discontinued or reduced when the innovator went on to other things.

This pattern can be contrasted with a second, much less common but more successful approach to innovation. In a small number of cases, instructional innovations were adopted collaboratively by groups of faculty members and an administrator — typically a department chair. The motivations for these adoptions were an identified need of the organization or of students. . . . The adoption decision was made by several people and the ownership of the innovation was shared. Dissemination resulted from informal, one-to-one, personal interactions among faculty members. With this form of adoption, the innovation was frequently continued, expanded, and institutionalized or formalized into programs, offices, or centers.

There were several organizational factors that influenced the adoption process. . . . First of all,

everyone . . . indicated the need for resources. To innovate, faculty members need some combination of money, released time, technical assistance, equipment. The lack of these was the reason cited most often by those who did not adopt.

Secondly, the innovations that were most successful involved the participation of others and evolved out of identified organizational need. All of them involved the department chair. . . . Instructional improvement centers also supported some of the successful projects in our study. . . .

Simon argues that for revolution to succeed in higher education it must be accompanied by improvements in our understanding of learning and teaching, and by changes in the organizational structure of our colleges and universities. The award-winning software described earlier clearly builds on an understanding of teaching and learning that goes well beyond the model of passive learning implicit in television. . . . [S]tudents become more active and engaged in the learning process; they learn for understanding and application rather than memorization; and they connect their new knowledge to that previously learned, to the ideas of other students, and to the real world outside the classroom. . . .

From isolated experiments to organizational commitment. We must move from the independent activities of early adopters to the integration of these activities into the academic community. . . . Department chairs and instructional improvement centers can play an important role here by pulling innovation into the organizational context, building a departmental base for it, and making it less egocentric and more collaborative. The organization must also provide the released time, technical assistance, and other resources that may be needed to support such innovations.

Models of implementation. We must move from developing exciting software packages to developing models for their implementation in the classroom. . . . Computers will have their ultimate impact only when faculty members are presented with vivid images of how computer use changes the classroom and changes what students do when they study. . . .

Systematic evaluation. Finally, we must move from innovation to the systematic assessment of the impact of computers on teaching and learning. . . .

Making the Most of a Slow Revolution

Steven W. Gilbert

For more than 25 years, I've been involved with information technology and education. During most of that time, I (and many of my colleagues) have believed that "the next 18 to 24 months" would bring revolutionary change in how people teach and learn, through the use of technology or otherwise. Yet we're still waiting for those widespread, dramatic improvements; and we're also still waiting for research results that definitively prove the educational merit of applications of these new technologies. Meanwhile, we have observed a gradual—perhaps accelerating—process in which individual faculty members find, try, discard, rediscover, adopt, adapt, and use applications of information technology to improve teaching and learning. Commitment to change based on accumulated experience is outpacing the availability of conclusive research results. . . .

. . . What I've seen and heard . . . suggests that 1995 was the year in which educational uses of information technology began passing from the "early adopters" to the "mainstream faculty" in many colleges and universities, and that for higher education in the 1990s, electronic mail and the World Wide Web are bringing computing into instruction in the way that word processing brought computing into personal use for students and faculty in the 1980s. . . .

For many colleges and universities, 1995 was also the year when student and faculty use of electronic mail exploded. . . .

Along with the e-mail explosion, more faculty members began offering their e-mail addresses to students and inviting them to ask course-related questions via e-mail, as well as during regular office hours. Although neither the faculty nor the students perceive this step as a marked departure from traditional practice, many faculty members report even this simple use of e-mail increases the participation from categories of students usually underrepresented in class discussions (women, minorities, speakers of English as a second language, shy people, and others). Some faculty report that classroom participation seems to increase along with e-mail participation, and others report that students continue discussing course-related ideas via e-mail even after the course has ended.

Faculty who use e-mail to supplement their communication with students report significant increases in their own workloads, but these reports are usually offered along with expressions of pleasure and pride about the changes in learning that seem to follow, and the improved quality of education. The quality changes even further as faculty and students discover how to use the World Wide Web. And it is difficult to ignore how rapidly that medium is growing in content, availability, and use.

An old idea—distance education—is also attracting new attention as more powerful forms of telecommunications (such as two-way video, electronic mail, and the World Wide Web) make it a more attractive option. However, no form of distance education or any other *widely applicable* educational use of information technology has yet proved so much more effective and/or less expensive than "traditional" forms of teaching and learning as to become a complete replacement for them. Meanwhile, more academic leaders believe they must offer better access to higher-quality information technology to compete for students and faculty. And still other forces (economic, political, philosophical) are pushing colleges and universities toward change. The signs and symptoms of this "slow revolution" are appearing more frequently.

■ Among faculty, students, academic leaders, and the general public, there is a growing recognition of the power of information technology to help improve the quality of teaching and learning, improve the motivation and attention of students, and improve students' career preparation.

■ . . . [I]n December 1995, the governors of the Western states unanimously endorsed the notion of a "virtual university" to serve the entire Western region. . . .

- Legislators and regents are pushing for productivity gains in higher education, . . . while reducing state funding and allowing only modest tuition increases.

- Faculty organizations are working not only to understand and support new technology options, but also to prevent the loss of jobs and tenure. . . .

- Colleges and universities . . . are extending their investments in computer- and video-related hardware. . . .

- Nationwide from 1994 to 1995, according to Kenneth Green's data, the percentage of faculty using several key instructional applications of information technology approximately doubled; the proportion of the faculty with direct personal access to computers grew past 50 percent; and the proportion of entering freshmen who had already had some academic experience with computing was also beyond 50 percent. . . .

. . . More and more faculty are using various applications of information technology to help their students through "instructional bottlenecks" in courses. . . .

. . . However, in spite of the rapidity with which exciting new computer-related technology applications continue to arrive from industry, the pace of faculty adoption of the most significant changes in teaching and learning is still measured in years or decades rather than months—and depends heavily on the accessibility of equipment, "software" in various media, and support services.

Education is being transformed, but the inertia of the system is enormous, and the costs associated with widespread, "deep" integration of information technology into teaching and learning are significant. In order for institutions to make difficult choices among strategies for change in the absence of conclusive data, each college and university must get the best advice it can from those within its own community who have relevant experience, knowledge, skills, and insights about teaching, learning, and technology. Implementing the best strategies requires institutionwide collaboration involving all key stakeholders. The cumulative impact will be "revolutionary," changing how people teach and learn, and what is taught and learned.

So now I believe that the next decade—not the next 18 to 24 months—will be critical. There seems to be rapidly growing acceptance that the ways in which information technology is used for teaching and learning will be a significant part of this transformation. What can colleges and universities do to prepare for this slow revolution? . . .

Unfortunately, the most common institutional strategy for integrating information technology into teaching and learning is CRISIS, LURCH, CRISIS, LURCH. . . .

What follows are 12 recommendations for . . . improving teaching and learning through more effective use of information technology.

1. *Fundamental Questions*
   Keep asking fundamental questions.
2. *Future Vision*
   Observe trends; shape the future; build a vision.
3. *Permanent Change*
   Adjust to new pace and depth of change.
4. *Judgment, Reductionism, Trust*
   Use judgment; resist reductionism; trust faculty and students.
5. *Dichotomies, Combinations*
   Reject dichotomies; find good combinations.
6. *Intellectual Property, Fair Use*
   Understand intellectual property law; help keep "fair use."
7. *Guidelines, Policies*
   Develop new guidelines quickly; develop new policies slowly.
8. *Support-Service Crisis*
   Prepare for your support-service crisis.
9. *Student Roles*
   Extend student roles as assistants, learning colleagues; form Faculty Student Support Service Teams (FSSSTs) and learning communities.
10. *Portfolio of Change Strategies*
    Develop a portfolio of change strategies.
11. *Realistic Expectations: More Time, Money*
    Invest more time and money.
12. *Institutionwide Collaboration*
    Develop institutionwide collaboration to improve teaching and learning. . . .

To create a climate that fosters and supports long-lasting, widespread, significant instructional change, most colleges and universities need to "de-fragment" the usual campus planning, policymaking, and support activities. One approach that is gaining acceptance and seems effective is to form a Teaching, Learning, and Technology

(TLT) Roundtable or an equivalent forum. (More than 100 institutions have already begun participating in the American Association for Higher Education's TLTR Program).

This advisory group, which includes representatives of all key stakeholders, facilitates communication, coordination, and collaboration within the institution — with a focus on teaching and learning first, technology second. The TLTR Program also encourages participants to exchange information with those conducting similar efforts at peer institutions nationwide. A long-term goal is for each college or university to achieve a balance among individuals' expectations, institutional priorities, and the availability of resources.

March/April 1996

Teaching and Learning in the Computer Age
Primacy of Process

Trent Batson and Randy Bass

We are particularly concerned in this article . . . with the implications of information technology for teaching and learning. . . . Computers, though welcome, have not been necessary to push us toward greater attention to the process of learning in any field or toward collaborative learning. . . .

Although . . . technology may not have been necessary for a focus on process or collaboration (or an appreciation of views of the social construction of knowledge), it may be necessary for the realization of those efforts. At the least, substantial affinity exists between newer pedagogical emphases and the capabilities of information technologies. . . .

. . . [M]any teachers have long expressed a desire that students experience more directly the process of how knowledge is discovered, created, shared, and shaped in their fields. . . .

Before new technologies began to alter the circumstances and means for developing knowledge, knowledge products (print elements such as books, articles, reports . . .) were not . . . apparently connected with the process of their own creation. Because of this separation, the products took on a solidity, permanency, and authority that belied the changeability of the knowledge domain behind them. Thus, our naive beliefs about thinking, teaching, and collaboration tend to be tied too much to the highly visible product and not to the almost invisible process of its creation. But as knowledge products become more apparently tied to their process of creation — because of Internet discussion lists, a much quicker publishing cycle, digital publishing on the Web that changes weekly or even daily, e-mail, videoconferencing, broader collaborative involvement, connection to new databases — the products will be perceived as less final and more tentative. They may be seen for what they are, a representation of a temporary coalescence of beliefs about what is true in any field.

Because information technologies have the ability to mediate and manage this knowledge "negotiation" process more dynamically, efficiently, inclusively, and at a much greater scale and reach than before, teachers can now bring their students into more direct contact with the process itself. That may mean — to name just a few examples — inviting them to

- "lurk" on a professional Internet discussion list,
- connect to databases formerly open only to professionals in the field,
- create simulations of reality that are almost as compelling as reality itself,
- "visit" foreign countries and "talk" to natives via Internet discussion lists or e-mail,
- create learning spaces on the Net where they and fellow learners grapple with problem-solving,
- "listen" via electronic mail or conferencing to experts in their field as they go about their daily work. . . .

Chart 1 indicates what teachers are now faced with as we find ourselves "astride the divide" be-

Chart 1 **Implications for Six Elements of Epistemology of a Shift Toward More Visible Processes**

Parameter	Print Culture (*Focus on Knowledge Products*)	Digital Culture (*Focus on Knowledge Processes*)
1. *Knowledge*	Knowledge products are not obviously connected to the process that created them.	Knowledge products are more immediately embedded within the knowledge community. Closure is harder to achieve, so knowledge seems to be more an ongoing process than an object.
2. *Teaching*	Working with disembodied knowledge objects (e.g., books). Products seem to be far removed from process of knowledge development.	More views of knowledge-in-process available. Easier to get students involved in co-creation of knowledge.
3. *Collaboration*	Harder to see social creation of knowledge: it occurs more one-to-one or in small groups. Distance discourages collaboration. Knowledge in many fields tends to be identified with an individual.	Communal collaboration more apparent. Easier to recognize social nature of knowledge. Collaboration more likely to be the norm. Knowledge more likely to be identified with community.
4. *Publication/Authority*	Print publication costly so access limited by gate keepers (editors); publication is thus the privilege of a few and therefore takes on powerful sense of authority.	Lower cost of electronic publication and shortening of print publication cycle through aid of information technology result in greater access to publishing. Co-publication of some print elements with publication on the Web. Sense of authority of print publication is therefore reduced.
5. *Thinking*	Cognitive skills needed to produce knowledge products more highly valued: structural (linear, logical) thinking skills are favored.	Cognitive skills to produce consensus in a collaborative process of knowledge-building also valued. Thinking skills leading toward conversational congruence as well as hypertextual and associational thinking gain credence.
6. *Classroom*	The place where students encounter knowledge products as explained to them by teachers and where they are given guidance (and/or the tools) to create their own knowledge products.	The place where students encounter knowledge-building processes and are given guidance about how to participate in them.

tween the print culture and the digital culture. Epistemologies are systems, and thus, if one part is radically changed, other parts are affected as well. . . .

As with any chart, one side looks "good" and the other "bad." This is the danger of this kind of simplified synoptic representation. We hope, instead, that each side will be taken to suggest tendencies of each primary technology. We know that most academics do not focus only on knowledge "products," but the tendency of print itself is to encourage that focus. Many teachers work hard to focus on the related processes of knowledge development and learning as well. Meanwhile, not all those dabbling with computers fully understand the potential impact of their explorations. Our interaction with this new technology, as individual faculty members, as students, as creative scholars, and even as a culture, will lead us to greater awareness of the primary processes of knowledge negotiation—and to the development of new ways of knowing, teaching, and learning.

The use of information technology and telecommunications and the growing importance and accessibility of process are influencing both the representation of knowledge "content" and the facilitation of knowledge "reproduction." The traditional distinction between these two processes may be dissolving.

The weakening of the distinction between the discovery and the representation of knowledge is evident in the changing nature of the faculty role and the impact those changes will have on the evaluation and rewarding of faculty. Traditional distinctions between product and process have underwritten the most prevailing categories (and hierarchies) of the evaluation and reward structure. Put simply, the evaluation of research is relatively easy because it entails the examination of the products of research, which can be measured by where they appeared, who published them, and how they were reviewed.

On the other hand, the evaluation of teaching is very difficult because teaching is about process, not products. Although there are a number of ways to argue and assess certain teaching outcomes, the heart and soul of teaching is the synthesis of the intellectual work that goes into preparation, the myriad choices of methodology and content, and then the dynamic process that unfolds as teacher and students together engage the course's content and methods. That process is dynamic because it is never the same twice, and it always requires a running negotiation between structure and improvisation. Teaching is primarily about process because it is only "in process" that its knowledge and skill are made manifest—in the process of discovery experienced by students and, in those precious moments, by teachers as well.

The increased involvement of faculty in electronic environments is helping to breach the tradi-
tional boundary between scholarship and teaching. Why? Because just as new technologies help make the process of knowledge creation more public, so too do they help faculty make their teaching more public. Whether in the case of distance education (through videotape, teleconferencing, cable television, or the Internet), or in the rapidly developing practice of mounting course materials on the World Wide Web, teaching materials and processes are becoming ever more public—and thus open to peer review.

That is, such efforts to use and integrate technology in teaching more obviously entail an explicit synthesis of content and pedagogical expertise.

In addition, information technologies are providing faculty new venues of publication and professional collaboration, including electronic journals, discussion lists and conferences, database application packages, subject-oriented CD-ROMS, and a variety of new forms of multimedia. The uses of these new formats do not fall neatly into our traditional categories of "teaching" and "research." Indeed, they represent a new borderland between the two.

As we move forward in seeing the points of contact between evolving ideas about collaborative process and the capabilities of new technologies, we need also to see the synergies between faculty work in new media and the important efforts of the last decade to rethink the question of faculty work. . . . Many of the new forms of faculty publication present new means for presenting and synthesizing knowledge that bear directly on Boyer's "scholarship of integration"; similarly, the "synoptic capacity" of teaching—the ability to draw the strands of a field together in a way that provides both coherence and meaning—is being realized in a whole host of electronic teaching venues. . . . These new forms and activities will contribute some new energy to the discussion of the "scholarship of teaching" as well. The changing landscape of higher education that spawned the calls for a more expansive and flexible notion of scholarship to begin with is being given fuller realization in the expansive, integrative, and collaborative spaces of digital culture. . . .

Universities in the Digital Age

John Seely Brown and Paul Duguid

... Colleges, Communities, and Learning

The delivery view of education assumes that knowledge comprises discrete, pre-formed units, which learners ingest in smaller or greater amounts until graduation or indigestion takes over. To become a physicist, such a view suggests, you need to take in a lot of formulas and absorb a lot of experimental data. But, on the one hand, knowledge is not a static, preformed substance: it is constantly changing. Learning involves active engagement in the processes of that change. And, on the other hand, people don't become physicists by learning formulas any more than they become football players by learning plays. In learning how to be a physicist or a football player—how to act as one, talk as one, be recognized as one—it's not the explicit statements, but the implicit practices that count.

Indeed, knowing only the explicit—mouthing the formulas or the plays—is often exactly what gives an outsider away. Insiders know more. By coming to inhabit the relevant community, they get to know not just what the standard answers are, but the real questions and why they matter. ... Learning involves inhabiting the streets of a community's culture. The community may include astrophysicists ... but learning involves experiencing its cultural peculiarities.

By describing universities in terms of community, we may seem to be putting academic disciplines somewhere on a cozy line running from neighborhood watch groups to football-team boosters—the sorts of communities that some communitarians have in mind. The communities we have in mind, however, are quite different. These hold together not through voluntarism but through the enduring interpersonal relations that form around shared practices. People come to share this sort of community by sharing the same tasks, obligations, and goals. ...

Communities of practice are, we think, essential and inevitable building blocks of society. ... It is the practice and the concepts they share that connect members of a community, not a warm glow of communitarian fellow feeling. So we are not claiming, as communitarians do, that it would be useful to form communities and that universities are a good place to form them. Rather, we claim that communities, with all their strengths and shortcomings, grow inevitably and inescapably out of ongoing, shared practice. Learning a community's ways always requires access to that community and that practice.

The real test of a school, then, is the quality of access it provides to academic communities—Toulmin's communities of concepts. A degree reflects not simply the quality of participation of a particular individual, but also the quality of access made available by the institution. That is why choosing a school is so important. Moreover, it's exactly because some schools give credentials without ever giving suitable access to knowing communities that the relationship between learning and credentials is always problematic. People can and do end up with the label but without having had the necessary experience. Consequently, the central thrust of any attempt to retool the education system must involve expanding direct access to communities, not simply to credentials.

But our concern about technological retooling also comes at this issue from the opposite direction. Those who have the label but not the experience present one problem. Those who might have the experience but not the label face another. This is a central problem for proponents of "open learning." Experience without a formal representation has very limited exchange value—as those whose experience comes from the university of life well know. Consequently, we believe that any retooling must be two-pronged: it must seek to provide wider access to communities, and not just to information, and it must expand ways to represent new forms of access and practice. ...

From Delivery to Interactivity

... [C]onventional boundaries such as those between "town" and "gown" or students and alumni will start to blur as schools extend their reach across space and time. New technologies will be increasingly important for doing this. So far, "distance learning," which primarily involves delivering instruction to people off campus, has been the center of attention. As schools consider their options, we think it's important that they look beyond traditional paradigms of distance and delivery. A college's core competency . . . involves a great deal more than simply delivering knowledge. . . .

. . . [W]hen distance learning shifts education on-line and off campus, it can damagingly restrict the essential access to . . . authentic communities. . . . Students in dislocated, virtual campuses are unable either to engage fully with a range of communities, as undergraduates should, or to participate in particular ones, as graduates must.

. . . [T]he focus on distance and delivery overlooks not only the needs of students, but all too often the strengths of new technologies, which are distinctive because they are interactive. Previous communications technologies — books, film, radio, television, telephones, video — have all supported distance and delivery, but they have primarily permitted only one-to-many or one-to-one communications. Knowledge communities, however, are built on more complex interactions, such as continuous conversation. Even in the technologically rich 20th century, such interactions have, for the most part, been possible only in face-to-face situations. The explosion of interactive and midcast (as opposed to broadcast or narrowcast distribution) technologies for the Internet argues that in the 21st century mediated communications will expand the possibility for rich, distal interactions — urging consideration of more than distance in distal education.

Already, innovative teachers and students are taking full advantage of the Internet to move from a paradigm of delivery to one of interactivity. We offer here a few examples of technologies and teachers that strike us as going in the right direction.

■ *Newsgroups, usenets, bulletin boards, and listserv mail lists* — all these are based on the rudimentary software of electronic mail. E-mail has proved very useful in keeping teachers and students in touch with one another in one-to-one exchanges, but these groups or lists move beyond that by allowing all their members to address the group as a whole (in much the way someone asking a question in class addresses the whole class). Anyone who subscribes to a group or list can broadcast or midcast. Furthermore, many lists and groups capture the apparently ephemeral exchanges and comments of members in an archive that outlives the transient status of classroom questions. In sum, these systems essentially embrace both the features of many-to-many, real-time, conversation-like interaction and those of more enduring, written exchanges. . . .

■ *Shared on-line environments.* Nowhere on the Net has conversation become as lively as in MUDs and MOOs, shared on-line environments that allow all participating to see whatever anyone writes, though the participants may be continents apart. MUDs (Multi-User Dungeons) allow several players on computers connected by modems to play the game "Dungeons and Dragons" together. MOOs (object-oriented MUDs) remove the game goals, turning the dungeons into a computationally manipulable set of "rooms" where people can meet for on-line discussions and programming. MOOs have become the clubs and coffee houses, pubs and cafés of the Internet.

For courses that have difficulty finding enough live bodies on one campus, a MOO offers an interesting medium for interactive distal learning. James O'Donnell's graduate course on Boethius, conducted in the fall of 1994 for credit from the graduate school at the University of Pennsylvania, is an early example. Graduate medieval Latinists are few and usually far between, but Penn's Latin-MOO allowed students from the United States and Asia to form a reasonable quorum. (The course on Boethius spanned some nine time zones.)

Penn's LatinMOO was much more than a simple chat line. It comprised a "complex" with a quadrangle, several classrooms, a Latin-only common room, and a virtual Coke machine around which people would gather to chat. O'Donnell opened the Boethius classroom to students enrolled in the class, while he made other parts of the MOO available for Latin students from his regular courses (including a "live" undergraduate class on Boethius) to get together more informally. To widen the conversation, O'Donnell combined other Net facilities with the MOO. In addition to putting the central text on a Web site with links to a commentary and other resources, he started a Boethius e-mail list that included all students in the MOO seminar and the live class, but essentially created space for virtual "auditors." This opened discussion to students and academics from around the world, while distinguishing levels of participation and access. . . .

We suspect that, though Net interactions offer profoundly useful means to support and develop existing communities, they are not so good at helping a community to form or a newcomer to join. Dan Huttenlocher agues that from his experience there is an important synergy between his live classes and their on-line interactions that the on-line exchanges alone couldn't provide. "The Net isn't a good place to form communities," he claims, "though it's a very good place to keep them going." Clearly, someone with only on-line access to Huttenlocher's course material would not benefit from this synergy.

The experience of LatinMOO at first seems to challenge Huttenlocher's claim. A cadre of Boethius scholars did appear to form wholly on-line. Yet even here on-line participation was significantly dependent on a deep base of off-line experiences. All the participants were graduate students, which by our earlier analysis makes them quite distinct from Huttenlocher's class. Graduate students have already been heavily socialized into the patterns of university and graduate work and behavior, whereas undergraduate classes have only started this difficult socializing process. Unlike Huttenlocher, O'Donnell didn't have to instill too many social conventions beyond those of MOO-ing itself, since participants had already picked up the niceties and the idiosyncrasies of scholarly behavior off-line. In short, O'Donnell's on-line class was inescapably enabled and enriched from the participants' background in off-line classes. . . .

March/April 1999

When Wishes Come True

Colleges and the Convergence of Access, Lifelong Learning, and Technology

Kenneth C. Green

. . . All around us we see the evidence that the wishful, if often ephemeral, themes of academic conferences of the past two decades are now, unexpectedly, part of our new reality—structural components of the emerging new world of postsecondary education. Academe's wish list, as drawn from these conference themes, is represented by the convergence of three key issues:

■ *Increased access.* In both developed and developing nations, we see growing demand for access to higher education. In the United States, the proportion of recent high school graduates entering college has risen from just over half in 1980 to 67 percent today. Rising demand—coupled with rising expectations—is pushed by an escalating set of demographic, social, and economic factors. . . .

■ *Lifelong learning.* We, and our students, confront a future of not one job or career, but many. Growing numbers of adults—many with college degrees, many without—are coming to colleges and other postsecondary providers for new rounds of education and certification. Individuals and employers alike have come to recognize that a bachelor's degree is not the end of the educational journey but just another milestone.

■ *Information technology.* Information technology is now ubiquitous, across and beyond higher education. It's not just computers, the Internet, or the Web; it's the *aggregated presence* of technologies in virtually all facets of daily life that has made the difference. Higher education's clientele—students from ages 17 to 67—now come to college expecting to learn *about* technology and also to learn *with* technology.

For the campus community, . . . *these are the things we have wished for . . . . Now what do we do?*

Truth be told, . . . as an "enterprise," higher education remains mostly unprepared for the consequences of this coming convergence. We *know* we confront more younger students, more adult learners, and more technology. Yet to date, much (if not most) of the writing and planning addressing these issues seems conventional, piecemeal, even dated. Like the old generals, much of academic leadership seems to be planning for the last war, not the current one. . . .

Today, . . . information technology has finally emerged as a permanent, respected (or at least accepted), and increasingly essential component of the college experience. . . .

However, significant questions remain . . . about IT that cluster into three key issues:

■ *Content.* How will information technology expand access to information and knowledge? What IT resources can or should be incorporated into teaching and curricula?

■ *Delivery.* How might technology be used to enhance instruction in both traditional and non-traditional contexts, for both traditional and non-traditional learners?

■ *Infrastructure.* What kind of infrastructure (hardware, software, networks, technical support, user support and training, financial planning) is required to make technology accessible, available, and effective in postsecondary education? . . .

Have we really witnessed a "computer revolution" or experienced a "technology transformation" of higher education? Clearly no! More accurately, we are participating in a steady process of evolution and change. It is still premature to talk about a technology-driven *transformation* of educational institutions because virtually all schools and colleges are still in the early stages of adopting and incorporating various kinds of IT resources into their instructional functions. And it is hyperbole to discuss a technological revolution in education, which implies a sudden and dramatic departure from past practices — practices that reflect, in part, academic traditions that are centuries old.

Yet technology, as a function and as a resource, has in fact entered the pedagogical mainstream in American colleges and universities. As of Fall 1998,

■ more than two-fifths of college courses used e-mail, while fully a third of college courses drew on content from the Web;

■ more than 40 percent of the nation's colleges had some sort of computer literacy or computer competency requirement;

■ over 60 percent of public four-year institutions had a mandatory IT fee;

■ more than three-fourths of the two- and four-

year colleges had IT support centers to assist faculty with instructional integration; and

■ almost half of the nation's colleges had a formal plan to use the Internet for marketing the institution to prospective students; more than half had some portion of the undergraduate application available to prospective students on the Web.

These indicators notwithstanding, we need to acknowledge that information technology has yet to transform classrooms, the instructional activities of most faculty, or the learning experiences of most students. Moreover, while we know that technology changes the learning experience, we do not have hard, consistent evidence documenting that it enhances academic achievement and learning outcomes. Our willingness to learn (or admit) what we *don't* know about IT impacts and learning outcomes becomes increasingly important as technology emerges as a driving force in the discussion about campus and corporate (business) plans under development for serving lifelong learners via distance-learning programs. . . .

American higher education is very much an organic enterprise. . . .

. . . At each step along the way, new kinds of colleges, new or specialized institutions — specialized cells — have emerged as derivatives of the existing enterprise, expanding the definition, the mission, and the clientele of the educational and social institution known as the American College. . . .

. . . [A]s we approach the 21st century, we are again witnessing a significant *evolutionary* event in American higher education. This event is the emergence of *distance education* and *distributed learning*, a phenomenon fostered to a large degree by the three convergence issues cited earlier: increased access, lifelong learning, and information technology.

This is a significant event — as significant as the 19th-century birth of the land-grant colleges and the early 20th-century emergence and subsequent postwar expansion and success of community colleges.

Land-grant institutions and community colleges were educational organizations born of new needs in a changing American society. To some degree, the land-grant institutions were accidents and experiments — a hybrid of the 18th-century English college and an American derivative of the 19th-century German research university. Similarly, community colleges were also clearly a response to specific education and training needs that emerged in American society in the middle of the present century. They were endorsed by many educational leaders and public officials at the time of their birth, similar to the official sponsorship of entities such as today's Western Governors University and California Virtual University. Yet these new forms of college each had their critics who raised questions about their quality and integrity. Does this sound familiar?

Distance learning is not new to the American college experience. Agricultural extension programs that began some 130 years ago in the early days of the American land-grant movement are the programmatic precursors of today's distance-education initiatives. . . . However, technology changes the instructional methodologies as well as the content, costs, and delivery of distance education. . . .

. . . Focus on the *instructional* mission of higher education . . . and three primary functions emerge: *content* (what is taught), *context* (the environment that fosters or supports instruction and learning), and *certification* (documenting outcomes). . . .

Higher education typically has addressed these three instructional functions concurrently: the classroom focuses on content, the campus fosters a learning environment, and the institution certifies educational and professional accomplishment. What's so very significant today is that technology makes porous the boundaries that traditionally separated content, context, and certification. Technology brings new, rich resources to the learning of content; creates new contexts for interaction between and among instructors and learners; and can fundamentally change the way students and institutions approach assessment and certification.

A careful look at the growing population of largely part-time adult learners who drive the current distance-learning market suggests that most are primarily interested in *content* and *certification*. Moreover, these (lifelong) learners want specific content, not a comprehensive offering: they need a course or two to acquire new knowledge and up-to-date skills, but not to obtain a degree (or yet another degree!).

Indeed, in distance learning we see that *convenience* has replaced *context* as a component of the educational experience. (This is clearly the mantra of the University of Phoenix.) Context, as traditionally offered as part of the college experience, has little priority in the educational aspirations or self-assessed educational needs of most adult learners.

Phoenix and Jones International (via Mind Extension University, now the College Connection), as the first national "brands" in this arena, have understood these issues better than most traditional institutions. Moreover, the for-profit companies coming into the distance- or distributed-learning market certainly understand this difference. These new, for-profit providers also understand the market disadvantages (and higher operating costs) of focusing on all three traditional instructional functions. And they recognize that there is significant money to be made in unbundled educational services like content (only) or certification (only). . . .

Just as Mark Twain once announced that reports of his death were premature, so too is it premature—even for Peter Drucker—to announce the coming demise of residential colleges, let alone of "traditional" higher education, as entities about to be swept under by the *tsunami* of online learning. . . .

. . . [A]ll parties would do well to view distance, distributed, and online learning as a new, fourth sector of higher education, residing alongside (and not behind) research universities, residential colleges, and commuter institutions. The boundaries that separate the sectors and their respective clientele are increasingly porous. Growing numbers of institutions firmly planted in one sector now serve (and indeed recruit!) students from other sectors: universities pursue part-time adult learners, while community colleges develop honors programs to serve the growing numbers of middle- and upper-ability, middle- and upper-income students who matriculate directly from high school. . . .

. . . Increased access, lifelong learning, and information technology are converging on American colleges and universities in ways that go well beyond the aspirations articulated in hundreds of conference speeches over he past three decades. The American postsecondary enterprise continues to evolve, changing slowly at the traditional center and faster on the perimeter. . . .

Conclusions

Deborah DeZure

During the past 30 years in higher education, significant changes have occurred in teaching and learning. These changes were propelled not by a single engine, but by many different developments acting as levers—shaping attitudes, creating opportunities, and promoting shifts in policies and practices. Together, they provided the critical mass of momentum to enable higher education to make unprecedented strides. This concluding chapter recaps the key developments we have witnessed in *Change*, explores major trends that emerge from them, and identifies unfinished agendas for the future.

Developments that Changed Higher Education (1969–1999)

The many developments that changed the world of higher education, particularly with regard to teaching and learning, included:

- introduction of publications like *Change* and the *Chronicle of Higher Education*, which provided a venue for discussion of issues, creating a common discourse about higher education and introducing new developments in teaching and learning;
- increased access to higher education through open admissions, affirmative action, and outreach to adult learners and those who work full- and part-time;
- remedial and developmental education, academic support services, and programs to support students underprepared for college work;
- addition of new fields: black studies, women's studies, ethnic studies, global studies, environmental studies, and interdisciplinary studies;
- models of living-learning communities, experimental colleges, residential colleges, and learning communities;
- changes in student values from social protest, to personal development, to vocationalism and consumerism, reflecting the values of the larger society;
- demographic shifts in the college population, particularly the reality of declining enrollments;
- curricular reform and revision of general education as well as emphasis on career preparation and the major;
- a large and growing body of research on college teaching and learning;
- multiculturalism and a commitment to diversity;
- new conceptions of knowledge, particularly the social construction of knowledge;
- new instructional approaches rooted in "active" learning;
- introduction of writing across the curriculum;
- national education reports, some of which shocked and provoked the nation, including *A Nation at Risk* (U.S. National Commission on Excellence in Education, 1983), *Involvement in Learning* (National Institute of Education, 1984), and *Integrity in the College Curriculum* (Association of American Colleges, 1985);
- market demands for graduates with skills in problem-solving, communications, working in teams, sensitivity to diversity, and ethical decision-making;
- accreditation and state mandates for outcomes assessment and the growth of the assessment movement;
- renewed concern for a commitment to civic life;
- development of co-curricular community service and academic-service learning;
- increased complexity and difficulty of teaching in a sustained period of social and educational transition;

- emergence of "faculty development" and establishment of support programs and centers for college teaching and learning;
- introduction of systematic methods to evaluate teaching, including student evaluations of teaching, teaching portfolios, and peer review;
- paradigm shift from teaching to learning;
- reconsideration of the nature of faculty work, including changing roles and rewards, and the publication of *Scholarship Reconsidered* (Boyer, 1990) and *Scholarship Assessed* (Glassick, Huber, Maeroff, & Boyer, 1997).
- developments in the "scholarship of teaching";
- changes in the training and socialization of new faculty;
- new technologies: media, distance learning, computers, the Internet and the World Wide Web; and
- competition from providers outside the academy.

Each of these factors can be seen as both causes and effects of the changes that occurred in teaching and learning during this period. None of them is discrete, and the interactive effects are profound and ongoing. The list is not in strict chronological order; some of these developments emerged concurrently, albeit in different sectors of higher education, gaining momentum and significance at different rates. Others have had an ongoing impact that is periodically energized by innovations in the field, as in the case of new technologies.

This collection explores all of these developments. Their elaboration is not my intent here. They are included to underscore the number and type of developments that contributed to the changes we see in higher education today. They affirm the degree to which significant changes were made possible by other shifts; some antecedent, some concurrent; some proactive, some reactive. They help to explain why, for example, many of the student-centered active learning methods advocated 30 years ago now are taking root and flourishing; there is readiness for these methods because a sufficient number of pre-conditions now exist, enabling innovations to be adopted, assessed, rewarded, and sustained. Taken together, these developments represent a cultural shift, one that increasingly promotes and supports an active culture of teaching.

Learning from *Change*: Trends

Beyond these developments, several trends emerge from the ongoing "conversations" in *Change* about teaching and learning: the thrust toward democratizing higher education; border crossings; collaboration, communication, and community; and using what we know.

Democratizing Higher Education

Of all the trends evident in this collection, the thrust toward democratizing higher education is the most important and pervasive. What do I mean by democratizing higher education? I mean that institutions of higher education, collectively if not individually, are actively engaged in efforts:

- to provide access and equity for all who wish to enter American higher education;
- to include representation of diverse constituencies, ensuring that their needs and viewpoints are heard and respected;
- to elicit input from all interested parties about the decisions that affect them;
- to maximize collaboration, cooperation, and consideration in power and authority relations;
- to promote community values, balancing the needs of individuals with those of the group.

While the quest has not been fully realized, progress has been made on these dimensions during the past 30 years.

Increased access, if not always equity, is most clearly seen in the waves of new students who have entered higher education since 1969. The policy of open admissions, begun in the early 1970s, provided access for high-school graduates regardless of their levels of achievement. They were primarily from blue-collar and white ethnic backgrounds. Many of them worked full- or part-time. As seen in the articles in "Portraits of Students" and "Teacher Narratives," these students were often poorly prepared for academic work. The influx of new students led to the further development of community colleges that were responsive to the needs of these students. Community colleges recognized and acted upon the need to provide support services, flexible schedules, integration of work experiences, credit for prior learning, active learning strategies, ongoing faculty-student contact, strong advising, community outreach, and high school/community college connections. All of these anticipated the approaches we use and advocate today (see Binzen, 1973; Cross, 1973; Maeroff, 1981; Marshak & Wurtemburg, 1981).

Affirmative action increased access for people of color while bringing new and diverse viewpoints and cultures to many predominantly white campuses. (See "Portraits of Students.") This interactive effect of affirmative action is critical to understanding the profound shifts that it set in motion not only for people of color, but also for white faculty and staff, for curriculum, for pedagogy, and, most important, for the learning outcomes of all students (see Astin, 1993).

Workers increasingly found access to higher education through their workplace, supported by union groups and employers (Barasch, 1981). In the mid-1970s, there was also a call for life-long learning and the role that higher education could take in serving the ongoing educational needs of adults throughout their lives (Mondale, 1976). With the aging of the baby boomers, we are bound to see more attention to these needs.

There was outreach made possible by distance learning. In 1971, *Change* featured the efforts of England's Open University. This groundbreaking model doubled the college population of England within a few years by offering college courses to adults through a combination of television, correspondence, and sites set up throughout England to provide tutoring and testing (Maclure). The United States already had a history of land-grant institutions reaching out to adults, particularly those in rural settings, through extension programs, but the last three decades saw a dramatic increase in adults seeking continuing education in both degree and non-degree programs. In recent years, the use of computers, and the Internet, has transformed the traditional concept of distance learning. By providing synchronous and a-synchronous learning experiences around the globe at all times of the day and night, the new technologies have expanded access dramatically by reducing the barriers of time and location.

The ubiquitous presence of computers and distance learning in higher education does not mean that access and equity now are assured. The cost of higher education continues to be a significant roadblock for many. Access to computers solves some problems while it creates others; there is cause for concern that those who cannot afford computers are denied access to skills in information literacy as well as the knowledge afforded by their use. This digital divide may reinforce rather than obliterate the gap between the haves and have-nots in our society.

Another critical dimension to democratizing higher education is evident in the curriculum: what is studied, whose stories are told, whose traditions are taught and reified in the process. During the student movement in the 1960s, the curriculum was one of the areas that fell under greatest attack. The curriculum was revised to provide more choice and more course offerings that reflected the interests of students (Hall & Kevles, 1980). While electives replaced requirements, the major was granted an increasing share of the collegiate experience, reflecting the interests of faculty.

Courses in black studies, women's studies, and ethnic studies took root. On some campuses, these courses were housed in separate programs or departments. On other campuses, they were infused across the curriculum through the efforts of interested and knowledgeable faculty members who saw the need to include diverse voices. These efforts were catalytic in forcing a re-examination of the curriculum, not simply to address student requests for relevance but also to legitimate the cultural variety within American society that was underrepresented in the traditional curriculum. This process served to further democratize higher education.

The transition has been long and arduous. The courses, programs, faculty and their scholarship were often marginalized. There were other faculty members who actively resisted these changes, charging that they watered down the curriculum, replacing the "great books" with those of lesser value. Thus began the culture wars that continue today. "Curriculum" captures many of these issues. (See, in particular, articles by Howe, 1982; Lester, 1979; Booth, 1988; Hirsch, Jr., 1988; Wong, 1991; Hill, 1991; and Cortés, 1991).

Enrolling diverse new learners was only part of the equation of access and equity. An equally important part was supporting their academic success by providing academic services for underprepared students. When it was ignored, the open door became the revolving door, resulting in low student retention rates and faculty demoralization. However, many institutions responded in productive ways: they offered academic support programs that provided tutoring and mentoring, and eventually, if reluctantly, they introduced developmental education. Although not offered for credit toward graduation, developmental courses enabled students to develop the skills necessary to succeed in their subsequent courses. Debates about remedial education continue today, often accompanied by finger-pointing at the K-12 schools. In other cases, institutions have addressed the issue by conducting diagnostic testing and referring underprepared students to community colleges. An increasing number of college students today exhibit academic deficiencies that require remediation, and colleges are finding it more difficult to limit admission to those who, upon enrollment, have all the academic skills necessary to succeed. Once again, these efforts reflect the democratization of higher education, albeit with growing pains along the way.

Another element of the curriculum and co-curriculum deserves particular mention: the overt and explicit efforts to prepare students for participation in a democratic society and to renew civic life (see Gabelnick, 1997; Gamson, 1997; Parks Daloz, Keen, Keen, & Parks Daloz, 1996). During the student movement in the 1960s, social and community needs had an important place. While some students looked inward in a personal quest for self-exploration, many others found ways to serve society. Throughout the 1970s and 1980s, however, self-interest and vocationalism became the prevailing values among students, perpetuated however unwittingly by institutions eager to maintain enrollment in the face of a declining student population. Programs increasingly took on vocational goals, with the liberal arts and electives redesigned to support careerism. As we moved into the 1990s, however, we saw calls to renew the commitment to civic life and a democratic society. In the 1990s, we also saw renewed emphasis on global and environmental studies. Efforts continue to ensure that students graduate as informed citizens who vote, contribute to their communities, and actively seek solutions to pressing social problems here and abroad.

The interest in community service, both co-curricular service and academic-service learning, reflects these concerns. Service learning literally and figuratively moves students and teachers out of the classroom and into the community. (See "Work, Service, and Community Connections" and "Learning Communities.") The trajectory of service learning in higher education is not yet clear. Service learning appears every few decades but disappears again because it has never been fully integrated into the goals of academic life. Zlotkowski (1996) argues that until faculty members make a commitment to integrate academic-service learning, it will remain on the margins of what we do in higher education, a noble but modest effort. For those who are involved, these activities bring students, faculty, staff, and members of the community together to work collaboratively on social problems—often with productive results. Surely this signals a democratization of higher education.

During this 30-year period, we witnessed progressive shifts in the relations between faculty and students, with subtle changes in the dynamics of power and authority. The image of the professorial "sage on the stage" has been increasingly replaced by the image of the "guide on the side"—or variations on that theme including "coach," "mentor," even "midwife," and "resource provider." In the context of distance learning and the World Wide Web, students and their teachers are often characterized as "co-learners." Methods of teaching increasingly engage students actively with faculty and with their peers. Lecture and discussion techniques are giving way to collaborative and cooperative learning, case studies, discovery-based methods, problem-based learning, and simulations. In the mid 1990s, we began to hear about the "paradigm shift from teaching to learning," from emphasis on what the teacher does to emphasis on what students do, from teacher-centered to learner-centered classrooms (see Barr & Tagg, 1995). In many cases, these changes resulted in shifting relations as faculty members began to share authority and power with their students much as they had done in the 1960s. Some faculty members introduced student management teams and invited student input in the preparation of syllabi, assignments, and assessments. Others introduced contract learning to empower students further by granting them some control in evaluation and grading. Most prevalent of all was the growing use of student evaluations of teaching, which fueled and reinforced the important role of student input in the teaching, learning, and assessment processes.

Let me not overstate the case here. While new teaching methods have been plentiful, and *Change* and other publications periodically featured their use and efficacy, lecture was still the predominant instructional method throughout this period. The emerging image of teacher as "coach" and "co-learner with students" is only now beginning to spread. Nonetheless, this shift is one more sign of changing power relations in teaching and learning, one that serves to democratize the classroom.

Assessment, too, has had a role to play in this process. Barbara Wright's "Commentary" on the democratizing effect of assessment bears repeating:

Democratization means a couple of things. It means, for example, respecting and including the voices of those who have traditionally been excluded. In the case of higher education, this has meant, almost as a point of pride, the voices of students as well as the voices from beyond the campus: everyone from K-12 educators or employers or policymakers to parents and the general public. Thanks to assessment, these voices now have avenues of input.

At the same time, democratic process requires a sense of civic responsibility and community effort. In that regard, the democratization of education on campus has meant pulling faculty back from anarchic individualism or from a survivalist focus on departmental turf. It's meant creating new communities of interest across boundaries seldom traversed in the past. . . The best assessment represents a new way to mesh education on campus with the requirements of the society that both supports it and depends on it. That's a challenge likely to keep us busy for decades.

It is somewhat ironic that a change *imposed* on the academy by state mandates and accrediting agencies has had such a democratizing effect on higher education.

Taken together, these shifts present a complex picture of changing demographics, curricula, methods of instruction and assessment—all of which affirm and support the ongoing process of democratizing higher education.

Border Crossings

Part of the evolutionary story of higher education during the last 30 years involves border crossings, that is, efforts to traverse the great divides once erected by higher education that may have outlived their usefulness and effectiveness. These border crossings are less obvious and less institutionalized than the changes we noted in the previous section, but they are appearing on the education horizon with increasing frequency. We do not hear about them as often perhaps because they are accomplished quietly. Discretion helps to protect the pathfinders in an academic world that still honors the old borders.

Where do we find these border crossings? We find them between and among curricula, department, and disciplinary structures, and administrative units. We see them in redefinitions of the traditional faculty roles of research, teaching, and service. We see them in personal acts of "going public" with one's teaching. Finally, we see them in interactions with the larger community—locally and globally. The walls of the ivory tower are not crumbling, but the doors are opening, both within the academy and to the outside world.

Prime examples of border crossings can be found in interdisciplinary teaching and learning and the scholarship that supports them. The movement to promote interdisciplinary studies has waxed and waned over the years (Klein, 1990, 1996). Interdisciplinary initiatives were well supported in the 1960s: students and faculty wanted courses that spoke to broad social issues whose solutions required the insights of many disciplinary ways of knowing. Funding for interdisciplinary programs declined in the 1970s and 1980s with the renewal of vocational interests that required graduates to have specialized training within the traditional disciplines. But in the last 10 years, interdisciplinary efforts are again on the rise (Edwards, 1996; Newell, 1998). There is a renewal of interest in providing connected learning, that is, learning that transcends disciplinary boundaries (Association of American Colleges, 1990). Once again, complex problems like AIDS, cancer, world hunger, violence, and genocide defy the solutions proffered by problem-solving within solitary disciplines. Employers want graduates who can demonstrate problem-solving, communication, and ethical decision-making skills that are not necessarily rooted in disciplinary training. "Connected learning" also supports the learning styles of many of the "new learners" in higher education today, particularly women, students of color, and adult learners (Belenky, Clinchy, Goldberger, & Tarule, 1986; Schroeder, 1993).

Interdisciplinary scholarship is also thriving. As Julie Klein (1990) notes, some of the most innovative research is emerging from the interdisciplines. Neuroscience, gender studies, bioengineering, and biomedical technology all exemplify this trend.

Interdisciplinary work has a long way to go, however. First, institutions continue to train, grant degrees, hire, evaluate, and reward faculty for their work in specializations within the traditional disciplines. Although progress has been made in finding administrative solutions, many institutions continue to struggle with how to integrate interdisciplinarians and their work into the rigid departmental structure of the academy. Second, faculty are reluctant to engage in interdisciplinary teaching because they are trained as specialists within a discipline: for many, interdisciplinary teaching flies in the face of their conceptions of expertise and competence. Third, we are only beginning to understand the nature of interdisciplinary integration and synthesis. All too often faculty who team-teach in interdisciplinary courses provide presentations of the course materials from their own disciplinary perspectives and leave the integration to the students — a task well beyond many of them. Nonetheless, interdisciplinary work is on the rise, both in teaching and in research, and more productive models are emerging.

A second model of border crossing involves learning communities, the newest incarnation of living-learning communities. One popular approach supported by research on student retention focuses on integrating the academic and social lives of students. This model relies on the participation of faculty and student affairs specialists. Although there are variations, many of these learning communities organize students in cohorts to provide ongoing peer support. They maximize faculty-student interaction and collaborative learning. They promote learning as a communal activity and offer support services where and when needed (see Gabelnick, MacGregor, Matthews, & Smith, 1990; Gabelnick, 1997; Singleton, Jr., R., Garvey, R.H., & Phillips, G.A., 1998). Whatever the specifics of the model, most of these learning communities involve border crossing, including the active collaboration of faculty and student affairs staff, overriding long-standing administrative and cultural separations.

Third, as noted in the discussion of democratizing higher education, assessment brings together faculty, administrators, and staff to evaluate student learning outcomes and to take collective responsibility for them. Assessment of student learning outcomes forces systematic examination of the collegiate experience of students, general education and the major, as well as attitudes and values learned throughout the curriculum and the co-curriculum. The work of assessment, whether driven by accreditation requirements, state mandates, or internal institutional research, requires the input and the attention of faculty and staff members working together toward a common goal.

Fourth, the gradual development of a culture of teaching in higher education not only opened classroom doors, but it also helped to build a community of scholars around their mutual concern for teaching. This development was reflected in and promoted by the publication of *Scholarship Reconsidered* (Boyer, 1990), a document that gave voice to the desire to reconceptualize faculty work beyond the traditional paradigm of teaching, research, and service. This new vision for faculty roles and rewards is rich with examples of border crossings and changing epistemologies. The scholarship of teaching, for example, borrows the concept, methods, and privileged status of scholarship and adapts them to teaching (see Hutchings & Shulman, 1999; Schön, 1995).

Fifth, there are efforts to engage with the larger local and global communities. Thirty years ago, students could study abroad for a semester. Today, thanks to distance learning, students from around the world can take on-line courses or participate in classes that use interactive video to bring together students and faculty members from multiple sites around the globe. The World Wide Web offers access to resources in other countries, updated to ensure access to breaking news as it is happening and to information as it is released. The Internet crosses borders unimaginable to most of us three decades ago.

Border crossing is part of the larger dialectic of change — breaking down barriers and creating others. Over time new interdisciplines often become interdisciplinary disciplines with new borders and paradigms — new silos in our midst. The border crossings we observed may be modest, marginalized, and sporadic, but they offer options we did not have in the past. Equally significantly, they both inspire and create new pathways to traverse the great divides so characteristic of higher education in the 20th century.

Communication, Collaboration, and Communication

College teaching has become increasingly more difficult and more complex, requiring us to take into account many more variables, each with its own challenges. The "new learners" often have different learning styles both from their predecessors who attended college several decades ago and from faculty who tend to prefer teaching methods that reflect their own learning style rather than those of their students (Schroeder, 1993). Faculty members are expected to understand and respect the diverse needs and cultures of all of their students and to ensure that students in their classrooms conduct themselves with civility and mutual respect. The "new learners," who are often first-generation college students, enter higher education with multiple learning needs. Many of these students are underprepared for college level work and require remediation in reading, writing, quantitative skills, and study skills. We are also seeing an increase in students with learning disabilities and students in need of support and accommodations in compliance with regulations of the Americans with Disabilities Act. Student attitudes also present challenges. Many students today reflect the consumerist values of the larger society, with expectations for college much like those they have for their banks and dry cleaners: service, convenience, ease of parking, and low cost (Levine, 1993, p. 4).

The knowledge explosion continues unabated, and the curriculum continues to expand exponentially. New views of knowledge and knowledge construction have emerged, challenging what, why, and how we teach. The goals for student learning outcomes are far more extensive and ambitious than ever before, including broad-based skills, such as communication skills, problem-solving skills, and ability to work with diverse others, often in teams, as well as discipline-based knowledge and abilities. Faculty members are required not only to teach these skills but also to assess them, using a range of formative and summative approaches to evaluation. There is an expectation that faculty will teach using new and active instructional methods, although they themselves were taught primarily by lecture methods. Many of these new strategies are labor intensive, requiring more planning and more time to respond to student work—as in the use of writing across the curriculum. Faculty members also are expected to learn and to use technology not only for professional communication and research but also in teaching, keeping abreast of each new form of technology as it emerges.

Faculty members are now evaluated on their teaching with input from students on regularly administered student evaluations and by peers as part of peer review. Faculty members are required to document their teaching as part of reviews for tenure and promotion— often being asked to produce a teaching portfolio or some variation of it, replete with a statement of their philosophy of teaching (Seldin, 1984, 1999). They are asked to engage in curricular and instructional reform, often requiring them to read and learn the extensive and growing body of research on college teaching and learning, and to adapt that research to their institutional context.

Teaching *is* more complicated than it was in the 1960s, 1970s, and 1980s. The profound irony of these challenges is that they have forced even the most private and reticent teachers to open their classroom doors and speak with their colleagues about the changes in teaching they have experienced. The result has been an increase in collaboration among colleagues to build community and to share their collective wisdom of practice.

The words *collaboration, communication,* and *community* echo through the pages of this collection as the response and often the solution to the difficulties of teaching and learning as we enter the new millennium. (See Astin, 1987; Palmer, 1992, 1997.) The challenges are too numerous and too complex to brave them alone. Even if it were possible, it is inadvisable. It is too lonely, too frustrating, and ultimately too ineffective. Most tasks of value today require the input and insight of many people — those diverse voices about which so much has been written. The challenges require ongoing dialogue among communities of learners, teachers, scholars, colleagues within departments and across the university, and with communities outside the academy.

In "Promoting a Culture of Teaching," we repeatedly see the invocation of *collaboration* and *community* as solutions to overcoming professional isolation, to enhancing reform efforts, and to fostering productivity as teachers and scholars. In "Portraits of Students: A Gallery Tour" and "Learning Communities," we see communities of learners as a critical feature of supporting diverse students as they make the transition into the brave new world of higher education. In "Curriculum," "Assessing Student Learning" and "Professional, Graduate, and Teacher Education: Criticism and Reform," we hear that working in teams and the ability to collaborate and communicate are among the most valued learning outcomes of employers, academics, and accrediting groups. In "Philosophy, Psychology, and Methods of Teaching" and "Teaching in the Disciplines: Visiting Across the Disciplines," we learn that cooperation, not competition, will produce the kinds of learning outcomes we most value and that knowledge construction is a social endeavor. We also learn that ongoing communication and dialogue are required for mutual understanding of diverse viewpoints. In "Evaluating College Teaching: Myth and Reality" and "Assessing Student Learning," we see that effective evaluation techniques involve collaborative efforts and input from several sources. In "Media and Technology: *Plus ça change*," we learn about on-line learning communities that engage learners from around the world. The use of technology not only promotes communication between faculty and students and among students; it also enables students to communicate with the larger world. The use of instructional technology requires collaborations with many individuals who support and maintain the technology infrastructure so critical to its effectiveness. Teaching with technology cannot be accomplished alone. It is an institution-wide commitment that requires continuous collaboration and communication.

In the readings in this collection, *collaboration*, *communication*, and *community* are not suggested lightly: they are seen as educational imperatives to meet the challenges of the future.

Using What We Know

The good news is that there is a large and growing body of research to guide us about effective approaches to teaching and learning. The disturbing news is that many academics are not familiar with the research; others who do know it do not use it to guide their practice (Svinicki, 1999; Terenzini & Pascarella, 1994). Three of the commentaries in this collection speak directly to the issue of prevailing myths about teaching and learning that continue unabated despite the availability of abundant research findings that dispel them. (See "Philosophy, Psychology, and Methods of Teaching," "Evaluating College Teaching, " and "Media and Technology.")

In "Assessing Student Learning," the National Center for Postsecondary Improvement (NCPI) report on the status of assessment on American campuses found that institutions are complying with assessment mandates. They are collecting data about student learning, but the vast majority of institutions are not using that data to inform their decision-making or practices (National Center for Postsecondary Improvement, 1999).

In the title of his section on "Media and Technology," Kenneth Green refers to the expression: *"Plus ça change, plus c'est la même chose,"* that is, the more things change, the more they remain the same. He is not commenting on the new technologies. He critiques the inability and unwillingness of institutions to respond effectively to each new technology as it appears. Institutions make the same mistakes, the same omissions, and the same commissions with the advent of each innovation without learning from the past. Time after time, institutions underestimate the needs for infrastructure and ongoing support services. He concludes his commentary with the observation that academics should attend more carefully to the research on higher education generally and on educational technology specifically because it offers productive approaches to the challenges we face.

In higher education, a field that reveres the dissemination of knowledge, it is terribly ironic that more academics have not been engaged in learning about this rich body of research and have not used it to improve their practice. Surely one key implication of this collection is to encourage those in leadership roles to get the word out systematically. The challenge of dissemination is not unique. The business world too had a history of collecting data that went underutilized. The business world responded by problem-solving and finding ways to ensure that research findings go to those who can best use them. We need to do the same.

Unfinished Agendas

As we enter the new millennium, there are several unfinished agendas:

Structures that need revision. In their recent essay, "Habits Hard to Break," Schneider and Shoenberg (1999) identify traditions that have outlived their utility in higher education. These "habits" need to be re-examined and adapted to current and future needs. They include the accrual of courses and credit hours as the basis for granting the baccalaureate degree; the hegemony of the disciplines and specialization in the training of faculty; and the continued separation of general education and the major in light of new types of learning outcomes. (See also Rudolph, 1984; Smith 1983.) These "habits" are unwieldly, deeply entrenched, and systemic problems. Rather than attempt systemic change, we have turned our attention to more manageable, self-contained problems, leaving these for another day. Nonetheless, they go to the heart of many of the challenges we face in higher education, and we have brought them with us into the next century.

Beyond assessment. The assessment movement has impelled us to define our goals and determine whether students are achieving them. Nonetheless, in many institutions there is little collective sense of responsibility to ensure that these goals will be reached. This is borne out by the recent NCPI (1999) report that indicates that campuses have been busy collecting assessment data but have not used the data to revise curriculum or improve instruction. If we keep the long view in sight, assessment has the potential to drive curricular change, and curricular change has the potential to drive instructional change, but we are only beginning this process — one which may be very protracted.

The hard work of interdisciplinarity. The promise of interdisciplinary ways of knowing, teaching, and learning also has a long road ahead. Jerry Gaff notes in his commentary in "Curriculum" that interdisciplinary efforts are still marginalized and may continue to be on the periphery of higher education. In the past decade, learning communities have emerged that are often described as interdisciplinary. The structures for team-teaching and linked courses are proliferating, and the infrastructure to support interdisciplinary initiatives are in place in many institutions (Edwards, 1996; Gabelnick et al., 1990), but the core intellectual and curricular issues are yet to be resolved. The curricular goals of interdisciplinary teaching and learning are ill defined. What do we mean by *interdisciplinary integration and synthesis*? How can we help students develop these integrative skills? How will we know when they are mastering them? These are not new questions. Members of the Association for Integrative Studies have asked these questions for decades. What is new is the wider audience waiting for answers, an audience schooled in assessment and eager to know whether this new wave of interdisciplinary initiatives deserves our continued support.

Training and development. In the last 30 years, opportunities for ongoing faculty development, particularly in relation to teaching and learning, have been integrated into higher education. These initiatives support faculty and instructional staff at all stages of their careers to explore new and effective teaching methods. They are increasingly important in efforts to implement both curricular reform and assessment of student learning. The field of faculty development itself has grown and developed, and there is now a large and growing body of research and expertise on best practices in the field.

Unfortunately, while we have come a long way, opportunities for training and development still reach only a fraction of those who teach. Units that provide instructional support are often underfunded, understaffed, and marginalized in subtle and overt ways. Nonetheless, the training and development function will be increasingly important, given rapid changes in instructional technology and other emergent instructional models. As Kenneth Green emphasizes, institutions have made serious errors in the past by consistently underestimating the needs and cost of creating and sustaining an adequate infrastructure and ongoing support personnel. Support structures enable innovations to thrive. Without them, they all too often fail. "Training and development" activities deserve to be center stage, where they can better support learning organizations in their efforts to grow and change.

Difficult dialogues. The goals for diversity in higher education will be ongoing, but the last 30 years have helped us to make "constructive adjustment[s] to new national circumstances" (Bonham, 1976, p. 13). Trosset's (1998) article in "Methods of Teaching" about the Grinnell College Study is a clear example both of the work that has been accomplished and the work that remains ahead of us. In this study, students explain that despite their participation in classroom discussions about diversity issues, they view these experiences primarily as opportunities to convince others of their own strongly held views — not as opportunities to listen and learn about or from each other. Others report that they retreat into silence to maintain comfort in the classroom. On one hand, we can celebrate the presence of students and faculty from diverse backgrounds in our classrooms, just as we can celebrate their participation in open discussions about diversity issues. On the other hand, many students — by their own admission — are not yet listening with open minds. There are also many groups that still have only limited access to higher education and struggle once they are admitted. Clearly, the quest to diversify and democratize higher education must continue.

Promoting a culture of teaching: To be continued. . . We have made significant strides in promoting a culture of teaching. We have begun to open classroom doors and "go public" with teaching. We have focused on redefining faculty roles and rewards and re-conceptualizing the scholarship of teaching. We are engaging in assessment of student learning and are seriously exploring the paradigm shift from teaching to learning. We are integrating active approaches to teaching and learning, particularly the use of technology. Innovative programs like Preparing Future Faculty are establishing new ways to acculturate faculty to the importance of their instructional role (Gaff & Lambert, 1996). Teaching centers and instructional development programs are proliferating, and higher education organizations and disciplinary associations are focusing on teaching and learning initiatives.

However, this emergent culture of teaching exists within the larger culture of higher education, and therein lies the greatest challenge. Bringing together those who care deeply about teaching is only part of the task; gaining and sustaining the support and interest of those who are primarily committed to the other missions of higher education is an equally important and difficult endeavor. That is the work of the 21st century. Larry Cuban's (1999) model of "strategic incrementalism," targeting "a series of small but high profile improvements" (p. 204), may serve us well as a plan for the future, building on what has been accomplished during the past 30 years. In the meanwhile, we can take heart that we are entering the new millennium to the sound of voices engaged in animated conversations about teaching and learning, voices that continue to be heard in the pages of *Change*.

***Change* as Change Agent**. The role of *Change* magazine and the American Association for Higher Education (AAHE) should not be underestimated in the transformations that have occurred in higher education. *Change* itself has played the role of "change agent" in several ways. First, it has provided a venue to articulate the need for change, to share models of reform, to air positions of advocacy and resistance, and to share research on effective practices in higher education. Early examples are provided by articles on active learning in the issues of *Change* devoted to the National Teaching Project; the diverse positions on open admissions in "Portraits of Students"; the culture wars in "Curriculum"; mandated assessment in "Assessing Student Learning"; and faculty roles and rewards for teaching in "Promoting a Culture of Teaching." Additional examples are found in the articles that present current research and debunk prevalent myths in higher education in "Philosophy, Psychology and Methods of Teaching" and "Evaluating Teaching."

Second, *Change* has helped to establish a common language that transcends disciplinary discourse, a point well made by Daniel Goroff in his Commentary on science education reform. It has not only helped both scientists and non-scientists to engage in discussions of science reform, but it also has helped to clarify concepts whose meanings have changed over time or have different meanings for different people. These include concepts such as "multiculturalism," "feminism," and "diversity."

Third, *Change* has identified the trends and reported them, for example, in the articles on the scholarship of teaching in "Promoting a Culture of Teaching," on learning communities in the section of the same name, and on reform efforts in "Professional, Graduate, and Teacher Education: Criticism and Reform."

Fourth, in collaboration with the AAHE, *Change* has helped to create and nurture movements, including service learning, assessment, and high school/college collaborations.

Fifth, *Change* has taken an active role in supporting trends, including the use of technology, a renewed commitment to civic life, and diversity.

Finally, *Change* has provided a vehicle to express the growing pains of a culture in transition, captured most dramatically in "Teacher Narratives." Each of these stories expresses the anguish and the joys of transformation that are personal, professional, and societal. They represent a form of "going public" with one's teaching that is cathartic for speaker and audience alike, helping us to make meaning of the changes we witness and experience.

It is not that *Change* tries to be all things to all people; it does not. Its leadership has understood that there are many voices in higher education, and it has made an effort to let those diverse voices be heard. In doing so, it fulfills the promise made years ago by George Bonham (1976) to provide us with an ongoing "national town meeting" (p. 13), one that reflects and supports democratic process in action.

References

Association of American Colleges. (1985). *Integrity in the college curriculum: A report to the academic community*. Washington, DC: Author.

Association of American Colleges. (1990). *The challenge of connecting learning*: Project on liberal learning, study in depth, and the arts and sciences major. Liberal Learning and the Arts and Science Major, Volume 1. Washington, D.C.: Association of American Colleges.

Astin, A.W. (1987, September/October). Competition or cooperation? Teaching teamwork as a basic skill. *Change, 19* (5), 12–19.

Astin, A.W. (1993, March/April). Diversity and multiculturalism on campus: How are students affected? *Change, 25* (2), 44–49.

Barasch, F. K. (1981, April). Learning in the workplace: Stronger support from the unions. *Change, 13* (3), 42–45.

Barr, R.B., & Tagg, J. (1995, November/December). From teaching to learning: A new paradigm for undergraduate education. *Change, 27* (6), 13–25.

Belenky, M., Clinchy, B.M, Goldberger, N.R., & Tarule, J.M. (1986). *Women's ways of knowing: The development of self, voice and mind*. New York: Basic Books.

Binzen, P. (1973, February). Education in a world of work: LaGuardia Community College. *Change, 5* (1), 35–37.

Bonham, G. (1976, June). Notes from the editor. *Change, 8* (5), 13.

Booth, W. (1988, July/August). Cultural literacy and liberal learning: An open letter to E.D. Hirsch, Jr. *Change, 20* (4), 10–21.

Boyer, E. L. (1990). *Scholarship reconsidered: Priorities of the professoriate*. Princeton, NJ: Carnegie Foundation for the Advancement of Teaching.

Cross, K. P. (1973, February). The New Learners. *Change, 5* (1), 31–34.

Cuban, L. (1999). *How scholars trumped teachers: Change without reform in university curriculum, teaching, and research, 1890–1990*. New York, NY: Teachers College Press.

Daloz, L.A. Parks, Keen, C.H., Keen, J.P., & Daloz Parks, S. (1996, May/June). Lives of commitment: Higher education in the life of the new commons. *Change, 28* (3), 11–15.

Edwards, A. (1996). *Interdisciplinary undergraduate programs: A directory* (2nd ed.). Acton, MA: Copley.

Gabelnick, F. (1997). Educating a committed citizenry. *Change, 29* (1), 30–35.

Gabelnick, F., MacGregor, J., Matthews, R.S., & Smith, B. L. (Eds.) (1990). *Learning communities: Creating connections among students, faculty, and disciplines*. New Directions for Teaching and Learning, No. 41. San Francisco: Jossey-Bass.

Gaff, J. G., & Lambert. L. M. (1996, July/August). Socializing future faculty to the values of undergraduate education. *Change, 28* (4), 38–45.

Gamson, Z.F. (1997, January/February). Higher education and rebuilding civic life. *Change, 29* (1), 10–13.

Glassick, C., Huber, M., Maeroff, G., & Boyer, E.L. (1997). *Scholarship assessed:*

Evaluation of the professoriate. Carnegie Foundation for the Advancement of Teaching.

Hall, W.H., & Kevles, B.L. (1980, January). Democratizing the curriculum. *Change, 12* (1), 43.

Hirsch. Jr., E.D. (1988, July/August). A postscript by E.D. Hirsch, Jr. *Change, 20* (4), 22–26.

Hutchings, P., & Shulman, L. S. (1999, September/October). The scholarship of teaching: New elaborations, new developments. *Change, 31* (5), 11–15.

Klein, J.T. (1990). *Interdisciplinarity: History, theory and practice.* Detroit, MI: Wayne State University Press.

Klein, J.T. (1996). *Crossing boundaries: Knowledge, disciplinarities, and interdisciplinarities.* Charlottesville, VA: University of Virginia Press.

Levine, A. (1993, September/October). Student expectations of college. *Change, 23* (5), 4.

Maclure, S. (1971, March/April). England's open university: Revolution at Milton Keynes. *Change, 3* (2), 62–68.

Maeroff, G.I. (1981, January). Ties that do not bind: The high school/college connection. *Change, 14* (1), 12–17, 46–51.

Marshak, R.E., & Wurtemburg, G. (1981, November/December). Open access, open admissions, open warfare I. *Change, 13* (8), 12–19, 51–53.

Mondale, W. (1976, October). The next step: Lifelong learning. *Change, 8* (9), 42–45.

National Center for Postsecondary Improvement. (1999, September/October). Revolution or evolution? Gauging the effect of institutional assessment. *Change, 31* (5), 53–56.

National Institute of Education (1984, October). Involvement in learning: Realizing the potential of American higher education. *Report of the NIE Study Group on the Condition of Excellence in American Higher Education.* Washington, DC: U.S. Department of Education.

Newell, W. (1998, March). *The place of interdisciplinary studies in higher education today.* Paper presented at the Association of American Colleges and Universities and the Association for Integrative Studies Annual Meeting. Chicago, Il.

Palmer, P. (1997, September/October). Community, conflict and ways of knowing: Ways to deepen our educational agenda. *Change, 29* (3), 20–25.

Palmer, P. J. (1992, March/April). Divided no more: A movement approach to educational reform. *Change, 24* (2), 10–17.

Rudolph, F. (1984, May/June). The power of professors: The impact of specialization and professionalism on the curriculum. *Change, 16* (4), 12–17, 41.

Schneider, C.G., & Shoenberg, R. (1999, March/April). Habits hard to break: How persistent features of campus life frustrate curricular reform. *Change, 31* (2), 30–35.

Schön, D.A. (1995, November/December). The new scholarship requires a new epistemology: Knowing-in-action. *Change, 27* (6), 26–34.

Schroeder, C.C. (1993, September/October). New students — New learning styles. *Change, 25* (5), 21–26.

Seldin, P. (1984, April). Faculty evaluation: Surveying policy and practices. *Change, 16* (3), 28–33.

Seldin, P. (1999) *Changing practices in evaluating teaching.* Bolton, MA: Anker.

Singleton, Jr., R., Garvey, R.H., & Phillips, G.A. (1998, May/June). Connecting the academic and social lives of students. *Change 30* (3), 18–25.

Smith, J.Z. (1983, July/August). Why the college major? Questioning the unexplained aspect of undergraduate education. *Change, 15* (5), 12–15.

Svinicki, M.D. (Ed.) (1999, Winter). Teaching and learning on the edge of the millennium: Building on what we have learned. *New Directions for Teaching and Learning,* 80. Jossey-Bass.

Terenzini, P.T., & Pascarella, E. T. (1994, January/February). Living with myths: Undergraduate education in America. *Change, 26* (1), 28–32.

Trosset, C. (1998, September/October). Obstacles to open discussion and critical thinking: The Grinnell College study. *Change, 30* (5), 44–49.

U.S. National Commission on Excellence in Education. (1983). *A nation at risk: The imperative for educational reform.* Washington, D.C.: U.S. National Commission on Excellence in Education.

Wong, F. F. (1991, July/August). Diversity & community: Right objectives and wrong arguments. *Change, 23* (4), 48–54.

Zlotkowski, E. (1996, January/February). Linking service-learning and the academy: A new voice at the table? *Change, 21* (1), 21–27.

Editor's and Contributing Editors' Biographies

Deborah DeZure is Coordinator of Faculty Programs and Publications at the Center for Research on Learning and Teaching at the University of Michigan. Previously she served as Director of the Faculty Center for Instructional Excellence, Education Consultant to the President, and Associate Director of the University Honors Program at Eastern Michigan University. Her publications on innovative and effective approaches to college teaching and faculty development and evaluation have appeared in *Change, The AAHE Bulletin, Academe, Thought and Action, Literature and Psychology, Changing Practices in Evaluating Teaching* (Ed., Peter Seldin, 1999) and publications of the NCTE, among others. She served as editor of *To Improve the Academy 1997* and is a member of the editorial boards of *The International Journal of Academic Development, Journal of Excellence in College Teaching,* and *Issues and Inquiry in College Teaching and Learning.* Deborah received her B.A., M.A., and Ph.D. from New York University in Interdisciplinary Humanities and Education. She is active as a consultant, workshop presenter, and keynote speaker on teaching and learning in higher education in the United States and abroad.

K. Patricia Cross is Professor of Higher Education, Emerita, at the University of California at Berkeley. She has had a distinguished career as a university administrator (Assistant Dean of Women, University of Illinois and Dean of Students at Cornell University), researcher (Distinguished Research Scientist at Educational Testing Service and Research Educator at The Center for Research and Development in Higher Education, University of California, Berkeley), and teacher (Professor and Chair of the Department of Administration, Planning, and Social Policy at the Harvard Graduate School of Education and Professor of Higher Education, University of California, Berkeley). The author of 10 books and more than 200 articles and chapters, Cross has been recognized for her scholarship by election to the National Academy of Education, and receipt of the E.F. Lindquist Award from the American Educational Research Association, the Sidney Suslow Award from the Association for Institutional Research, and the Howard Bowen Distinguished Career Award from the Association for the Study of Higher Education. Elected Chair of the Board of the American Association for Higher Education twice (1975 and 1989), she has received many awards for her leadership in education as well as 15 honorary degrees. She is listed in *Who's Who in America.*

Alfredo G. de los Santos Jr. served as Vice Chancellor for Student and Educational Development at the Maricopa Community Colleges for more than 21 years, until he retired in October 1999. Currently, he serves on the Board of Trustees of the Tomas Rivera Policy Institute; the Carnegie Foundation for the Advancement of Teaching; Multicultural Education, Training, and Advocacy; the United States Open University; and the Council for Higher Education Accreditation.

He has previously served on the Board of Directors of the American Council on Education, the American Association of Community Colleges, the American Association for Higher Education, and the Partnership for Service-Learning. He also served on the Board of Trustees of The Educational Testing Service, the College Board, and American College Testing.

Jerry G. Gaff is Vice President of the Association of American Colleges and Universities, which serves as the national voice of liberal learning. He received a B.A. from DePauw University in 1958 and a Ph.D. in psychology from Syracuse University in 1965. Through his publications, projects, and related professional activities, he has contributed to many efforts to improve undergraduate education. He has directed national projects to strengthen undergraduate general education programs and to foster the professional development of faculty members. He is the founding Director of the Network for Academic Renewal that assists administrators and faculty members in improving their academic programs in such ways as internationalizing the curriculum, using diversity and technology to aid learning, and developing more quality and coherence in general education curricula. He also directs the Preparing Future Faculty program, which has awarded grants to research universities to develop new programs that prepare graduate students for research, teaching, and service roles in colleges and universities. His most recent book is *Handbook of the Undergraduate Curriculum: A Comprehensive Guide to Purposes, Structures, Practices and Change* (1996).

Zelda F. Gamson is the founding Director of the New England Resource Center for Higher Education at the University of Massachusetts-Boston, where she also founded and taught in the Higher Education Leadership program. As a sociologist who has applied sociological concepts to higher education, she has been active throughout her career in promoting the study and practice of change. She has published widely on a variety of subjects related to change: *Academic Values and Mass Education* (with David Riesman and Joseph Gusfield) and *Liberating Education* are her best-known works. For more than 20 years, she held research, faculty, and administrative positions at the University of Michigan at the Institute for Social Research, the Center for the Study of Higher Education, and the Residential College. She served as vice-chair of the Board of Trustees at Antioch, on the visiting committee on general education at Harvard College, and as executive editor of *Change*. She is currently Senior Associate at the New England Resource Center for Higher Education and a member of the Board of Directors of the Center for Campus Organizing, a resource center for student activists.

Diane Gillespie is currently Professor of Interdisciplinary Arts and Sciences at The University of Washington, Bothell. Until 1998, she was an original member of the Goodrich Scholarship Program at The University of Nebraska at Omaha. The program provides an academically rigorous, culturally relevant curriculum to its culturally diverse students. Through grants from the Spencer Foundation and the Ford Foundation in the early 1990s, she was part of a team that developed "Critical Moments," a project that uses diversity case stories to enhance students' critical thinking. She is currently working with the Washington Center for the Improvement of Undergraduate Education to implement the project in the state of Washington. Contributing articles to *Change, Innovations in Higher Education*, and the *Journal of Excellence in Higher Education*, she has been active nationally in promoting a culture of reflective teaching practice. From 1990-1995, she was Faculty Consultant to the American Association for Higher Education's Forum on Exemplary Teaching. Her book *The Mind's We: Contextualism in Cognitive Psychology* argues for a contextual understanding of human cognition in which narrative plays a constituent role. She has won numerous awards for her teaching, including the 1992 CASE Nebraska Professor of the Year.

Daniel L. Goroff is Professor of the Practice of Mathematics at Harvard University and Associate Director of the Derek Bok Center for Teaching and Learning. He earned his A.B.-M.A. summa cum laude from Harvard University, an M.Phil.

in Economics as a Churchill Scholar at Cambridge University, and a Ph.D. in Mathematics as a Danforth Fellow at Princeton University. Winner of a Phi Beta Kappa Teaching Prize in 1988, Goroff worked for the National Research Council during 1996–1997 and for the President's Science Advisor at the White House during 1997–1998. In 1998, *Change* named him one of its "Young Leaders in Academia."

Kenneth C. Green is the founder and Director of The Campus Computing Project, the largest continuing study of the role of information technology in U.S. colleges and universities. The project is widely cited by campus officials and corporate executives as the definitive source for information about information technology issues affecting American higher education. Green is also is a visiting scholar at The Claremont Graduate University. His column on technology and higher education issues, DIGITAL TWEED, appears monthly in *Converge* Magazine (www.converg emag.com). The author/co-author or editor of 12 books and published research reports and 36 articles in academic journals and professional publications, Dr. Green is frequently quoted on higher education, information technology, and labor market issues in *The New York Times, The Washington Post, The Los Angeles Times, The Chronicle of Higher Education,* and in other print and broadcast media. Additionally, he is an invited speaker at numerous academic conferences and professional meetings each year. Green's research and consulting activities focus on information technology, campus planning and policy issues, and higher education marketing.

Pat Hutchings is a Senior Scholar with The Carnegie Foundation for the Advancement of Teaching. She co-directs, with Lee Shulman, the Carnegie Academy for the Scholarship of Teaching and Learning (CASTL), which works with individual faculty, campuses, and scholarly societies to foster learning for all students, enhance the practice and profession of teaching, and bring to faculty's work as teachers the recognition and reward afforded to other forms of scholarly work in higher education. Previously, Pat served as Director of the Teaching Initiative at the American Association for Higher Education (AAHE), working with faculty, administrators, and others to foster a campus culture in which teaching and learning are talked about, inquired into, evaluated, and rewarded. Several publications resulted from this project, the most recent of which is *The Course Portfolio: How Faculty Can Examine Their Teaching to Advance Practice and Improve Student Learning* (AAHE, 1998). Before directing the Teaching Initiative in 1990, Pat served as founding Director of the AAHE Assessment Forum. From 1978–1987 she was a faculty member and chair of the English Department at Alverno College in Milwaukee, Wisconsin. Her Ph.D. is from the University of Iowa.

Malcolm A. Lowther is Professor Emeritus of Education in the Center for the Study of Higher and Postsecondary Education and in the Educational Studies Program in the School of Education at the University of Michigan. He was also a senior researcher with the National Center for Research to Improve Postsecondary Teaching and Learning. His research and publications have focused on professional education programs and faculty members, professional career patterns and transitions, and course-planning activities of higher education faculty members.

Wilbert J. McKeachie is in his fifty-fifth year of teaching at the University of Michigan (in recent years at no salary) where he is Professor Emeritus of Psychology, former Chairman of the Department of Psychology, and past Director of the University of Michigan Center for Research on Learning and Teaching. He has served as President of the American Psychological Association and the American Association for Higher Education (AAHE) and has been an avid reader of *Change* since its inception. He has also served as Chairman of the Committee on College and University Teaching, Research and Publication of the American Association of University Professors. He has written numerous books and articles related to undergraduate education and college teaching. He is author of *Teaching Tips: Strategies, Research, and Theory for College and University Teachers,* (1999), now in its 10th edition.

Joan S. Stark is Professor in the Center for the Study of Higher and Postsecondary Education, School of Education, The University of Michigan. At Michigan she has been Dean of the School of Education, Editor of *The Review of Higher Education,* and Director of the National Center for Research to Improve Postsecondary Teaching and Learning. She has also taught and administered in a liberal arts college, a community college, and other universities. Professor Stark's research and teaching interests include curriculum development, evaluation and assessment, and undergraduate professional education in colleges and universities. Her recent book, *Shaping the College Curriculum: Academic Plans in Action,* (1997) is a comprehensive treatment of curriculum development in colleges and universities.

Peter Seldin is Distinguished Professor of Management at Pace University, Pleasantville, New York. His most recent books include: *Changing Practices in Evaluating Teaching* (1999) and *The Teaching Portfolio* (2nd edition, 1997). He has contributed numerous articles on the teaching profession, student ratings, educational practice, and academic culture to publications including *The New York Times, The Chronicle of Higher Education, Change,* and the *AAHE Bulletin.* A specialist in the evaluation and development of teaching performance, he has been a consultant to nearly 300 colleges and universities throughout the United States and in 27 countries around the world.

James Wilkinson has been Director of the Derek Bok Center for Teaching and Learning and Lecturer in History and Literature at Harvard University since June 1988. He received his B.A. from Harvard College in 1965 in French History and Literature, an M.A. in Comparative Literature from Harvard in 1970, and a Ph.D. in History from Harvard in 1974. From 1974 until 1983, he taught modern European history at Harvard. From 1985 until 1988, he was Visiting Associate Professor of History and Coordinator of Instructional Development at Boston University, where he founded that University's first teaching center. He is the recipient of a National Endowment for the Humanities Senior Research Fellowship, a Guggenheim Fellowship in the field of European history, and a Japan Society for the Promotion of Science Fellowship in higher education. He has written on both history and education and has lectured and conducted teaching workshops widely throughout the United States and abroad.

Barbara D. Wright is an Associate Professor of German at the University of Connecticut. Though she was hired to teach Renaissance, Baroque, and Expressionist literature, her interests over the years have expanded to include Women's Studies, second-language acquisition, and general education. From 1988 to 1990, she headed a FIPSE-funded project at the University of Connecticut to assess a new general education curriculum. From 1990 to 1992 she served as Director of the American Association for Higher Education Assessment Forum, organizing three national conferences, editing publications, and making frequent visits to campuses. She has remained active in assessment and continues to give workshops and presentations. Since 1995, she has served on the commission of the New England Association of Schools and Colleges, the regional accreditor for New England. She also reviews manuscripts on assessment for *Change,* the *Journal of General Education,* Jossey-Bass, and other educational resources.

Article Index by Author

---

* Copyright © Heldref Publications

Index

border crossings, 428–430

Boyer, Ernest, 172; *Scholarship Reconsidered: Priorities of the Professoriate*, 20, 23, 32

British Open University, 399–400, 406

Brodsky, Joseph, 219–220

Brookwood Labor College, 128–129

Bruner, Jerome, 386

California, Partnership Program, 154

California State College, 373–376; Social Systems Research Center, 222–223

Cambridge University, 136

Campus Compact, 162, 170–171

campus, role of, 196–197

canon, versus faculty competence, 7

career orientation, 70, 95–96, 267, 269

Carnegie Foundation for the Advancement of Teaching, 19–20, 93–94, 160

cases, on teaching and learning, 23–24, 255–257

challenge, by great teachers, 363–364

change. *See* educational reform; innovation

character: Dewey on, 202–203; education for, 95–96, 139, 273–274

chemistry education, 235–236

citizenship: education for, 140–141, 172–176, 201–204; in information society, education for, 99

City University of New York, 64–67, 71–74; open admissions at, 58–61; Richmond College, 119–120; teacher narratives on, 378–381; and work and education, 149–150. *See also* LaGuardia Community College

civility, in academy, 174

classroom visitation, in evaluation, 356

Clinton administration, and education, 168, 332

cognitive-developmental theory, 207

collaboration, 430–431

college major: and curricular reform, 109; questioning, 96–97

College of the Holy Cross, 141–143

collegiality, 24–26, 31; at community colleges, 8; hollowed, 31–32; lack of, 8–9

comfort, versus discussion, 215–216

commitment: characteristics of, 173; education for, 172–174

communication, 183, 430–431; Dewey on, 202; great teachers and, 365

community: Dewey on, 202–203; diversity and, 79–82, 108–109; education for, 95–96; epistemology and, 204–205; and science education, 241–242, 244; and value systems, 281–282

community-college connections, 145–148, 155–156, 176–177

community colleges, 8, 119–120, 149–156

community of teaching, 24–32

competency education, 305–306

competition, versus cooperation, 182–186

computers, 33–34, 404–406, 408–411, 414–416; and epistemology, 415; and institutions, 417–419; in mathematics education, 404; in science education, 245, 247–248

connoisseurship, 328

consciousness-raising, 77, 94

consensus decision-making, 31, 99

consensus, search for, 213–214

construction, in science education, 244

continuing education, 150–151; technology and, 419–421

continuity, in science education, 244

continuous improvement, 324–325

conversation, and teaching, 27–28

cooperation: versus competition, 182–186; and quality, 325; in teacher training, 384; technology and, 403

cooperative learning, 149–150, 205–212; definition of, 205–206; in discussion method teaching, 190–191; dynamics of, 207–208; research on, 208–210; in science education, 245; theory of, 206–207; uses of, 210–211

core curriculum, 88–89, 103–105

Cornell University, 220–222

educational methods, open admissions and, 59

educational reform, 284–287; and academic freedom, 6–7; assessment and, 318; barriers to, 109–111; *Change* and, 434–435; changes in, 156–158; culture of teaching and, 2; cumulative, 252; effects of, 129–131; versus excellence, 6–7; future of, 432–435; in general education, 105–106; language of, 44–45; movement approach to, 15–19; pessimism regarding, 15; in science, 227–258; standardized testing and, 332; teacher narratives on, 381

Education Commission of the States, 162

Ehrlich, Thomas, 14, 170

Elementary and Secondary Education Act, 332

e-mail, 412, 418

English, remedial, 91

environment, Dewey on, 201

epistemology: of computer learning, 415; in scholarship of teaching, 32–35

equilibrium, Dewey on, 203

ethics: education for, 106, 139, 270–275, 285; relativism and, 279–284

ethnic minorities. *See* students of color

ethnic studies, 106

evaluation of faculty performance, 339–349; at Antioch, 121–122; changes in, 340–342; and culture, 2; learning to live with, 351–352; myths of, 339–343; by peers, 358–360; policy and practices on, 353–358; recommendations for, 21, 25–26; student, 31, 340, 344–346, 352–353; teacher narratives on, 381. *See also* assessment of student outcomes

Evergreen College, 118–119

excellence: approaches to, 182; versus reform, 6–7; in teaching, market for, 42–44

experience: Dewey on, 202; and distance learning, 407; and knowledge, 214; of learning, 376

faculty: and accountability, 326–328; and accounting education reform, 278; at Antioch, 121–122; and assessment, 312, 315–316; and character education, 95–96; competence of, and canon, 7; and competency education, 306; and cooperation, 185; in cooperative education, 150; and cooperative learning, 207–208; and curriculum, 97, 110; and discussion method teaching, 186–192; education of, 279–287; and ethics education, 270, 274; at Hampshire College, 127; influence of, 195–196; market for, 41–44; at New College, 126; and new learners, 84; on physics education, 257–258; and public service, 164–166, 170–171; at Santa Cruz, 131–132; in science education, 243; and science education reform, 253; senior versus junior, 5–7, 19, 30; and teacher training reform, 297; and undergraduate teaching, 35–38. *See also* teachers

faculty development, 8, 106

faculty morale, spirit and, 45–47

faculty rewards, 1–2, 391; and curricular reform, 109–110; and educational reform, 7; equity in, 31; memory and, 11; in movement approach to educational reform, 16, 18–19; and quality, 326; recommendations on, 21; re-examination of, 19–22; and spirit, 45–46

faculty roles, 5–7, 289; importance of, 390; in instruction versus learning paradigms, 199; open admissions and, 72–73; and undergraduate teaching, 36

feminism: and women's colleges, 77–78. *See also* women

feminist scholarship, 94–95

funding: and assessment, 312; and educational reform, 251–252. *See also* accountability

Gaff, Jerry G., 85–87

Gamson, Zelda F., 113–116

Geertz, Clifford, 1

general education, 93–94; and curricu-

176–177; in science, 241–243; types of, 59–60

noncognitive development, assessment of, 310

nonteaching organizations, and education, 156–157

open admissions, 52–53, 58–61, 71–74; case for, 64–67; and competency education, 306; and curriculum, 62; evaluation of, 73–74; and faculty roles, 72–73; and work and education, 149–150

open universities, 406–408

organizational approach to change, 16

organizational learning, 325

otherness, engagement with, 173

Oxford University, 136

participation: Dewey on, 201; in information society, 98–99

Partnership Program, California, 154

pedagogical colloquium, 26

peer evaluation, 358–360

peer review: and culture of teaching, 3; departmental culture and, 30–31; and recognition of teaching, 43; recommendations for, 21, 25

perennialism, 107

performance assessment, 331, 333

Personalized System of Instruction, 193–194

perspective-taking, 173–174

Phi Beta Kappa, 44

philosophy of teaching, 179–216

physics education, 247–249, 255–257

pluralism, 107–108; cultural, 203–204; and ethics, 280–281

poetry, and teaching, 219–220

politics, discussion of, 377

postmodernism: and discussion, 215; and science, 253–254

power, information and, 98–99

practice teaching, 289–290

Preparing Future Faculty project (PFF), 37–38

process learning, computers and, 410, 414–416

professional education, 259–279; ethics in, 271; recommendations for, 265–266

professionalization, and curriculum, 97

Project Athena, MIT, 33–34

Project Discovery, 275

psychology education, 220–222

psychology of teaching, 179–216

public: learning in, 46; reform efforts in, 17–18

public service, 164–166; and academy, 169–172; awards for, 162–164; on campus, 168–169; and community-college connections, 176–177; low-income students in, 166–167; required, 160–161

quality: management for, in institutions, 324–326, 329–331; recognition of, 192–193; in teacher training, 335–336; of teaching, 28–32, 313–314, 316

questions: on assessment, 313; in discussion method teaching, 187, 189–190

racial diversity, 76–78

racial issues, discussion of, 387–388

racial segregation, 61

recognition of teaching, 21, 43–44, 360–361; causes of lack of, 24

Reed College, 127–128

relativism, 107; myth of, 279–284; radical, 215

relevance, 5, 10, 379–380; in mathematics, 239–240; responses to, 269; versus rigor, 32–33; at Santa Cruz, 132; and vocationalism, 62–64

remedial education, 73, 91; versus prevention, 154

reputational view of excellence, 182

research: action, 33; on cooperative learning, 208–210; definition of, 36; in sociology, 222–223; on standardized testing, 332; on subject mastery, 288–289